9.27.01

Literature and
Its Times

VOLUME 5

**Civil Rights Movements
to Future Times
(1960-2000)**

Literature and
Its Times

Profiles of 300 Notable Literary Works and
the Historical Events that Influenced Them

Joyce Moss • George Wilson

GALE

DETROIT   NEW YORK   TORONTO   LONDON

Literature and Its Times

Profiles of 300 Notable Literary Works and the Historical Events that Influenced Them

VOLUME **5**

Civil Rights Movements to Future Times (1960-2000)

JOYCE MOSS • GEORGE WILSON

STAFF

Jeff Hill and Lawrence J. Trudeau, *Production Editors*
Susan Trosky, *Permissions Manager*
Kimberly F. Smilay, *Permissions Specialist*

Mary Beth Trimper, *Production Director*
Evi Seoud, *Production Manager*
Shanna Heilveil, *Production Assistant*

Cynthia Baldwin, *Product Design Manager*
Mary Claire Krzewinski, *Senior Art Director*

Barbara J. Yarrow, *Graphic Services Supervisor*
Randy Bassett, *Image Database Supervisor*
Robert Duncan, *Scanner Operator*
Pamela Hayes, *Photography Coordinator*

ISBN 0-7876-0606-5 (Set)
ISBN 0-7876-0611-1 (Volume 5)

Printed in the United States of America
10 9 8 7 6 5 4 3

Library of Congress Cataloging-in-Publication Data

Literature and its times : profiles of 300 notable literary works and the historical events that influenced them / [edited by Joyce Moss and George Wilson].
        p.   cm.
    Includes bibliographical references and index.
    Contents: v. 1. Ancient times to the American and French Revolutions, (pre-history-1790s) -- v. 2. Civil wars to frontier societies (1800-1880s) -- v. 3. Growth of empires to the Great Depression (1890-1930s) -- v. 4. World War II to the affluent fifties (1940-1950s) -- v. 5. Civil rights movements to future times (1960-2000).
    ISBN 0-7876-0607-3 (vol. 1 : alk. paper). -- ISBN 0-7876-0608-1 (vol. 2 : alk. paper). -- ISBN 0-7876-0609-X (vol. 3 : alk. paper). -- ISBN 0-7876-0610-3 (vol. 4 : alk. paper). -- ISBN 0-7876-0611-1 (vol. 5 : alk. paper)
    1. Literature and history. 2. History in literature. 3. Literature--History and criticism.
I. Moss, Joyce, 1951- . II. Wilson, George, 1920- .
PN50.L574 1997
809'.93358--dc21

                                                                                            97-34339
                                                                                            CIP

Contents

Preface

~

"Even a great writer can be bound by the prejudices of his time ⁄. . we cannot place Shakespeare in a sealed container. He belonged to his time," notes Alexander Leggatt in his essay "*The Merchant of Venice*: A Modern Perspective" (William Shakespeare, *The Merchant of Venice* [New York: Washington Square Press, 1992], 217). This reasoning, applicable to any work and its author, explains why *Literature and Its Times* fixes a wide range of novels, short stories, biographies, speeches, poems, and plays in the context of their particular historical periods.

In the process, the relationship between fact and fantasy or invention becomes increasingly clear. The function of literature is not necessarily to represent history accurately. Many writers aim rather to spin a satisfying tale or perhaps to convey a certain vision or message. Nevertheless, the images created by a powerful literary work—be it the Greek poem *Iliad,* the Spanish novel *The Adventures of Don Quixote,* or the American play *The Crucible*—leave impressions that are commonly taken to be historical. This is true from works that depict earlier eras to ones that portray more modern occurrences, such as the world wars or race relations. The fourteenth-century poem *Inferno* from the *Divine Comedy* by Dante Alighieri is probably the most powerful example. So vividly does *Inferno* describe Hell that for more than two centuries people took its description as truth, going so far as to map Hell according to the details of the poem.

In taking literature as fact, then, one risks acquiring a mistaken or an unverified notion of history. Yet, by the same token, history can be very well informed by literary works. An author may portray events in a way that for the first time aptly captures the fears and challenges of a period, enabling readers to better understand it and their own place in the historical continuum. This is easily illustrated by tracing novels that feature women's issues, from Nathaniel Hawthorne's *The Scarlet Letter* (1640s setting) to Leo Tolstoy's *Anna Karenina* (1870s) to Alice Walker's *The Color Purple* (1920s–40s) and Amy Tan's *The Joy Luck Club* (1940s–80s).

Placing a given work in historical context involves pinpointing conditions in the society in which it was written as well as set. Stephen Crane's *Red Badge of Courage* is set in the early 1860s. Published three decades later, it was written in a different social context and, in this case, in response to a literary trend of Crane's own era. Only by gaining insight into this era as well as the one in which the work takes place can it be fully appreciated; *Literature and Its Times* therefore addresses the author's time frame too.

The task of reconstructing the historical contexts of a work can be problematic. There are stories—the tales of England's King Arthur, for example—that defy any attempt to fit them neatly into a particular time. Living in a later era, their authors, consciously or not, mixed events that actually belong to two or more different periods. In some cases, this is an innocent mistake by a writer who did not have the benefit of accurate sources. In other cases, fidelity to the actual events of the time is of little concern to the writer; his or her main interest is the fictional world to be portrayed. In still other cases, the mixture of times is intentional. Happily, present-day knowledge makes it possible for this series to begin unweaving the historical mixture in these types of works.

Literature and Its Times relates history to literature on a case-by-case basis, intending to help readers respond fully to a work and to assist them in distinguishing fact from invention in the work. The series engages in this mission with a warm appreciation for the beauty of literature independent of historical facts, but also with the belief that ultimate regard is shown for a literary work and its author by positioning it in the context of pertinent events.

Selection of Literary Works

Literature and Its Times includes novels, short stories, plays, poems, biographies, essays, speeches, and documents. The works chosen for inclusion have been carefully selected on the basis of how frequently they are studied and how closely they are tied to pivotal historical events. Reflected in the selection are works not only by classic and still widely read authors but also by noteworthy ethnic and female authors. To finalize the selection, the complete list of titles was submitted to a panel of librarians, secondary teachers, and college professors. Please see "Acknowledgments" for a specific listing of these reviewers.

Format and Arrangement of Entries

The five volumes of *Literature and Its Times* are arranged chronologically from ancient times to the present. The set of entries within each volume is arranged alphabetically by title. As the series progresses, the range of years covered in each successive volume grows narrower due to the increasing number of works published in more recent times.

Each entry is organized according to the following sections.

1. ***Introduction***—identifying information in three parts:

   The literary work—describes the genre, the time and place of the work, and the year(s) it was first performed or published;

   Synopsis—summarizes the storyline or contents;

   Introductory paragraph—introduces the literary work in relation to the author's life.

2. ***Events in History at the Time the Literary Work Takes Place***—describes social and political events that relate to the plot or contents of the literary work and that occurred during the period the story takes place. Subsections vary depending on the literary work. The section takes a deductive approach, starting with events in history and telescoping inward to events in the literary work.

3. ***The Literary Work in Focus***—describes in brief the plot or contents of the work. Generally this summary is followed by a subsection on one or more elements in the work that illuminate real events or attitudes of the period. The subsection takes an inductive approach, starting with the literary work and broadening outward to events in history. It is usually followed by a third subsection detailing the sources used by the author to create the work.

4. ***Events in History at the Time the Literary Work Was Written***—describes social, political, and/or literary events in the author's lifetime that relate to the plot or contents of the work. When relevant, the section includes events in the author's life. Also discussed in the section are the initial reviews or reception accorded to the literary work.

5. ***For More Information***—provides a list of all sources that have been cited in the entry as well as sources for further reading about the different issues or personalities featured in the entry.

If a literary work is set and written in the same time period, sections 2 and 4 of the entry on that work ("Events in History at the Time the Literary Work Takes Place" and "Events in History at the Time the Literary Work Was Written") are combined into the single section "Events in History at the Time of the Literary Work."

Additional Features

Whenever possible, primary source material is provided through quotations in the text and material in sidebars. There are also sidebars with historical details that amplify issues raised in the main text and with anecdotes that give readers a fuller understanding of the temporal context. Timelines appear in various entries to summarize intricate periods of history. To enrich and further clarify information, historically noteworthy illustrations have been included in the series. Maps as well as photographs provide visual images of potentially unfamiliar settings.

Comments and Suggestions

Your comments on this series and suggestions for future editions are welcome. Please write: Editors, *Literature and Its Times,* Gale Research, Inc., 835 Penobscot Building, Detroit, Michigan 48226-4094; or call toll-free: 1-800-877-4253.

Acknowledgments

For their careful review of entries in *Literature and Its Times*, the following professors and lecturers from the University of California at Los Angeles (UCLA) deserve the deepest appreciation:

English Department

Robert Aguirre
Martha Banta
Lynn Batten
A. R. Braunmuller
Daphne Brooks
King-Kok Cheung
Michael Colacurcio
Ed Condren
Jack Kolb
Jinqui Ling
Chris Mott
Michael North
Barbara Packer
David Rodes
Karen Rowe

Comparative Literature Department

Eric Gans
Kathryn King
Mary Kay Norseng
Ross Shideler

Slavic Languages and Literature Department

Micheal Heim
Peter Hodgson

Gratitude is also extended to professors from other institutions for their valuable review of selected entries, and to history department chairman Robert Sumpter for his guidance and reviews:

Rabbi Stanley Chyet, Hebrew Union College
Agnes Moreland Jackson, Pitzer College, English and Black Studies
Michael McGaha, Pomona College, Romance Languages and Literatures— Spanish Section
Robert Sumpter, Mira Costa High School, History Department

A host of contributers assisted in collecting and composing data for the entries in *Literature and Its Times*. Their painstaking hours of research and composition are deeply appreciated.

Diane R. Ahrens
Eric A. Besner
Suzanne C. Borghei
Luke Bresky
Anne Brooks
Corey Brettschneider
Thomas Cooper
Patricia Carroll
Terence Davis
Mark Druskoff
Shelby Fulmer
Betsy Hedberg-Keramidas

Acknowledgments

Ryan Hilbert
Lisa Gabbert
Anne Kim
Amy Merritt
Michael Le Sieur
Barbara A. Lozano
Michele Mednick
Michelle Miller
Larry Mowrey
Evan Porter
Edward R. OþNeill
David Riemer
Monica Riordan
Jane E. Roddy
George Ross
Rita Schepergerdes
Roberta Seid
Shira Tarrant
Benjamin Trefny
Pete Trujillo
Lorraine B. Valestuk
Colin Wells
Sandra Wade-Grusky
Allison Weisz
Jeannie Wilkinson
Denise Wilson
Brandon Wilson
Antoine Wilson

A special thank you is extended to Lorraine B. Valestuk, Ph.D., for her refinement of data and to Cheryl Steets, Ph.D., for her deft copy editing. Anne Leach indexed the volumes with proficiency and literary sensitivity. The editors also thank Larry Trudeau and Jeff Hill of Gale Research for their careful editorial management.

Lastly the editors express gratitude to those who guided the final selection of literary works included in the series:

Neil Anstead, Director of Humanities,
    Los Angeles Unified School District
William Balcolm, Librarian,
    Villa Park Public Library, Villa Park, IL
Marth Banta, Professor,
    University of California at Los Angeles
Carol Clark, Head Librarian,
    Robert E. Lee High School, Springfield, VA
Chris García, Head Librarian,
    Beverly Hills Children's Library, Beverly Hills, CA
Nancy Guidry, Young Adult Librarian,
    Santa Monica Public Library, Santa Monica, CA
Kenneth M. Holmes, Ph.D.,
    Educational Consultant,
    Educational Concepts Unlimited, Bellville, IL
Carol Jago, Mentor Teacher,
    English Department, Santa Monica Public High School, Santa Monica, CA
Jim Merrill, Instructor,
    Oxnard Community College, Oxnard, CA
Mary Purucker, Head Librarian,
    Santa Monica High School, Santa Monica, CA
Karen Rowe, Professor,
    University of California at Los Angeles
Hilda K. Weisburg, Librarian,
    Sayreville War Memorial High School, Parlin, NJ
Dr. Brooke Workman, Teacher,
    West High School, Iowa City, IA
Richard Yarborough, Professor,
    University of California at Los Angeles

Introduction to Volume 5

Volume 5 of *Literature and Its Times* opens with works set amid the domestic turmoil of the civil rights movement in the United States and the international tension of the ongoing Cold War between the Soviet Union and the Western democracies. The volume closes in future worlds with science fiction stories that extrapolate from the present to speculate about forthcoming societies. Covered in between are a mix of literary works that portray realities of life for minority populations in the United States, that tackle harsh issues facing modern-day adolescents, and that deal with social structure and upheaval in some Latin American lands.

Concentrating almost exclusively on foreign relations, President John F. Kennedy's 1961 Inaugural Address managed, at least momentarily, to unify different factions of American society and to present a strong front to Soviet foes in the Cold War. Kennedy's mettle would be put to the test in the coming years, first in the 1962 Cuban Missile Crisis, a standoff that brought the globe to the brink of World War III. Then, after Kennedy's death, came the Vietnam War, which U.S. troops entered in 1965. At the time of the war, politicians tended to view the world in terms of the opposing forces of democracy and communism. Vietnam, as they understood it, was predominantly a struggle for power between the procommunist North and the anticommunist South. In the end, the cost to both sides was enormously high. Altogether

the war killed 58,000 American soldiers, 210,000 South Vietnamese soldiers, and 900,000 soldiers on the side of North Vietnam. Caught in the crossfire were more than a million civilians whose lives were also lost in the fighting. Several of the era's novels portray the war's impact on young men, including Walter Dean Myers's *Fallen Angels* and Cynthia Voigt's *The Runner*.

While in Southeast Asia war was being waged, in Latin America deadly military regimes emerged and civil disturbances erupted. Works by Isabel Allende (*The House of the Spirits*—set in Chile), Mario Vargas Llosa (*Time of the Hero*—in Peru) and Lawrence Thornton (*Imagining Argentina*—in Argentina) portray various power struggles in Latin American lands, while Barbara Kingsolver's *The Bean Trees* looks at the plight of Central American refugees who risk everything by seeking sanctuary across the border in the United States.

From the 1960s to the 1980s, the United States experienced a nonviolent civil rights movement, witnessed its evolution into a movement with leaders who sanctioned violence, and saw its contagious effects on other ethnicities in the United States. In the 1960s, black activists and white ones took to the streets, conducting marches, sit-ins, and freedom rides to protest racial segregation in the South. Writers like Alex Haley (*Roots*) and Ernest J. Gaines (*The Autobiography of Miss Jane Pittman*) helped contextualize the plight of blacks in the South by delving into cultural and personal history. In his "I Have a Dream" speech, Martin Luther King, Jr. reminded listeners of the high-minded principles on which the nation was founded and shared a vision of social harmony that many citizens— white as well as black— not only dreamed of but dedicated their personal safety and futures to attaining. All ideas of how to achieve equality were not equal, however. While King advocated nonviolent protest to achieve an integrated society, Malcolm X (see *The Autobiography of Malcolm X*), at least initially, championed separatism and denigrated the idea of not fighting back with physical force, messages that would be echoed in the Black Power movement of the late 1960s. James Baldwin, another prominent black American of the time, evaluated all the ferment and warned in his essay *The Fire Next Time* that violence would certainly erupt unless America changed the conditions of life that it imposed on African Americans, a prediction borne out by the riots of the late 1960s. Both the threat and reality of this violence lie at the heart of Flannery O'Connor's short story "Everything That Rises Must Converge."

The civil rights movement scored victories in the mid-1960s, when Congress passed new laws guaranteeing greater equality for African Americans. Following these successes, other victimized groups argued that they too deserved equal rights, and people heeded their complaints as legitimate ones. These other minorities garnered attention not only in law but also in literature, as demonstrated by Latino stories like Sandra Cisneros's *House on Mango Street* and Richard Rodriquez's *Hunger of Memory*; by American Indian tales such as Louise Erdrich's *Love Medicine* and Michael Dorris's *A Yellow Raft in Blue Water*; and by Asian American novels like Amy Tan's *The Joy Luck Club* and Frank Chin's *Donald Duk*. Within African American literature, female authors began registering the black woman's experience in works like Ntozake Shange's *for colored girls who have considered suicide / when the rainbow is enuf*, while females in other ethnic groups conveyed their experiences as well. These works expanded on the contemporary women's movement of the 1960s and '70s, giving definition to its grievances by relaying specific plights of females in the majority and the minority populations of the United States.

One result of all this social turmoil was that the familiar assimilation model of the past, the "melting pot,"—according to which newcomers from around the world shed their previous identities to become American— gave way to a sociological trend in which cultural differences are celebrated and nourished. The literary works mentioned above, as well as many others covered in the volume, are part and parcel of this trend. So are stories that have dared to feature previously neglected subcultures within white America, both in literary works written for the general population (for example, Tony Kushner's *Angels in America*, a pair of plays that focuses on homosexual characters) and in young-adult novels (see S. E. Hinton's *The Outsiders*, which focuses on white teen gangs, and Paul Zindel's *The Pigman*, which features the elderly).

The 1960s saw the widening of a gap between America's generations. More Americans than ever before were fifty years of age or older, while American youth, to varying degrees, rejected the traditional values of their elders. This is evident in works throughout the volume, from Robert Anderson's *I Never Sang for My Father* and W. P. Kinsella's *Shoeless Joe*—whose basically well-meaning protagonists struggle to define themselves in the context of traditional social standards— to the drug-involved and violent youth in Jervey Tervalon's *Understand This*. In fact, such works portray more than the generation gap; they convey the struggle to adjust to the changing realities of late twentieth-century life, with its increasing violence, its drug abuse, and its increase in single-parent as well as step-parent families. Various novels portray these realities, and include young-adult characters who make positive rather than self-destructive choices, as in Robert Lipsyte's *The Contender* and Alice Childress's *A Hero Ain't Nothin' but a Sandwich*. Glendon Swarthout's *Bless the Beasts and Children* features some conservation-minded if troubled youths. In the adult world, Ernest Gaines's *A Gathering of Old Men* includes a law-abiding white Southern sheriff who learns from and defends from mob justice the old black men in the story.

Perhaps because of the approaching millennium and the astounding technological advancements associated with space exploration (see Thomas Wolfe's *The Right Stuff*), writers since 1960 have turned increasingly to the genre of science fiction and have tried, often by observing life in their own times, to imagine what the future might hold. The relationship of the individual to government (Margaret Atwood's *The Handmaid's Tale* and George Orwell's *Nineteen Eighty-Four*), the ethical limits of experimentation (William Sleator's *House of*

Stairs), and the role of technology in human life (Aldous Huxley's *Brave New World*) are issues that have stimulated the imaginations of writers across the continents. As suggested in Annie Dillard's essay, *Pilgrim at Tinker Creek,* at the close of the twentieth century people are focusing on the heavens and the possibility of new worlds—on life in other times, on other planets, under different cultural circumstances.

Chronology of Relevant Events

1960–2000

CIVIL RIGHTS MOVEMENT

The 1960s and early 1970s in America were characterized by political and social unrest. African Americans, women, American Indians, Chicanos—all these groups and others staged protests in the streets and at universities in a struggle to guarantee equal rights for all. Initially, though, it was the quest of the African American community to achieve equality that dominated the nation's literature and news headlines. Though activists scored some successes in the 1960s, poverty and drug use persisted in the community, pointing to more deeply seated problems than overt segregation. The black community also gave rise to individuals who achieved distinction in education, the performing arts, the military, and sports. Professional boxing made a comeback during the 1960s and '70s, with African American boxers winning world championships.

Historical Events	Literary Works Set in the Period
	1750–1967 *Roots* by Alex Haley
	1860s–1960s *The Autobiography of Miss Jane Pittman* by Ernest J. Gaines
	1925–65 *The Autobiography of Malcolm X* as told by Malcolm X to Alex Haley
	1950s–60s *The Fire Next Time* by James Baldwin
	late 1950s? "Everything That Rises Must Converge" by Flannery O'Conner
1960 1960 Black students in Greensboro, North Carolina, sit down at segregated lunch counter and refuse to move until served	
1961 1961 Freedom riders take buses through the South to test its compliance with national laws that desegregate bus stations	
1962 1962 James Meredith, a black student, enrolls at all-white University of Mississippi, leading to a riot on campus in which 2 are killed and 375 injured; boxing star Sonny Liston becomes world's heavyweight boxing champion	

Historical Events	Literary Works Set in the Period
1963 1963 In April, Martin Luther King, Jr. leads peaceful demonstration in Birmingham, Alabama, at which cattle prods, high-pressure hoses, and dogs are used against children and other protesters in televised incidents that horrify nation; in August, 250,000 people participate in March on Washington for civil rights law against racial injustice—Martin Luther King, Jr. delivers "I Have a Dream" speech	1963 "I Have a Dream" by Martin Luther King, Jr.
1964 1964 Civil Rights Act outlaws segregation in public facilities and in private businesses that serve the general public; Martin Luther King, Jr. receives Nobel Peace Prize; in Mississippi civil rights activists conduct "Freedom Summer," in which more than 1,000 activists, including blacks and whites, conduct African American voter registration drive; Muhammad Ali wins world's heavyweight boxing championship	
1965 1965 Voting Rights Act forbids the obstruction of registration of black voters; Watts race riots in Los Angeles leave 34 dead and 1,000 injured	mid-1960s *The Contender* by Robert Lipsyte
1966 1966 Black leader Stokely Carmichael calls for "Black Power," signalling new militant wing of civil rights movement; race riots throughout America's cities; Robert Weaver becomes first black American to serve in Cabinet; riots in Atlanta, Cleveland, Milwaukee, San Francisco, and other U.S. cities	
1967 1967 Thurgood Marshall becomes the first African American Supreme Court Justice; riots in 128 cities, with major clashes in Newark and in Detroit	
1968 1968 Civil Rights Act prohibits discrimination in sale or rental of housing; Martin Luther King, Jr. is assassinated; his widow, Coretta Scott King, leads march of welfare mothers from 20 cities of U.S. during Poor People's Campaign in Washington, D.C.; Robert Kennedy is assassinated	
1969	
1970 early 1970s Use of heroin claims 1 of 6 residents in Harlem, New York	1970 *His Own Where* by June Jordan
	early 1970s *A Hero Ain't Nothin' but a Sandwich* by Alice Childress
1971 Supreme Court decides that desegregation of American schools should be accomplished by busing if necessary	
1975 Supreme Court-mandated busing helps desegregate American schools	late 1970s *A Gathering of Old Men* by Ernest J. Gaines

RISE OF MULTICULTURAL AMERICA

In the 1960s women also became active on their own behalf, protesting against earning less pay for doing the same job as a man and other injustices. Their movement grew as the decade progressed, fanned by the experience of young women in the civil rights movement, who were often relegated to menial positions by its males leaders. Ethnic groups other than African Americans became more vocal too about the injustices visited upon them because of their ethnicity. In the process, Americans began to reconsider the value of a uniform American culture. The diversity of the "cultural mosaic," as opposed to the assimilation of the "melting pot," began to emerge as a potent image of a new American society, in which minority groups as well as female Americans celebrated their own particular history—and their differences—with pride.

	Historical Events	Literary Works Set in the Period
		1850–1975 *The Woman Warrior: Memoirs of a Girlhood among Ghosts* by Maxine Hong Kingston
		1918–49 *The Joy Luck Club* by Amy Tan
		1940s–70s *A Hunger of Memory* by Richard Rodriguez
	1952 Puerto Rico becomes American commonwealth—Puerto Ricans can travel freely to and work in the United States	
1955		
1960	1960s Chicano movement insists on public recognition of Mexican American accomplishments and inclusion of Mexican American cultural, social, and political material in school curricula; thousands of Cuban refugees from Castro's regime flee to Florida	1960–70s *for colored girls who have considered suicide / when the rainbow is enuf* by Ntozake Shange
1965	1965 Congress passes Immigration Act of 1965, opening doors to Asian immigrants and admitting, without regard to quotas, applicants with family in America as U.S. citizens; Luis Valdez founds El Teatro Campesino, which stages plays documenting the abhorrent conditions of migrant farm workers	
	1965–70 Farm workers mount nationwide strike against grape industry, led by César Chávez	
	1966 Betty Friedan and others form National Organization of Women (NOW), which agitates for women's rights	
	1967 United Nations adopts Declaration of Women's Rights, stating that discrimination based on gender violates U.N. Charter	
	1968 President Lyndon Johnson signs Bilingual Education Act to aid children educationally disadvantaged by their inability to speak English; 10,000 Chicano students walk out of Los Angeles high schools to protest inadequate educational facilities and standards; they inspire similar demonstrations across the West	
	1969 *El Espejo* (*The Mirror*), the first anthology of Chicano literature, is published; University of California at Berkeley launches nation's first Chicano studies program; Vietnam War drives thousands of Asians to America	
1970	1970 30 percent of Chinese American husbands and 22 percent of Chinese American wives have non-Chinese spouses (in sixteen- to twenty-four-year old age group)	1970 *In Nueva York* by Nicholasa Mohr
	1971–80 Latin American immigrants comprise 40 percent of the legal immigrants to the U.S.; Asians comprise 35 percent	

	Historical Events	Literary Works Set in the Period
	1972 Gloria Steinem founds *Ms.* magazine; Congress passes women's Equal Rights Amendment (it is never ratified)	
	1973 5 million Puerto Ricans migrate annually to American mainland, not all of them permanently	
	1974 Supreme Court rules in *Lau v. Nicols* that "education on equal terms," a right of American students, is not provided by merely giving everyone the same textbooks, teachers, and curriculum; the case is used as justification for more strident bilingual education provisions	
1975	1975 Agricultural Labor Relations Act gives California farm workers right of collective bargaining; 40 percent of college graduates are women; 50 percent of women hold jobs outside the home	
	1978 Congress amends Bilingual Education Act to read that a language other than English could be used "only to the extent necessary to allow a child to achieve competence in the English language"	
1980	1980–88 Under Ronald Reagan, funding for education drops 8 percent and spending related to bilingual education drops 46 percent	
	1981 Senator S. I. Hayakawa (California) sponsors bill that would make English the official language of the United States (bill is never passed)	
1985		
1990	1990s San Francisco's Chinatown has 30,000 inhabitants within 24-block area, the second densest population in America (after parts of Manhattan)	early 1990s *Donald Duk* by Frank Chin

RESURGENCE OF NORTH AMERICAN INDIANS

Associated with the rise of multicultural America was the growth of a movement championing the native populations of North America. Beginning in the late 1960s, American Indians commanded the attention of the mainstream population. Political activists brought the plight of the urban Indian as well as the reservation dweller to the forefront while culturally oriented activists conveyed the strengths of tribal cultures and the Indian experience in works that informed the general public in both Canada and the United States.

	Historical Events	Literary Works Set in the Period
		1934–84 *Love Medicine* by Louise Erdrich
1960		1960s *I Heard the Owl Call My Name* by Margaret Craven
	1966-67 In Canada, government report (the Hawthorn report) documents poverty of Indians, advises that Indians not be pressured to adopt non-Indian values of Canadian society.	
	1968 In United States, American Indian Movement (AIM) is founded to protect and promote Indian civil rights, becomes the spokesgroup especially for off-reservation, urban Indians	
	1969 Indians begin a "Red Power" movement, seizing control of Alcatraz Island in San Francisco Bay	
1970		1970s–80s *A Yellow Raft in Blue Water* by Michael Dorris

Historical Events	Literary Works Set in the Period
1972 Red Power activists occupy Washington, D.C., office of Bureau of Indian Affairs	
1973 Red Power activists occupy the town of Wounded Knee, South Dakota—armed conflict follows	
1975 Indian Self-Determination and Education Assistance Act supports tribal independence and Indian management of benefits received from U.S. government	
1978 American Indian Religious Freedom Act guarantees the right of Indians to practice traditional religions	
1980 1980s Tribes take U.S. government to court over water, resources, and fishing and mineral rights	
1984 Survey indicates that of the 182,000 American Indian families living on or near reservations, 33,097 are homeless	
1985 Survey shows that three times as many Indians as non-Indians in the United States die from alcohol-related causes—35 percent of Indian deaths are related to alcohol	
1990 1990 Museums across the nation are required by law (Native American Grave Protection and Repatriation Act) to return tribal remains and historical artifacts	

MID- TO LATE TWENTIETH-CENTURY LATIN AMERICAN UNREST

South of the American border, the Spanish-speaking nations of Central and South America underwent politically and socially tumultuous times in the mid- to late twentieth century. War, intrigue, and human rights abuse characterize much of this period, as demonstrated by literary works set in Argentina, Chile, Guatemala, and Peru. Continuing to view the world in terms of the opposing forces of communism and democracy, the United States supported anticommunist activities Cuba in the early 1960s. Continuing to take this approach in Latin America, the U.S. government proceeded to support some shockingly undemocratic and unpopular regimes over the ensuing decades.

Historical Events	Literary Works Set in the Period
	1910–1973 *The House of the Spirits* by Isabel Allende
1940	
1946–55 Juan Perón elected president of Argentina	
1947 Women are given full voting rights in Argentina	
1948–56 General Manuel Odría takes over government of Peru, forms a military junta, and initiates eight-year rule characterized by oppression and brutality	
1950	1950s *The Time of the Hero* by Mario Vargas Llosa
1952 Chilean women are given full voting rights	
1954 CIA-sponsored coup in Guatemala deposes left-leaning leader Jacobo Guzmán, puts army in charge; anti-U.S. sentiment takes strong root in Latin America	
1955–83 Government leadership changes in Argentina sixteen times	

Historical Events	Literary Works Set in the Period
1960	
1961 President John F. Kennedy promises in his inaugural address to oppose communist aggression in the Americas; United States backs Bay of Pigs fiasco in Cuba, in which 1,400 Cuban exiles fail to depose Fidel Castro; Castro makes Cuba the first communist nation in Western hemisphere	1961 Inaugural Address by John F. Kennedy
1962 Soviets construct launching sites and place missiles in Cuba, leading to Cuban Missile Crisis, a Soviet-U.S. standoff that after a tense period, is resolved peacefully	
1970 1970 Salvador Allende becomes president of Chile, forming first Marxist government to be elected in Western Hemisphere	1970s–80s *Imagining Argentina* by Lawrence Thornton
1971 Chilean poet Pablo Neruda wins Nobel Prize for Literature; in the "March of the Empty Pots," 5,000 Chilean women protest food shortages	
1971–72 Antigovernment agrarian protests in Chile; strikes paralyze county; massive protests of government economic reform	
1973 Chilean economy is on brink of collapse; President Allende dies in political coup by Chilean army under General August Pinochet; 3,000–30,000 Chileans killed; concentration camps appear in the north and south of the nation	
1973–74 Juan Perón becomes president of Argentina again in September 1973 but dies the following July	
1976 Argentine president Maria Estela Perón forced out of power by Argentine generals, who dismiss Congress and legalize use of death penalty for political purposes	
1976–84 Argentine generals cause up to 10,000 people to disappear	
1977 Mothers of the Plaza de Mayo gather in front of Argentine government headquarters to protest the disappearance of their children and relatives; they meet there every Thursday for ten years, demanding information about the disappeared	
late 1970s–80s Return to civilian rule in Argentina, Ecuador, Peru, Brazil, and Uruguay	
1980 1980 In Peru, Fernando Belaúnde becomes president again, after a dozen years of military rule	1980s *The Bean Trees* by Barbara Kingsolver
1982-83 Efraín Ríos Montt rules in Guatemala until he is overthrown by Oscar Humberto Mejia Victores, who promises to grant all citizens voting rights and to respect human rights; mass killings, kidnappings, and disappearances, directed at the intellectual and native communities, become legion; thousands of Guatemalans flee to Mexico and the U.S.	
1983 Argentina loses Falkland War to Britain; generals forced to schedule democratic election that fall	
1985 Argentine generals are put on trial for genocide; seven receive light sentences, two receive life in prison	
1990 1990 Three Argentine generals still in prison are pardoned by Argentine president Carlos Menem; Mario Vargas Llosa wins presidency in Peru	
1991 Jorge Serrano Elías elected Guatemalan president; political mayhem in that country subsides	

VIETNAM WAR

Committing itself to fighting the Cold War not only in Latin America but also in Southeast Asia, for nearly a decade the United States committed troops to the fight against the communist forces in Vietnam. Becoming the longest war the United States had ever waged, the Vietnam War took the lives of some 58,000 Americans. Great controversy surrounded questions of the wisdom and rectitude of American participation. Thanks to television coverage, the war entered the living room of every American family, and increased passions and tensions between those who opposed participation in the war and those who favored it.

1950

1954 French forces are defeated at Dien Bien Phu in Vietnam; international conference in Geneva, Switzerland, divides Vietnam into North and South, arranges for cease-fire

1960 1960 National Liberation Front (or "Vietcong") challenges rule of U.S.-supported government of Ngo Dinh Diem

1961 Kennedy administration sends vice president Lyndon Johnson from U.S. to South Vietnam to bolster government morale; by December American advisers begin to arrive in the country

1963 President Kennedy is assassinated; 16,700 American so-called "advisers" in Vietnam

1964 Alleged North Vietnamese attacks on U.S. vessels in Gulf of Tonkin; Congress passes Tonkin Gulf Resolution to declare support for President Lyndon Johnson's policy in Vietnam; America begins bombing North Vietnam

1965 United States builds U.S. force in Vietnam to 184,000

1966 U.S. steps up bombing of Vietnam

1967 Martin Luther King, Jr. leads anti-Vietnam War protest at United Nations building in New York City; for refusing to fight in Vietnam, Muhammad Ali is stripped of heavyweight boxing title

1968 Half a million American troops in Vietnam

1969 First American troops are withdrawn from Vietnam; G. I. Movement of soldiers against the Vietnam War reaches peak

1970 1970 In Ohio, National Guardsmen kill four students during an antiwar protest at Kent State University

1973 Paris Accord—U.S. signs peace treaty with Vietnam

1975 South Vietnam surrenders; war ends

1976 Vietnam is unified under communist rule

1977 President Jimmy Carter pardons Vietnam draft evaders

1980

1982 Vietnam War Memorial is erected in Washington, D.C.

1990

1991 One-quarter to one-third of American's homeless (approximately half a million people) are Vietnam veterans

1967–68 *Fallen Angels* by Walter Dean Myers

1967–69 *The Runner* by Cynthia Voigt

COUNTERCULTURE MOVEMENT AND ITS AFTERMATH

Preoccupied with racial relations and the Vietnam War in the 1960s, a great many of America's young people agitated for change. Critical of mainstream society, they rejected conventional ways of thinking and behaving, registering their discontent politically through demonstrations, boycotts, and speeches and artistically through song, story, and artwork. A growing number of the young experimented with drugs and alternative lifestyles, affecting other youths who rebelled in less overt ways and encouraging mainstream society to be more critical of itself. The teenage subculture that had first appeared in the 1950s grew more distinct, while the generation gap between young and old grew more pronounced. In mainstream society, the American family underwent fundamental change as divorce rates climbed, a trend that, along with drug use, would continue to affect the young in subsequent generations.

	Historical Events	Literary Works Set in the Period
1940		1940s–80s *The Prince of Tides* by Pat Conroy
1950	1950s 70 percent of American families consist of working father, at-home mother; adolescent psychotherapy becomes accepted field of study	mid–late 1900s *Watership Down* by Richard Adams
1960	1960s American youth protest racial segregation and the Vietnam War, which many feel to be an old men's war in which young men will die; members of counterculture movement advocate drug use, free love, and rejection of traditional American capitalist values	1960s *The Outsiders* by S. E. Hinton
	1960s–70s Discontent with established churches leads to rise of evangelical preachers and to growth of religious sects like the Hare Krishna	
	1960 1,300 American teens attempt suicide	
	1962 *Silent Spring* by Rachel Carson is published, alerting Americans to the deadly effects of their use of pesticides	
	1964 Congress passes Land and Water Conservation Fund Act; students at University of California at Berkeley stage most publicized campus protest	
		mid-1960s *I Never Sang for My Father* by Robert Anderson
	1966 Congress passes Endangered Species Preservation Act	
	1966–76 Divorce rate doubles in the United States	
	1968 Democratic National Convention in Chicago disrupted by anti-Vietnam war protesters; police unleash brutal attack	late 1960s *The Pigman* by Paul Zindel
		late 1960s *Bless the Beasts and the Children* by Glendon Swarthout
1970	1970s Counterculture social protest evolves into "do your own thing" philosophy of early 1970s—the period is labeled "the Me Decade"; people embrace solitary activities like jogging; affirmative action admits minority students into universities	1970 *His Own Where* by June Jordan
		early 1970s *The Chocolate War* by Robert Cormier
		mid-1970s *Ordinary People* by Judith Guest
	1970s–80s Environmental activists campaign against nuclear power	late 1970s *Carrie* by Stephen King
	1979 Accident in nuclear reactor at Three Mile Island, Pennsylvania, helps ignite opposition to nuclear power	
	1980s Divorce rate is 50 percent in American marriages	
	1986 Accident at nuclear power plant in Chernobyl in Soviet Union further reduces confidence of U.S. public in nuclear power	

Historical Events	Literary Works Set in the Period
1989 President George Bush calls drug abuse severest U.S. problem	
1990	early 1990s *Understand This* by Jervey Tervalon

REAGAN'S AMERICA

Serving as president of the United States from 1981–89, Ronald Reagan ushered in a highly conservative era in American politics and culture. Reagan cut social welfare, education, environmental spending, and funds for the arts, also initiating tax cuts that were of most benefit to the rich. Meanwhile, he increased the defense budget astronomically, halted antitrust investigations against big business, and proposed a nuclear defense system, called "Star Wars" by scientists who doubted that it could work and protested that such a system would only heighten Cold War tensions. Changing his attitude at the end of his term, Reagan entered an agreement that reduced Cold War tensions.

	Historical Events	Literary Works Set in the Period
1980		1980s *Angels in America* by Tony Kushner
		1980s *Sweet Whispers, Brother Rush* by Virginia Hamilton
1981	1981 Congress approves Reagan's request to cut over $35 billion from welfare, Medicare, and other domestic programs; researchers discover the AIDS virus	
	1981–86 16,000 Americans die of AIDS	
1982	1982 American economy suffers a recession; unemployment is at 10.8 percent, black unemployment exceeds 20 percent	
1983	1983 U.S. increases aid to Guatemala and El Salvador; American marines invade island of Grenada and depose its leftist government	
	1983–88 10 million Americans lose their jobs	
1984	1984 Reagan is elected to second term; Congress votes to cut off aid to rebel *contras* in their effort to overthrow leftist government in Nicaragua; Reagan proposes "Star Wars" defense system	
1985	1985 Reagan secretly endorses Iran-Contra plan (release of American hostages in Lebanon linked to American sale of weapons to Iran, with profits being funneled to the *contras* in Nicaragua)	
1986	1986 Poverty plagues 33 million Americans—14 percent of population; Iran-Contra scandal is made public	
1987	1987 Stock market crashes	
	1987–88 U.S.-Soviet reach first agreement to destroy deployed nuclear weapons—agreement bans shorter- and medium-range missiles	

Historical Events	Literary Works Set in the Period

ERA OF THE SPACE RACE AND FUTURE TIMES

The Cold War between the United States and the Soviet Union took to the heavens in the late 1950s as the superpowers competed to achieve firsts in space. All eyes turned to the skies while men orbited the earth, walked on the moon, and sent probes to neighboring planets. These efforts, as well as alleged sightings of Unidentified Flying Objects (UFOs), fed the imaginations of many. Drawing on experience as well as their imaginations, science fiction writers envisioned future worlds in which technology often played a dominant role.

1940

1945 Science fiction gains widespread respectability after U. S. drops atomic bombs on Hiroshima and Nagasaki

1945–46 Major publishers print anthologies of science fiction stories

1947–63 *The Right Stuff* by Tom Wolfe

1950

1950s Number of science fiction magazines soars; stories focus on scientists and gadgetry; most science fiction writers are men

1957 Soviet Union launches Sputnik I, the first artificial satellite, which begins the "space race"; panicked, the U.S. founds the National Aeronautics and Space Administration (NASA)

1958 U.S. launches first satellite, Explorer I

1960

1960s New type of science fiction emerges—focus shifts from scientists and gadgetry to average people and the effects of science on them; an increasing number of science fiction writers are women

1961 Soviet cosmonaut Yuri Alekseyevich Gargarin, aboard Vostok I, is first man in space; American astronauts Alan Shepard and John Glenn follow him up shortly; upon election, President Kennedy emphasizes the importance of beating the Russians in space

1961 Inaugural Address by John F. Kennedy

1963 Vostok 6 takes first woman into space

1965 Soviet cosmonaut is first man to walk in space; Americans succeed in replicating the feat in the same year

1966 U.S. makes unmanned landing on the moon

1967 Aboard Soyuz I, the first man, a Soviet, is killed in space

1969 American astronaut Neil Armstrong is first man to walk on moon

1970

1970s–future *Childhood's End* by Arthur C. Clarke

1972 U.S. launches Pioneer 10, which will send back photos of Jupiter by 1973; Mariner IX completes a year-long mapping mission of Mars; the Russians land Venera 8 on the surface of Venus

1973 Russians land probe on Mars; Mariner X sends pictures of Venus to U.S.; American "Skylab" project, which will photograph earth and sun, begins

1973 *Pilgrim at Tinker Creek* by Annie Dillard

1975 First U.S.-Soviet joint mission occurs—crews of Apollo 18 and Soyuz 19 share meals

Historical Events	Literary Works Set in the Period
1976–82 Viking 1 and Viking 2 spacecraft, sent to search for life on Mars, map the planet's surface and transmit 56,500 photographs to U.S.	
1980	
1983 Challenger spaceflights (STS-7 and STS-8) take first U.S. woman astronaut and first African American astronaut into space	
1984 Soviet crew spends record 237 days in space on Soyuz T-10	1984 *Nineteen Eighty-Four* by George Orwell
1988 Soviets spend record 355 days in space on Soyuz TM-7	
1990	
1997 U.S. lands Pathfinder spacecraft on Mars, from which robot car (Sojourner) emerges, becoming first vehicle to wander over the surface of another planet	
2000	early 2000s *The Handmaid's Tale* by Margaret Atwood
	early 2000s *Stranger in a Strange Land* by Robert A. Heinlein
2500	2500s *Brave New World* by Aldous Huxley
future	future *Dune* by Frank Herbert
	future *Fahrenheit 451* by Ray Bradbury
	future *Foundation* by Isaac Asimov
	future *House of Stairs* by William Sleator
	future *Left Hand of Darkness* by Ursula K. Le Guin

Historical Events	Literary Works Set in the Period

Contents by Title

Contents by Title

Contents by Author

Contents
by Author

Photo Credits

Joseph McCarthy and Roy Cohn, photograph. By Walter Bennett. Time-Life Syndications. Reproduced by permission. —Tony Kushner, photograph. AP/Wide World Photos, Inc. Reproduced by permission. —Nation of Islam National Convention, photograph. UPI/Corbis-Bettmann. Reproduced by permission. —Martin Luther King, Jr., and Malcolm X, photograph. AP/Wide World Photos, Inc. Reproduced by permission. —Freed slaves leaving the South in ox-carts, photograph. The Library of Congress. —Civil Rights protester attacked by policeman and dog, Birmingham, Alabama, photograph. AP/Wide World Photos, Inc. Reproduced by permission. —Barbara Kingsolver, photograph. AP/Wide World Photos, Inc. Reproduced by permission. —Dust Jacket of *The Bean Trees* by Barbara Kingsolver, illustration. Harper & Row. Reproduced with permission. — Buffalo kill, photograph. National Audio Visual Center. Reproduced by permission. —Model T Assembly line, photograph. AP/Wide World Photos, Inc. Reproduced by permission. —Henry Ford, photograph. —Sissy Spacek in a scene from the 1976 film adaptation of *Carrie* by Stephen King, photograph. Archive Photos/United Artists. Reproduced by permission. —Gloria Steinem and Betty Friedan signing ER-Agram, photograph. UPI/Corbis-Bettmann. Reproduced by permission. —Cover of *Fate* magazine, November 1954, illustration. Mary Evans Picture Library. Reproduced by permission. —UFO, photograph. AP/Wide World Photos,

Inc. Reproduced by permission. —Robert Cormier, photograph. By Beth Bergman. Reproduced by permission. —Woodstock, photograph. UPI/Corbis-Bettmann. Reproduced by permission. —Elijah Muhammad, photograph. AP/Wide World Photos, Inc. Reproduced by permission. —Muhammad Ali and Leon Spinks, photograph. UPI/Bettmann Newsphotos. Reproduced by permission. —Chinese New Year, photograph. AP/Wide World Photos, Inc. Reproduced by permission. —Chinese laborers employed by the Central Pacific in the Sierra Nevada, 1880, photograph. Association of American Railroads. Reproduced by permission.

Edwin E. Aldrin, Jr. on the moon's surface, photograph. U.S. National Aeronautics and Space Administration. —Allen Ginsberg, photograph. AP/Wide World Photos, Inc. Reproduced by permission. —Ralph Abernathy and Martin Luther King, Jr., photograph. AP/Wide World Photos, Inc. Reproduced by permission. —Flannery O'-Connor, photograph. The Library of Congress. —Ray Bradbury, photograph. By Thomas Victor. Reproduced by permission. — Captain Oliver Murray, Brigadier General F. Davison, and soldiers, South Vietnam, 1968, photograph. AP/Wide World Photos, Inc. Reproduced by permission. —Vietnam Memorial Wall, photograph. By S. Scott Applewhite. AP/Wide World Photos, Inc. Reproduced by permission. —Martin Luther King, Jr. arm in arm at March on Washington, photograph. AP/Wide World Photos, Inc. Reproduced by permission. —James Baldwin, photograph. AP/Wide World Photos, Inc. Reproduced by permission. —Toussaint L'Ouverture, drawing. —Laurie Carlos and Ntozake Shange, photograph. UPI/Bettmann. Reproduced by permission. —Atomic explosion, photograph. UPI/Corbis-Bettmann. Reproduced by permission. —Early UNIVAC mainframe computer, photograph. The Library of Congress. —Ernest J. Gaines, photograph. © Jerry Bauer. Reproduced by permission. —Phyllis Schlafly, photograph. AP/Wide World Photos, Inc. Reproduced by permission. —Jerry Falwell, photograph. AP/Wide World Photos, Inc. Reproduced by permission. —Stokely Carmichael, photograph. AP/Wide World Photos, Inc. Reproduced by permission. —Alice Childress, photograph. © Jerry Bauer. Reproduced by permission. —June Jordan, photograph. AP/Wide World Photos, Inc. Reproduced by permission. —B. F. Skinner, photograph. The Library of Congress. —John W. Dean, photograph. UPI/Corbis-Bettmann. Reproduced by permission. —Salvador Allende, photograph. UPI/Bettmann. Reproduced by permission. —August Pinochet, photograph. AP/Wide World Photos, Inc. Reproduced by permission. —Américo Paredes, photograph. By Ralph Barrera. Reproduced by permission.

Sandra Cisneros, photograph. AP/Wide World Photos, Inc. Reproduced by permission. —Mural "The Great Wall of Los Angeles" by Judith Baca, photograph. By Jacinto Quirarte. Reproduced by permission. —Richard Rodriguez, photograph. National Catholic Reporter/Arthur Jones. Reproduced by permission. —Martin Luther King, Jr., photograph. AP/Wide World Photos, Inc. Reproduced by permission. —Martin Luther King, Jr., photograph. AP/Wide World Photos, Inc. Reproduced by permission. —Kwakiutl Indian aboard the H.M.S. Boxer, photograph. By Richard Maynard. Royal British Columbia Museum. —Goods gathered for a potlatch at Alert Bay, British Columbia, photograph. Royal British Columbia Museum. —Michael Landon and Lorne Green, on "Bonanza," photograph. AP/Wide World Photos, Inc. Reproduced by permission. —Theodore Roosevelt, photograph. Theodore Roosevelt Collection, Harvard College Library. Reproduced by permission. —Eva and Juan Perón, photograph. AP/Wide World Photos, Inc. Reproduced by permission. —Mothers of the Plaza de Mayo, Buenos Aires, Argentina, photograph. From *The Disappeared and the Mothers of the Plaza: The Story of the 11,000 Argen-tineans Who Vanished* by John Simpson and Jana Bennett. St. Martin's Press. Copyright © 1985 by John Simpson and Jana Bennett. Reproduced by permission of Robson Books, Ltd. —Children playing in a vacant lot, Brooklyn, New York, photograph. By Geoffrey Biddle. From *Alphabet City* by Geoffrey Biddle. University of California Press, 1992. © 1992 by Geoffrey Biddle. Reproduced by permission of the author. —Nicholasa Mohr, photograph. By Larry Racioppo. Courtesy of Nicholasa Mohr. —John F. Kennedy and Lyndon Johnson, photograph. Photograph No. SC5789902 in the John F. Kennedy Library. —John F. Kennedy, photograph. The Library of Congress. —Meeting of the Workingmen's Party in California, photograph. The Library of Congress. —Kiev Chinh, in a scene from the film adaptation of *The Joy Luck Club* by Amy Tan, photograph. Fotos International/Archive Photos, Inc. Reproduced by permission.

John F. Kennedy and Robert McNamara, photograph. Photograph No. ST-A26-23-62 in the John F. Kennedy Library. —Ursula K. Le Guin, photograph. UPI/Bettmann. Reproduced by permission. —Rocky Boy (Stone Child), photograph. National Archives and Records Administration. —Clyde Bellecourt, photograph. AP/Wide World Photos, Inc. Reproduced by permission. —Map of the world as depicted in *Nineteen Eighty-Four* by George Orwell, illustration. Stanford Alumni Association. Reproduced by permission. —John Hurt in a scene from the 1984 film adaptation of *Nineteen Eighty-Four* by George Orwell, photograph. The Kobal Collection. Reproduced by permission. —Mary Tyler Moore and Timothy Hutton in a scene from the 1980 film adaptation of *Ordinary People* by Judith Guest, photograph. The Kobal Collection. Reproduced by permission. —Judith Guest, photograph. AP/Wide World Photos, Inc. Reproduced by permission. —S. E. Hinton, photograph. By Thomas Victor. Reproduced by permission. —Police struggling with youth at the Democratic National Convention in Chicago, photograph. UPI/Corbis-Bettmann. Reproduced by permission. —Old woman sitting on a veranda, photograph. By Ann Zane Shanks. From *Old Is What You Get: Dialogues on Aging by the Old and the Young.* By Ann Zane Shanks. Viking Press, 1976. Copyright © 1976 by Ann Zane Shanks. Reproduced by permission of Ann Zane Shanks. —Mariner X space probe, photograph. U. S. National Aeronautics and Space Administration. —Annie Dillard, photograph. © Jerry Bauer. Re-

Angels in America

by

Tony Kushner

Born in 1956 in New York City, Tony Kushner moved with his family to Louisiana shortly thereafter. Kushner's mother was an actress, and he credits her performances with inspiring him to go into theater. Kushner studied theater back in New York, graduating with a master's in fine arts from New York University in 1984. He went on to write several plays before creating *Angels in America,* a seven-hour drama separated into two parts that deal with, among other issues, the experiences of being gay and contracting the disease AIDS in the United States during the 1980s and 1990s.

> ## THE LITERARY WORK
>
> A pair of plays (*Part One, Millennium Approaches* and *Part Two, Perestroika*) set primarily in New York City 1985-90; *Part One* first performed in 1991, *Part Two* in 1992.
>
> ## SYNOPSIS
>
> Set against a backdrop of politics and religion in the 1980s, a disparate group of people—gay and straight—face the specter of AIDS and learn to support one another.

Events in History at the Time the Plays Take Place

Reagan's America. The two-term presidency of Republican Ronald Reagan (1981-89) set the tone for American life in the 1980s. Riding a wave of conservatism in religion, social policy, and international relations, Reagan made cuts in federal social welfare, education, and environmental spending and in funds for the arts. At the same time, his administration increased the defense budget astronomically and halted antitrust investigations against big business. Among Reagan's major achievements was the passage of two landmark tax bills, reducing the personal income tax rate, in some cases by up to 42 percent. Americans rejoiced, but not for long.

By 1982, America was in the middle of a serious recession: bank failures rose, as did the unemployment rate. Nearly 10 million Americans lost their jobs between 1983 and 1988. Throughout it all, the social message was clear: individuals had to take responsibility for their own welfare and not rely on the government to come to their rescue. One view that was often voiced held that government aid was demeaning to the recipients and hampered them from participating in the American dream of one day becoming rich.

Federal courts in the Reagan years. Three of the main characters in *Angels in America*—Roy Cohn, Louis Ironson, and Joe Pitt—work in some capacity for the American justice system during the Reagan presidency; Roy Cohn is a famous Republican lawyer, Joe Pitt is the chief clerk for a federal appeals court judge, and Louis Ironson is a word processor for the Second Circuit court of appeals. Throughout the plays, the Republican Party is taken to task for its social programs (or lack thereof) and for its callous judicial record.

Some historians have argued that in fact Reagan-appointed Supreme Court judges "voted together to strike at civil rights laws adopted for minorities, women, and the disabled" (Schwartz, p. 131). And indeed a number of cases decided during the Reagan administration had this effect. *Grove City College vs. Bell,* for example, concerned Title IX of the 1972 education act, which banned sex discrimination in federally funded education programs. Until the case, the ban was applied generally to all programs at any school that received federal aid. Reagan's position, approved by the Supreme Court in a 6-3 vote, was that the ban should apply not to an entire school but only to the program that received the aid.

TONY KUSHNER ON THE AMERICAN CULT OF THE INDIVIDUAL

In the Afterword of *Perestroika,* Kushner reflects on some of the people and the social forces that compelled him to write *Angels in America.* Chief among the social pressures was individualism, which became the dominant social model of the Reagan years in America.

We pay high prices for the maintenance of the myth of the Individual: we have no system of universal health care, we don't educate our children, we can't pass sane gun control laws, we elect presidents like Reagan, we hate and fear inevitable processes like aging and death, and on and on.

(Kushner, Afterword, p. 150)

Roy Cohn. Kushner writes a disclaimer at the beginning of both *Millennium Approaches* and *Perestroika,* in which he acknowledges that he at least partially fictionalizes Roy Cohn in his plays. The real-life Roy Cohn, the inspiration for the character in the plays, rose to prominence in the early 1950s and by his death in 1986 had become an infamous figure. His illegal manipulations of the spy case against Julius and Ethel Rosenberg, the case that made him famous, are a matter of historical record. The Rosenberg trial is now recognized as one of the lowest points in America's judicial history.

In 1949 the United States was shocked to learn that Joseph Stalin's Soviet Union suddenly had an atom bomb to match America's. Reliable sources had reported the Soviets to be still ten years away from creating an atomic bomb: the

American government suspected treason. Their investigation finally settled on Ethel Rosenberg, a Jewish housewife from the Lower East Side of Manhattan, and her husband Julius; both were known to have communist leanings. The chief witness for the prosecution was David Greenglass, Ethel's younger brother, who claimed to have divulged to the Rosenbergs the secrets of the atom bomb that he had learned while stationed at Los Alamos (a nuclear testing sight in the New Mexico desert) during World War II. Although they pleaded innocent, the Rosenbergs were executed in 1953 for the crime of passing on atomic secrets to the Soviets.

At the time of the Rosenberg trial, Roy Cohn was a twenty-three-year-old assistant U.S. attorney. During the trial, he questioned prosecution witnesses on the stand, and he later claimed to have written the opening and closing statements for the prosecution. As it turned out, Cohn also communicated privately with the judge on the case—one-sided contacts labeled *ex parte* and branded as unethical because they were unknown to the other side. Cohn's discussions with Judge Kaufman reportedly influenced the judge's decision to sentence the Rosenbergs to death.

The larger cultural context for the Rosenberg affair was the "red scare" that gripped America in the 1950s. In the wake of World War II, and the Soviet domination of Eastern Europe, people feared that communists were infiltrating the highest echelons of society in preparation for a takeover of America. The most prominent person fanning the flames was Wisconsin senator Joseph R. McCarthy, who transformed himself from an obscure and shady opportunist into the nation's most powerful politician, primarily by making groundless accusations about other people being communists. McCarthy accused numerous government officials and famous Americans (generally actors, writers, and artists) of having communist sympathies. In February of 1950 the American public heard on the radio the first of what came to be known as McCarthy's "witch-hunts": those suspected of having communist sympathies or ties were questioned before McCarthy's Subcommittee on Un-American Activities. Chief counsel to Senator McCarthy was none other than Roy Cohn.

In his later years, Cohn became a high-profile lawyer who specialized in representing glittering society names in divorce proceedings. Also he dealt covertly with the elite and powerful in New York and Washington, D.C. Shortly before his death in 1986, Cohn was disbarred for profes-

Senator Joseph McCarthy and Roy Cohn during the House Un-American Activities Committee
Meetings.

sional misconduct. It later became well known that Cohn was a closeted homosexual who died from AIDS.

Mormonism and Joseph Smith Jr. *Angels in America* makes liberal use of the story about the inception of the Mormon faith (also known as the Church of Jesus Christ of Latter-Day Saints). It is a story that features angels; golden books of prophecy; emphasis on the family, order, and tradition; and faith in the approaching millennium. In particular, Kushner draws on the legendary experiences of Joseph Smith Jr., the founder of Mormonism, to create Prior Walter's apocalyptic vision in *Perestroika.*

Mormon tradition has it that on September 21, 1823, a blinding light awoke eighteen-year-old Joseph Smith Jr. in his family's Palmyra, New York, cabin. Hovering in the air was the Angel Moroni, who quoted prophecies from the Bible about the last days of Earth and the coming of Christ. The angel told Smith that he was to do God's work, then graced him with a prophetic vision.

ROY COHN ON ETHEL ROSENBERG

In *Millennium Approaches,* Roy Cohn tells Joe Pitt proudly what he did to get ahead as a lawyer. The tale, which involves illegality and murder, sums up the role of individualist extraordinaire: "That sweet unprepossessing woman, two kids, boo-hoo-hoo, reminded us all of our little Jewish mamas—she came this close to getting life; I pleaded till I wept to put her in the chair. Me. I did that. I would have fucking pulled the switch if they'd have let me. Why? Because I fucking hate traitors. Because I fucking hate communists. Was it legal? Fuck legal. Am I a nice man? Fuck nice. . . . You want to be Nice, or you want to be Effective?" (Kushner, *Millennium Approaches,* p. 108).

The next day, Smith visited the Hill Cumorah, three miles southeast of the Smith farm. He dug up a box made up of five stones set in cement, just as the Angel Moroni had shown him. Inside the box were gold plates upon which was written a Gospel—*The Book of Mormon.* Also inside the box were the Urim and Thummim—two stones set in silver frames, like spectacles (such as those Prior Walter is given by his angel), and fastened to a breastplate. The stones were to be used in translating the plates, although Smith was

not instructed to translate them for another four years. The inscribed plates were allegedly written by Mormon, a military figure who led his people, the Nephites, from 327 to 385 A.D. Additional sections of *The Book of Mormon* were composed by Mormon's son Moroni, (who became the visitation angel), and by Nephi, in Mormon tradition one of the first migrants from Palestine to America back in 600 B.C. Included in the plates that Joseph Smith Jr. received were pages on which was written a vision of the world's end.

According to Smith, the *Book of Mormon* provided a history of ancient America that showed how Christianity and the Bible had become corrupted. (Among other assertions, it records that the Indians, originally from the tribes of Israel, were brought by God to America, the new promised land.) He believed he had been given the authority to restore the true church of God to the world. As one historian describes the movement:

> Reading *The Book of Mormon* it seems clear that many Americans wished, in the depths of their hearts, to believe in a new, purified order of humanity in the United States. They wished to be free of the burden of history. . . . They wished to solve the dilemma of sexuality and to preserve the family inviolate against the disintegrative forces of the insatiable land.
> (Smith, p. 568)

Thousands of disaffected Americans joined the Mormon church and moved west to find land on which they could live together peacefully. They were driven by fearful or scornful neighbors from Kirtland, Ohio, to Independence, Missouri, to Far West, Missouri, to Illinois, and finally to the Great Salt Lake in Utah, where they remained. Joseph Smith himself was killed in Carthage, Illinois, by a mob who stormed the jail cell where he was locked up for advocating, among other things, the practice of polygamy, or having multiple wives. His religion lived on, though, growing to include 7 million members by 1990, becoming the only worldwide religion to have begun in the United States.

Mormonism and homosexuality. According to D. Michael Quinn, a former history professor at Brigham Young University, until the mid-1950s Mormons accepted intimate same-sex relationships. The year 1958 proved pivotal in their attitude, beginning with a series of arrests of men in Salt Lake City for same-sex crimes. Later that year Allen Drury's *Advise and Consent* was published. The Pulitzer-Prize winning novel features a Mormon senator from Utah, a family man who once had an affair with another man and is now so publicly humiliated over it that he commits suicide. Not at all happy about such links between their faith and homosexuality, Mormon leaders started talking about this "growing problem" (Quinn, p. 377). Brigham Young University began aversion therapy to "cure" the same-sex impulses of young men, showing them erotic pictures and punishing them with 1,600-volts to the arm for eight seconds if they responded improperly (Quinn, p. 379). By 1974 Mormon Church president Spencer W. Kimball was speaking publicly against homosexuality, and his talks gained fame through newspapers outside Utah, including the *New York Times*. In 1976 a person's "homosexuality," rather than "homosexual acts," became grounds for excommunication from the Mormon Church; also that year one of the Mormon leaders advised young men to beat up male missionaries who showed homosexual interest (Quinn, pp. 382-83).

The Plays in Focus

The plot—*Part One: Millennium Approaches*. The plays unfold in a nonlinear fashion, with scenes often overlapping and occurring out of chronological order. Act 1 of *Part One* opens in late 1985, during the middle of the Reagan presidency. In his Manhattan law office, Roy M. Cohn, an attorney facing disbarment for professional misconduct, attempts to entice Joseph (Joe) Pitt, clerk for a federal justice, to move to Washington and work for the Justice Department under Attorney General Edwin Meese; Cohn secretly hopes that once in his new position, Joe will be able to help him out in his disbarment hearings. While Joe is flattered to have gained the support of a power broker as famous as Cohn, he hesitates, and insists that he consult with his wife.

Harper Pitt, Joe's wife, has emotional problems that her faith in Mormonism and her Valium addiction cannot cure. She hallucinates about travelling to international destinations, and it is during one such "trip" that her husband, Joe, also a Mormon, suggests that they move to Washington, D.C., so he can take up the lucrative post offered him by Cohn. Harper instead dwells on the poor state of their marriage, and she asks about the walks Joe takes every evening in their neighborhood.

Joe finds a fellow worker, Louis Ironson, crying in the men's room of the Brooklyn courthouse at which Joe clerks. Joe tries to comfort him, and Louis teases Joe about being that most

unlikely of creatures: a gay Republican lawyer. Startled, Joe denies that he is gay, and Louis returns to his live-in lover, Prior Walter. Prior has recently confessed to Louis that he now has fully developed AIDS, complete with bodily lesions. Although he does love Prior, Louis is frightened and revolted by Prior's illness, and his anguish leads to several bitter confrontations between them. Prior is hospitalized for a time, at which point Louis, despite his self-loathing for what he does, leaves the relationship.

In one of Harper's hallucinations, Prior inexplicably appears and tells her that Joe is homosexual. Harper confronts her husband about his sexuality; at first, he denies that he is gay, but eventually breaks down and admits that he takes his late-night "walks" in order to find anonymous male sex partners.

Roy Cohn's doctor, Henry, informs Cohn that he has contracted the HIV virus, which causes AIDS, and that the cause of the infection was homosexual intercourse. Cohn admits to having sex with men, but denies being "homosexual" and threatens to destroy the doctor's career should he reveal Cohn's disease to be anything other than liver cancer.

At Cohn's second and third meetings with Joe regarding the Department of Justice position, he adopts a paternal attitude and encourages Joe to leave his wife behind and move to Washington. However, Joe learns that hearings about Cohn are about to begin in Washington, and realizes that his mentor wants to use him somehow to prevent disbarment. Joe thinks that interfering with Cohn's disbarment hearings would be unethical, and he stalls yet again.

Joe calls his mother, Hannah Pitt, one night late from a pay phone in Central Park. He informs her that he is gay, but she pretends to ignore the news. Soon, however, she arranges to sell her house in Salt Lake City and heads for New York. Meanwhile, Harper has a hallucination in which she disappears to Antarctica. In fact, she really disappears, and Joe informs Cohn that, with his mother arriving and his wife missing, he can't possibly take the position in Washington. Cohn blows up at him and explains what it takes to "make it" in the world—revealing how Cohn himself illegally influenced the prosecution of Ethel Rosenberg and her husband for treason.

After Joe departs, Cohn doubles over in pain from his virus, and the executed Ethel Rosenberg appears and dials 911. Joe, meanwhile, follows Louis to a park bench and persuades Louis to take him home. As *Part One* concludes, some visions that Prior has had—including a great book on whose steel pages burns an inscribed Hebrew letter Aleph—culminate in the fabulous yet horrifying appearance of an Angel in Prior's own bedroom.

The plot—*Part Two: Perestroika.* It is now January 1986. Joe and Louis are having an affair, while Prior is preoccupied with his Angel and his own failing health. Prior calls a male nurse at the hospital and tells him of the Angel's visit from the end of *Part One*. The Angel shows Prior some Sacred Implements—a pair of bronze spectacles

---

PRINCE OF THE ALPHABET

In *Millennium Approaches*, Prior Walter, dying of AIDS, is visited by an angel who gives him a book on which burns the first letter of the Hebrew alphabet, Aleph (א). In the Hebrew tradition, the Hebrew alphabet, the "Alpha-Beis," is the very foundation of the universe. God is believed to have rearranged different combinations of the alphabet's letters, and the different spiritual forces created thereby brought the world's variety into existence, much as different combinations of atoms create different substances. Aleph is the first letter, the prince and best of the letters. It is regarded as the symbol of God, the letter that denotes God's oneness, sovereignty, and infiniteness. In fact, the Aleph is seen as a direct connection between heaven and earth. Its form resembles a ladder placed on the ground reaching heavenward, where the upper yud (an apostrophe-like character) denotes the celestial, the lower yud denotes the mundane, and the diagonal line connecting them is said to link man's physical and spiritual inclinations. The Aleph ultimately "conveys to man that—in order to free himself from earthly bondage—he must infuse his physical existence with spirituality so that he can ascend to the summit: the Divine" (Munk, p. 54).

---

with rocks where lenses should be, a direct allusion to the "seer stones" that enabled Joseph Smith to read *The Book of Mormon*. With the spectacles, Prior sees the end of the world and can read the magnificent book with steel pages that accompanies the glasses—a sacred text. The Angel tells him that God has abandoned heaven because the creation of humans unleashed a virus for change; humans explore, grow, and reproduce, which destabilizes both heaven and earth. Change rocks heaven (portrayed as a version of

San Francisco, complete with "heaven quakes") and threatens to destroy the entire universe. It is now Prior's job as prophet to tell the world to stand still until God returns to heaven.

Henry, Cohn's doctor, informs the male nurse that, even though Cohn's charts indicate he has cancer, Cohn is to be hospitalized on the floor for AIDS patients. Understanding the ruse, the nurse—his name is Belize and he is a former drag queen and homosexual himself—attends to Cohn and expresses his hatred for the homophobic, racist, anti-Semitic Jew. Nonetheless, Belize feels sympathy for the fellow gay man and advises Cohn to pull whatever strings he can to get a hold of the experimental drug AZT to fight the AIDS virus, which Cohn does.

Hannah Pitt now resides in her son's apartment in Brooklyn and works at the Mormon Visitors Center. When she receives a call that Harper has been taken into police custody for gnawing down a pine tree in the park, she retrieves her daughter-in-law and allows her to stay in the Diorama Room at the Center while Hannah works. It is there that Prior, researching angels, meets Harper in the flesh (they had met once before in each other's dream/hallucination), and they both fantasize that the Mormon dummies in the diorama come to life. Louis and Joe appear among the dummies, squabbling because Louis cannot fathom that Joe is a Mormon.

Louis tells Joe he must see Prior again. There is no reconciliation between the former lovers, however; Prior can only express his bitterness and anger at Louis, then flee. Prior drags Belize, who happens to be a former lover of his, to the courthouse to get a look at Louis's new lover, Joe, whereupon the male nurse reveals that Joe has come to visit Cohn at the hospital. Later Belize meets Louis at the Bethesda Fountain in Central Park and informs him that Joe is Cohn's "boy." Louis in turn confronts Joe with the gay-bashing legal decisions Joe has ghost-written as clerk for his mentally infirm Justice, and Joe punches him.

The dying Cohn learns from Ethel Rosenberg that he has been disbarred. While she enjoys his misery, Cohn pretends that he thinks Rosenberg is his mother. He tricks her into singing him a Yiddish love song and dies, smug that he has made Rosenberg, whom he sent to the electric chair, sing for him. Belize and Louis sneak into Cohn's room and steal the remaining AZT for Prior.

Elsewhere in the hospital, the Angel has returned—this time to Hannah as well as to Prior. In a scene that recalls the Genesis story of Jacob wrestling an angel to get a blessing from him,

Tony Kushner

Prior wrestles the Angel to make it renounce its prophecy regarding the end of the world, and wins ascent to heaven to return the sacred text. In heaven, Prior runs into Harper, then appears before the Council of Continental Principalities, a gathering of Angels who represent the continents of the world. He returns the prophetic book and insists that humans can't just stop and wait for God to return—they must continue to live. On his way home to earth, Prior spies Roy waist-deep in a smoldering pit, working out a legal defense for God's abandonment of mankind.

Back in his hospital bed, Prior receives the AZT pills from Louis and Belize. Louis tells Prior he wants to come back to him. After they profess their love for each other, Prior refuses Louis. Harper flies off to San Francisco as Joe sits alone in Brooklyn. The play closes four years later, as the still-living Prior, accompanied by Louis, Belize and Hannah, sits underneath the stone fountain of an angel:

> PRIOR: The fountain's not flowing now, they turn it off in the winter, ice in the pipes. But in the summer it's a sight to see. I want to be around to see it. I plan to be. I hope to be.
>
> This disease will be the end of many of us, but not nearly all, and the dead will be commemorated and will struggle on with the living, and we are not going away. We won't die secret deaths any more. The world only spins forward. We will be citizens. The time has come.
>
> Bye now.
>
> You are fabulous creatures, each and every one.
>
> And I bless you: *More Life.*
>
> The Great Work Begins.
>
> (*Perestroika,* p. 148)

Perestroika. In 1987 the Russian leader Mikhail Gorbachev wrote a book entitled *Perestroika,* which means "restructuring" in Russian. The process of social and political change had been taking place in the Soviet Union since Gorbachev came to power in 1985, and American publishers convinced Gorbachev to write a book explaining his reforms for an American audience. Gorbachev's stated desire is that two peoples who have historically disliked and mistrusted each other can somehow set aside their differences to ensure that the one world they share is not permanently destroyed by their hatred:

> [I]f the Russian word "perestroika" has easily entered the international lexicon, this is due to more than just interest in what is going on in the Soviet Union. Now the whole world needs restructuring . . . a fundamental change.

People feel this and understand this. They have to find their bearings, to understand the problems besetting mankind, to realize how they should live in the future. The restructuring is a must . . . for a world ridden with serious economic and ecological problems; for a world laden with poverty, backwardness and disease; for a human race now facing the urgent need of ensuring its own survival.

(Gorbachev, p. 254)

Kushner uses *Perestroika* as the title for the conclusion of *Angels in America* perhaps to suggest the idea of a revolutionary community—of people who traditionally fear and hate one another coming together to support and love each other. In the final scene of the play, just such a community has gathered: Louis and Prior, ex-lovers who have finally come to an understanding of what they mean to each other; Belize, the black drag queen who disliked Louis for his treatment of Prior; and Hannah, the Mormon mother of Louis's ex-lover, Joe, are all sitting together in a park, four years after the main action of the play.

Reactions to homosexuality and AIDS in modern America. Five of the eight principal characters in *Angels in America* are gay. Among them are a male nurse, a judicial clerk, and a high-powered attorney based on an actual person. One suffers from AIDS, and another dies from AIDS before the plays conclude. The five characters' perceptions and relationships reveal in microcosm how America deals with sexuality and AIDS as the millennium approaches.

Roy Cohn refuses to accept that he is gay, even after his doctor, Henry, tells him he has been infected with AIDS from years of having sex with men. Cohn feels that he can distinguish himself from "homosexuals" by virtue of his social status and influence in the halls of power. As Cohn tells Henry, being gay isn't an issue of sexual orientation, but of "clout" (*Millennium Approaches,* p. 45). Cohn perceives homosexuals as having no clout, and since he is a man of status, he cannot by his own definition be gay.

The case of the Mormon Pitt family invokes other societal responses to homosexuality and AIDS: religious disapproval and turning a blind eye. Joe Pitt has tried to live his life for years without acknowledging his homosexuality because his sexual orientation violates the principles of his religious upbringing. But Joe's hidden homosexuality helps propel Harper into madness and leaves Joe desolate and alone. Both Harper and Hannah, Joe's mother, prefer at first to ignore the problem and hope that it will just go away. This does not, of course, work.

Like Joe, Louis loathes himself, but not for his homosexuality. Louis feels intense guilt at having deserted Prior when his lover required his help the most. His tortured reaction to Prior's AIDS is an indication of how dreadful the disease is physically, and of the high emotional price that the families of AIDS patients must pay as they watch their loved ones slowly weaken and decay.

Like Belize, who promotes healing and understanding, Prior is more or less at ease with his sexuality. What he will not accept is the death sentence that AIDS seems to promise. He struggles against the illness and against the isolation and the bitterness; in the final scene of the play, Prior asserts that life goes on even in the face of a terrible illness. In his brave fight—against death and for a loving community of friends—Prior confirms what the real blessing is: more life.

Sources and composition. Impressed in 1985 by another Kushner play, *A Bright Room Called Day,* Oskar Eustis, then the artistic director for the Eureka Theater in San Francisco, California, commissioned Kushner to craft a new work. Initially the play was to be a short (90-minute) funny piece about Jews, Mormons, and homosexuals and their common migratory experience. The idea had its basis in an earlier poem by Kushner about Mormons, or more exactly about the paradox of their biases and their good works. "The poem . . . was bad enough, Kushner says, that he won't show it to anyone now. But it contained the seeds of the play he began writing in 1987, commissioned by his friend Oskar Eustis" (Weber, p. 30).

Kushner drew on firsthand knowledge to compose the work. He had recently become open about his own homosexuality and admits that he drew heavily on this personal experience in his depiction of several of the plays' gay characters. Joe Pitt's phone call to his mother in Salt Lake City to inform her he is gay, for instance, is modeled on a similar phone call Kushner made at a pay phone in Central Park to his own mother. Also affecting the creation of the plays was Kushner's friendship with Kimberly Flynn. Kushner discussed contemporary issues with her, and she otherwise affected the play when a taxicab accident left her brain-injured. Her injury, from which she fortunately recovered, became Kushner's most direct contact with a serious health condition, and elements of it found their way into his two plays.

Events in History at the Time the Plays Were Written

AIDS. Acquired Immune Deficiency Syndrome (AIDS), from which Prior Walter and Roy Cohn suffer, is caused by a virus spread from one person to another when the blood or semen of a person infected with the human immunodeficiency virus (HIV) comes into contact with the blood of an uninfected person; it is also transmitted from pregnant mother to child. In the early 1980s, AIDS was considered by many to be a homosexual disease that posed little risk to the heterosexual community. Perhaps because of its conservative leanings, the Reagan administration did next to nothing about the AIDS epidemic that swept through the nation during the decade. Meanwhile, while high-risk groups continued to include gays, bisexuals, prostitutes, and intravenous drug users, it became clear that AIDS poses a significant risk to the general public. By June 1992, 141,223 Americans had died of AIDS. To date, no cure exists, although the drug azidothymidine (AZT), which the plays' Roy Cohn procures for himself through masterly pulling of strings, slows the progression of HIV infection.

Reviews. *Millennium Approaches* won Tony Kushner a Pulitzer Prize for drama in 1993. Both plays won him consecutive Tony Awards in 1994 and 1995 for Best Play. Internationally, the critical reception to both parts of *Angels in America* has been uniformly enthusiastic.

When *Millennium Approaches* premiered in London in January 1992, Frank Rich wrote in the *New York Times* of that first major production: "Mr. Kushner finds an ingenious vehicle for examining the twisted connections between power, sexuality, bigotry, and corruption in an America that has lost its moral bearings" (Rich, "The Reaganite Ethos," p. 15). By the time both parts opened in Los Angeles in November 1992, Rich wrote in the *New York Times:*

> Some playwrights want to change the world. Some want to revolutionize the theater. Tony Kushner, the remarkably gifted 36-year-old author of Angels in America, is that rarity of rarities: a writer who has the promise to do both.
>
> (Rich, "Marching Out of the Closet into History," p. 15)

For More Information

Biskup, Michael D., and Karin L. Swisher, eds. *AIDS: Opposing Viewpoints.* San Diego, Calif.: Greenhaven Press, 1992.

Angels in America

Gorbachev, Mikhail Sergeevich. *Perestroika: New Thinking for Our Country and the World.* New York: Harper & Row, 1987.

Kushner, Tony. *Angels in America, Part One: Millennium Approaches.* New York: Theatre Communications Group, 1992.

Kushner, Tony. *Angels in America, Part Two: Perestroika.* New York: Theatre Communications Group, 1992.

Munk, Michael L. *The Wisdom in the Hebrew Alphabet.* Brooklyn, N.Y.: Mesorah, 1983.

Quinn, D. Michael. *Same-Sex Dynamics among Nineteenth-Century Americans: A Mormon Example.* Urbana: University of Illinois Press, 1996.

Rich, Frank. "The Reaganite Ethos with Roy Cohn as a Dark Metaphor." *The New York Times* (March 5, 1992): sec. C, p. 15.

Rich, Frank. "Marching Out of the Closet into History." *The New York Times* (November 10, 1992): sec. C, p. 15.

Schwartz, Herman. "Civil Rights and the Reagan Court." In *Culture in an Age of Money: The Legacy of the 1980s in America.* Chicago: Ivan R. Dee, 1990.

Smith, Page. *The Nation Comes of Age: A People's History of the Ante-Bellum Years.* New York: Penguin, 1981.

Weber, Bruce. "Angels' Angels." *The New York Times Magazine* (April 25, 1993): 29-30, 45, 48.

The Autobiography of Malcolm X

as told by
Malcolm X to Alex Haley

In the late 1950s Alex Haley (1921-92) was a struggling African American magazine writer. His research for an article on the Nation of Islam led, in turn, to Haley's writing of an autobiography as told to him by one of the most controversial African Americans of his day, Malcolm X. When approached about the idea, the thirty-seven-year-old Malcolm hesitated but then agreed, deciding that the story of his life might be of benefit to others.

Events in History at the Time of the Autobiography

Passive resistance. On December 1, 1955, the civil rights-era tenet of passive resistance was born in Montgomery, Alabama, when Reverend Dr. Martin Luther King Jr., a pastor in the city, organized a boycott of the Montgomery city buses. King was responding to the arrest of Rosa Parks, a black seamstress who had refused to give up her seat to a white passenger. Over a year after the boycott began, the federal courts ruled that the law requiring blacks to sit at the back of Montgomery's buses was unconstitutional.

The success of the boycott made King the subject of international headlines. In eloquent orations, sprinkled with quotes from famous documents like the **Declaration of Independence** (also covered in *Literature and Its Times*) and the Emancipation Proclamation, he decried the injustice of segregation. Denouncing the hypocrisy of a nation founded on the ideals of freedom and equality yet remaining overtly racist, he challenged state and

THE LITERARY WORK

An autobiography set mainly in the United States but also in the Middle East and Africa from 1925 to 1965; published in 1965.

SYNOPSIS

Malcolm X, a renowned minister in the Nation of Islam, also known as the Black Muslim movement, recounts his life story for Alex Haley. The activist journeyed from poverty and prison to become one of the most controversial speakers on race relations in the United States before his assassination in 1965.

federal legislators to rescind laws that discriminated against minorities. Inspired by his example, blacks throughout the South not only participated in resistance actions organized by King but also staged their own sit-ins and protests.

Yet it was not until 1963, after a pivotal clash between civil rights protesters and local authorities in Birmingham, Alabama, that King finally received the limited support of the federal government. Theophilus "Bull" Conner, an infamous Southern law enforcement official, directed the police to use attack dogs and fire hoses to disperse the protesters, among whom were black schoolchildren. Television footage of German shepherds snapping at children's faces outraged the nation. The demonstrations had been nonviolent, but the response of the local officials was

THERE IS NO GOD BUT ALLAH. MUHAMMAD IS HIS APOSTLE

The National Convention of the Nation of Islam in Chicago, 1963.

not. It was a very apprehensive President John F. Kennedy who intervened. Federal officials convinced the white businessmen of Birmingham to integrate their stores.

Throughout his fight for integration King exhorted his followers never to consider violent retaliation against whites. When his own house in Montgomery was firebombed, he pacified an incensed crowd. "If you have weapons," he pleaded, "take them home; if you do not have them, please do not seek to get them" (King in Fairclough, p. 25). He firmly believed that "non-violent resistance is the most potent weapon available to oppressed people in their struggle for freedom and human dignity" (King in Clark, p. 23).

The Nation of Islam. While many blacks in the South applauded King's triumphs, blacks in the slums of the North rallied around a different set of leaders. In the years prior to World War II, the Nation of Islam, a black nationalist movement, had captured the attention of thousands of blacks in the Northern cities. Whereas King encouraged peaceful demonstrations to further integration, leaders for the Nation of Islam advocated separatism and militancy.

In 1930, when Malcolm was just five years old, a mysterious peddler, W. D. Fard, wandered the streets of Detroit's black community. He sold raincoats and umbrellas, but also silks and arti-

facts that, he explained, were the same kind used by the peoples of Africa and Middle East. Fard enchanted his audiences with tales about Asia and Africa and the first people, black people, to roam the earth.

As his popularity grew, Fard delivered vitriolic condemnations of both Christianity and white people. He declared that he had come to arouse the black people of the United States and vanquish the "blue-eyed devils" who oppressed them. Stirred by his daring, dejected blacks living in the slums of Detroit flocked to hear his speeches.

Fard founded a movement originally called the Lost-Found Nation of Islam. He contended that Islam was the true religion of the black race, and that Christianity had been foisted upon blacks to keep them under control. Christian whites promised a blissful hereafter, he explained, to ensure that blacks remained docile and submissive in the present. Blacks were not Americans and owed no loyalty to a government that, Fard argued, offered them no protection from "the depravities of the white devils" (Fard in Lincoln, p. 16).

In 1934, after having won over eight thousand adherents, Fard disappeared. His followers insisted he had died in prison as the result of police brutality, whereas some policemen insinuated he had been ousted by competing factions within the Nation of Islam. In any case, he was succeeded by Elijah Muhammad, one of his most zealous adherents.

Muhammad's unrestrained condemnations of the white race and his assurances that the superior black race would soon rise to take its rightful place as the ruler of the earth captivated his audiences. "The Caucasian race is a race of devils," he proclaimed (Muhammad, p. 26). "Their days of success are over; their rule will last only as long as you remain asleep" (Muhammad, p. 34).

Muhammad advocated the formation of a separate black nation. He demanded that the U.S. government cede territory to his followers in recompense for the degradation of slavery. "[Black people] worked 300 years without a pay day," Muhammad asserted. "We feel that we've got something due us, and I don't mean this phony integration stuff" (Muhammad in Lincoln, p. 96).

The Nation of Islam grew to number over one hundred thousand members. Inspired by its spokesmen, who visited prisons and reformatories, rehabilitated criminals swelled the ranks of Muhammad's following. Heroin addicts, obeying Muhammad's injunction against drugs, kicked their habits and began lives of moderation and restraint. Although many of the members of the Nation of Islam had appeared incorrigible to social workers, once they came under Muhammad's influence few were ever arrested again.

Nevertheless, the Nation of Islam had many detractors. Other Islamic groups in the United States insisted that Elijah Muhammad merely borrowed words and sometimes tenets from the Islamic religion to disguise his fanatic nationalism. Skeptics insisted that Muhammad exploited the frustration of blacks in the United States to finance his pursuit of fame. Yet even the most derisive critics could not deny that Elijah Muhammad had accomplished impressive goals.

The appeal of separatism. Many of the blacks living in the North were the children of migrants who had fled the hostile racism of the South, where Jim Crow laws made segregation legal. In the North, according to law, blacks supposedly enjoyed the same rights as whites. Such equality, however, was only theoretical. Most blacks could afford to live only in the overcrowded and segregated slums. The public schools, which were paid for in part by local taxes, were underfunded and hardly comparable to schools attended by white children in affluent neighborhoods. Slums were often homes to infamous drug and prostitution rings, yet bigoted policemen

ventured into such areas more often to harass blacks than to protect them.

To many blacks in the North, the separation prescribed by Elijah Muhammad seemed a more practical solution to the problems of racism than integration. Their own contact with white society and their observation that laws did not necessarily guarantee civil equality convinced many that the movement for integration was both misguided and futile.

Malcolm X versus Martin Luther King Jr. Malcolm X became one of the most successful recruiters for the Nation of Islam. His talent for oration, along with the fact that he had used drugs and even served time in prison, won him enormous audiences in the largely black district of Harlem in New York City. He seemed to prove by example that the teachings of Elijah Muhammad could transform a criminal into a leader. But Malcolm's transformation is not what caught the eyes and ears of followers and the general American public.

THE IMPACT OF ELIJAH MUHAMMAD AND THE NATION OF ISLAM

"Mr. Muhammad may be a rogue and a charlatan," one black journalist wrote, "but when anybody can get tens of thousands of Negroes to practice economic solidarity, respect their women, alter their atrocious diet, give up liquor, stop crime, juvenile delinquency and adultery, he is doing more for the Negro's welfare than any current leader I know" (Lincoln, p. 142).

Instead he won both for himself and the Nation of Islam numerous headlines in the media because of his daring assertions that Martin Luther King Jr., a leader respected even by many whites, had hindered the emancipation of blacks in the United States. "You don't have to criticize Reverend Martin Luther King," Malcolm sneered:

> His actions criticize him. . . . Any Negro who teaches other Negroes to turn the other cheek is disarming that Negro. . . . [M]en like King—their job is to go among Negroes and teach Negroes "Don't fight back." . . . "Don't fight the white man." . . . White people follow King. White people pay King.
>
> (Malcolm X in Clark, p. 42)

Martin Luther King, Jr., and Malcolm X.

Estrangement and reconciliation. After his release from prison in 1952, Malcolm X became a minister in the Nation of Islam, and in a matter of only a few years he distinguished himself as its most prominent and controversial speaker. He was, despite this success, suspended from the Nation in 1963, supposedly because of a flippant remark concerning Kennedy's assassination. Malcolm always suspected, however, that Muhammad had become jealous of his success. Largely because of Malcolm's tireless efforts, membership in the Nation of Islam in New York City had increased from an estimated four hundred when he joined to forty thousand when he was suspended.

Malcolm's estrangement from the Nation of Islam and the subsequent journeys he took to the Middle East and Africa caused him to reexamine his views and shift to a more positive outlook on the possibilities for race relations in the United States. Malcolm also reevaluated Martin Luther King Jr., with whom he had so stridently disagreed. He journeyed to Selma, Alabama, in 1965, where King was imprisoned for organizing protests, and told King's wife that he was "trying to help" (X with Haley, *The Autobiography of Malcolm X,* p. 434). Malcolm acknowledged, at the close of his autobiography, that "it is anybody's guess which of the 'extremes' in approach to the black man's problems might *personally* meet a fatal catastrophe first—'non-violent' Dr. King, or so-called 'violent' me" (*The Autobiography of Malcolm X,* p. 385).

Meanwhile, it was not only Malcolm who reevaluated his understanding of race relations in the United States. King, too, would come to appreciate Malcolm's contribution when, in the years following Malcolm X's assassination, he would attempt to tackle the racial injustices in the urban North. Abortive campaigns in cities like Chicago and race riots in places like Los Angeles's Watts section would convince King that the South was by no means the last bastion of racism. King would even admit that legislative changes like the Civil Rights Act of 1964 were "at best surface changes" that did little for the "millions of Negroes in the teeming ghettoes of the North" (King in Fairclough, p. 110).

Eventually most civil rights activists, including Malcolm himself, would come to regard Malcolm's attitudes and King's attitudes as complementary, rather than contradictory. Malcolm once observed that *integration* between blacks and whites is really assimilation for blacks, the giving up of their distinctive ways, and that it should be fought tooth and nail by those blacks who want to preserve their heritage. His observation presaged a dramatic turn in the civil rights movement, a turn that was barely perceptible at the time of his death in 1965. Ethnic minorities would begin to stress that, while they sought civil equality, which included integration, they did not intend to assimilate. A movement among black Americans described as an "ethnic revival" would flower in the years after Malcolm's death, a movement sparked in part by him.

The Autobiography in Focus

The contents. Malcolm X was born Malcolm Little on May 19, 1925, in Omaha, Nebraska, the son of Reverend Earl Little, a Baptist minister and an organizer for Marcus Garvey's Universal Negro Improvement Association, and of his wife Louise Little. Malcolm spent most of his early youth with his parents and many siblings in Lansing, Michigan.

In 1931, when Malcolm was six years old, his father died, supposedly as the result of a streetcar accident. Although the police had concluded that the death had been accidental, both Malcolm's mother and her friends and relatives believed that Reverend Little had been killed by racist whites who had subsequently laid his body across streetcar tracks to be mutilated.

With the burden of raising her many children, Malcolm's mother tried to survive by taking jobs as a seamstress or housekeeper for white families. Unable to earn even a meager income, Louise Little had no choice but to go on welfare. Each month state welfare inspectors would come to her house to inspect her and her children and draw conclusions concerning her competency to raise her family. This insult to her pride, combined with poverty, led to her collapse. Malcolm's mother suffered a mental breakdown; she was committed to a state mental hospital and her children became wards of the state.

Malcolm was sent to the Michigan State Detention Home, where he became the favorite of the supervisors. Rather than being sent on to a reform school with the other wards, he attended a normal public school. He was an outstanding student, popular with both teachers and classmates, and was elected president of his seventh grade class.

His faith in the schools were crushed, however, by a remark made by his English teacher. When Malcolm said he was thinking about becoming a lawyer, the teacher replied with consternation. "Malcolm, one of life's first needs is for us to be realistic. . . . A lawyer—that's no realistic goal for a nigger. . . . Why don't you plan on carpentry" (*The Autobiography of Malcolm X,* p. 38). Although Malcolm conceded that the advice might have been well intended, the remark convinced him to drop out of school.

In 1941, at the age of sixteen, Malcolm left Michigan to move in with his half-sister, Ella, in Boston, Massachusetts. Although Ella encouraged Malcolm to socialize with her middle- and upper-class friends, Malcolm was attracted to a more unwholesome crowd. He took a job as a shoeshine boy at a ballroom only to learn that the shoeshine boys made their real money by connecting white customers with drug dealers and pimps. Malcolm himself began selling drugs and procuring women for prostitution. He moved to Harlem for a time, then returned to Boston, where he joined a burglary ring with another black man and two white women. When the four were caught breaking into an apartment, the two white women were sentenced to one to five years in a women's reformatory. The black men were sentenced to eight to ten years to be served in Charleston State Prison. Later Malcolm concluded that the average burglary sentence for a first-time offender was around two years; probably his more grievous crime in the eyes of the court had been his involvement with white women.

Between 1946 and 1952, the years Malcolm spent in prison, he underwent an enormous change. A self-educated prisoner named Bimbi convinced Malcolm of the value of knowledge. Malcolm began not only to read the books in the prison library, but also to take correspondence courses in Latin and English.

Of greatest import during this period was Malcolm's decision to read the teachings of Nation of Islam leader Elijah Muhammad on the evils of whites. Malcolm's knowledge of history and the experiences of his own life provided sufficient evidence of the white man's fundamentally evil nature. Dropping the surname Little, which had been bestowed on Malcolm's forefathers by their enslavers, Malcolm adopted the name by which he became famous, Malcolm X.

In 1952 Malcolm was paroled. After living with his brother in Detroit for a few months, he went to Chicago to meet Elijah Muhammad in person. In 1953 and 1954, at the behest of Elijah Muhammad, he journeyed to Boston and Philadelphia to found temples for the Nation of Islam. Because of his success in attracting adherents in these cities, he was appointed minister of Temple Seven in Harlem.

Between 1953 and 1962 the Nation of Islam flourished, largely because of Malcolm's tireless efforts and dramatic orations. In 1959 the television documentary, *The Hate That Hate Produced,* brought national attention to Malcolm X and the Nation of Islam. The documentary depicted Malcolm as an angry separatist fomenting unrest in the ghettos of the North. Because Malcolm often decried the passive resistance protests organized by Martin Luther King Jr., he was cast as a hatemonger. In dramatic speeches he called for blacks in the United States to unite in their demand not for integration, but for separation.

It may have been Malcolm's fame that brought him into conflict with Elijah Muhammad. In 1963 Malcolm was suspended from the Nation of Islam, supposedly for having remarked that President Kennedy's assassination was a case of "chickens coming home to roost" (*The Autobiography of Malcolm X,* p. 307). Malcolm believed, however, that Elijah Muhammad had grown jealous of his prodigy and sought to discredit him. His fears were confirmed when a member of his Temple confessed that he had been given orders to assassinate Malcolm.

Confident of his popularity among the poor blacks of Harlem, Malcolm formed his own organization, the Muslim Mosque, Incorporated. In 1964, he resolved to make the obligatory pilgrimage to Mecca, Saudi Arabia—one of the essential duties of a follower of Middle Eastern Islam. During his journey Malcolm sat in a crowded airplane alongside pilgrims of all colors, all journeying together to Mecca to worship the same God. He discovered that the racism he had decried in the States as an innate evil of whites was in fact not a matter of color, but a matter of culture. "The white man," he admitted, "is *not* inherently evil, but America's racist society influences him to act evilly" (*The Autobiography of Malcolm X,* p. 378).

Malcolm returned to the United States with a new message. Although he still believed that people of different races tend to segregate themselves voluntarily, he admitted to panels of scribbling reporters, peaceful coexistence between blacks and whites was still possible.

Another journey to the Middle East and to Africa, where Malcolm was welcomed by state officials, revealed the presence of blacks in international politics and inspired Malcolm with the idea of approaching the United Nations on the matter of race relations in the United States. On his return to the United States he founded the Organization of Afro-American Unity (OAAU) with the hope of convincing blacks in America that they had, in their struggle against racism, the support of many of the peoples of Africa.

During the last months of his life, Malcolm felt betrayed and saddened by the threats of assassination by members of the Nation of Islam. When he discovered that Elijah Muhammad planned to evict him and his family from their home—which, Muhammad contended, actually belonged to the Nation of Islam—he armed himself and insisted that his wife know how to use the firearms he kept in the house.

In spite of this pressure, Malcolm managed to give speeches on college campuses around the nation in support of the OAAU. A scheduled journey to France was canceled because the French government deemed him an incendiary speaker. Malcolm began to suspect that a group other than the Nation of Islam was behind the death threats he often received.

On February 21, 1965, as he took the podium to speak at a ballroom in Manhattan, Malcolm was shot and killed. Three Black Muslims were convicted of the murder, although many contested the validity of the convictions. Years later, Talmadge X Hayer, one of the three convicted, said that he had committed the murder, but that the other two men were innocent.

Malcolm X's appeal. Malcolm enjoyed recounting to Haley an incident that occurred as he strolled through Harlem with another influential black man. The two men were approached by a hustler who said:

> Hey, baby! I hear you holding this all-originals scene at the track. . . . I'm going to lay a vine under the Jew's balls for a dime—got to give you a play. . . . Got the shorts out here trying to scuffle up on some bread. . . . Well, my man, I'll get on, got to go peck a little, and cop me some z's.
> (*The Autobiography of Malcolm X*, p. 317)

When Malcolm noticed that the other influential black man was bewildered, he explained that the hustler was going to pawn a suit for $10 in order to patronize a Muslim-organized bazaar, that he had little money though he was trying hard to make some, and that he was going to go eat and then get some sleep. "The point that I'm trying to make," Malcolm explained to Haley, "is that, as a leader, I could talk with the so-called 'middle class' Negro and with the ghetto blacks (whom all the other leaders just talked about)" (*The Autobiography of Malcolm X*, p. 317).

One reason that speakers for the Nation of Islam, and Malcolm X in particular, won the trust and devotion of blacks in the North (where King would later fail to inspire any large following) was that many of them had themselves once turned to drugs or crime. Poor and uneducated blacks, who may have felt alienated by social workers or even a leader as brilliant as King, trusted members of the Nation of Islam because, Malcolm explained, "The Muslim talks . . . straight" (*The Autobiography of Malcolm X*, p. 272). Malcolm elaborated that, whereas most black civil rights leaders could not even understand street speech, he could approach an addict and honestly say:

> Daddy, you know I know how you feel. Wasn't I right out here with you? Scratching like a monkey, smelling all bad, living mad, hungry, stealing and running and hiding from Whitey. Man, what's a black man buying Whitey's dope for but to make Whitey richer—killing yourself.
> (*The Autobiography of Malcolm X*, p. 266)

This commonality, Malcolm explained, was the key to his appeal to so many black Northerners; his experience at the bottom of the social order made him a credible speaker, one who knew whereof he spoke and one whose advice might therefore be worth heeding.

Sources. Alex Haley first met Malcolm X in 1959 as he was working on an article for *Reader's Digest* about the Nation of Islam. "You're another one of the white man's tools to spy" (*The Autobiography of Malcolm X*, p. 390), Malcolm snapped when Haley requested an interview. However, when Haley's article, "Mr. Muhammad Speaks," was published, Malcolm telephoned Haley to thank him for having been "objective" (*The Autobiography of Malcolm X*, p. 391).

Three years later Haley approached Malcolm and suggested he write an autobiography. "I will have to give it a lot of thought," Malcolm cautioned, but two days later he consented. "I think my life story," he explained, "may help people to appreciate better how Mr. Muhammad salvages black people" (*The Autobiography of Malcolm X*, p. 393). Malcolm insisted that all the profits from the sale of the book go to the Nation of Islam. He later changed this decision and asked that the profits go to his wife and children.

In spite of his break with the Nation of Islam, Malcolm did not regret the decision to publish an autobiography. Rather than help inform people about how Elijah Muhammad salvaged the lives of black people, Malcolm hoped simply that "the objective reader, in following my life—the life of only one ghetto-created Negro—may gain a better picture and understanding than he has previously had of the black ghettoes which are shaping the lives and the thinking of almost all of the 22 million Negroes who live in America" (*The Autobiography of Malcolm X,* p. 386).

Reception. Disparaging reviews of portions of Malcolm's autobiography appeared before his assassination. An editor for the *Saturday Evening Post* wrote "[i]f Malcolm X were not a Negro, his autobiography would be little more than a journal of abnormal psychology, the story of a burglar, dope pusher, addict and jailbird . . . who acquires messianic delusions and sets forth to preach an upside-down religion of 'brotherly' hatred" (*The Autobiography of Malcolm X,* p. 426).

After the assassination, one critic described the autobiography as a moving account of Malcolm's own experiences with racism. Another critic, reviewing the autobiography in the *Nation,* regarded it as

> a monument to the most painful of truths: that this country . . . has practiced unspeakable cruelty against . . . an individual who might have made its fraudulent humanism a reality.
>
> (Nelson in Davison and Samudio, p. 585)

A third critic contended in the *New York Review of Books* that Malcolm's story had won "a permanent place in the literature of the Afro-American struggle" (Stone in Davison and Samudio, p. 828), a contention borne out by the continuing popularity of the autobiography over the past three decades.

For More Information

Clark, Kenneth. *King, Malcolm, Baldwin.* Middletown, Conn.: Wesleyan University Press, 1985.

Davison, Dorothy, and Josephine Samudio, eds. *Book Review Digest.* Vol. 61. New York: H. W. Wilson, 1966.

Fairclough, Adam. *Martin Luther King, Jr.* Athens: University of Georgia Press, 1990.

Lincoln, Eric. *The Black Muslims in America.* Boston: Beacon, 1961.

Muhammad, Elijah. *The Supreme Wisdom.* Chicago: University of Islam, 1957.

Silberman, Charles. *Crisis in Black and White.* New York: Random House, 1964.

X, Malcolm, with the assistance of Alex Haley. *The Autobiography of Malcolm X.* New York: Ballantine, 1965.

The Autobiography of
Miss Jane Pittman

by
Ernest J. Gaines

In the fall of 1962, surrounded by more than 2,000 jeering white protesters, James Meredith entered the University of Mississippi as its first African American student. This event, a landmark in United States history, was also a turning point in the life of the then twenty-nine-year-old Ernest Gaines. At the time an aspiring writer in San Francisco, California, Gaines said to himself, "if James Meredith can go through all this—not only for himself, but for his race—, [then I] should go back to the source that I [am] trying to write about" (Gaines in Babb, p. 5). This source, rural Louisiana—where Gaines had been born in 1933 and was raised until age fifteen—is the setting for his novel *The Autobiography of Miss Jane Pittman*. Narrated by a 110-year-old former slave, the novel tells the long story of her struggle—and the greater African American struggle—for justice after the Civil War and into the 1960s.

Events in History at the Time the Novel Takes Place

Life after slavery. The months following the end of the Civil War were a time of great uncertainty for the freed slaves of the South. Although they rejoiced at their emancipation, many also felt fearful and confused about what lay ahead. A scene Miss Jane describes early in the novel is typical of what many newly freed slaves experienced. "What's we to do?" one slave asks on hearing that they have been freed.

> "Slavery over, let's get moving," somebody said. "Let's stay," somebody else said. "See if old

> Master go'n act different when it's freedom."
> "Y'all do like y'all want," I said. "I'm headed North." I turned to leave, but I stopped. "Which way North?"
>
> (Gaines, *The Autobiography of Miss Jane Pittman*, p. 13)

For a group that had been forced into dependency on white masters for hundreds of years, the transition to freedom was difficult. In fact, the prospect of leaving home to start a new life was often too much for former slaves. While some moved out of the South, many chose to stay in the same area—sometimes even on the same plantation—where they had worked as slaves; others returned after failed attempts at starting anew. Although these freedmen and freedwomen often performed the same functions they had before emancipation—plowing fields, picking cotton, cooking meals, caring for white children—they were paid for their work (in land, harvest, or wages) and expected to pay for their

Freed black slaves lead a wagon train out of the South after the Civil War.

food and shelter. To many former slaves, however, these differences seemed insignificant. As one Mississippi slave put it:

> I used to think if I could be free I should be the happiest of anybody in the world. But when my master come to me, and says—Lizzie you is free! it seems like I was in a kind of daze. And when I would wake up in the morning I would think to myself, Is I free? Hasn't I got to get up before daylight and go into the field to work?
>
> (Litwack, p. 220)

Violence and unequal justice. Although the years of slavery were infamous for the horrible treatment African Americans received at the hands of slave traders and masters, the years of Reconstruction (the period immediately following the Civil War) were actually crueler to blacks in many areas of the South. Before the war, slaves were whipped and otherwise abused, but because they were considered valuable property, their masters were usually careful not to wound them so badly that they could not work. After the war, however, slaves belonged only to themselves; if they were hurt or killed, no white man suffered (except, of course, by losing an employee, whom he could easily replace). As a result, during Reconstruction African Americans were often the victims of savage, even deadly, attacks by white Southerners, angry and demoral-

ized after losing the war. The fictional massacre described by Miss Jane in the novel is no worse than many real attacks reported in the South in the decades following the war. In this scene former Confederate soldiers and "patrollers" (poor white men hired to find runaway slaves) surround the camp where Jane and other newly freed slaves have stopped on their way to Ohio.

> They moved in with sticks now to look for us. I could hear them hitting against the bushes and talking to each other. Then when they spotted somebody, a bunch of them would surround the person and beat him till they had knocked him unconscious or killed him. . . . Now, you heard screaming, begging; screaming, begging; screaming, begging—till it was quiet again.
>
> (*The Autobiography of Miss Jane Pittman,* pp. 21-2)

Although attacks like this were technically illegal, few Southern whites were punished for crimes against blacks. The white culture of violence was far more powerful in the postwar era than laws, judges, or Freedmen's Bureau officers (those appointed by the federal government to ease the transition from slavery to freedom). As a result, white witnesses to such crimes were more inclined to protect guilty fellow whites—especially those who demanded such protection with threats of violence—than to stand up for the rights of African Americans. African American witnesses were also subject to violence if they spoke out against whites, and they faced major legal obstacles as well.

To lodge an official complaint against a white person for any crime, African Americans were required either to pay bail to the court or to stay in jail for days or weeks to insure that they would show up to testify during the trial of the accused white person. With such unfair social and legal advantages for whites, it is no surprise that events like the massacre of Miss Jane Pittman's African American traveling companions and the murder of her adopted son, both perpetrated by white men, went unpunished. Such episodes were a common occurrence during Reconstruction.

White, Cajun, Creole, and African American. In the century following the Civil War, Louisiana was a typical Southern state in many ways, but also a region with a distinctive culture. The Cajun settlers of this area, French exiles from an earlier settlement in Canada, influenced it with their language, food, and customs. During the one hundred years Gaines depicts, though, Cajuns as a group were poorer and less powerful than other white Louisiana residents. They were often hired to do the dirty work for more powerful whites, as in the novel when Albert Cluveau, Jane's Cajun fishing buddy, is paid to kill her adopted son Ned. "I must do what they tell me," he says when she asks if he plans to kill Ned (*The Autobiography of Miss Jane Pittman*, p. 105). Creoles of color, such as the "almost white" Mary Agnes LeFabre (*The Autobiography of Miss Jane Pittman*, p. 164), shared some of the French heritage of the Cajuns but usually looked different because of their mixed African and European ancestry. (In *Miss Jane Pittman* the term "Creole" is used for those with mixed French and African heritage, but it has also been used as a term for the exclusively white descendants of Louisiana's original French and Spanish settlers.) The mixed-heritage Creoles generally kept away from Cajuns as well as other whites and from African Americans, speaking their own French-based language and maintaining a unique, sophisticated culture. Before the Civil War, most free people of color were Creole. At the bottom of the Louisiana social ladder during this century were African Americans like Jane Pittman, whose dark skin marked them as inferior in the eyes of most whites, Cajuns, and Creoles.

A long struggle for equal rights. After the United States government won the Civil War and outlawed slavery in 1865, national legislators spent the next five years writing laws to improve the political standing of African Americans. While some of these laws resulted in dramatic changes—like the ability of former slaves to vote and run for office—most had a very limited effect on the real lives of African Americans. This was partly because the United States government did not enforce the laws effectively and partly because Southern state lawmakers soon found ways around them.

HATE GROUPS

The Ku Klux Klan and the Knights of the White Camellia were founded after the Civil War by white Confederates who turned their anger and shame at being defeated by the Union into violence against former slaves. Many members of these groups feared a black revolt against the white people of the South and concluded that the way to prevent it was to beat, maim, or lynch those blacks who sought to exercise their political rights (or in any way disobeyed the order of a white person). Although these acts of terrorism became less common after a federal crackdown in the 1870s, the Ku Klux Klan experienced a huge revival during the civil rights movement of the 1960s.

In fact, not until the 1960s would laws passed a century before finally begin to be fully enacted and enforced. The time line below describes a dozen of the most important political and legal developments in the century of African American history portrayed in *The Autobiography of Miss Jane Pittman*.

1865: Thirteenth Amendment to U.S. Constitution
Outlawed slavery in the United States.

1865-66: Black Codes
Passed by Southern state legislatures; granted African Americans limited rights (e.g., to marriage and property) but denied them the right to bear arms, marry whites, possess alcohol, sit in the passenger car of a train, gather in large groups, or be on city streets at night.

1867-68: Fourteenth Amendment to U.S. Constitution
Defined African Americans as citizens entitled to "the equal protection of the laws."

1870: Fifteenth Amendment to U.S. Constitution
Gave African Americans the right to vote, prohibiting states from denying the vote to

anyone because of "race, color, or previous condition of servitude."

1890: Mississippi Plan

Duplicated by other Southern states between 1890 and 1920; established a poll tax, literacy test, and other measures aimed at preventing African Americans from voting.

1890s: Jim Crow laws

Passed by Southern state legislatures; set up separate schools, train cars, hotels, restaurants, water fountains, bathrooms, hospitals, parks, prisons, sidewalks, and cemeteries for African Americans and whites.

1896: *Plessy v. Ferguson* Supreme Court ruling

Declared that "separate but equal" facilities for African Americans and whites were legal, endorsing segregation.

1954: *Brown v. Board of Education* Supreme Court ruling

Outlawed segregation in public schools, reversing *Plessy v. Ferguson* decision.

1957: Civil Rights Act

Created a Civil Rights commission and directed the U.S. Justice Department to sue anyone interfering with African Americans' right to vote

1964: Twenty-fourth Amendment to the U.S. Constitution

Outlawed poll taxes in national elections

1964: Civil Rights Act

Outlawed segregation in public buildings and racial discrimination in hiring

1965: Voting Rights Act

Outlawed literacy tests and other tests for voters

Louisiana's first civil rights movement. With new laws and the Freedman's Bureau slow to improve the lot of former slaves, African Americans in the South and elsewhere began to realize that if they were to achieve the goals most important to them at the time—the acquisition of land, education, and equal civil rights—they would have to work together on their own behalf. Meeting in churches and schoolhouses, African American groups provided training and education for one another, published newspapers, and got involved in politics.

In Louisiana, African American political action was especially effective in the decade from 1867 to 1877. During that time, newly elected black lawmakers and community leaders led a successful fight to outlaw segregation in public schools, streetcars, bars, and hotels.

Unfortunately, passing laws against segregation did not make it disappear. Although many African Americans in Louisiana tried to exercise

the new rights granted to them by law, the risk of violent responses from angry whites kept most from crossing the color boundaries erected by white society.

Soon, with the victory of anti-integration Democrats in Louisiana's 1877 elections and the *Plessy v. Ferguson* Supreme Court decision (see time line), even the political gains made by Louisiana's African Americans were canceled out. However, the segregation struggle of the 1860s and 1870s had helped pave the way for the civil rights movement of the 1960s, when not only laws but also actions began to change.

The Novel in Focus

The plot. Miss Jane's story begins when she is ten or eleven years old and meets a Union soldier passing by the plantation where she works as a slave. This soldier, a Colonel Brown, refuses to use what he calls her "slave name," Ticey; instead, he gives her his daughter's name, Jane. Although the Civil War is not over yet, this soldier inspires the girl to insist that her master and mistress call her "Miss Jane Brown," a move that angers them enough to have her whipped severely.

A year later, the war has ended, and Jane sets out with some other newly freed slaves to head north and start a new life. On the second day of their journey, though, the group is surrounded by white patrollers and most of its members are beaten to death—all perish but Jane and an orphaned toddler, Ned.

Jane and Ned continue walking until they meet a Northerner from the Freedmen's Bureau who brings them to a shelter and school for freed slave children. Jane soon decides, though, that the strict atmosphere of this school is not the kind of freedom she is looking for, and she and Ned resume their journey. Tired, hungry, and still in Louisiana, Jane and Ned eventually end up on another plantation, where Jane works in the fields for a wage while Ned goes to school.

Life on this plantation is little better than life under slavery, but Jane and Ned stay there for a number of years. Eventually, however, because of death threats from local white terrorists, Ned—now grown and involved in a betterment project for the African Americans in his area—is forced to leave for Kansas. Soon after his departure, Jane marries Joe Pittman, a horse trainer, and moves with him to another plantation with similar conditions. Eight years later, Joe is killed by a wild horse and Jane sets up a small laundry

A civil rights protester is attacked by a policeman and his dog.

business in another part of Louisiana, where Ned soon settles with his new family. The school Ned founds there and the politics he teaches make him a target once again for local whites, and he is murdered by Albert Cluveau, a hired gun and Cajun fishing buddy of Jane's.

The murder of her adopted son leads Jane to leave her independent life and join an old friend who works at a nearby plantation. This plantation, Samson, is where Jane is to spend most of the last fifty years of her life. There she lives through a huge flood, joins the church, and sees the black schoolchildren on her plantation given free books by governor Huey Long. She also witnesses a failed love affair between the white plantation owner's son and a Creole schoolteacher—an affair that ends in the son's suicide. Most importantly, though, in her last years she braves threats and violence to lead a group of co-workers from Samson to a civil rights demonstration in nearby Bayonne.

What it means to be free. Although Jane Pittman is freed from slavery as a young girl, her remaining lifetime is spent testing and pushing the limits of this freedom. Freedom does not give her the privileges of being white or even Creole in Louisiana; as an African American, she must put up with prejudice and mistreatment for the length of her 110-year life. Still, Jane struggles to assert her freedom—often in small ways, but sometimes in more noticeable ways—throughout the novel. Although she may not know at first what it means to be free, she is determined to find out—and to make this true freedom her own.

The first symbol of freedom Miss Jane seizes is the right to choose her own name. Her insistence on claiming this right, even before the war is over, shows how anxious she is to find freedom in whatever form she can. When her mistress calls her by her old name, Jane ignores her. "You little wench, didn't you hear me calling you?" the woman asks. "I raised my head high," Miss Jane says,

and looked her straight in the face and said: "You called me Ticey. My name ain't no Ticey no more, it's Miss Jane Brown. And Mr. Brown say catch him and tell him if you don't like it." (*The Autobiography of Miss Jane Pittman,* p. 9)

At the end of the war, Jane is given two more substantial choices—where to go and what to do. Though her options are limited by her skin color and lack of money and education, she still follows her instinct to leave, believing that true freedom could only exist somewhere other than

Louisiana. When her attempt to reach the North with Ned fails, however, Jane begins to search for freedom in the same place where she knew slavery.

Jane finds small examples of freedom in Louisiana through many things we might take for granted today: choosing where to work, marrying the man she loves, growing what she wants in her garden, fishing in her spare time, riding her own horse to pick up laundry for her business, stubbornly staying on the Samsons' land after she is too old to work for them, even eating vanilla ice cream (Gaines, p. 207). A part of her, though, is never completely free from the fear of mistreatment by whites, a fear we see, for example, when she urges Ned to stop teaching because of death threats from local whites. At the end of the novel, though, Jane's support for the civil rights movement shows that she is ready to confront this fear and risk losing her simple pleasures. By fighting for broader freedom for African Americans—freedom from racial prejudice and discrimination—Jane demonstrates that she has also found freedom from the fear she calls "worse than any death" (*The Autobiography of Miss Jane Pittman,* p. 228).

Sources. Although the introduction to *The Autobiography of Miss Jane Pittman* is signed by an "editor" who claims to have constructed the book from taped interviews with a real Jane Pittman, the character of Miss Jane and the "autobiography" itself are actually fictions. These fictions, however, are based on true stories and experiences Ernest Gaines was exposed to in his childhood. Born on a Louisiana plantation in 1933, Gaines worked in its sugarcane fields as a boy. There he heard tales about life during and after slavery—tales that he remembered as a young writer in California years later.

Because *The Autobiography of Miss Jane Pittman* was based so heavily on historical events, Gaines could not rely just on his memories of plantation stories to write the novel. Before he started writing, he traveled to Louisiana to research Southern history, both by reading in libraries and by talking to people in the fields about their memories of local and national events.

In addition to this research, Gaines used his knowledge of American and European literature to help construct *Miss Jane Pittman*. He credits the work of Southern writer William Faulkner with helping him learn to write like his characters would talk and to capture a great deal of meaning in just a few words. The works of Russian writers Ivan Turgenev and Leo Tolstoy, which deal with Russia's poor farmers, also influenced Gaines's writing, showing him how to create realistic characters that are poor but still have dignity.

Events in History at the Time the Novel Was Written

The 1960s civil rights movement in Louisiana. The 1960s was a time of great social and political upheaval in the United States, especially for African Americans. Sit-ins, freedom rides, and civil rights demonstrations like those described in *Miss Jane Pittman* were helping to bring centuries-long practices like segregation and racial discrimination to an end. Louisiana became famous during the 1960s for two events: the New Orleans school integration crisis and the Bogalusa movement.

In 1960, six years after the *Brown v. Board of Education* decision, in which the Supreme Court outlawed segregation in public schools, the New Orleans school board had still taken no steps toward integrating its schools. Frustrated with this lack of movement, Judge Skelly Wright forced the board to enact an integration plan in November of 1960. Although this plan allowed only four black students (all first-grade girls) to attend white schools, opposition from local whites was tremendous. Most parents of white students at the two schools chosen for integration pulled their children out; those who did not were taunted and terrorized by anti-integration neighbors. Politicians who supported the integration were also harassed by threatening phone calls, slashed tires, and stone-throwing. Most disturbing, though, was the treatment of the four young black students. Every day they went to school, they were bombarded by spitting, screaming crowds of angry white faces. One of the black students stopped eating after hearing a woman shout, "We're going to poison you until you choke to death" (Fairclough, p. 249). Without the bravery of these four first-grade girls and the support of the African American community and organizations like the NAACP (National Association for the Advancement of Colored People)—which organized a letter-writing campaign to give the four students moral support—the terrorism of these white protesters might have continued to prevent school integration.

Instead, gradual improvements were made in integrating schools and other public facilities across Louisiana. More and more African Americans, inspired by the example of the four girls, began to stand up for their right to equal treatment and an integrated society. Bad publicity about the New Orleans school crisis—and a resulting loss of business—also helped the civil rights movement in Louisiana. Local businesspeople lent their support to integration policies, hoping to drum up lagging business by improving Louisiana's image.

Although slow improvements in civil rights were made in New Orleans and across the state, the racist hatred of many white Louisianians was not easily overcome. In the rural mill town of Bogalusa, for example, movements to register African Americans to vote and to integrate local establishments were met with extreme violence. White and black civil rights workers from the North and politically active Bogalusa blacks were repeatedly threatened, beaten, and even shot by Ku Klux Klan followers. Soon members of Bogalusa's African American population, many veterans of World War II or the Korean War, formed an armed self-defense corps to protect themselves from the KKK threat because local police would not. This corps eventually attracted enough national attention to force President Lyndon Johnson to declare "war on the Klan" (Fairclough, p. 377), providing Bogalusa and other Southern towns and cities with the military and legal support to finally enact and enforce civil rights laws.

Reception. Reactions to *The Autobiography of Miss Jane Pittman* were overwhelmingly positive. Gaines was praised by one reviewer for joining good writing to politics, or in his words, making "imaginative literature" compatible with "political speculation" (Bryant in Samudio, p. 468). Another liked the balance of his writing, noting that whether black or white, his characters all had their strengths and weaknesses. Most of all, Gaines's reviewers were struck by the realistic feel of *Miss Jane Pittman*—the sound of Louisiana dialects, the believability of the characters, and the convincing blending of history with fiction. Gaines's novel was so popular, in fact, that three years after its publication, it was made into a television movie. The success of *Miss Jane Pittman* suggests that Gaines did what he set out to do in the novel: "to go back, back, back into our experiences in this country to find some kind of meaning to our present lives" (Gaines in Rowell, p. 34).

For More Information

Babb, Valerie Melissa. *Ernest Gaines.* Twayne's United States Authors Series, no. 584. Boston: Twayne, 1991.

Brasseaux, Carl A., Keith P. Fontenot, and Claude F. Oubre. *Creoles of Color in the Bayou Country.* Jackson: University Press of Mississippi, 1994.

Fairclough, Adam. *Race and Democracy: The Civil Rights Struggle in Louisiana, 1915-1972.* Athens: University of Georgia Press, 1995.

Fischer, Roger A. *The Segregation Struggle in Louisiana, 1862-1877.* Chicago: University of Illinois Press, 1974.

Gaines, Ernest J. *The Autobiography of Miss Jane Pittman.* New York: Bantam, 1971.

Litwack, Leon F. *Been in the Storm So Long: The Aftermath of Slavery.* New York: Alfred A. Knopf, 1979.

Rowell, Charles H. *Callaloo* l, no. 3 (May 1978).

Samudio, Josephine, ed. *Book Review Digest.* Vol. 67. New York: H. W. Wilson, 1972.

Stalcup, Brenda, ed. *Reconstruction: Opposing Viewpoints.* San Diego: Greenhaven, 1995.

The Bean Trees

by

Barbara Kingsolver

Born in 1955 in Annapolis, Maryland, Barbara Kingsolver later settled in Tucson, Arizona, attended graduate school, and worked at the university there. Eventually she married and had a daughter, Camille—real-life experience for the fictional mother-daughter relationship created in her first novel, *The Bean Trees*. Prior to its writing, Kingsolver worked as a freelance journalist and before that as a technical writer. Her novels portray an especial sensitivity to everyday Americans—the shop-owners, the unemployed, the single parent fighting to survive—and expose the strength that can be gained by their mutual support of one another.

Events in History at the Time of the Novel

Guatemalan refugees. *The Bean Trees* examines, in part, the lives and fates of a pair of young Guatemalan refugees, Estevan and Esperanza, who benefit from a sanctuary run secretly from Tucson, Arizona, to help them and other Central Americans avoid being sent back to their strife-ridden homelands. While official U.S. policy on political refugees has long been that no one should be forced to return to a nation in which his or her life or safety are judged to be in jeopardy, the reality at the time that Kingsolver was writing the novel was that Guatemalan citizens fleeing that country's horrific human rights abuses were but rarely admitted to the United States. Between June 1983 and September 1989, only 2 percent of the

asylum petitions filed by Guatemalans with the U.S. Immigration and Naturalization Service (INS) were approved; during that same period, the overall approval rate for all nationalities seeking asylum in the United States ranged between 20 percent and 39 percent (*Reasonable Fear*, p. 19).

The situation has immediate historical roots almost half a century long. In 1954 the American government sponsored the overthrow of Guatemalan president Jacobo Arbenz Guzman, ushering in military rule that, with some exceptions, continued to control the country into the late 1980s, even while a democratically elected president was nominally in power. The Americans had originally supported the Guatemalan army in the hopes of staving off the spread of communism through Cuba and nearby Nicaragua, a goal to which the Reagan administration stuck for most of the 1980s. In the mid-1970s, however, the political alliances in

Guatemala shifted decisively. The government became more oppressive toward the poor, the Indians, the intelligentsia. American support for the Guatemalan military nevertheless remained in place, despite copious evidence that the human rights record of the Guatemalan government was appalling. Guatemala's native Indians, of Maya heritage and traditionally passive in nature, began to join revolutionary forces with the intention of overthrowing the government that had ruled with an iron fist for so many years. Government retaliation was swift, prolonged, and horrifying. Whole villages were burned and the people slaughtered. Kidnapping, torture, and other violations of international standards on human rights became everyday occurrences. The violence was not confined to Guatemala's Indian-populated highlands either, but rapidly descended into the cities and, indeed, into every corner of the country. More than one million people were displaced, and a quarter of that number fled the country for their lives, many of them to Mexico and the United States.

In January 1986, Vinicio Cerezo Arevalo became the first Guatemalan civilian to be made president of that country in twenty years. Observers noted that this apparently new state of affairs meant almost nothing to the average citizen of Guatemala —the military continued to kill and spirit away people at the rate of one hundred a month as late as 1988. Freedom of the press was almost nonexistent; people were held in military camps; student activists, human rights workers, union members, and teachers, among others, were regularly threatened with death or violence if they continued to agitate for improved living and working conditions. Despite all this, the U.S. government, pleased that the civilian-led rule was still in place and choosing to take this for evidence that the country was being run democratically and with respect for human rights, almost doubled the amount of its aid to the Guatemalan military and police. The Watch Committee, an American human rights advocacy group, had the following to say about the Reagan administration's 1986 stance on Guatemala:

> Though it may be impossible for President Cerezo himself to acknowledge publicly his lack of control, it does not help him to have the most powerful external force [the United States] simultaneously insisting that he is fully in control; that abuses by the armed forces are at an end; and that abuses actually committed by the military were committed by common criminals.
>
> (*Reagan Administration's Record,* p. 65)

Barbara Kingsolver

Based on its judgment that Guatemala was well on the way to recovering from its most dismal period in human rights abuses, the Reagan administration consequently refused to admit Guatemalans as refugees into the United States on the grounds that there was nothing to seek refuge from in their homeland. On the contrary, according to Amnesty International, violations of human rights in Guatemala escalated in 1988 and 1989.

American laws on immigration and refugee status. The Immigration Act of 1980 was written to broaden the scope of America's definition of a refugee; previously, a refugee was considered to be a person fleeing primarily communist or Middle Eastern regimes. The 1980 legislation put the United States in line with the 1951 United Nations Convention Relating to the Status of Refugees, which states that a refugee is a person who,

> owing to a well-founded fear of being persecuted for reasons of race, religion, nationality, membership of a particular social group or political opinion, is outside the country of his nationality and is unable or, owing to such fear, unwilling to avail himself of the protection of that country.
>
> (*Reasonable Fear,* pp. 6-7)

In 1968 the United States had signed the United Nations Protocol Relating to the Status of Refugees, a binding international law that in part legislates against "refoulement," or return of a person to a dangerous situation in his or her homeland. A 1987 United States Supreme Court case, *INS v. Cardoza-Fonseca,* defined "well-founded fear" of persecution as a reasonable person's fear of likely death or danger if he or she is forced to return to the land of origin.

Sanctuary. If Washington refused to admit that there was something wrong with its immigration and asylum policies with regard to Central American refugees, many of America's churches and synagogues did not agree. The Sanctuary movement was born among American religious workers in Arizona in the early 1980s to give assistance to Guatemalans and Salvadorans fleeing oppression in their native lands. The movement officially began in March 1982 at the Southside Presbyterian Church in Tucson, Arizona; four years later the Sanctuary movement boasted more than 400 participating congregations—65,000 participants in Mexico, Canada, and the United States (Cunningham, p. xiii). At first, the members would post bail for jailed illegal immigrants, and then arrange for them to have legal representation at their asylum and deportation hearings, but this type of aid quickly escalated to helping such people evade detection in the first place. Eventually news of what the Sanctuary providers were doing came to the attention of the INS, which threatened legal action.

The leaders of the movement decided to go to the media about what was happening; according to their version of events, the United States was breaking its own laws about not sending people back to dangerous situations in their homelands, and the Sanctuary volunteers were merely doing what was perfectly legal. As a result of several high-profile national television shows, word about the Sanctuary movement spread across the country, and volunteers descended upon Tucson to help out. By 1984 federal authorities began arresting Sanctuary workers crossing the Mexico-United States border with illegal aliens. The situation escalated with the 1985 indictment of sixteen Sanctuary workers, among them Catholics, Quakers, Methodists, and Presbyterians. Each was given a three- to five-year suspended sentence, after the judge was flooded with letters in their support from Democratic members of Congress, housewives, students, professors, schoolchildren, lawyers—a broad spectrum of people from the length and breadth

of the nation. The publicity generated by the trial increased the popularity of the Sanctuary movement across the United States, as churches, synagogues, and city councils throughout the nation declared themselves official sanctuaries for fleeing Central Americans.

Cherokee removal. Taylor Greer, the novel's heroine, is descended from a Cherokee man who was too old to be force-marched from the southeastern United States to the flat expanses of Oklahoma, the fate of thousands of his people in 1838. The Cherokee, one of the five "Civilized Tribes," had a well-developed agricultural culture and ran profitable plantations (sometimes with

---

SANCTUARIES

By June 1986 twenty-two city councils across the United States had declared their cities official sanctuaries for Central American refugees:

California:	Berkeley, West Hollywood, Santa Barbara, San Francisco, Sacramento, Davis, Santa Cruz
Minnesota:	St. Paul, Duluth, Minneapolis
Pennsylvania:	Swarthmore
New York:	Rochester, Ithaca
Massachusetts:	Cambridge, Brookline
Wisconsin:	Madison
Maryland:	Tacoma Park
Washington:	Olympia, Seattle
New Mexico:	Santa Fe
Vermont:	Burlington
Michigan:	East Lansing

---

the help of African slaves) in the southeastern United States. Unfortunately, they were thriving in areas desired by white settlers—especially after gold was discovered on Cherokee land in the mid-1820s. In 1827 the Cherokee adopted a constitution, modeled upon the U.S. document, that declared they had sovereign rights over their own land; the United States government was not impressed and on May 28, 1830, Andrew Jackson signed into law a removal bill mandating that the Cherokee were to be given land west of the Mississippi River in exchange for the land on which they were living. While some of the Cherokee signed the Treaty of New Echota in 1835 and agreed to move west, others refused. The rebels, despite their earnest efforts, failed to prevent the move. In 1838 the majority of the Cherokee Nation were rounded up and forced to begin the arduous trek to their new home. Bad summer weather delayed their departure and they were caught in winter weather before they reached their destination. Thousands died of cold, fatigue, and other hardships in the detention camps before departure and on the journey that became known in American history as the "Trail of Tears."

In the 1980 census, 7 million Americans claimed to have some American Indian ancestry, without designating themselves as racially American Indian. Taylor Greer, the novel's heroine, is one such American—her great-grandfather was a full-blooded Cherokee. One historian points out that a lot of people claim Cherokee ancestry, a practice he calls the "Cherokee grandmother phenomenon" (Thornton, p. 172). The label is connected to the fact that the Cherokee trace their family lineage matrilineally, through the mother. If a child is born to a Cherokee woman and a non-Cherokee man, the child is considered a Cherokee. If the mother was not a Cherokee, the child is not either, no matter who the father was. In any case, in Oklahoma particularly, it is socially prestigious to have Cherokee blood, for the Cherokee were long considered the elite class of sophisticated warriors, farmers, and scholars long before other settlers arrived in the area.

The Novel in Focus

The plot. Taylor Greer escapes a dead-end hospital job in Pittman County, Kentucky, and heads west in a beat-up car. A few nights into her trip, in the midst of Cherokee land in central Oklahoma, her car breaks down and she pulls into a roadside garage and bar. On her way back into the parking lot, a strange woman from the bar follows her into the parking lot and deposits a toddler, an Indian child, in the car. Claiming that no one cares about the toddler, she disappears into the night. For lack of a better idea, Taylor takes the child with her to a roadside motel to clean the child up and put her to bed; Taylor has to haggle with the woman at the desk for a room, offering to trade a place to sleep for housework. The clerk reluctantly agrees. Once safely in their room, Taylor discovers to her horror that the little girl has been abused.

The action then shifts to Tucson, Arizona, where Lou Ann Ruiz, originally from Kentucky

and seven months pregnant, has just been deserted by her husband, Angel. He vacates their apartment on Halloween, taking half of their belongings with him.

Back in Oklahoma, Taylor, who has stayed on at the motel through the Christmas holidays to earn cash as a chambermaid, finally heads back on the road. She still has the Indian girl, whom she has named Turtle because of her habit of hanging on fiercely to things around her, much like a mud-turtle does. A flat tire in Tucson takes them to the ramshackle "Jesus Is Lord Used Tires" store, just around the corner from Lou Ann's place. The store's proprietor, Mattie, delivers the bad news that Taylor in fact has two flat tires; in fact, they are so damaged that they will need to be completely replaced. The two women share a cup of coffee while Taylor, who is very short of money, decides what to do. The car is obviously going to take them nowhere, so Taylor and Turtle move into the nearby Hotel Republic, frequented by prostitutes and the destitute. Taylor contemplates taking a minimum-wage job at the Burger Derby.

Six days at the Burger Derby turn out to be all that Taylor can stomach, so she quits her job and starts hanging out in coffee shops, reading other people's abandoned newspapers. In one of them she sees an ad seeking a roommate. It had been placed by Lou Ann, and upon meeting the two women become fast friends. Taylor and Turtle move into Lou Ann's apartment.

Taylor takes a job at Mattie's used tire shop, despite fears of being blown up by an exploding tire, an incident with which the book opens. At Jesus Is Lord Used Tires, she meets a young Catholic priest, Father William, who with Mattie is involved in operating a "sanctuary" for Central American refugees who have fled persecution in their homelands and seek to avoid being deported by U.S. immigration officials. At a picnic in a desert oasis with Lou Ann and Mattie, Taylor meets Esperanza and Estevan, a young refugee couple from Guatemala. Estevan was once an English teacher in Guatemala City, but now works as a dishwasher in a Chinese restaurant in Tucson. For an unknown reason, Esperanza is shaken by the sight of Turtle and Lou Ann's son, Dwayne Ray, and remains withdrawn for the day. On the way home that night, Turtle makes the first sound Taylor has ever heard her utter—a laugh. Shortly thereafter, she says her first word: bean, then goes on to name a whole list of other vegetables.

When Taylor takes Turtle to the doctor for her first checkup, she discovers that the little girl has had multiple compound fractures all over her body. Taylor's situation is compromised slightly by the fact that she has no papers for Turtle—no documents to prove that she is the child's legal guardian. A parallel incident then occurs with regard to the health of Esperanza—severely depressed, the young woman has swallowed a bottle of aspirin and has had to be rushed to a clinic where no papers will be required of her.

Estevan visits Taylor at her home while his wife is in the hospital; he tells her about the horrors of their life in Guatemala. Their daughter, Ismene, was stolen in a government raid that took the lives of Esperanza's brother and two of their friends, who were tortured before they died. The officials who took Ismene were trying to get Estevan and Esperanza to reveal the names of the seventeen other people in Estevan's teachers' union, an underground organization. The parents refused to bargain for Ismene by betraying the lives of their friends, and the child disappeared forever, probably to be adopted by a childless government or military couple.

One night Taylor returns to find that something awful has happened to Turtle. The child had been out in the park with one of the kindly neighbor women, who is blind, and someone assaulted Turtle. A social worker and medical examiner are sent to investigate, and Taylor withdraws into herself, unable to cope with this development. She also withdraws from Turtle, overwhelmed by all the cruelty and injustice that she has heard about in the last few days. To make matters worse, Child Protection Services has figured out that Taylor has no legal claim to Turtle and is launching proceedings to either return her to her home or place her in foster care. A sympathetic social worker gives Taylor the name of a lawyer in Oklahoma City who might be able to help her establish that the child has been abandoned.

Mattie, meanwhile, has been trying to smuggle Estevan and Esperanza out of Tucson to safer ground—Tucson was a hotbed of sanctuary activity, and authorities there were very suspicious. As luck would have it, she has arranged for them to be taken in at another sanctuary at a church in rural Oklahoma. Taylor decides to risk jail by acting as an accomplice to their flight; apart from her wish to help, she has fallen in love with Estevan. So the three adults and Turtle head north, retracing Taylor's earlier steps. They take a one-day holiday at Lake o' the Cherokees, where Estevan and Esperanza are transformed, finding themselves among people—the Cherokees—

Dust jacket to Kingsolver's novel about Central American refugees.

who look like them. Now that they do not stand out so much, they relax; Esperanza especially thaws, looking truly happy for the first time in Taylor's experience, playing with Turtle, who returns her affection. The three of them hatch a plan, which works, whereby Esperanza and Estevan pretend to be the parents of Turtle, and sign legal documents in Oklahoma City to the effect that they give her to Taylor. For Esperanza especially, the action is important. Turtle looks like her lost daughter, and when Esperanza pretends to give Turtle to Taylor it helps her lay to rest her disquiet and despair at having lost her own child to nameless forces. Taylor then delivers the couple to the Presbyterian church that will help them melt into the masses of America, bearing new names: Steven and Hope Two Two. Taylor and Estevan exchange tendernesses and sorrow over what might have been, and then part forever. Taylor loads Turtle back into the car and they head home to Lou Ann.

Oral Roberts. In contrast to the dedicated religious workers who man the Sanctuary movement is the omnipresent face and voice of Oral Roberts, Oklahoma's famous television and radio evangelist. Part Cherokee (he won the Indian of the Year award in Oklahoma in 1963), Roberts began as a traveling preacher and faith healer, and eventually parlayed his talent for self-promotion and drama into a $60 million-a-year religious and financial empire. One ex-employee of high standing in Roberts's organization estimated that Roberts received 20,000 pieces of mail every day and that 90 percent of those contained a donation of, on average, $5. Roberts is perhaps most famous for the notion of "Seed-Faith," a fundraising tactic by which Roberts stated that it was

---

FOUNTAIN OF FAITH

∼

At the end of her adventures, with the legal adoption of Turtle virtually completed, a relieved Taylor decides to call 1-800-THE-LORD, something she half-jokingly held out as a last resort if things ever got hopeless. She finds that the operator on the other end of the line is in the business of taking contributions, not offering comfort or hearing testimonials of faith.

"No pledge," I said. "I just wanted to let you know you've gotten me through some rough times. I always thought, 'If I really get desperate I can call 1-800-THE-LORD'." . . .

[The operator] didn't know what to make of this. "So you don't wish to make a pledge at this time?"

"No," I said. "Do you wish to make a pledge to me at this time? Would you like to send me a hundred dollars, or a hot meal?"

She sounded irritated. "I can't do that, ma'am," she said.

"Okay, no problem," I said. "I don't need it, anyway. Especially now. I've got a whole trunkful of pickles and baloney."

"Ma'am, this is a very busy line. If you don't wish to make a pledge at this time."

"Look at it this way," I said. "We're even."

(Kingsolver, *The Bean Trees*, p. 226)

---

the desire of God that people should enjoy spiritual, physical, and financial prosperity; he convinced millions of his television and radio listeners that the way to guarantee themselves a better job, a better home, and a more affluent lifestyle was to give money to the Oral Roberts ministry. By sowing such a monetary "seed," the donor would reap a rich harvest.

Roberts used the money he gleaned from his audience to construct the gleaming Oral Roberts

University in Tulsa, various shots of which Taylor sees on the television in the bar outside of which she is given Turtle. In the early 1980s, Roberts conceived a plan to build the "City of Faith" hospital, hotel, and research center. When he got into some financial difficulties involved with the multimillion dollar project, he claimed to have had a miraculous visitation from a 900-foot Jesus, who assured him that the City of Faith could be built. After making this information public, Roberts was besieged by letters and articles of ridicule and scorn from the media and other religious leaders; he also raked in $5 million almost instantly from his faithful. Roberts continued his fundraising campaigns on television; the toll-free number 1-800-THE-LORD that flashes constantly on the screen that Taylor watches is likely connected with this project, which continued into the late 1980s.

Sources. *The Bean Trees* is highly autobiographical. Kingsolver herself moved from Kentucky to Tucson and came into contact with the Sanctuary movement that sprang up there. Roosevelt Park, which stands at the center of the neighborhood in which the characters central to the novel live, is a composite of the many neighborhoods in which Kingsolver herself has lived. She explains her attraction to a marginally poor community populated almost exclusively by women and children as deriving from her "rural outlook on life": "That's why I found community in a place that more jaded folks would call bad real estate" (Kingsolver in Trosky, p. 287). Kingsolver also explains that the characters of Taylor and Lou Ann are drawn from her own life:

> The two principal characters, both women, are very different: one is adventurous and the other is terrified of life. They were drawn from disparate aspects of my personality that have long been at war. As I wrote the novel, the characters grew to be close friends, and I realized how much these two sides of myself depend on one another for survival.
>
> (Kingsolver in Matuz, p. 68)

Reviews. *The Bean Trees* was a commercial success and also won praise from critics, both especially noteworthy considering that it was a first novel. Margaret Randall, in the *Women's Review of Books*, writes that the book "bolsters my belief in an isolated but essentially generous American people. . . . [A]s long as books like this one are written to help us recreate our common memory, we will be able to leave worthy lives to those coming along behind us" (Randall in Matuz, p. 68). The book "gives readers something that's increasingly hard to find today—a character to believe in and laugh with and admire," said Diane Manuel in the *Christian Science Monitor* (Manuel in Matuz, p. 66). Jack Butler of the *New York Times Book Review* found that the novel decreased in interest after a gripping first third, but stated nonetheless that *The Bean Trees* was "a remarkable, enjoyable book, one that contains more good writing than most successful careers" (Butler in Matuz, p. 66). *Ms.* magazine's reviewer, Karen FitzGerald, looked at how well Kingsolver negotiated the tensions between the book's political and social commentary and its ability to draw the reader into the characters' lives:

> Given [its] ostensible contrivances of plot and character, *The Bean Trees* would seem to be on a collision course with its own political correctness. But Barbara Kingsolver has resisted turning her characters into mouthpieces for the party line. Instead, she has written a vivid and engaging novel that is concerned more with love and friendship than with the perils of single motherhood and the politics of the sanctuary movement.
>
> (FitzGerald in Matuz, pp. 64-5)

For More Information

Coutin, Susan Bibler. *The Culture of Protest: Religious Activism and the U.S. Sanctuary Movement.* Boulder: Westview, 1993.

Cunningham, Hilary. *God and Caesar at the Rio Grande: Sanctuary and the Politics of Religion.* Minneapolis: University of Minnesota Press, 1995.

Harrell, David Edwin, Jr. *Oral Roberts: An American Life.* Bloomington: Indiana University Press, 1985.

Kingsolver, Barbara. *The Bean Trees.* New York: HarperPerennial, 1988.

Manz, Beatriz. *Refugees of a Hidden War: The Aftermath of Counterinsurgency in Guatemala.* Albany: SUNY Press, 1988.

Matuz, Roger, ed. *Contemporary Literary Criticism.* Vol. 55. Detroit: Gale Research, 1988.

The Reagan Administration's Record on Human Rights in 1986. New York: The Lawyers' Committee for Human Rights and the Fund for Free Expression, 1987.

The Reagan Administration's Record on Human Rights in 1988. New York: Human Rights Watch and The Lawyers' Committee for Human Rights, 1989.

Reasonable Fear: Human Rights and United States Refugee Policy. Amnesty International: New York, 1990.

Sholes, Jerry. *Give Me That Prime-Time Religion: An Insider's Report on the Oral Roberts Evangelistic Association.* New York: Hawthorn, 1979.

Thornton, Russell. *The Cherokees: A Population History.* Lincoln: University of Nebraska Press, 1990.

Trosky, Susan, ed. *Contemporary Authors.* Vol. 134. Detroit: Gale Research, 1992.

Washburn, Wilcomb E., ed. *Handbook of North American Indians.* Vol. 4: *History of Indian-White Relations.* Washington: Smithsonian Institution, 1988.

Bless the Beasts and Children

by
Glendon Swarthout

Before becoming a full-time author, Glendon (Fred) Swarthout taught English at various universities. He wrote his first novel in 1943, going on to create short stories, film scripts, and plays as well. His bestselling novel, *Bless the Beasts and Children,* is a coming-of-age story about the pains of adolescence; it also serves as a social and ecological commentary about animal preservation in the United States. Published in 1970 and written shortly before, the novel mirrors America's growing concern for conservation at this time by emphasizing the cruel but legal method of buffalo hunting in the United States. Also raised in the novel are other contemporary issues of the day, such as the war in Vietnam.

Events in History at the Time of the Novel

The buffalo. At the turn of the century, the North American bison, a type of buffalo, was in danger of becoming extinct. The American Bison Society was established in 1905 and proceeded to lobby for laws that would protect and restore the population of American buffalo; it enjoyed the support of President Theodore Roosevelt. By 1930 efforts to rescue the species had met with success. Set aside in the southwestern and midwestern regions of the country were several buffalo preserves. One such preserve was the Raymond Ranch in Arizona, between the cities of Flagstaff and Winslow, in the same area where the novel's Box Canyon Boys Camp is located.

> **THE LITERARY WORK**
>
> A novel set in a boy's camp in Arizona in the late 1960s; published in 1970.
>
> **SYNOPSIS**
>
> A group of teenage misfits in a summer camp for boys attempt to rescue a herd of buffalo destined for slaughter.

Because of the successful preservation efforts of the American Bison Society, the population of buffalo grew so strong and numerous that it became necessary for the herds to be "thinned" in order to maintain a healthy population within the perimeters of the preserves. State-approved gaming licenses were allocated for the slaughter of a specified percentage of buffalo. Part of the slaughter served commercial purposes through the sale of hides, meat, and other such products obtained from the animals. One method of reducing the population of herds came from game sportsmen, who would hold buffalo hunts similar to the hunt the boys witness in *Bless the Beasts and Children.* In the novel the boys are horrified at how the buffalo hunts are conducted. The story describes bloody, violent, and cruel killings in which there is no regard or compassion for the animals relegated to this fate.

> Three animals were released from the pens each half hour, and the shooting began . . . strange things happened to Americans when they

attempted to fix in their sights the most American of all species. Shooting from less than a hundred yards at enormous stationary targets, firing heavy .30-06 and .30-30 caliber weapons, they were somehow emotionally or psychically incapable of killing well.

They gutshot.

They blasted horns from heads.

They blinded.

They crippled, shattering hocks and fetlocks.

They bled buffalo to death before striking a vital organ.

> (Swarthout, *Bless the Beasts and Children,*
> pp. 108-09)

Such passages inspired an already growing awareness of wildlife conservation in the country at the time.

General conservation and preservation of animals. Although buffalo were no longer considered an endangered species by the late 1960s, they were still of concern to the national wildlife conservation movement, which was dedicated to the preservation and treatment of wild animals in the United States. Others, such as Tom McHugh in his book *The Time of the Buffalo,* warned that the crisis had not passed.

> With each passing year man draws his world of concrete and steel more closely around him. In the fight to reverse this trend, the rescue of the buffalo has been a dramatic and encouraging success, but it marks no more than a beginning. If man cannot make a passionate commitment to the preservation of his fellow creatures, many more will vanish in time.
>
> (McHugh, p. 314)

In 1962 an essay entitled **Silent Spring,** (also covered in *Literature and Its Times*), by Rachel Carson, alerted Americans to the deadly effects of pesticides on man, animals, and vegetation. A renewed conservation movement arose from this book's message, and in subsequent years it produced legislation aimed at protecting and preserving wildlife and endangered species. The year 1964 saw the creation of the Land and Water Conservation Fund Act, which allowed for the use of federal funds to acquire property needed for conserving endangered species and a variety of wildlife. In 1966 the Endangered Species Preservation Act was instituted, a land acquisition program created to conserve, protect, restore, and propagate selected species that were in danger of extinction in the United States. In 1969 this legislation was expanded even further in the Endangered Species Conservation Act, which listed specific types of wildlife under protection.

The Novel in Focus

The plot. *Bless the Beasts and Children* takes place near Flagstaff, Arizona, at the Box Canyon Boys Camp during a summer in the late 1960s. The camp hosts boys from the ages of thirteen through sixteen. Parents are encouraged to send their adolescent male offspring to the camp to help the boys through their difficult passage into manhood. The camp advertising slogan is, "Send us a boy—We'll send you a Cowboy!" (*Bless the Beasts and Children,* p. 24).

To promote ambition and pride in oneself, camp authorities have designed a program in which steep competition plays a major role in the day-to-day activities. The boys are encouraged to divide themselves up into cabins and are then assigned counselors, after which the groups are labeled best to worst. By the end of the first week, the misfits of the camp, the boys who have reputations for being less adept in sports or who generally have problems fitting in with the rest, end up together in one cabin. While the other cabins excel in the various sports and activities, these outcasts, who are unceremoniously labeled "The Bedwetters," come in last in every event. The other cabins have mascots of a lion's head, an elk's head, and a buffalo head; the Bedwetters are given a chamber pot. The leader of the Bedwetters, a fifteen-year-old named Cotton, is an honest and just boy with a cherished dream—to lead a troop of Marines through rice paddies in war-torn Vietnam. Also among this group of misfits are Goodenow, an introverted, sensitive boy with a stepfather and a genuine bed-wetting problem; Teft, a wealthy juvenile delinquent who gets caught driving without a license; Shecker, the attention-starved son of a comedian; and lastly, the Lally brothers (called Lally 1 and Lally 2), whose parents have jetted off to Kenya after reconciling their own unstable relationship. Interjected throughout the novel are glimpses of each of the boys' dysfunctional family background. All coming from less than happy home lives, the boys support one another during their period of growth into manhood.

Since the Bedwetters are deemed delinquents and losers by their peers, they decide to live up to the reputation by pulling various pranks throughout the summer. In one incident, they sneak out on horseback in the middle of the night to see a drive-in movie. They try to capture a rival cabin's mascot but are caught and humiliated. Trying again at this prank, they let loose the camp horses as a diversion while they steal the mascots from the other cabins. Teft then shoots

A nineteenth-century buffalo kill. Widespread slaughter of the buffalo nearly led to its extinction.

a round into each mounted animal head and the Bedwetters are thereafter feared by the other campers and considered beyond reproach. One day, on the way back from a camp-out, they talk their counselor into letting them watch a buffalo hunt. The boys are all sickened at how cruelly and inhumanely the animals are slaughtered for sport. Lally 2 leaves camp that night and the others follow. All six boys embark on a mission to save what is left of the buffalo herd, whose remaining animals are tagged for slaughter in the next day's hunt. In the middle of the night, they release the buffalo from their pen, taking horses and hot-wiring cars until they manage, in the end, to carry out their noble task of making the buffalo stampede a couple of miles to the wilderness area beyond the preserve, where they would be safe from the shooters.

The changing family. Tough enough to lead his "troops," the other Bedwetters, teenager Cotton nevertheless shows a vulnerable side when it comes to his family. "His mother had been married three times and divorced three times and was now keeping a man ten years younger than she" (*Bless the Beasts and Children,* p. 94). Cotton liked her second husband, who took the boy fishing.

> "Will you and her get divorced?" the boy asked.
> "Probably. She needs a younger man. And money even more, her own money."

> "I wish you wouldn't."
> "Perhaps she'll sell you to me."
> (*Bless the Beasts and Children,* p. 95)

The conversation reflects values and trends in larger society—money and the increasing number of broken or unstable marriages—that resurface in the background information about the other Bedwetters. Goodenow has problems relating to his stepfather, while Shecker's father pays a counselor $50 so that his son will always have a friend at the camp. The unstable marriage of the Lally parents prompts one of the boys to retreat "into a world of fantasy, self-created, into an isolation to which he admitted no one" (*Bless the Beasts and Children,* p. 73). The majority of boys in the Bedwetters' group do not hail from the traditional two-parent home with working father, housewife mother, and children.

The story is, in fact, set in a time of tremendous transition in the American family, a period that began around 1960. Within a decade (1966-76) divorce rates doubled in the country and there was at the same time a rapid increase in the number of stepfamilies. Meanwhile, scores of married women pushed beyond the limited housewife and mother role that they had filled in the past, and instead joined the work force. All this had a great impact on their offspring. Television grew in importance; watching it occupied youngsters' time until it became "the single most important caretaker of children in the United States" (Hawes and Nybakken, p. 196). And the medium began to present shows that portrayed young people as wise and independent, sometimes more knowing than their parents, as Cotton seems to be in relation to his mother in the novel. Teenagers became a group more separate from children and adults than they had been in the past. Meanwhile, people worried about the harmful effects of divorce on children and of their constant exposure to drugs, violence, and sex on television. There were, in fact, detrimental consequences. Teenage suicide and juvenile delinquency rose, factors reflected in the novel by young Goodenow's threats to commit suicide and by Teft's brazen actions such as his expertise at hot-wiring cars.

Another influence of the era came from the counterculture, the name given to a movement of rebellious American teenagers and young adults who criticized the nation in protests, art, and the music of the 1960s. The boys' rebellion at society's policy regarding the buffalo echoes the rebellious stance that had been taken earlier in the decade by the counterculture youth against policies they identified as unjust, such as segregation.

Vietnam on television. The fact that the head of the Bedwetters, Cotton, aspires to be a Vietnam war hero is due in part to what he has viewed of the war on television and also to his natural inclination to be a leader.

> Cotton's generation grew up with war in the house. . . . A boy had but to turn a control to be totally involved in the violent distention of experience that was Vietnam on television. Cotton became addicted to it. . . . His former fantasies, being the first man on the moon . . . he put away as childish, preferring instead to slog through a rice paddy with a decimated platoon. . . . His only fear was that Vietnam might be over before he could get there.
> (*Bless the Beasts and Children,* pp. 144-45)

Although visions of war were captured on film and shown before mass audiences in movie houses in the form of newsreels during World War II, the Vietnam War became the first major conflict to be internationally televised and shown daily on local and national news programs. Sometimes called "the living-room war," no other war has been so written about, filmed, or documented by the media as the one in Vietnam. The networks spent millions of dollars to provide television viewers with a bird's-eye view of the

battle in Indochina from the mid-1960s through its final days in 1975. Critics debated whether the coverage of the war on television was more effective in provoking antiwar sentiment or in rallying support for the cause. In 1967 *Newsweek* magazine commissioned a poll regarding the media impact on public opinion concerning the war. The survey found that only 31 percent of those polled said that they were moved to oppose war by what they viewed of Vietnam on television. The same group also indicated that the television coverage made them more inclined to support the troops rather than oppose American intervention in the conflict.

"GAS HIM"

Along with the rise in juvenile delinquency and suicide among teenagers after 1960 came an increase in childhood obesity. In *Bless the Beasts and Children,* the camper Sammy Shecker has an overeating disorder. He also overdoes it, as far as the other Bedwetters are concerned, in his attempts to be funny, an understandable strategy given that his father is Sid Shecky, the comedian. The boys find a way to control their campmate's annoying habit of trying to be a comic—they resort to the refrain "gas him," a reference to the murder of 6 million Jews in Nazi Germany's concentration camps during World War II, and he quickly cuts out the comedy. It is a sobering chant that shows the influence of the times on communication among young people as well as on family relations.

Sources. In addition to his many accomplishments as an author and a professor of English, Glendon Swarthout was also a World War II veteran who served in the U.S. Army infantry from 1943 to 1945. He became a sergeant and was awarded two battle stars. Cotton's dreams of the glories of war and his aptitude for leadership may have been drawn from Swarthout's own experiences; the view is expressed in the novel that the broadcasting of the Vietnam War on television made it seem glorious to potential soldiers like Cotton.

Swarthout lectured in English at Arizona State University, Tempe, from 1959 through 1963, after which he retired from teaching and pursued his writing career full-time. The novelist died in Scottsdale, Arizona, in 1992. His familiarity with the state of Arizona contributed directly to the settings used in *Bless the Beasts and Children.*

Reception. *Bless the Beasts and Children* received praise from critics upon its publication in 1970. Glowing reviews came from Brian Garfield in the *Saturday Review* and from Richard Schickel in *Harper's* magazine:

> Mr. Swarthout's taste in simile and metaphor is a little richer than mine, but the novel needs simplifying intelligence like his right now if it is to retain its hold on the general populace. . . . He is a stylist who also entertains and instructs and I say good for him. It is not as easy as it sounds.
>
> (Schickel, p. 107)

Considered Swarthout's most popular novel, since its publication in 1970 *Bless the Beasts and Children* has since sold more than 2 million copies worldwide. In 1980 the Arizona Game and Fish Department published the following in its annual report issue of *Wildlife Views:*

> In 1971 the Department received a lot of public sentiment against the buffalo hunt, largely as the result of a novel which told a gory fictional account of Arizona's annual buffalo removal program. The procedures of the hunt were subsequently changed in 1973, and within a few more years the buffalo hunt became a true hunt with hunters stalking the huge animals across seemingly miles of prairie.
>
> (*Arizona Game and Fish Department Wildlife Views,* p. 30)

Although *Bless the Beasts and Children* was not specifically named in this report, it is safe to assume that it probably was the novel indicted by the Arizona Game and Fish Department.

For More Information

Allen, Thomas B. *Guardian of the Wild: The Story of the National Wildlife Federation, 1936-1986.* Indianapolis: Indiana University Press, 1987.

Arizona Game and Fish Department Wildlife Views 23, no. 1 (January 1980): 30-1.

Hallin, Daniel C. *"The Uncensored War": The Media and Vietnam.* New York: Oxford University Press, 1986.

Hawes, Joseph M., and Elizabeth I. Nybakken, eds. *American Families: A Research Guide and Historical Handbook.* New York: Greenword, 1991.

McHugh, Tom. *The Time of the Buffalo.* New York: Alfred A. Knopf, 1972.

Schickel, Richard. Review of "Bless the Beasts and Children," by Glendon Swarthout. *Harper's* 240, no. 4 (April 1970): 107.

Swarthout, Glendon. *Bless the Beasts and Children.* New York: Doubleday, 1970.

Brave New World

by
Aldous Huxley

THE LITERARY WORK

A novel set in the year 632 A.F. (defined in the novel as after Ford, or occasionally Freud); published in 1932.

SYNOPSIS

In a dystopian world in which mass production techniques are applied to human biology, a young man tries to deal with a society in which population and social rank are determined by the state and true happiness is achieved only at enormous cost to individual freedom.

Aldous Huxley was born in 1894 into one of England's most distinguished intellectual families. His grandfather, Thomas Henry Huxley, was a brilliant biologist nicknamed "Darwin's bulldog" for his staunch support of the theory of evolution during the *Origin of Species* debates in the mid-Victorian period. His father, Leonard Huxley, was a respected editor and essayist, and his mother, Julia Frances Arnold, was the niece of the poet and literary critic Matthew Arnold as well as granddaughter of Dr. Thomas Arnold, a pioneer of English public education. Huxley's brother, Julian, was a noted geneticist. A product of the combined Huxley and Arnold strains, Aldous Huxley possessed a heritage that was literary as well as scientific. Although this marriage of ideas is found in many of Huxley's writings, it is especially evident in *Brave New World,* the novel for which he is most famous.

Events in History at the Time of the Novel

Despair in England. Huxley wrote much of *Brave New World* in 1931, during a difficult period in England: "The Labour Government fell, the pound fell, productivity fell, unemployment rose, riots broke out in London and Glasgow, the Navy mutinied at Invergordon, long lines formed everywhere, and the depression settled down over Britain like an ominous cloud" (Firchow, p. 77). Filled with despair, people "were seriously contemplating and frankly discussing the possibility that the Western system of society might break down and cease to work" (Toynbee in Bradshaw, p. xvii).

In October of 1930, Huxley visited a mining village in Willington; what he saw there contributed greatly to his sense of gloom and decay. In Willington, the miners continued to face unemployment and diminished living conditions as a result of a general strike in 1926. In the years immediately following World War I, England's coal industry had fared unexpectedly well because its European competitors were still recovering from the effects of the war. However, when production in neighboring countries resumed at the middle of the decade, British mine owners decided that the only way to remain viable was to implement longer hours and lower pay for their work-

Ford Model T assembly line.

ers. In protest, nearly 3 million union members from the railroad industry and the iron, steel, and building trades officially went on strike on May 3, 1926. Their action was short-lived. Not only did the government devise an emergency system of transportation, which weakened the impact that the work stoppage had on the general population, but, unlike previous protests, the general strike of 1926 was not violent. As a result of these conditions, the strikers were unable to secure the widespread support necessary to elicit change, and the strike came to a close after only nine days, with the two sides failing to come to an agreement. When Huxley happened upon the miners some five years later, his contact with them convinced him that England was at its nadir in the 1930s. In a letter dated January of 1931, he described the despair permeating the lives of the unemployed miners that he met in Willington:

> The human race fills me with a steadily growing dismay. I was staying in the Durham coalfield this Autumn, in the heart of English unemployment, and it was awful. The sad and humiliating conclusion is forced on one that the only thing to do is to flee and hide. Nothing one can do is any good and the doing is liable to infect one with the disease one is trying to treat. So there's nothing for it but to make one's escape while one can, as long as one can.
>
> (Huxley in Bradshaw, p. xv)

Huxley's sense that it was futile to attempt to rectify what has gone wrong with English society is expressed in *Brave New World,* in which the effort to build a perfect society leads only to a different strain of the original sickness, and in which the final option exercised by John, the "Savage" who has been introduced to the "modern" society, is to "flee and hide."

Huxley's travels. In the decade preceding publication of *Brave New World,* Huxley found himself in an enviable position. After spending his post-Oxford years working first as a schoolmaster at Eton and then as a journalist for the *Athenaeum* in London, he signed what would be the first of a series of three-year contracts with the Chatto & Windus publishing house in January of 1923. For the first time, Huxley now had the opportunity to write what he wanted and, more importantly, where he wanted. Taking advantage of this new freedom, Huxley and his wife, Maria, traded the familiar comforts of London for the poetic allure of Italy. The couple would remain there for the next two years, traveling extensively and observing firsthand the rise of Benito Mussolini's Fascist Party.

In the fall of 1925, the Huxleys embarked upon a world tour, which took them from India to Indonesia, Japan, and finally to the United States. America left its indelible mark upon the author; *Brave New World,* in fact, takes its inspiration in large part from a uniquely American style of industrial manufacturing. The factory in which children are produced, for example, is modeled upon Henry Ford's manufacturing plant, where Model T automobiles were built with speed and efficiency using assembly-line techniques. Ford himself becomes a sort of religious figure within the future society that Huxley envisions.

Brave New World recalls the culture of 1920s and early 1930s America, a culture of which Huxley—like many other European philosophers and social critics of the day—was highly critical (although Huxley himself would live for many years in California). In 1927, he wrote an essay entitled "The Outlook for American Culture: Some Reflections in a Machine Age," in which he theorized that American culture represented the future of civilization. In his view, this was a dim prospect indeed. In America's capitalist system, Huxley saw the privileging of quantity over quality—the system would cater to the masses, and not to the wishes and needs of the best and brightest citizens. The average citizen thus becomes the focal point of the civilization:

> This tendency to raise the ordinary, worldly man to the level of the extraordinary and disinterested one seems to me entirely deplorable. The next step will be to exalt him above the extraordinary man, who will be condemned and persecuted on principle because he is not ordinary—for not to be ordinary will be regarded as a crime. In this reversal of the old values I see a real danger, a menace to all desirable progress.
>
> (Huxley in Firchow, p. 35)

The "real danger" of which Huxley speaks in this essay appears as standardization in *Brave New World;* although he by no means condemns it outright, Huxley clearly perceives American popular culture as a threat to individuality and intellectual development.

Eugenics. *Brave New World* opens in the Central London Hatchery, where test-tube babies are incubated and "decanted," and where their genetic development is carefully manipulated in order to produce predictable results. Huxley's fantastical setting was but a foreshadowing of future developments in reproductive technology; practices such as amniocentesis, cloning, and test-tube babies would eventually come to pass. This scene at the Central London Hatchery is based on theories of eugenics, a school of thought that was both popular and respected in Huxley's day. Sir

Francis Galton, an English statistician and amateur biologist (and cousin of Charles Darwin), coined the term *eugenics* in 1883 from Greek words that mean "well born" (Degler, p. 41). People later applied the term to a movement to regulate the inheritance of traits in order to "improve" society. Proponents of the movement argued that "scientific proof" linked undesirable social traits such as mental deficiency, criminality, and other forms of deviant behavior to inherited characteristics. Such arguments led to an increase in the popularity of eugenics around the turn of the twentieth century, although it had been discussed in scientific circles for some two decades

---

AN INTRODUCTION TO FASCISM

One of the prevailing themes in *Brave New World* is the extent to which an authoritarian government stifles the individuality of its people. Huxley learned this lesson during his sojourn in Italy in the early 1920s. One morning in June 1925, he and his wife were accosted by four ruffians clad in the uniforms of the Fascist Party, who insisted on searching the Huxley home. Apparently, they believed that the Huxleys were hiding Gaetano Salvemini, an Italian professor wanted for writing material against the fascist regime. Huxley refused to let the ruffians in and demanded to see their warrant (which they did not have). The men ignored his protests and went ahead with their search. They found no sign of their suspect and left rather shamefaced. Their blatant disregard of his rights made a strong impression upon Huxley. Later he would say with some authority: "One cannot imagine how the Italian population suffers an entirely irresponsible private organization . . . sometimes usurping powers that should belong to the state, sometimes resorting to incredible acts of violence and brutality" (Huxley in Bedford, p. 119).

---

before that. The original intent of eugenics was to produce "socially desirable" people and to prevent the spread of the "undesirable" by such means as sterilization and legal restrictions on marriage. Conceived of as a responsible social reform movement, eugenics proved immensely popular in both England and America in the early 1900s. The first world congress of the Eugenics Society was held in 1912, with Winston Churchill as vice president of the English delegation and prominent university directors and philanthropists at the head of the American faction. Less prominent citizens also showed keen interest in the idea of regulating human breeding to bring the masses up to the intellectual and moral level of the elite. So high was the demand for 10,000 pamphlets printed by the English Eugenics Society to explain the benefits of sterilizing certain people that an extra 10,000 were produced. Huxley himself favored compulsory sterilization for the "feeble-minded," for adults who had a mental age of six to eight (Huxley in Bradshaw, p. 151).

I'M *SO* GLAD I'M A BETA

In the dormitory visited at the beginning of *Brave New World,* young Betas—second in rank among the five classes of people—are undergoing training as they sleep regarding how to act and think. Recordings are played over and over again in the ears of slumbering children. The Betas hear the following message:

> Alpha children wear grey. They work much harder than we do, because they're so frightfully clever. I'm really awfully glad I'm a Beta, because I don't work so hard. And then we are much better than the Gammas and Deltas. Gammas are stupid. They all wear green, and Delta children wear khaki. Oh no, I *don't* want to play with Delta children. And Epsilons are still worse.

(Huxley, *Brave New World,* p. 21)

Although it began as a liberal reform movement, eugenics quickly became markedly racist. In America, some eugenicists used scientific theory and I.Q. tests to assert that blacks and some minority whites were inferior to other Caucasians and should be dealt with accordingly. Criminals and juvenile delinquents were sometimes sterilized without legal authorization. This violation of rights reached extreme measures in Nazi Germany, where the desire to "purify" German lineage eventually resulted a program of genocide. Beginning in the 1930s the Nazis began implementing a range of tactics based on eugenic theories, such as forced sterilization of the disabled; eventually their campaign against "non-Aryans" would decree the outright slaughter of Europe's Jewish population.

Modernism. From the early to the mid-twentieth century, a revolutionary movement preoccupied the world of literature and the arts. Termed

"modernism" because of its stark break from traditional forms and subjects, the literary strain of this movement is represented by well-known writers like Ezra Pound, Virginia Woolf, Franz Kafka, James Joyce, and T. S. Eliot. These authors ushered in a new era of writing that reflected contemporary breakthroughs in the social sciences—predominantly in anthropology, psychology, philosophy, and political theory. The psychoanalytic theories of Sigmund Freud and Carl Jung assume great importance in the works of these writers, as does comparative anthropology's collection and comparison of mythic systems from around the world. Abandoning traditional chronology and narrative technique, modernist literature often played with individual forms of expression: sharing a character's thoughts, for example, just as he or she would have thought them, unmodified by grammar and punctuation. At its onset, modernist writing exhibited a lively energy and utopian spirit, which World War I seriously dampened. Postwar literature conveyed an overwhelming sense of disillusionment and despair, a bitter realization of humanity's most savage instincts.

By the early 1930s, when *Brave New World* was published, Aldous Huxley had come to epitomize the skepticism and sophistication of the late modernist movement. To an entire generation of younger people, he was a brilliant literary figure. According to one source: "[Huxley] seemed to represent the kind of freedom which might be termed *freedom from:* freedom from all sorts of things such as conventional orthodoxies, officious humbug, sexual taboos, respect for establishments" (Spender in Julian Huxley, p. 19). Although the modernist movement would come to a close by the start of World War II, the influence of Huxley and his predecessors would linger for decades to come.

The Novel in Focus

The plot. As the novel opens in the year 632 A.F. (after Ford), or 2540 A.D., the Director of Hatcheries and Conditioning is taking a group of students on a tour of the Central London Hatchery and Conditioning Centre. "Viviparous," or natural, childbirth is a thing of the past. Nowadays, test-tube fetuses are delivered by decanting, a process that is carefully regulated by the state. People destined to be leaders—Alphas— are produced from a single ovum and are therefore capable of individual thought; those meant to be followers and workers are mass-produced by causing a single ovum to "bud" into multiple embryos. Each person is engineered to remain content with his or her position in society: no one wishes to be other than who he or she is. From the fetal stage people are conditioned to become one of five basic varieties: Alpha, Beta, Gamma, Delta, or Epsilon (after the first five letters of the Greek alphabet). A variety of scientific techniques is used to produce each of the five types. For example, at the bottom of the social hierarchy, Epsilon fetuses are deprived of oxygen at various stages of their development to render them "fit" (i.e., mentally and physically deformed) for the type of position they will fulfill during their lifetime.

Later, the tour group goes to a dormitory where several young children are undergoing hypnopaedia, or sleep-teaching. The tour ends with a quick trip to the outdoor playing facility where naked children engage in erotic games designed to adequately prepare them to enter their sexually promiscuous society.

Mustapha Mond, the Resident Controller for Western Europe (one of ten world controllers), then appears, and delivers a lecture on the history of Utopia. As Mond is speaking, the novel races back and forth between several other conversations occurring simultaneously. One of these takes place between Lenina Crowne, a nurse from the Hatchery, and her friend, Fanny. Apparently, Lenina has been spending too much time with only one man, an act of behavior discouraged in modern society. As Fanny begins to scold her friend for not being promiscuous enough, the reader is whisked away to another scene in which two men, Henry Foster and the Assistant Predestinator for the Centre, are casually discussing "having" Lenina. "Yes, I really do advise you to try her," the former suggests to the latter. "Every one belongs to every one else, after all" (*Brave New World,* pp. 46-7). Eavesdropping on their conversation is yet another figure, a member of the Psychology Bureau named Bernard Marx, who silently objects to their discussing Lenina "as though she were a bit of meat" (*Brave New World,* p. 45). Rumor has it that Bernard's embryo was tainted with alcohol prior to his birth, thereby offering an explanation for his strange glumness.

A few days after the scenes at the Hatchery, the story focuses on Bernard and Lenina. As a member of the scientific community, Bernard has secured passage to the Savage Reservation in New Mexico, one of the last bastions of primitive society left on earth. He invites Lenina to join him;

Henry Ford

in an attempt to cure herself of her previous bout with monogamy, she readily accepts. Neither can predict what awaits them.

The pair are guided to a mesa where a penitent ritual involving snakes and flagellation is taking place. Lenina is disgusted, and the sight of dirt, disease, and old age on the faces around her—none of which occur in the modern world—does little to assuage her contempt. After the ceremony, a young savage named John approaches the couple with an interesting tale. His mother, like Bernard and Lenina, is a product of the outside world, abandoned in the reservation by her male partner many years earlier. John introduces Bernard and Lenina to his mother, Linda, who not only corroborates his story but also adds insight into the difficulties she experienced adapting to primitive ways. Upon hearing all this, Bernard decides to bring both John and his mother back into the folds of modern society and, after a few phone calls, the quartet are on their way to London.

The two people from the reservation find life in the civilized world far from accommodating. Linda, whose return to the society she once adored is marred by her visible aging and the disparaging rumor that she bore a child naturally through "viviparous" birth rather than by decanting, eventually seeks solace in the wonder-drug known as "soma." She spends the rest of her days in soma-induced bliss until her death near the novel's end.

WHERE DID THE NAMES COME FROM?

Although Huxley does not state the exact origins for his characters' names, they are clearly derived from among the world's most famous politicians and scientists. The following is a list of some of Huxley's cast and the identities of the real-life persons their names invoke.

1. Benito Hoover: Benito Mussolini (1883-1945)—founder of Italian fascism; Herbert **Hoover** (1874-1964)—U.S. president at the onset of the Great Depression.

2. Bernard Marx: Claude **Bernard** (1813-78)—French physiologist; credited with launching the science of experimental medicine; Karl **Marx** (1818-83)—political theorist, sociologist, and economist, and author of the *Communist Manifesto* (1848).

3. Mustapha Mond*: Kemal Atatürk **Mustapha** (1881-1938)—founder and first president of the Turkish republic; Ludwig **Mond** (1839-1909)—a founder of Britain's chemical industry and one of the first to establish an eight-hour workday in England, as well as homes and recreational facilities for his employees.

4. Helmholtz Watson: Hermann Ludwig von **Helmholtz** (1821-94)—German scientist-philosopher who held that all knowledge is based upon experience (either hereditary or acquired); John Broadus **Watson** (1878-1958)—founder of behaviorism, which decreed that all human behavior was learned.

* Since this is the name of Huxley's World Controller, it has also been suggested that it serves as a pun, as in "must staff a world" (*monde* being the French word for "world").

John is also unable to adjust to his new surroundings, despite the support given him by his new friends Bernard and an "emotional engineer" named Helmholtz Watson. Even the affections of Lenina are not enough to make him feel welcome; he is repulsed by her lust for him and spurns her attentions. Eventually John's dissatisfaction leads to the inevitable: a meeting with Mustapha Mond, the Resident Controller.

John and Mustapha Mond engage in a compelling debate regarding the status of Utopian society. Armed with his knowledge of Shakespeare (who is quoted sixty-five times in the novel), whose works are banned in the modern world but accessible on the reservation, John challenges the restrictive policies of his new culture. Arguing against the insulating effects of soma, he quotes *Othello* as proof that emotions, however harsh, are beneficial to human life: "If after every tempest came such calms, may the winds blow till they have weakened death," he says (*Brave New World,* p. 244). John asks to be sent to one of the islands to which Bernard and Helmholtz are being exiled, but it is decided that he will remain in modern society in the vain hope that he may one day realize the error of his ways. Balking at this decision, John flees to an abandoned lighthouse outside London, where he attempts to lead a life of solitude until the press locates him. Soon after being discovered, and after a savage ritual in which he whips Lenina, John decides to end his life as the only means of escape.

Our Ford. The name of Henry Ford ("Our Ford") is used religiously by the characters in *Brave New World,* as though a person today might say "oh God"; the whole society, in fact, takes its dating system from the year in which Ford first starting producing the Model T automobile in the same way people have commonly used the date of the birth of Christ. Ford's writings are treated within the novel as though they were holy scripture, and characters cross their stomach with a "T" (after the Model T) when invoking Ford's name. The novel clearly means to indicate that the "brave new world" in fact had its birth in Ford's industrial philosophy.

Although he seems something of a sinister influence in Huxley's novel, the real-life Ford has been described as someone motivated by the best of intentions. He was a believer in making business benefit the consumer and the employee, and in the ability of machinery to improve the quality of life. His assembly-line technique for building cars lowered the price and sped up the rate at which cars could be produced; by mass-producing a single identical item over and over again, with workers repeating the same simple task over and over, Ford made it possible for almost every family in America to be able to own a car. He also paid high wages to his employees, although this practice has been described by some historians as mere business sense and not compassion. Furthermore, Ford's system relied on a "hierarchical authoritarian organization of industry," beginning a trend that seems to have greatly troubled *Brave New World*'s author (Bradshaw, p. 242).

Sources. In *Brave New World,* one of the steps in producing children perfectly suited to their destined roles in society takes place in the "Neo-Pavlovian Conditioning Rooms." For example, children who are to work indoors in a nonintellectual capacity are conditioned as infants to respond negatively to books and flowers by associating these things with frightening sounds (shrieking sirens and alarm bells) and a mild electric shock. This scene was modeled closely on the theories of John Broadus Watson (1878-1958), an American psychologist who, influenced by Ivan Pavlov's theory of conditioning, believed that instinct had little to do with human behavior, and that conditioned responses, such as those that the children in Huxley's books-and-flowers incident undergo, explained everything that people did. In a book entitled *Behaviorism* (1921), Watson wrote what one historian has called "the most famous single passage in the history of American psychology":

> Give me a dozen healthy infants, well-formed, and my own specified world to bring them up in and I'll guarantee to take any one at random and train him to become any type of specialist I might select—doctor, lawyer, artist, merchant-chief and, yes, even beggar-man and thief, regardless of his talents, penchants, tendencies, abilities, vocations, and race of his ancestors.
> (Watson in Degler, p. 155)

Such theories were in direct contrast to principles of eugenics. Huxley opposed Watson and the "behaviorists" who followed him, and agreed with his geneticist brother Julian's theory that human life could not be so easily and mechanically explained. In *Brave New World,* the "emotional engineer," Helmholtz Watson, is named, in part, as a disparaging allusion to John Watson.

Reviews. *Brave New World* was published on February 2, 1932, and received mixed reactions; some public libraries chose to ban it from their shelves. But a review in *Punch* magazine praised the book: "Never has Mr. HUXLEY'S intelligence been more lucid, his wit more mordant or his style more competent than in this remarkable book" ("Grim Future," p. 166). The novel sold 13,000 copies in England in the first year and 10,000 the next.

The American reviewers were far less polite, perhaps because the work was so obviously a satirical disparagement of their own culture. Its poor sales (only 3,000 immediately after publication) may also have reflected the wave of pessimism that was flooding American society in the years following the Great Depression: people simply did not care to experience such a dismal attitude in the literature they read. Instead, they wished to escape reality. One representative American review in the *New York Herald Tribune* notes: "*Brave New World* is intended to be the Utopia to end Utopias, the burlesque of grandiose modern schemes for futurity. It is described by the publishers as 'witty and wickedly satirical,' but unless the substitution of Ford for God . . . and the introduction of . . . scintillating nursery rhymes can be relied on to stop the show, it must stand on its merits as a lugubrious and heavy-handed piece of propaganda" (Dawson in Draper, p. 284). Huxley recounts the fate of his book in a 1932 letter to an American friend thus: "I'm glad you liked *Brave New World.* I gather that it's been rather badly received by the critics on your side [of the Atlantic]. Which is a pity from the business point of view. In England, surprisingly, they have chirped up most laudatorily and the book is selling hard" (Huxley in Smith, p. 358).

For More Information

Bedford, Sybille. *Aldous Huxley: A Biography.* London: Chatto & Windus, 1973.

Bradshaw, David. *Aldous Huxley: Between the Wars.* Chicago: Ivan R. Dee, 1994.

Degler, Carl. *In Search of Human Nature: The Decline and Revival of Darwinism in American Social Thought.* Oxford: Oxford University Press, 1991.

Draper, James, ed. *Contemporary Literary Criticism.* Vol. 79. Detroit: Gale Research, 1994.

Firchow, Peter Edgerly. *The End of Utopia: A Study of Aldous Huxley's Brave New World.* Lewisburg, Pa.: Bucknell University Press, 1984.

Huxley, Aldous. *Brave New World.* London: Chatto & Windus, 1932.

Huxley, Julian, ed. *Aldous Huxley.* London: Chatto & Windus, 1965.

Kevles, Daniel J. *In the Name of Eugenics: Genetics and the Uses of Human Heredity.* New York: Knopf, 1985.

"Grim Future." In *Punch* 182 (February 10, 1932): 166.

Schultz, Harold J. *British History.* 4th ed. New York: HarperCollins, 1992.

Smith, Grover, ed. *Letters of Aldous Huxley.* New York: Harper & Row, 1969.

Carrie

by
Stephen King

Born in 1947, Stephen King came of age during an era in which many praised the achievements of science but also feared its potential for destruction. The author himself has noted that the tenor of American life at the time lent itself to horror fiction. Between the wonders of technology and the fears raised by the Cold War, potential terrors seemed to lurk around every corner. King has utilized these subconscious fears in his creation of a phenomenally successful body of horror fiction, of which *Carrie* was his first commercial triumph.

Events in History at the Time of the Novel

Modern American horror. Although it arose out of a long literary tradition, the modern American horror novel only emerged in the years following World War II. At this time, writers began to break from the gothic elements that had dominated horror writing in the past. Rather than focusing on the menacing individual, novelists started to associate horror with modernization, American society, and the threat of aliens to human existence. Moreover, the potential destruction affected not just a fictional individual or family, but was global in scope. This shift resulted from the cultural and social conditions of the times.

After the stock market crash of 1929 and the subsequent depression that followed, many argued that the capitalist system required economic and political management. They bolstered their argument by pointing to the apparent success of Fordism, a way of organizing labor that extended beyond the business environment to management of other areas of employees' lives. Many of

---

THE LITERARY WORK

A novel set mainly in the late 1970s in the fictional town of Chamberlain, Maine; published in 1974.

SYNOPSIS

Subjected to the torment of her mother and her peers, a female adolescent, Carrie, uses her telekinetic powers to exact revenge.

Fordism's tenets were based on the principles of automotive pioneer Henry Ford, whose company employed a Sociological Department that made inspections into workers' homes to ensure that cleanliness and sobriety were being practiced and that the workers were saving their money. Investigators reviewed the personal bankbooks of employees. Although some people applauded these principles of Fordism and general attempts to legislate social behavior, others feared the potential for social domination by a powerful elite. Books such as *Invasion of the Bodysnatchers* (1954) reflected a fear of the loss of American individualism.

By the next decade, the horror writer's criticism of American society had reached even further. Many critics identify the release of Robert Bloch's novel *Psycho* in 1959 as a major shift in the direction of horror fiction. Rather than expressing the "monster" as an invader from another planet or country, *Psycho* pointed toward American institutions as instigators of evil. In *Psycho,* this threat is traced back to the most basic of all institutions, the family. A "normal" teenager, Norman Bates, takes on a murderous personality when he becomes sexually excited. Raised in a matriarchal household, Norman blames his family for his disturbed mental state, and refers to his alternate persona as "mother." *Psycho* did not stand alone in its critique of the American family. In Shirley Jackson's *The Haunting of Hill House* (1959), for example, the main character, Eleanor, spends her life caring for her domineering mother. Eventually she takes her own life, frustrated with her conflicting desire for individuality and her fear of vulnerability. This concern with the family and the instability of the individual became a prevailing theme in horror fiction of the 1950s and 1960s.

By the late 1960s, however, horror writing had taken on apocalyptic dimensions. Novels such as Michael Crichton's *The Andromeda Strain* explored the potential for destruction contained inside the human mind itself. In this book, a satellite sent from earth returns, bringing with it a pestilence that threatens human existence. Originally sent into orbit by the U.S. military, the explicit purpose of the satellite had been to discover a plague that the military could use as a weapon. The real-life fear of nuclear and biological weaponry at the time, as well as the contemporary mistrust of the military, are clear factors in this work and others like it. King's novel falls in line with the popular horror tales of the day. Like its predecessors, *Carrie* explores the complications that can result from a dominating, matriarchal household. The resulting destruction, moreover, not only affects its title character and her mother but also encompasses the entire town. With its psychological and apocalyptic elements, King's novel combines the most significant components of modern horror fiction.

Psychokinetic research. The late 1960s saw a boom in the public's general interest in parapsychology. This field includes two general categories. The first, extrasensory perception (ESP), incorporates such phenomena as telepathy, clairvoyance, and precognition. Persons possessing such powers can transmit, sense, or foretell knowledge of a general state of affairs independent of the known senses. The second category, called psychokinesis (PK), literally translates as "motion produced by the mind" (Braude, p. 26). Also known as telekinesis, this ability enables a person to move objects without the use of physical force. The novel's Carrie White demonstrates this talent.

Studies of paranormal behavior have taken place throughout the course of modern history.

Between the late 1800s and 1930, exploratory efforts attempted to establish scientifically the existence of such powers. Because most researchers linked the paranormal and spiritual worlds, experiments assumed that persons with PK acted as mediums between the earthly and metaphysical realms. Most PK phenomena cited at this time occurred during séances. At these sessions, a medium and several attendees would sit around a table in a dimly lit room. Entering a trancelike state, the medium would call on the spirits to offer signs of their presence. There were reports of such spectacular events as the levitation of furniture, the feeling of hot or cold sensations, or the manipulation of musical instruments. While many fraudulent mediums were exposed as charlatans, other experiments gave the public cause for wonder. In one series of studies, for instance, Harry Price recorded the actions of the medium Stella C. Situated in his laboratory, Price maneuvered all controls of the room. Despite the use of "foolproof" devices, Stella still managed to significantly manipulate the temperature of the room as registered on a wall thermometer. On one occasion, she flipped a light switch located in a cup sealed by a soap bubble covering. Without disturbing the cup or breaking the seal, Stella turned the light on and off.

Inspired by these and other such claims, the focus of PK research underwent a shift in 1930. That year the Parapsychology Laboratory of Duke University, under the helm of J. B. Rhine, initiated a series of groundbreaking experiments. These studies used more scientific approaches than had been attempted in the past. Rhine and his co-workers standardized the apparatus used to determine PK ability, and they employed rigorous statistical standards of research. With the use of dice, Rhine asked his subjects to attempt to mentally manipulate the numbers that would come up in a series of rolls. He began by letting the subjects throw the dice from their hands, then moved to a cup, and finally on to a mechanical apparatus. Since each of the six faces of a given die should turn up, on average, in one-sixth of the throws, Rhine looked for runs of twenty-four where a target number turned up greater than four times. While his studies did little to conclusively determine the presence or absence of PK, in his research he nevertheless managed to pioneer a scientific approach toward parapsychological research.

Although experimentation with PK declined during the early 1960s, a series of PK "stars" excited the public's interest in the phenomenon.

Psychokinetic individuals such as Ted Serios, Nina Kulagina, Felicia Parise, and Uri Geller grabbed headlines with tales of their powers. Geller, arguably the most famous of the telekinetics, astounded researchers with his ability to bend keys and platinum rings with the influence of his mind. Unfortunately for the field of parapsychology, however, Geller preferred the role of showman over that of subject. As such, he submitted himself to few controlled experiments. Given the climate of the era, it is little wonder that in the novel, Carrie White emerges as a star of infamous proportions. Indeed, compared with the bending of keys, the depth of Carrie's alleged psychokinetic abilities far outreaches those of her real-life contemporaries.

Religion and parapsychology. In the novel Carrie's mother, Margaret White, violently opposes her daughter's use of telekinesis. Although Margaret herself does not possess any such power, her familial line carries a history of it. Nonetheless she refuses to allow Carrie to exercise her talents. When Carrie first evidenced telekinetic ability at the age of three, Margaret White physically beat her daughter into suppression. Only when Carrie begins to mature into womanhood does she gain the self-awareness that allows her to explore her psychokinetic powers. Much of Margaret White's fear and abhorrence stems from her fanatical involvement with religion. She views her daughter as an incarnation of the devil, and thus seeks to destroy her own offspring. Unfortunately for Carrie, her mother does not subscribe to a line of reasoning in real life at the time; this reasoning acknowledged a connection between religion and parapsychology.

Virtually all religions assume the existence of a realm beyond that which we physically perceive. Through ceremonies involving prayer, song, or dance, most religions of the world attempt to bridge the gap between earthly existence and the spiritual realm. Parapsychology likewise attempts such connections. Because the presence or absence of God cannot physically be confirmed, religion relies on faith. While the wonders of parapsychology certainly cannot prove or disprove the existence of God, they do shore up the argument for forces beyond human recognition for people of the mid- to late twentieth century. One sees this especially in the case of miracles. The Christian Bible recounts the tale of the woman of Samaria to whom Jesus spoke. With no knowledge of her personal history, Jesus tells the woman that she has five husbands, and that she currently resides with a man who is not one of these husbands.

Taken aback by his powers of perception, the woman declares Jesus a prophet. In the language of parapsychology, his ESP powers have led her to this claim of faith. Such miracles are furthermore not limited to Western religion. In Buddhism, there is a tale that upon meeting a disbelieving hermit, Buddha exercised his powers of the mind to convince the doubting man to have faith. In fact, the pages of religious texts tell countless tales of healings, prophecies, and telekinesis.

While connections between parapsychology and religion certainly do not appear in mainstream discussions of faith, interest in them did begin to develop during the latter half of the twentieth century. Michael Perry's *The Easter Enigma* (1959) suggests that parapsychology's experimentation with apparitions lends credence to the belief in the actual resurrection of Jesus Christ. Other works, such as J. D. Pearce-Higgins and G. S. Whitby's *Life, Death, and Physical Research* (1973), sought to educate religious students on parapsychological findings. The early 1970s also saw the emergence of several groups whose purpose was to outline the implications of parapsychology for religious teachings. Organizations such as the Churches' Fellowship for Physical and Spiritual Studies, and the Spiritual Frontiers Fellowship began to meet to discuss these themes. In fact, in 1969, Sir Alister Hardy founded the Religious Experience Research Unit at Oxford University with the express purpose of studying religion and parapsychology from a biological standpoint. Hardy suggests that the mind's ability to communicate with another mind relates to the belief in contact with an entirely alternate plane of consciousness. While humans have yet to unequivocally prove the validity of parapsychology, the interest that has sprung up over the last fifty years suggests that a sizable number of people are willing to entertain the possibility of its validity. This popular interest provides a ready audience for stories like King's *Carrie*.

The Novel in Focus

The plot. *Carrie* opens in Chamberlain, Maine, during the 1980s, but quickly flashes back to detail the horrific story of Carrie White, which transpired a decade earlier. Carrie, a senior at Chamberlain's public high school, had suffered throughout her life as the butt of her peers' jokes. Ostracized from the company of her contemporaries, she endures the rigors of school only out of necessity. Carrie's home life is equally abysmal. A religious fanatic, Carrie's mother takes Christ-

Sissy Spacek in the title role of the 1976 film adaptation of *Carrie.*

ian worship to dangerous extremes. She rejects most social behavior as the temptation of the devil, and both physically and emotionally abuses her daughter into following this same belief system. Without a father or sibling, Carrie has no allies at either home or at school. Despite this unusual upbringing, however, Carrie leads a fairly normal existence until one fateful afternoon in gym class.

While showering with her peers in the locker room, Carrie begins to menstruate. Her mother has always viewed the menses as outward evidence of female impurity, and thus has never educated Carrie regarding puberty. Seeing the blood running down her leg, Carrie assumes that she has suffered a hemorrhage and flies into a state of panic. Her classmates, giddy with the opportunity to deride their favorite victim, encircle her and throw sanitary napkins while taunting her. In her confusion and humiliation, Carrie experiences a unique sensation. She serendipitously discovers that by focusing her rage, she can manipulate objects. In the locker room, she causes doors to slam and makes light bulbs burst, all without the use of physical force. After this introduction to her telekinetic powers, Carrie begins to exercise and thus improve her mind's control.

Carrie leaves school that afternoon and does not return for the rest of the week. The other girls involved in the incident receive reprimands for their behavior. Forced to either endure detention or to miss their senior prom, most of the young women choose to stay after school in detention hall. However, one of the more popular girls, Chris Hargensen, refuses to suffer from a trick played on such an inconsequential person as Carrie White. She opts out of detention, and although she can no longer attend the prom, she intends to exact her own revenge. Meanwhile, another of Carrie's tormenters, Sue Snell, undergoes a change of heart. Embarrassed by her actions, Sue tries to right her wrong by befriending the ostracized Carrie. The separate plots of Sue and Chris coalesce in disaster on prom night.

Knowing that no boy is likely to ask Carrie to the prom, Sue talks her boyfriend, the popular Tommy Ross, into inviting Carrie. He hesitantly agrees, and though she is initially suspicious, Carrie accepts. Meanwhile, Chris, busy with plans of her own, convinces her boyfriend to obtain a bucket of pig's blood that she intends to dump onto Carrie's head at the dance. Carrie, by now elated at the prospect of going to the dance with Tommy, begins preparations for the big

night, oblivious to the events transpiring. When she informs her mother of her plans to attend the prom, Margaret White shudders in rage. Although she pleads, threatens, and even attempts to force her daughter into submission, Carrie no longer suffers under the control of her mother. With the use of her telekinetic powers, Carrie makes it clear to her mother that she will be making her own decisions from now on.

On the night of the dance, Carrie emerges as a young woman transformed. She has sewn a fashionable dress for herself, a far cry from the nondescript clothing that she usually wears. Both outwardly and inwardly, Carrie appears more beautiful than she has ever looked. In fact, when Tommy picks her up, he is taken aback by the makeover that has occurred. The prom begins as a magical evening, with Carrie finding acceptance from classmates who had always teased her. The stars of the event, Carrie and Tommy even win the votes of their peers as queen and king of the prom. When they take the stage, however, disaster ensues. Having previously rigged the set of the prom, Chris and her boyfriend release the pig's blood during the ceremonial crowning. Covered in blood, humiliated before the entire school, Carrie flies into a blind rage. As her classmates laugh, Carrie telekinetically locks the doors of the gym and opens the emergency sprinkler systems. When water comes into contact with the band's electrical equipment, the sparks set off a fire. Mayhem ensues as the high school seniors find themselves trapped in a burning building. Carrie calmly walks away from the school, but her reign of terror has only just begun. As she walks through the town, she causes electrical lines to fall, and sparks the explosion of the local gas station. Her wake of destruction follows the same path that leads from her high school back to her home. When she arrives, Carrie kills her mother and then dies herself from the strain of the event. In total, 444 residents of Chamberlain die on the fateful prom night. Although investigations into the incident found no conclusive evidence of telekinetic powers at play, the remaining residents of Chamberlain feared for the day when another Carrie would release the same unchecked fury.

Carrie and women's rights. Perhaps the most memorable scene from *Carrie* occurs during the prom's crowning ceremony. At last the recipient of her peers' admiration, Carrie finds herself on stage, accepting her school's nomination as prom queen. So frequently the target of cruel jokes, Carrie can hardly believe her newfound popu-

Gloria Steinem and Betty Friedan at a rally in support of the Equal Rights Amendment.

larity. Unfortunately, the moment of bliss does not last long. Like a Cinderella story gone awry, Carrie's coronation ends in tragedy when the bucket of pig's blood is dumped over her head. The subsequent mayhem suggests just how important the prom had been to Carrie.

Carrie is an adolescent who rarely finds acceptance among her own peer group, and prom night gives her the opportunity to finally belong at school. Despite her unique abilities, she seeks approval just like any other teenager. In the microcosm of high school, a victory in a popularity contest such as the one for prom queen symbolizes the quintessential achievement of such approval. The cruel way in which Carrie is stripped of this moment devastates her beyond emotional repair.

In terms of the historical context of the novel, the emphasis on the prom crown is particularly revealing. Most women remember the early 1970s as a time of activism for the women's liberation movement and a quest for equal rights. The Civil Rights Act of 1964 had guaranteed that employers could not discriminate on the basis of gender, ethnicity, or religion. Seven years later, the Supreme Court determined that unequal treatment based solely on sex violated the Fourteenth Amendment to the United States Constitution. Through these legal victories, women be-

gan to realize their long-sought goals of equal treatment in the eyes of the law. They struggled to break through social and legal gender barriers, to be regarded less as simply homemakers or ornamental objects. The early 1970s ushered in the debate over the Equal Rights Amendment, which, had it passed into law, would have outlawed any and all legal definitions based solely on sex. Discontented with such limitations, women began acting to change old barriers and notions. They organized feminist theater groups and set up day-care centers for infants so mothers could join the work force. In New York City women picketed the offices of *Ladies' Home Journal* and demonstrated in Atlantic City against the Miss America pageant for reinforcing notions that beauty and wifely and motherly duties should take top priority in a woman's life. In 1973 the Supreme Court case *Roe v. Wade* made abortion legal across the country regardless of restrictive state laws, sanctioning the notion that an adult woman possessed absolute control over her body. Female activists seemed to be fighting tooth and nail to lose the "delicate sex" label that modern history had long placed upon them. Yet in Carrie's self-focused teenage world, traditional desires and values—being sought after by boys, looking pretty, and being crowned as queen of an event—still reign supreme.

Sources. Clearly much of the novel's origin comes from Stephen King's imagination, but elements of *Carrie* are rooted in the author's own past. Like Carrie White, King grew up without a father figure, and the small New England town where he lived provides much of the setting for his novel. The author attended Lisbon High School in Lisbon Falls, Maine. Because the district could not afford a bus for the few students that required transportation, it hired a local limousine service to drive students to school. King, one of the passengers, found inspiration for the title character of *Carrie* in one of his fellow riders. A classmate of King's remembers, "When the limo arrived, there was a rush to get the best seat. You didn't want to ride all the way to Lisbon with Carrie on your lap" (Hall in Beahm, p. 29). King often pondered what might have happened if the real-life Carrie had sought revenge.

Carrie, the novel, began as a short story. The author noted that the publishing world seemed taken with supernatural fiction, so he wanted to craft a novel that would capitalize on the popularity of this genre. Intending to write a Cinderella tale with a twist, King seemed disappointed with his initial attempt. In fact, the novel might not have come to fruition had King's wife, Tabitha, not fished some discarded papers from the garbage can. At his wife's urging, King persisted with his efforts and ended up with a 25,000-word tale. With a piece of fiction too long for a story and too short for a novel, King reworked his plot structure. He inserted bogus historical documentation— news articles, for example, on the destruction of the town—that added to the authentic feel of the text as well as to its length. Although he considered his attempt a failure, his publisher at Doubleday did not. Doubleday offered the author a $2,500 advance and published the book in 1974.

Reception of the novel. While *Carrie* drew some rave reviews, it did not reach the bestseller chart when it hit the bookstores in April of 1974. *School Library Journal* called it "a terrifying treat for both horror and parapsychology fans," while *Publishers Weekly* referred to the book as a "fine, eerie, haunting tale" (Beahm, p. 66). Other critics commended the work as a superb attempt by the young writer, since King was only twenty-five when he created the novel. On the other hand, King himself commented that "as far as *Playboy, The New Yorker, The Saturday Review, Time,* and *Newsweek* were concerned, it didn't exist at all. Ditto book clubs" (King in Beahm, p. 67). In fact, King was not pleased with his effort. Of the novel he stated, "Oh yes, it's just some old trash I put together" (King in Beahm, p. 236). Nevertheless, *Carrie* did eventually achieve commercial success, and it was made into a well-received film in 1976.

For More Information

Banner, Lois W. *Women in Modern American History.* New York: Harcourt Brace Jovanovich, 1974.

Beahm, George W. *The Stephen King Story.* Kansas City: Andrews & McMeel, 1992.

Braude, Stephen E. *ESP and Psychokinesis.* Philadelphia: Temple University Press, 1979.

French, Warren. *Stephen King.* Boston: Twayne, 1988.

Jancovich, Mark. *American Horror from 1951.* Staffordshire, England: Keele University Press, 1994.

King, Stephen. *Carrie.* 1974. Reprint. New York: Dutton Signet, 1975.

Krippner, Stanley. *Advances in Parapsychological Research.* New York: Plenum, 1977.

Childhood's End

by
Arthur C. Clarke

Arthur C. Clarke was born on December 16, 1917, in Minehead, England, a small coastal town on the Bristol Channel. At the age of twelve, he read his first science fiction magazine, a November 1928 issue of *Amazing Stories.* Four years later, he joined the British Interplanetary Society, a group founded on the common desire for space exploration. For the next two decades, his interest in this group would endure, through his tenure as a radar instructor in the Royal Air Force during World War II and later as a student in physics and pure and applied mathematics at King's College in London. The influence of the interplanetary society is apparent in *Childhood's End,* the novel most responsible for placing Clarke's name among the foremost science fiction authors.

THE LITERARY WORK

A science fiction novel set primarily on Earth from the mid-1970s to nearly a century into the future; published in 1953.

SYNOPSIS

Members of an alien race known as the Overlords mysteriously appear over Earth's major cities and promise to eliminate war, hunger, and poverty. Only later is it discovered that they are preparing Earth's children to transcend into a superhuman entity known as the Overmind.

Events in History at the Time of the Novel

Life in the fifties. "We have arrived at the point . . . where there is just no real alternative to peace" (Constable, p. 25). With this one brief phrase, United States President Dwight D. Eisenhower summarized the prevailing mood of the fifties. Despite an exterior of unprecedented material bliss, beneath the surface lay the fear of impending doom at the hands of the Soviet Union.

In the closing days of World War II, many longed for a return to the peaceful stature of prewar society. But as early as the Yalta Conference in 1945, Britain's Prime Minister Winston Churchill knew that this would not be the case.

Already the British statesman could see the world dividing into two separate spheres, with Communist Russia leading the East and the United States leading the West. Throughout the 1950s, these two superpowers and their respective allies engaged in fierce competition both on the world's surface (the Korean War, 1950-53) and above it (the launching by the Soviets of Sputnik 1 on October 4, 1957, followed by the United States's own Explorer 1 four months later). The tension between the two superpowers was so sharp at times that though their forces never clashed directly, people came to refer to the competition as the "Cold War."

The birth of the United Nations. One of the most intriguing characters in Clarke's novel is

Rikki Stormgren, the sixty-year-old Secretary General of the United Nations who serves as the human mediator with the Overlords when they first arrive on Earth. It is primarily through Stormgren's conversations with Karellen, an Overlord, that the reader gains several insights into the Overlords' actions.

At the writing of the novel, the United Nations was still a fledgling organization, less than a decade old. The world officially gave birth to the United Nations with the signing of its charter in San Francisco's War Memorial Opera House on June 26, 1945. In January of the following year, the United Nations held its inaugural session of the General Assembly in London, England. Soon after, in 1947, the world organization experienced its first encounter with war.

After several unsuccessful attempts by Britain to assuage the violence in its mandate Palestine, an appeal was made to the United Nations' General Assembly for a possible solution. Under the latter's auspices, it was determined that Palestine would be partitioned into two distinct sectors—one Jewish, the other Arab—with an internationalized Jerusalem. But this settlement was not to everyone's liking, and war soon broke out. The fighting would continue for two years until a cease-fire was established by U.N. representative Ralph Bunche, who earned the 1950 Nobel Peace Prize for his efforts.

Preoccupied with the Arab-Israeli conflict in the Middle East, the United Nations had a difficult time choosing a permanent location for its headquarters. After moving from one temporary location to another, it was decided in 1952 that the headquarters would be built on an eighteen-acre site of Manhattan's east side donated by John D. Rockefeller Jr. The architect Wallace K. Harrison was chosen to design the new structure, a "soaring Secretariat Building, flanked by a low-lying domed Assembly" (Janello and Jones, p. 25). Over the years the building would come to be recognized across the globe as a beacon of peace in a sometimes chaotic world.

The space age. Historians hesitate to attach an exact date to the start of the space age. But its three founding fathers can be named with more certainty. From the first father of the space age, Robert Goddard (1882-1945) of the United States, came contributions to rocket theory that were rivaled only by his launching of the first liquid-fueled rocket in 1926. The second, Konstantin E. Tsiolkovsky (1857-1935) of Russia, solved theoretically the problem of escaping the Earth's atmosphere and introduced the concept of multistage rockets. Finally Herman Oberth (1894-1989) of Germany wrote books on rocketry that tackled everything from maneuverability in space to the abnormal effects of pressure on the human body. Working independently, each of these men contributed significantly to the study of rocket science. The results of their experiments helped lay the foundation upon which later studies about rockets and space would be built.

During World War II, the ideas originally proffered by Goddard and his colleagues were elevated to new heights. While up to this time there had been little continuity of development among the world's greatest minds, the advent of war brought with it a rejuvenated interest in the study of rocketry, particularly with regard to use of rockets for military weaponry. All the major powers—Germany, Japan, Russia, Great Britain, and the United States—used rockets and missiles of various sizes throughout the course of the war. The most influential of these was the German V-2, which would become the ancestor of all major postwar designs.

Also to emerge from World War II was the idea of using satellites in space to create a worldwide communication network, first posited by Clarke when he was only twenty-eight years old. In a letter written in 1945 to the English magazine *Wireless World,* Clarke suggested using modified versions of the same German V-2's that were raining on London to launch into orbit instruments capable of broadcasting information across the globe. At the time of the letter's publication, few paid attention. Clarke nevertheless expanded the scope of his ideas into a full-length article for the same magazine nine months later. When the first communication satellite was launched in 1958—five years after the publication of *Childhood's End*—Clarke was credited as being the "father of telecommunications."

Postwar science fiction. When the United States dropped its atomic bombs on the Japanese cities of Hiroshima and Nagasaki on August 6 and August 9, 1945, respectively, many of the world's inhabitants wondered about the dangers technology had created. Those writing in the realm of science fiction were no different. Whereas before the focus had been on a limitless future made possible by scientific means, now, in a post-Holocaust era dominated by the threat of nuclear weapons, many began to subscribe to a more pessimistic view, replacing "the vision of an earthly paradise with the nightmare of an earthly hell" (Clareson, p. 45).

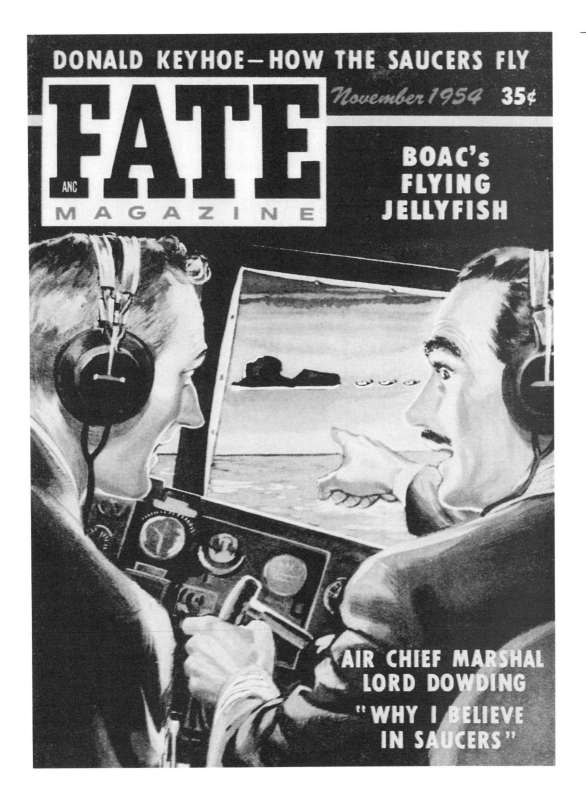

DONALD KEYHOE—HOW THE SAUCERS FLY

November 1954 35¢

FATE
ANC
MAGAZINE

BOAC's
FLYING
JELLYFISH

AIR CHIEF MARSHAL
LORD DOWDING
"WHY I BELIEVE
IN SAUCERS"

Cover of a science fiction magazine from the 1950s focusing on UFOs.

In addition to the new perspectives World War II had given science fiction literature in the postwar years, this period also served as a major turning point for many of the genre's authors. In the early 1950s nearly all of the science fiction literature was still being put out by small magazines. According to Scott Meredith, an American agent who represented Arthur C. Clarke, "In this period none of the major publishing companies . . . were doing science fiction. So several basement operations, cottage industries like Gnome Press and Fantasy Press, had sprung up, and they were started by fans of science fiction. These small presses were the only markets for science fiction novels in the early 1950's" (Meredith in McAleer, p. 78). In 1952, however, things began to change. Thanks in part to Donald A. Wollheim becoming the science fiction editor of Ace Books and Ian and Betty Ballantine founding Ballantine Books (the latter being the first to publish, along with Clarke's *Childhood's End,* such classics as Ray Bradbury's **Fahrenheit 451** [also covered in *Literature and Its Times*]), science fiction made the transition to book format. From that year on, the novel would increasingly become the medium by which science fiction reached out to larger audiences.

Paranormal activity. For centuries, paranormal activity has captivated the imaginations of people everywhere. Included under this label are a number of categories from psychokinesis to astrology, dowsing (searching for underground water with a forked tree branch), card-reading, palmistry, and ouija boards. In more recent times, the study of Unidentified Flying Objects (UFOs) has been added to this list. Clarke was quick to disregard UFOs (one of his favorite lines for would-be UFO observers was: "It's not a spaceship unless you can read the Mars registration plate" [Clarke in McAleer, p. 135]). The novel, however, suggests that he may have had an interest in other phenomena; in particular, the ouija board. Used for paranormal communication, this apparatus is a board with a pointer that spells out messages. Although the ouija board is said to have been in use as early as 540 B.C., it wasn't until 1889 that William Fuld of Baltimore, Maryland, and his brother Isaac came up with the format commonly seen today. Based on their inspiration, most boards contain the alphabet as well as the numbers 0 through 9. The Fulds added also the words *yes, no,* and *good-bye.* To use the board, people thought of as mediums lightly touch the pointer (sometimes called a

"planchette"), allowing it to slide over the board's surface, forming responses to questions. How the pointer manages to compose these messages has long been the subject of controversy. While some believe that it is the result of conscious muscle movement, usually performed by some joker in the group (one of the characters in *Childhood's End,* George Greggson, certainly subscribes to this theory), others believe the movement to be unconscious in origin, either a supernatural occurrence or a display of one's inner psyche.

The Novel in Focus

The plot. *Childhood's End* is a novel told in three separate parts: "Earth and the Overlords," "The Golden Age," and "The Last Generation." Before these parts begin, a brief prologue introduces the reader to two ex-German rocket scientists, Konrad Schneider and Reinhold Hoffman. The year is 1975 and both men are vying for the opportunity to be the first to launch a rocket into space. As Clarke cuts from one man to the other, providing the reader with glimpses of how close each truly is to reaching his goal, the first of the Overlords' great ships arrives on the horizon. It is a moment of self-realization, particularly for Reinhold, who, upon learning that his whole life's work has now been instantly surpassed, can only offer one prophetic thought: "The human race [is] no longer alone" (Clarke, *Childhood's End,* p. 11).

Part 1, "Earth and the Overlords," opens several years later. By now the Overlords have established themselves in the world's skies. Their only spokesperson is an enigmatic figure named Karellen who relays the wishes of his race to the humans on Earth through Rikki Stormgren, the Secretary General of the United Nations.

The Overlords constitute a race far superior to anything humankind has to offer. As a result of the shroud of mystery that seems to cloak both them and their motives (not even Stormgren knows what they look like) there are those such as the Freedom League, a group of dissidents led by a clergyman named Alexander Wainwright, who view the Overlords as a threat. But when members of this group orchestrate the kidnapping of Stormgren in the hope that they can interrogate him for information regarding Karellen, the Overlords respond merely by temporarily freezing the Secretary General's captors and identifying them in case of further subversive activity. Part 1 comes to a close with a promise by Karellen that the Overlords will reveal themselves in fifty years' time. Unfortunately Stormgren knows that by then he will be dead; only future generations will have the pleasure of seeing the two races—human and Overlord—walk side by side.

Fifty years have passed when Part 2 begins. True to his word, Karellen emerges from his space ship as the whole world watches in anticipation. In the half century since the Overlords' arrival, humankind has made tremendous strides, exhibited by the crowd's general acceptance of their alien spokesperson despite his overt resemblance to the devil. "There was no mistake," says the novel. "The leathery wings, the little horns, the barbed tail—all were there. The most terrible of all legends had come to life, out of the unknown past" (*Childhood's End*, p. 68).

Thanks to the Overlords' direct influence, Earth has steadily moved toward Utopia over the years, erasing ignorance, disease, poverty, and fear from the world. Also absent is the concept of war, "[Its] memory . . . fading into the past as a nightmare vanishes before dawn; soon it would lie outside the experience of all living men" (*Childhood's End*, p. 71). The only problem that remained was boredom, which plagues most, but not all, of the earthlings.

Some guests attend a dinner party hosted by Rupert Boyce, a man well-known for his collection of books on the occult. Among his guests is an Overlord named Rahaverak. Despite the Overlords' recent acceptance on Earth, many at the party have never seen one up close and thus much of the evening's conversation revolves around the unusual guest. The highlight of the party occurs near the end when a small group of individuals engages in a seance with a ouija board. In the course of the seance, the question is asked "Which star is the Overlord's sun?" (*Childhood's End*, p. 100). After receiving the cryptic reply of "NGS 549672," one of the participants faints, allowing another one, an African American physicist named Jan Rodricks, to secretly grab the piece of paper upon which the answer is written.

After the dinner party, Jan contemplates his next move. Unbeknownst to the rest of Rupert's guests, "NGS 549672" is the identification number of a star found in an astronomical catalogue Jan had come in contact with during his days as a student. Convinced that it is indeed the location of the Overlords' home, he sets in motion an intricate plan to become a stowaway on their space ship when it returns for supplies. The end of Part 2 finds Jan putting his affairs in order before he departs for a galaxy four light years away.

At the start of Part 3, the reader is reintroduced to George Greggson and Jean Morel, who were guests at Rupert's dinner party. The pair are now happily married with two children, a son named Jeffrey and an infant daughter named Jennifer. In their search for a place that recalls the democratic ideals and individuality of the past, the family has moved to the island of New Athens, a place the novel describes as "what old Athens may have been had it possessed machines instead of slaves, science instead of superstition" (*Childhood's End*, p. 148). The family resides here peacefully and productively, at least for the time being.

THE OVERLORDS AS DEVILS

Scholars tie the concept of the devil, or Satan, as the embodiment of pure evil almost entirely to the Hebrew and Christian faiths. In various other religions, good and evil have been regarded not as two contrary forces but rather as polar opposites of a larger divinity. This affects how one views the devilish-looking Overlords in the novel. By the time they show themselves in the story, all religions have disappeared, except for Buddhism, a faith that subscribes to the notion of a larger divinity. Yet, says the novel, although on the surface people accept the Overlords, many can never face such a satanic-looking creature. "In the Middle Ages, people [had] believed in the Devil and feared him. But this was the twenty-first century; could it be that, after all, there was such a thing as racial memory?" the novel wonders. (*Childhood's End*, p. 70)

The first sign that something strange is happening to the Greggson children occurs when their son Jeffrey is miraculously rescued from an impending tidal wave moments before it comes crashing down. Soon afterward, Jeffrey begins to experience recurring dreams that seem to make no sense. For their daughter Jennifer, the change in behavior is more drastic. One evening Jean is awakened from a deep sleep by the sound of a constantly changing rhythm emanating from her daughter's bedroom. After investigating the sound, she immediately calls out for her husband. Not in her wildest dreams could she have imagined the scene that awaits her.

> It was the sight of that commonplace, brightly colored rattle beating steadily in airy isolation half a meter away from any support, while

Jennifer Anne, her chubby fingers clasped tightly together, lay with a smile of calm contentment on her face.

(*Childhood's End*, p. 174)

It is during the course of a meeting that George has later with the Overlord Rashaverak that much of the explanation in the novel is presented. According to Rashaverak, what is happening to the Greggson children is not an isolated event. All around the globe, the world's children are gradually metamorphosing into a benevolent supreme being known as the Overmind. It is an event as inevitable as the seasons; the purpose of the Overlords' presence was merely to facilitate the transformation. As George leaves, Rashaverak can only offer him one bit of advice regarding his children. "Enjoy them while you may. They will not be yours for long" (*Childhood's End*, p. 177). The words echo in George's mind, especially when the transformation has been completed and he must bid his son a fond farewell before the boy departs into a world the elder Greggson will never be able to enter.

IN THE NAME OF THE FATHER

Clarke's father died prematurely when Clarke was only thirteen years old (of lung complications resulting from poison gas inhalation suffered in World War I). Some scholars believe that the impact the tragedy had on Clarke is evident in his writings, citing in particular the scene in *Childhood's End* in which George Greggson imparts a silent farewell to his son Jeff.

Meanwhile, several light years from the earth, Jan Rodricks awakens from his self-induced slumber, his dream of making it aboard the Overlords' vessel now a reality. To his surprise, the Overlords are not angry with him for joining them uninvited; rather, they treat him almost like a child, intervening only in those rare cases in which he may harm himself or serve as a nuisance, or both. Once on the Overlords' planet in a system they call Carina, Jan is shown the wonders of Overlord society, from marvelous towers built for a race capable of individual flight, to pragmatic buildings, each serving a unique purpose. One day, after riding in an elevator to a height far above the city's peaks, he experiences the climax of his journey.

Right before his very eyes, a large mountain undergoes a transformation of brilliant colors before changing shape into a huge, perfectly circular ring of the most beautiful hue of blue. Little does Jan realize that what he is actually seeing is none other than a physical manifestation of the Overmind. After seeing this and other wonders, Jan is advised to board the next available ship toward earth. He soon finds himself traveling at unheard-of speed back to the planet he calls home.

In the four months that Jan has spent traversing the galaxy, eight decades have passed at home. Since his departure, the children of the Overmind have enveloped much of the world as he knew it through the sheer magnitude of their mental powers. Jan is now the earth's sole survivor.

After assuming his new role gracefully, Jan seeks out remnants of the human race (such as a villa and a piano) with which to bide his time until the inevitable occurs. Eventually he is summoned by Rashaverak, who explains the Overlords' appearance on Earth. Although much of their purpose was to facilitate the metamorphosis of the Overmind, they also sought to understand the transformation. Despite their advanced technology and superior intellect, the Overlords are unable to join the Overmind like the children of the Earth and are envious. At the end of Rashaverak's explanation, Jan is offered a proposition: even though the time has come for the Overlords to depart, he may remain on Earth to inform them of transpiring events. Jan agrees and is soon beaming reports up to Karellen in the Overlords' ship. The death of his signal's emission coincides with the death of the Earth. As the novel draws to a close, Karellen sits six thousand million kilometers away, gazing into a suddenly darkened screen. "No one dared disturb him or interrupt his thoughts: and presently he turned his back upon the dwindling sun" (*Childhood's End*, p. 218).

***Childhood's End* and the Cold War.** In the opening pages of *Childhood's End*, the reader is introduced to two ex-German rocket scientists, Konrad Schneider and Reinhold Hoffman, as they both vie for the opportunity to be the first to launch a rocket into space. In addition to the personal pride that goes along with such an accomplishment, there are also pervading feelings of nationalism. While the former represents the Soviet Union in the East, the latter serves the United States in the West. It is a division born out of the rubble of World War II. Speaking from

Photograph of a purported UFO.

the point of view of Reinhold, the novel describes the division's genesis vividly:

> He could still see Konrad's tired blue eyes, and the golden stubble on his chin, as they shook hands and parted in that ruined Prussian village, while the refugees streamed endlessly past. It was a parting that symbolized everything that had since happened to the world—the cleavage between East and West.
>
> (*Childhood's End,* p. 8)

The two men go about pursuing their goal diligently, backed by the resources of the governments they represent. Then, just as they are about to see their dreams fulfilled, into the novel come the Overlords. In one brief second, the hopes and desires of both men seem instantly defeated: "Reinhold Hoffman knew, as did Konrad Schneider at this same moment, that he had lost the race. And he knew that he had lost it, not by the few weeks or months that he had feared, but by millennia" (*Childhood's End,* p. 11).

In the months following the Overlords' appearance, they create a sort of Utopia on Earth by effectively eradicating war, hunger, and poverty. Although there is uncertainty about the novel's intentions in setting up the U.S-Russian competition and then rendering it meaningless, some scholars have posited that the author is making a statement about the futility of the Cold War. As a member of 1950s society, in which material comfort was offset by the fear that one could perish from nuclear weapons at any moment, Clarke realized that such need not be the case. Rather than use technology to create weapons that inspire fear in the world, these same advancements could be used to promote peace and prosperity, as shown by the Overlords. "[The] novel," says one scholar, "becomes a magnificently desperate attempt to continue to hope for a future for the race in the face of mounting evidence to the contrary. It becomes, in fact, a sometimes brilliant attempt to turn the contrary evidence to the positive. It becomes nothing less than an effort to make positive the destruction of the race" (Hollow, p. 66).

Sources. The origins of *Childhood's End* hark back to July of 1946 when Clarke wrote a short story entitled "Guardian Angel." Although in its original format, it met with little success—"I submitted it to *Astounding,* [and] it was promptly rejected" (Clarke in McAleer, p. 88)—it would eventually provide the basis for Part 1 of *Childhood's End.*

The novel drew also on issues and influences affecting Clarke's own life at the time. Writing in the midst of the Cold War, Clarke was clearly cognizant of the nuclear threat that existed between the opposing superpowers and their allies.

Also reflected in the novel are the author's personal beliefs about religion. Ever since his days as a teenager in England, Clarke had maintained an aversion toward organized religion. In the novel the Overlord Karellen makes the following statement to Secretary General Stormgren: "You will find men like [Wainwright] in all the world's religions. They know that we represent reason and science, and, however confident they may be in their beliefs, they fear that we will overthrow their gods" (*Childhood's End,* p. 23). Finally, Clarke's membership in the British Interplanetary Society, or BIS, influenced the novel. Founded in 1933 by Phillip E. Cleator, an astronautical expert, the BIS was devoted to the study of space travel. Not only did the group provide avenues for publishing Clarke's stories, including *Childhood's End,* but also the ideas that Clarke fostered during his participation with the group served as a main source of his inspiration.

THE LAST MAN STANDING

While visiting the United States in the early 1950s, Clarke spoke with Ian Macauley, publisher of the science fiction magazine *ASFO* (Atlanta Science Fiction Organization). Apparently, the two had much to talk about. "We got to know one another and discussed all kinds of ideas—life, marriage, racial problems, and so on," Macauley later recalled. "At that time, I was very concerned with the racial problems in the South. . . . [Clarke] was writing *Childhood's End* . . . and these discussions about racial problems may have influenced him. I'd like to think that perhaps this is why he chose to make the last person on Earth [Jan Rodricks] a black person" (Macauley in McAleer, p. 92). Clarke himself admitted that this was "perfectly possible. I never met any blacks before I went to America." (Clarke in McAleer, p. 92)

Reviews. Clarke's novel was immediately hailed as a major literary success. The first 210,000 copies sold out in less than two months and by November, an order for another 100,000 was already being placed with the printer. His science fiction novel won all this attention despite being part of a genre that was still years away from major respectability.

Critically speaking, the novel garnered almost entirely rave reviews. Basil Davenport, critic for the *New York Times Book Review,* argued that "In *Childhood's End,* Arthur C. Clarke joins Olaf Stapledon, C. S. Lewis, and probably one should add H. G. Wells, in the very small group of writers who have used science fiction as the vehicle of philosophic ideas. Having said that, one must hastily add that it is as readable a book, from the point of view of pure narrative, as you are likely to find among today's straight novels" (Davenport in McAleer, p. 99). Not all critics shared Mr. Davenport's sentiments. Some, such as H. H. Holmes, a reviewer for the *New York Herald Tribune Book Review,* chose to fault Clarke for what Holmes saw as his overzealous desire to tackle so many themes at once. According to Holmes, "*Childhood's End* is . . . fascinating, but the awkward imbalance between the vast major plot and a series of smallscale subplots makes for a diffuse and distracting novel" (Holmes in James and Brown, p. 185). Generally, however, the praise for *Childhood's End* far outweighed the negative comments, inspiring one scholar to declare thirty years after its publication, "in my opinion [it is] the best SF novel ever written" (DeWeese in May and Lesniak, p. 109).

For More Information

Clareson, Thomas D. *Understanding Contemporary American Science Fiction.* Columbia: University of South Carolina Press, 1990.

Clarke, Arthur C. *Childhood's End.* New York: Ballantine, 1953.

Constable, George, ed. *This Fabulous Century: 1950-1960.* Virginia: Time-Life Books, 1970.

Hollow, John. *Against the Night, the Stars: The Science Fiction of Arthur C. Clarke.* New York: Harcourt Brace Jovanovich, 1983.

Inglis, Brian. *The Paranormal: An Encyclopedia of Psychic Phenomena.* London: Granada, 1985.

James, Mertice M., and Dorothy Brown, eds. *Book Review Digest.* Vol. 49. New York: H. W. Wilson, 1954.

Janello, Amy, and Brennon Jones, eds. *A Global Affair: An Inside Look at the United Nations.* New York: Jones & Janello, 1995.

May, Hal, and James G. Lesniak, eds. *Contemporary Authors New Revision Series.* Vol. 28. Detroit: Gale Research, 1990.

McAleer, Neil. *Arthur C. Clarke: The Authorized Biography.* Chicago: Contemporary Books, 1992.

The Chocolate War

by
Robert Cormier

Robert Cormier, born in Leominster, Massachusetts, in 1925, would later raise a family of three daughters and a son there. During his adolescence, Robert Cormier's own son objected to participation in his school's candy sale. While the boy did not suffer the extreme humiliation that the novel's Jerry Renault undergoes, he did feel a certain amount of alienation from his peers. Building on this premise, the elder Cormier created his fourth novel, *The Chocolate War,* a work that focuses on the sometimes cruel nature of adolescent societies and the consequence of individual choice in a communal world.

Events in History at the Time of the Novel

Adolescents and popular fiction. Although adolescent novels such as *The Chocolate War* now line the shelves of bookstores and libraries nationwide, young readers did not always have such literature at their disposal. In fact, relative to the history of the written word, the teenage novel is a new genre. During the 1930s, secondary education enrollments nearly doubled, giving rise to a new and powerful class of readers. Prior to this period, teachers and authors had, for the most part, ignored the tastes of adolescents, choosing instead to rely on the so-called "literary classics" for reading fare. While these sufficed for some children, educators found that the mandatory reading of formalized literature often turned young minds away from literary experiences that they might have enjoyed later in their intellectual

THE LITERARY WORK

A novel set in Boston, Massachusetts, during the early 1970s; published in 1974.

SYNOPSIS

A young boy defies his teachers and his peers by refusing to participate in the school's annual chocolate sale.

careers. With the burgeoning enrollments, teachers began to consider alternative methods of instruction. Researchers compiled psychological studies of adolescents and discovered that, contrary to popular opinion, older children did seek to broaden their experiences through reading. During this same time, May Lamberton Becker, an educational literature editor, compiled a survey of almost eight hundred young adults. Through their letters she found that most preferred romance and adventure tales such as *Lorna Doone, Ramona,* and *Ben Hur.* These results indicated that the adolescent reading problem stemmed not from a resistance to learning, but rather from a paucity of appealing material. Although educators debated over what types of new reading materials should be promoted, they nevertheless initiated a move toward the acceptance of popular young adult fiction.

By the 1960s, adolescent literature had matured into its own genre with three primary areas of concern: the individual and his or her growth;

social problems and responsibility; and the youth's concern with world events. Librarians, authors, and educators noted that teenagers increasingly sought out books that portrayed honest visions of the world, with all of its virtues and vices. When first published in 1951, for instance, J. D. Salinger's **Catcher in the Rye** (also covered in *Literature and Its Times*) created quite a controversy for its depiction of a character in need of psychological help. The censorship debate that ensued suggested that adolescents might not have the capabilities to deal with negative portrayals of the world. By the late 1960s, however, most educators had accepted the growing teenage interest in novels that dealt honestly with personal or social problems. For example, a 1960 survey cites such political novels as **Animal Farm** (also covered in *Literature and Its Times*) and *The Ugly American* as current favorites for young adults. With the mid-century spread of television, the American youth was exposed to the same mature, often violent images that the previous generation had encountered only later in life. By the late 1960s, for the first time in history the American public could view on a daily basis, through the nightly newscasts, the bloodshed occurring as a result of warfare—in this case, the war in Vietnam. Given such an environment, adolescents seemed no longer to need shielding from the harsh worlds that might await them between the covers of a novel.

Also during this era, the civil rights movement spawned a growth in minority literature. Librarians actually pleaded with editors to provide youths with books that offered realistic portrayals of ghetto life and for ones that used regional or ethnic vernacular. Robert Cormier's *The Chocolate War* aptly represents this turn to realistic fiction for youth. It does not deal with racial issues, but it does concern an individual's painful struggle to defy the status quo. Like other popular novels of its day, Cormier's book paints a realistic image of the sometimes harsh world in which adolescents live.

Private education. The private, all-male school of the novel differs vastly from the typical public institution. While the classes offered at the novel's Trinity High School certainly compare to the curricula of public schools, its social atmosphere is entirely unique. In addition to its single-sex composition, Trinity's Catholic affiliation sets it markedly apart from public high schools. The fictional school does, however, resemble many other private religious schools of modern times.

A 58 percent majority of Catholic schools are located in cities. With enrollments much smaller

Robert Cormier

than in public institutions, private schools offer more compact classes with lower student-to-teacher ratios. In the 1970s, the average enrollment for Catholic high schools was about five hundred. By contrast, many urban public schools boasted student bodies of several thousand. In many cases minority enrollment was low, so the composition of these schools was generally homogeneous.

Trinity is a fictional Catholic day school catering to the children of local blue- and white-collar workers. In real life, wealthier families have tended to send their children instead to prep (preparatory) schools that board them away from home. At the other end of the spectrum, the poorer families of the community are unable to afford even Catholic day school tuition. The ability to pay tuition, however, is not the only challenge to enrollment. As private entities, Catholic schools can refuse admission to applicants for a variety of reasons. Typically the administration relies on school records, achievement test scores, and personal references when deciding whether or not to accept a prospective student. These rigorous standards do not relax once a student enters the school.

Catholic high schools emphasize college preparation in setting academic goals. While the schools offer such typical core classes as physics, mathematics, and foreign languages, they also provide students with opportunities in independent study and off-campus college courses. Naturally schools also insist on a schedule of religious classes as a graduation requirement. Students need not practice Catholicism to attend Catholic schools, but the majority do.

A concern of the first order for private schools is, of course, their own survival. Although current statistics indicate that America's 20,000 private schools account for 10 percent of the secondary education sector, enrollments in Catholic schools are on the decline. This translates into significant monetary losses for these institutions. In Cormier's novel, Brother Leon expresses concern over the financial future of Trinity. With enrollments down, the annual chocolate sale serves an important role in augmenting the school's income. As Trinity earns a percentage of every chocolate sold, the success or failure of the sale directly impacts the budget of the high school. A student refusing participation in the sale would appear to have little or no concern for the welfare of the school in general. For this reason, Jerry's rejection of the sale is not viewed as an individual decision. By refusing to work with his classmates for the welfare of the school, he appears indifferent to the future of Trinity altogether. At a public school funded by tax dollars, this issue would take on less significance. Trinity, however, is a private Catholic school that demands loyalty from the students that it instructs. In the novel Jerry is ostracized, which certainly does not reflect the kindest of Christian values. It does, however, reflect the reality of financial hardship, when in some cases hard-line capitalism often defeats the "love thy neighbor" principle.

High school athletics. Far from being a mere sport, football plays a consequential role in Jerry Renault's life at Trinity. While trying out for the freshman team, he suffers humiliation from his coach as well as physical abuse from older players. He nonetheless competes for a spot on the roster. By the novel's close, the sport ironically forms a safe haven for Jerry. Ostracized by the entire campus for his lack of participation in the chocolate sale, the freshman turns to football as a measure of normalcy in his suddenly confounded life. Jerry, like many other high school athletes, embraces sports as an integral core of the educational experience.

Across the United States, communities share similar enthusiasm for the high school competitions of their local athletes. The American obsession with sports has as much to do with the principles taught through games as it does with the game at hand. In one comprehensive survey, three out of five respondents agreed that athletes provide the best overall role models for children (Cavallo in Miracle and Rees, p. 16). Through sports, adolescents can learn many of the social values necessary for success in work and other aspects of life. They come to understand fair play, respect for authority, and good sportsmanship. Last, but certainly not least, they realize the thrill of victory. All this emphasis on athletics has spawned such telltale American slogans as "winning isn't everything, it is the only thing" (Lombardi in Miracle and Rees, p. 14) and "A tie is like kissing your sister" (Theodore Roosevelt in Miracle and Rees, p. 15). Fostered in schools, the competitive drive, many believe, serves adolescents well not only in teaching them these principles but also in generating school spirit.

Played during the fall season, football kicks off the school year, so to speak. In fact, the sport provides an overall example of the educational institutionalization of athletics. At the turn of the century, football was an incredibly hazardous sport with many injuries and deaths reported annually. Although some schools sought out coaches, faculties originally resisted this move. They feared any type of official association between the school and such an "abusive" sport. The institutionalization of football, however, solved these problems. With adults rather than students leading the field practice and play, rules were adhered to, training facilities were improved, and injuries declined. In 1919 the National Education Association issued a report entitled "The Cardinal Principles of Secondary Education," which extolled the virtues of organized school athletics. By 1932 sociologist Willard Waller had concluded that "Of all activities, athletics is the chief. . . . It is the most flourishing and the most revered culture pattern" (Waller in Miracle and Rees, p. 66). Within a relatively short time, organized athletics had proved their importance in the educational arena.

The Novel in Focus

The plot. When Jerry Renault begins his freshman year at Trinity, the local all-boys Catholic day school, he does not intend to earn an infamous reputation. Still recovering from the recent death of his mother, Jerry wants only to lead a normal high school life. He and his father are not very close, and so Jerry's life has been quite lonely for the past year. Within the first week of school, Jerry earns a position on the football team and seems poised to begin a successful freshman year. However, Archie Costello, the leader of a secret society known as the Vigils, has other plans for Jerry.

THE COUNTERCULTURE AND *THE CHOCOLATE WAR*

Made up largely of young, middle-class white youth, the counterculture movement swept through America in the 1960s. Its members refused to conform to conventional ways. Called "hippies," many of them let their hair grow long if they were male or donned more distinctive clothing such as long flowing dresses if they were female. A trademark for both sexes became blue jeans and muslin shirts. Along with the new styles came a willingness to engage in daring behaviors, such as taking hallucinogenic drugs or engaging freely in sex. On the whole, the movement fostered a general mood of dissent, often expressed by groups of rebels at concerts or political protests. As the 1970s dawned, however, this dissent developed into a more individual trend of following one's own inclinations, popularly described as "doing your own thing." In the novel Jerry encounters a group of hippies; a youth of the 1970s meets youths of the 1960s. The fact that after the encounter Jerry persists in doing his own thing in the chocolate sale, despite tremendous pressure from authorities and peers, brings to mind this real-life societal backdrop.

The Vigils, through their underground student body network, run the social order at Trinity. Every few months or so, Archie and his cohorts choose various students to burden with Assignments. They summon their victims to secluded Vigil meetings, where Archie hands down a sentence. Those chosen cannot refuse their tasks, nor can they tell anyone about their activities when they execute them. In one session, for instance, Archie commands a new freshman to loosen all the furniture screws in a classroom. The following day, mayhem ensues as the class literally falls to pieces. No one dares to defy the Vigil Assignments, as the students fear the wrath of the society. Unfortunately for Jerry, he catches Archie's eye one afternoon at football practice. The Vigil leader singles him out for an Assignment, and orders Jerry to refuse participation in the school chocolate sale.

Each year, Trinity sponsors a schoolwide sale of chocolate candy. A private institution, Trinity relies solely on tuition income to fund its facilities. The proceeds from the annual sale serve as a necessary supplement to the school budget. This year, however, the sale brings with it an added anxiety. With the principal of the school temporarily hospitalized, one of the other teachers, Brother Leon, has taken over the administrative duties at Trinity. Unbeknownst to the other faculty members, Leon signs for twice the normal amount of chocolates. The monk quickly panics over his fiscal risk and, in his desperation, enlists the aid of the Vigils. Recognizing the opportunity to join forces with a faculty member, Archie quickly agrees. The arrangement signifies an unprecedented alliance between the Vigils and the administration of Trinity.

Although the Assignment only mandates that Jerry refuse to sell the chocolates for ten days, he extends the sentence of his own accord. Inspired by a poster that asks, "Do I dare disturb the universe?" Jerry decides to keep refusing to participate in the sale. At first, Jerry's refusal to sell causes only minor tensions at the school. Some of the students even support his independent stance. When chocolate sales fall well behind statistics of years past, however, Brother Leon and the Vigils single out Jerry as a symbol of insolence. The monk puts pressure on the Vigils to pick up the pace of the sales, and the Vigils, in turn, transfer this pressure onto Jerry. They begin to torment him by making prank calls to his house, vandalizing his locker, and beating him up. Nevertheless, Jerry refuses to submit. Angered by the freshman's defiance, Archie rallies his group to sell chocolates like never before. In this manner, they hope to humiliate Jerry for his audacity in challenging the Vigils. As chocolate sales escalate, the school turns on Jerry, accusing him of apathy and disregard for the welfare of the school. Jerry ironically finds himself ostracized for carrying out an "assignment" that he originally undertook for fear of not fitting in.

Eventually the chocolate sale ends with Brother Leon and Trinity successfully meeting the school quota. Still the Vigils refuse to relax in their pursuit of Jerry. They arrange for an after-school fight at which spectators both choreograph and bet on the physical blows that Jerry must endure. Brother Leon appears as an invited guest to watch the event. Jerry suffers such harm that an ambulance must be called to take him away. Although he loses the physical bout, he maintains his dignity in becoming the first stu-

The Woodstock Music and Art Fair (1969), perhaps the culmination of the counterculture movement of the 1960s.

dent to defy the school, the Vigils, and his educational universe in general.

Peer pressure. A turning point in Jerry's life occurs one afternoon as he waits for his bus following football practice. Standing at the stop in his school uniform and tie, he stares at a group of hippies across the street. One man confronts him, asking, "Hey, man, you think we're in a zoo? That why you stare?" (Cormier, *The Chocolate War,* p. 19). Unable to respond, Jerry boards the bus. The man continues stating, "Square boy. Middle-aged at fourteen, fifteen. Already caught in a routine. . . . You're missing a lot of things in the world, better not miss the bus" (*The Chocolate War,* p. 20). For some reason unknown to Jerry at the time, the event haunts him. He questions his own blind acceptance of peer pressure and authority. Later in the novel, Jerry recalls the hippie as he stares at a poster lining his locker. The picture shows a lone figure on a stretch of beach with the caption "Do I dare disturb the universe?" Although he had never done so before, Jerry decides to answer in the affirmative by the way he acts in regard to the chocolate sale.

By refusing to sell Trinity's chocolate, Jerry not only defies his teachers, but he also counters the wishes of the school's "in crowd." In fact, he alienates himself from his own peer group. In the world of a modern-day teenager, this type of self-imposed separation is not easy to endure. As part of a group separated from other generations, typical teens spend the majority of their time with their own peer group and learn to conform to it. This is especially true in private schools like Trinity. With their familiar environments being classrooms, shopping malls, playing fields, and automobiles, adolescents virtually invent their own society. This, in turn, places a great deal of importance on the judgment of one's peers. With few other influences that matter as much to them at this point in their lives, teens look to one another for social approval.

In the novel, the Vigils virtually run the school—and, as often the case, a natural leader has emerged. Teenage "in" groups tend to gravitate toward leaders who possess good personality, nice hair, good grooming, fine clothes, and money. Mentioned far less frequently as a factor among teens is academic success. As the novel opens, Jerry hopes to attain these symbols of popularity, but he loses his enthusiasm for group acceptance by the book's close. Perhaps the hippie, a symbol of the counterculture movement, inspires him. Or perhaps Jerry reaches this state of independence because he was forced to grow up quickly after the death of his mother. The novel remains ambiguous as to the impetus for the young man's defiant stance. Even Jerry himself cannot say why he does what he does, and in the end, even he questions the intelligence of his choice. For whatever reason, however, Jerry does opt to go against the grain. In doing so, he becomes a target for those who govern the social structure.

Sources. *The Chocolate War* emphasizes self-reliance and self-respect of the individual. Because of his decision, Jerry must learn to survive alone within his society of peers. Much of Cormier's interest in individual independence comes from his own experience. While still a young boy, Cormier lost his father to cancer. Like Jerry in the novel, the author matured through adolescence in a single-parent household. Later in life, his son refused participation in a school candy sale. Although the boy did not undergo the extreme harassment that Jerry suffers, his actions nonetheless inspired the elder Cormier to develop the defiance into a novel.

Reception. While many critics found the novel disturbing for its "distorted view of reality and . . . feeling of absolute hopelessness" (Bagnall in Stine and Marowski, p. 84), others praised the work for its stark realism. One critic opined that "Robert Cormier does not leave his readers without hope, but he does deliver a warning: they may not plead innocence, ignorance, or prior commitments when the threat of tyranny confronts them" (Carter and Harris in Stine and Marowski, p. 86). Clearly a dichotomous opinion of the book exists. In spite of or perhaps because of this critical debate, *The Chocolate War* is now considered by many to be one of the more important adolescent novels of modern times.

For More Information

Abramowitz, Susan, and E. Ann Stackhouse. *The Private High School Today.* Washington, D.C.: National Institute of Education [1981?].

Cormier, Robert. *The Chocolate War.* New York: Bantam Doubleday Dell, 1974.

Miracle, Andrew W., and C. Roger Rees. *Lessons of the Locker Room.* New York: Prometheus, 1994.

Stine, Jean C., and Daniel G. Marowski, eds. *Contemporary Literary Criticism.* Vol. 30. Detroit: Gale Research, 1984.

Varlejs, Jana. *Young Adult Literature in the Seventies.* New Jersey: Scarecrow Press, 1978.

The Contender

by
Robert Lipsyte

Robert Lipsyte began his writing career as a copy boy on the *New York Times* sports section at age nineteen. After working several years for the *Times,* Lipsyte earned the privilege of writing his own sports column for the paper in 1967. The inspiration for his first novel came from his coverage of the heavyweight boxing title fight between Muhammad Ali and Floyd Patterson in Las Vegas in 1965. During the fight, Cus D'Amato, an aging boxing manager, told Lipsyte stories about his gym on New York's Lower East Side. As soon as he returned to New York, Lipsyte began building on the conversation with D'Amato to write *The Contender,* which would become a major stepping stone in Lipsyte's career as a young-adult novelist.

Events in History at the Time of the Novel

Growing up in Harlem. By World War I, the black population of New York City was centered largely in Harlem, an area in the northern part of the city. Harlem had been overbuilt, abounding in new structures, but the city's transportation systems had not extended into the area at the same pace. Partly as a result of this situation, inexpensive housing suddenly became plentiful, and the growing black population of New York settled the area. In time whites left Harlem completely, and property values dropped. Landlords either sold their buildings at a loss or simply refused to maintain them, allowing the structures in the area to fall into disrepair. The relative

THE LITERARY WORK

A young-adult novel set in Harlem in the mid-1960s; published in 1967.

SYNOPSIS

Alfred Brooks, a seventeen-year-old living in Harlem, overcomes the negative forces of the ghetto to become a "contender" in the amateur boxing world.

poverty of the black community propelled a further decline in the area. In 1961 six out of every ten black families had an income of less than $4,000 a year. In white families, the statistic was reversed—six out of ten white families had an income of more than $4,000 a year.

Poverty was simply one of numerous difficulties facing residents of ghettos such as Harlem in the 1960s. Adolescents growing up in these areas were surrounded by gambling, excessive drinking, drug abuse, sexual promiscuity, violence, crime, and broken families. In the novel, Alfred encounters almost every one of these situations. His circle of friends engages in the burglary of the Epstein store and steals a car; Alfred drinks and smokes marijuana while at an illicit hangout known as the clubroom; he is beaten by Major and the other boys; and his parents are both gone, leaving him to be raised by his aunt. Even though Alfred is intelligent, hard-working, and honest, the conditions have taken a toll on him. When the novel begins, Alfred has dropped out of high school and really has no plans for the future. The question that arises is whether Alfred can overcome his surroundings through the positive influence of Donatelli and the other men from the gym.

The black family and the Johnson administration's War on Poverty. The number of young blacks living in poverty was on the rise in the mid-1960s, when *The Contender* takes place. So was the number of young blacks living in female-headed households, as Alfred does in the novel. Yet contrary to reports of the time, the black family was not in danger of disappearing altogether. The majority of black young people still lived in two-parent households, as they would continue to in the 1970s and '80s. Those who did not belong to this majority were often supported by friends and relatives who joined forces to replace the nuclear family. These friends and relatives formed "domestic networks, making it their business to help out mothers, stand in for fathers, and share their resources with those in need" (Mintz and Kellogg, p. 213). The existence of such networks is portrayed in the novel by Alfred's aunt, who raises him after his mother dies and his father leaves, and Alfred's brother-like concern for the fate of his friend James. Despite such support systems, though, many people's lives were adversely affected by the rising poverty rate and the increasing number of broken homes.

AMATEUR BOXING

Like Alfred in the novel, boxers begin their careers as amateurs, receiving no money for fighting. Amateur boxing matches have only three rounds, which can be either one, one and a half, or two minutes long. Each round is scored on a point system, with victory going either to the fighter who wins two out of three rounds or to the fighter who is able to knock out his opponent. The fighter decides when he wants to move on to the professional level, usually waiting until he has gained experience and several victories before doing so. Alfred's amateur career lasts for only three fights before he retires, realizing that he doesn't have what it takes to move on to the professional level.

The government made an effort to tackle the growing problems. President Lyndon B. Johnson began a "War on Poverty" in 1964, committed

to strengthening the family in America. One of the first efforts in this war was the opening of an Office of Economic Opportunity to furnish education and training to unskilled young people so that they could break out of the cycle of poverty. Under Johnson, Congress established Medicaid to provide health care for poor people under sixty-five years of age; it passed a housing act that gave rent supplements to the poor; and it increased the federal money for education from about $1.5 billion in 1960 to close to $7 billion in 1968. Young people benefited from such projects as the building of new schools, for example. And by the decade's end the War on Poverty had scored some successes. The 20 percent of the population that the government classed as poor in 1960 dropped to 12 percent of the population in 1969. Also there was a decline in the number of families living in sub-standard housing—that is, housing without indoor plumbing—from 20 percent in 1960 to 11 percent by the end of the decade. But problems persisted. One was the high-school dropout rate, which continued to rise, swelling with the increase of young minority dropouts such as Alfred in the novel.

Boxing and its hopes. For many young men growing up in America's poorer neighborhoods in the 1960s, boxing seemed to be one of the few possible escape routes. Newspaper headlines describing the massive paychecks of champion boxers encouraged members of lower-income communities to try their hand at the sport.

In reality, boxing offered little chance of escape. One nationwide study, spanning the years 1938 to 1951, showed that only six hundred fighters actually earned enough money to sustain themselves and only sixty became headline fighters. Succeeding years offered little improvement. Close to the time of the novel, the experiences of Malik Dozier of Washington, D.C., are representative of the false hopes and broken dreams common in the sport. Earning only $150 per fight, Dozier's purse on one occasion was not even enough to cover his medical costs for a broken jaw and chipped teeth. Like many other boxers, Dozier had to supplement his boxing income with money from a full-time job. In many cases, such fighters would drive several hundred miles for a $75 or $150 fight, sleeping in their cars to limit expenses.

Even the more successful boxers seldom found long-term prosperity in the sport. Generally speaking, prizefighters were mostly from low socioeconomic backgrounds and had little education; thus, they were easily victimized by dishonest managers and promoters. Because the average boxing career only lasted six to eight years, it was nearly impossible for fighters to establish a sufficient amount of money for retirement. With few practical skills, many boxers had to return to menial professions even after attaining near-celebrity status. Beau Jack, a famous fighter, became a shoeshine man following his boxing career, and Kingfish Levinsky, another former great, became a traveling tie salesman.

Another aspect of boxing that its eager entrants failed to acknowledge was its physical dangers. After automobile racing, boxing is the next most dangerous sport. There are an average of 3.8 deaths in boxing for every 1,000 participants, a statistic that dwarfs college football's 0.3 deaths per 1,000. Furthermore, deaths and serious injuries in the ring reveal only a small percentage of boxing's potential for danger. The repeated blows to the head that are part and parcel of boxing can cause brain damage as well as increase the risk of neurological diseases. In the novel, Alfred realizes these dangers during his second fight when he refuses to finish off his opponent out of fear of hurting the weakened boy, and during his last fight when he realizes that Hubbard is strong enough to injure him severely.

Black Muslims. The Black Muslim movement began as a small religious sect, the Lost-Found Nation of Islam, established by Elijah Muhammad. Muhammad's central message was black redemption, and his followers were called Black Muslims. He preached that the black man's poor condition in the United States was due to white oppression, and that improvement could only come after blacks relinquished the white man's ways and adopted the true religion of Islam. Muhammad believed that the degradation of blacks could be stopped if blacks would rediscover their African heritage. They should unite and maintain strict separation from whites. Progress would depend, he believed, on the thrift, business enterprise, and economic independence of his followers. The motivating force behind all of these ideas was the belief that blacks were superior to whites and that they would eventually be restored to their rightful place of predominance in the world. In the novel, Major, Hollis, and even James hold attitudes that resemble this idea. While trying to convince Alfred to help in committing a robbery, James tells him, "Whitey been stealing from us for three hundred years. We just going to take some back" (Lipsyte, *The Contender,* p. 5).

Nation of Islam leader Elijah Muhammad

The Black Muslim movement gained momentum with the rise of a new leader named Malcolm X. Born Malcolm Little, Malcolm X was introduced to the teachings of Elijah Muhammad while serving a prison sentence for burglary. Malcolm studied Muhammad's ideas, and by the time he left prison in 1952 he was fully converted and had pledged to serve Muhammad and the movement. As was customary in the movement, he replaced his surname with an "X" to mark the abandonment of his "slave name" (Little) and the renunciation of his earlier way of living (Blair, p. 31).

Malcolm rose quickly in the Black Muslim hierarchy and in December of 1954 was given the ministry of Temple No. 7 in Harlem. It soon became the most prominent Black Muslim congregation in the country, and Malcolm became one of Muhammad's most trusted disciples.

Malcolm declared to his congregation that African Americans were descended from an original Black Nation whose members differ completely from, and are superior to, the Caucasian race. By trickery, Malcolm claimed, the Caucasians had conquered the Black Nation and transported its people to America as slaves. The Christian religion had further reduced the status of blacks through treachery and falsehood. Malcolm preached that blacks must give up the Bible, take up the Koran—the Muslim holy book—and embrace Islam, "the black man's religion" (Blair, p. 33). Malcolm taught that blacks could benefit from their suffering by following Muhammad's teachings and giving up the evil ways they had learned from white people, such as eating unhealthy food, drinking, smoking, carrying weapons, using drugs, and gambling. By exacting retribution for past abuses in the form of land and reparations from the U.S. government, they could start a new life under the leadership of Muhammad.

MUHAMMAD ALI AND THE MUSLIM MOVEMENT

The heavyweight boxer and 1960 Olympic gold medal winner Cassius Clay met Malcolm X in 1963. Malcolm convinced Clay that he could become a powerful tool for the movement, and Clay converted to Islam shortly after his involvement with the group became public in 1964. In 1965 Elijah Muhammad gave Clay the Muslim name *Muhammad Ali* in recognition of his faith. Robert Lipsyte spent much of his career for the *New York Times* covering Ali and actually became a member of Ali's entourage. The author's experience with the fighter and his own conversion to Islam provided background experience for the fictional character Alfred's encounters with the Black Muslims in *The Contender*.

In the novel, Alfred and his Aunt Pearl are confronted by Black Muslims on their way to church. Alfred is ridiculed for going to a Christian church and encouraged to join the movement. One of the Muslims says about Alfred, "Ain't that sweet? On his way to pray to Whitey's God, learn to Tom and turn the other cheek . . ." (*The Contender*, p. 30). Despite their intention of conveying a feeling of empowerment to blacks, the Muslims in the novel make Alfred feel even more alienated and confused, presenting another hurdle he must overcome on his path to success.

The Novel in Focus

The plot. Alfred Brooks, a seventeen-year-old African American, lives with his widowed Aunt Pearl and her three young daughters in a small Harlem apartment. Alfred is an orphan; his father deserted him when he was ten, and his mother died of pneumonia when he was thirteen. After

dropping out of high school, Alfred began working as a stockboy at a local grocery store run by a white family, the Epstein brothers.

After work on a Friday, Alfred waits for his friend James to meet him so they can go to the movies. When James fails to show up, Alfred realizes that he must be hanging out with some local troublemakers at their "club" in a neighborhood basement. Alfred finds James there and tries to get him to leave, but James refuses. The other club members—Major, Hollis, and Sonny—make fun of Alfred for working like a "slave" for the Epsteins, calling him "Good Old Uncle Alfred." When Alfred defends the Epsteins, he inadvertently mentions that they leave the money in the store over the weekend for religious reasons (they are Jewish and do not handle money after sunset on Friday, when Sabbath begins). Major immediately wants to rob the store, and the other boys, including James, follow him. They ridicule Alfred when he refuses to go.

Henry, a teen crippled by a childhood case of polio, whose family lives above the clubroom, finds Alfred alone in the club. Alfred is distracted and barely listens as Henry tells him about his new job working for Mr. Donatelli, the owner of a nearby boxing gym. Worried about James, Alfred leaves the club. On the street, a police cruiser passes by and Alfred suddenly remembers the new silent alarm the Epsteins have installed in the store. He starts to run, but sees the police respond to a call and realizes it is too late. A crowd has gathered outside the store, and Alfred learns that James has been arrested, though the others got away. Walking home, Alfred runs into Major, Hollis, and Sonny, who beat him unconscious for not telling them about the alarm. Henry and his father find Alfred and carry him home to his Aunt Pearl.

The next day, after recovering, Alfred walks around the neighborhood and sees Donatelli's gym and remembers Henry talking about it. Remembering his father saying that Joe Louis had worked out there once, he decides to enter. Inside he finds Mr. Donatelli alone in the darkened gym. Alfred tells him he wants to box, that he wants to become a champion, to which Donatelli responds that he has to become a contender before he becomes a champion. He has to be willing to work hard, even knowing that he may never reach the top. Alfred leaves feeling inspired by Donatelli's words.

Monday morning, Alfred follows Donatelli's advice and gets up at 5:30 a.m. to run through the park. After his exercise, Alfred goes to work at the grocery. Lou Epstein, the oldest Epstein brother, asks Alfred if he knows who the other boys were who tried to rob the store. Alfred says he knows nothing. Still liking Alfred, but wary because they know he is James's best friend, the Epsteins no longer let Alfred take the deposit to the bank in the afternoon.

After work Alfred begins his training at the gym. One night Donatelli gets him a ticket to a fight at Madison Square Garden so he can watch one of their fighters box. After several weeks of training, Alfred begins to doubt his ability to become a boxer. He goes to the clubroom to see if he can find James, who has been released by the police because robbing the store was his first offense. Major and the other club members treat Alfred with more respect now that he is boxing. James hasn't yet arrived, but Major says he is coming and invites Alfred to stay. Eventually Alfred is coaxed into drinking, and he also smokes marijuana with the others as the party lasts through the night. James shows up late in the evening and Alfred is shocked to learn that he has become a heroin addict. The next day, feeling terrible, Alfred again lets himself be persuaded by Major and the other boys to forgo his boxing and go with them in Major's white Cadillac to Coney Island. When it turns out that the car is stolen, Alfred and the others run from the police and escape.

Alfred finally makes his way home by himself, feeling more depressed than ever. He visits Donatelli with the intention of clearing out his locker and giving up. When he asks Donatelli if he thinks Alfred could have become a contender, Donatelli responds that only Alfred can answer that question. Newly inspired, the boy decides to continue his training.

Over the next few months Alfred works diligently and finally gets his first amateur fight. Supported by Donatelli, Henry, and Bill "Spoon" Witherspoon, a former fighter turned schoolteacher, Alfred wins this first fight. During his second amateur fight, he wins but shows that he does not have the killer instinct necessary to become a champion. Despite his two victories, Donatelli wants him to give up the sport. Alfred refuses; he needs to fight again to see if he has become a contender. When he is matched against a heavy-hitting amateur in the next bout, Donatelli again wants him to stop, but Alfred is determined to fight. During the three-round fight he is thoroughly beaten and loses, but proves to himself that he has finally become a contender and can now give up the sport knowing he has succeeded.

Inspired by the example of "Spoon," who has used his discipline in boxing to become a success as a teacher and mentor, Alfred decides that he wants to help his community as well and thinks about working at a local recreation center. When he gets home after the fight, Aunt Pearl tells him that James broke into the Epsteins' store again, this time on his own, and that the police are after him. Remembering a hiding place they shared as children, Alfred finds James there and convinces him to turn himself in. Now stronger than he has ever been, Alfred assures James that they can overcome anything together. Alfred is indeed a contender.

Negativity and peer pressure in the ghetto. One of the greatest difficulties faced by Alfred as he struggles to succeed is the negative influence of people around him. The primary negative influence faced by Alfred comes from other boys in his neighborhood. Out of the five boys in the group, Alfred is the only one who has a job. For working and responsibly giving the money to his Aunt Pearl, Alfred is teased by the other boys. Major mocks Alfred by saying, "You such a good sweet boy. Old Uncle Alfred" (*The Contender*, p. 3). When Alfred refuses to go along with the other boys to rob the Epsteins' grocery, Major scorns Alfred for his loyalty and for working, saying "You just a slave. . . . You was born a slave. You gonna die a slave" (*The Contender*, p. 4). Alfred's best friend James also pressures him to go along, telling him, "Look, Alfred, you don't owe them anything" (*The Contender*, p. 5).

The boys from the neighborhood plan to rob the store a second time, again trying to enlist Alfred's help. But he refuses to disconnect the burglar alarm for them, so Major threatens him with a knife. When that fails to persuade Alfred to help them, Major tries to impress his own perception on the boy: "The Epsteins don't care about you, you just a black nigger slave to them" (*The Contender*, p. 73).

Once Alfred starts boxing in an attempt to better himself, he receives negative feedback from other people around him. Even Reverend Price from his church fails to see the positive side in Alfred's quest. The reverend talks with Alfred about his boxing and tells Aunt Pearl, "This is a passing phase. He'll soon grow tired of this meaningless pursuit" (*The Contender*, p. 81). Although the people in Donatelli's gym provide positive role models for Alfred, the rest of the neighborhood offers no support. Alfred becomes discouraged when he looks around the

Heavyweight boxing champion Muhammad Ali.

neighborhood and realizes that everyone else is out cruising and having fun while he is training. Losing his resolve, he goes to the clubroom where he drinks wine and smokes marijuana. While this is a major lapse for Alfred, it is the normal routine for the rest of the neighborhood teens. Though Alfred does eventually achieve success, he must first overcome the negative influence of people around him. The novel's depiction of Alfred's struggle shows how difficult it is to become successful while living in a negative environment.

Sources. The basic premise of *The Contender* came from a conversation Robert Lipsyte had with Cus D'Amato in 1965 while the two men were in Las Vegas for the heavyweight title fight between Muhammad Ali and Floyd Patterson. Lipsyte was particularly fascinated by D'Amato's story of how he used to sit in his gym on New York's Lower East Side, waiting to hear the sound of footsteps on the three flights of steep stairs outside. Lipsyte recalled D'Amato saying, "If a kid came up those dark, narrow, twisting flights of stairs alone and running scared, there was a chance he might stay with it, hang tough, find himself through dedication and sacrifice" (D'Amato in Cart, p. 1). D'Amato also told Lipsyte, "Fear is like fire. It can burn you or keep you warm; it can destroy you or make you a

hero, a contender in the ring and in life" (D'Amato in Cart, p. 2). Lipsyte recalls that after this conversation, "I sat up the rest of that night aflame. To me becoming a contender meant writing a novel" (Lipsyte in Cart, p. 2). For Lipsyte, who had spent a great deal of time in the boxing world as a sportswriter for the *New York Times,* the creation of *The Contender* was a natural process. D'Amato's gym became Donatelli's gym in the novel, and D'Amato's philosophies inspired the words of wisdom that Donatelli imparts to Alfred in the story. Lipsyte's own experience and journalistic attention to detail became further sources used to make *The Contender* a complete novel.

Critical reception of the novel. There were two predominant critical responses to *The Contender.* Many critics praised the novel for its uplifting portrayal of Alfred's struggle for success, but others argued that Lipsyte is too heavy-handed in his presentation of moral issues, which detracts from the characters and story of the novel. Edward B. Hungerford commented that "Lipsyte writes from deeply within the boy's self and the life of the ghetto. The reader suffers with Alf's humiliations, is stirred by his strivings. Mechanics disappear, and between reader and struggling boy no obstacle stands. A fine book in which interest combines with compassion and enlightenment" (Hungerford in Senick, p. 207). In contrast, journalist Nat Hentoff maintained that while there are flashes of inspired writing, much of the novel is overly didactic. Hentoff wrote: "Far too many writers of fiction for the young seem to believe their primary function is to teach rather than to create textures of experience which are their own reasons for being" (Hentoff in Senick, p. 207). Despite this initial criticism, Hentoff continued that "in several of its parts, however, didacticism recedes, and lo, there is life! In particular, whenever Lipsyte writes about boxing itself he indicates how intensely evocative he can be and he moves the reader beyond maxims into participation" (Hentoff in Senick, p. 207). Despite this and other remarks that *The Contender* was too moralizing in tone, most reviewers agreed that it succeeded in telling a moving story of one young man who overcomes the challenges of his surroundings to become a true champion.

For More Information

Blair, Thomas L. *Retreat to the Ghetto: The End of a Dream?* New York: Hill & Wang, 1977.

Cart, Michael. *Presenting Robert Lipsyte.* New York: Twayne, 1995.

Lincoln, C. Eric. *The Black Muslims in America.* Boston: Beacon, 1961.

Lipsyte, Robert. *The Contender.* New York: Harper Collins, 1967.

Meier, August, and Elliott Rudwick. *The Making of Black America: Essays in Negro Life & History.* New York: Atheneum, 1969.

Mintz, Steven, and Susan Kellogg. *Domestic Revolutions: A Social History of American Family Life.* New York: Free Press, 1988.

Nash, Gary B., et al., eds. *The American People: Creating a Nation and Society.* Vol. 2. New York: Harper & Row, 1990.

Sammons, Jeffrey T. *Beyond the Ring: The Role of Boxing in American Society.* Chicago: University of Illinois Press, 1988.

Senick, Gerard J., ed. *Twentieth-Century Literary Criticism.* Vol. 23. Detroit: Gale Research, 1982.

Donald Duk

by
Frank Chin

Born in Berkeley, California, in 1940, Frank Chin has been called the "conscience of Asian American writing" (Wand in Chan, p. 529). He is a critic, an essayist, a fiction writer, and a playwright. In Chin's view, much of traditional Chinese American literature has stereotyped the Chinese as timid and passive, and has departed from the truth of Chinese history and philosophy. His own writing aims to show Chinese culture in its "real" form, a form that attempts to break away from the stereotypes of the past.

Events in History at the Time of the Novel

San Francisco's Chinatown. Since its origins as a city, San Francisco has included a large Chinese community within its population. The original surge of Chinese immigration came as a result of numerous events in both China and the United States. In the 1840s, China's ruling Manchu dynasty was declining into a state of corruption and injustice. Increases in population, which limited available land, coupled with a terrible cycle of flood, famine, and drought, drastically affected the living conditions for the majority of China's population. The Taiping Rebellion (1850-1864) and the conflicts of the Opium War (1839-42) created even greater discord and hardship in the country. When news of California's gold discovery reached the Canton province in China in 1848, the United States became an attractive destination to thousands of Chinese men eager to improve their lives and

THE LITERARY WORK

A novel set in San Francisco's Chinatown in the early 1990s; published in 1991.

SYNOPSIS

As the Chinese New Year approaches, a twelve-year-old Chinese American boy, Donald Duk, tries to deal with his feelings about his cultural heritage.

those of their families as well. In 1850, 500 men left Hong Kong for California. By the end of 1851, there were an estimated 25,000 Chinese in California, working in the mining industry and other manual labor occupations. By 1890 the Chinese population in the United States reached its peak at more than 107,000, with the majority on the West Coast. The Chinese Exclusion Acts of 1882 and 1902 caused this number to dwindle, but after their repeal in 1943, new waves of immigration revitalized San Francisco's Chinatown and other Chinese American communities. A 1965 revision of U.S. immigration law further stimulated movement from China to the United States.

From its earliest years, San Francisco's Chinatown has existed as a virtually self-sufficient political community through a complicated system of interconnecting organizations. Its ability to handle its own problems has allowed Chinatown to maintain a unique existence, almost independent of the city surrounding it. Chinatown became almost a city unto itself, growing by the 1990s to include 30,000 inhabitants within a twenty-four block area, a population density exceeded in the United States only by some areas of Manhattan. Chinatown continues to be the first home in the U.S. for many immigrants from southern China; they tend to leave the inner city for the surrounding suburbs after achieving some economic success.

Chinese New Year. The New Year is the main festival in the Chinese calendar. It occurs on the second full moon of the winter solstice, which places it either in late January or early February. The celebration of the holiday spans two full weeks. Countless superstitions and traditions are associated with the holiday. For example, it is believed that one shouldn't wash one's hair on New Year's Day for fear of washing away good luck for the coming year. Business transactions are settled and debts are paid before the New Year because it is considered bad luck to begin the year owing money. Another important tradition of the New Year involves giving away *lay see,* or lucky money. The lay see consists of dollar bills folded and enclosed in small red envelopes which are doled out to children and unmarried family members. In *Donald Duk*, Donald receives lay see from his uncle, his aunts, and even from a few family acquaintances.

Food is also a major part of the New Year's celebration. Families come together to share large meals; the overabundance of food symbolizes the hope that the coming year will yield prosperity and happiness. Customary foods also play a part in the New Year's holiday. In the novel, Donald's father cooks a traditional dish, "ho see fot choy," which translates as oysters with noodles and vegetable casserole; the dish is eaten on New Year's because "ho see fot choy" sounds identical to the expression for typical holiday greeting, "happy new year," in Chinese. Similarly, lettuce and cabbage are eaten because their names also sound like the words "fortune" and "riches." Another common New Year's dish is a whole fish, which symbolizes togetherness and abundance for the year to come. The majority of these New Year's dishes are prepared the night before so that nothing is cut on New Year's Day out of fear that the luck of the new year might be cut.

During the New Year's holiday, San Francisco's Chinatown assumes a colorful and carnival-like atmosphere. Vendors sell flowers and candy, and of course, a variety of lay see envelopes all decorated with calligraphy or charac-

ters printed in gold. At the end of the two-week holiday comes the Chinese New Year parade, which includes a colorful sixty-foot dragon operated by more than fifty dancers who carry it on poles as it weaves its way through the streets. The parade is one of San Francisco's largest celebrations and typically draws a crowd of more than 500,000. In the novel, Donald and his friend Arnold carry the dragon through the parade with other members of their kung-fu martial arts school.

Chinese opera. When Chinese immigrants left their homeland to establish a Chinese American community in California, they brought many elements of their culture with them. One of these elements was the musical theater, or Chinese opera. Many of the stories staged in Chinese opera are based on Chinese folktales and mythology. The opera consists of a small orchestra with no more than seven or eight members and elaborately dressed actors who perform the key roles, which are typically limited to a few characters.

IMMIGRATION ACT OF 1965

In 1965 the United States replaced its immigration policy, which set quotas by nation of origin, with an act establishing a yearly limit of 170,000 newcomers from the Eastern Hemisphere and 120,000 from the Western Hemisphere. Family members of U.S. citizens could be admitted regardless of these limits, as could political refugees.

When the Chinese imperial government banned the opera in 1854, San Francisco's Chinatown became one of the greatest refuges for Chinese opera performers. This ban was lifted in 1868, which drew many of the greatest Chinese opera stars back to China; opera was again banned in the twentieth century during the Cultural Revolution of the communist era. Small Chinese American groups like the one led by Donald's uncle in the novel work to keep the traditional opera alive. Other members of the main character's family have been involved in Chinese opera too. Donald is shocked to learn that his father was once a famous opera star, known for playing the role of Kwan Kung, a Chinese immortal whose eyes could kill with a glance.

Chinese railroad workers. After Donald's uncle tells him that one of his ancestors worked on the

Chinese New Year celebration.

railroad, Donald begins having dreams about the Chinese railroad workers who built the Central Pacific tracks through the Sierra Nevada mountain range. The Chinese had been recruited to work on the Central Pacific in the early 1860s. Congress had approved financial subsidies for the railroad, but only under the condition that the Central Pacific would complete its line from Sacramento, California, to an undetermined location in Utah (where it would connect to the Union Pacific tracks), by July 1, 1869. The Chinese laborers spent the winter of 1866-67 hacking tunnels through the dense granite of the Sierra Nevadas. Much of the work was done with explosives, which the Chinese were highly proficient in using; this had been one of the skills that made them desirable employees to the owners of the Central Pacific. As the Chinese struggled through the snow and ice in the Sierras, they were urged to work even harder by their Caucasian supervisors. Finally, the Chinese went on strike, demanding a raise in pay from $30 a month to $45 a month and an end to their twelve-hour workdays. After bitter negotiations, the Chinese received a $5 a month raise but were forced to maintain a twelve-hour day.

With the arrival of spring in 1867, many of the Chinese workers moved on to the Nevada desert to continue laying the rails toward Utah.

Though the fact that the ground was level made much of the work easier, the extreme desert heat, scorpions, and rattlesnakes kept the working conditions difficult. Despite the inhospitable Nevada desert, the Chinese made dramatic progress throughout the next year, completing 362 miles of track in 1868.

Early in 1869, the Central Pacific workers came in sight of the Union Pacific track crew, which consisted almost entirely of Irishmen. Because they were being paid by the mile, a fierce competition arose between the two railroad crews as each tried to lay more track than the other. Fearing that the quality of the rails would suffer as a result of the competition, Congress designated Promontory Point, Utah, as the meeting place for the two railroads, beyond which neither one could go. Despite this mandate, the competitive spirit between the two companies continued. Charles Crocker, one of the owners of the Central Pacific, bet William Durant of the Union Pacific that the Central Pacific crew could lay 10 miles of track in a single day. Durant readily accepted the wager; his Irish crew had only finished 6 miles of track on their most productive day of work, and he doubted that Central Pacific could exceed that. On April 28, 1869, 5,000 Central Pacific rail workers laid 10 miles and 56 feet of track in twelve hours. In that single day the Chinese crews had placed 25,800 ties, laid 3,520 rails, sledged 28,120 spikes, and fastened 14,080 bolts. The record has never been matched, even by the machines now used by the railroads. The tracks were joined with those of the Union Pacific on May 10, 1869, with great fanfare. Two golden spikes, one silver spike, and one spike of gold, silver, and iron were hammered into place at the juncture of the two rails.

In the novel, Donald dreams about many details in the lives of the Chinese railroad workers, including the arduous working conditions, poor treatment, and the record-setting effort of the workers. His dreams and his study of the events at the library instill in Donald his first feelings of pride in his people as he realizes the courage and tenacity it took for them to complete their work on the railroad. Donald also feels frustrated and cheated when he looks at photographs of the Golden Spike ceremony and realizes that not a single Chinese appears in the picture.

The Novel in Focus

The plot. Donald Duk, a twelve-year-old Chinese American boy growing up in San Francisco's Chinatown, hates his name. He also hates being Chinese; after all, his history teacher at public school constantly describes the early Chinese in America as "passive," "nonassertive," and "timid" (Chin, *Donald Duk,* p. 2). Matters are made even worse by the approach of the Chinese New Year. Now Donald will have to tell his whole class about the things the Chinese do during the holiday. Donald's uncle, also named Donald, comes to Chinatown with his Cantonese opera group and performs for Donald's class, embarrassing Donald even further.

A non-Chinese friend of Donald's, Arnold Azalea, gets permission to stay the night at Donald's house. Donald is amazed that Arnold likes Chinese food and is interested in Donald's father's stories. Besides telling stories, Donald's father makes model planes that he plans to fly on New Year's day. Uncle Donald explains to Donald that each of the 108 planes is painted to represent a hero from the Chinese Water Margin story, a legend concerning 108 outlaws who stand against a corrupt dynasty.

Donald is shocked to learn that his father, recognizing the impermanence of all dynasties, plans to burn each of the planes when he flies them. In the middle of the night, Donald takes one of the planes and flies it off the roof of his building. The tiny plane flies a short distance and

the firecracker inside it explodes. As Donald prepares to go back to his family's apartment below, he is confronted by American Cong, a strange man dressed in army fatigues who seems to live on the roof. American Cong claims to be a Vietnam veteran who has a lasting illness from the war, which he describes as "orange" (*Donald Duk,* p. 19). Downstairs Donald finds his Uncle Donald waiting for him. His uncle had seen him take the plane and tells him that he must make another to replace it and that he must tell his father what he's done.

LEGEND OF THE WATER MARGIN

The story of the Water Margin is one of the most popular pieces of Chinese folklore. The legend tells of 108 good men who have been outlawed by dishonest officials of a corrupt government. Led by Song Jiang, known as "Timely Rain," the 108 outlaws combine forces and form an army in the "Water Margin," or Leongshan swamp, an area of impenetrable marsh. They then overthrow the corrupt Song Dynasty. One of the most interesting of the 108 heroes is Lee Kuey, also known as "the Black Tornado." Lee Kuey fights naked, with a gigantic battle ax in each hand. In *Donald Duk,* it is this character who is painted on the model plane that Donald pilfers from his father's collection and flies by himself from the rooftop.

As the Chinese New Year gets closer, Donald researches the history of the Chinese, and he begins having dreams each night about the Chinese workers who built the Central Pacific railroad. Donald begins to appreciate the accomplishments of the early Chinese immigrants who worked through the grueling winters, cutting tunnels and pathways through the mountains for the railroad.

Each day, Donald and his family visit relatives and friends in anticipation of the holiday, giving gifts and *lay see,* lucky money, to children and their unmarried friends. One night, Donald's father gives away fifty-pound sacks of rice to his neighbors. On another night he cooks a banquet for family, friends, and members of Uncle Donald's opera troupe.

Donald and his family watch the news and see that Homer Lee, whom Donald recognizes as American Cong, has been arrested for killing a local gang member, Fisheyes Koo. Donald realizes that he was with Lee at the time of the mur-

Chinese laborers employed by the Central Pacific in the Sierra Nevada Mountains.

der and insists that they go to the police station to prove him innocent. Homer Lee is released and the family feels that they have done their good deed for the New Year.

Finally, New Year's Day arrives, and Donald and Arnold help carry the ceremonial dragon in the Chinese New Year parade. All of Chinatown grows boisterous with the celebration. After the parade, Donald, Arnold, and both of their families go to Angel Island in San Francisco Bay to fly the 108 model airplanes. The tiny planes, which have taken years to build, are all destroyed in just a few minutes. Donald starts to understand the idea his father has shared with him: that nothing lasts forever. He also begins to accept his Chinese heritage and begins to see that it is something of which he can be proud.

Donald's anti-Chinese feelings in the novel. Throughout the novel, one of the most compelling themes that continues to surface is Donald's anti-Chinese sentiment. At several points in the story Donald has fantasies that he is white. He also does everything he can to throw off his Chinese background and remove himself from the Chinese culture surrounding him. On the first page of the novel, Donald is already fantasizing about becoming different than what he is. Chin writes, "Donald Duk wants to live the late night life in old black-and-white movies and talk with his feet like Fred Astaire, and smile Fred Astaire's sweet lemonade smile" (*Donald Duk*, p. 1). Later in the novel, Donald can't understand why his father is happy being Chinese. After all, Donald's grandparents did everything they could to become Americanized, even rejecting their culture when they immigrated to the United States, so why doesn't his father do the same? As the novel points out, "Dad's parents didn't want to be Chinese. Donald Duk doesn't want to be Chinese. Why does Dad want to be Chinese? Doesn't he know everybody talks about him funny?" (*Donald Duk*, p. 47). Donald's father, who realizes how Donald feels about his heritage, comments on the inner turmoil: "I think Donald Duk may be the very last American-born Chinese-American boy to believe you have to give up being Chinese to be an American" (*Donald Duk*, p. 42). This tension between Donald and his father over Donald's anti-Chinese feelings resurfaces later in the novel during one of Donald's dreams. In the dream, Donald's father says, "I can't believe I have raised a little white racist. He doesn't think Chinatown is America. I tell you one thing, young fella, Chinatown is America" (*Donald Duk*, p. 90).

The root of Donald's shame in being Chinese seems to lie in the stereotypes presented in the world around him. At school, the history teacher Mr. Meanwright constantly makes unfavorable remarks about the Chinese. When describing early Chinese immigrants, Meanwright says, "From their first step on American soil to the middle of the twentieth century, the timid, introverted Chinese have been helpless against the relentless victimization by aggressive, highly competitive Americans" (*Donald Duk*, p. 2). Even in Chinatown, Donald is surrounded by images that make the Chinese seem inferior or dependent on American white culture. Donald's dance teacher dubs himself "the Chinese Fred Astaire" (*Donald Duk*, p. 66) and a local Chinese actress calls herself "the Chinese Marilyn Monroe" (*Donald Duk*, p. 134). Instead of simply existing independently as Chinese citizens of the United States, these figures in the novel seem in this way to subordinate their own talents to those of non-Chinese role models. Fortunately for Donald, he begins to understand more about his culture and ancestors through both his dreams and his conversations with Uncle Donald. After learning about the heroic actions of the nineteenth-century railroad workers and the daring deeds and bravery of the 108 heroes of the Water Margin stories, Donald seems much more at ease with his culture and begins to feel proud of his Chinese heritage.

Sources. Frank Chin was born in Berkeley, California, and grew up in the San Francisco Bay Area. Much like Donald Duk, whose great-great-grandfather worked on the Central Pacific, Frank Chin's own grandfather worked in the steward-service of the Southern Pacific railroad. Frank Chin himself worked as the first Chinese American brakeman on the Southern Pacific railroad, an experience that, along with the experience of his grandfather, most likely inspired Chin's interest in the early Chinese immigrants' role in building the railroads. Donald's feelings of inferiority and shame in being Chinese are inspired by the author's own feelings of frustration that so much of Asian American culture seems to focus on the American aspect alone. In his essay, *Come All Ye Asian American Writers,* Chin writes, "What do we Asian Americans, Chinese Americans, Japanese Americans, Indo-Chinese, and Korean Americans have to hold us together? What is 'Asian American,' 'Chinese American,' and 'Japanese American'? . . . no matter how white we dress, speak, and behave, we will never be white" (Chin in Chan, p. 2). This same sentiment prompts the invention of characters in the novel whose personas rely on white America—the dancer called the "Chinese Fred Astaire," the actress identified as the "Chinese Marilyn Monroe," and a photographer known as the "Chinese Richard Avedon." The novel refutes such stereotypes of mainstream white American culture as well as negative attitudes held by some Chinese Americans toward their own heritage.

Critical reaction. *Donald Duk* made a favorable impression on critics because of the issues it raised, and critics felt moved by Donald's plight in the novel. However, some pointed out a certain roughness in other areas. In his *New York Times* review, Tom De Haven writes of the novel: "Throughout 'Donald Duk,' Mr. Chin's energy is high and his invention lively, but all too often the narrative seems rushed, filled with first-draft bursts of staccato prose." De Haven also finds the novel inconsistent. In the same review, he writes, "For every scene that reads true or funny, there's another that seems arbitrary or forced, and occasionally . . . meanspirited" (De Haven, p. 9). Another reviewer, Janet Ingraham, commented on elements of the novel that make it entertaining as well as politically potent. She notes that "Chin spices his first novel with a flip, clipped, present-tense narrative voice, slapstick dialog, and kinetic dreamscapes. The result is a tart social comment packed into a cartoon, with verbal energy verging on hyperactivity" (Ingraham, p. 220).

For More Information

Chan, Jeffrey Paul et al., eds. *The Big Aiiieeeee!: An Anthology of Chinese American and Japanese American Literature.* New York: Penguin, 1991.

Chin, Frank. *Donald Duk*. Minneapolis: Coffee House, 1991.

De Haven, Tom. "Not by Shakespeare Alone." *The New York Times Book Review* (March 31, 1991): 9.

Fong-Torres, Shirley. *San Francisco Chinatown: A Walking Tour*. San Francisco: China Books, 1991.

Ingraham, Janet. Review of *Donald Duk*. *Library Journal* 116, no. 3 (February 15, 1991): 220.

Riddle, Ronald. *Flying Dragons, Flowing Streams: Music in the Life of San Francisco's Chinese*. London: Greenwood, 1983.

Sinnott, Susan. *Chinese Railroad Workers*. New York: Franklin Watts, 1994.

Walters, Derek. *Chinese Mythology: An Encyclopedia of Myth and Legend*. London: Aquarian, 1992.

Dune

by

Frank Herbert

The first novel in a series of five, *Dune* introduces its readers to the Atreides family
and the world of Arrakis. Frank Herbert
creates in the *Dune* novels not merely a fictional
setting but an entire world, complete with its
own ecology, history, religion, and social customs. Winner of both the Hugo and Nebula
awards for science fiction writing, *Dune* bridges
the gap between the fictional future and the realistic present. Herbert's themes, while set in the
future, clearly relate to the social and historical
issues of his own day.

> **THE LITERARY WORK**
>
> A novel set in the unspecified future on the
> fictional desert planet Arrakis; published in
> 1965.
>
> **SYNOPSIS**
>
> A young duke, Paul Atreides, discovers his
> destiny and that of his people on the planet
> Arrakis.

Events in History at the Time of the Novel

Space travel. In the appendices to *Dune,* Herbert notes that "mankind's movement through
deep space placed a unique stamp on religion.
. . . Immediately space gave a different flavor and
sense to ideas of Creation" (Herbert, *Dune,* p.
501). The novel's sacred regard for the space
frontier is a reflection of the author's own times.
On October 4, 1957, the Soviet Union launched
the world's first manmade satellite, *Sputnik.*
America looked on this aeronautic achievement
as a challenge to its own struggling space program. On July 29, 1958, after months of congressional debate, President Dwight D. Eisenhower signed the National Aeronautics and Space
Act of 1958, thereby establishing the National
Aeronautics and Space Administration (NASA).
NASA's first project, the Vanguard satellite,
added 150 researchers from the Naval Research
Laboratory to its own staff of 8,000 and paved
the way for the Mercury space program (1958-63).
The strong scientific component formed the base

for NASA's technical leadership. By the end of
1960, the organization had built a relatively comprehensive space program.

In 1959 NASA began preparations for a
manned space flight to the moon. By October of
1960, three aerospace firms had received contracts from NASA to deliver plans for a lunar-
bound vehicle dubbed Apollo. Even so, Congress
refused to make a definitive effort toward turning the dream into a reality. It would take another Soviet advance—this time the manned
space flight of Major Yuri A. Gagarin—to spur
the government into action. On May 25, 1961,
President John F. Kennedy made his position
clear to Congress. "I believe," declared Kennedy,
"that this nation should commit itself to achieving the goal, before this decade is out, of landing a man on the moon and returning him safely
to the earth" (Kennedy in Compton, p. 6). The
space race had officially begun.

Throughout the decade, NASA officials
worked toward achieving the goal set for them
by Kennedy's dream. His assassination in 1963
seemed to heighten the purpose of the space

Apollo 11 astronaut Edwin E. Aldrin, Jr. stands next to the U.S. flag on the moon's surface.

program, which launched the Gemini series in 1964-66. Although the United States made great strides toward the goal of reaching the moon, sending groups of two or three men into orbit between the years of 1965 and 1968, NASA also suffered severe setbacks. On January 27, 1967, three astronauts were killed on the ground in a fire that started during a test of their spacecraft. Nonetheless, the space program continued. On July 20, 1969, two American astronauts, Neil A. Armstrong and Edwin "Buzz" Aldrin Jr. became the first men to set foot on the surface of the moon. At 9:56 p.m., Central Standard Time, Armstrong declared in a transmission that was televised around the world, "That's one small step for man, one giant leap for mankind" (Armstrong in Compton, p. 144). Indeed, once man set foot on the moon, the future possibilities for the human race seemed almost limitless. Although Herbert had published his book a few years before NASA's landmark feat, he conveys in *Dune* the same sense of awe that surrounded the space program at this time.

Psychedelic drugs. The production and use of drugs plays an important role in the novel. In the story, the mining and transport of the melange spice forms the whole economic base of Arrakis. With an entire galaxy addicted to melange, Arrakis holds the key to political and economic

power. The spice offers its users powers of insight that even the hero Paul cannot control.

Lysergic acid diethylamide (LSD) was first produced in 1938 by a Swiss chemist, Dr. Albert Hofmann. Hoping to use the drug in the treatment of headaches, Hofmann was disappointed when LSD proved ineffective in laboratory experiments. He left the drug in his lab untouched for five years. On April 16, 1943, Hofmann decided to attempt further experimentation. While handling the LSD, the doctor unwittingly ingested an unknown quantity. He records in his journal, "Last Friday . . . I was forced to stop my work in the laboratory in the middle of the afternoon and to go home, as I was seized by a peculiar restlessness associated with a sense of mild dizziness" (Hofmann in Trulson, p. 20). He notes later on in his journal that the sensation developed into a series of hallucinatory images with a kaleidoscope of colors.

LSD first came to the United States in 1949. Confined to medical and military experiments, the drug remained in research laboratories. During the 1960s, however, Dr. Timothy Leary, an assistant professor of psychology at Harvard University, brought LSD to mainstream culture. Dr. Leary had experimented with psilocybin, an LSD-like substance, and had been impressed with the drug's ability to produce psychological effects. Convinced that the ingestion of LSD could expand consciousness, Leary became an advocate of the drug. He held sessions with his students during which everyone would take LSD and describe their experiences. With a Harvard associate, Dr. Richard Alpert, Leary founded the International Federation for Internal Freedom (IFIF). He soon gained national acclaim, with stories on the IFIF appearing in the *New York Times.* When Harvard fired both Leary and Alpert, it only accelerated their popularity, and LSD quickly became a recreational drug.

With no known medical value, LSD was primarily used in social settings. Looking to Dr. Leary as an example, others formed their own LSD groups. They developed a drug-related lingo, referring to LSD as "acid," to LSD users as "acid heads," and, more specifically, to experienced users as "gurus." The hallucinatory experience was called a "trip," and someone on a "bad trip" was said to be "freaking out." This jargon developed during the social gatherings at which users consumed LSD. Within time, a small counterculture comprised mostly of young people rebelling against mainstream values and behaviors would embrace the drug. Rock lyrics referred to the virtues of LSD. In 1967 the Beatles released their *Sergeant Pepper's Lonely Hearts Club Band,* an album thought to be influenced by the drug or to contain veiled references to drug experiences. Hippies congregated at rock concerts, love-ins, be-ins, and rallies where much of the crowd used the drug. Like the melange spice of *Dune*'s Arrakis, LSD seemed to permeate almost every corner of American culture. While it certainly was not the only catalyst for the social revolution of the 1960s, the drug did play a major role in it. In 1967 President Lyndon Johnson passed a bill making the drug illegal. While some contended that psychedelic drugs were a definite health hazard, others felt that the laws against LSD were prompted by a fear that LSD users would engage in anti-establishment activities.

The dangers of hero worship. The concept for *Dune* began with a longing "to do a novel about the messianic convulsions which periodically inflict themselves on human societies. I had this idea that superheros were disastrous for humans" (Herbert in O'Reilly, p. 38). Within the novel, there is a cloud hanging over Paul Atreides's rise to power. *Dune* concerns itself with the dangers of hero worship, of which Paul is mindful. Although he earns the reputation of a religious leader, Paul feels uncomfortable in this position.

Indeed, he envisions death and destruction when he looks into a possible future as a political and religious messiah. He struggles internally over the issue, not wanting to abuse his power.

The 1960s saw the appearance of cults and cult leaders in America. During this decade, youth dominated American society; in 1964 the median age was twenty-nine. The large number of young people coming of age in the 1960s possessed a good deal of idealism and optimism. They tended to place less emphasis on traditional Judeo-Christian religion because many of them felt that these religions were based on fear and pessimism. A group of intellectuals known as the "Death of God theologians" asserted that the Judeo-Christian God had no place in a modern world. Led by such scholars as William Hamilton, these men and women held that the decade of the 1950s, with its Cold War fears of nuclear devastation, had been a time of angst, and that with the arrival of the sixties "a new spirit [was] in the land" (Ellwood, p, 139). The traditional concepts of God were pushed aside during this time, and others lined up to replace them.

Several bodies of iconoclastic worship sprung up across the country. In 1966 Anton LaVey formed the Church of Satan in his San Francisco home, appropriately colored black. Through his Hollywood affiliations and his role as the devil in the movie *Rosemary's Baby* (1968), LaVey found quite an audience. He and his followers saw the conventional God as a tyrant of repression, while Satan represented freedom and self-expression. LaVey, however, did not stand alone in his quest for an alternative figure of worship. In 1965 A. C. Swami Bhaktivedanta Prabhupada emigrated from India to New York. Embarking on a spiritual mission to spread the love of the Hindu god, Krishna, Swami Bhaktivedanta offered his followers a communitarian lifestyle and a spiritual high. The poet Allen Ginsberg described his Krishna experience stating, "I started chanting to myself, like the Swami said . . . and suddenly everything started looking so beautiful . . . like I'd taken a dozen doses of LSD. . . . [But] there's no coming down from this" (Ginsberg in Ellwood, p. 143). In this time of innovative spirituality, other movements such as Nichiren Shoshu, Scientology, and the Unification Church found followers as well. In fact, a study conducted at Brooklyn College concluded that between the years of 1965 and 1980, 1300 new cults appeared in the United States, boasting a membership of between 2 and 3 million individuals.

Poet Allen Ginsberg in 1969, the height of the counterculture movement.

Although these cults initially seemed like inviting alternatives to a distressed society, some proved dangerous. The 1970s saw a rise in so-called religious groups that exploited followers in a manner similar to what happens in *Dune.* Using techniques of peer pressure, sleep deprivation, indoctrination, and diet control, cults attracted and maintained followers using less-than-holy motives. They isolated their members from the outside world and confiscated all money and personal possessions. In this manner, cults themselves became quite rich and powerful. The People's Temple, led by Jim Jones, for instance, held over $10 million in several bank accounts at its peak of popularity. When the government and other agencies began investigating this group, death and destruction ensued. In 1978 a United States congressman traveled to Guyana to look into claims that the People's Temple, ensconced in a compound in the jungle, was holding members against their will. After killing the congressman and his party, Jim Jones led 911 women, men, and children to their own deaths by drinking cyanide-laced Kool-Aid. Obviously this example represents an extremity of cult violence, but Herbert's warnings of the dangers of hero worship had merit. The future that he foretells in *Dune* was perhaps closer at hand than even he imagined.

The Novel in Focus

The plot. On the lush, tropical planet of Caladan, Duke Leto Atreides prepares his family for their impending geographical and political move. As head of one of the Great Houses of the Landsraad galaxy, Leto will soon assume leadership of the desert planet Arrakis. Although barren in landscape, the dunes of Arrakis house the galaxy's supply of the valuable spice melange. Because of this resource, the House that obtains leadership of Arrakis also holds the key to a bounty of wealth and power. Leto enters this position knowing, however, that danger lies ahead. The House Harkonnen, the previous masters of Arrakis, had reigned there for over eighty years. Its leader, Baron Vladimir Harkonnen, is not prepared to abandon Arrakis without a fight. The Padishah Emperor, who rules above both these leaders as head of the galaxy, wants the baron replaced.

The move to Arrakis represents a political plan that developed over many generations. Nothing concerning the Atreides clan occurs by happenstance. Duke Leto's son, Paul, for instance, has received training throughout all fifteen years of his life from various masters of arts. From Thufir Hawat, Leto's Master of Assassins, Paul learns how to survive an assassin's attack. From Gurney Halleck, Paul receives schooling in man-to-man combat. From Dr. Wellington Yueh, Paul learns about poisons and eventually treachery. Perhaps the most effective teacher, however, is Paul's mother, Jessica. A Bene Gesserit "witch," Jessica has had her own schooling in various forms of sorcery. Although only women typically receive such training, Jessica nonetheless passes on her knowledge to her son. Such a multifaceted upbringing has molded Paul Atreides into a noble heir, and a formidable foe.

After settling into the new quarters on Arrakis, Duke Leto begins to show Paul the world of his inheritance. Although it promises great wealth, the planet requires a strong, determined hand to gain control of it and guide it. From its climate to its predators, Arrakis proves difficult to conquer. When Paul and his father travel out to the desert mine stations where the sand gets stripped of the melange spice, they catch their first glimpse of the enormous sand worms that patrol the desert. Often reaching hundreds of meters in length, the worms render the deep desert uninhabitable for most humans. They move toward and attack vibrations in the earth, and their size allows them to swallow entire mining stations whole. Although the miners have their own defense mechanisms for dealing with the worms, a lone man would probably perish. In addition to the worms, the desert also promises harsh storms and a deadly lack of water. The few cities on Arrakis stand behind Shield Walls that protect them from these dangers. Only the Arrakeen natives, the Fremen, seem fit to survive in the outer reaches of the wasteland. Through the use of still-suits, garments made to recycle the body's own water and waste, the Fremen thrive in the dry climate. They live in sietches, or small communities spread far throughout the deep desert.

The arrival of the Atreides clan on Arrakis marks the beginning of a new way of life for some and the end of life for many. Unbeknownst to Duke Leto, Dr. Yueh has turned against him and joined forces with Baron Vladimir. During a carefully planned ambush, Dr. Yueh captures the Duke and turns him over to the Harkonnens. Both the Duke and Dr. Yueh perish in this battle. Although the others escape, only Paul and his mother remain together. The other surviving members of the House of Atreides scatter to avoid the Harkonnen onslaught. Baron Vladimir and his men believe erroneously that the entire House of Atreides has been exterminated. The Duke's Master of Assassins, Hawat, falls into the hands of Baron Vladimir, who keeps him alive as an as-sistant. Meanwhile, another one of Paul's teachers, Halleck, joins a band of spice smugglers and remains on Arrakis to plot revenge against the Baron. Eventually Paul and Jessica meet up with a group of Fremen. Although the natives do not initially welcome the two Atreides, they ultimately decide to aid the foreigners. An ancient Fremen legend tells of Lisan Al-Gaib, a prophet from another world who will bring bountiful water to the land of Arrakis. Because of Paul's unique abilities, including a kind of extrasensory perception, the Fremen come to believe that he is Lisan Al-Gaib. Even Jessica senses that her son may fulfill a destiny more significant than just assuming the duchy of Arrakis.

Over the next two years, Paul and the Fremen leaders train their people as skilled combatants. Gurney Halleck serendipitously meets up with Paul and joins with the Fremen army. Together Paul, Halleck, and the Fremen plan their attack against the House Harkonnen. Disabling the Shield Wall that surrounds the capital city, the Fremen army invades the Baron's headquarters. Baron Vladimir meets his demise in the ensuing battle, and Paul gains control of the planet. His plot, however, involves more than the reclaiming of Arrakis. Through the Fremen he learns that the precious melange spice, on which the whole galaxy depends, is a byproduct of the sand worms. Killing the worms would mean ending the spice production. Paul uses this threat to gain control of the galaxy's throne. The close of the novel promises a marriage between Paul and the Padishah Emperor's daughter, sealing Paul's place as the future Emperor. With this deal, Paul avenges his father's death and brings peace to the land of Arrakis.

An ecological message. Herbert takes great pains to describe the ecological makeup of Arrakis. The planet's desert environment provides both a backdrop and an impetus for much of the action within the novel. Although the desert-dwelling Fremen come to regard Paul Atreides as a godlike figure, their first leader occupied a role other than that of a statesman. This first leader, the ecologist Liet-Kynes, delivers an environmental sermon to his followers. He states, "There's an internally recognized beauty of motion and balance on any man-healthy planet. . . . Its aim is simple: to maintain and produce coordinated patterns of greater and greater diversity" (*Dune*, p. 493). This reflects a reverence for the environment that appears throughout Herbert's works and recalls the author's own heritage as well.

Born in Tacoma, Washington, Herbert's family resided in a rural area. This country upbringing, according to the author, produced a certain self-reliance that a city lifestyle would not provide. During his retirement, in fact, the author maintained a small farm in Port Townsend, Washington. Regarding the farm as an "ecological demonstration project" (Herbert in O'Reilly, p. 15), Herbert and his wife envisioned a five-year-plan that would show how a high quality of life could be sustained with minimal stress to the environment. The couple grew their own vegetables and raised their own poultry; Herbert also built an electricity-generating windmill that earned him a patent from the federal government in 1978. The manure that the Herberts recovered from their chickens provided enough methane gas to generate their own power supply. Any additional energy needed came from solar panels. The author even maintained a vineyard that produced grapes for wine. Although this ecologically sound plan won Herbert an almost cultlike following of environmentalists during this time, he shied away from a public lifestyle and instead tried to communicate his ideas through the pages of his novels.

Perhaps the most climactic moment of Paul Atreides's career occurs during his test of ascension to Fremen manhood. In order to prove himself worthy of his adoptive culture, Paul must harness and ride one of the sand worms. Unlike the other denizens of Arrakis, the Fremen do not fear or seek to destroy the sand worms. They understand the creatures' value in the environmental cycle and learn to coexist with these virtual monsters. As the only society on Arrakis that survives in the deep desert with little water and in constant contact with the worms, the Fremen represent Herbert's notion of a self-sufficient people. They sustain their lifestyle with minimum stress to the environment, and eventually earn the reward of ascending to political power on Arrakis.

Sources. Although the planet of Arrakis is an entirely fictional world, Herbert does draw some of its inhabitants from his own life. For instance, the author's paternal grandmother, while unschooled and illiterate, possessed an uncanny memory for dates, names, and places. Herbert built on this family trait, developing some superhuman characters for *Dune* called the Mentats, whose brain power is phenomenal. Derived from the Latin word *mentis,* meaning "of the mind," the Mentats embody logic and reason. As a lead counselor to Duke Leto, Thufir Hawat

earned the reputation as the greatest Mentat of the Imperium. Herbert's grandmother offered inspiration in other areas as well. When excited, she would break into a dialect that resembled Elizabethan English. From this childhood exposure to other languages, Herbert developed his own interest in dialects. He uses the notion of other tongues throughout the *Dune* series. Paul, for example, has to learn various languages. Other family members also proved influential. For instance, Herbert's ten maternal aunts provided the idea for the Bene Gesserit witches, who speak their own special language.

The author did not rely solely on his immediate family for inspiration. For models of the Fremen characters, Herbert turned to biographies of American Southwest Indians and North African nomads. Like the American Indians, the Fremen exist as foreigners in their own land. Their knowledge of the environment and their mastery of weaponry, however, makes them formidable foes. Also like the Southwest Indians, the Fremen practice a religion that incorporates a psychedelic-based sacrament. Even more than the American Indians, however, the Fremen resemble seventh-century Bedouin nomads. Their language, clothing, and customs seem Arabic in nature while their environment closely resembles the African desert. Herbert felt that a figure such as his prophet, Lisan Al-Gaib, would be more readily accepted in a desert environment historically related to such faiths as Islam, Judaism, and Christianity. Finally, though Herbert did study the two aforementioned cultures as preparation for the novel, with the Fremen he certainly creates his own society. The characters of Arrakis, from wherever they originate, come to full fruition in the author's own mind.

Reception of the novel. Published in 1965, *Dune* found immediate critical and popular success. As mentioned, the novel earned both the 1966 Hugo Award and the 1965 Nebula Award for its author. In fact, science-fiction aficionados often point to the *Dune* chronicles as evidence that the science fiction genre should receive more credibility as serious writing. Herbert cultivated the unique ability to fuse his writing with current social issues. One critic commented that "[One] of the most spectacularly successful science-fiction novels of recent years, Frank Herbert's *Dune,* [is a good example] of how public concerns and infatuations catch up with the science fiction imagination" (Sheppard in Bryfonski, p. 270). A second reviewer remarked: "It is the unstultified vigor of Herbert's imagination which is responsible for the complexity, the depth, and the symbolic virtuosity of his novel" (Owner in Bryfonski, p. 273). Aside from its entertainment value, the novel succeeded as a vehicle for thought-provoking social commentary.

For More Information

Bryfonski, Dedria, ed. *Contemporary Literary Criticism*. Vol. 12. Detroit: Gale Research, 1980.

Compton, William David. *Where No Man Has Gone Before*. Washington D.C.: National Aeronautics and Space Administration, Science and Technical Information Division, 1989.

Ellwood, Robert S. *Spiritual Awakenings*. New Brunswick, N.J.: Rutgers University Press, 1994.

Herbert, Frank. *Dune*. New York: Ace Books, 1965.

McNelly, Willis Everett. *The Dune Encyclopedia*. New York: Berkley, 1984.

O'Reilly, Timothy. *Frank Herbert*. New York: Fredrick Ungar, 1981.

Trulson, Michael E. *LSD: Visions or Nightmares*. New York: Chelsea House, 1985.

Dune

"Everything that Rises Must Converge"

by
Flannery O'Connor

Mary Flannery O'Connor (1925-64) was born in Savannah, Georgia, to a middle-class Catholic family, and devoted her literary career to portraying the culture of the South with all of its macabre social and religious tensions. "Everything that Rises Must Converge" dramatizes civil rights activism surrounding public transportation in the South and the strong undercurrent of violence that runs beneath race relations in the region. O'Connor wrote the short story near the end of her life; she had long suffered from lupus and died of kidney failure on August 3, 1964.

THE LITERARY WORK

A short story set in the mid-twentieth century American South; written and first published in 1961; reissued in a posthumous short story collection in 1965.

SYNOPSIS

The ingredients of race, class, and family history culminate in tragedy as a white woman and her son learn the hard way about the complexities of Southern society during the era of the civil rights movement.

Events in History at the Time of the Short Story

Freedom rides. O'Connor's "Everything that Rises Must Converge" concerns an interracial encounter on a city bus. The modern era of civil rights history in the United States is often referred to as beginning on December 1, 1955. On that day, an African American department store saleswoman in Montgomery, Alabama, was told to give up her seat on a bus to a white person—as was customary at the time—but she refused to do so. The woman, Rosa Parks, was sent to jail for her obstinacy and her act in essence launched the civil rights movement into the modern age. The local chapter of the National Association for the Advancement of Colored People (NAACP), of which Parks was the secretary, and another political group with which she was associated, the Women's Political Council (WPC)

of Montgomery, sprang to her defense. Parks's lawyer began to develop a test case that would challenge the constitutionality of segregated buses, but the WPC started something even more significant—a black boycott of Montgomery's public transit system. Originally, the boycott was to last only one day—December 5, 1955—but the black population of Montgomery was so incensed with the prejudice and restrictions with which they were forced to live that they decided to extend the boycott indefinitely. Dr. Martin Luther King Jr., a young Baptist minister, emerged as their leader, and under his direction the Montgomery bus strike lasted thirteen months.

Montgomery's buses had been patronized primarily by the city's African American population, almost all of whom began walking to work or us-

Ralph Abernathy (front row, left), Martin Luther King, Jr. (second row, left), and others ride in the front of a bus, ending the Montgomery bus boycott.

ing carpools, winter and summer, an act which brought public transit in the city to its knees. Without African American passengers, the buses were practically empty. The first goal of the boycotters was not desegregated buses, but merely a more fair system of segregation in which there were clearly marked black and white sections of the bus that could not be waived according to the whim of the driver and the number of white riders. The bus company agreed to certain modifications of the system, but the city's white administration refused to approve them. The black leadership countered with the demand that now they would settle for nothing less than desegregated public transit. City officials resisted even further, even forbidding black cab drivers from giving groups of black workers a ride to work for a lower rate than usual. Yet this new obstacle did not serve to drive African American riders back to public transit, especially when money poured in from private sources to purchase station wagons for carpools. Montgomery's police force then became the embodiment of the official white power structure, issuing traffic tickets to black drivers. King himself was pulled over on January 26, 1956, and, until a large crowd of African Americans gathered outside the police station, it appeared that he might be held indefinitely. King

was released, but two days later his house was bombed. In November 1956 the U.S. Supreme Court ruled that Montgomery's segregated buses were in fact unconstitutional; on December 20, 1956, Parks, King, and others—accompanied by a host of journalists and photographers— boarded a Montgomery bus and sat in the front, legally. "I believe you are Reverend King," said the pleasant white driver. "We are glad to have you with us this morning" (quoted in Halberstam, p. 562).

In May 1961, two months after O'Connor finished "Everything that Rises Must Converge," another civil rights crisis occurred that also revolved around public transportation. This crisis involved interstate buses. Some so-called "freedom riders," both black and white, left Washington D.C. in two buses and headed south to challenge segregation and test federal rulings. In 1946, in *Morgan v. Commonwealth of Virginia*, segregation on interstate buses had been ruled unconstitutional. Nine years later the federal Interstate Commerce Commission banned segregated buses and bus stations involved in interstate travel. Freedom riders were testing this last ruling in particular. The civil rights protesters were now adept at using the media to make public their causes, and soon the freedom rides became a press event. Their transit through the South was peaceful enough until the buses reached the Alabama center of Anniston. A mob shot out the tires of one of the two buses and dragged the nonviolent and unarmed protesters from their buses, beat them, set fire to the buses, and mobbed the hospital where they were taken for treatment. The second busload met much the same fate in Birmingham, Alabama, and yet another attack occurred some days later in Montgomery, Alabama. Up to this point, authorities had done nothing or little to protect the lives of the freedom riders. But when Martin Luther King Jr. phoned U.S. Attorney General Robert Kennedy from a church gathering in Montgomery organized in support of the freedom rid-

---

BUSES BEFORE ROSA PARKS

In the early 1950s in the South, it was customary that most bus systems were segregated. In Montgomery, Alabama, however, they were segregated in a way in which black riders were not guaranteed courtesy or even a clearly designated section of the bus. The bus driver could decide if white people were being inconvenienced by having to stand or having to sit next to a black person. In such situations, the driver had the power to order black riders to move. An entire row of black riders would have to leave their seats if a white person needed to sit in that row. Furthermore, black riders were forced to disembark from the front of the bus after having paid their fare, and then reboard through the "black door" at the back of the bus. Rosa Parks herself had once been forcibly removed from a bus for refusing to get off and then get back on at the back. The black passenger suffered not only the indignity of it all but sometimes even the loss of a ride. It was not uncommon for a black person to pay the fare and then have the bus driver zoom off before he or she could get back through the rear entrance.

---

ers, he informed Kennedy of the mob outside that seemed ready to burn down the church and everyone in it. The Kennedy administration, which supported civil rights in the South but was hesitant about convincing states to enforce them, finally persuaded Alabama governor John Patterson to take appropriate action, and National Guard troops arrived at the scene. Further freedom rides throughout the state were supervised by the Guard. Upon arriving in Mississippi, however, the riders were arrested, supposedly for

their own good, to keep them safe. Three hundred of them served sentences in Mississippi jails. As media coverage of their plight spread both across the country and the globe, the federal government began to more actively support the demand for black rights.

Separate but equal. The policy of separating areas of use by black and white Americans was customary in more facets of daily life than just public transit. The late 1880s gave rise to a system in the South called "Jim Crow" (after a comic stage character, a figure based on an old black stableman who sang and danced). The system, which depended on separate facilities for the two races, effectively deprived the black population of its civil rights. Blacks were made to patronize establishments, or parts of the same, reserved specifically for them, and were expected to behave in certain deferential ways. "Jim Crow involved formal codes, restrictions written into law, and informal codes, unwritten but understood forms of behavior" (Cooper, p. 545). It was asserted that African Americans were naturally "inferior" to whites. When such a state of affairs was challenged in the 1896 Supreme Court case of *Plessy v. Ferguson* (which had confirmed that Louisiana's policy of racially segregated public transportation was constitutional), the phrase "separate but equal" was first uttered. This legal philosophy involved, among other things, the sanctioning of racially segregated parks, hospitals, schools, churches, libraries, phone booths, drinking fountains—even a separate Bible on which to swear in the courtroom. Yet "separate but equal" was in reality "separate and unequal" the majority of the time. In 1946 black activists took the University of Texas to court over the decidedly unequal law schools available on campus to white and black students. As a result, the Supreme Court heard and rejected an argument that "separate but equal" was unconstitutional, but did uphold the contention of African Americans that their law school was in fact illegal because it was unequal to the white school. In 1954, however, the high court reversed this decision in *Brown v. Topeka Board of Education,* which declared segregated schools unconstitutional. Desegregation in the South now gained a legal basis and was officially on its way to becoming reality.

The 1950s proved to be a tumultuous time in the United States, as the black population and many sympathetic whites fought hard to achieve equality before the law for people of all races. The battle was difficult, as the white supremacist strain of Southern society fought sometimes viciously to keep African Americans from exercising their voting rights and from achieving equal protection under the law. In 1957 President Dwight D. Eisenhower signed the Civil Rights Act, which created a federal commission for investigating and correcting abuses of civil rights. O'Connor's story dramatizes the tension between outright integrationists like the character Julian and more reluctant people like his mother, who claimed that black people should remain separate from and perhaps equal to white society.

Declining upper class. Julian, the main character in "Everything that Rises Must Converge," has a conflicted relationship with his mother, who descends from a wealthy Southern family that has fallen into decline. She tries to keep up appearances, convinced that her heritage is something that sets her apart from the others in her run-down neighborhood, but Julian claims to see things differently. Still, he fantasizes about the family mansion that his mother knew as a child; it was sold long ago as the Chestny family fell into social and economic decline.

The fictional Chestnys of O'Connor's story had many real-life counterparts; in fact, an entire way of life—that of the old-style family landowners—began to disappear by the early years of World War II as the South started to invest heavily in agricultural industrialization. Long after the slave-supported plantations belonging to Southerners such as Julian's great-grandfather had ceased to exist, a privileged lifestyle was still enjoyed by landowners who ran the family estate. Replacing the plantation was a system of sharecropping and tenant farming, whereby black or white farmers leased land from a white owner, or worked it in exchange for a percentage of the yield. Improved industrialization in the South brought with it larger farming enterprises that put these smaller concerns out of business, just as human labor itself shrank with the introduction of industrial technology. Unemployed rural residents, black and white, streamed to the cities in the South, or moved north in search of an improved way of life.

Between 1940 and 1980, approximately 14 million Southerners, black and white, left Southern farms for cities. Julian and his mother are the short story's representatives of an entire displaced class of Southerner—the wealthy rural population suddenly ousted from its comforts with the advent of technology. The civil rights movement further hastened the whirl-

wind of change that swept through the previously monied classes. As Julian's mother reminisces in "Everything that Rises Must Converge," the farm or plantation life shared by white landowners with their black employees often bred a kind of paternalism; "I've always had a great respect for my colored friends," she said. "I'd do anything in the world for them" (O'Connor, "Everything that Rises Must Converge," p. 488). The empowerment of black laborers and the granting to them of improved civil rights made them less dependent upon the goodwill of their white employers. In keeping with this trend, as O'Connor's story testifies, interracial relations in the South as a whole became less dependent on the economic and social condescension of white citizens.

The Short Story in Focus

The plot. Julian, a typewriter salesman who has finished college and wants to be a writer, accompanies his overweight mother to her weight-loss class at the downtown YWCA. She is dressed in a ridiculous hat that cost her more than they can afford, but she is very concerned about keeping up appearances. Julian's great-grandfather was once governor of the unnamed Southern state in which they live, and the mother and son come from a once-privileged family that has fallen onto hard times. The pair live in an apartment building in a shabby part of town; both fantasize about returning to the family mansion, which is now completely run-down and inhabited by poor blacks. Julian's mother, though, is proud of her struggle to remember who she is despite her economic and social decline; Julian, on the other hand, is bitter and convinced that his life will not amount to much.

The two start up an old argument on their way to the bus stop; Julian's mother claims that she has always respected her colored friends, but feels that the civil rights movement is unrealistic in its aims toward integration: "They should rise, yes, but on their own side of the fence" ("Everything that Rises," p. 488). Julian despises his mother for her attitudes on race and class, and fantasizes about teaching her a good lesson. The matter is taken out of his hands when, on the bus, a black woman, wearing the same hat as Julian's mother, sits beside Julian and across from his mother. The black woman's boy is taken with Julian's mother and she plays peekaboo with him, to the irritation of the black mother, who orders him to behave. Julian sees what his mother

Flannery O'Connor

does not—that this woman will not suffer a condescending attitude from white people like Julian's mother. As the four of them—the two women and their sons—get off the bus at the same stop, Julian tries to prevent his mother from handing the little black boy a penny—she has no larger change—but she persists. The black woman hits Julian's mother angrily with her purse and knocks her down, yelling, "He don't take nobody's pennies!" ("Everything that Rises," p. 498). Julian is smug about what has happened to his mother, feeling that she got exactly what she deserved and hoping that she will have learned her lesson:

> "Don't think that was just an uppity Negro woman," he said. "That was the whole colored race which will no longer take your condescending pennies. . . . [T]he old world is gone. The old manners are obsolete and your graciousness is not worth a damn."
> ("Everything that Rises," p. 499)

To his horror, Julian then discovers that his mother has been badly injured by the blow; she picks herself up off the sidewalk but doesn't know where she is or even when it is. She calls out for the black nurse of her childhood and the stunned Julian breaks off his righteous lecture about a just new social order to notice that she is barely conscious. As the story comes to a close,

she crumples to the sidewalk again and he runs off frantically into the night to find help:

> [H]is feet moved numbly as if they carried him nowhere. The tide of darkness seemed to sweep him back to her, postponing from moment to moment his entry into the world of guilt and sorrow.
> ("Everything that Rises," p. 500)

Tensions. In "Everything that Rises Must Converge," it is the unexpected act of violence between two women, one black and one white, with which the story culminates. This focus upon the actions of women in particular in a story about civil rights marks the contemporary emergence of women—black and white—as vocal demonstrators for equality across racial and gender lines. Young white middle-class Southern (and eventually Northern) women took notice of the effective organizational and protest skills of the civil rights marchers and showed evidence of their own spirit of rebellion. Many became tireless agents for the cause of liberation in general, at first working to mobilize the white community to the cause but, as time progressed, eventually moving within black communities themselves. The modern feminist movement grew from these conditions, not just because women were learning how to articulate their feelings of oppression, but because they came together, black and white; white women rethought the basic tenets of femininity as they watched black women take to the streets in protest, become community leaders, and refuse to be cowed by the potential brutalities their actions sometimes brought. As one Southern woman explained, "For the first time, I had role models I could respect" (Evans, p. 169).

Unfortunately, the relationship between black and white women involved in the civil rights cause was not to proceed altogether smoothly. The flooding of white women into black communities brought a commensurate number of interracial relationships with it, something that historians point to as the greatest of Southern social taboos: "The presence of hundreds of young whites from middle- and upper-middle-income families in a movement primarily of poor, rural blacks exacerbated latent racial and sexual tensions beyond the breaking point" (Evans, p. 173). The civil rights movement began to show signs of stress, as those involved tried to manage the new social realities brought on by white women living and working in black communities. Some black women accused their white counterparts of doing all the indoor safe work while they themselves confronted an angry public, and ascribed the growing tensions within the civil rights movement to white women's inability to work with black people of both genders. Partially as a result of all this, white women were gradually phased out of the civil rights movement in the South, their services no longer required or desired. Black women continued to fight to strengthen their social position, linking racial and gender issues, and participating in the surge of black nationalism that took off in the mid-1960s. Meanwhile, many of the middle-class female activists went north, and eventually allied with the university student protest movements that also emerged in the mid-1960s.

If, in "Everything that Rises Must Converge," Julian and his mother are taken aback by the attack that occurs at the end of the story, O'Connor's readers, both at the time the short story appeared on its own and much more so when the collection was released, would have probably been less so: tensions between black and white women in the South were a well-documented part of the civil rights-era climate.

Sources. O'Connor took the title of her story from the works of the modern Jesuit theologian Pierre Teilhard de Chardin (1881-1955):

> I'm much taken . . . with Pere Teilhard. I don't understand the scientific end of it or the philosophical but even when you don't know those things, the man comes through. He was alive to everything there is to be alive to and in the right way. I've even taken a title from him "Everything that Rises Must Converge" and am going to put it on my next collection of stories.
>
> (Letter to Thomas Strich, September 14, 1961, in O'Connor, p. 1152)

The French priest and paleontologist Teilhard de Chardin spent much of his time between 1923 and 1946 in China, where in 1927 he was part of the team that discovered Peking Man, a Stone Age hunter from the Pleistocene era. But Teilhard is more properly famous for his efforts to reconcile science, particularly evolution, with Christianity. He discussed the specific idea of convergence, or moving toward a common end. As his editor explained, Teilhard saw it as "the tendency of mankind, during its evolution, to superpose centripetal [moving toward a center] trends, so as to prevent . . . fragmentation" (Huxley in Johansen, p. 71). What O'Connor means in her use of the phrase "everything that rises must converge" as the title for her story, and for the story collection that was to be her last, has been debated among her critics. In each of the short stories in the collection O'Connor seems to write about a rise to a higher level of consciousness through a coming together of people or forces temporarily at odds with one another. In the short story "Everything that Rises Must Converge," both Julian and his mother, worlds apart in their racial attitudes, both end up stunned and hurt by the violence that erupts from the black woman who strikes out against what she sees as condescension.

Reviews. "Everything that Rises Must Converge" won the O. Henry award for short fiction in 1962. Robert Fitzgerald, editor of the 1965 collection bearing the same title as the short story, points enthusiastically to O'Connor's "austere" vision, which "will hold us down to earth where the clashes of blind wills and low dodges of the heart permit any rising or convergence only at the cost of agony" (Fitzgerald in Johansen, p. 180). The general consensus seems to be that the title story is perhaps not the finest of those collected in *Everything that Rises Must Converge,* but is nevertheless an important exploration of the "sexism, false nationalism, classism and other destructive attitudes . . . [that] are all part . . . of the attitude of a proud individualism which prevents humanity from rising and converging" (Spivey, p. 144).

For More Information

Cooper, William J., and Thomas E. Terrill. *The American South: A History.* New York: Alfred A. Knopf, 1990.

Evans, Sara. "Women's Consciousness and the Southern Black Movement." In *A History of Our Time.* Edited by William H. Chate and Harvard Sitkoff. New York: Oxford University Press, 1984.

Grimshaw, James A., Jr. *The Flannery O'Connor Companion.* Westport, Conn.: Greenwood, 1981.

Halberstam, David. *The Fifties.* New York: Villard, 1993.

Johansen, Ruthann Knechel. *The Narrative Secret of Flannery O'Connor: The Trickster as Interpreter.* Tuscaloosa: University of Alabama Press, 1994.

O'Connor, Flannery. "Everything that Rises Must Converge." In *Collected Works.* New York: Literary Classics of the United States, 1988.

Spivey, Ted. *Flannery O'Connor: The Woman, the Thinker, the Visionary.* Macon, Ga.: Mercer University Press, 1995.

Fahrenheit 451: The Temperature at Which Books Burn

by

Ray Bradbury

When Ray Bradbury (1920—) graduated from high school, he was already committed to a writing career in science fiction. From the beginning his short stories and novels showed a personal concern about what Bradbury perceived as the dehumanizing effect of the rapid growth of technology. Themes of evil, or at least misused technology, and victory of the human spirit are the focus of *Fahrenheit 451*.

Events in History at the Time of the Novel

An uncertain era. Bradbury wrote the story that would grow into *Fahrenheit 451* in 1950, a time when relations between the world's two most powerful nations were uneasy. In what would come to be known as the Cold War, the tensions between the Soviet Union and the United States—essentially a battle between capitalism and communism—were played out on numerous economic, political, and territorial fronts around the world, but primarily in Europe. The end of World War II five years earlier and the resulting disagreements about how to divide the spoils of war in a devastated Europe, and which system would win out there, had launched the Cold War. A scramble for spheres of influence, beginning with Germany, divided Europe and set in motion a world competition that was to last

---

THE LITERARY WORK

A science fiction novel set in a large American city in the near future; published in 1953.

SYNOPSIS

A fireman lives in an era when the fire department has the task of starting fires to destroy books. One day he encounters a teenaged girl, and their chance meeting leads the fireman to reexamine his life.

---

through the century. In 1945, the provisional French president Charles de Gaulle had allowed the country's communist party to be included in its newly recreated political system. Only a year later, the West, to its alarm, discovered that the communist party was one of the three largest political parties in France. In another part of the world, China's communist party—in control of 100 million people in North China by the end of the war—grew until it overwhelmed its opponents in 1949 and proclaimed the country the People's Republic of China, a communist nation.

Back in 1946, the wartime prime minister of Great Britain, Sir Winston Churchill, speaking in the United States, warned that an "iron curtain" had closed Eastern Europe to the view of the West. Behind this curtain, Josef Stalin, leader of the Soviet Union, bolstered communist ideology by destroying books that depicted life and history in the non-communist West in a too-favorable light, and by forbidding future publication of such books. It was a policy that had been practiced with some success by Adolf Hitler during the 1930s as he created a fascist dictatorship in Germany. Soviet censorship made the events behind the iron curtain difficult or impossible for the Western world to monitor, and as a result average citizens of the noncommunist world had a fearful view of the communist system. Distrust among the former wartime allies grew partly as a result of what was unknown on each side.

Censorship. *Fahrenheit 451* is a story built around book-burning, but that action is representative of all sorts of censorship. As the author states in a coda to the novel, "The point is obvious. There is more than one way to burn a book. And the world is full of people running about with lit matches" (Bradbury, *Fahrenheit 451*, p. 176).

After World War II, the threat of communism led to a panic in the United States as rumors surfaced about communist spies active in Canada. A U.S. House of Representatives member from California, Richard Nixon, had won election in 1946 by suggesting communist leanings of his opponent. In Washington he gained prominence on the House Un-American Activities Committee (HUAC), an investigative body set up to look into possible communist elements in the government. Prodded by Congress, President Harry Truman directed the Federal Bureau of Investigation and Civil Service Commission to investigate the loyalty of all federal employees. Some 3 million workers came under the inspection of government agencies—yet just 300 were dismissed for disloyal ideas while 2,900 resigned their positions in protest. The government desire to weed out any "foreign" ideas grew as Whittaker Chambers, an editor of *Time* magazine and a confessed Soviet spy, accused Alger Hiss, a former State Department official, of providing classified documents for transmittal to the Soviets during this decade. Hiss denied the charges but in 1950 was convicted of lying under oath, for which a federal court sentenced him to five years in prison. Back in Congress, Wisconsin Senator Joseph McCarthy carried on and escalated the virtual witchhunts that had begun with Nixon and the HUAC. McCarthy became especially focused on finding communists in the State Department and then the U.S. Army.

There was a frenzy to eliminate any ideas suspected of socialist or communist leanings, and as a result some ninety mostly harmless or even useful organizations were listed by the U.S. attorney general as wellsprings of communist doctrine. Attempts to censor news sources resulted in blacklists of writers and performers in the motion picture, radio, newspaper, and fledgling television industries. These frantic attempts to censor ideas grew from 1950 to 1953 as Senator McCarthy continued to pursue his destructive investigation of almost everyone with whom he disagreed and produced long lists of people with imagined connections to communism. *Fahrenheit 451* stands as a type of protest against such activity and the threat it poses of establishing the "Tyranny of the Majority" and enforcing conformity (Mogen, p. 107).

The atom bomb. The end of World War II was hastened by the Allied use of the atom bomb, a new device of mass destruction dropped on the Japanese cities of Hiroshima and Nagasaki. In a single bombing of Hiroshima, some 60,000 people were killed, allegedly saving many times that number of lives that might otherwise have been lost in an extended war. The bombings, however, left nations with a lingering fear that an enemy might develop a similar weapon and use it elsewhere. The United Nations, formed in 1945 as an international political body to maintain world peace, addressed the issue of regulating atomic weaponry soon afterward. In 1949, Cold War tensions increased dramatically when the Soviet Union successfully detonated an atomic bomb of its own.

Meanwhile wartime advances in technology led to improved aircraft and rocketry, making the delivery of atomic bombs possible from nearly every place on earth to any target. U.S. and Soviet scientists raced to improve both the weapons and the speed with which they could be delivered. In the Soviet Union, fighter planes reached speeds of 684 miles an hour. The United States countered with reconnaissance planes capable of flying at more than 500 miles per hour at very high altitudes.

The aircraft carrying weapons to the city in *Fahrenheit 451* fly at speeds of 5,000 miles per hour and carry such bomb loads that war, once declared, is over in a few seconds.

Television. After World War II, what had been only experimental forays into television broadcasting evolved into a full-scale industry, and the popularity of the new medium grew astronomically. In 1946 there were about a dozen broadcasting stations in the entire United States and a few thousand viewers, who viewed the programs on screens so small that most required a magnifying glass mounted in front of the picture. Within ten years, there were about 450 stations in the United States broadcasting programs to 34 million receiving sets watched by more than 100 million viewers.

To the citizens of *Fahrenheit 451,* television is as big as life and disseminates all knowledge the government allows creating a "family" that comes to include the viewers. Television has become so pervasive that one resident of the fictional city, ex-professor Faber, longs for and builds a miniature receiver—one that he can cover with his hand. *Fahrenheit 451,* as well as other stories by Ray Bradbury, have conveyed his concern that such services as television and computers could fall into powerful hands that would use them to manipulate the human population. Indeed, early television appeared at first to be headed in that direction. Licensing became a tool for restricting television in the United States, while Great Britain, Canada, the Soviet Union, and Japan established government-controlled networks.

Fahrenheit 451 carries television technology into the future. The time setting for the story is unspecified but clues in the story suggest that it is a not-too-distant future. Trains, for example, no longer exist in the city but the tracks are still whole and identifiable. People show great enthusiasm for television, much as they did in the 1950s. Their sets, however, grow beyond the dimensions of sets in the 1950s or even the 1990s. In the story, some screens serve as an entire wall inside private homes, while more prosperous citizens build television rooms that resemble cinerama, surrounding the viewer on four sides.

Other technologies. In 1950 computers were still almost novelties. Enormous, room-sized configurations of vacuum tubes and switches were beginning to solve complex mathematical problems. The computers were bulky and large. Still, *Fahrenheit 451* imagines a computer so small that it can be used to direct a robot's movements and be programmed to sense and track a million different human scents.

Between 1950 and the future time of *Fahrenheit 451,* video and computer technologies have advanced to challenge the old ways of delivering information that once appeared only in book form. *Fahrenheit 451* reveals a concern for this change. Television is the sole source of information in Ray Montag's city, and a computerized dog tracks down book lovers so that books can

be destroyed by fire. In the real world, however, the newer technologies seem to have made books more accessible than in 1950. The number of books published in 1985, for example, was more than four times the number published thirty-five years earlier.

THE PACE OF TELEVISION'S DEVELOPMENT

1930: Station W2XBS begins experimental broadcasts

1931: CBS begins regular broadcasts over station W2XAB

1936: TV receivers on sale in England

1939: TV receivers on sale in the United States

1941: First licensed commercial transmitters, WNBT and WCBW, in New York

1946: First TV sets on sale after World War II

1949: First color TV broadcast

1950: About 120 TV stations broadcast to 75 cities

1951: First coast-to-coast TV broadcasts

Furthermore, censorship of ideas has relaxed somewhat with the passage of time. There had been various laws against publishing so-called traitorous or lewd printed matter in the United States since colonial times. In force at the time of the writing of *Fahrenheit 451* was the Smith Act. Passed in 1940, the act outlawed printed matter that urged or advocated the overthrow or destruction of the national government or any of the state governments by force or violence. A 1951 Supreme Court ruling (*Dennis v. United States*) declared the Smith Act to be constitutional, and it was invoked in the virulent anticommunist campaign that swept the nation in the early 1950s. In 1957, a few years after the publication of *Fahrenheit 451,* the Supreme Court would modify the Smith Act, ruling that it could not be used to punish someone who merely advocates prohibited activities; to break the law a person actually had to engage in them. Senator McCarthy's anticommunist campaign was discredited and the emptiness of his charges exposed in 1954. With his downfall, the anticommunist fervor lessened in the United States. In Bradbury's view, though, the danger of censorship lurked elsewhere in the world, and so the novel's relevance seems to be timeless: "For while Senator McCarthy has long been dead, the Red Guard in China comes alive and . . . books are thrown to the furnace all over again. So it will go, one generation printing, another generation burning, yet another remembering what is good to remember so as to print again" (Bradbury in Mogen, p. 107). Communist China under Mao Zedong (Tse-Tung) was an especially apt model of censorship practices over the decades. Authorities suppressed writing that did not further government aims or that expressed "Western" ideas, and book banning and burning reached a fevered pitch during the late 1960s and early 1970s. Restrictions were relaxed over the decade, then reimposed in the 1980s; one generation printing books and the next one "burning" them, so to speak, just as Bradbury predicted.

The Novel in Focus

The plot. Ray Montag, the story's protagonist, is a fireman in a large city. The role of firefighter, however, has become very specialized. The city's buildings are sheeted with fireproof materials so that firemen no longer need to worry about extinguishing blazes. Instead Ray and his co-workers, including a robot dog, ferret out books and burn them under orders from the government. This the firemen do with great pleasure—even as the city is threatened with total destruction by greatly expanded nuclear bomb loads carried by supersonic planes capable of speeds of 5,000 miles an hour.

For most of the citizens, the book-burning seems acceptable, even desirable. They receive all the information that the government feels is good for them through state-run television. The only acceptable thoughts come from the television "family," for whom books are the enemy. The players on television become very real members of the family in each household (which, more often than not, lacks children—children have become unpopular in this society). Relief from the monotony of this television-locked world comes in the form of mind-numbing drugs. In this atmosphere, Ray's wife, Millicent, along with many of her friends, becomes a pill addict.

The drug problem has grown so that the city's medical workers respond to a dozen calls each day to rescue people, mostly women, who have overdosed. It is such a common occurrence that doctors do not respond to the calls but send medical mechanics to do the work. Two technicians frequently rescue Millie. In the end, she lives to denounce her own husband, calling the firemen to report his cache of books.

Ray Bradbury

On one occasion, the firemen are tipped that an old woman has books stored in her attic. A raid proves that to be true, and the books are burned. The law requires that the old woman be taken away and the entire house be set ablaze. But the woman resists by deliberately setting fire to the home and to herself. Ray is very shaken by the sight of the old woman burning to death in defense of her own ideals. He begins to wonder how the book-burning began and why most of the people of the city came to believe in it.

A chance acquaintance with Clarisse McClellan, an almost-seventeen-year-old girl who wants to live freely and question everything, changes Ray's life. He becomes curious about books and how their censorship began. An answer comes from a least likely source. Captain Beatty is at the moment a dedicated fireman, but he has obviously read books and, sometime in his life, loved them. It is Beatty who explains how the practice begins over and over throughout history. First there is conditioning—by television in his own city and by picture books and sports. People are inundated with nonthinking activities. "More sports for everyone, group spirit, fun, and you don't have to think, eh? . . . More cartoons in books. More pictures. The mind drinks less and less" (*Fahrenheit 451*, p. 57).

Another issue, according to Captain Beatty, made books expendable or even undesirable, at least items that no one cared about enough to purchase.

> Now let's take up the minorities in our civilization, shall we? Bigger the population, the more minorities. Don't step on the toes of the dog lovers, the cat lovers, doctors, lawyers, mechanics, chiefs, Mormons, Baptists, Unitarians, second-generation Chinese, Swedes, Italians, Germans, Texans, Brooklynites, Irishmen, people from Oregon or Mexico. . . . The bigger your market, Montag, the less you handle controversy, remember that! All the minor minor minorities with their navels to be kept clean. Authors, full of evil thoughts, lock up your typewriters.
>
> (*Fahrenheit 451*, p. 57)

In the frenzy to appease everyone, books become empty shells and no one cares when they are banned or burned.

Ray grows more curious and begins to read. This is permitted of a fireman for a short time, but Ray becomes committed to saving books. He soon falls victim to the robot; his stolen books are discovered and his home destroyed. Even as enemy bombers approach the city, Ray is forced to run from his fellow firemen, choosing to follow a river and then an abandoned railroad track out of the city. From a distance he watches the entire city explode under the superbombs. Ray follows the abandoned tracks away from the city until he finds a group of scholars who have a unique way of preserving the information in the destroyed books.

Book burning and the human spirit. In the decade before the novel was published, there was plenty of evidence of "people running about with lit matches," as Bradbury discussed in the novel's coda. Adolf Hitler in Germany and Josef Stalin in the Soviet Union had used book-burning demonstrations to rally supporters and intimidate those with opposing views. Authors had been suppressed through state-directed writers' organizations. Persistent writers with challenging views were thrown into jails or exiled. Then, in the United States, "book-burning" took the path of psychological persecution as meted out by Senator Joseph McCarthy in his anticommunist campaign.

No matter how oppressive the book bannings, however, there were always those who resisted censorship. Prominent writers and actors, for example, resisted McCarthy by refusing to testify

before his Senate committee at the risk of being banished from their trade. The people of *Fahrenheit 451* accept book-burning—except for a few citizens of the city. The firemen's official activities provide brief diversions when flames shoot up and the robot hound equipped with a hypodermic-needle tongue paralyzes the offending book-lover. Yet even under these conditions humane people of courage and intellect appear again and again in *Fahrenheit 451*. The story tells of a future world dominated not only by electronic media and superweapons, but by the indomitable human spirit capable of ultimate victory over machines and technology. The human spirit is revealed by Clarisse, the teenager who refuses to stop thinking, enjoying nature, and questioning. Ray, the fireman, is infected by this free spirit, and her mysterious disappearance is a stimulus to him and leads to his daring to collect books.

DRUGS IN MID-TWENTIETH-CENTURY AMERICA

The abuse of pills in *Fahrenheit 451* raises the question of how prevalent drugs had become in mid-twentieth-century America. In fact, the 1950s saw a nationwide scare, especially in regard to increases in heroin use. Popular journals such as *Newsweek* reported in 1950 and 1951 on the revival of drug use, and people feared that it threatened to spread throughout American society. To counteract the perceived threat, Congress passed the 1951 Boggs Act, which laid out increasing fines and prison sentences for first-time, second-time, and third-time offenders in drug trafficking. State and local regulation also increased to the extent that it permitted narcotics agents to carry firearms. At the same time pockets of society began to call for medical rather than police-type control and to regard drugs as an option for people outside of its traditional user base, the underclass: "The events of the 1950s demonstrated that some drug experiences appealed to people who seemed normal. They took drugs . . . for mere pleasure or relaxation. The delinquency model that had reigned since the 1920s . . . was not the final word" (Morgan, p. 147).

Another encounter with the undying human spirit comes when Ray meets the elderly ex-professor Faber. He has kept his mind active by inventing useful electronic tools such as miniature radio receiver-transmitters and small television receivers. This old gentleman helps Ray plot to revive the printing of books and, when that endeavor comes too late, to escape punishment for his book-reading. The ultimate victory of humanity over technology, however, is reflected in Ray's encounter with a group of campers along the railroad tracks. They are scholars dedicated to a single purpose. Members are admitted to this impressive group if they have committed to memory any part of the world's great literature. Collectively, they plan to preserve the world's knowledge in the face of government persecution and nuclear holocaust.

Sources. Direct sources for *Fahrenheit 451* are Bradbury's own tales. In 1947 he wrote the short story "Bright Phoenix" about a small town whose inhabitants defy government book-burnings by each committing to memory one of the texts. This idea of government book-burners grew into a novella called *The Fireman,* which appeared in the magazine *Galaxy Science Fiction* in 1951 before finally being developed into the novel *Fahrenheit 451.*

Horror at the rise of Adolf Hitler is what inspired the novel's original premise. In Bradbury's view, burning books was burning people. "When Hitler burned a book," said Bradbury, "I felt it as keenly, please forgive me, as burning a human, for in the long sum of history they are one and the same flesh" (Bradbury in Mogen, p. 107).

That Bradbury's concern was more about the suppression of ideas than the destruction of books per se is evident from his attitude to new technologies. Over the years, Bradbury seems to have softened his position on technology, although he still refuses to learn to drive an automobile. In an interview in the 1990s, Bradbury was asked if he thought books were in danger from the new computer and television technology. By then Bradbury had accepted the electronic medium. Books, audiotapes, videotapes—in his view, they were all forms of literature.

The novel's reception. *Fahrenheit 451* was published in 1953. Ray Bradbury had already gained writing fame with a series of stories called *The Martian Chronicles.* The new novel, therefore, had a ready audience of science fiction addicts and Bradbury fans.

Critics, however, were only mildly positive toward the book. Its publication only a few years after the birth of the atomic age placed it in the realm of dystopian literature, works about wretched or miserable imaginary places. *Fahrenheit 451* was soon being compared with other books in this genre, notably with George Orwell's **Nineteen Eighty-Four** (also covered in *Literature and Its Times*). Critics focused on a perceived weakness in the novel—too rapid and inadequate character development and identification of events. But finding positive elements in the novel as well, they generally accepted it as a worthwhile work. In a review, critic Kingsley Amis wrote, "The book emerges quite creditably from a comparison with *Nineteen Eighty Four* as inferior in power, but superior in consciousness and objectivity" (Amis in Bryfonski, p. 68). A review in the *Nation* (December 19, 1953) praised the novel as one of the most brilliant social satires to be published in recent times. Perhaps most importantly, Bradbury succeeded in meeting his own goal—to rewrite the original novella, *The Fireman,* into a longer story that retained the intense pace of his shorter fiction. The result, again in Amis's words, is a "fast and scaring narrative" (Amis in Mogen, p. 110).

For More Information

Bradbury, Ray. *Fahrenheit 451: The Temperature at Which Books Burn.* New York: Ballantine, 1953.

Bryfonski, Dedria, ed. *Contemporary Literary Criticism.* Vol. 10. Detroit: Gale Research, 1979.

Flem, Penna Frank. *The Cold War and Its Origins, 1917-1960.* Garden City, N.Y.: Doubleday, 1961.

Mankiewicz, Frank, and Joel Swerdlow. *Remote Control: Television and the Manipulation of American Life.* New York: Times Books, 1978.

McClellan, Grant S., ed. *Censorship in the United States.* New York: Wilson, 1967.

Mogen, David. *Ray Bradbury.* Boston: Twayne, 1986.

Morgan, H. Wayne. *Drugs in America: A Social History, 1800-1980.* Syracuse, N.Y.: Syracuse University Press, 1981.

Thomas, Lately. *When Even Angels Wept: The Senator Joseph McCarthy Affair—A Story without a Hero.* New York: Morrow, 1973.

Fallen Angels

by
Walter Dean Myers

W alter Dean Myers was born on August 12, 1937, and after his mother died during his infancy, he was raised by family friends in Harlem, New York. In his third year of high school, Myers realized that he would not be able to attend college for financial reasons. He proceeded to join the army at the age of seventeen. After returning to civilian life and to Harlem, Myers began writing books for young adults. He created the novel *Fallen Angels* as a tribute to his younger brother, who was killed in the Vietnam War. The novel's descriptions of the interactions among soldiers and the long periods of inactivity they experience are based on its author's own military background.

Events in History at the Time the Novel Takes Place

The Vietnam War. American concern over Vietnam began in the 1940s, when the French colonial powers, who had held the Southeast Asian land since the nineteenth century, began to experience resistance from Viet Minh revolutionaries. Led by Ho Chi Minh, the Viet Minh was a coalition of nationalists and communists united against the French. Elections in 1946 brought Ho Chi Minh a landslide victory over conservative opponents in northern Vietnam. Later that year, French attempts to reassert control in the north sparked an all-out war for independence.

The U.S. State Department feared yet another communist regime in Asia and began looking into how devout a communist Ho Chi Minh was

---

THE LITERARY WORK

A young-adult novel set in war-torn Vietnam in 1967; published in 1988.

SYNOPSIS

A seventeen-year-old African American learns about life and death while serving as an infantry soldier in the jungles of Vietnam.

---

and how strong his connections to the Soviet Union were. In 1949, U. S. Secretary of State Dean Acheson abandoned any thoughtful research into the issue, stating that Ho Chi Minh was an "outright Commie" because he "fails to unequivocally repudiate Moscow connection and Commie doctrine" (Acheson in Young, p. 23). As the war continued between the French and Vietnamese, the United States granted aid to the French. This aid increased dramatically after Chinese communist insurgency leader Mao Zedong (Tse-tung) won a substantial victory that same year and proclaimed the People's Republic of China. Feeling that French control of Vietnam was the last wedge against the spread of communism in Southeast Asia, the United States assured the French that every resource, except for American combat troops and nuclear weapons, would be at their disposal. Despite this promise, U.S. aid did not materialize at the crucial moment, and the French were crushed by the Viet Minh at Dienbienphu in May 1954. Following

Captain Oliver E. Murray (left), Brigadier General F. Davison (right), and others, southwest of Saigon, South Vietnam, 1968.

this loss, the French declared a cease-fire and withdrew from Vietnam. The country was partitioned into the communist North and nationalist South, with national elections to determine a final outcome.

The South, however, proclaimed its independence in 1955, and won the support of the United States despite the regime of Ngo Dinh Diem. The South Vietnamese leader was an unpopular ruler whose cruel tactics against the growing number of communist sympathizers and outright rebels in South Vietnam increased in proportion to his lack of solid support. In 1961 the Kennedy administration, worried about the possible fall of South Vietnam to the communists, sent Vice President Lyndon B. Johnson there on a mission to bolster the morale of Diem's government by promising American aid. By December of 1961 there were 675 so-called "advisers" (troops) from the United States in Vietnam; this number increased to 11,000 in 1962. When President Kennedy was assassinated in November 1963, there were 16,700 American troops in Vietnam.

When he assumed the presidency Johnson also inherited the war in Vietnam and immediately became determined that South Vietnam would not fall to the communists during his term. Johnson said of the conflict, "If I left the war and let the Communists take over South Vietnam, then I would be seen as a coward and my nation would be seen as an appeaser, and we would both find it impossible to accomplish anything for anybody anywhere on the entire globe" (Johnson in Young, p. 106). Johnson's attitude led to an increase in the U.S. military presence in Vietnam, which prompted further deployment of North Vietnamese troops, causing the conflict to escalate rapidly.

Black soldiers in Vietnam. During the Vietnam War, 2.15 million men went to Vietnam; 1.6 million experienced combat. The soldiers who fought and died in the war were disproportionately poor, uneducated, and minority. Especially during the years 1965 to 1967—the year in which the novel is set—black Americans suffered more than their fair share of combat horror, injuries, and death. Responsible for much of these hardships was a special U.S. government program called Project 100,000. Between 1966 and 1972, this program called to service over 300,000 young men previously considered ineligible for the military because of their low written test scores. Many supporters of the project extolled the benefits it brought to young black Americans. One supporter, Harvard sociologist and presidential advisor Daniel Patrick Moynihan, spoke highly about the project's opportunities for blacks, saying:

> Given the strains of disordered and matrifocal family life in which so many Negro youth come of age, the armed forces are a dramatic and desperately needed change, a world away from women, a world run by strong men and unquestioned authority, where discipline, if harsh, is nonetheless orderly and predictable, and where rewards, if limited, are granted on the basis of performance.
>
> (Moynihan in Young, p. 320)

Of the new recruits brought in by Project 100,000, 41 percent were black. Most of these men had dropped out of high school, could read only at less than sixth-grade level, and were sent directly into combat. These men were also court-martialled at twice the normal rate, and most emerged from the military with no practical training, skills, or benefits. The characters of Richie Perry, Peewee Gates, and most of the other soldiers in *Fallen Angels* share a similarly disadvantaged background.

Combat in Vietnam. Every war has unique and terrifying battlefields: World War I was riddled with the muddy trenches and foxholes, while World War II featured the bloody beaches of Normandy and Iwo Jima, among others. The Vietnam War had its own horrifying battleground—the endless jungles of Southeast Asia. Sitting water from heavy rainfall turned the jungles into nightmarish worlds of mud and ceaseless mosquitoes. Long exposure to the climate resulted in severe discomfort, rashes, and other more serious skin disorders commonly called "jungle rot." Another difficulty experienced by American combat troops was the blurry lines of combat. The Vietnam War was a war of intense guerrilla fighting, with few conventional front-line maneuvers. During many battles, American troops did not even see the enemy, and outside of combat American soldiers were not even sure who the enemy was. The farmer in the rice paddy could be a guerrilla fighter by night, and "friendly" villages could be secret havens for the Viet Cong. Because of this, soldiers in the field lived in a constant state of nervousness, wondering who their enemies were and where they would strike next.

When soldiers engaged enemy troops in the jungles, the battles were fierce and chaotic. Small squads of American troops were sent into the jungles to find enemy targets. In some cases, once Viet Cong soldiers were located, American ground troops would be assisted by air support or artillery fire that would rain heavy explosives on enemy positions. Unfortunately, however, in most cases such small squads of American troops were forced to face the enemy on their own. These squads, which sometimes numbered as few as five men, were typically armed with automatic rifles and one heavy M-60 machine gun known as the "pig." In addition to engaging in direct combat, American soldiers faced countless dangers from landmines and other booby traps laid by Viet Cong. The most infamous type of trap set by the Viet Cong was a small pit set with sharpened bamboo stakes and then concealed. Soldiers would fall into the hole and onto the stakes, or "punji sticks," which were often coated with excrement in an attempt to immediately infect the wounds.

In the novel, Perry is involved in numerous combat skirmishes in the jungle, and in almost every case while on patrol with a small five-man squad. Perry also witnesses the uncertainties of Vietnam's jungle combat, finding hostile Viet Cong soldiers in a "friendly" village and seeing a soldier from his unit die in a Viet Cong landmine explosion. While simply fighting in the tangled jungles was horrifying enough, such additional dangers particular to the guerrilla nature of this war made life a living hell for American combat troops.

The Novel in Focus

The plot. Richie Perry, a seventeen-year-old black soldier, is sent to Vietnam via plane along with other military personnel. During the flight he meets Judy Duncan, a young army nurse, and Peewee Gates, a tough black youth from Chicago. In Vietnam, Perry and Peewee are assigned to Alpha Company along with several other soldiers: Johnson, Monaco, and Jenkins. Perry, who has a bad knee from a basketball injury, is worried when his medical papers exempting him from combat duty fail to arrive. Alpha Company is transported to a small base in the jungle, or "deep boonies," as the soldiers call it. At the base, they meet their commanding officer, Lieutenant Carroll, and at their barracks they meet Sergeant Simpson, who is counting down his last 120 days. During Perry's first guard patrol, Jenkins is killed when he steps on a Viet Cong landmine just outside the base. The death troubles Perry when he realizes that even though he feels sorry for Jenkins, he feels relieved that it was Jenkins instead of him.

Perry and the other Alpha Company soldiers get their first taste of combat when a news crew comes to the base and goes out on patrol with them. After a wild gunfire fight, they find one dead body. Ironically, Perry later realizes that the dead soldier is not the enemy but from South Vietnam's army, the ARVN, or Army of the Republic of Vietnam. Following this initial encounter, Alpha Company is sent out constantly on patrols. Perry realizes that Captain Stewart, one of the base commanders, is volunteering Alpha Company for combat in an attempt to get promoted to major before his tour of duty is over.

During a night patrol, Lieutenant Carroll is killed when Alpha Company's ambush on a group of Viet Cong soldiers fails. Asked to write a letter to Carroll's wife to inform her of her husband's death, Perry finds it a painful experience. On another patrol, the Alpha Company raids a village suspected of aiding enemy Viet Cong troops. Perry kills a Viet Cong soldier in self-defense and is disturbed by the incident, his first confirmed kill. The raid becomes chaotic, culminating in the destruction of the entire village. The worst fighting occurs when Alpha Company is sent into combat with several ARVN companies. Ambushed by large companies of Viet Cong, the ARVN soldiers and Alpha Company are forced to retreat, suffering heavy casualties all the way. During another patrol, Perry and Peewee are both wounded and hospitalized. While in the hospital Perry finds out that Judy Duncan, the young nurse with whom he flew into Vietnam, was killed when her hospital got hit by mortars. Perry and Peewee both receive Purple Heart medals and learn that they are being sent home; Peewee needs additional surgery, and Perry's original medical papers have finally arrived. They leave Vietnam on the same plane, happy to be returning to their homes, and to life.

Why are we in Vietnam? One of the more prominent issues in the novel is the uncertainty felt by the soldiers about their role in Vietnam. After Lieutenant Carroll's death, Perry struggles to understand the reasons for the death and destruction in Vietnam. He also begins to question what his role is there as a soldier, and if this role is right or wrong. Perry tries to understand the reason for Carroll's death, musing that he "wanted to talk to everybody about it, but nobody could deal with it. Lobel had thought it was his fault. He said if he had shot more maybe he would have got the guy that got Carroll" (Myers, *Fallen Angels,* p. 138). Perry continues his self-questioning: "But why was Carroll even here? What was he doing so far from Kansas City? So far from his bookstore on Minnesota Avenue?" (*Fallen Angels,* p. 138).

Later in the novel, Perry talks to Johnson about their purpose for being in Vietnam. As he tries to sort it out he tells Johnson, "You talk about Communists—stuff like that—and it doesn't mean much when you're in school. Then when you get over here the only thing they're talking about is keeping your ass in one piece" (*Fallen Angels,* p. 149). After killing the Viet Cong soldier in the village, Perry continues to think about the reasons for his being there. Finally he writes a letter to his younger brother Kenny: "I just told him that the war was about us killing people and about people killing us, and I couldn't see much more to it. . . . I had thought that this war was right, but it was only right from a distance. . . . But when the killing started, there was no right or wrong except in the way you did your job, except in the way that you were part of the killing" (*Fallen Angels,* pp. 269-70).

These feelings and questions faced by Perry were common among American troops in Vietnam. The war was ostensibly being fought for the purpose of preventing the spread of communism and protecting the South Vietnamese, yet many American soldiers found themselves hated by the South Vietnamese people and fighting battles that seemed to accomplish nothing. In her essay "A Different War," Myra MacPherson quotes an American GI asking, "What am I doing here? We don't take any land. We don't give it back. We just mutilate bodies" (MacPherson in Sevy, p. 53). One Vietnam scholar, Marilyn B. Young, poses this same question in her book *The Vietnam Wars,* and writes, "There was no conceivable justification for the horrors daily inflicted on

The Vietnam Memorial.

and suffered in Vietnam" (Young, p. ix). In *Fallen Angels,* Perry, Peewee, and the other members of Alpha Company arrive at the same conclusion.

Sources. *Fallen Angels* was inspired by the death of the author's younger brother, Thomas Wayne Myers, in Vietnam in 1968. To create a realistic story, Walter Dean Myers based many details in the novel on his own experiences in the army in the mid-1950s. Myers was not in Vietnam and never in combat, but he understood the bond between enlisted men. Thinking back on his military service, Myers recalls learning "something about killing. I learned something about dying. I learned a lot about facilitating the process, of making it abstract" (Myers in Senick, p. 185). Myers instills some of this attitude in the character Richie Perry, who struggles to come to terms with his feelings about death throughout the novel.

Myers's army background also taught him about the long periods of waiting that separated action in the military and incorporated this reality into the novel; it pays a great deal of attention to the interactions between the men of Alpha Company as they wait for their next assignment. Another real-life parallel arises from the fact that Myers spent much of his noncombat time in the army playing basketball, just as Perry does in the novel.

Events in History at the Time the Novel Was Written

Postwar experience. American troops returning from the war in Vietnam experienced a homecoming different from any in American history. Unlike the soldiers of the two world wars or the conflict in Korea, Vietnam veterans were not welcomed back with parades or celebrations honoring their sacrifice. Instead, they returned to the United States to encounter apathy and sometimes even hostility. In "A Different War" Myra MacPherson writes, "Ticker tape parades and the generous GI Bills of the past were forms of absolving the soldier of anything he may have done in the course of battle, as well as signs of societal commitment. . . . All of this was absent after Vietnam" (MacPherson in Sevy, pp. 54-5). As MacPherson explains, "Societal indifference was a form of punishment instead; this was symbolized in the punitive attitude toward everything from meager GI benefits" to the Pentagon's inattention to the dangers of Agent Orange, a chemical that had been used to defoliate trees in Vietnam and that was linked to subsequent medical problems (MacPherson in Sevy, p. 55). So angry were antiwar activists about U.S. participation in the fighting that some of the veterans were spat upon by war protesters when they returned from Vietnam. By 1991 one-quarter to one-third of

America's homeless population would consist of Vietnam-era veterans, approximately 500,000 men. Returning from the war with no skills or training of use in their own country, many came to realize that their service in Vietnam had even put them at a disadvantage. Many were plagued by post-traumatic stress disorder (PTSD), which causes an estimated 700,000 veterans to suffer from symptoms including flashbacks, severe sleep disorders, depression, and rage. Related to this psychological trauma is the inordinately high suicide rate among Vietnam veterans. More veterans have committed suicide since the war than died in it, at least 60,000 in contrast to the 58,000 known to have been killed in action. Over a thousand more have been classified as missing in action in Southeast Asia.

Attitudes toward Vietnam veterans have slowly changed for the better, as indicated by the dedication of the Vietnam Veterans Memorial in Washington, D.C., in 1982. The monument, consisting of two black granite walls in the shape of a V, lists the names of all 58,152 Americans in the armed forces who died or disappeared in Vietnam between July 1959 and May 1975. Unfortunately, this gradual change in opinion has occurred too late for many Vietnam veterans, who may never be able to overcome their experiences both in Vietnam and the United States. In the novel, as Perry prepares to leave Vietnam, he thinks about himself and Peewee: "We had tasted what it was like being dead. We had rolled it around in our mouths and swallowed it and now the stink from it was coming from us. We weren't all right. We would have to learn to be alive again" (*Fallen Angels,* p. 304).

Reception. Since its publication in 1988, *Fallen Angels* has received high praise from the general public and critics alike. Reviews lauded Myers's ability to create sympathetic characters to whom the reader can easily relate and situations that draw the reader directly into the story. Maria V. Salvadore writes about Richie Perry, the novel's central character, "His first-person narrative provides an immediacy to the events and characters revealed. His experiences become readers' experiences, as do his fears and his insight about this war, any war" (Salvadore in Senick, p. 191). Ethel L. Heins, writing for *Horn Book Magazine,* praises Myers's "skill, maturity, and judgement" and compares the novel to a classic: "With its intensity and vividness in depicting a young soldier amid the chaos and the carnage of war, the novel recalls Stephen Crane's ***The Red Badge of Courage***" (also covered in *Literature and Its Times*) (Heins in Senick, p. 192). Another critic, Alison Hurst, applauds Myers's technique in creating characters. "The dialogue is so convincing," she confesses, "that American accents rang around my head as I read" (Hurst in Senick, p. 193). A general critical consensus described as the novel's chief merit its clear and realistic portrayal of the lives of America's young soldiers in the Vietnam War. The story, noted some reviewers, captures these soldiers' greatest hopes and fears as they struggle to become men and to survive.

For More Information

Appy, Christian G. *Working-Class War: American Combat Soldiers and Vietnam.* Chapel Hill: University of North Carolina Press, 1993.

Goff, Stanley, and Robert Sanders. *Brothers: Black Soldiers in the Nam.* Novato, Calif.: Presidio, 1982.

Myers, Walter Dean. *Fallen Angels.* New York: Scholastic, 1988.

Senick, Gerard J., ed. *Children's Literature Review.* Vol. 35. Detroit: Gale Research, 1995.

Sevy, Grace, ed. *The American Experience in Vietnam.* Norman: University of Oklahoma Press, 1989.

Taylor, Clyde, ed. *Vietnam and Black America: An Anthology of Protest and Resistance.* Garden City, N.Y.: Anchor, 1973.

Young, Marilyn B. *The Vietnam Wars: 1945-1990.* New York: HarperCollins, 1991.

The Fire Next Time

by
James Baldwin

James Baldwin was born in 1924 in Harlem, New York. As a youth he dodged the perils of his rough neighborhood by preaching in a local church. When he heard his father proclaim that his Jewish friends were damned, however, James grew wary of Christian dogma. Abandoning the church, he moved to Greenwich Village to pursue a career as a writer. His first novel, *Go Tell It on the Mountain,* recounts his disillusionment with religion. After its publication, Baldwin went to France hoping to escape the racism that he felt poisoned the United States. A decade later he returned home to join the budding civil rights movement. In *The Fire Next Time* Baldwin expressed both his frustration with the reluctance of the federal government to deal effectively with segregation in the South and his fear that militant separatists such as Elijah Muhammad might persuade black Americans that integration was a farce.

Events in History at the Time of the Essay

The civil rights movement. During the Second World War, the United States had fought alongside Great Britain to defend the self-determination of European countries against Nazi Germany. As the war ended, British officials were forced to concede that the British colonial administrations in countries like India and Nigeria infringed on the native peoples' right to govern themselves. Reluctantly the British responded to protests within these countries by dismantling

THE LITERARY WORK

An essay set in the United States in the 1960s; published in 1963.

SYNOPSIS

After meeting with Elijah Muhammad, the leader of the Nation of Islam, Baldwin reflects on the civil rights movement and the future of race relations in the United States.

the colonial governments. As many of the peoples of Africa and Asia wrested their independence from Britain, blacks in the United States, inspired by changes abroad and dissatisfied with the sluggish rate of progress at home, struggled to change the restrictive laws and customs that divided black Americans and white Americans.

Although the Emancipation Proclamation of 1863 had put an end to chattel slavery, state laws mandating segregation reduced the citizenship of blacks to little more than a sham. In 1896 Homer Plessy had challenged these laws by defying a Louisiana state statute requiring railroad companies to provide separate cars for whites and blacks and making it a crime for any passenger to take a seat in a car reserved for the other race. Plessy had argued that the law violated his constitutional rights. He appealed to the U.S. Supreme Court to enjoin the judge in his case, John Ferguson, from continuing proceedings against him. The Supreme Court rejected Plessy's appeal and dismissed his argument on the grounds that separate, but supposedly equal, facilities were constitutionally legal. This landmark decision temporarily gave federal sanction to state laws requiring or allowing segregation.

In 1952, Linda Carol Brown, a black girl living in Topeka, Kansas, challenged the precedent set by *Plessy v. Ferguson*. Denied admission to an all-white school, Brown appealed to the federal courts, contending that the denial violated her constitutional rights. Because of the significance of the case, the Supreme Court took jurisdiction. In 1954 the court overturned *Plessy v. Ferguson* in *Brown v. the Board of Education of Topeka*, agreeing with the student that separate facilities were inherently unequal. This monumental ruling heralded a decade of unprecedented changes in the legal rights of minorities in the United States.

Martin Luther King Jr. and passive resistance.
Atlanta, Georgia, native Martin Luther King Jr. would become the most celebrated leader of the U.S. civil rights movement in the twentieth century. Ordained as a minister in 1947, King attended Crozer Theological Seminary in Chester, Pennsylvania, and then Boston University, where he earned a doctorate in philosophy. King married and, in 1952, returned with his wife to the South. In 1954 King accepted the pastorate of a church in Montgomery, Alabama.

Soon after King's arrival in Montgomery, racial tensions erupted. On Montgomery's city buses, the seats in the front rows were reserved for whites and the back rows, located over the engines, for blacks. In a bus crowded with blacks, the black passengers who could not sit in the back had to stand—even if all the seats in the front rows were empty. It was furthermore not allowed for blacks and whites to sit in the same row. On December 1, 1955, Rosa Parks, a black seamstress, took a seat in the first row of the black section. Several whites then boarded the bus, and one was left standing. When the driver noticed this, he instructed the four blacks in Parks's row to stand up and let the white man take a seat. Parks alone kept refusing to stand up, whereupon she was arrested and jailed.

Responding to Parks's arrest, a coalition of black ministers created the Montgomery Improvement Association (MIA), with King as the organization's president. King delivered fiery orations, framed in the cadences of a preacher, that roused the black community of Montgomery. Recalling a lecture he had attended at the Crozer Seminary on Mohandas Gandhi, an Indian leader who led a peaceful revolt against British rule in India, King organized a nonviolent boycott of the Montgomery buses. Tensions escalated.

The boycott started on December 5, 1955. When the boycotters organized a voluntary car-pool to provide transportation, Montgomery police began to stop and arrest black automobile drivers. On January 26, 1956, police arrested King himself, and four days later hooligans bombed his house. Standing outside his ruined house, King entreated his angry supporters to remain calm. "If you have weapons," he pleaded, "take them home; if you do not have them, please do not seek to get them" (King in Fairclough, pp. 24-5). This show of fortitude reassured the boycotters. The MIA made its boldest demand, insisting that buses be completely desegregated.

On November 13, 1956, nearly a year after the boycott began, the Supreme Court ruled that Alabama's bus segregation law discriminated against blacks and was therefore unconstitutional. This landmark decision suggested that the federal courts might eventually invalidate all state laws that allowed discrimination. For King this was the first of a number of triumphs.

The success of the boycott propelled King to the forefront of national politics. He became the unofficial spokesman for the movement for integration. Inspired by King's example, blacks throughout the South staged sit-ins to protest segregation. King's eloquent orations, sprinkled with quotes from famous documents such as the Declaration of Independence and the Emancipation Proclamation, continued to turn the nation's attention to the plight of blacks.

Yet it was not until 1963, after a pivotal clash between civil rights protesters and local authorities in Birmingham, Alabama, that King finally received the committed support of the federal government. Hoping to provoke Sheriff Theophilus "Bull" Conner, an infamous official who never hesitated to use force, King organized an enormous demonstration composed of black schoolchildren. Conner directed the police to use attack dogs and fire hoses to disperse the crowds. Telecasts of German shepherds snapping at children's faces outraged the nation, and President John F. Kennedy intervened. Persuaded by federal officials, the white businessmen of Birmingham agreed to integrate their stores. King's success in Birmingham seemed to prove his contention that "non-violent resistance is the most potent weapon available to oppressed people in their struggle for freedom and human dignity" (King in Clark, p. 23).

Dr. Martin Luther King, Jr., leading the March on Washington, August 28, 1963.

Later in 1963, King led the March on Washington, an assembly of over 250,000 people, in support of a civil rights bill before Congress. The bill, passed in 1964, banned segregation in all public accommodations, including hotels, restaurants, shops, and theaters. Another piece of legislation, the Voting Rights Act of 1965, outlawed the discriminatory measures used in the South to prevent blacks from voting.

The Nation of Islam: Militant resistance. While blacks in the South applauded King's triumphs, blacks in the slums of the North rallied around a different set of leaders. Prior to World War II, the Nation of Islam, a black nationalist movement, had captured the attention of thousands of blacks in Northern cities. Whereas King encouraged peaceful demonstrations to further integration, leaders for the Nation of Islam advocated separatism and militancy.

The Nation of Islam's roots stretched back to the early 1930s, when a mysterious peddler named W. D. Fard wandered the streets of the black community in Detroit. He sold raincoats and umbrellas, but also silks and artifacts that, he explained to his clients, were the same kind used by the peoples of Africa and the Middle East. Along with his exotic wares he carried a copy of the Bible, which he used to expound on the history of mankind.

Fard did not, however, preach traditional Christianity. He used the Bible because it was the only religious text with which his audience was familiar. Carefully interpreted, he explained to his listeners, it could serve until they were acquainted with the Holy Koran, the genuine text of the black man's religion.

Fard enchanted his followers with tales about Asia and Africa and his version of the first people, black people, to roam the earth. As his prestige grew, Fard delivered vitriolic condemnations of both Christianity and white people. He declared that he had come to arouse the black people of the United States and vanquish the whites who oppressed them.

Fard called his movement the Lost-Found Nation of Islam. He contended that Islam was the true religion of the black race, and that Christianity had merely been foisted upon blacks to subdue them. Christian whites promised a blissful hereafter, he elaborated, to ensure that blacks remained docile and submissive in the present. Furthermore, Fard argued, blacks were not Americans and owed no loyalty to a government that offered them no protection from "the depravities of the white devils [who] by their tric-

knology . . . keep our peoples illiterate to use as tools and slaves" (Fard in Lincoln, p. 16).

In 1934, after having won over eight thousand adherents, Fard disappeared. His followers insisted he had died in prison as the result of police brutality, whereas some policemen insinuated he had been ousted by competing factions within the Nation of Islam. Fard was succeeded by Elijah Muhammad, one of his most zealous adherents.

Muhammad's unrestrained condemnations of the white race and his assurances that the superior black race would soon rise to take its rightful place as the ruler of the earth captivated his audiences. Muhammad advocated the formation of a separate black nation. "To integrate with Evil," he warned his followers, "is to be destroyed with evil. . . . We want, and must insist upon an area in this land that we can call our own" (Muhammad in Lincoln, p. 95). He demanded that the U.S. government cede territory to his followers in recompense for the historical crime of slavery. "[Black people] worked 300 years without a pay day," he pointed out. "We feel that we've got something due us, and I don't mean this phony integration stuff" (Muhammad in Lincoln, p. 96).

The Nation of Islam grew to number over a hundred thousand members. Inspired by spokesmen for the Nation who visited prisons and reformatories, rehabilitated criminals swelled the ranks of Muhammad's following. Heroin addicts, obeying Muhammad's injunction against drugs, kicked their habits and began lives of moderation and restraint. Once they came under Muhammad's influence, few were ever arrested again.

Nevertheless the Nation of Islam had many detractors. Skeptics insisted that Muhammad exploited the frustration of blacks in the United States to finance his pursuit of fame. Baldwin himself believed that Muhammad merely gave his followers a "false morale by giving them a false sense of superiority." "It will always break down in a crisis," he warned. "That's the history of Europe simply; it's one of the reasons that we are in this terrible place" (Baldwin in Clark, p. 60).

Yet even the most derisive critics could not deny that Elijah Muhammad had accomplished impressive goals. "Mr. Muhammad may be a rogue and a charlatan," one black journalist wrote, "but when anybody can get tens of thousands of Negroes to practice economic solidarity, respect their women, alter their atrocious diet, give up liquor, stop crime, juvenile delinquency and adultery, he is doing more for the

Negro's welfare than any current leader I know" (Schulyer in Lincoln, p. 142).

Malcolm X. The Nation of Islam won national attention when the eloquent and charismatic spokesman Malcolm X dared to challenge the more moderate tenets of Martin Luther King Jr. His assertions that King, a leader revered throughout the country, had hindered the emancipation of blacks in the United States sparked debates that divided civil rights activists.

Upon his release from prison on parole in 1952, Malcolm X went to Chicago to join Muhammad's movement. He soon emerged as the Nation of Islam's most prominent speaker. Malcolm X decried King's support of nonviolence, and dismissed King's campaign in Birmingham. "Any time dogs have bitten black women, bitten black children," he protested, "and the one who advocates himself as their leader is satisfied in making a compromise or a deal with the same ones who did this . . . it's a sellout" (Malcolm X in Clark, p. 43).

In response to Malcolm's allegations that his approach pleased whites, King rejoined, "If anyone has ever lived with a non-violent movement in the South . . . and seen the reactions of many of the extremists and reactionaries in the white community, he wouldn't say that this movement makes . . . them comfortable. I think it arouses a sense of shame within them" (King in Clark, p. 26).

Baldwin's view. James Baldwin explained some of the conflicts between the two leaders. He pointed out that many of the blacks living in the North had fled the South during the first half of the century hoping to find a promised land free of racism. When they found instead crime-ridden slums terrorized by bigoted policemen, it shattered their optimism. King's quest for integration could hardly appeal to them. Most blacks of his day, Baldwin explained, "dismiss white people as the slightly mad victims of their own brainwashing" (Baldwin, *The Fire Next Time*, p. 116). "Do [blacks]," Baldwin wondered, "really *want* to be integrated into a burning house?" (*The Fire Next Time*, p. 108).

"Martin's a very rare, a very great man," Baldwin insisted, "[but] he has [no moral authority] whatsoever in the north" (Baldwin in Clark, p. 60). Although he applauded King's use of nonviolence, Baldwin admitted "you can only survive so many beatings, so much humiliation, so much despair, so many broken promises before something gives" (Baldwin in Clark, p. 58). Baldwin pointed out that the protesters represented only a fraction of the black population of the United States. "There [are] many, many, many, many more," he warned, "who [have] given up, who [are] desperate and whom Malcolm X can reach" (Baldwin in Clark, p. 59).

Nevertheless, Baldwin did not approve of Malcolm's campaign. He thought it dangerous to build pride on a foundation of lies. He agreed with Malcolm that blacks should be proud of being black, but did not agree that blacks were innately superior to whites. "What [Malcolm] does," Baldwin explained, "is say 'You're better *because* you're black.' Well, of course that isn't true. That's the trouble" (Baldwin in Clark, p. 59).

> ## MALCOLM'S BREAK WITH THE NATION OF ISLAM
>
>
> Malcolm X's views changed after 1963, the year Baldwin's essay was published. He broke with the Nation of Islam and took a trip to the Middle East, where he learned about genuine, orthodox Islam. Upon his return, Malcolm tempered his anti-white rhetoric and encouraged blacks to unite with sympathetic whites. He denounced Elijah Muhammad as a racist and a fraud. On February 21, 1965, as he took the podium to speak at a ballroom in Manhattan, Malcolm was shot and killed. Three black Muslims were convicted of the murder, although many contested the validity of the convictions. Years later, Talmadge X Hayer, one of the three convicted, said that he had in fact committed the murder, but that the other two men were innocent.

In sum, Baldwin saw merits and flaws in the strategies of both King and Malcolm X, and they themselves adjusted their viewpoints over the years. Malcolm is said to have often remarked in private that he respected King immensely and felt that his own antagonistic presence made it more possible for King's movement to reach its goals. King, on the other hand, developed a new appreciation for the obstacles faced by Malcolm and other Northerners after living in Chicago for a while and campaigning for civil rights there. Affected by their separate experiences, the viewpoints of the two black leaders grew closer together toward the end of their lives.

The Essay in Focus

The contents. Before describing his encounter with Nation of Islam leader Elijah Muhammad, Baldwin retells the story of his own break from the Christian church. As a child in Harlem he suffered a religious crisis when he was fourteen. Not only had the developing forms of schoolgirls tempted his eyes away from the pages of the Bible, but his friends were beginning to drink, use drugs, and drop out of school. Watching the hookers and drug dealers on the corner, Baldwin had realized that for his generation crime was not "*a* possibility, but . . . *the* possibility" (*The Fire Next Time*, p. 35).

Desperate to find some escape from this fate, he took refuge in religion. Avoiding the church where his own domineering father preached, Baldwin began attending services with a school friend. Although he enjoyed the music and drama of the ceremony, he realized "I could not remain in the church merely as another worshipper. I would have to give myself something to do" (*The Fire Next Time*, p. 46). Out of a "deep adolescent cunning" (*The Fire Next Time*, p. 46), he became a young minister, preaching from the pulpit for over three years. He enjoyed the attention, especially when people left his father's church to come hear him.

THE FIRE

On April 5, 1968, President Lyndon B. Johnson ordered the flag flown at half-mast and proclaimed the following Sunday to be a day of national mourning. A day earlier, Martin Luther King Jr., standing on the balcony of a motel room in Memphis, Tennessee, discussing plans to support striking city workers, had been shot and killed. Blacks poured into the streets of the nation's cities and, in an eruption of grief and rage, looted and burned places of business. More than 40,000 police, joined by over 30,000 soldiers, suppressed the riots. By April 11, 46 people had been killed and over 35,000 injured. "I remember the sick feeling that came over me," President Johnson wrote, "as I saw black smoke from burning buildings fill the sky over Washington" (Johnson in Fairclough, p. 124).

Some of Baldwin's Jewish school friends, however, questioned him about his faith. They pointed out that, according to Christianity, blacks were descendants of Ham and therefore predestined to be slaves. "As I taught Sunday school," Baldwin confesses, "I felt that I was committing a crime in talking about the gentle Jesus, in telling [the children] to reconcile themselves to their misery on earth in order to gain

the crown of eternal life" (*The Fire Next Time*, p. 53). Baldwin admitted to himself that his bursts of eloquence in the pulpit were not moments of sincere inspiration, but rather attempts to outdo his father.

The essay recounts how distancing himself from the pulpit allowed Baldwin to consider Christianity within a historical context. He realized that the Christian church had been used to sanctify not only European conquests in Africa but also slavery in America. "Whoever wishes to become a truly moral human being," the essay counsels, "must first divorce himself from all the . . . hypocrisies of the Christian church" (*The Fire Next Time*, p. 61).

Baldwin had heard of Elijah Muhammad long before he finally met him. "I paid little attention," he explains, "because the burden of his message did not strike me as very original" (*The Fire Next Time*, p. 61). It was not until he noticed that the police in Harlem were hesitant to disperse the crowds gathered around spokesmen for the Nation of Islam that Baldwin began to listen.

The spokesmen insisted that white people were devils whose reign over the earth would soon come to an end. God is black, they explained, and black people are superior to whites. It was not the theology, however, that impressed Baldwin, but rather the fact that the Nation of Islam had done what decades of political wrangling and social reform had failed to achieve. It had helped drug addicts break their habits, kept ex-convicts from returning to prison, and invested blacks with a sense of pride.

When Elijah Muhammad invited Baldwin to dinner at his stately mansion in Chicago, Baldwin accepted. The two were joined by several of Muhammad's adherents who, as their leader spoke, chimed in "Yes, that's right. . . . The white man sure *is* a devil" (*The Fire Next Time*, p. 79). Baldwin listened while Muhammad explained that Allah—the Islamic God—allowed the devil to create the white man, but has grown anxious to restore peace to the world by destroying him.

In Baldwin's eyes, "there is nothing new in this merciless formulation except for the explicitness of its symbols and the candor of its hatred" (*The Fire Next Time*, p. 81). He felt inclined to disagree with Muhammad, and to point out that Baldwin himself has white friends. He hesitated, however, knowing that this assertion would seem flimsy when weighed against the horrors of the black experience in the United States.

Leaving Muhammad's mansion, Baldwin could not escape the sense that Muhammad re-

James Baldwin at work in his home.

garded him with skepticism. Baldwin felt he had failed some sort of test. For his part, although he admired Muhammad's charisma and conviction, he did not accept his views. He admitted that it was hardly surprising that hundreds of thousands of blacks, having endured insufferable humiliations, were eager to believe that they are superior to whites. Elijah Muhammad, who insists that whites are devils, deserved no more censure than the preachers who for hundreds of years alleged that the descendants of Ham were destined for slavery. But Baldwin cautions that "the glorification of one race and the consequent debasement of another . . . has been and always will be a recipe for murder" (*The Fire Next Time*, p. 96).

Baldwin concludes his essay with another caution. The rise of the Nation of Islam, he warns, should have alerted white legislators to the fact that there is a dangerous faction of American blacks who are not content to limit themselves to passive resistance. "The intransigence and ignorance of the white world," he warns, "might make . . . vengeance inevitable . . . no more water, the fire next time!" (*The Fire Next Time*, p. 120).

Baldwin's view of black-white relations. In an introductory note addressed "to my nephew" (*The Fire Next Time*, p. 15), Baldwin warns that one must beware of the words *acceptance* and *integration.* "There is no reason for you to try to become like white people," he explains, "and there is no basis for their impertinent assumption that *they* must accept *you*" (*The Fire Next Time*, p. 22). Warning that many white Americans are too cowardly to abandon the notion that they are somehow superior, Baldwin warns his nephew "the really terrible thing . . . is that *you* must accept *them*" (*The Fire Next Time*, p. 22).

Baldwin contends that too many whites have misunderstood the drive for integration. "There appears to be a vast amount of confusion on this point," he maintains, "but I do not know many Negroes who are eager to be 'accepted' by white people, still less to be loved by them; they, the blacks, simply don't wish to be beaten over the head by whites" (*The Fire Next Time*, p. 35).

Integration, Baldwin explains, is not a matter of blacks merging with the white majority, for the white majority has already proven itself to be corrupt and spineless. Rather it is up to whites to rise to the standards blacks have set for them by reminding them of the founding principles in the Declaration of Independence and other significant legal documents. Civil rights leaders strove not simply to free blacks from unjust civil codes, but to free whites from the shackles of their own prejudices. The sentiment and ideas he expresses here convey the tenor that underlies the subsequent essay.

Sources. Baldwin's experience with Elijah Muhammad inspired the writing of *The Fire Next Time*. More specifically, Baldwin's perspective on race has been attributed to his time abroad. Baldwin's experience in France may have caused him to differ with Elijah Muhammad. As he adapted to life in a foreign country, Baldwin realized how much he had been shaped by American culture. He noticed, as he watched Algerians and French mingle, that in Europe he was no longer different because he was black, but rather because he was American. "I began to see [America] for the first time," he admitted (Baldwin in Standley and Louis, p. 15). "If I hadn't gone away, I would never have been able to see it" (Baldwin in Standley and Louis, p. 15). He returned to the United States to express his conviction that "the Negro has been formed by this nation, and does not belong to any other—not to Africa and certainly not to Islam" (*The Fire Next Time*, p. 95).

Reception. By 1963 Baldwin had already won renown as well as censure for his fiction. The publication of *The Fire Next Time*, however, made him both a political as well as an artistic figure. President Kennedy invited Baldwin to join other prominent black artists and leaders in a discussion of race relations in the United States. Baldwin didn't hesitate to castigate Kennedy for failing to quicken the pace of integration.

Many critics, however, were more impressed with Baldwin's style than his politics. "Despite its still formidable reputation as a central document in the struggle for equality," one critic complained, "*The Fire Next Time* turns out to have little of interest to say about the question of racial politics. Its impact comes solely from the fact that it is so exquisitely written" (Teachout in Stine and Marowski, p. 19). Another critic dismissed the essay as "an apologia for Black Muslim theology (or demonology) [which] ends with a mixture of real threats and unreal demands" (Gross in Stine and Marowski, p. 17).

Militant black activists contended that Baldwin's essay had betrayed his race. They accused him of perpetuating "the self-contempt which for generations the whites had subtly forced Negroes to suffer" (Campbell in Stine and Marowski, p. 15). Baldwin's entreaties, they asserted, amounted to little more than a sheepish apology for the unpardonable crimes whites had committed.

For More Information

Baldwin, James. *The Fire Next Time*. New York: Dial, 1963.

Clark, Kenneth, interviewer. *King, Malcolm, Baldwin: Three Interviews*. Middletown, Conn.: Wesleyan University Press, 1985.

Fairclough, Adam. *Martin Luther King, Jr.* Athens: University of Georgia Press, 1990.

Lincoln, Eric. *The Black Muslims in America*. Boston: Beacon, 1961.

Muhammad, Elijah. *The Supreme Wisdom*. Chicago: University of Islam, 1957.

Standley, Fred, and Pratt Louis. *Conversations with James Baldwin*. Jackson: University Press of Mississippi, 1989.

Stine, Jean, and Daniel Marowski, eds. *Contemporary Literary Criticism*. Vol. 42. Detroit: Gale Research, 1984.

for colored girls who have considered suicide / when the rainbow is enuf

by

Ntozake Shange

Paulette Linda Williams, born October 18, 1948, is now known by the Zulu name she took in 1971: Ntozake Shange (En-toe-ZAK-kay SHONG-gay). As a child, she was exposed to music, literature, and art in a home environment that fostered pride in her African American heritage, and the future seemed full of promise. Later, however, Shange discovered that the jobs she wanted to fill were closed to her. She turned to writing and became an accomplished poet and novelist, but ultimately it was a dramatic piece—*for colored girls who have considered suicide / when the rainbow is enuf*—that made her famous. Besides winning the Obie Award and Tony, Emmy, and Grammy award nominations, the work introduced a new theatrical form called the choreopoem.

Events in History at the Time of the Choreopoem

"Colored girls." Any generalization about such a large segment of the population—young women of color—would be understandably difficult. As with most other groups, their experiences vary depending on where and how they live. Nevertheless, Ntozake Shange's choreopoem tries to address experiences that such young women probably have in common as a result of their racial identity. The term "colored girls" in the title refers to all females of color,

---

---

though Shange's focus in the choreopoem is particularly on black girls.

In the only monologue spoken from a child's point of view, the speaker does not find it easy to be a young black girl in St. Louis in 1955. The character, who has no name, decides to run away from her integrated school, street, and home. Her distaste for integration is a reminder of the harsh treatment received by real black children entering previously all-white schools in the 1950s and 1960s. One Missouri woman remembered how it felt to be a black girl who was transferred suddenly to a predominantly white school in the mid-1950s. She was unhappy "because when you live in a racist society you learn your place. . . . We didn't know what to expect and we did not expect acceptance, in fact we expected rejection" (Greene, p. 174).

And in fact, despite orders to desegregate, the authorities of many school districts in Missouri and elsewhere either refused to integrate their schools or else met only the minimum requirements. For example, black children in St. Louis who were bussed to new schools in the early 1960s still studied in separate classrooms and were restricted to separate parts of the playground.

Mixed signals like these made black girls intensely aware of race problems in America at an early age, and at times, some of these girls seemed confused about their racial identity. Around the time that Shange wrote *for colored girls,* studies were being conducted to learn about the development of racial self-concept in white and black children. Researchers noticed that a surprising number of young black girls were prone to identify themselves with white dolls rather than black ones. This was one finding among many that led researchers to believe that black girls were sometimes inclined to reject their racial identity (Porter, p. 133).

Shange's childhood seems to have provided ample opportunity for personal development and the reinforcement of a positive racial identity. Famous black Americans like Dizzy Gillespie, Chuck Berry, Miles Davis, and W. E. B. Du Bois visited her parents regularly. Shange described the encouragement and cultural background she received as a child and the impact of her family life on her development as an artist. As evident in the description below, this emphasis on personal development affected not only what she said but the mechanics she used to say it.

> my mama wd read from dunbar, shakespeare, countee cullen, t.s. eliot. my dad wd play congas & do magic tricks. my two sisters & my brother & i wd do a soft-shoe & then pick up the instruments for a quartet of some sort: a violin, a cello, flute & saxophone. we all read constantly. anything. anywhere. we also tore the prints outta art books to carry around with us. sounds / images, any explorations of personal visions waz the focus of my world.
>
> (Shange in Dear, p. 411)

Even so, Shange later thought that she grew up "living a lie," since on the one hand she felt like she could do something with her life, but on the other, it seemed that no one expected her to because she was black and female (Shange in Dear, p. 411). In her case, it appeared that even under relatively favorable circumstances, black

Toussaint L'Ouverture

girls could not escape the limitations placed on them because of their race and gender.

Toussaint L'Ouverture. In the process of constructing a positive racial and gender-based identity, black girls were much more likely to encounter white heroes than black ones in their school books and in the media. In the choreopoem, the girl who struggles with integration in St. Louis faces this problem. She sneaks into the adult section of the library and finds comfort in reading about Toussaint L'Ouverture, a famous black leader in the fight to liberate the French colony of Saint-Domingue (modern-day Haiti) from white rule. He becomes her imaginary friend and helps her plan ways to recreate his success in miniature by removing white girls from her hopscotch games. In her long monologue, she calls him "my first blk man," a phrase that indicates he is probably important to the development of her concept of black manhood (Shange, *for colored girls,* p. 26). In the view of critics, the portrait of Toussaint was also singled out as a positive example of a black man in the choreopoem—of his abilities and his racial pride.

The historical Toussaint L'Ouverture was a brilliant strategist who deserves much of the credit for leading Saint-Domingue to independence and its slaves to freedom. He reputedly had an impressive capacity for work and fairness. He was perceived as a humanitarian by some, in part because of his willingness to grant amnesty to even his worst enemies. He had the foresight to include all three castes—black, mulatto, and white—in his plans for Saint-Domingue, but infrequently his vengeful side prompted him to attack the mulattos, whom he distrusted because of their reluctance to help free the blacks (Ott, p. 128).

The girl in the choreopoem asserts that Toussaint "held the citadel gainst the french," but this point of view requires some explanation (*for colored girls,* p. 27). He was a lieutenant governor in the French army in the 1790s, but his alliance with France was a duplicitous one, intended to increase his military power and help free the slaves. By the turn of the century, he was in control of the whole island, and he guided the drafting of the Constitution of 1801. Among other things the Constitution abolished slavery and appointed Toussaint governor-general for life. In Europe, Napoleon was finally aware that the black leader had duped him by pretending allegiance to France while really preparing the island for independence. Toussaint was arrested and shipped secretly to France, where he soon died, only months before the French were forced to grant Saint-Domingue its freedom.

Women's studies. In the 1960s and 1970s, efforts to honor women by studying their accomplishments and making them well-known role models intensified. Shange's *for colored girls* was also born out of the need to establish a more accurate legacy of women's experiences. Like the scholars who were formally discussing women's issues at the time, Shange tried to have an effect on later generations by talking about past and present examples set by adult women.

The activism of female students in the 1960s led to the creation of women's studies programs at many colleges and universities. Students and faculty in the new programs reconsidered the traditional ways in which mythological women and heroines in fiction had been perceived. They also researched the lives of real women, whether famous or ordinary, for the purpose of obtaining a more complete picture of women's struggles and contributions to society. Shange had taken such courses and would later go on to teach in women's studies programs herself.

The choreopoem addresses many of the issues that are central to the field of women's studies because they are of common concern to almost all women. These issues include pregnancy, sexuality, abortion, dependency, rape, and emotional abuse. But black women inside the movement made it clear that their experiences as females were often markedly different from the experiences of white women in various respects. Government statistics, for example, corroborated the black women's claims that they were more likely to become victims of rape than any other group, and that half of their households were headed by single females.

The majority of scholars attracted to women's studies programs were feminists themselves, and demanded equal rights for women in society and academics. Here again, black women strove to distinguish their experiences from those of white women, who sometimes tried to build support for the cause of women's liberation by speaking of the "common oppression" suffered by blacks in general and white women; one black feminist scholar refuted the comparison by writing in 1970:

> [L]et us state unequivocally that, with few exceptions, the American white woman has had a better opportunity to live a free and fulfilling life, both mentally and physically, than any other group in the United States, with the exception of her white husband. Thus, any attempt to analogize black oppression with the plight of the American white woman has the validity of comparing the neck of a hanging man with the hands of an amateur mountain climber with rope burns.
>
> (Linda La Rue in Guy-Sheftall, p. 164)

As white and black feminists fought for equality on campus and in society, they advocated alternatives to traditional work roles like homemaker, secretary, and nurse. They argued that women should rely on themselves and put their own needs ahead of men's needs for a change. Shange dramatically asserted herself as a black woman by rejecting her given name of Paulette Williams, which she felt was too reminiscent of her father's name (Paul T. Williams), as well as of Anglo-Saxon culture and the heritage of slavery. Instead, she let friends from the Xhosa tribe in South Africa give her the Zulu names *Ntozake,* meaning "she who comes with her own things," and *Shange,* meaning "who walks like a lion" (Lester, p. 10). This personal renewal announced that Shange, for one, would gladly overturn traditions that made her feel oppressed as a woman.

The choreopoem. Shange's willingness to defy convention is evident the moment one sees *for* *colored girls* in print or on the stage. The new form that Shange calls "choreopoem" is a clear departure from traditional play act divisions and linear plot structure. It consists of occasional music, dance, and song accompanying a series of poems that eventually fuse into one statement or voice. In keeping with these elements is Shange's background as a poet and a dancer, which prompted her to point out that she was not a playwright and that *for colored girls* was not a play.

This innovative theatrical form drew on African-style storytelling, in which the performer passes along cultural information and images in a dynamic way. In this sense, *for colored girls* had something in common with much black poetry of the 1960s and early 1970s, since many of the black poets performed their pieces at large public gatherings. Shange tried also to preserve this dynamic connection between artist and listener in the text by avoiding capital letters, spelling things phonetically, leaving out letters, and using obliques (/) to manipulate the flow of the lines. She wanted to energize the appearance of the words on the page as well as "attack deform n maim the language that i was taught to hate myself in" (Shange in Dear, p. 414).

The Choreopoem in Focus

The contents. The poetry is shared among seven women who are each associated with a color and a city: the lady in brown (Chicago), yellow (Detroit), purple (Houston), red (Baltimore), green (San Francisco), blue (Manhattan), and orange (St. Louis). Historically, each of these cities has attracted a large number of black residents, and the fact that Shange has selected locales spread evenly throughout the United States makes the stories seem representative of black women's experiences in America. This impression is reinforced by the fact that the same actor can appear in different cities and that often the stories have no specific setting.

The women rush onstage and freeze. The lady in brown appeals for someone to "sing a black girl's song" as a way of voicing what black girls have long been unable to say (*for colored girls,* p. 4). The other characters join in, identifying themselves and invoking childhood through rhymes and a game of tag. Swiftly, the mood changes, and the lady in yellow delivers a monologue about the wonderful experiences of cruising, dancing, and losing her virginity on graduation night. The other women comment on her story until the lady in blue recalls a time when she,

too, was the center of attention on the dance floor. Her talent and the "hints of spanish" in her heritage had prompted her to travel to the South Bronx for a Puerto Rican dance contest (*for colored girls,* p. 11). The Spanish she speaks at the end of her story translates to "Listen, black (man), I love you more than. . . ."

The lady in red follows with a monologue about loving a man too much, lavishing care on him, and deciding to end the affair because she feels unwanted. All of the characters dance, after the lady in orange proposes the idea. The lighting changes, the women list off rationalizations for rape, and the conversation turns to the difficulty of pressing charges against a rapist who was a friend instead of a stranger. The lady in blue then delivers an anguished monologue about undergoing an abortion when "once i waz pregnant & shamed of myself" (*for colored girls,* p. 23).

Next the lady in purple tells the story of Sechita, an exotic dancer in a redneck bar in Natchez, Mississippi. Sechita's life is juxtaposed with that of an innocent young black girl in St. Louis. The lady in brown describes the girl's discovery of Toussaint L'Ouverture in books and the admiration she feels for him. In southwest Los Angeles, a woman portrayed by the lady in red flaunts her sexuality, hurting as many men as possible but crying herself to sleep too. On the other coast, the lady in blue talks about feeling vulnerable and demoralized in Harlem.

The story of three friends who desire the same man—and are ultimately disappointed by him—is told by the lady in purple and finishes with a dance. The lady in orange recalls wanting to avoid the stereotype of being a nagging black woman, but by always keeping up a good front, she has "died in a real way" (*for colored girls,* p. 43). The lady in purple also talks about having shut out her feelings and come to an impasse, telling her lover, "lemme love you just like i am / a colored girl / i'm finally bein real / no longer symmetrical & impervious to pain" (*for colored girls,* p. 44). A possible solution would be to make life dry and abstract, the way white people do, suggests the lady in blue.

The women's need for love is reiterated by the lady in yellow, who initiates a sequence in which all of the characters dance and assert that their love is worth more than the response it gets from their men. The lady in green complains that she almost let a lover walk off with the things that make her special but caught herself in time, saying "ntozake 'her own things' / that's my name / now give me my stuff" (*for colored*

Laurie Carlos (left) and Ntozake Shange (right), in a scene from *for colored girls.*

girls, p. 50). The women trade with one another men's excuses, which they are tired of hearing, and the lady in blue suggests that her ex-lover admit he is good-for-nothing and be happy with himself instead of apologizing for his behavior all the time.

The lady in red tells the story of a woman named Crystal and her partner of nine years, a returned Vietnam veteran who ultimately takes his problems out on her and their children. After this particularly disturbing portrayal of a woman who has been brutalized, the characters identify the spiritual void that has left all of them aching. The lady in red tells about wanting to "jump up outta my bones & be done wit myself," only to be embraced by nature until she found god in herself, and loved her (*for colored girls,* p. 63). The refrain "i found god in myself & i loved her" becomes a song of joy for all of the characters (*for colored girls,* p. 63). The lady in brown finishes the piece by repeating a version of the title: "this is for colored girls who have considered suicide / but are movin to the ends of their own rainbows" (*for colored girls,* p. 64).

The title. The choreopoem's long title—*for colored girls who have considered suicide / when the rainbow is enuf*—is rich in meaning, offering clues about the work, its author's views, and the intended audience. In particular, the title alerts the

audience to Shange's perception—developed over the years in 1950s to 1970s America—of the relationship between skin color and the development of a healthy self-image. "Colored" was no longer the standard word used in reference to black Americans when the choreopoem was written. The term called to mind the "For Colored Only" signs prevalent in public places in the era of segregation, for example; when used by whites, its implications were often derogatory. At the same time, it could be a term of endearment and cultural solidarity when used by blacks. Shange was struck by the fact that her grandmother had called her a precious "little colored girl" (Lester, p. 25). Consequently, Shange believed that the phrase "colored girl" in the title would have resonated with her grandmother, whom she would not have wanted to alienate with a more modern phrase. Shange was writing not only "for colored girls" but for anyone who had been a girl of color or was raising one.

Furthermore, the word "colored" draws attention to Shange's interest in the problems of all women of color, not just black women. The title proceeds to the image of the rainbow, in which many colors coexist in nature. This emphasis on a variety of hues is a reminder that there are many shades of skin tone and a great diversity of experience among people of color—

facts that society often tends to overlook. Shange includes the color brown in her rainbow of colors worn by the characters in her choreopoem. The inclusion is worth noting because it reinforces the idea that brown skin tones belong to and beautify the world. This celebration of brownness and blackness would have called to mind the cultural "Black Is Beautiful" movement of the 1960s and 1970s, which intended, among other purposes, to strengthen racial pride in blacks.

COLORED, NEGRO, BLACK, AFRICAN AMERICAN

In 1974 the title *for colored girls* called to mind the various names that most blacks have embraced and rejected in the twentieth century. Early in the century, the fact that blacks preferred the term "colored" was reflected in the name of the NAACP (National Association for the Advancement of Colored People), which was organized in 1909. "Colored" fell out of favor during the 1920s, but many older blacks continued to use it. From about 1930 to the 1960s, "Negro" often replaced "colored" and "black" among the middle class, intellectuals, and whites, since it was supposedly insulting to refer to the color of a black person's skin. The 1960s and 1970s saw the revival of "black" in slogans like "Black Power" and "Black is Beautiful," expressions that helped turn "Negro" into a negative term applied by blacks to blacks who shied away from the identity asserted by the slogans. There was also by the early 1970s already a precedent for using the term "African American," which would become interchangeable with "black" and widely adopted after 1988.

As used in the title, "rainbow" also refers to the variety, depth, and richness to be found within each "colored girl," whatever troubling circumstances might affect her. Shange believed that when a girl found these colors inside herself, she would have recognized her own beauty and found the tools to survive her pain. A real rainbow had inspired the image when Shange saw it at the end of a depressing day and remembered that every rainbow is, after all, the product of a storm.

With this significance of the rainbow in mind, the title makes the most sense if the first and second halves are thought of as separate ideas instead of as two ideas joined in time by the word "when." In other words, the choreopoem is in-

tended "for colored girls who have considered suicide," and it also hints at the emotional and spiritual health that are achieved "when [one recognizes that] the rainbow is enuf."

Sources and writing. The poems in *for colored girls* are based in part on Shange's own experiences. She had tried to commit suicide four times, including episodes after an abortion and an attempted rape. The suicide attempts—drinking Drano, taking alcohol and Valium, driving her Volvo into the Pacific Ocean—were intended as acts of taking control, although Shange also found them "ridiculous and humorous even at the time" (Shange in Lester, p. 29).

Courses in the women's studies program at Sonoma State College in California also nurtured her views as a feminist. She studied women and female archetypes from antiquity to the present day, finding inspiration and information which enhanced *for colored girls*. For example, Shange mentions female archetypes represented in the character Sechita, who is "perceived as deity, as slut, as innocent & knowing" (Shange in the front matter to *for colored girls*, p. x). Then, in the summer of 1974, Shange began writing a series of seven poems modeled on the poet Judy Grahn's book, *The Common Woman,* and these later provided the foundation for the choreopoem. The poems were revised constantly over the next two years, until Shange was satisfied that the final production at the Booth Theater on Broadway was "as close to distilled as any of us in all our art forms can make it" (Shange in *for colored girls,* p. xv).

Although *for colored girls* was written primarily with girls and young women of color in mind, Shange recognized that adults were more likely to attend the performances than girls. Still, she hoped that the choreopoem would eventually find its way onto school and public library shelves and into the hands of those who needed to read it most.

Production and reviews. "We just did it," said Shange about the first performance of *for colored girls* (Shange in *for colored girls,* p. ix). In December of 1974, she and five other women had presented it at the Bacchanal, a women's bar outside Berkeley, California. About twenty patrons were on hand to witness the dance, music, and poetry that night. "We were a little raw, self-conscious, & eager," recalls Shange (Shange in *for colored girls,* p. ix). In the months that followed, the cast incorporated more dance and varied the selection of poems to suit their mood or the audience. They worked on the show in cafés, bars, poetry centers, and women's studies departments before taking it to Minnie's Can-Do Club in San Francisco. There they played to standing-room-only crowds of poets, dancers, and members of the women's community, and they were called a must-see act. Finally, they felt ready to take *for colored girls* to New York.

In New York, they had to start all over again: only a few friends and family came to the first performance, and the actors quickly realized that the show would have to become more sophisticated if it was to attract New York audiences. They worked with any poets and dancers they could; some new performers joined the cast, while others left it.

Finally, in September 1976, *for colored girls* opened at the Booth Theater on Broadway, and it quickly provoked sharp disagreement among the critics. Both female and male reviewers lavished praise on the poetry and the images of sisterhood presented in the choreopoem. Some found it a wonderfully complete statement of the issues faced by women, and especially by women of color. But black feminist writer Michele Wallace cautioned against the feeling that the discussion of these issues was complete:

> There is so much about black women that needs retelling. . . . Shange's *For Colored Girls* should not be viewed as the definitive statement on black women, but as a very good beginning.
> (Wallace in Dear, pp. 412-13)

Although many critics felt the structure was rough and the style unrefined, most of them found something to praise warmly. Others could not, and one reviewer was so turned off by the show's unconventionality that cultural sensitivity fell by the wayside:

> Is this poetry? Drama? Or simply tripe? Can you imagine this being published in a serious poetry journal? Would it have been staged if written by a white?
> (Simon in Lester, p. 14)

In addition to crimes against style, Shange was accused of tarnishing the image of black men. Wallace suggested that some black women focused on the issue of male-bashing as a front for the real source of their anger: resentment that *for colored girls* had exposed black women's fear of rejection and anger at being rejected. But Shange made no apologies for the choreopoem. After all, her first priority was to break what she called a conspiracy of silence and give young black women "information that I did not have. I wanted them to know what it was truthfully like to be a grown woman" (Shange in Dear, p. 413).

For More Information

Churgin, Jonah R. *The New Woman and the Old Academe: Sexism and Higher Education.* New York: Libra, 1978.

Collins, Patricia Hill. *Black Feminist Thought: Knowledge, Consciousness, and the Politics of Empowerment.* New York: Routledge, Chapman & Hall, 1991.

Dear, Pamela S., ed. *Contemporary Authors New Revision Series.* Vol. 48. Detroit: Gale Research, 1995.

Greene, Lorenzo J., Gary R. Kremer, and Antonio F. Holland. *Missouri's Black Heritage.* Rev. ed. Columbia: University of Missouri Press, 1993.

Guy-Sheftall, Beverly, ed. *Words of Fire: An Anthology of African-American Feminist Thought.* New York: New Press, 1995.

Lester, Neal A. *Ntozake Shange: A Critical Study of the Plays.* Critical Studies in Black Life and Culture. Vol. 21. New York: Garland, 1995.

Ott, Thomas O. *The Haitian Revolution: 1789-1804.* Knoxville: University of Tennessee Press, 1973.

Porter, Judith D. R. *Black Child, White Child: The Development of Racial Attitudes.* Cambridge, Mass.: Harvard University Press, 1971.

Shange, Ntozake. *for colored girls who have considered suicide / when the rainbow is enuf: a choreopoem.* 1977. Reprint. New York: Collier Books, 1989.

Foundation

by
Isaac Asimov

B orn in Russia in 1920, Isaac Asimov moved to New York at the age of three. A self-proclaimed child prodigy, he began to write science fiction as a teenager and by 1950 had become a successful writer, published mostly by Doubleday. His repertoire by then included eight interconnected science fiction magazine stories. In 1951 he organized this 200,000-word beginning into a science fiction trilogy—which the Doubleday publishing company promptly rejected, as did the house of Little, Brown. An obscure press, Gnome, published the three books—*Foundation* (1951), *Foundation and Empire* (1952), and *Second Foundation* (1953). Not until approached by a Portuguese publisher for rights to these books did Doubleday acquire the trilogy and republish it in 1961. The series marked Asimov as one of the premier science fiction writers of this century. Eventually the stories of the Foundation were expanded to three additional volumes: *Foundation's Edge* (1982), *Foundation and Earth* (1986), and *Forward the Foundation* (1993).

Events in History at the Time of the Novel

Shifting powers. The stories in *Foundation* were written in the midst of the turmoil of World War II and the subsequent Cold War, or competition for world leadership between the Soviet Union and the United States. Isaac Asimov was born in the Soviet Union, a nation that at that point had just survived the crisis of the world's first communist revolution and now faced a new crisis in government and economic changes instigated by Vladimir Lenin and his

followers. The writer's parents found the change, particularly the effects on Russian Jews like themselves, so unbearable that they moved to the United States and then even refused to speak Russian in their new home.

The Russian Revolution of 1917 had overthrown the czarist leadership and brought to power the first communist government under Lenin. When Lenin died in 1924, he was replaced by Josef Stalin, who proceeded to eliminate his opponents, radically change agriculture by collectivizing it (which led to the deaths of millions of peasants), and industrialize the economy. He also purged millions of dissenters and aggressively added land to the new Union of Soviet Socialist Republics, formed officially in 1922. Stalin's goal was first to establish a dictatorship in the Soviet Union and then introduce communism throughout the world.

By the 1930s, another dictator, Adolf Hitler, with designs for world power, had used a few initial followers to become a local politician in

THE CONQUESTS OF HITLER, STALIN, AND TOJO

Hitler	Stalin	Tojo
Austria	Estonia	Burma
Belgium	Finland (part)	China (part)
Czechoslovakia	Latvia	Indonesia
Denmark	Lithuania (part)	Korea
France	Poland (part)	Manchuria
Hungary	Romania (part)	Philippines
Lithuania (part)		
Netherlands		
Norway		
Poland (part)		
Sweden		

the southern German city of Munich and then rose to control Germany. He had shrugged off the yoke of armaments agreements imposed on Germany after World War I, abandoning them altogether by 1935 in favor of building a German army of 500,000 soldiers equipped with new weapons capable of striking swiftly in quest for land. In 1939 Hitler used this force to attack Poland, after having coerced other European nations into accepting his occupation of Austria and Czechoslovakia.

For a short time, Stalin and Hitler joined each other in dividing such eastern European lands as Poland, but then the German leader set his sights on Russian territory. This new crisis resulted in a Soviet policy shift. Stalin's government aligned itself with two nations who were becoming more resistant to German takeovers —France and England. On the other side, Japan joined Hitler, who was contending for European control. Hideko Tojo, prime minister of Japan, likewise had plans to conquer other nations and entertained the idea of becoming emperor of all Asia.

The Cold War. The first human-controlled nuclear reaction took place in an assemblage of materials at a top-secret project at the University of Chicago in 1942. Immediately following this success, a massive effort was organized under the name of the Manhattan Project to apply atomic energy to wartime uses. Four years later, the atom bomb was ready for action; the United States used it to destroy Hiroshima and Nagasaki in Japan, bringing an earlier end to the war than might have otherwise have been the case. The atomic bombs brought an end to traditional international armed conflict, but a new struggle rose in its place. The competition for world leadership known as the "Cold War" began between the United States and Soviet Union. The weapons used were primarily economic.

United States President Harry Truman, through a plan administered by General George Marshall, offered to supply the economically and emotionally devastated nations of Europe with financial aid, technical advice, and materials to rebuild their war-torn economies. Over a course of several years, an amount of money, goods, and services—estimated variously from $12 billion to $30 billion—was distributed to nations from Greece to France on the condition that the recipients would become trading partners with the United States. The Truman Doctrine (the policy of helping democratic nations repel potential communist takeovers) and Marshall Plan (the plan of U.S. aid to Western European nations for postwar recovery) succeeded in their goals. Western European nations soon prospered while becoming indebted to the United States and bound to it by trade.

The American strategy to maintain a friendly, democratic alliance in Western Europe was so successful that the trade agreements were later

The July 26, 1946, atomic bomb test at the Bikini atoll in the South Pacific. The development of nuclear weapons was an important aspect of the Cold War.

expanded to military assistance, and various nations banded together to form the North Atlantic Treaty Organization (NATO) to defend Western Europe from Soviet expansion. Meanwhile, the Soviet Union also employed trade to consolidate its power. Neighbors of the Soviet Union were required to trade exclusively with U.S.S.R. and thus became economically dependent on its management. The weapons of war were used to enforce trade agreements on such nations as Czechoslovakia, Hungary, and Romania. Of course, the Soviet economic system was entirely different from the one promoted by the United States. Even before World War II, the Soviet Union and the Western nations had diverged onto separate economic paths. The Soviets had set out to control all the means of production for the good of all the people, an idea known as centralized planning. Ideally their goal was to progress from temporary control by a few leaders to government and economic control by the masses. At the end of World War II, the Soviet Union had not yet succeeded to a level beyond control by a few, and in fact, it never did before the demise of Soviet communism in 1991.

Nuclear energy. After World War II, many applications were found in the military for the new nuclear technology. Ships and submarines

gained nuclear-powered engines. Missiles carrying nuclear warheads became the arsenal with which the major Cold War opponents—the Soviet Union and the United States—threatened each other. Eventually nuclear reactors supplied electric power to homes and industries, although the first of these reactors so used in the United States would not appear until 1958. In 1946 President Harry Truman removed control of atomic energy from the military to a civilian Atomic Energy Commission. It appeared that the uses for nuclear energy might be endless.

The Novel in Focus

The plot. An entire unnamed galaxy has been united into one massive Galactic Empire for many ages. Its ruler, grown complacent and now largely a figurehead, is protected by his ancient fleet of nuclear spaceships while the real power lies with a "commission of public safety." Meanwhile, some of the more distant parts of the empire are doing little to support the emperor with wealth and thus are being neglected by the government. Controlling the knowledge of nucleonics (the study of atomic nuclei), the emperors over the years have concentrated government on a single planet, Trantor. Forty billion workers on this planet, sheltered mostly underground in metal buildings, gather taxes from the galaxy and enforce its rules. Into this situation steps the university professor Hari Seldon, creator of the new science of psychohistory, a man whom the government fears but cannot overtly eliminate because of possible political repercussions.

Psychohistory is a highly mathematical science through which Seldon can predict the future with a high degree of certainty. His science has indicated that the empire will fall within 500 years and be followed by 30,000 years of unbearable chaos as a new government builds. Nothing can be done to avoid the collapse, which will proceed in a series of unalterable crises. Seldon intends only to ease or reduce the period of chaos. He aims also to shorten the whole transitional era to just 1,000 years. With this in mind, Seldon has convinced the government to initiate a massive encyclopedia project, for which he has assembled 100,000 workers who will supposedly record all of human knowledge. It is to be a cover behind which he can proceed with his real plans. A good portion of these so-called "encyclopedists" are actually experts in nucleonics, a branch of science necessary for building a new world.

Through a series of machinations executed over a period of two years, Seldon has engineered his own exile, and that of his workers, to a deserted planet, Terminus, on the outskirts of the empire. Once there, Seldon's group, otherwise known as the Foundation, turns away from the encyclopedia project, eventually revealed to have been a smokescreen from the beginning, concealing a far more complicated imperative for their actions. The group begins to develop a wide array of nuclear-powered tools, some with power plants that can be held in a walnut-sized lead jacket. The knowledge of the Seldon "Foundation" comes to be used by rulers of nearby planets on the fringe of the galaxy. The Foundation is able to create nuclear weapons as well as hundreds of nuclear tools for household uses—all constructed so that specialists from the Foundation can maintain and control them. The Foundation's science takes on the aspect of a religion, initially because Seldon feels that this makes it easier for the "barbarians" who "looked upon our science as a sort of magical sorcery" (*Foundation*, p. 59) to accept its tenets.

Eventually those who can make, repair, and operate the nucleonic tools—the traders entrusted to deliver them from Terminus—dominate space politics. When the power of these traders falls into the hands of a few, the way is paved for a new empire operated by a single merchant prince, Hober Mallow.

Trade. As the plot reveals, Hober Mallow is a master salesman, a merchant prince who is quite familiar with the old but still existent Galactic Empire. The old Empire has constructed items on a large scale—giant nuclear power plants that are immobile and two-mile-long spacecraft that are fully armed and shielded from the weapons of rebels. Mallow and traders before him take the small Foundation in a new direction, searching for power through trade.

ASIMOV ON RELIGION

Personally Asimov has described himself as someone who never in all his life has been "tempted toward religion of any kind"; his philosophy of life "does not include any aspect of the supernatural," for he believes only "what reason tells [him] is so" (Asimov, *I. Asimov: A Memoir*, p. 13).

The Foundation scientists are encouraged to test new ideas for nuclear use. The result is that nuclear power can soon be installed nearly anywhere. Mallow and his men thus build up a brisk trade with neighboring planets and extend their trade, though within a limited area initially, since they feel gradual expansion is wiser than attempting too much too quickly. Many of the tools and gadgets they sell are intentionally short-lived, and the nuclear power plants need continual servicing—with repairs and replacements available only through systems that Mallow controls. In fact, Mallow's engineers have found ways to turn off important power sources at will. Thus trade provides the avenue by which Hober Mallow comes to rule the Empire.

> The whole war [between the Terminus "Foundation" and the old empire] is a battle between those two systems; between the Empire and the Foundation; between the big and the little. To seize control of the world, they bribe with immense ships that can make war, but lack all economic significance. We [Mallow speaks for the Foundation], on the other hand, bribe with little things, useless in war but vital to prosperity and profits.
>
> (Asimov, *Foundation*, p. 193)

This notion of conquering through trade works in the Foundation era. Hober Mallow can command loyalty and cooperation through his trade goods. Societies that become accustomed to his nuclear gadgets cannot tolerate periods when servicing and resupplying are neglected. Whole planets become dark and the machines lifeless as Mallow wishes. In history, trade has in fact been used as a tool of war and as a means of regulating distasteful crises. Mallow's strategy parallels the real-life use of trade in lining up allies for the United States and the Soviet Union during the Cold War.

THE RISE OF THE SCIENCE FICTION NOVEL

According to Asimov, science fiction readers of the 1930s and 1940s favored magazine stories over novels. It was only during the post-World War II era—because of the nuclear bomb, German rocket science, and the electronic computer developments—that the genre became a respectable one. In 1949 Doubleday publishers decided to release a line of science fiction novels and bought the rights to Asimov's first one, *Pebble in the Sky*.

Sources. Isaac Asimov sold his first science fiction story in 1938 to *Amazing Science Fiction Magazine* but shortly thereafter began writing letters and sending stories to *Astounding Science Fiction Magazine* (later *ASF*). Through the editor of *ASF*, John Campbell, he became acquainted with other science fiction writers who wrote for the magazine and kept up a lifetime acquaintanceship with such giants in the field as Robert Heinlein, Clifford Simak, and L. Sprague de Camp. In 1938 he joined a splinter group of a large science fiction fan club. The splinter group came to be known as the Futurians and included later science fiction writers and critics such as Frederik Pohl, Cyril Kornbluth, and Donald Wollheim. Asimov credits Pohl with encouraging and advising him in his science fiction writing and John Campbell with providing a guiding hand. Much of Asimov's early science fiction writing was published in *ASF* with John Campbell's guidance. The stories that made up the *Foundation* trilogy were first published by Campbell and it was at his insistence that they concluded in an open-ended fashion to provide opportunities for sequels.

Asimov and his literary analysts ascribe some of the organization of the whole *Foundation* trilogy to the epic *Rise and Fall of the Roman Empire* by Edward Gibbon. *Foundation* and the other

books that followed seem organized, as Gibbon's book was, on the notion that history is a spiral of events—one crisis after another. If so, and past history can cast some light on the present because of the near repetition of events, perhaps ancient and modern history will be reflected in the future. *Foundation* is organized in this way; the evolution of the encyclopedists and their successors follows unalterable paths through crisis after crisis in all-too-familiar sequences. Events occur and their consequences follow in a logical fashion, in much the same way that events progress in the real world.

Events in History at the Time the Novel Was Written

Ideological conflict and military might. World War II had come to an end with the United States unveiling an awesome new weapon of mass destruction—the atom bomb. The devastation of Hiroshima and Nagasaki stirred international consciousness regarding the capacity for large-scale destruction now within human reach. The United States itself took the initiative to suggest a worldwide surveillance of the uses of atomic energy. The newly formed United Nations took the idea under submission, but action was thwarted by a Soviet veto. Both the United States and the Soviet Union continued their experimentation to develop nuclear weapons. In 1949 the Soviet Union exploded its first test bomb, and by 1951, the year *Foundation* was published, the United States had detonated nine more atomic devices. In 1950 the United States announced that its scientists were developing a new and even more powerful bomb, the hydrogen bomb. With this weapon, the United States established nuclear superiority over the Soviet Union and other nations then developing nuclear technology, but it was a war of numbers and stockpiles rather than actual destruction.

A crisis of economics arose instead. The Soviet Union continued to behave in some ways much like Asimov's old Galactic Empire. Control over production and distribution was held centrally and by force. The Soviets appeared unable to act quickly or efficiently. One example was its inability to work with its former allies in setting occupation policies in the conquered territories—Germany, Austria, and Korea. It seemed likely that a repeat of the same turmoil over redistricting Europe and Asia that occurred after World War I would ensue. In 1951, the

An example of an early computer: the UNIVAC, which revolutionized computer science.

that two years later they became the first spies ever to be executed in peacetime.

The new crisis of technology. A bright new tool appeared that would revolutionize the world as the Foundation's miniature nuclear gadgets had changed the old empire. In 1946, ENIAC, a gigantic and slow computer, was unveiled. Though primitive, ENIAC proved able to perform mathematical and engineering tasks much more quickly than the best human workers. By 1951 there were more than a thousand computers solving mathematical puzzles around the world. These would soon prove useful in managing the new peacetime applications of nuclear reactors to provide energy for homes and factories. The year of *Foundation*'s first publication, 1951, also saw the first successful generation of electricity from nuclear reactions. By the second publication of *Foundation* in 1961, civilian nuclear power plants were operating in New York State, Pennsylvania, and Cumberland, England.

Reception. The stories in the *Foundation* trilogy were first published between 1942 and 1948 in *Astounding Science Fiction.* Among the Asimov contributions to this magazine, they were second in acclaim only to his series of robot stories. Yet they were still initially rejected by publishing houses until Gnome Press showed interest. Asimov was delighted by its suggestion that it publish his series of related *Foundation* stories in three volumes, because the stories were the most ambitious ones he had ever done and "the best received by the readers" (Asimov, *In Memory Yet Green*, p. 618). A decade later, Doubleday decided to buy the copyright and republish the three *Foundation* books in 1961. Sales indicated that there was still reader interest. In 1982, thirty years after *Foundation,* Asimov revived the series with the publication of a fourth novel—*Foundation's Edge*—and Doubleday celebrated by reissuing the *Foundation* books once more. The novels received the 1982 Hugo Award as the Best All-Time Science Fiction Series. Asimov was hailed as the inventor of a new science fiction form—future history—and for his persistence in maintaining a logical progression in his stories.

frustrated United States made its own peace agreement with Japan and a year later with West Germany.

The communist scare. During the early 1920s, a new strain of communist politics appeared in many countries, including the U.S., buoyed in part by the success of the Soviet revolution. J. Edgar Hoover's Federal Bureau of Investigation had begun massive files on those suspected of harboring communist tendencies. In the late 1940s and 1950s a communist scare arose once more. In the aftermath of World War II and the paranoia of the Cold War, U.S. authorities deemed it wise to crack down on such "red" political affiliations. Members of Congress such as Senator Joseph McCarthy were quick to assign the communist label to their foes. In Asimov's novel the enemies of the Galactic Empire are questioned and disposed of by death or exile. In real life, suspected communists were questioned, blacklisted, and banished from their jobs. The furor raged during the year Asimov's novel was published. In 1951 two New York communists, Julius and Ethel Rosenberg, were found guilty of passing nuclear secrets to the Soviets. Such was the terror of the communist threat in the U.S.

For More Information

Asimov, Isaac. *I. Asimov: A Memoir.* New York: Bantam Doubleday Dell, 1994.

Asimov, Isaac. *Foundation.* Garden City, N.Y.: Doubleday, 1951.

Asimov, Isaac. *In Memory Yet Green.* Garden City, N.Y.: Doubleday, 1979.

Gibbon, Edward. *The Decline and Fall of the Roman Empire.* New York: Modern Library, 1932.

Gunn, James. *Isaac Asimov: The Foundations of Science Fiction.* New York: Oxford University Press, 1982.

Marshall, Richard, ed. *Great Events of the Twentieth Century.* Pleasantville, N.Y.: Reader's Digest, 1977.

Olander, Joseph D., and Martin Harry Greenberg, eds. *Isaac Asimov.* New York: Taplinger, 1977.

Patrouch, Joseph F. *The Science Fiction of Isaac Asimov.* Garden City, N.Y.: Doubleday, 1974.

A Gathering of Old Men

by

Ernest J. Gaines

Ernest J. Gaines was born January 15, 1933, in Oscar, Louisiana, and began his life among cotton pickers in the old slaves' quarters at River Lake Plantation. Although he moved as a teenager to California and now lives most of the year in San Francisco, Gaines returns in real life each year and repeatedly in his fiction to southern Louisiana. Following the highly successful *The Autobiography of Miss Jane Pittman,* (also covered in *Literature and Its Times*), *A Gathering of Old Men* continues the exploration of race, gender, and color central to Gaines's writing.

THE LITERARY WORK

A novel set in the fictional St. Raphael's Parish in rural Louisiana on a Friday afternoon in October in the late 1970s; published in 1983.

SYNOPSIS

The murder of a Cajun farmer brings together a group of elderly black men eager for revenge.

Events in History at the Time of the Novel

Agricultural revolution in the South. *A Gathering of Old Men* takes place on a former Southern sugarcane plantation run by a white man, Marshall, and his daughter, Candy. The only people left on the plantation seem to be the elderly: "[t]he young ones had all gone away" observes one character (Gaines, *A Gathering of Old Men,* p. 58). In fact, they had gone away from farms all over the South in droves; between 1940 and 1980, statistics show that around 14 million Southerners left farms for cities, and Southern small farm life virtually disappeared. This was a result of increased mechanization, which brought with it an increase in the average size of farms. Within time, the family-run properties were swallowed into huge agricultural interests, and the (usually black) tenant farmers and sharecroppers who lived on those

family farms found themselves out of a home and a job.

Paradoxically, the civil rights movement also hastened the end of agricultural employment for black workers. As *A Gathering of Old Men* demonstrates, a kind of paternalism often existed between black laborers and a white landowner; Candy Marshall, the young white woman who organizes the bizarre obstruction of justice in Gaines's novel, is the epitome of such an employer. The tensions that surface between her and the black laborers, to whom she refers as "her" people, demonstrate that this type of landowner-laborer relationship, even when it involved people of good will who liked and respected each other, promoted a strong sense of white superiority. While the empowerment of black laborers and the granting to them of improved civil rights made them less dependent upon the good will of their white employers, it seems also to have made interracial relations less close and personal in many ways. "Them white folks got a lot more interested in machinery after the civil rights bill was passed," observes one black farmer in Alabama (Cooper, p. 766).

The industrialization of the Louisiana farms is often attributed to the ambitions of a particular class of Louisianans, the Cajuns. In *A Gathering of Old Men,* Miss Bea, a member of the Marshall clan, whose plantation is now farmed by a Cajun family, distinctly approves of Candy's story about having shot Beau Boutan: "About time she shot one of them Cajuns, messing up the land with those tractors. . . . Why we ever let that kind on this land, I don't know. The land has not been the same since they brought those tractors here" (*A Gathering of Old Men,* p. 23). The Marshalls' oldest black employee is Tucker, who recounts the story of how his brother Silas, the last sharecropper on the Marshall place, was pitted in a contest against a tractor driven by a white Cajun farmer. Silas won, but in an episode that captures the hard change in Southern agricultural practice, the black man is beaten to death in retaliation for upstaging Cajun mechanization.

Shades of difference. The simple dualism of black versus white is not the only issue that divides people on and near the novel's Marshall plantation; other more complex social codes come into play as well. Old Mathu, for example, in whose yard the body of Beau Boutan lies, has always looked down on most of his neighbors, holding himself apart from both black and white people. Clatoo, ringleader of the old men, explains:

> He acted like he didn't care if we was even there. Mathu was one of them blue-black Singaleese niggers. Always bragged about not having no white man's blood in his veins. He looked down on all the rest of us who had some, and the more you had, the more he looked down on you.
>
> (*A Gathering of Old Men,* p. 51)

Gaines's novel in fact emphasizes the variegated shades of the people who live in and around the old slave quarters on the former plantation. The "black" men and women there come in shades of yellow, brown, and black, depending on their genetic background. But the white men in the novel also come in different shades; the Boutans, for example, are Cajun, not Creole, for which they are scorned by certain members of the Marshall clan. The distinctions might seem insignificant to an outsider, but Louisianan society has historically subscribed to a hierarchical rank-

ing of racial heritage based on one's ancestry, dating back to the era of European colonization in the sixteenth to eighteenth centuries. Louisianans continue to debate, for example, whether or not there can be such a thing as a black Creole, or, for that matter, a white Creole, depending on the color of the person to whom one speaks. The white community in Louisiana defines a Creole as being a white descendant of the French or Spanish people who colonized Louisiana, while a Cajun is a white descendant of Acadian colonists (French inhabitants of what is now eastern and maritime Canada), roughly 3,000 of whom settled in the southern regions of Louisiana between 1764 and 1803. Among the nonwhite community, however, the words can mean something else; *Cajun* still means that a person's ancestors came from the Acadians, but not necessarily from white people exclusively, and *Creole* means that a person comes from a racially mixed background. One researcher suggests that in contemporary Louisiana, the term *Creole* now defines everyone in the state who has at least one French or Spanish ancestor (Dominguez, p. 151).

Gaines is very careful throughout the novel to note subtle distinctions among people's color and ancestry. This is in keeping with the social and legislative atmosphere both in the Louisiana he was trying to evoke and the Louisiana in which he lived at the time he was writing. In 1970 the state of Louisiana enacted a law stating that anyone with 1/32 Negro blood was to be considered legally black; it was the only legislation in the United States written to calculate a person's race. The statute was repealed in 1983, the year in which *A Gathering of Old Men* was published, perhaps in part because of a famous 1982 Louisiana trial in which Susie Phipps, a woman with a black great-great-great-great grandmother, tried to have herself declared legally white.

Lynching. "Boy, boy, boy, we haven't had a good stringing in these parts in quite a while," states one of the white characters in the novel (*A Gathering of Old Men,* p. 157). He makes the statement in anticipation of what old Fix Boutan might plan to avenge the death of his son, Beau, at the hands of one of the old black men gathered at the Marshall plantation. The "stringing" to which he refers is lynching, or the act of white mob retribution used to instill fear among the black community in the South for decades following the Civil War; it is generally associated with the Ku Klux Klan. The term "lynching" usually refers to the act of hanging a person without trial; the term can also apply to other punishments such as flogging or even tarring and feathering; in Gaines's novel, it clearly refers to hanging. The number of lynchings in the United States peaked in 1892, when 230 people met their end at the hands of mobs. Between 1882 and 1968, an estimated 3,445 black Americans were lynched; by the 1940s, the number of blacks lynched in Arkansas alone since the 1880s exceeded 200. The practice was not to die out completely until the late 1960s, but fear of it survived beyond these years. Gaines's novel is set in the late 1970s, when memory of such terror was clearly present in the minds of both black and white people.

Angola. At the beginning of *A Gathering of Old Men,* Sheriff Mapes threatens an ancient black man with the electric chair if he doesn't break down and "un-confess" to the crime of killing Beau Boutan:

> When that juice hit you, I've seen that chair dance. You see, Uncle Billy, we don't have a permanent chair in Bayonne. When we need one, we go to Angola to pick it up. And we don't waste time screwing it down—not just for one killing.
>
> (*A Gathering of Old Men,* p. 79)

Later in the novel, another character recounts the terrible story of how his son was killed in the electric chair, the execution having been botched several times before the young man was eventually given a lethal jolt. Despite the fear of capital punishment that runs throughout the work, at the time that Gaines was writing it, Louisiana had not killed a prisoner since 1961, although the statute remained on the books; as a nation, America saw no capital punishment at all between 1968 and 1972.

Historically, the Louisiana penal system stood to gain more by *not* killing prisoners—in fact, the state prisons were expected to turn a profit for Louisiana, primarily by making use of prisoner labor in the fields and in some basic industries. Between 1940 and the mid-1950s, the Angola prison to which Mapes refers, which sits on 18,000 acres just north of Baton Rouge, was universally recognized as the worst prison in the entire nation—rife with beatings, poor food, and brutal working conditions for its inmates. Angola inmates were housed in a series of work camps, rather than in a formal prison, which contributed to the many abuses they suffered; with the building of a cell-block prison in the mid-1950s, conditions improved somewhat. Just the same, the Louisiana penal system was compromised deeply by an entrenched system of graft and political corruption, which combined to make the idea of going to prison there a fearful one indeed. When the judge at the end of the novel threatens to send all the old men involved in the trouble over Beau Boutan's killing to jail if they don't behave, the threat consequently bears more than usual weight.

School segregation in Louisiana. In *A Gathering of Old Men,* Fix Boutan's son Gil is a football star at LSU, the Louisiana State University in Baton Rouge, and hopes to make the All-American squad by doing well in a game that is to take place the day after his brother is killed. His success on the field depends largely on a teammate of his, a black youth; together they are known as Salt and Pepper.

Racial integration in Louisiana schools proved difficult, more so in some respects than was the case for black students nationwide as they attempted to attend the same schools attended by white students. The graduate school at Louisiana State University was integrated in 1950, by order of the United States Circuit Court of Appeals. The Supreme Court followed that ruling with a 1954 decision that it was unconstitutional to segregate students in Louisiana public schools; six years later, in 1960, black students first entered previously all-white public schools. This groundbreaking event took place in New Orleans, the first city in the Deep South that, as the result of a federal lawsuit launched eight years previously, was forced to integrate its schools; integration of schools in rural areas would not occur until 1964.

Yet the integration of the New Orleans school system did not happen effortlessly. On November 14, 1960, four black students tried to enter first grade in two previously all-white schools.

Ernest J. Gaines

Candy and a group of eighteen old black men who all live in the immediate area have gathered at Mathu's place, and each of them confess to the murder of Beau Boutan. In turn, each person explains why she or he had motive, and the men describe the shooting as the product of years of hostility and oppression not just from the Boutans but white people in general; one man recounts the story of the rape and murder of his sister, another tells about the beating of his brother, yet another describes the botched execution of his son. Despite her protestations to the contrary, Mapes knows full well that Candy didn't do it, and most of the old men can't even see well enough to aim a rifle at someone, nor have the strength to hoist a weapon in the first place; Mapes is certain that the killer is Mathu, still strong and a man who has established himself as someone not to be pushed around.

Everyone gathered in Mathu's front yard expects the imminent arrival of old Fix Boutan, Beau's father—a notoriously racist and violent man who is sure to avenge his son's death. Actually, all the old men sitting on Mathu's porch with their rifles hope fervently that Fix shows up with his cronies, because they have been waiting a lifetime to settle a score with him. The story of what has been happening in St. Raphael's Parish over the last forty or fifty years emerges gradually, as each chapter is devoted to the viewpoint of one of the people involved on the day when Beau Boutan dies. Eventually, Charlie Biggs, a laborer who has always run away from his problems and submitted to the abuses of the Boutan family and other white people all his life, finally admits the truth—he shot Beau. Just then, from the darkness that has gathered outside, comes the voice of Luke Wills, a white man who is determined to find and murder Beau Boutan's killer, even if Beau's own father won't. Luke demands that Mapes hand Biggs over, but Mapes refuses. The sheriff has come to respect the old men and he has no inclination to abandon the law for the mob justice of Luke Wills and the band of armed rednecks he has brought along. A gun battle ensues, in which Charlie Biggs and Luke Wills are both killed. The novel ends in the courtroom, as a judge decrees that none of the men—black or white—who have been involved in the trouble at the Marshall place may touch a weapon for five years or before their death, whichever comes first, or even be within ten feet of someone carrying a firearm.

Defense of white womanhood. In *A Gathering of Old Men,* one of the old black men, Gable,

Their attempt led to white (and eventually black) rioting in the city's downtown streets; white students began refusing to attend the two schools involved; and a near-economic disaster seemed imminent when the state legislature refused to pay teachers and other education workers until matters could be straightened out. With the help of extensive legal and legislative negotiations, the issue was relatively settled within a year. Peaceful desegregation began in some schools in September 1961, though the whole process was attended by armed groups of police.

The Novel in Focus

The plot. In the parish of St. Raphael—the county-type district by which Louisiana is organized—the body of a young white man, Beau Boutan, lies in the yard of old Mathu. Mathu is a black plantation worker who is the special favorite of Candy Marshall, the young white woman who runs her family's land on which the crime has taken place. Old Mathu helped raise her. By the time that Sheriff Mapes, an old-fashioned Southern law enforcement official, arrives on the scene, he is met by an unlikely sight.

recounts his son's death in the electric chair: "[T]hey put him in the 'lectric chair on the word of a poor white trash. . . . [T]hey put him in that chair 'cause she said he raped her" (*A Gathering of Old Men,* p. 101). Another of the men recalls the fate of a young black soldier who returned from World War II with the picture of his white girlfriend in his wallet: "Look what happened to Curt's boy when he come home from World War II. Because they seen him with that German girl's picture, they caught him— and all y'all remember what they did to him with that knife" (*A Gathering of Old Men,* p. 104). As the incident shows, German enemy or not, the girl was white and so Curt's black son was made to pay the price for a love affair conducted an ocean away. One of the old black men, Jacob, has a sister Jessie, a mulatto (half white and half black), who has many white boyfriends. They warn her not to have anything to do with black men, and when she is found in the company of black men, the white ones kill her. The trumped-up charge of rape, leveled against black men throughout Southern history, proved to be one of the most powerful forces behind lynch mobs who were supposedly rising in defense of white womanhood. This so-called defense of white women reached its peak in the 1920s and 1930s. So bad was the problem that the Association of Southern Women for the Prevention of Lynching (43,000 strong) was formed in 1930 to formally dissociate Southern white women from the claims of white men that lynching was practiced as a means of protecting them from predatory black men. Of course, the much more common scenario was that of a white man raping a black woman, but such action was not the subject of any organized protest; historians note that it is clear that the Klan and other organizations of white males were less interested in preventing racial mixing than in enforcing the dependency of women upon men.

Sources. Repeatedly in his fiction Gaines returns to Pointe Coupee Parish, in the West Baton Rouge area of southern Louisiana where he was born and raised. His personal experience informs his work, as do the influences of other authors. Gaines points to his own debts to William Faulkner, particularly when it comes to writing dialogue, to Mark Twain for the ability to transform an oral storytelling tradition into written fiction, and to Ernest Hemingway for his model of writerly discipline. Still, the most potent source of Gaines's creativity is the talk that he

heard among the men and women of his community. "I come from a long line of storytellers. I come from a plantation where people told stories by the fireplace at night. . . . They would talk and talk and talk, and I'd listen to them" (Gaines in Laney, p. 3).

COMMUNITY OF MEANING

The novel's plot advances through monologues by a string of first-person narrators. Readers are left to fill in the gaps and piece together the story gradually for themselves. Sparsely narrated, the novel's style has been influenced by the environment in which Gaines was raised: "The leanness of his narrators' accounts descends from his recollection of storytellers who needed to provide little elaboration because they shared a community of meaning with their listeners. In his world and the world of his novel, histories are told and retold from person to person, from generation to generation. Within this oral continuum a silent second text gives unspoken meaning to stated meaning" (Babb, p. 11).

Reviews. *A Gathering of Old Men* was a bestseller and was translated into many foreign languages, including German and Russian. Critics praised Gaines's ear for the characteristic language of the South: "He has a marvelous ear for speech rhythms, context, and dialect; a deep knowledge of the people, black and white, of the region; and a rich fund of humor, compassion and understanding" (Charney, p. 134). Like *The Autobiography of Miss Jane Pittman, A Gathering of Old Men* was turned into a successful made-for-television movie. The 1987 production received some trenchant criticism from the author himself, including some which addressed the film's use of regional language; Gaines felt that the German director did not understand the centrality of genuine southern Louisiana diction to the whole story:

> They want the camera to do the work. . . . But there are certain damned things that a camera can't do, and a camera can't speak lines. . . . That camera cannot repeat rhythm. . . . This is not just a narrative thing, but it's a spoken thing.
> (Gaines in Gaudet and Wooton, p. 102)

The film reduced the novel's fifteen first-person voices to four, which also tended to reduce the story to its narrative elements rather than explore its psychological depths.

For More Information

Babb, Valerie Melissa. *Ernest Gaines.* Boston: Twayne, 1991.

Carleton, Mark T. *Politics and Punishment: The History of the Louisiana State Penal System.* Baton Rouge: Louisiana State University Press, 1971.

Charney, Mark J. "Voice and Perspective in the Film Adaptations of Gaines's Fiction." In *Critical Reflections on the Fiction of Ernest J. Gaines.* Edited by David C. Estes. Athens: University of Georgia Press, 1994.

Cooper, William J., and Thomas E. Terrill. *The American South: A History.* New York: Alfred A. Knopf, 1990.

Dominguez, Virginia R. *White by Definition: Social Classification in Creole Louisiana.* New Brunswick, N.J.: Rutgers University Press, 1986.

Gaines, Ernest J. *A Gathering of Old Men.* New York: Alfred A. Knopf, 1983.

Gaudet, Marcia, and Carl Wooton. *Porch Talk with Ernest Gaines: Conversations on the Writer's Craft.* Baton Rouge: Louisiana State University Press, 1990.

Laney, Ruth. "A Conversation with Ernest Gaines." *Southern Review* n.s. 10 (1974): 3.

The Handmaid's Tale

by

Margaret Atwood

THE LITERARY WORK

A fantasy set during the first decades of the twenty-first century in the former United States; published in 1986.

SYNOPSIS

Sterile women toil as domestics and fertile women live only because they can bear children for men of high rank in the Gilead regime. Offred, a childbearer in the service of an elderly commander, struggles both to preserve as well as forget the painful memories of her life before the Gilead regime.

Born in 1939 in Ottawa, Ontario, Canada, Margaret Atwood worked as a cashier, waitress, market research writer and film script writer before publishing her own poetry in 1961. The publication of *The Edible Woman* in 1969 won her fame as a novelist. Atwood's novels became part of a new wave of fiction writing by feminists who wrote both to entertain and to dramatize the plight of women. In 1986 Atwood published *The Handmaid's Tale*. In part, the novel was a response to the decade's rise of right-wing politicians and preachers who had fomented a backlash against the gains made by the feminist movement in the 1960s and '70s.

Events in History at the Time of the Novel

Feminism before the 1960s. After women gained the vote in Canada in 1918 and in the United States in 1920, the feminist consciousness seemed eclipsed by other issues. During the Great Depression of the 1930s, clamor for economic reform took precedence over questions of discrimination, and during World War II, women, whether feminists or not, joined the work force as men left their jobs to fight overseas. During the late 1940s and the 1950s, most women across North America returned to the traditional gender roles of mother and housewife.

Although the 1950s may have seemed to have been a tranquil decade—in regard to conventional notions of the family—various trends and events contributed to the evolution of the women's liberation movement that would gain momentum in the 1960s. In both nations the number of college graduates swelled in the years following World War II, although many women who had achieved some degree of higher education married soon after graduation or even before. In their new roles as housewives, these women often found themselves bored and frustrated with the repetitive domestic routines and unsatisfied in their roles as mothers. It was these educated women who helped form the core of the feminist movement in the 1960s. Secondly, though conventional wisdom preached that a woman's place was in the home, a growing percentage of wives supplemented their husbands' incomes by taking jobs. In fact, *Life* magazine reported that in 1956 women held one-third of all jobs in the United States. Many of those who enjoyed their work and sought advancement and equal pay were dismayed to find that women had few chances for these rewards and even less legal recourse. Such discriminatory practices also led to an increase in the number of women who became involved in the feminist movement. Finally, successes in the civil rights movement—for example, the 1954 *Brown v. Board of Education of Topeka* ruling that outlawed segregation in public schools—convinced women that reform was indeed possible.

Feminism during the 1960s and 1970s. In 1963 Betty Friedan published *The Feminine Mystique,* which divulged the frustrations of women who suffered from a sense of emptiness rather than the contentment that being a mother and housewife supposedly conferred on them. Friedan was the first author to frankly declare that she found housework dull and mind-numbing. She castigated educational institutions, the mass media, and other parts of society that, she argued, had limited women's opportunities as well as their ambitions.

Friedan influenced thousands of North American women. In the U.S., some of them banded together, forming the National Organization for Women (or NOW) to campaign against discrimination in the workplace and in politics. Other women, many of whom had joined in the civil rights movement, participated in loosely organized protests at colleges and universities.

The activists won significant triumphs. Title VII of the Civil Rights Act of 1964 prohibited employers from discriminating on the grounds of sex. Title IX of the Higher Education Act of 1972 prohibited discrimination on the grounds of sex in educational institutions funded by the federal government. In the mid-1970s, as public support for feminism increased, the Justice Department forced communications giant AT&T to establish affirmative action programs and to pay women who had worked for the company $15 million in back wages. This monumental ruling constituted an acknowledgment of discriminatory hiring and pay practices. The establishment in 1972 of the first shelter for battered wives and the first rape crisis center indicated that activists had convinced at least some part of the public that rape and wife-beating were significant problems and deserved attention. In 1973 the U.S. Supreme Court addressed the issue of abortion, ruling in *Roe v. Wade* that abortion was legal in

the first three months of pregnancy and that women's rights included the right to control their own bodies.

A recital of legal victories does not, however, give a comprehensive understanding of how the feminist activists of the 1960s and '70s influenced political and social attitudes throughout North America. These activists had sought not merely to reform the laws and practices that confined women to the home, but also to explode myths about women's natural inclination to serve men and children. It was this daring attempt to debunk age-old stereotypes that earned feminists both admiration and strident reproach.

The reaction against the movement. Throughout the first half of the 1970s the feminist movement continued to gather strength. Public opinion polls indicated that a majority of U.S. citizens supported the ratification of the Equal Rights Amendment (ERA), a bill that had been proposed before Congress every year since 1923 and said simply "Equality of rights under the law shall not be denied or abridged by the United States or by any state on account of sex" (Radl, p. 106). In 1972 the U.S. Congress passed the amendment. It then needed only to be ratified by three-fourths of the states in order to become law. Within a month fourteen states had ratified the ERA. The likelihood of passage seemed promising, but then activists for the New Right, a faction of religious zealots and proponents of traditional values, helped turn the public against the ERA.

The New Right was not exclusively a reaction against feminism. Members of the New Right rallied to combat a myriad of trends that they thought threatened traditional values. Among the trends that caused alarm were the rise in the number of single mothers, the liberalism pervading college campuses, and a growing acceptance of homosexuality. Feminism was linked to these trends and targeted as a prime enemy.

Perhaps the most influential leader of the antifeminist campaign in the U.S. was Phyllis Schlafly, the mother of six children and a long-time Republican Party activist. Schlafly contended that the ERA threatened the traditional family because it relieved a husband of the obligation to provide for his wife and children. "The women's liberation movement is antifamily," she claimed. "The Equal Rights Amendment . . . would take away the marvelous legal rights of a woman to be a full-time wife and mother in the home supported by her husband" (Schlafly in Falwell, p. 151). Schlafly also objected that feminists aimed to give a mother of an illegitimate baby the same respect as a mother of a child born in wedlock. She founded and appointed herself chairman of STOP ERA, an organization that staged nationwide rallies to foment opposition to the ERA. "Fight," she urged voters, "against the ERA and . . . win this battle for God" (Schlafly in Falwell, p. 152).

Schlafly galvanized a campaign against the ERA. Across the nation women spoke out against the amendment. Most insisted that the government could not legislate the equality of the biologically different sexes. Women had been ordained by nature, went one argument, to spend their energy meeting the needs of others. Hundreds of thousands of letters from such organizations as Pro-Family United, Concerned Women for America, Women United to Defend Existing Rights, and Citizens for God, Family and Country helped convince a sufficient number of elected officials not to vote for ratification of the ERA.

Such antifeminist rhetoric appealed to women who felt they had been belittled by the feminist movement. Many stay-at-home wives and mothers resented the contention that housework was mindless or demeaning. In fact, as indicated by articles in the popular press during the 1980s, the antifeminists convinced many women that the women's liberation movement had brought them nothing but grief. One of them claimed that "[although] women's lib has given my generation high incomes, our own cigarette, the option of single parenthood, rape crisis centers, personal lines of credit, free love, and female gynecologists[,] in return it has effectively robbed us of the one thing upon which the happiness of most women rests—men" (Charon, p. 25). In reality, what had happened was that many women now shouldered dual burdens—rushing home from low-paying jobs to cook and clean for their families. In return, they blamed their frustrations on the feminist movement that had encouraged them to seek employment.

Religious fundamentalism. Schlafly was helped in her campaign by religious leaders who denounced the feminist movement. Television evangelists used scriptural excerpts to convince millions of voters that feminism was not only antifamily, but anti-Christian. One of the most influential of these evangelists was Jerry Falwell. Like Schlafly, Falwell believed that "the Equal Rights Amendment strikes at the foundation of

our entire social structure. If passed, this amendment would accomplish exactly the opposite of its outward claims. By mandating an absolute equality under the law, it will actually take away many of the special rights women now enjoy" (Falwell, p. 151). Falwell insisted that the ERA violated the biblical mandate that "the husband is the head of the wife, even as Christ is the head of the Church" (Falwell, p. 151). Like Schlafly, Falwell believed that God had created men and women with differing needs and to fill different roles; husbands should be the decisionmakers.

PARADOX FOR WORKING WOMEN

Jerry Falwell contended that the majority of women who left their homes to find jobs did so not out of economic necessity, but because they were "overly concerned with material wealth" (Falwell, p. 126). One woman responded to these types of assertions by insisting, "I work because we need the money to maintain a decent lifestyle. I'd rather be home because it would be easier. And I feel so guilty leaving my daughter. But one of the reasons we need some of the money I earn is that we send our daughter to church school, something we're told we must do. But my working has caused friends in the church to treat me differently—with disapproval. And whenever our pastor talks about men's and women's roles, I feel he's speaking directly to me. The result is guilt on guilt" (Radl, p. 7).

The notion of the working woman was repugnant to Falwell and religious fundamentalists like him. He cautioned his followers that the goal of feminists was to take jobs from men and thus undermine their authority as the head of the family. "In a drastic departure from the home," he lamented, "more than half of the women in our country are currently employed." "The answer to stable families," Falwell asserted, "will come only as men and women in America get in a right relationship to God and His principles for the home" (Falwell, pp. 124, 128).

Religious fundamentalists like Falwell also opposed the Equal Rights Amendment on the grounds that it would legitimize homosexual marriages. To convince others that homosexuality was a sin, Falwell quoted Scripture—"Thou shalt not lie with mankind, as with womankind: it is an abomination" (Falwell, p. 181). He went on to connect it to the feminist movement, con-

Phyllis Schlafly, antifeminist activist and ERA opponent.

tending that it had spawned a rise in homosexuality by challenging traditional gender roles. "We would not," said Falwell, "be having the present moral crisis regarding [homosexuality] if men and women accepted their proper roles" (Falwell, p. 183). Elaborating on these proper roles, he again quoted the Bible—"wives submit yourselves unto your husbands, as unto the Lord" (Ephesians 5:22).

Fundamentalists also objected to the teaching of secular humanism in the public schools. They decried the fact that the biblical tale of the creation of the world found in the Book of Genesis had been replaced by Darwin's theory of evolution. Implicit faith in the teachings of God as recorded in the Bible, they insisted, should not be supplanted with theories formulated by humans.

Pro-family movement. The American family has undergone some dramatic changes in the later years of this century:

- Divorce rates have risen sharply, as has the number of unmarried couples living together.

- Female-headed, single-parent households, once regarded as "broken homes," doubled from 1960 to the late 1980s.

- Nearly 60 percent of married women were working outside the home by the late 1980s.

Alarmed at these changes, religious fundamentalists and antifeminists banded together to form a pro-family movement. Its members blamed the feminists for encouraging wives and mothers to work outside the home. They asserted that modern children receive less support and guidance than in the past and yet are exposed to a permissive society replete with sex, alcohol, drugs, and violence. The solution, argued the pro-family movement, lay not only in reversing *Roe v. Wade* but also in restoring prayer to the public schools and in monitoring the content of young people's textbooks.

Experts outside the pro-family movement agreed that feminism had indeed made a significant impact on family life. Women exhibited more concern with personal fulfillment than in prior generations and were now more reluctant to sacrifice their own happiness and goals for someone else's. Such self-determination grew in part from a growing public acceptance that the traditional family was not without its serious flaws behind closed doors. Often, wives and mothers who found themselves victims of abuse, alcoholism, and mental illness had no real options for leaving prior to the era of feminist legal gains. By urging women to consider their own needs and abilities, the feminist minority has influenced the majority of females in the

United States. "This is true," maintain two of the experts, "even among women who claim to reject feminism. Polls have shown . . . a far greater unwillingness to subordinate personal needs and interests to the demands of husbands and children. A growing majority of women now believe that both husband and wife should have jobs, both do housework, and both take care of children" (Mintz and Kellogg, p. 208). In essence, the experts suggest, the pro-family movement may be alarmed at what only seems to be a breakdown of the American family. The family has not in fact collapsed; rather it is undergoing a transition beyond the old standard of husband as breadwinner and wife as housewife. In other words, it is the survival of the traditional family, not of the family altogether, that appears to be at risk.

The Novel in Focus

The plot. "Maybe I'm crazy," Offred thinks to herself, "and this is some kind of therapy" (Atwood, *The Handmaid's Tale*, p. 94). She is reclined on a luxurious bed, her head cradled in the crotch of a fat, leathery-faced women, her skirt pulled up around her waist, her cotton underwear on the floor. Propped on his elbows above the two women lies the commander. The ceremony goes as always. Without exchanging a kiss, the commander and Offred copulate, while the commander's infertile wife lies beneath them and feigns pleasure. When he has finished, the commander withdraws, zips up his pants, and leaves the two women alone. "Get up and get out now," his wife snaps (*The Handmaid's Tale*, p. 95). Offred disentangles herself from the older woman's body. "Which one of us is it worse for," she wonders, "her or me?" (*The Handmaid's Tale*, p. 95).

Offred lives in what was a college town in New England before religious fanatics established the Protestant theocracy of Gilead. In official parlance she is a "handmaid," a fertile woman living in the house of a commander and his wife. As a handmaid, she is referred to not by her actual name, which she often fears she may forget, but by the name of her commander, Fred, prefixed with the preposition "of." She is attended to by two "Marthas," sterile women who cook and clean, and guarded over by "Aunts," older women who have proven their devotion to the regime. Offred's purpose is to copulate with the commander so that he and his infertile wife may raise a family. Periodically she is called upon by the commander and his wife so that he may attempt to impregnate her. If, after a few months, she is not pregnant, she will be declared barren and shipped to distant war-ravaged cities to join other so-called "unwomen" as they clean toxic and nuclear waste to prepare the cities for colonization.

As a handmaid, Offred is confined to the house of her commander except to take brief walks with another handmaid. The handmaids are expected to walk past a wall each day where various criminals, Catholics, homosexuals, doctors who had performed abortions before the rise of the regime, and other offenders are hanged to provide an example for all. (Jews were not hanged but told they could emigrate to Israel. Taking advantage of this option, they had been drowned en route.) Offred is tempted to commit suicide to escape the monotony and humiliation of her life, but the prudent authorities have removed all sharp objects from her room.

Offred struggles both to repress and to preserve the troubled memories of her life before the Gilead regime. She lived, with her husband and daughter, in what had been the United States at the close of the twentieth century. Like the rest of the nation, she had been shocked on the day that the President was assassinated and Congress machine-gunned. Although the Constitution had been suspended and the nation governed by the military, Offred and her husband had trusted the authorities and assumed they were working to restore constitutional law.

Life seemed to continue as normal. The frequent police raids on libraries or even people's homes were, Offred assumed, merely reasonable security measures. Yet strange laws began to be passed. Homosexuality was declared illegal and a few supposedly subversive books were banned. Some universities and libraries were closed. Offred has difficulty remembering how quickly the changes took place.

What she remembers vividly, however, was the day the government declared it illegal for women to work or have their own bank accounts. She was sent home from her job. All accounts with an "F" next to the name for "female" were simply frozen by computer overnight. In the months that followed most women remained in their homes for fear that if they wandered the streets the police might arrest them as protesters. There had been a few riots against the police. A post office was blown up, but one could never be sure if the police themselves hadn't done it merely to justify further raids.

Jerry Falwell, a prominent fundamentalist spokesman and television minister who founded the Moral Majority.

Offred and her husband resolved to flee with their daughter. They obtained forged passports to cross the Canadian border for an afternoon. They were apprehended, however, and separated from one another. What happened after her capture Offred remembers only dimly. She recalls long nights spent awake on a cot in the gymnasium of what had been a high school. There she endured a sort of retraining. She and hundreds of other fertile women were informed that they were to be the mothers of the next generation. They were to serve as worthy vessels for the children of high-ranking officials.

Now Offred's only hope is that the commander, who, she fears, may be sterile, will impregnate her. However grim her life as a handmaid may seem, she dreads being sent to work as a slave in the colonies. To avoid that fate she risks execution by sleeping with the commander's chauffeur in the hopes that he will impregnate her.

Offred is terrified, though not surprised, when police come to the house to arrest her because, she thinks, of her affair with the chauffeur. "It's all right," the chauffeur assures her. "It's [the resistance]" (*The Handmaid's Tale,* p. 293). Offred resigns herself to her fate with the one hope that these policemen are indeed traitors to Gilead come to ferret her to safety across the Canadian

border. She disappears behind the closed doors of the van, while the commander's wife watches and mutters, "Bitch . . . after all [we] did for you" (*The Handmaid's Tale,* p. 294).

Parallels between Gilead and religious fundamentalism. The closing pages of the novel are a transcription of the proceedings of a "Symposium on Gileadean Studies," (*The Handmaid's Tale,* p. 299), supposedly held on June 25, 2195. They reveal that the Gilead regime fell sometime during the mid-twenty-first century, and in its place arose a society more like that of the twentieth-century United States. The Gileadean police destroyed almost all written material, leaving little record of life under their regime. Offred's tale, which was unearthed in an old footlocker, has become a resource for historians eager to research the Gileadean period.

"Certain periods of history," one of the speakers cautions, "quickly become, both for other societies and those that follow them . . . the occasion for a good deal of hypocritical self-congratulation" (*The Handmaid's Tale,* p. 302). He intends to warn his audience against passing hasty judgment on the Gileadean society. Religious intolerance, sexism, and perverse and brutal rituals, he insists, were common long before Gilead. "There was little," he points out, "that was truly original with or indigenous to Gilead" (*The Handmaid's Tale*, p. 307). The novel's attachment of these remarks to the end of Offred's tale intimates that although the surreal story takes place in the future, it borrows ideas from the present. Presently, for example, a married woman is often referred to by her husband's last name. The practice of referring to a handmaid by her commander's name can be viewed as an extension of such a custom.

Like modern religious fundamentalists, officials in Gilead contend that a woman's place is in the home. The majority of women, left sterile because of wars and nuclear and toxic waste, serve as nothing more than domestics who prepare food, maintain a clean house, or worse, clean the waste and debris from wars and nuclear accidents. The few fertile women are procured by the commanders to bear children.

The policies of Gileadean regime, like the convictions of religious fundamentalists, are founded on interpretations of the Bible. Homosexuals are hanged because the Bible decreed homosexuality immoral. To justify the use of handmaids, officials cite the story of Rachel, from Genesis 30:1-3. An infertile woman, Rachel instructed her husband to have children by her maid. The Bible provides the infallible source for all law in fictional Gilead. Offred mentions that "[the wives of commanders] can hit [handmaids], [because] there's Scriptural precedent" (*The Handmaid's Tale*, p. 16).

In a confession ceremony, Aunts harass the handmaids, encouraging them to admit their sins and become worthy vessels for the seed of a commander. When one handmaid confesses that she was, as a girl, raped by several men and subsequently became pregnant and had an abortion, an Aunt remonstrates, "But *whose* fault was it?" Other handmaids chant, "*Her* fault, *her* fault, *her* fault." When the Aunt asks, "*Who* led them on?" the handmaids reply, "*She* did, *she* did, *she* did" (*The Handmaid's Tale*, p. 72).

The notion that a victim of rape provoked the attack is not peculiar to Gilead. Even during the era in which the novel was written, many Americans held the belief that a woman's dress or comportment might tempt a man to rape her. According to this view, the woman's indiscretion is as much to blame as the rapist. It was argued that "virtuous women are seldom accosted by unwelcome sexual propositions or familiarities" (Schlafly in Radl, p. 119), intimating that only an immoral woman could be harassed or raped.

Sources. Although Atwood's novel is set in the future, she herself has described it as "speculative fiction" rather than science fiction because it extrapolates from the existing world rather than inventing an entirely new one. "A lot of what writers do is they play with hypotheses," she commented during a discussion of her novel. "The original hypothesis [of *The Handmaid's Tale*] would be some of the statements that are being made by the 'Evangelical fundamentalist right'" (Atwood in Bouson, p. 135). Atwood asserted that she "didn't invent a lot" and described the novel as merely a "logical extension of where we are now" (Atwood in Bouson, p. 136). Her decision to set the novel in the United States rather than Canada was influenced by her perceptions that "the States are more extreme in everything," and, as she explained to one U.S. interviewer, that "our television evangelists are more paltry than yours" (Atwood in Ingersoll, p. 223).

Reception. Most critics welcomed *The Handmaid's Tale* as a gripping dystopian novel in the tradition of Orwell's *1984* and Huxley's *Brave New World*. One critic found the novel "disquieting and not nearly as futuristic nor fantasmatic as we might wish" (Bouson, p. 136). Another observed that Atwood's projections, though startling, were not illogical. But a few critics complained that Atwood's novel taxed their credulity. "I just can't see the intolerance of the far right," one critic commented, ". . . leading to a super-biblical puritanism" (McCarthy in Hall, p. 150). Another reviewer dismissed the whole novel as "paranoid folklore about what the future may hold for women" (Ehrenreich in Hall, p. 155). While these critics felt that Atwood's vision of the future was a far-fetched exaggeration, even they found Offred's story engaging. One of their reviews, for example, described Offred as a "sappy stand-in" for the hero of *1984* yet admitted that Atwood had nevertheless written "an absorbing novel" (Ehrenreich in Hall, p. 156).

For More Information

Atwood, Margaret. *The Handmaid's Tale*. Boston: Houghton Mifflin, 1986.

Bouson, J. Brooks. *Brutal Choreographies*. Amherst: University of Massachusetts Press, 1993.

Charon, Mona. "The Feminist Mistake." *National Review* (March 23, 1984): 24-7.

Conover, Pamela, and Virginia Gray. *Feminism and the New Right*. New York: Praeger, 1983.

Falwell, Jerry. *Listen, America!* New York: Doubleday, 1980.

Hall, Sharon, ed. *Contemporary Literary Criticism.* Vol. 44. Detroit: Gale Research, 1987.

Ingersoll, Earl. *Margaret Atwood: Conversations.* Princeton, N.J.: Ontario Review Press, 1990.

Mintz, Steven, and Susan Kellogg. *Domestic Revolutions: A Social History of American Family Life.* New York: Free Press, 1988.

Radl, Shirley. *The Invisible Woman.* New York: Dell Publishing, 1982.

The Handmaid's Tale

A Hero Ain't Nothin' but a Sandwich

by

Alice Childress

Alice Childress was born in Charleston, South Carolina, but grew up in the racially segregated Harlem district of New York City in the 1920s and 1930s. By the early 1970s, when Childress's novel takes place, the civil rights movement had improved the political situation of African Americans. Living conditions, however, remained just as squalid in Harlem and other urban areas of the United States as they had been before the movement. Furthermore, opportunities for African Americans were still severely limited by racism. Some of the era's young people, as shown in *A Hero Ain't Nothin' but a Sandwich,* escaped from its harsh pressures by turning to heroin.

THE LITERARY WORK

A novel set in the Harlem section of New York City in the early 1970s; published 1973.

SYNOPSIS

An African American teenager is drawn to use heroin because of the pressures of being black and living in poverty in urban United States.

Events in History at the Time of the Novel

Urban blacks in the early 1970s. The gains made by African Americans as a result of the civil rights movement of the 1950s and 1960s lay mostly in the realm of their *status* as citizens. The Civil Rights Act of 1964 and the Voting Rights Act of 1965 legally abolished segregation and discrimination, but "legal equality in principle did not make for justice in *practice*" (Pinkney, p. 62). Despite the victories of the civil rights movement, many blacks still resided in segregated areas with a far lower standard of living and more limited life options than whites.

Urban blacks felt this especially keenly. In the early 1970s, nearly half of black America lived in segregated city ghettos in dangerous, rundown buildings with constantly interrupted water and heating services. Schools had few materials, including textbooks, and often there was not even enough room for students to sit. Throughout black urban areas the infant mortality rate was twice as high as for white infants. Jobs were scarce and often menial, a situation that, combined with the substandard housing, contributed to the breakup of the black family unit. However, this type of breakup was far from always the case. In fact, the majority of black families in the 1970s included both a husband and a wife.

The civil rights movement and Black Power. The civil rights movement awakened the political consciousness of urban blacks. "It's nation time!" Nigeria Greene, the novel's schoolteacher, says repeatedly to anyone who will listen. In real life, the idea of black nationhood took many forms and meant many different things to urban blacks of the early 1970s. One aspect of "nation" was the concept of Black Power, that is, self-empowerment achieved by blacks taking control of civil rights organizations as well as other elements in their lives. Some Black Power advocates demanded a separate nation within the United States, while others encouraged blacks to keep their money within their own community by shopping only at black-owned businesses. Still other Black Power champions attempted socialistic collectives, whose black resident members would pool both their resources and their wealth.

In keeping with the concept of Black Power, black communities began to demand more control over their institutions, such as local schools and police departments. Their efforts were often met with great resistance. One Harlem teacher wrote in his diary of a rift that developed between black parents and the Board of Education in the selection of a new principal for a predominantly black school:

> The parents are preparing for a long fight to get the [black] acting principal appointed principal . . . the Board will react in its customary manner. It will sit on this problem, wait until the parents grow weary, and then act against them. The Board can wait. It is never in a hurry to do anything in this area.
>
> (Haskins, pp. 25, 28)

THE CONCEPT OF BLACK POWER

Civil rights leader Stokely Carmichael, who is credited with coining the term "Black Power" at a rally in Mississippi, explained the rationale behind the slogan: "The concept of Black Power rests on a fundamental premise: *Before a group can enter the open society, it must first close ranks*" (Carmichael in Pinkney, p. 64).

Another reason for the growth of the Black Power movement was a suspicion that the civil rights movement, which called for integration with whites, was increasingly shutting out working-class blacks. Middle-class blacks were accused of not caring about the liberation of *all* African Americans, but only about liberation insofar as it affected their status and acceptance by whites. In the novel, Nigeria Greene, a middle-class black, feels torn between the urge to make a better life for himself by integrating into white culture, and the temptation to join the Black Power call for separating from white culture and any "help" it offers. He attends a ben-

efit sponsored by middle-class blacks and whites:

> We so-called "high achievers"—doctors, lawyers, teachers . . . most of us now makin a buck offa either "puttin down the nigga" or "upliftin the nigga" on some specially "funded" gigs . . . we're the upper strata welfare recipients, dig? . . . drinkin our mash outta long-stem champagne glasses . . . we have turned into the most insensitive bunch you'll find anywhere west of hell.
>
> (Childress, *A Hero Ain't Nothin'
> but a Sandwich,* p. 98)

Nigeria's dilemma of feeling as if he must abandon his black roots to reap the rewards of integration into a higher economic strata pricked the conscience of many upwardly mobile blacks.

Conspiracy to quell Black Power with heroin?
Charles Rangel, a Harlem congressman in the early 1970s, said of his district, "Walk along any street uptown and you'll see Harlem's great addict army—slumped over in doorways, stumbling along in a trance, nodding in front of bars, standing in the cold without enough clothes on" (Rangel in Kunnes, p. 83). Officials and residents of Harlem and other slum areas across the country sought to combat heroin use by trying to identify the source of it. Did the problem lie in the individual weakness of every user? Was society's racism causing users to quit on life and nod away until they died? Or did the trouble start with the drug dealers, the ones who, as Benjie's stepfather says, "livin offa Benjie's veins, while they ride round in limousines" (*A Hero Ain't Nothin' but a Sandwich,* p. 126)? Many believed that poverty, racism, and the sense of alienation they produced made people likely addicts. Some suggested a more sinister cause of the heroin epidemic, which by the early 1970s was claiming one out of every six Harlemites. Social scientist Michael Rossman spoke of a white conspiracy to put blacks into an eternal daze. "Before each 'long hot summer' and in each period of ghetto political tension, heroin becomes increasingly available to the ghettoes" (Rossman in Kunnes, p. 87). He contended that the black urban uprisings of the late 1960s frightened white officials, who reacted by upping the flow of heroin into ghettoes. He was not alone in this suspicion. A *New York Times* article in 1971 quoted a police informer as saying that "the police had allowed and encouraged narcotics to be sold in black . . . communities to create a dependency on heroin and undercut political movement" (Kunnes, p. 88).

Stokely Carmichael addressing a Black Power rally in 1966.

African and American roots. In an effort to re-define themselves as something other than second-class citizens, American blacks began to investigate the history of their African ancestors. They also studied modern African culture in search of a unifying and positive identity that the experience of slavery in America had acted to erase. In the novel, teacher Nigeria Greene takes this idea to heart as he fights for a class at his school in an African language, Swahili. Real-life blacks similarly attempted to develop a stronger sense of self by rejecting white standards of beauty, such as straight hair. There was an effort to express a sense of "blackness" by wearing Afro hairstyles and adopting African-style dress to show pride in the ancestry of American blacks.

Speaking Black English was another way of expressing blackness and declaring allegiance to the group in the 1970s. The "street culture" language, which developed in insular communities, helped blacks distinguish themselves from others. When Benjie uses phrases in the novel like "Then I decide to sound on him" rather than "I told him what I think," he's subscribing to a dialect of Black English; speaking the dialect knits him to his community and his history (*A Hero Ain't Nothin' but a Sandwich,* p. 13).

Though dialects of Black English have consistent rules and grammar of their own, the language has not been readily accepted as an alternative to standard English. In the 1970s tension mounted between blacks promoting solidarity through language and others demanding conformity to standard English. Teachers were alarmed by the use of Black English and the seeming disregard for standard English: "They attribute mistakes [in standard English] to laziness, sloppiness or the child's natural disposition to be wrong" wrote researchers (Labov, p. 4). Educators questioned how students would ever learn to communicate past the ghetto. Some recommended that they be forced to abandon their dialects of English, while others urged teachers to accept and learn them, so that the students would be encouraged to regard standard English as a possible form of expression as well.

The black family. The breakup of the traditional black nuclear family has its roots in the forced separation of families during slave days, when members were sold to different slaveowners. But, as social scientists have pointed out, "family destruction and dispersal did not erode family and kinship ties" (Mintz and Kellogg, p. 69). Instead, African Americans developed extended networks between more distant relatives and other community members as they cooperated to improve their living conditions.

45

In black ghettos of the 1970s a redefinition of "the family" became necessary as a growing number of fathers, under the strain of unemployment or underemployment, left the family unit. Often such a man's sense of self as one who should provide for his family was undercut by his lack of access to jobs with reasonable pay, and this burden on his pride was sometimes too much to bear. In the novel, after his father leaves, we see Benjie's family reconfigured to form a unit that is "a source of mutual assistance and support . . . sharing resources and responsibilities" (Mintz and Kellogg, p. 79). Ranson Bell, Benjie's grandmother, lives with the family, taking care of Benjie when his mother is working. Then the family structure shifts again when Benjie's stepfather joins the household. The final unit, a single mother living with a man who is not the father of her children, was not uncommon for families in urban areas affected by racism, poverty, and unemployment.

The Novel in Focus

The plot Thirteen-year-old Benjie Johnson lives with his mother, grandmother, and stepfather in a rundown tenement building in New York City's Harlem. Benjie tells the reader right off that, "My block ain't no place to be a chile in peace . . . you on your own and [adults] got they things to do, like workin, or goin to court, or seein after they gas and letrit bills" (*A Hero Ain't Nothin' but a Sandwich*, p. 9). He describes his apartment building as a place where men sexually assault children in the unlit hallway. Benjie's real father left the family when Benjie was a baby—Benjie struggles to shake off the feeling of abandonment that plagues him. He also feels replaced by his stepfather, Butler, in being a companion to his mother. "I'm wonderin in my mind, what they need with me?" (*A Hero Ain't Nothin' but a Sandwich*, p. 70).

Benjie senses hypocrisy and desperation all around him in the black community. He likes his stepfather but when Butler starts talking about how things are going to get better for African Americans, and how there will be more opportunities, Benjie thinks he's all talk. "I don't see im doin nothin but bein a janitor in one of the [whi]tey's downtown buildins. Hear *him* tell it [he a] *maintenance* man . . . ain't nothin but a [fancy] name for janitor" (*A Hero Ain't Nothin' but [a Sandw]ich*, p. 13). Benjie is also confused by all [that he] hears at school from a teacher, Nige[ria] who claims to be a black nationalist.

He thinks Greene is a hypocrite who talks about black people uniting and working together yet buys his clothes not from blacks but from British tailors in London. Although Benjie hasn't given up on the world yet and wants to concentrate on his education, he cannot see a day in the future when blacks will be free.

Benjie first tries heroin on a dare at the apartment of a fifteen-year-old drug dealer. Soon he's shooting it into his veins every other day but denying to himself that he's on his way to being hooked—he claims he just wants something for his nerves. He begins to steal to get money for another fix and lies for the first time in his life when he takes $3 from his grandmother. His teachers, Greene and Cohen, notice Benjie is falling asleep in class all the time, and the teachers, although they don't trust each other, unite to bring Benjie's addiction to the attention of his mother and stepfather.

Benjie recovers from his addiction in the hospital, but falls back into the habit within a week, paying for his fix by stealing Butler's clothes. This is the final straw for Butler, who goes to live in another apartment. Finally, Benjie and Butler are forced to reckon with each other when Butler chases Benjie onto the roof after Benjie steals a toaster from Butler's new apartment. Benjie slips on ice and Butler grabs him in time to save him from falling off the roof into an airshaft—Benjie begs Butler to let him go, "Let me be dead" (*A Hero Ain't Nothin' but a Sandwich*, p. 110). Butler is struck with the truth as he's holding on to Benjie: "His eyes locked on mine, we lookin right at each other. . . . Then I know *I was runnin from him* . . . I went off cause he wasn't mine." Butler proceeds to pull Benjie up with all his strength as he echoes Nigeria Greene's battle cry, "Come on, goddamit! It's nation time!" (*A Hero Ain't Nothin' but a Sandwich*, pp. 110, 111).

Searching for a strong adult, not a "hero." Feeling abandoned by his real father, imagining he's a fifth wheel at home, and getting the message at school and from society at large that "Nobody digs niggas, not even other niggas" (*A Hero Ain't Nothin' but a Sandwich*, p. 88), Benjie yearns for an adult male with enough pride to instill some pride in him. When Benjie recovers from his addiction in the hospital and is sent home, he senses and resents the discomfort of his mother and stepfather, who don't know how to approach him. Benjie baits Butler to see if he will go away when the talk gets tough: "Relax pal, you just a maintenance man—so don't strain yourself tryin to prove nothin" (*A Hero Ain't*

Nothin' but a Sandwich, p. 76). After Butler storms out of the apartment, Benjie prays on the bathroom floor, "Please God . . . send me a friend, someone to be crazy bout *me*" (*A Hero Ain't Nothin' but a Sandwich*, p. 76). When he gets no response, he steals Butler's suit to sell for more heroin and justifies the act to himself: The man is taking his mama, he thinks, so he'll take the man's clothes. Benjie's theft of Butler's suit for a fix finally sends Butler away to live in another apartment in the same building.

While he's recovering from his addiction in the hospital for the second time, Benjie is counseled by a white social worker, but the boy seems to know he needs something different, not such a distant adviser. Benjie wants a real person, someone who is living in the ghetto—and surviving—to believe in him. When he finally steals the toaster to sell for heroin right in front of Butler, Benjie takes his last shot at getting Butler's undivided attention. Butler reacts by using his final ounce of strength to keep Benjie from falling down the airshaft on the roof of the building, at which point Benjie begins to accept that Butler, although not his real father, is someone who will make a fine substitute:

> I'm lookin up into Butler's face, veins in his face all swole out. I tried to think of my real father's face . . . Butler's face kept wipin out the real father . . . Voice inside my head say, 'Butler you are my father.' Thassa weird trip, Jack.
> (*A Hero Ain't Nothin' but a Sandwich*, p. 113)

Butler insists that although Benjie wants someone to believe in him, "you gotta do it even if nobody believe in you, gotta be your own man, the supervisor of your own veins, the night watchman and day shift foreman in charge-a your own affairs" (*A Hero Ain't Nothin' but a Sandwich*, p. 120). For his part Butler realizes he's been running from taking on the full responsibility of treating Benjie like a real son. He also realizes that when Nigeria Greene says "It's nation time!" he means that fighting for civil rights isn't something you only do in court or in marches. Mutual support among blacks needs to be expressed everywhere, in the workplace, in the street, and at home, whether you're living with your birth family or your family by choice. With this new attitude, he tells Benjie's social worker, who is counseling Butler to take Benjie to movies and ball games so he can see more heroes, "Yall gotta learn to identify with *me*. . . . I'm supportin three adults, one chile and the United States government on my salary . . . and can't claim any of em for tax exemptions. So explain

Alice Childress

me no heroes" (*A Hero Ain't Nothin' but a Sandwich*, p. 126).

Schoolroom controversy. The beliefs of teachers Nigeria Greene and Bernard Cohen collide when considering what should be taught to students about the history of African Americans and racism. Cohen, a white teacher, faults Greene for filling students with so much rage about "their" history that they resent Cohen. "Was *I* ever a slave master? Did *I* bring slaves over here? Am *I* the one?" (*A Hero Ain't Nothin' but a Sandwich*, p. 35). He says that black students *should* know some of "their" history, but doesn't understand why Greene wants to teach black children about their African heritage: "At the moment [Greene's] in a big hassle to get a Swahili class started. What in the hell do they need with Swahili? Well, maybe they can use it to ask for a welfare check in two languages" (*A Hero Ain't Nothin' but a Sandwich*, p. 37). Also, Cohen is afraid that if the schools hire more and more African Americans to teach their students, white teachers will be run out of the system.

Nigeria Greene is angered by Cohen's views and amused by Cohen's own frustration with him,

> It shakes Cohen to his boots when he hears me ask, 'What time is it?' and the class hollers out,

'It's nation time!' I'm teachin that it's high time to straighten up and hold hands because my inner clock is tellin me that now is only half past slavery.

(*A Hero Ain't Nothin' but a Sandwich,* p. 46)

Nigeria Greene has resolved to teach what could not yet be found in books. When he came to teach in Harlem he was horrified to find a picture on the wall of George Washington. He found it impossible to see a picture of Washington, who was a slaveholder, hanging over his blackboard and not discuss this.

Benjie, it turns out, has ambivalent feelings toward both teachers. He feels that Greene's talk inspires pride in him, but he questions Greene's emphasis on ancient black cultures. Greene, muses Benjie, speaks of the queens and kings in Africa as being the forefathers and foremothers of American blacks, but as the father of his friend Jimmy Lee says, blacks have no kings and queens now and they haven't yet figured out how to deal with this.

Benjie recognizes that the other teacher Bernard Cohen's emphasis on skills have helped Benjie become a better reader. But Benjie takes issue with Cohen's views and with his ability as a communicator. "He say, 'You can be somebody if you want.' How the shit he don't know I'm somebody right now? He think *he* somebody and I'm not" (*A Hero Ain't Nothin' but a Sandwich,* p. 90).

Sources. A playwright by trade, Alice Chidress came to write *A Hero Ain't Nothin' but a Sandwich* when a book editor suggested she had something to say to young people about drugs and Harlem. Childress may have been moved to write about the infiltration of heroin into the Harlem community as she compared the Harlem of her childhood and the Harlem of the 1970s: "[In the past] a boy would not dream of killing his grandmother or hurting his mamma or her friends in order to pour cooked opium dust through a hole in his arm" (Childress in Commire, p. 52).

The characters in the novel are likely composites of the scores of people Childress knew growing up on 118th Street, and as an adult. She gives most of the credit to these people for writing themselves into her work, using her as a conduit:

[M]en in love with 'nothing to offer' . . . women who . . . wouldn't hold back their emotions for the 'sake of the race' . . . the poor genteel and sensitive people who are seamstresses, coal-carriers, vegetable peelers, who are somehow able to sustain themselves within the poet's heart sensitivity and appreciation of pure emotion . . . they tap at the brain and move a pen to action in the middle of the night.

(Childress in Commire, p. 52)

Reviews. According to one reviewer *A Hero Ain't Nothin' but a Sandwich* conveys "a grim picture that holds little or no promise for the children's future," (Rogers in Bryfonski, p. 106). But others have argued that the novel ends on an upbeat note with "a suggestion of hope" and have praised the story for its fearless look at, as one reviewer writes, "a segment of society seldom spoken of above a whisper" (Bullins in Bryfonski, p. 106).

Many reviewers comment that Childress does a brilliant job in avoiding the portrayal of any character as evil, not even the pusher, Walter. Nor, say the reviewers, is the Benjie character treated like a complete victim just because he is a child; Childress empowers the character by recognizing the thirteen-year-old's own responsibility for his descent into drugs.

In 1973, however, the novel was the first book banned in the Savannah, Georgia, school system since **Catcher in the Rye** (also covered in *Literature and Its Times*) in the 1950s. *A Hero Ain't Nothin' but a Sandwich* was also one of only nine books that has ever been taken to the Supreme Court for the question of whether to allow a community to banish it from school. Despite the controversy, *A Hero Ain't Nothin' but a Sandwich* won many awards; it was, for example, named one of the Outstanding Books of the Year by the *New York Times Book Review* in 1973.

For More Information

Bryfonski, Dedria, ed. *Contemporary Literary Criticism.* Vol. 12. Detroit: Gale Research, 1980.

Carlisle, Rodney. *The Roots of Black Nationalism.* Port Washington, N.Y.: Kennikat, 1975.

Childress, Alice. *A Hero Ain't Nothin' but a Sandwich.* New York: Avon, 1973.

Commire, Anne, ed. *Something about the Author.* Vol. 48. Detroit: Gale Research, 1987.

Haskins, Jim. *Diary of a Harlem Schoolteacher.* New York: Grove, 1969.

Kunnes, Richard, M.D. *The American Heroin Empire.* New York: Dodd, Mead, 1972.

Labov, William. *Language in the Inner City: Studies in the Black English Vernacular.* Philadelphia: University of Pennsylvania Press, 1972.

Mintz, Steven, and Susan Kellogg. *Domestic Revolutions: A Social History of American Family Life.* New York: Free Press, 1988.

Pinkney, Alphonso. *Red, Black and Green.* Cambridge: Cambridge University Press, 1976.

His Own Where

by

June Jordan

June Jordan was the only child of parents who emigrated from Jamaica to New York City. Born in Harlem on July 9, 1936, Jordan was raised in a section of Brooklyn called Bedford-Stuyvesant, the majority of whose residents were black. As a young adult, however, she spent several years enrolled in schools populated almost completely by whites. Jordan's parents opposed her desire to become a poet, an obstacle with which she had to come to terms. After publishing some of her poetry, Jordan wrote her first novel, *His Own Where,* which addresses some of the problems faced by black adolescents. Jordan's story broke new ground in young adult literature, becoming one of the first novels for the audience to portray realistically the life of black youths.

Events in History at the Time of the Novel

Brooklyn ghetto. *His Own Where* takes place in Brooklyn, a borough of New York City that is officially divided into more than a dozen sections. At the time of the novel, much of the borough's black ghetto was heavily concentrated in Bedford-Stuyvesant, 84 percent of whose residents were African American, with a large number coming from the West Indies, as Jordan's parents had. Some 12 percent of Bedford-Stuyvesant's remaining residents were Puerto Rican; 4 percent were white. Other sections with large black populations were East New York and Brownsville, areas that by the early 1970s were showing signs of greater urban decay than Bedford-Stuyvesant.

> ### THE LITERARY WORK
> A young adult novel set in a predominantly black Brooklyn neighborhood around 1970; published in 1971.
>
> ### SYNOPSIS
> A sixteen-year-old boy and his fourteen-year-old girlfriend try to create a better life for themselves in the ghetto.

Residents of Brooklyn's ghetto communities were plagued by a variety of ills, including segregation, unemployment, lack of education, poor economic conditions, overcrowding, deplorable housing, and exorbitant rents. The conditions created an oppressive environment that some residents felt unable to cope with and that others resolved to improve. In the novel the protagonist's mother has fled without a trace, leaving her son and husband in the process. Her son, Buddy, believes she has moved on in order to escape life in a place that breaks her heart, and he does not seem to resent her going. Instead he remembers her simply as a "strange lovely woman warm and hungering and gone" (Jordan, *His Own Where,* p. 19).

There were historical reasons for the decay that plagued Brooklyn's sections. In the case of Bedford-Stuyvesant, for example, the decay resulted partly from price gouging that began when real estate agents purchased homes for next to nothing (e.g., $2,000) during the 1930s, then turned around and resold them for many times the amount (e.g., $20,000). Black residents began to trickle into the area in the 1930s, then streamed into it during the 1940s, when the nearby Brooklyn Navy Yard hired blacks for wartime work. By then owners had already taken to subdividing their houses and then renting them out to several families at the same time. Many renters found themselves paying exorbitant sums for cubicles in dilapidated buildings that lacked adequate plumbing, heating, or sanitation. One Bedford-Stuyvesant girl told an interviewer about the rat problem in the slum where she lived: "We had a cat, but he was afraid of the rats and we had to get rid of him. So we got a dog. And even him is so scared of the rats that he gets in bed with us at nights" (Manoni, p. 16).

Health care. Overcrowding in Brooklyn's ghetto hospitals in the 1960s and 1970s resulted in long waits for service from overworked doctors. In the novel Buddy praises the clean, comfortable hospital environment he encounters, yet he also comments on the long wait. In real life, at the area's Kings County Hospital, it was common to wait eight to twelve hours for emergency room service. The long waits were blamed partly on the shortage created when many private doctors fled the ghetto. On average, the doctors remaining in 1970 were over the age of sixty; they faced a monumental task—practicing not only family medicine but also providing all the services expected from emergency rooms, public health department facilities, and large municipal outpatient clinics. Moreover, there were too few in-patient hospital beds to meet the ghetto's needs. Kings County, the largest of five hospitals in Bedford-Stuyvesant, had half the ghetto's total of 2,795 sick beds for a population of a quarter million residents.

Activism in the ghetto. All these problems caught the attention of activists in the ghetto, who joined forces in efforts to combat them. Youth in Action was one of Bedford-Stuyvesant's most generously funded community action programs at the time. Established in the mid-1960s as part of President Lyndon B. Johnson's national War on Poverty program, Youth in Action offered more than a dozen services, from Headstart for preschoolers to a young and unwed mothers program, job training for adults, and an emergency home repair service. A second organization, the Bedford-Stuyvesant Restoration Corporation, became the largest community de-

velopment program in the United States. Its main goal was to create jobs and ownership opportunities for local residents. The corporation oversaw still another group, the Neighborhood Improvement Program, which employed high school students to clean up and repair the area. To be sure, crime continued to plague Bedford Stuyvesant, including offenses by young truants, runaways, and drug addicts, but according to one researcher the area's crimes were committed by a minority of the population:

> Rapes continue to happen, shootings are not infrequent occurrences, and murders are still reported. Yet this is only a part—and not the major part—of today's real Bed-Stuy scene. And, taken on balance, the major segment of the community is upward bound.
>
> (Manoni, p. 112)

There were individual efforts too. State assemblywoman Shirley Chisholm, whose home community was Bedford-Stuyvesant, raised nearly a half million dollars for the Consumer Action Program in Bedford-Stuyvesant. Another effort was Jordan's writing of *His Own Where,* a novel that addresses real-life problems, especially the need for quality housing and for neighborhoods that nurture the spirit instead of breaking the heart. Some suggestions implied by the novel are that (1) residents could create attractive communal open space by tearing down the fences separating their backyards; (2) people could be brought together by local barbecues, sand piles for child play, and efforts to landscape open spaces; and (3) residents could gradually make improvements that personalize their living space and render it more satisfying.

Ghetto schools. Like the hospitals, Brooklyn's ghetto schools suffered from overcrowding and inadequate resources in 1970. They were also frequented by students who voiced their discontent more often than in the past, as did students in other areas of the United States. Two years earlier, for example, at Howard University in Washington, D.C., students demanded that their school adjust the curriculum to include more black studies. Violence, even the killing of a demonstrator, sometimes resulted from such confrontations, which helps explain why they made authorities uneasy. In the novel Lane High School and Boys' High School project images of fear among adults and unrest among the students. Lane has a reputation for fights, and at Boys' High it seems that school officials are overly anxious about controlling their students at all times. Buddy voices the students' resentment of such treatment when he confronts a lunchroom monitor in the novel:

> Mr. Jenkins, why you scrunch up all the tables one side of the lunchroom? . . . You pack us in like animals, and then you say, they act like nothing more than animals. To hell with your control.
>
> (*His Own Where*, p. 44)

Lane and Boys' high schools actually existed in Brooklyn at the time of the novel and thereafter, although Boys' merged with Girls' High School in 1976. This development is particularly interesting in light of the fact that *His Own Where* was published five years before the merger took place, and in the novel some boys hold a rally demanding that girls be admitted to their high school.

Young adults, sexuality, and parents. For many young people in the 1960s and 1970s, the demand for more freedom was a call to new experiments with sex, drugs, and fashion. Rejecting the conventions of society, these young people formed the so-called hippie movement, whose psychedelic music, tie-dyed clothing, and freer sexual ways created an even wider generation gap between parents and their teenagers than had existed in the 1950s, when youth culture first came into its own in the United States.

It was in the sixties that young people started carrying blaring portable radios the way Buddy does in the novel. The Afro hairstyles of Buddy and his girlfriend are also a sign of the times. Above all, *His Own Where* embraces the then newly popular notion that sex was something natural, wonderful, and permissible before marriage. Premarital sex became more common among the general population, and black women tended to have more children out of wedlock than whites. In 1970 ten times as many babies were born to unwed female black mothers as to unwed white ones. Furthermore, the highest incidence of such births happened among teenagers.

In the novel Buddy and Angela are protective of and devoted to each other. Although they are underage teens engaging in premarital sex, there is nothing unsavory about their relationship, and it is one to which they both show an earnest commitment. Yet, despite their willingness to take responsibility for sex and parenthood, most of their elders are by no means prepared to sanction sexual relations between a sixteen-year-old and a fourteen-year-old. This reflected the attitude of real-life adults; in fact, sexual relations between two such youths would have constituted a misdemeanor under New York law.

The Novel in Focus

The plot. At its opening *His Own Where* skips back and forth in time between later and earlier events. (In fact it starts with a scene that, chronologically, occurs near the end of the action.) The novel ultimately moves into a straight chronological progression, during which the daydreams of characters periodically cause a blurring of the line between fantasy and reality in the story.

UNREST AT LANE HIGH SCHOOL

The following real-life events of 1969 help explain why black students might have felt resentful toward the school, why teachers and school officials probably felt afraid, and why a principal might be quick to suspend a student the way Buddy is suspended in *His Own Where*:

Jan. 10: Police are stationed in the halls of Lane High School.

Jan. 14: It is recommended that 1,100 black students be transferred in order to achieve a 50-50 racial balance at Lane.

Jan. 20: A white chemistry teacher is beaten and set on fire by black students. Lane is closed for three days while officials discuss overcrowding at the school.

Jan. 27: 678 black students—all supposedly truants—are ordered to leave Lane.

May 1: A judge orders these students to return to Lane.

Oct. 23: Black students replace the United States flag with a black liberation banner; five students are suspended.

Oct. 24: Two more students are suspended following a fight in the cafeteria.

Oct. 30: Another fight in the cafeteria prompts another temporary closure of the school.

A sixteen-year-old black boy named Buddy Rivers has discovered a place of refuge in an overcrowded, broken-down Brooklyn neighborhood. He finds tranquillity in a cemetery among a group of trees that also surrounds a reservoir and an abandoned brick house. The first time he shows this place to his fourteen-year-old girlfriend Angela Figueroa, they wonder what it would be like to live together in the small brick house, far from their personal problems and the dangers of the city. Buddy is particularly wary of street traffic since his father was hit by a car while standing on a corner. Because of the accident, Mr. Rivers is in the hospital, unconscious and dying, and his son visits him daily.

The story returns to a time before Buddy first met Angela. While visiting his injured father, Buddy contemplates the hospital environment and wishes the city were like a hospital, with "everybody taking turns to heal the people. People turning doctor, patient, nurse. Whole city asking asking everybody how you are, how you feel, what can I do for you, how can I help" (*His Own Where,* p. 16). The bleakness of the city had saddened his mother so much that she fled from it, leaving her son and husband behind. Buddy's father then began rebuilding their house to suit the two of them, a project that strengthened their love for home and each other, until the car accident took him away too.

Angela's mother, Mrs. Figueroa, is a nurse at the hospital, and she takes a special interest in Buddy and his father. Each evening, Angela must come to the hospital in order to receive instructions from her mother and answer questions about household chores and the four younger siblings she babysits after school. Buddy feels guilty about being attracted to this girl while sitting with his dying father, but he cannot stop thinking about her. An efficient nurse, Angela's mother can also be an accusing, hostile parent who verbally abuses her daughter and even slaps her in public. After one of these confrontations, Buddy intercedes on Angela's behalf and walks her home.

As days pass and they get to know each other better, Buddy and Angela compare high schools, music interests, and family lives. Walking Angela home and then returning to the hospital becomes a routine for Buddy, but one evening after he drops her off he goes home instead. Angela's parents already suspect their daughter is running wild, and when Mrs. Figueroa sees that Buddy does not return to the hospital, she believes the girl must be up to no good with him. Angela's father happens to be drunk when his wife calls him and paints a bleak picture of their daughter's behavior, whereupon he wakes Angela and beats her until she passes out.

Later Angela staggers in the rain to Buddy's house, and he drives her to the emergency room. When confronted by the police, Angela's parents seem indifferent to their daughter's condition. Meanwhile, Buddy is nearly in shock in the wait-

June Jordan

ing room, worried that the two people he cares about most could both be dying. To Buddy, "the whole city of his people [is] like a all-night emergency room. People mostly suffering, uncomfortable, and waiting," and he imagines himself doing little things to lift the spirits of the patients and the people in the waiting room (*His Own Where,* p. 35). When Angela has recovered, the police place her in a shelter in Manhattan, away from her parents.

Buddy cannot concentrate in school because Angela's shelter prohibits visits from boys and his father's condition has worsened. At school Buddy organizes his friends, who in turn organize their friends, and so on, until fifteen hundred boys congregate in the gym to present the principal with several demands: they want thorough sex education, contraceptives, and the admission of girls to the school. Buddy leads the negotiation process, and a wary principal satisfies the boys by agreeing to some of their terms. Jubilant, the boys head to the cafeteria for lunch, where they cajole the staff into letting them turn on some music. They dance with the "Big Mommas" who work in the lunchroom, and everyone has a good time until the police arrive (*His Own Where,* p. 45). The police see no harm in the situation, but the principal suspends Buddy.

The last time the reader sees Buddy visit the hospital, Angela's mother refuses to speak to him. The authorities have transferred Angela to a Catholic home for girls outside the city; she and Buddy stay in touch by writing letters. Unable to go to school, Buddy works on his father's house and plants a garden behind it. During a visit to Angela he is troubled by the strictness of the nuns, and he imagines ways to challenge their repressive mentality. Buddy and Angela plan to meet again the next weekend, when she will visit her parents.

Angela's mother starts to harass her the moment they are in the same house, which prompts Angela to leave home for good. She goes to meet Buddy, and they buy food, he gives her a tour of his house and garden, and they sleep together for the first time. In the morning Buddy is excited at the possibility that Angela could be pregnant, and they decide to run away together before Angela is missed.

They drive to the reservoir and, with a little money and a few supplies, set up housekeeping in the abandoned brick house. Buddy worries about his father, then settles into sketching some changes for the abandoned house. He and Angela eat, listen to the radio, and make love. While they sleep Buddy dreams about enabling people to inhabit skyscrapers at night and Angela dreams that the city is organized according to kinds of music. The novel's end celebrates the happiness they have created and their intention to start a family.

Setting aside stereotypes. In her writings Jordan presents a version of reality different from much of what passes for realism in novels and newspapers. Instead of overemphasizing problems, she creates potent characters who concern themselves with taking steps in the right direction. In doing so Jordan challenges a variety of common stereotypes. For example, the high number of female-headed households in the black community is frequently discussed in the same breath as the supposedly unreliable or flighty black male. Rather than invoking such stereotypes Jordan offers the case of Buddy's father, Mr. Rivers, who is left by his wife. Mr. Rivers is the breadwinner and is an excellent parent, a father who works two jobs and takes responsibility for fixing up a home for his son and himself. In another move that might surprise many readers, Jordan has Buddy accept and even sympathize with his mother's sudden abandonment of them.

Stereotypes that characterize adolescents as selfish, irresponsible pleasure-seekers do not find expression in *His Own Where* either. Angela behaves like a responsible parent by caring for her siblings, and Buddy takes on the burdens of life willingly, whether they be coping with crises or addressing neighborhood problems. The two adolescents discuss birth control, pregnancy, feminine hygiene products, and sex. And in contrast to the usual statistics about unwanted teenage pregnancies, they delight in the prospect of caring for a family soon.

When fifteen hundred high school boys congregate and sound belligerent in their demands for sex education and girl students, one might expect a dangerous situation to develop. Certainly the incident could have mushroomed out of control. Instead Buddy moves to the lunchroom, where he finds the usual low quality food and close supervision. Rebellious, objecting to these conditions, Buddy leads his male schoolmates in dancing with the women who work there. "Must be some women in this lunchroom," says Buddy; "Find the women!" He then jumps over a counter and grabs one (*His Own Where*, p. 45). The fact that such behavior would usually arouse considerable fear and provoke punishment in real life makes it doubly unexpected when, in the novel, the police and a lunchroom monitor later side good-naturedly with the boys.

In Jordan's view, most authors who claim to write realistically dwell too much on problems, conflicts, and character flaws, and as a result their stories present a skewed, overly negative picture of reality. Consequently she has vowed to provide young readers with uplifting alternatives:

> I will attempt, in all of my written work, to devise reasonable alternatives to this reality, and to offer these alternatives particularly to young readers. . . . [T]hey are the ones we have failed, in these so many ways, and we are the ones who owe our children something else, right now— some good news, a chance, a story of love gracing an entire family or an entire community for thirty to forty years, a manual for the assertion of human rights versus private property rights, more reference sources clearly listing the groups and the individuals who are busy doing . . . urgently required, humane work, on behalf of other lives. . . .
>
> (Jordan in Varlejs, p. 149)

Sources. Like Many of Jordan's other works, *His Own Where* incorporates details about ghetto life and the author's relationship with her parents. In this novel, it is Angela's parents, the Figueroas, who resemble the real-life Mr. and Mrs. Jordan. Both Figueroas work night shifts, as did the Jordans. Like Mrs. Jordan, Angela's mother is a nurse who takes a personal interest in the well-being of others in the community. Unfortunately Angela's family also resembles Jordan's in a less positive way—the author, says one biographical essay, was beaten by her father, and her mother bore "complicity in this violence" (Davis and Harris, p. 147). More biographical information can be found in *Civil Wars* (1981), a collection of Jordan's essays that explores further the connection between her life experiences and her development as a writer.

Particularly influential were Jordan's experiences with urban planning and her high regard for Black English. Jordan proposed to join with designer R. Buckminster Fuller in making a plan to renovate Harlem, but their ideas were never implemented. Behind the plan, though, was an energy for inner-city redesign that found its way into her fiction. In the novel Buddy first remodels a house with his father, then by himself. He successfully persuades his neighbors to improve the area by tearing down the fences that separate their backyards and making a park out of the freed-up space. Jordan would win the Prix de Rome in Environmental Design for the novel,

one goal of the story having been to familiarize youths with simple ways to rebuild and improve a neighborhood. Jordan also sought to make a point by having Buddy and many other characters speak in Black English. The aim in this case was to attract teenage readers by speaking their language, a very viable one in Jordan's view. She has elsewhere described Black English as not a verbal deficiency but "a communication system" with internal consistency. Jordan explains, for example, that its speakers logically use multiple negatives to make the meaning of a statement clearer or more emphatic, as in: "You ain gon bother me no way, no more, you hear?" (Jordan, *Civil Wars*, pp. 67-8).

Reception. The novel's use of Black English, along with elements of the plot, caused a stir in some black communities. African American parents in Baltimore, Maryland, moved to ban *His Own Where* from public school libraries, one of their fears being that it would encourage young people to shun standard English. There were also objections to what was deemed a cavalier approach to the subjects of teenage sex, pregnancy, and cohabitation. According to one critic, making role models out of Angela and Buddy was "an act of social as well as literary irresponsibility" that could only hurt the black community if others followed their example (Tremper in Senick, p. 118). The critic objected also to the absence of talk about racism and the struggle to combat it in the novel and to the "sometimes impenetrable prose" (Tremper in Senick, p. 118).

On the other hand, a number of reviews showered unqualified praise on the novel. They complimented Jordan on her sensitive portrayal of two adolescents and their world. Particularly pleasing to some of these critics was the example Buddy set by his concern for the community and for his girlfriend. They admired the novel for its positive portrait of the teenager characters:

> This novel is no cop-out pseudo-case study of a confused kid or of kids "in trouble." Buddy's not guilty, hostile, mixed-up and ineffectual, or prodded on the road to self-discovery by a well-meaning adult. He really loves Angela (for how long is an adult concern) and the two of them can't wait to make a baby and share love with it (what its precise future will be is also not their concern now).
>
> (Goddard in Senick, p. 117)

Finally, these reviewers expressed appreciation for the language of the novel, or, as one these critics expressed it, for "Jordan's uncanny ability with words" (Goddard in Senick, p. 117).

For More Information

Connolly, Harold X. *A Ghetto Grows in Brooklyn.* New York: New York University Press, 1977.

Davis, Thadious M., and Trudier Harris, eds. *Dictionary of Literary Biography.* Vol. 38. Detroit: Gale Research, 1985.

Green, Charles, and Basil Wilson. *The Struggle for Black Empowerment in New York City: Beyond the Politics of Pigmentation.* New York: Praeger, 1989.

Jordan, June. *His Own Where.* New York: Laurel-Leaf Library, 1971.

Jordan, June. *Civil Wars.* Boston: Beacon, 1981.

Manoni, Mary H. *Bedford-Stuyvesant: The Anatomy of a Central City Community.* New York: Quadrangle, 1973.

Senick, Gerard J., ed. *Children's Literature Review.* Vol. 10. Detroit: Gale Research, 1986.

Sex Education in Schools. Washington, D.C.: National School Public Relations Association, 1969.

Varlejs, Jana, ed. *Young Adult Literature in the Seventies.* Metuchen, N.J.: Scarecrow, 1978.

House of Stairs

by
William Sleator

Born February 13, 1945, William Sleator pursued first music and then English at Harvard University. In 1974, when Sleator wrote *House of Stairs,* he was wavering between a career as a writer—he had already had a few stories for young adults published—or as a pianist for the Boston Ballet Company. *House of Stairs* was his fourth of more than seventeen books for this audience. The novel's main themes, a questioning of authority and an illustration of the dangers of behavior conditioning, reflect the counterculture sentiment of many young people during the early 1970s.

Events in History at the Time of the Novel

The science of behavior modification. Russian scientists at the turn of the twentieth century conducted research into an aspect of behavioral science known as conditioning—that is, the practice of teaching a subject to behave in a certain way. The American scientist B. F. Skinner, among others, greatly extended this research in the 1940s and 1950s. Skinner focused on the conditioning of behavior through some type of response being reinforced by a positive result—such as the act of pressing a lever being rewarded with food. The repeated appearance of the reward reinforces the particular behavior—in this case, pressing the lever. By the late 1950s and early 1960s scientists were applying this type of conditioning in psychology to clinical treatment of people with behavior problems and using it for educational pur-

poses. In psychology the goal was to alleviate or remedy a maladaptive behavior such as excessive drinking, for example. Behavior specialists agreed, however, that conditioning could lead to a positive or negative end: "This, they said, is because behaviors are learned, maintained, and modified by the same principles independent of whether the actions are . . . 'normal' or 'abnormal,' 'healthy' or 'sick'" (Kazdin, p. 204).

As this field of research expanded, behavior specialists proceeded to experiment with different techniques and evaluate the results of their experiments. Various approaches developed, all attempting to change a person's overt behavior. One of these approaches concentrated on altering the normal assumptions and thought processes of the person, an approach that seems to be used in the *House of Stairs*. By the end of the novel, fighting, an activity once considered negative and something to refrain from, is regarded by most of the subjects of the fictional experiment as positive and something to engage in because fighting elicits the reward of food.

Real-life behavior specialists have noted that a person's drive to maintain control of his or her own behavior is strong. In fact, it is so strong that "[a]n individual may respond in a way counter to obtaining some tempting and immediately reinforcing consequences" (Kazdin, p. 329). In other words, a person determined to maintain self-control may do so at the expense of forgoing a reward—even one as desperately needed as food. The two rebels who fail to conform to the machine's wishes in the *House of Stairs* do so despite the threat this poses to their survival.

Behavior modification therapy became widespread by the mid-1960s, but also raised some disturbing ethical questions. Should a person have the right, for example, to agree to or refuse these types of treatment? While scientists discussed the legal and ethical issues, novelists created stories that raised such issues as well and carried the process to some devastating hypothetical conclusions. There was a fear that detractors and ill-intended individuals could misuse the research to reshape society to their own diabolical ends. Popular books such as *Brave New World* postulated a world in which progress in behavioral research would lead to minority control over the behavior of the majority. Meanwhile, terms used by the specialists—*control, conditioning,* and *modification*—helped feed such fears.

There are, however, checks in place to prevent the misuse of behavioral methods. Court cases have rendered some key decisions to protect the rights of people being subjected to these methods. In 1972 *Wyatt v. Stickney* specified that conditions to which a person is subjected must be humane, including the right to a comfortable bed, well-balanced meals, and one's own clothes. Protective measures mounted. In 1974, the year *House of Stairs* appeared, the U.S. Congress arranged for a special commission to draft ethical guidelines for research with human subjects; child subjects were considered deserving of special attention. Meanwhile, the American Psychological Association issued guidelines of its own, declaring that "experimenters must avoid exposing subjects to physical and mental discomfort, harm, or danger, and must secure consent if the

B. F. Skinner

possibility of experiencing such risks exists" (Kazdin, p. 381). Though the theory behind the scenario created in *House of Stairs* had a basis in reality, such a heinous experiment would have been impossible to carry out given the guidelines existent at the time Sleator wrote it.

The Vietnam War and American protesters. To use military language, in *House of Stairs* five orphans are drafted into a strange behavior-conditioning experiment. The goal of this experiment is to turn the five undisciplined young people into obedient soldiers who follow orders without questioning them. If the experiment proves successful, the participants will conform to some clearly defined, strict group rules. They will respond to the conditioning imposed upon them with the aid of a machine. This belief in conformity and behavior conditioning reflects the principles followed by the United States Armed Forces in conditioning its soldiers for warfare at the time.

By 1974, U.S. military involvement in Vietnam had largely ended, with a complete U.S. retreat by 1975. But in the years leading up to the publication of *House of Stairs,* the war in Vietnam was in the forefront of American concerns. During the post-World War II Cold War, American military and intelligence forces sought to limit the spread of communism worldwide. As early as 1950, communist North Vietnam had been viewed as a threat to its democratic neighbor, South Vietnam. And in the early 1960s, when communist-supported guerrillas aggressively invaded the South Vietnamese jungles, President Kennedy took action and sent advisors, and then troops, to South Vietnam. By the time Kennedy was assassinated in November of 1963, there were 16,500 American troops in South Vietnam to fight communist aggression there (Smith, p. 41). During this period, casualties were relatively small and the American public had not yet focused its attention on this overseas conflict. But when President Lyndon B. Johnson's administration dramatically increased the number of American troops in Vietnam, they began to draw international attention, and a national debate over the U.S. presence in Vietnam began. Johnson's administration increased the U.S. presence in Vietnam to 184,000 troops in 1965. The number climbed to 385,000 in 1966. Over the next few years sometimes violent antiwar demonstrations would erupt across the United States.

Many antiwar protesters felt that the U.S. had no business intervening in a small country that was thousands of miles away and represented no immediate threat to their own nation. Protesters also condemned the killing of thousands of innocent women and children through air-raid bombings and vicious ground attacks. There was discontent, too, over the fact that the war was largely being fought by poor and undereducated Americans. "Those from disadvantaged backgrounds were about twice as likely as their better-off peers to serve in the military, go to Vietnam, and see combat" (Becker, p. 127). In Sleator's book, the "drafted" group of teenagers are likewise disadvantaged—all are parentless. And two of the orphans, Lola and Peter, rebel against the dictates of the machine. These rebels, in effect, parallel the real-life protesters of Sleator's day, who rebelled against "the system" and conformity to values, including the commitment to the Vietnam War, that society had chosen for them.

The counterculture. Sleator's pair of dissenters resemble members of the American "counterculture" that developed in the 1960s. Comprised mostly of the swelling number of teenagers and young adults born during the prosperous "baby boom" era following World War II, the counterculture movement renounced mainstream goods, goals, language, and dress. The movement had its origins in the "beat generation" of the 1950s, whose leaders—for example, poet Allen Ginsberg—were critical of society and its emphasis on materialism and consumption. In keeping with this position, members of the counterculture outspokenly rejected establishment values and prejudices.

Typically, members of the counterculture and the related student movement spoke out against the Vietnam War and violence of any kind; the word "peace" became a common greeting as well as a frequent subject for contemporary songwriters and poets. Attempting to create a nonviolent society set apart from what they perceived as a violence-ridden establishment, many members of the counterculture joined communes and "dropped out" of society at large. They set out to live in harmony and peace, abiding by their own values rather than submitting to the values of others—which were primarily those of the previous generation.

In Sleator's novel, Lola, a tough and independent leader, teams up with Peter, who is peaceful and introspective, and together the pair stands apart from the majority, who submit to the demands of the machine for violence. It is Lola who realizes that they must stand up against the machine if they are to retain control over their own lives. At the end of the novel, the society that created the machine judges Lola and Peter as "misfits"—much as American society at large commonly judged members of the student movement and the counterculture—without considering the worthiness of the choices the "misfits" made for self-determination. They were risky choices. In the novel Lola and Peter are in danger of starving to death because of their defiance. In real life two protesters were, for example, shot to death (along with two bystanders) at an antiwar demonstration at Kent State University in Ohio in 1970.

Watergate and Nixon's operatives. In the early 1970s the Republican administration of President Richard Nixon became embroiled in what would eventually be called "a national nightmare," the Watergate scandal. If the war in Vietnam prompted Americans to question their government and the politicians who ran it, the Watergate scandal of 1974 created an environment of complete distrust and, in some cases, even contempt for national leaders. For the first time in U.S. history, a president was forced to resign in disgrace because of his involvement in a series of illegal actions that included politically motivated spying and an attempted cover-up at the highest levels.

White House counsel John Dean, shown here taking the oath before the Senate Committee, was the most important witness in the investigation into the Watergate cover-up.

In *House of Stairs,* scientists oversee a sometimes cruel experiment that has one goal: to produce conditioned subjects who blindly follow orders based on intense conditioning and behavior-control techniques. A 1974 review of the novel by Pamela D. Pollack connects it to the Watergate scandal. The novel has someone orchestrating the training of an elite corps who will "follow unquestioningly any order given to them and not get caught" (Pollock in Senick, p. 200). In the real-life Watergate scandal, Nixon re-election aides behaved like obedient foot soldiers in an orchestrated scheme; only they were caught, and Nixon's tape-recorded links to them led to his downfall.

The Watergate scandal began in 1972, when, at the end of his first term in office, Nixon faced a re-election campaign against Democratic challenger George McGovern. In June of 1972, five men were arrested when they were caught breaking into the Democratic National Committee Headquarters at Washington's ritzy Watergate office building and residential complex. They were attempting to gather information about the McGovern campaign by wire-tapping the telephone of McGovern's campaign manager. Initially the burglary attempt was viewed by the public as an insignificant, almost laughable incident meaning little. But as revelations emerged over the months

that followed, a complex paper trail led aggressive journalists at the *Washington Post* and led governmental investigation committees to the Oval Office itself. Nixon and some of his top aides, it appeared, had been somehow involved in the political espionage. In time, the president was forced to turn over audio tapes he had made of conversations that implicated him in blatant cover-up attempts.

By mid-1974, the president was aware that the House of Representatives, led by public outrage and ever-increasing indications of Nixon's involvement in Watergate, would move toward a constitutional impeachment. But he thought he still might have a chance to win over the Senate. On August 7, 1974, Senate and House members met privately with the president, and grim-faced, told him that the Senate, too, would be voting to impeach him. The president summoned his family and staff, and tearfully informed them of his decision to resign. On August 8, President Nixon addressed a stunned American television audience and announced his resignation, which officially occurred at noon the next day.

The Novel in Focus

The plot. Peter is the first of a group of five sixteen-year-old orphans mysteriously deposited into a strange world of white stairs. As his unknown captors remove Peter's blindfold, he sees dozens of flights of steps that seem to be interconnected and stand as one large entity that floats in a white spacious void. The stairs go up, down, and sideways, but don't seem to lead anywhere. In the distance, all Peter can see are more stairs, and no doorways or exits. He can't tell how high he is off the ground, but he has fears of falling down. Peter proceeds to cling to any flat landings he can find and forces himself to sleep. He dreams of better times at the orphanage with his best friend, Jasper. Peter seems lost and hopeless, until another person arrives.

Lola appears in the stair world. Tough and independent compared to Peter, she quickly explores the stairs in an effort to find her way out. She proves to be a dominant, leader type, her personality contrasting greatly with Peter's quiet submissiveness. The two become friends and decide to find an escape together.

At this point, they encounter another abandoned orphan—an obese girl named Blossom with curly locks of hair and a frilly dress. She appears to be obsessed with a machine that she's facing. Although she doesn't understand why, when Blossom sticks out her tongue, the machine flashes a light and then dispenses a small piece of food. Lola, who is quite hungry at this point, forces Blossom to hand over some of the food for her and Peter. Lola's bossy manner upsets Blossom, and the two quickly become enemies. Blossom, it turns out, knows as little about this strange stair world as Lola and Peter do.

Suddenly a new female voice is heard coming down from the steps above. The voice belongs to Abigail, another sixteen-year-old orphan who has been left in the stair world. The group acquaint themselves with one another, and Lola heads off on her own to find a source of water and a bathroom.

Once she's out of earshot, Blossom starts to tell the others how mean she thinks Lola is and tries to turn the rest against her. She then starts to talk about her secret life with her family. While she is, in fact, an orphan, her parents died only a month ago in a car crash. Before her parents died, she says, her family "lived in a *house*. With real grass around it, and a live growing tree" (Sleator, *House of Stairs,* p. 32). Blossom further explains that her mom used to cook real food, and that the family even had a dining room and swimming pool. This contrasts sharply with the backgrounds of the others, who have lived in massive residential megastructures and eaten synthetic foods.

Finally, Oliver, a new boy, appears and explains to the group that he somehow was dumped into this stair world as well. Abigail instantly notices that Oliver is good-looking. He also exudes an air of confidence and strength that the others find attractive. Even Peter finds himself staring at Oliver in admiration. Lola returns and finds Oliver dancing and singing with the rest of the group. Oliver seems like a born leader, but Lola somehow threatens his sense of superiority. Lola's investigation has been successful. She has located a toilet, which can also serve as a source of water for them, since there is no other. Oliver is angry that her return to the group has disrupted their fun; tension grows between the two.

Blossom's tongue trick is now failing to make the machine dispense food. Oliver takes stock of their plight. He decides that to be dominant in the group, he *must* be the one to make the machine work. Having nothing to eat for nearly one full day, the group is now hungry. They try to make the machine give them food—but nothing works. By accident, the group notices that they have the power to make the machine dispense food by dancing for it after it starts humming. Soon the group's around-the-clock job is to wait for the machine to start humming. When it does, they begin to dance and they usually get fed. When the machine does flash its light and give them food, they eat ravenously—especially Blossom. As weeks pass, members of the group develop coping patterns that reflect their personalities. For example, Peter retreats into a dream world in which he sleeps most of the time and thinks about his good friend Jasper. Blossom barely moves and spends all her time staring at the food machine and fighting with Lola. Oliver starts to become slightly abusive with Abigail. Highly independent, Lola begins each day by exercising up and down the stairs. She is determined to stay in top shape, both mentally and physically.

The group starts to sense that the machine wants more than mere dancing. In time they are no longer rewarded for this activity. Disagreeing over whether they should continue their dancing, they notice that the machine starts rewarding them for their contentious behavior. It seems to reward them with extra food whenever they are fighting. Picking up on this, the group decides to experiment. Blossom tells the group that Lola has been saying cruel things about them. By revealing these secrets, Blossom makes everybody feel bad, and Lola becomes the object of their hatred. After this outpouring of negative feelings and hatred, the food machine gushes forth with rewards for the hostages. Everyone realizes what they must now do. Lola thinks about the implications of the machine's violent urges. She decides that the only intelligent thing to do is to get away from the machine. She retreats to her own area and urges the rest to join her in a strike against the machine.

Peter soon follows her. He says that he's tired of always daydreaming and going along with the group. He wants to fight the machine the way Lola is doing. He suggests that a united front of two people will be more effective than just one. Lola and Peter attempt to get the other three participants to partake in their strike. But the others refuse.

The three orphans remaining near the machine try to find creative new ways to be cruel to one another. Oliver slaps Abigail's face. Blossom steals Abigail's food from her lap and throws a shoe at her. Soon the three are bruised and battered, and they run out of cruel tricks to play on one another.

They proceed to torment Lola and Peter, who by now are near complete starvation. Oliver, Blossom, and Abigail taunt the two rebels with food and begin to actually beat them up. The three return to their bountiful food supply and are rewarded with more food, while Lola and Peter, quite weak, draw closer to death.

At this point, Dr. Lawrence, the scientist conducting the experiment, decides to end it. He sends an elevator to rescue the five orphans and brings them to his lab, where they are all nursed back to health. He explains that they were, in fact, part of a behavior-modification group. According to Dr. Lawrence, the participants who fought for the food are successes. Lola and Peter, who fought the system, are "misfits" and will be confined to a misfit camp.

As the novel ends, the three "successes," who have been released, see a flashing red street light (like the machine's light) and instantly, they start to dance for their food. Lola and Peter look on sadly.

Lola and Peter fight authority. In Sleator's novel, Lola and Peter wage a hunger strike against the powerful lure of the food machine. They do this in spite of near-fatal starvation and brutal physical violence inflicted on them by the other young people. But they seem to be driven by a force that is more powerful than hunger and violence—their own determination to maintain control over themselves rather than forfeit it to an outsider—in this case, a machine.

At one point, Lola tries to explain to Peter the power of the unknown forces that are controlling the food machine:

> This thing we're fighting, this place, the people who are doing it, whatever the hell it is, it's tricky, it's real tricky. And it's in control. Everything is on its side. They have all the machines in the world and they've got us trapped, and they can do whatever they want to us. And we don't have anything. We have nothing to fight with except ourselves, our own bodies and our brains.
>
> (*House of Stairs,* p. 105)

Using their bodies, their brains, and their resolve, Lola and Peter emerge from the experiment as individuals who cannot be conditioned or brainwashed. They are viewed as failures by the scientist who conducts the experiment. But the reader is led to understand that Lola and Peter are in fact the real winners, for they have retained self-control. The so-called winners—Oliver, Abigail, and Blossom—are portrayed as pitiful slaves to their conditioning. The sad image of the three dancing even for a flashing street light at the end of the novel shows a bias toward the attitude demonstrated by the two rebels—Lola and Peter—in resisting the machine's conditioning. This same preference is conveyed through positive attributes attached to their characters. Throughout the story, Lola is presented as strong and self-reliant, and Peter is portrayed as kind and loving. Though he retreats into sleep and his dreams to escape the horrors of the stair world, he ultimately shows strong resolve by joining Lola's hunger fast. The three "winners" on the other hand, possess negative or unattractive attributes. Oliver abuses Abigail—even before the machine rewards him for doing so—and Abigail submits to his abuse, while Blossom proves to be gluttonous, greedy, and manipulative. In the end, the novel presents conditioning as a potentially destructive force and suggests a relation between its impact and the character traits of its subjects.

Sources. William Sleator says that "*House of Stairs* was an attempt to get away from where I've been and it was a totally different setting" (Roginski, p. 201). He adds that he prepared for the book by doing extensive research in the field of behavior modification. In writing the novel, he started by carefully planning each of his five teenage characters: "I did sit down and map out each character way ahead of time and figure out who each character was" (Roginski, p. 199). As with some of his other novels, in *House of Stairs* Sleator uses a strange, fantastic setting to highlight the inner workings of adolescent social relationships.

Reviews. Looking back at the 1974 novel, many critics refer to *House of Stairs* as a youth classic and a career highlight for Sleator, who went on to write more than twenty books. Upon its original publication, many critics spoke highly of the book. Pamela D. Pollack called the novel "an intensely suspenseful page-turner par excellence" (Pollack in Senick, p. 200). A *Publisher's Weekly* review referred to the book as "extremely interesting" and noted that "Sleator is saying some deep things here about privacy and courage and the rights of the individual" (*Publisher's Weekly* in Senick, p. 200). Finally, critic Sheila Egoff termed *House of Stairs* "Kafka-like" and added that "the story is one of the most brutal in science fiction, all the more sickeningly compelling because of its finely controlled, stark writing" (Egoff in Senick, p. 200).

For More Information

Becker, Elizabeth. *America's Vietnam War: A Narrative History*. New York: Clarion, 1992.

Dickenson, William B., ed. *Watergate: Chronology of a Crisis*. Vol. 1. Washington, D.C.: Congressional Quarterly, 1974.

Kazdin, Alan E. *History of Behavior Modification*. Baltimore: University Park Press, 1978.

Roginski, Jim. *Behind the Covers: Interviews with Authors and Illustrators of Books for Children and Young Adults*. Chicago: Libraries Unlimited, 1985.

Senick, Gerard, ed. *Children's Literature Review*. Vol. 29. Detroit: Gale Research, 1993.

Sleator, William. *House of Stairs*. New York: Penguin, Puffin Books, 1974.

Smith, Nigel. *The United States since 1945*. New York: Bookwright, 1990.

The World in 1974. Associated Press, 1975.

The House
of the Spirits

by
Isabel Allende

B orn in 1946, the novelist Isabel Allende, goddaughter and niece to Chile's future president Salvador Allende, was raised in the lavish home of her grandparents in Chile's capital city, Santiago. Her grandfather—described as a conservative and passionately violent yet endearing old patriarch—came of marriageable age in the early 1900s, when her novel *The House of the Spirits* opens.

THE LITERARY WORK

A novel set in a Latin American country, much like Chile, from about 1910 to 1973; published in 1982.

SYNOPSIS

Four generations of an upper-class Latino family experience social and political changes that greatly affect the course of their lives.

Events in History at the Time the Novel Takes Place

Chile in the early 1900s. From the 1890s to 1920, Chile experienced a great rise in prosperity as a result of a boom in the copper and nitrates mines of its northern deserts. Mining was one of the few ways a poor man could make a fortune in the country, as the character Esteban Trueba sets out to do in *The House of the Spirits*. It was possible for tough, hardworking miners to amass huge wealth, though they might search for years in poverty before a find catapulted them into Chile's tiny pool of millionaires. The few who struck such good fortune became part of the oligarchy, the small upper class of larger landholders and business proprietors who virtually ruled the nation. At the time, Chile's small oligarchy—whose ancestry was strictly Spanish—lorded over a large mass of poor mestizos of mixed Spanish-Indian heritage; there was little middle ground.

Turn-of-the-century politics in Chile was similarly limited, with a few major parties competing for power. A Socialist Party emerged in 1933, but it would not become a leading player until forty years later. During those forty years, principles of democratic rule became firmly entrenched in Chile; it was often described as one of South America's most stable nations. Though enfranchisement was wide, elections were sometimes fraudulent. During this same period, the government took on an increasing role in the economy, concentrating less on exports and more on bringing industry to Chile's cities. As a result, radical transformations took place in urban centers like Santiago and Valparaiso over the four decades, while the haciendas, or rural agricultural estates, experienced little change.

The hacienda. The average hacienda usually covered more than 1,000 acres, much of which lay untilled. Its owner, called the *patrón,* employed mestizo peasants as tenants (known as *inquilinos*) and hired an overseer to manage them. It was common for the owner to reside in a house in the city while entrusting the hacienda to the overseer. The inquilinos labored in their patrón's fields, and in return received their own small parcels to farm when they were not working in the patrón's fields; they also received pink slips of paper as pay. They "spent" these slips at the hacienda's general store, which carried goods that a patrón would buy wholesale and resell at cost to his workers. Such an arrangement encouraged them to depend on the patrón, and at the same time fostered a rather paternal attitude toward them on the patrón's part, evidenced by Esteban Trueba's musings in the novel.

A PATRÓN'S VIEW OF HIS TENANTS

As I've always said, they're like children. There's not one of them can do what he's supposed to do without me there behind him driving him on. And then they start in on me with the story that we are all equal! It's enough to make you die laughing.

(Allende, *The House of the Spirits,* p. 65)

As a result of this mindset, each hacienda essentially became its own separate society, with the patrón as absolute monarch and the tenants as his subjects. It was a setup that contributed to corruption in politics. Though Chile prided itself on being run by an elected government rather than a dictatorship like so many of its neighbors, there was forced voting in elections. A patrón would promise his peasants that if they voted for his favorite candidate they would receive bonuses; on the other hand, if that candidate lost they would lose their jobs. As it was, they barely earned enough to survive.

From country to city. Bouts of economic instability forced some peasants off the land, and in turn they drifted into Chile's capital, Santiago, and the seaport city of Valparaiso. The 1950s was an especially heavy time of internal migration, with thousands forming slum settlements such as the Misercordia District in *The House of the Spirits.* Urban mansions, like the novel's "house on the corner," contrasted sharply with these squalid *populaciones callampas* or "mushroom communities," named for how rapidly they grew. The gap between the rich minority and the impoverished majority widened, and the middle-class urban shopowners, teachers, entertainers, and military personnel—became more visible.

From time to time, wealthier women embarked upon charity projects to help slumdwellers, but it was to little avail; as the females realize in the novel, the poor "don't need charity; they need justice" (*The House of the Spirits,* p. 136).

There was increasing pressure for government reforms to cure Chile's social ills and to forcibly increase the slow pace of its economic growth. In 1969 a left-wing alliance of socialists, communists, and radicals united to form a new political party, the Unidad Popular. The alliance named Salvador Allende, the author's uncle, as its candidate for president.

Salvador Allende. Salvador Allende had already run for president of Chile three times and lost. In 1969, however, he felt confident he would win. The people were fed up with foreign ownership of so much of their wealth (Chile's copper mines were owned mainly by two American firms, Kennecott and Anaconda). Determined to free the economy from outside control, Allende was concerned also with Chile's antiquated agricultural system. Most of the nation's wines and cereals were raised for export while many people within Chile's borders went hungry. The problem, felt Allende supporters, was in the semifeudal system of agriculture that still prevailed. Aside from bringing industries under government control, Allende set out to reform the hacienda system.

Poems and protest songs. Allende had two famous Chilean supporters: the poet Pablo Neruda and the singer Victor Jara. Neruda would win the Nobel Prize for Literature in 1971; among his poetry were lines that addressed the widespread misery and injustice in his country and on his continent. Meanwhile, Jara sang of Chile's urban poor and forgotten peasants in stirring tunes that lambasted the rich who smugly ignored the misery surrounding them. He helped popularize the New Chilean Song, or music by politically committed, innovative folksingers such as himself. Making personal appearances, both Neruda and Jara sent potent messages to the people in lyrics far more memorable than a politician's speech. Their words are said to have converted many to Allende's side.

Brief victory. Allende won the election. But instead of the usual six-year term, his presidency would end abruptly. He was the first Marxist president to be elected in the Western Hemisphere, which greatly alarmed the Nixon-occupied White House. For years the United States had been engaged in an ideological and often economic battle to discredit its main rival, the communist Soviet Union. If Allende succeeded, conservatives feared, how many other South American nations might follow in Chile's footsteps? Allende had pledged to introduce Marxist changes while preserving democracy in Chile, but Nixon, Secretary of State Henry Kissinger, and the Central Intelligence Agency were skeptical. Allende was seen as a foe.

After Allende took office, around 3,500 haciendas were appropriated by the government in the first two years. At first much of the acreage and buildings were simply converted into cooperatives run by their former tenants. But there was great disagreement about the best way to reform the countryside. Not content with the cooperatives, the government decided to meld adjoining properties into new units—Agrarian Reform Centers. Each was to turn over to the government 90 percent of the profits, and the government, in turn, would pay the peasants' wages. To the peasants, this sounded suspiciously as if the government was taking over the role of the patrón, and a mood of discontent arose. In 1971 and 1972 agrarian unions marched on Santiago, demanding that the settlements be divided into individual plots as promised. Unrest mounted, for although the government made some sweeping changes under President Allende, the result was only limited progress.

There were nongovernment takeovers in the economy too. The MIR (Movimiento Izquierdista Revolucionario), a radical group, encouraged employees to seize small businesses and farms. Chilean workers staged a truckers' strike, copper miners' strike, cab drivers' strike, shopkeepers' strike, and more. About 5,000 women participated in the March of the Empty Pots in Santiago on December 1, 1971, beating pots with spoons and sticks to protest food shortages. And there was talk of civil war; "the country had split into two irreconcilable groups, a division that began to spread within every family in the land" (*The House of the Spirits,* p. 341).

Meanwhile the Conservatives—men like the novel's Esteban Trueba—did what they could to help topple Allende's Marxist government. By mid-1973, the economy in Chile was close to collapse. Prices soared and there was a shrinking supply of locally produced goods. Many went on anxious buying binges to protect themselves from future shortages and inflation, which only further depleted the supply. There were disputes about what course of action to take, but all became moot on September 11, 1973, when the army turned on President Allende, staging a violent coup that cost him his life and became the climax of his niece's *House of the Spirits.*

The Novel in Focus

The plot. *The House of the Spirits* first introduces the wealthy del Valle family around the time of the engagement of their breathtakingly beautiful daughter Rosa to Esteban Trueba. Rosa's father, Severo, decides to run for a position in Congress, and poison intended for him by his enemies winds up killing her. Nine years later her clairvoyant younger sister, Clara, predicts, with her usual uncanny foresight, that she will soon marry Rosa's fiancé, which she does.

CHARITY OR JUSTICE?

In vain Pedro Segundo García [the overseer in the novel] . . . tried to suggest to [his patrón, Esteban Trueba] that it was not little brick houses or pints of milk that made a man a good employer . . . but rather giving his workers a decent salary instead of slips of pink paper, a workload that did not grind their bones to dust, and a little respect and dignity. Trueba would not listen to this sort of thing: it smacked, he said of Communism.

(*The House of the Spirits,* p. 63)

The novel follows the growth of their family and the fiancé's fortune. Attempting to strike it rich in the Chilean mines, the not-yet-wealthy Trueba inherits a dilapidated hacienda, Tres Marías. He retreats to Tres Marías after Rosa dies, and succeeds in turning it into a lucrative estate. Trueba prides himself on being a good patrón, the only one to build his tenants little brick houses. Yet he is an arrogant and a ruthless overlord who rapes peasants' daughters with little care for the consequences. As a result, he does not know the exact number of the children he has fathered.

Trueba's practice of forcing himself on the daughters of peasants ends when he marries the gentle, whimsical Clara del Valle, whom he comes to love desperately and whose mystical, distracted, humanitarian nature contrasts sharply with his own. She is a main repository of magical powers in the novel; Clara, for example, can make saltcellars move on a table without touching them. In her marriage, Clara bears three children: twin boys named Nicolás and Jaime, and a

Salvador Allende

daughter, Blanca. Blanca falls deeply in love with Pedro Tercero García, the son of the overseer at Tres Marías. This infuriates her father, since Pedro Tercero is not only a peasant but also a revolutionary, spreading socialist notions on the hacienda and promoting the formation of a peasant union to insist on rights such as Sundays off and a minimum wage. Pedro Tercero plays the guitar and sings about weak hens who join forces to defeat a strong fox, and his melody catches on, foreshadowing his later fame as a folksinger. He is fired from the hacienda for stirring up the peasants with his socialist ideas, which silently pleases his father, who "preferred to see his son as a fugitive than one more of the peasants planting potatoes and harvesting poverty like everyone else" (*The House of the Spirits*, p. 175).

Though fired, Pedro Tercero continues to love Esteban Trueba's daughter, Blanca. The patrón becomes murderously furious with Pedro Tercero when he learns Blanca is pregnant, and mutilates the guitar player's hand. When the gentle Clara chides her husband for his hypocrisy in the matter, he vents his rage by striking the wife he adores, who afterward never speaks to him again. Clara takes Blanca and leaves the hacienda for their house in the city, where they are eventually joined by Trueba. Trueba forces his pregnant daughter into a loveless marriage with a French count, Jean de Satigny, but Blanca finally escapes the marriage. She bears Pedro Tercero's child, a little girl named Alba, whom the gruff old Trueba comes to adore.

As Alba grows up, her father, Pedro Tercero, now also living in the capital city, gains fame for his singing and supports a socialist called "the Candidate" for president. One of Esteban's twin sons, Jaime Trueba, sides with the Candidate as well. Politics divides the family; Esteban Trueba becomes a senator for the opposing Conservative Party. Meanwhile, a large number of guests visit his house on the corner, including "the Poet," on whose knee little Alba sits without suspecting the gruesome fate that awaits them both.

Much to the surprise of the conservatives, the socialist candidate wins the presidency. His opponents, including Senator Trueba, meet with the military and with "gringos sent by their intelligence service to map a strategy for bringing down the new government: economic destabilization, as they called their sabotage" (*The House of the Spirits*, p. 342). More Chileans have jobs now than before, but suddenly there are shortages of goods—the conservatives have helped foment conditions that will breed disharmony in the nation:

> Women woke at dawn to stand in endless lines
> where they could purchase an emaciated

FICTIONAL NAME	REAL-LIFE SOURCE
The capital	Santiago, Chile
House on the corner	Home of Allende's maternal grandparents
Esteban Trueba	Allende's grandfather
Rosa the beautiful	Rose, fiancée to Allende's grandfather
Clara Trueba	Allende's grandmother
Count de Satigny	Allende's father, Tomás Allende
The Poet	Pablo Neruda
The Candidate	President Salvador Allende, an uncle
Gringos	Central Intelligence Agency operatives
A Nordic ambassador	Harold Edelstram (Swedish ambassador; marshaled over 900 Chileans to safety)

chicken, half a dozen diapers, or a roll of toilet paper. They stood in line without even knowing what was being sold, just so they would not lose a chance to buy something.

(*The House of the Spirits*, p. 347)

The shortages worsen, and unrest mounts. One day Trueba's tenants seize his hacienda and hold him hostage. After being released, Senator Trueba becomes the first to openly call for a coup to topple the socialist government. The military stages the coup, a more violent one than anybody expected. Both the President and Trueba's son Jaime die in the process. Later, Trueba's precious granddaughter, Alba, now grown, is captured and tortured by an officer of the coup, who turns out to be one of Trueba's own illegitimate grandsons. Her "crimes" include smuggling refugees into foreign embassies from which the refugees flee the country. Among the escapees are her own mother and father, Blanca Trueba and Pedro Tercero García. The now-famous folksinger escapes with the help not only of Alba but also of a chastened Esteban Trueba, who regrets his role in bringing about the brutal coup and reconciles with his one-time enemy Pedro Tercero.

The future brings more pain to the increasingly broken man, who strives in vain for his granddaughter Alba's release after her capture by the agents of the coup. Finally he collects on a debt owed to him by a clever prostitute, who effects the young girl's release. Afterward, with the help of her grandfather, Alba records the events of the past sixty odd years that comprise the novel, bringing it to a close by pointing to the connection between the past, present, and future. It may be, says Alba, re-evoking the magical element that infuses the first part of the novel, "that everything happens simultaneously" (*The House of the Spirits*, p. 432).

Clara vs. Esteban. Though male-dominated societies have long prevailed in Latin America, there are strong female characters in *The House of the Spirits*. Clara's mother, Nívea, chains herself to the gates of Congress so that women can gain the vote; not until 1952 did women actually gain full voting rights in Chile. Clara speaks about male-female equality to her husband's tenants at Tres Marías. Clara's daughter, Blanca, insists on bearing a child out of wedlock rather than being trapped in a loveless marriage. Blanca's daughter, Alba, withstands political torture. And the prostitute Tránsito Soto manages to escape poverty and to retain her dignity despite her experiences. These female characters, in one way or another, counteract the violence and searing inequality in their nation. Not only are they strong and humane, but one of them, Clara, keeps in the foreground a magical, spiritual dimension to life.

During the course of the novel, women act in ways that reflect the progress of women's rights in Chilean society. Clara's mother, described as the first feminist in the country, lived in an era when women were confined by tight-fitting corsets and the notion that a woman's duties were motherhood and the home. Clara defies these bounds. She refuses to let her husband name either of their twin sons after himself, appropriating this long-held masculine right for herself, for example. Her daughter Blanca also crosses a boundary in her love for the peasant Pedro Tercero. By the time Clara's granddaughter comes of age, women not only vote but also participate in politics. Many of them wear pants instead of corsets and otherwise ignore the previously suffocating confines placed on women. All four women, from Clara's mother Nívea down to Clara's granddaughter Alba, play increasingly daring and public roles. By the novel's end even old Senator Trueba, whose reactionary ways make him the butt of political cartoons, comes to accept that "not all women are complete idiots" and that his beloved granddaughter can one day enter a profession and "make her living like a man" (*The House of the Spirits*, p. 301). For a man who believed fervently in the sexism of his generation, this is a startling shift, achieved in large part by the actions of women across the generations in his own family.

EARTHQUAKES, VOLCANOES, AND TIDAL WAVES

Natural disasters, such as the devastating earthquake of January 1939, find their way into *The House of the Spirits*. Attacking rich and poor alike, says the novel, the quake "removed whole villages, roads, and animals. . . . The salt water from the sea ruined the crops, and fires razed whole regions of cities and towns" (*The House of the Spirits*, pp. 161-62). In real life, this quake killed at least 5,600 and left 70,000 homeless (Collier and Sater, p. 241). Earthquakes also shook Chile in 1922, 1936, 1938, 1960, 1965, and 1971 during the time of the novel. None of these, however, was as destructive as the quake of 1939.

Sources. Isabel Allende began *The House of the Spirits* as a letter to her grandfather, the model for Esteban Trueba and an old patriarch whom she loved dearly. "He had reached almost one hundred years of age and decided that he was too tired to go on living . . . I wanted to tell him that he could go in peace because all his memories were with me. I had forgotten nothing. I had all his anecdotes, all the characters of the family, and to prove it I began writing the story of Rose, the fiancée my grandfather had had" (Allende in Zinsser, pp. 41-2).

Isabel Allende experienced the 1973 coup firsthand; around a year and a half later she fled with her husband and children to Caracas, Venezuela. Living in exile, Allende began *The House of the Spirits* in 1981 both to come to terms with her own experience and as a gift for her grandfather. He died a short while after Allende began her letter to him, which grew into the five-hundred page novel that she completed in 1982.

Aside from the earthquake of 1939, there are many other parallels between episodes in the novel and real events in Chile. The folksinger Pedro Tercero has three fingers chopped off by an ax in a violent scuffle in the novel. Similarly, the famous Chilean folksinger Victor Jara lost his hands during the coup, after which he led other prisoners who had been marshalled into the grandstands in a defiant, revolutionary song. The soldiers promptly shot him, then turned their machine guns on the grandstands and began to shoot into the crowd at random. Another of the novel's characters, the Poet, lays grievously ill in his house by the sea after the coup. Soldiers break in and ransack his possessions; he dies a few days later in the capital. In real life, soldiers ransacked the Nobel prize-winning poet Pablo Neruda's house by the sea in Valparaiso. Neruda was taken to a hospital in Santiago, where he died on September 23, 1973. The coup, friends say, hastened his death. Thousands attended his funeral, an event that finds its way into the novel. In real life, in full view of the coup's machine-gun-armed soldiers, funeralgoers vowed to remember Victor Jara, Pablo Neruda, and Salvador Allende.

> ¡Pablo Neruda!
> ¡Presente! (Here!)
> ¡Ahora y siempre! (Now and forever!)
> ¡Compañero Salvador Allende!
> ¡Presente!
> ¡Ahora y siempre!
>
> (Spooner, p. 54)

Later it would be forbidden to mention the folksinger, the poet, or the former president in Chile.

Allende died on September 11, 1973, the first day of the coup. The military prepared to bomb La Moneda, the presidential palace, to smithereens. Allende insisted on making his last stand there. He ordered all the women at the palace, including his two daughters, to vacate the premises, just as the President in the novel "had to order his daughters to leave" (*The House of the Spirits*, p. 367). The military stormed the palace. "At around two o'clock that afternoon, Salvador Allende—physician,

August Pinochet

freemason, socialist, and president of the republic—shot himself through the head with a machine gun" (Collier and Sater, p. 358).

Events in History at the Time the Novel Was Written

Dictatorship. The military junta was still ruling Chile when Isabel Allende began *The House of the Spirits*. Estimates of the number killed as a result of the coup ranged from 3,000 to 30,000. Others were tortured and then dispatched to twenty concentration camps in the far north and desolate south. Yet much of the population, disbelieving the stories of the disappeared and tortured, rejoiced at the government overthrow and the new leadership of General August Pinochet. Conservative politicians, who had helped engineer the coup, presumed that Chile would shortly return to democracy or that Pinochet would at least share power with them. This was not to be the case. Haciendas were, as expected, given back to their old owners, but the government remained in Pinochet's hands with the help of the DINA, a secret police that quashed any opposition. Pinochet named himself president, and a new constitution drafted in 1980 assured

him this government position for the rest of the decade.

Decline. Chile's economy began to decline, however, and many grew dissatisfied. Under Allende people had had more money and jobs were more plentiful, though food and other goods had grown scarcer and scarcer. After the coup, these goods had miraculously reappeared on shopowners' shelves. Over the course of the Pinochet regime, however, unemployment skyrocketed, and the prices of bread, sugar, and oil soared. The population rose up, despite the brutality of the Pinochet state. In 1980 homeless families tried to set up a tent city on unused public land; they were confronted by police clubs, tear gas, and arrests. In 1981, when Allende began her novel, anti-junta activity broke out on university campuses. Roman Catholic authorities took a strong stand against the regime that same year, ruling that it would excommunicate anyone "who tortures or is an accomplice to torture" (Spooner, p. 8). Meanwhile, the economy continued to decline. Unemployment escalated to 30 percent in 1982, and monthly demonstrations began in 1983. Again thousands were arrested, beaten, and subjected to electrode torture. At the same time, some began to smuggle *The House of the Spirits* into Chile. The novel, says Allende, "entered like a pirate, hidden in suitcases of daring travelers. . . . The few issues . . . this way multiplied as if by magic" (Allende in Flores, p. 29).

Reception. A number of critics faulted Allende's novel, arguing that it bore too close a resemblance to elements in the South American masterpiece *One Hundred Years of Solitude* by Gabriel García Márquez (also covered in *Literature and Its Times*). Other critics countered that Allende's novel was "an original and important work . . . one of the best novels of the postwar period, and a major contribution to our understanding of societies riddled by ceaseless conflict and violent change" (Bruce in Hall, pp. 37-8). Generally the book impressed critics as a worthy, compelling read.

A few reviewers criticized the novel for weaving elements of magic into the first few hundred pages, then breaking off into more journalistic writing in the chapters during the coup. P. Gabrielle Foreman argues, however, that the novel astutely maneuvers within the realms of magic and politics. While it engages the reader in a family saga with elements of magic—a familiar form for Latin American novels—its ultimate allegiance "is to the political and historical" (Foreman in Zamora and Faris, pp. 294-95).

For More Information

Allende, Isabel. *The House of the Spirits.* Translated by Magda Bogin. New York: Bantam, 1982.

Chavkin, Samuel. *Storm over Chile: The Junta under Siege.* Chicago: Lawrence Hill, 1982.

Collier, Simon, and William F. Sater. *A History of Chile: 1808-1994.* London: Cambridge University Press, 1996.

Davis, Nathaniel. *The Last Two Years of Salvador Allende.* Ithaca, N.Y.: H. W. Wilson, 1992.

Flores, Angel. *Spanish American Authors: The Twentieth Century.* New York: H. W. Wilson, 1992.

Hall, Sharon K., ed. *Contemporary Literary Criticism.* Vol. 39. Detroit: Gale Research, 1986.

Spooner, Mary Helen. *Soldiers in a Narrow Land: The Pinochet Regime in Chile.* Berkeley: University of California Press, 1994.

Zamora, Lois Parkinson, and Wendy B. Faris, eds. *Magical Realism: Theory, History, Community.* Durham, N.C.: Duke University Press, 1995.

Zinsser, William, ed. *Paths of Resistance: The Art and Craft of the Political Novel.* Boston: Houghton Mifflin, 1989.

The House on Mango Street

by
Sandra Cisneros

Sandra Cisneros was born in Chicago in 1954. Though she traveled often to Mexico City, she was raised primarily in Chicago barrios that "appeared like France after World War II—empty lots and burned out buildings" (Telgen and Kamp, p. 99). Life in the impoverished neighborhoods of Cisneros's youth revealed both hard truths and windows of opportunity: the social and economic hurdles faced by Mexican Americans, especially women, and the possibilities of surmounting those hurdles and changing the lives of individuals and the community. In *The House on Mango Street* Cisneros illustrates the development of an individual and a community. The novel exposes the adversity and prejudice encountered on a daily basis and also reveals the ability of individuals to combat these obstacles without relinquishing cultural identity.

Events in History at the Time of the Novel

Chicano movement. In the 1960s there arose a cultural, political, and social revolution in the Mexican American community. The decade's intense focus on civil rights issues in an effort to change attitudes and win equal treatment under the law for minorities in the nation evolved into distinct movements, as was the case with Spanish-speaking residents of the United States. Though its roots stretched back to the 1940s, the Chicano movement came to flourish during the 1960s under the leadership of activists like César Chávez, founder of the National Farm Workers

Association in 1962 (later known as the United Farm Workers). The very name given to the movement signified an affirmation of Mexican American heritage, the term "Chicano" (masculine) or "Chicana" (feminine) deriving from the ending of *Mexicano* as pronounced by the ancient Aztecs ("Mech-i-ca-no"). With this name, asserts author Rudolfo Anaya, the Chicanos "took on a new awareness of their place in society" (Anaya in Lopez, p. 6). No longer willing to accept roles as outsiders in an Anglo-dominated nation, Chicanos took pride in their heritage and promoted public awareness of their history and contemporary concerns.

Prior to the Chicano rights movement, U.S. history was taught almost exclusively from a European male perspective. This perspective excludes the long history of the native Indians in the Southwest, Mexico, and Central America, the population that, along with Spanish settlers, eventually gave rise to a mixed Spanish American civilization. This mixed civilization, which

Chicanos claim as their heritage in the Americas, predates the first Anglo settlements of the late 1500s and early 1600s.

Chicano consciousness-raising efforts during the 1960s centered on public recognition of Chicano accomplishments and on inclusion of Chicano cultural, social, and political material in school curricula. Bilingual education, Chicano studies programs in public schools, and affirmative action employment practices emerged as important battlefronts. Other Chicano activists protested unfair labor practices; staged hunger strikes, sit-ins, and boycotts; and lobbied for political and social changes such as increased Chicano representation in Congress and minimum-wage guarantees for migrant workers.

Mestizo or mixed-race heritage. In the early 1500s, Spanish explorers and conquistadores arrived in present-day Mexico and the southwestern United States. The conquistadores vanquished the native inhabitants, toppled the Aztec empire, and spread their influence throughout the Americas. They imposed Roman Catholicism on the local populations and instituted Spanish as the primary language. There followed a blending of Indian and Spanish cultures to form a new "mestizo" or mixed race, whose members played a large part in colonizing today's southwestern United States from central Mexico. They established their first colony in Sante Fe (present-day New Mexico) in 1598.

The Spanish crown's control over its colonies had disintegrated by the nineteenth century, and independence was awarded to Mexico in 1821. The new Mexican empire included the formerly Spanish-held areas in what is now the southwestern United States. Eventually this territory became an issue of dispute between the United States and Mexico. The Treaty of Guadalupe Hidalgo, which was signed at the end of the Mexican American War in 1848, had the immediate result of ceding the Southwest to the United States; its more long-term effect was to fragment the Mexican community across an imposed border. Though the Southwest became U.S. territory, its language ties and cultural identity remained strongly Spanish, Mexican, and native Indian.

As the United States became more industrialized and prosperous, Mexican Americans from the Southwest and Mexican immigrants from Mexico migrated to cities and farms across the nation. Most, however, remained in the Southwest, living in California, Texas, New Mexico, Colorado, and Arizona. Today's Chicano com-

Américo Paredes, one of the pioneers of the Chicano literary renaissance.

munity includes descendants of the early immigrants from central Mexico and of later Spanish, native Indian, and mestizo immigrants.

Chicano Renaissance. During the 1960s and 1970s a Chicano literary renaissance emerged as a result of the Chicano civil rights movement. Américo Paredes and José Antonio Villarreal were two pioneers of this renaissance. Their work was among the first to document the Chicano experience in America and to bring Chicano social and political concerns to the forefront in the nation. Luis Valdez, who founded El Teatro Campesino in 1965, contributed to the movement by staging plays documenting the abysmal working conditions endured by migrant farm workers. The first anthology of Chicano literature—published by Chicanos—was produced in 1969. Called *El Espejo* (The Mirror), the compilation includes work of Chicana writers and features Chicano legends and myths rather than those of Anglo-American society. This Chicano literary and artistic renaissance exposed mainstream American society to Chicano perspectives and experiences; its end result was to profoundly influence race relations as well as the political and social status of those in the Mexican American community.

Chicana writers. While writings by Chicanos gained prominence in literary circles, works by Chicanas were largely unpublished until the 1980s. Facing race- and gender-based discrimination both within and outside their community, Chicana writers were slow to reach a mainstream readership. Through the 1970s most Chicana literature was published by small presses or in regional magazines. Author Marta Sánchez explained how Chicana women have been faced with a double set of social restrictions: Chicanas, like Chicanos, had to contend with racial discrimination in general society, and both there and within their own community the Chicanas had to deal with sexual discrimination. They took on the formidable task of overcoming these dual restrictions in the 1980s. Chicana writers "explored the social and the political, looked for role models in their literary heritage, fought back at what they saw as an oppressive dominant society, and came together as a consciously awakened group of women" (Rebolledo and Rivero, p. 24).

Sandra Cisneros is one of the pioneering authors whose work brought Chicana concerns to light and opened the door for others. First published in 1984 by Arte Público Press, *The House on Mango Street* did not, despite its critical acclaim, lead to a major publishing contract until 1991, when Random House contracted for the novel. Though Cisneros has been designated as the first Chicana to land such a contract, her long wait in achieving it illustrates the continuing struggle of Chicanas to succeed in an Anglo- and male-dominated society.

Machismo and women's roles in the Chicano community. The term *machismo* has been defined as the need of the male to prove his virility or courage by daring action. Patriarchal cultures, such as both Mexican and American societies, have been natural conduits for the perpetuation of machismo behavior. Promotion of machismo sentiment subtly encourages women to take submissive roles and to let men dictate action. The imposition of Roman Catholicism by Spanish conquerors, and the devout nature of many Mexicans, has been a significant element in perpetuating this attitude. Particularly in the Mexican culture women have been expected to marry, bear children, tend to the home and family, and in general assume a subordinate position in relation to the men of the household. Despite strides made in the Chicano civil rights movement, such limitations were slow to die out. If women attended college, it was to find "a nice

professional" man to marry—as was expected of Cisneros (Telgen and Kamp, p. 100).

Yet machismo attitudes also retain a less obvious facet. While the machismo behavior promotes an outward appearance of male dominance, women have generally been the ones to head households in Mexican families. They nurture other family members, attend church in the largest numbers, and preserve cultural traditions. Meanwhile, machismo has served to separate men and women, preventing extensive social interaction between them. This is shown repeatedly in *The House on Mango Street*. The book's protagonist, Esperanza Cordero, almost exclusively associates with other women and girls.

Two archetypical role models for women in Mexican culture are the Virgin de Guadalupe and La Malinche. They both illustrate strong positive and negative images in the culture and show the limited stereotypes attached to women. The Virgin de Guadalupe (an incarnation of the Virgin Mary) is the patron saint of the underclass; she is associated with positive attributes—unselfishness and devoted motherhood. According to legend, her origins date back to 1531 when Juan Diego, an Indian convert to Christianity, visited a site once devoted to the Aztec Mother of the Gods and had a vision of the brown-skinned Virgin that would replace her. La Malinche, an Aztec woman, was the mistress of the sixteenth-century Spanish explorer Hernando Cortés; her name became associated with the conqueror, and she came to symbolize someone who betrays his or her people. These archetypes have long perpetuated the misidentification of women as either wholly pure and good or wholly tainted and evil. Progressive ideas have served to loosen the absoluteness of the images somewhat. The Virgin de Guadalupe, an advocate of the acceptance of one's lot, has in more recent times come to be viewed with some disfavor as not being active enough on behalf of the underclass. Meanwhile, the other archetype, La Malinche, has been reappraised and newly admired for her shrewdness and ability to survive.

Through their stories, Chicana writers such as Sandra Cisneros, while acknowledging the strength of these female archetypes, are combating the one-dimensional notion of Mexican American women and demolishing the good-or-evil stereotype. In her story "Woman Hollering Creek," Cisneros has a woman leave her abusive husband in order to preserve herself, and in so doing conveys a more complex image of women than the stereotypes allow. *The House on Mango Street* also helps redefine the old myths and create new ones, shattering the illusion of the one-dimensional Chicana. It is part of a more general goal the author aims to reach through her stories. As Cisneros explained to *Publishers Weekly,* "I'm trying to write the stories that haven't been written" and describe "as many different kinds of Latinos as possible so that mainstream America [can] see how diverse we are" (Cisneros in Telgen and Kamp, p. 99).

Chicago barrio life. After World War II, Chicago experienced a surge of immigration, with Mexicans comprising its fourth largest immigrant group. Over time, urban decay came to plague large sections of the city. In the 1940s, twenty-three acres of slums had been cleared but never rebuilt. Other blighted areas endured, and the problem grew. Dr. Martin Luther King Jr. chose the ghettos of Chicago as the rallying point for his 1966 civil rights campaign in the North. He called the city's slums evidence and cause of the Northern race problem because they segregated society and allowed the working and lower classes to live in abysmal surroundings while the upper and middle classes could afford to retreat to the safety of the suburbs. In the 1970s Chicago's inner city population declined by more than 10 percent as the upper and middle classes fled to the suburbs. In *The House on Mango Street* Esperanza describes this trend, noting that the white neighbors "move a little farther north from Mango Street, a little farther away every time people like us keep moving in" (Cisneros, *The House on Mango Street*, p. 13).

College and increased opportunities for women. The women's movement coincided with the Chicano and general civil rights movements during the 1960s and 1970s. Equal opportunities for the female half of the population stood at the forefront of the movement, especially in the areas of education and employment. Arguing that women need meaningful careers, recognition as primary caretakers of children, and equal pay for equal work, a group of three hundred men and women—led by Betty Friedan—formed the National Organization for Women (NOW) in 1966. In 1967 the United Nations adopted a Declaration of Women's Rights, which states that discrimination based on gender violates the UN charter. Among other provisions, the declaration calls for universal suffrage, the right for women to hold office, protection of the family, guarantee of women's property rights, and equal pay for

equal work. As a result of the women's movement, college enrollment and the awarding of advanced degrees among women increased sharply. By 1975, 40 percent of college graduates were women and 50 percent of women held jobs outside the home.

Chicana activism. Modern American feminism arose out of the dissatisfaction of a cross-section of women who were primarily white, educated, and middle-class. In its early days the movement paid relatively little attention to the concerns of working-class and minority women. Consequently Chicanas developed their own power base by forming groups, and also by writing. They held meetings (such as 1971's National Chicana Conference), organized into groups (for example, Texas's Mexican American Business and Professional Women of Austin), and started journals (*Regeneracion, Fuego de Aztlan,* and *Imagines de la Chicana,* among others).

Chicana activists, it has been argued, perhaps do not reject long-established female roles as vehemently as non-Chicana feminists. In keeping with this argument, one writer contends that evident in Chicana society today is "an emphasis on a new female ideal, a woman who respects men, the family, and the home but combines this with better opportunities for work outside the home and active social and political commitment to the larger Mexicano community" (Mason in Melville, p. 106).

The Novel in Focus

The plot. Told in a series of vignettes, *The House on Mango Street* chronicles the childhood development of Esperanza Cordero. The novel moves from a tale about Esperanza's family to other vignettes about friends and neighbors to still others about the changes in Esperanza's body and her first job. Through these short anecdotes, Esperanza shares her world in bits and pieces that convey a cumulative impression of herself and her community.

Esperanza is a young Chicana growing up in a Chicago barrio. Her family of six lives in a house on Mango Street that is anything but the home of her dreams. Better than her family's previous flat on Loomis Street, "the house on Mango Street is [nonetheless] not the way they told it at all," Esperanza says. "They always told us that one day we would move into a house, a real house that would be ours for always and so that we wouldn't have to move each year. . . . But this isn't it. . . . For the time being, Mama says. Temporary, says Papa. But I know how those things go" (*The House on Mango Street,* pp. 4-5).

From the outset the reader realizes that Esperanza—whose name literally means "hope"—is a dreamer, wise beyond her years and determined to better her life. She lives on Mango Street but refuses to be restricted by the limitations of poverty, gender, or race. Very aware of her surroundings, Esperanza finds hope and takes comfort in simple aspects of life—even in something as simple as her mother's hair:

> My mother's hair, like little rosettes . . . sweet to put your nose into when she's holding you, holding you and you feel safe, is the warm smell of bread before you bake it, is the smell when she makes room for you on her side of the bed still warm with her skin.
>
> (*The House on Mango Street,* pp. 6-7)

Esperanza grows up fast. She attends Catholic school and experiences shame and shyness associated both with her age and her economic status. But she refuses to be subdued by either. For the time being she is "a red balloon, a balloon tied to an anchor" but one day she will be free to fly wherever she wishes and show her brilliant colors to the world (*The House on Mango Street,* p. 9).

Esperanza is searching for her identity. She wonders who she is and who she will become. All around her are examples of what others have chosen. She sees the women on her street, trapped in their houses, always looking out their windows. She sees her friend, Marin, who marries to get away from Mango Street but winds up being equally repressed in another neighborhood. She sees a neighbor, Alicia, who is attending college. At first she considers Alicia somewhat snooty, but later changes her opinion:

> Alicia, who inherited her mama's rolling pin and sleepiness, is young and smart and studies for the first time at the university. Two trains and a bus, because she doesn't want to spend her whole life in a factory or behind a rolling pin.
>
> (*The House on Mango Street,* pp. 31-2)

Closer to home, Esperanza sees the hard work of her parents and listens to the regrets of her mother, who quit school and laments "I could've been somebody" (*The House on Mango Street,* p. 90). Finally, Esperanza witnesses domestic violence in her neighborhood and at first concludes, "I don't belong. I don't ever want to come from here" (*The House on Mango Street,* p. 106). But then she recognizes that she does come from Mango Street and that she can be the one who

Sandra Cisneros

improves life there. Surely, she decides, the mayor will not.

As Esperanza enters womanhood, she is both pleased and discouraged by this development. "Who here is ready?" she asks, and soon becomes very disheartened by her first encounters with the opposite sex (*The House on Mango Street,* p. 50). A boy attacks her, and she loses her virginity. Male-female relations are not at all like the fairy tales promised they would be, and she feels deceived. "They all lied," she cries. "All the books and magazines, everything . . . told it wrong" (*The House on Mango Street,* p. 100).

Her years of observation and questioning lead Esperanza into determining her own fate. She refuses to accept a life of poverty or subordination, deciding instead to make a house—in other words, a life of her own choosing. Her writing, she realizes, is her way out. It releases her sometimes even while she is still in the barrio. Esperanza resolves one day to pack up her bags of books and papers and leave the neighborhood. As the novel explains, she was a girl who didn't want to belong but then recognized how strongly she does. In the end Esperanza decides to go "away to come back. For the ones I left behind. For the ones who cannot out"—that is, for the ones who cannot leave the barrio as easily as Esperanza (*The House on Mango Street*, p. 110).

The power of naming. *The House on Mango Street* calls attention to the power of naming. Naming is a symbol of ownership, of power over circumstances and situations, an activity that confers cultural and social identity on the named. Historically women and minorities have been deprived of it, and *The House on Mango Street* returns it to them. The vignette entitled "Geraldo No Last Name" shows the anonymity and negative stereotypes produced from lack of familiarity with a name and therefore a person. Geraldo is a recent immigrant. He has no identification, no friends with him. He is killed in an auto accident and no one can identify him. He is called "a brazer [worker] who didn't speak English" and "just another wetback" (*The House on Mango Street*, p. 66). Bystanders wonder why he was out so late at night and insinuate that he

---

CISNEROS REVEALS WHAT DRIVES HER

I write about those ghosts inside that haunt me, that will not let me sleep, of that which even memory does not like to mention. . . . Perhaps later there will be a time to write by inspiration. In the meantime, in my writing as well as in that of other Chicanas and other women, there is the necessary phase of dealing with those ghosts and voices most urgently haunting us, day by day.

(Cisneros in Matuz, p. 144)

---

was doing something wrong. Because he is unnamed, he is unknown. Because he is unknown there is little sympathy for his death. The novel shares with the reader details withheld from others in the novel.

> They never saw the kitchenettes. They never knew about the tworoom flats and sleeping rooms he rented, the weekly money orders sent home, the currency exchange. How could they?
> (*The House on Mango Street*, p. 66)

"They" didn't even know his last name. The episode shows the importance of claiming identity and the vital role it plays in eliminating stereotypes and prejudice, a point emphasized throughout the novel. Elsewhere in *The House on Mango Street* Esperanza and her friends talk about cultural identities and about how each so-

ciety names things differently, according to tradition and importance of the person or object to the culture:

> The Eskimos got thirty different names for snow, I say. . . .
>
> I got a cousin, Rachel says. She got three different names.
>
> There ain't thirty different kinds of snow, Lucy says. There are two kinds. The clean kind and the dirty kind. . . .
>
> There are a million zillion kinds, says Nenny. No two exactly alike. . . .
>
> She got three last names and, let me see, two first names. One in English and one in Spanish. . . .
> (*The House on Mango Street*, p. 35)

In the nineteenth and early twentieth centuries, distinct or hard-to-pronounce foreign names of immigrants were often altered by U.S. immigration officials, or were later Americanized by the immigrants themselves in an effort to assimilate. For years the "melting pot" cliché had become part of popular American mythology, the idea that many cultures combined and became homogenized into a larger American society, creating a standard "American" identity. In the 1960s and 1970s, there was a backlash against this idea. Reformers encouraged Americans to embrace individuality, to recognize society as a "salad bowl" rather than a melting pot, to celebrate the cultural differences among its inhabitants. *The House on Mango Street*, written during an era of growing acceptance of cultural differences, reflects the pride Americans had begun to take in their own ethnicity, and their acknowledgment of their ethnic roots as an integral part of their identity.

Sources. *The House on Mango Street* is based on the author's own childhood. Cisneros grew up in the barrios of Chicago with seven older brothers who generally "teamed up and excluded me from their games" (Cisneros in Telgen and Kamp, p. 99). The family moved frequently and, feeling like an outcast from her relations and friends, Cisneros retreated inside herself. To escape, she read a great deal, and wrote poetry and stories. One of her favorite books was *The Little House* by Virginia Lee Burton. The idea of writing about her own house and childhood experiences dawned on her in college while she was attending the Iowa Writers' Workshop. As the class was discussing Gaston Bachelard's *The Poetics of Space*, she observed: "Everyone seemed to have some kind of communal knowledge which I did not have" (Cisneros in Matuz, p. 143). Her fellow students came from upper-class backgrounds and had attended some of the best schools in the country. They described lavish childhood houses with attics and garages and sprawling lawns. Cisneros's childhood homes were a far cry from those the other students described. It was at this point that she realized she was in a very unique position to write about her experiences as a Chicana from the barrios of Chicago.

Reviews. Despite its original publication by the small Arte Público press of New Mexico, *The House on Mango Street* received a relatively fair amount of media attention and garnered positive reviews for its style and content. Writing in *Booklist,* Penelope Mesic called it "refreshing and authentic, vivid in its metaphors . . . exact in its observations, and full of vitality" (Mesic in Matuz, p. 144). Julian Olivares commented that Cisneros had managed to treat an unpoetic subject "poetically" (Olivares in Matuz, p. 145). More than one reviewer has praised Cisneros's ability to tell a fine story with a spare use of prose. On the whole, her stories would later be described as essential to American society for the inside view they provide of Chicano lives.

For More Information

Cisneros, Sandra. *The House on Mango Street.* 1984. Reprint. New York: Random House, Vintage Books, 1991.

Cisneros, Sandra. *Woman Hollering Creek and Other Stories.* New York: Random House, 1991.

Lopez, Tiffany Ana. *Growing Up Chicana/o.* New York: William Morrow, 1993.

Matuz, Roger, ed. *Contemporary Literary Criticism.* Vol. 69. Detroit: Gale Research, 1992.

Melville, Margarita B., ed. *Twice a Minority: Mexican American Women.* St. Louis: C.V. Mosby, 1980.

Rebolledo, Tey Diana, and Eliana S. Rivero, comps. *Infinite Divisions: An Anthology of Chicana Literature.* Tucson, Ariz.: University of Arizona Press, 1993.

Shorris, Earl. *Latinos: A Biography of the People.* New York: W. W. Norton, 1992.

Telgen, Diane, and Jim Kamp, eds. *Notable Hispanic American Women.* Detroit: Gale Research, 1993.

Hunger of Memory

by
Richard Rodriguez

Richard Rodriguez was born on July 31, 1944, to Mexican immigrants Leopoldo and Victoria Rodriguez. In spite of the difficulties he faced as a Spanish-speaking child in the United States, Rodriguez excelled in school and eventually earned a Ph.D. in English literature. In 1976, rather than accept one of many job offers from prestigious universities, Rodriguez postponed a career as a professor. Although confident in the quality of his work, he could not quiet the suspicion that universities sought him primarily because he was a member of an ethnic minority. Rodriguez spent the next six years writing his autobiography, *Hunger of Memory*.

Events in History at the Time of the Autobiography

The postwar Mexican American community. Like many other segments of American society, Mexican American culture experienced numerous changes as a result of World War II. The drafting of an enormous segment of the male population sent many Mexican American youths to war, but since such a large number of American soldiers were sent overseas, a vacuum in the labor force was created. This caused a sudden growth in Mexican immigration to the United States. They came under the Bracero Program, which permitted Mexican laborers to enter the United States temporarily to join work crews on farms and in urban industries.

Both the permanent residents and the braceros suffered anti-Mexican discrimination

THE LITERARY WORK

An autobiography set in California, New York, and England from the 1940s to the 1970s; published in 1982.

SYNOPSIS

As he pursues his academic career, Richard Rodriguez, a child of Mexican immigrants to the United States, ponders how his education has distanced him from his parents. In the course of his reflections he articulates his attitude toward the debates concerning both affirmative action and bilingual education programs in education.

that persisted in the postwar years. Public facilities like swimming pools denied access to Mexicans or limited their and other minorities' use of the pool until the day before the water was drained to prevent "contamination" (Camarillo, p. 79). Movie theaters at the time restricted Mexican Americans to separate seating sections, and schools practiced segregation. In California the school segregation lasted ostensibly until it was outlawed by *Méndez v. Westminster* in 1946, yet little could be done after that to end de facto segregation. Mexican American families mostly lived in segregated neighborhoods, and so their children continued to attend segregated schools as the decades progressed. Meanwhile, more than two-thirds of the community's males and almost

"The Great Wall of Los Angeles": mural by Judy Baca.

as many females continued to labor in unskilled or semiskilled jobs, making only modest progress in the 1950s, when Richard Rodriguez was coming of age.

The 1960s promised to hasten change. While Mexican Americans had begun organizing on their own behalf in earlier decades, they did so in much greater numbers in the 1960s, giving birth to a genuine Chicano movement. Statistics were published showing that the high school dropout rate for Mexican Americans had reached 50 percent in many areas, while the poverty level in Spanish surname households was twice that of Anglo households. Community activists resolved to change these realities.

From the 1960s into the 1970s Chicano artists and writers championed their Mexican heritage and exposed the plight of Mexican Americans, painting murals on barrio walls and performing plays such as Luis Valdez's *Zoot Suit* (also covered in *Literature and Its Times*). Determined to win decent working conditions, farm laborers, led by César Chávez, went on strike in 1965 in a protest that received great public attention and support. At the same time there arose numerous Chicano community organizations that addressed immediate concerns such as job training and education. In the 1970s the Mexican American Legal Defense and Education Fund (MALDEF), un-

der the leadership of Vilma Martínez, battled a number of issues in the courts over school desegregation, job discrimination, and bilingual education. Other activists, expressing concern about the relatively few Chicanos among the country's college and university population, pressed for special admission programs and federal grants or loans. And at the high school level, the Los Angeles teacher Salvador Castro led a protest in 1968 against overcrowded classrooms, too few Mexican American teachers, and a curriculum that ignored the contributions of Mexican Americans. Nearly 10,000 students joined him.

All these efforts produced results. Chicano studies programs appeared on college campuses and the number of Chicano faculty increased. Nevertheless, the high school dropout rate remained high, with nearly half of all Chicano students leaving high school before graduation and less than 20 percent continuing on to the college or university level in the mid-1970s, which is the last decade in which *Hunger of Memory* takes place.

Bilingual education. During the late 1960s and throughout the 1970s educators and legislators in the United States debated the issue of bilingual education. Whereas some recent immigrants, most of Hispanic or Asian decent, argued that the nation had an obligation to educate their children in their own native language, advocates of "English only" responded that English is the nation's official language and that new immigrants to the United States should, like those who came before them, learn English. It is, in fact, a misconception that English is the nation's official language—the United States has no official language, though English is dominant.

During the early decades of the twentieth century, an influx of immigrants from southern and eastern Europe as well as China and Japan roused xenophobic sentiment in the United States. There was a reactionary debate about the potentially "harmful" effect of such immigration on American culture. During World War I, as anti-German sentiment swept the nation, advocates of a law making English the official language exploited this paranoia to convince legislators to pass decrees banning the use of German in classrooms, public meetings, and even in church. (These decrees affected laws that had been passed by various states in the 1800s, allowing schools to hold classes in German, Norwegian, or Spanish.) Wartime anxiety fomented an intolerance of all minority languages. Thirty-four states forbade the use of any language other than English in the classroom. Several states even outlawed foreign language study in the elementary grades. In 1924 Congress went so far as to establish immigration quotas favorable to applicants from northwestern Europe and to explicitly bar immigration from Asia.

In 1965, however, immigration reform legislation was passed by Congress that revoked the edicts of 1924 and raised the ceiling on the number of immigrants; it also gave preference to applicants with relatives already residing in the United States. The result was a dramatic increase in the number of immigrants from Latin America and Asia. Between 1971 and 1980, Latin American immigrants comprised 40 percent of the legal immigrants to the United States, and Asian arrivals comprised 35 percent.

During the political and social turmoil of the 1960s many of politically conscious Hispanics and Asians, encouraged by the civil rights movement among African Americans, began to emphasize, rather than downplay, ethnic solidarity and cultural differences. The Hispanic activists argued that there was a need for either bilingual education in the public schools or at least supplementary English classes for minority language students. Bolstering their argument was a 1965-66 survey by the National Education Association that documented the high failure and dropout rates among Hispanic American students in Tucson, Arizona.

In 1968 President Lyndon B. Johnson responded by signing the Bilingual Education Act to aid children who were "educationally disadvantaged because of their inability to speak English" (Crawford, p. 40). Although Senator Ralph Yarborough, the sponsor of the act, had insisted that his intention was to make children fully literate in English, many Hispanic activists viewed the ruling as an endorsement of bilingual programs. A debate arose between sides—one who favored children's attending classes in both English and their parents' tongue until graduation, and the other who favored programs that stressed rapid acquisition of English.

In 1974 the Supreme Court set the legal precedent on the matter with the ruling on the *Lau v. Nichols* case. Kinney Lau, a Chinese father distressed because his son was failing in school, had, with the help of attorney Edward Steinman, filed a class-action suit claiming that his child had been denied the "education on equal terms" (Crawford, p. 44) guaranteed by the *Brown v. Board of Education* ruling of 1954. The court agreed unanimously that, in the words of Justice William O. Douglas, "there is no equality of treatment . . . merely by providing students with the same facilities, textbooks, teachers and curriculum; for students who do not understand English are effectively foreclosed from any meaningful education" (Douglas in Crawford, p. 45).

By the time the Supreme Court decided the case, the plaintiffs had dropped their original demand for bilingual education, so the court never proceeded to delineate or deal with the question of what steps local schools should take to effect it. The Department of Education, however, issued guidelines in favor of a bilingual curriculum, which were used by the Office for Civil Rights to negotiate with local schools when they perceived the curriculum inadequate for minority language students. Faced with the prospect of losing federal funding, local schools had little choice but to comply. In various schools through the nation, and particularly in California, students began to attend classes in both English and another language, usually Spanish.

By the late 1970s, attitudes toward bilingual education had shifted. Various surveys suggested that bilingual programs did not help language minority students; moreover, they led to voluntary segregation among the students. In 1978 Congress responded to this and other disturbing news about the programs by passing amendments to the Bilingual Education Act. A language other than English could be used, Congress specified, only "to the extent necessary to allow a child to achieve competence in the English language" (Crawford, p. 51). All language programs were to be strictly transitional, rather than actually bilingual.

Bilingual education suffered even greater setbacks during the eight-year conservative administration of President Ronald Reagan.

> "I think it is proper," said the president, "that we have teachers equipped who can get at them in their own language and understand why it is they don't get the answer to the problem and help them in that way. But it is absolutely wrong and against American concepts to have a bilingual education program that is now openly, admittedly dedicated to preserving their native language and never getting them adequate in English."
>
> (Reagan in Crawford, p. 53)

During the Reagan years, funding for education in general would drop 8 percent and spending related to bilingual education would drop 46 percent.

Affirmative action. The Supreme Court's ruling in the 1954 *Brown v. Board of Education* case not only abolished segregation in the nation's public schools, but also paved the way for a proliferation of civil rights legislation, including the Civil Rights Act of 1964. The culmination of a decade of protests and activism, this act made illegal virtually all forms of discrimination in public places on the basis of color, race, religion, sex, or national origin. The 1972 amendments to the act ensured that, from a legal standpoint, such discrimination was an injustice of the past.

Yet despite the legislation and other legal measures, discrimination still remained a problem within American society. Indeed, as civil rights activists shifted the focus of their movement from the South to the North, they began to perceive that legal equality hardly guaranteed practical equality. They realized, as Rodriguez points out, that even though no official restrictions denied blacks access to northern universities, for example, this freedom was mostly theoretical. Universities such as Princeton had long been open to blacks. "But the tiny number of nonwhite students . . . at such schools suggested that there was more . . . to consider" (Rodriguez, *Hunger of Memory*, p. 144)

To remedy this problem, civil rights activists and legislators devised "affirmative action" programs. This mandated that universities receiving public funds (and likewise, government contractors) give preferential treatment to minorities and women in admissions and hiring; it also specified that the institutions set timetables to eventually achieve a level of campus integration proportionate to the general population. The intention was to compensate for past discrimination.

Advocates of affirmative action met strident opposition. Skeptics disparaged the programs, calling affirmative action "reverse discrimination." They insisted that both colleges and employers were simply filling quotas with sometimes unqualified candidates. Moreover, they argued that it was unfair for contemporary Caucasians to be forced to compensate for the crimes of their forefathers.

In 1977 the Supreme Court addressed some of this debate over affirmative action in the case of *University of California Regents v. Bakke*. Allan Bakke, a white, middle-class engineer, had applied to medical school at the University of California at Davis and been rejected. Angered, Bakke challenged the legality of the admissions program at UC-Davis, which reserved sixteen out of one hundred slots for minorities. The Supreme Court ruled that, in this particular case, Bakke had been unfairly discriminated against because of his race. The practice of setting aside a number of slots exclusively for minorities was, according to the court, unconstitutional. This ruling did not, however, challenge the legitimacy of all affirmative action programs. The court agreed, in a split decision, that a culturally deprived or disadvantaged applicant may, in spite of low scores on standardized tests, show more promise than an applicant from an affluent or educated background. Thus, affirmative action programs remained legal for the time being, though the *Bakke* ruling would stay controversial long after the publication of *Hunger of Memory*.

The Autobiography in Focus

The plot. Richard Rodriguez grew up the son of Mexican immigrants in Sacramento, California. His parents had settled in the United States hoping to find prosperous work and build a home for their children. They soon discovered that both their lack of formal education and the pervasive stereotypes concerning Hispanic Americans made it difficult for them to secure comfortable jobs. Rodriguez's mother worked as a typist, and his father at a succession of warehouse, cannery, and factory jobs.

As the only Hispanic student in his Roman Catholic elementary school, Richard remained more than normally timid and hesitated to speak when called upon. Disturbed by the boy's silence, one of the teachers met with his parents to suggest that they speak English at home in order to improve their children's chances of doing well in school. Richard's parents resolved to follow the teacher's advice, though they feared English would be more difficult for them than for their children.

The strategy worked. Yet while the clever children learned quickly, their parents stumbled over difficult words. Growing confident, Richard even began to volunteer to speak in class. His parents, however, encumbered by their years, did not pick up the language as rapidly. Richard noticed that when speaking English, he had to talk to his father slowly and select simple words.

As they grew older the Rodriguez children often challenged their parents' ideas. "It's what we were taught in our time to believe" (*Hunger of Memory*, p. 57), their mother answered when her kids disputed her convictions. She often mumbled that little children ought not to play with big ideas. More acute than these complaints was her objection that the children were growing distant. Often they would excuse themselves from the dinner table to retreat to their rooms and study, or pass their afternoons at the homes of white school friends. "Why aren't we close anymore," Richard's mother would wonder, "more in the Mexican style?" (*Hunger of Memory*, p. 57). What Richard began to understand is that he had grown fluent not only in a language but also in a lifestyle that would remain foreign to his parents.

After graduating high school, Richard elected to study at Stanford, a university about 100 miles away. He completed an undergraduate degree in English literature, then enrolled at Columbia University in New York, where he earned a master's degree. He subsequently returned to the West Coast, earning a Ph.D. at the University of California at Berkeley.

In order to do research for his dissertation, Richard journeyed to England. During his stay he began to realize that his decision to pursue an academic career was to some extent an act of social withdrawal. He was writing with a handful of academics throughout the world. "We formed an exclusive—eccentric!—society," he realized (*Hunger of Memory*, p. 66). Richard felt particularly distant from his parents, who, he thought, might chuckle if they read the title of his dissertation on genre and Renaissance literature.

One day, a pang of nostalgia swept over Richard as he overheard some scholars at the British Museum speaking in hushed Spanish whispers, and he resolved to return home to visit his parents. Back in Sacramento, Richard took comfort in the many similarities between his parents and himself, which he had not previously noticed. He realized that he laughed like his mother and that he had his father's watchful eyes. Yet he remained troubled by another realization—this very practice of noting the similarities between himself and his parents indicated how much he remained an academic. He was behaving like "a kind of anthropologist in the family kitchen, searching for evidence of our 'cultural ties' as we ate dinner" (*Hunger of Memory*, p. 160).

Richard returned to the academic world to find that, although he had not yet finished his dissertation, he had received job offers from prestigious universities. He had become the beneficiary of affirmative action programs. Hiring committees were vying for the qualified minority candidates in an effort to comply with affirmative action, which troubled him because he felt that he "was not really more socially disadvantaged than the white graduate students in [his] classes" (*Hunger of Memory*, pp. 146-47).

Yet it was not until a confrontation with a Caucasian colleague that he considered in detail the impact of affirmative action. "It's just not right," his colleague complained,

> None of this is fair. You've done some good work, but so have I. I'll bet our records are just about even. But when you go looking for jobs this year, it's a very different story. You're the one who gets all the breaks . . . it's all very simple. You're a Chicano. And I am a Jew. . . . Once there were quotas to keep my parents out. . . . Now there are quotas to get you in. And the effect on me is the same as it was for them.
> (*Hunger of Memory*, pp. 170-71)

Richard proceeded to reject the many job offers he had received. More difficult was the telephone call he made to his parents. All their lives they had toiled, goading their children to study hard and at the same time holding down jobs to provide for them. Richard had excelled and now had the chance to achieve his ambition of becoming a university professor. "I don't know why you feel this way," he father said. "We have never had any of the chances before."

"*We,* he said," Richard thought. "But he was wrong. It was *he* who had never had any chance before" (*Hunger of Memory*, p. 172).

Richard Rodriguez

Rodriguez's perspective. At the time Rodriguez was composing his autobiography, educational institutions in the United States were embroiled in the controversy surrounding bilingual education and affirmative action. Rodriguez himself participated in the debate, publishing articles in which he offered his ideas on the premises and impact of these programs. In his autobiography, *Hunger of Memory,* he articulates his objections to both bilingual and affirmative action programs. These objections were to remain, even long after the publication of the autobiography, the fundamental arguments against affirmative action and bilingual education.

Although Rodriguez was suspicious of the opponents of bilingual education who vehemently decried the use of a language other than English in the public schools, he agreed that whatever classes might be taught in a language other than English should be offered with the goal of eventually integrating the students into classes taught in English. He believed that programs that promoted the use of two or more languages in school would only encourage the students to segregate themselves. Indeed, he argued, students who did not finish high school with a firm command of English could legiti-

mately complain that they had been denied a sound education.

Rodriguez felt that affirmative action was a simplistic approach to a complex problem. The architects of affirmative action, he alleged, had failed to acknowledge that there existed significant class differences among the nation's various ethnic minorities. Although he agreed that there were minority students in the United States who performed poorly in school because their parents were uneducated and offered no encouragement or because white teachers failed to encourage them, he pointed out that there were also well educated, affluent Hispanics who were not handicapped by poverty or prejudice. As Rodriguez explained,

> The policy of affirmative action . . . [does not] distinguish someone like me (a graduate student of English, ambitious for a college teaching career) from a slightly educated Mexican-American who lived in a barrio and worked as a menial laborer, never expecting a future improved. Worse, affirmative action made me the beneficiary of his condition.
> (*Hunger of Memory,* pp. 150-51)

Furthermore, Rodriguez pointed out, once admitted to a university, the beneficiaries of affirmative action programs floundered. Minority students who earned mediocre grades in high school were unprepared for the challenges of the university. Admissions officers would promote these students while ignoring this truth. "The conspiracy of kindness," Rodriguez wrote, "became a conspiracy of uncaring."

> Cruelly, callously, admissions committees agreed to overlook serious academic deficiency. I knew students in college then barely able to read . . . bewildered by the requirement to compose a term paper . . . humiliated when they couldn't compete with other students in seminars. There were contrived tutoring programs. But many years of inferior schooling could not be corrected with a crowded hour or two of instruction each week. Not surprisingly, among those students with very poor academic preparation, few completed their courses of study. Many dropped out, most blaming themselves for their failure.
> (*Hunger of Memory,* p. 155)

Rodriguez finally concluded that, rather than help poor and uneducated minorities who suffered because of past and continuing racism, affirmative action merely obscured their plight. With a few blacks or Hispanics being pampered on college campuses across the nation, he contended, people would fail to notice the appalling state of the public schools in crime-ridden ghettos. The strategy of affirmative action did not in his view seriously address the educational dilemma of disadvantaged students. The most urgent need, as Rodriguez saw it, was for good early schooling.

Sources. After his last year at Stanford University, Rodriguez took a summer job in construction. Having planned to attend graduate school, he now welcomed an interlude of physical labor. Not only was he eager to meet the challenges of his friends who warned him, "You only *think* you know what it's like to shovel for three hours a day" (*Hunger of Memory*, p. 131), but he also gleefully anticipated telling his father, after the summer was over that, in fact, he did know what "real work" was like.

Yet he came to realize that his summer excursion into the world of the menial laborer would not teach him what his father had meant by "real work." He was not bound to the job as others were; in his case, it was a brief interlude and he, unlike his father, could foresee the day it would end.

Later that summer, the contractor hired a group of Mexican immigrants. Rodriguez realized that these Mexican immigrants were workers as his father had been. Listening to the loud, confident voice of the contractor speaking to the Mexicans, Rodriguez grew angry with himself. He could not, he concluded, shorten the distance he felt from them with a few weeks of physical labor. They were different from him.

Whatever his other intentions in writing an autobiography, Rodriguez meant to draw attention to poor people like these workers, minority members who had been overlooked by the architects of affirmative action. "You who read this act of contrition," he writes, referring to his autobiography, "should know that by writing it I seek a kind of forgiveness" (*Hunger of Memory*, p. 152). It is not the forgiveness of the reader he seeks, but that of the minority members outside the universities, whose absence from them re-

sulted in Rodriguez's being classed as a minority student. He wishes they would read *Hunger of Memory* but doubts they ever will.

Reception. Readers disparaged or praised *Hunger of Memory* depending upon their own political opinions. However, most reviewers lauded Rodriguez's talent as a writer. "Because Richard Rodriguez is an artist," one critic wrote, "he has managed to tell a specific American story in a way that draws easily into the light certain universal truths about the process of growing up" (Donohue in Mooney, p. 1138). One critic found the chapters Rodriguez devoted to his childhood "uncannily sensitive to the nuances of language learning, the childhood drama of voices, intonations" (Zweig in May, p. 430). Particularly moving, according to another review, was Rodriguez's insight that although his schooling had separated him from his parents, it gave him ways of speaking about and caring about that fact. "Beautifully written," the critic asserted, "wrung from a sore heart, 'Hunger of Memory' bears eloquent witness to this truth" (Comey in Mooney, p. 1138).

For More Information

Camarillo, Albert. *Chicanos in California: A History of Mexican Americans in California.* San Francisco: Boyd & Fraser, 1984.

Crawford, James. *Bilingual Education: History, Politics, Theory and Practice.* Los Angeles: Bilingual Education Services, 1995.

Lang, Paul. *The English Language Debate.* Springfield, N.J.: Enslow, 1995.

May, Hal, ed. *Contemporary Authors.* Vol. 110. Detroit: Gale Research, 1984.

Mooney, Martha, ed. *Book Review Digest.* Vol. 78. New York: H. W. Wilson, 1983.

Rodriguez, Richard. *Hunger of Memory.* New York: Bantam, 1982.

Simmons, Ron. *Affirmative Action.* Cambridge, Mass.: Schenkman, 1982.

Stavans, Ilan. *The Hispanic Condition: Reflections on Culture and Identity.* New York: HarperCollins, 1995.

"I Have a Dream"

by
Martin Luther King, Jr.

Martin Luther King, Jr., (1929-1968) accepted his first position as pastor of a Baptist congregation in Montgomery, Alabama, in 1954, after receiving his doctorate in philosophy from Boston University. A year later he rose to national fame by advocating nonviolent civil disobedience in his organization of a successful boycott of Montgomery's segregated buses. King, determined to advance black equality in the United States, soon became the de facto leader of the new civil rights era, and proceeded to travel, write books, and deliver speeches for this cause. He delivered his climactic "I Have a Dream" speech before a crowd of more than 200,000 onlookers, 60,000 of whom were white. King's speech inspired a wide audience, galvanizing many to believe in the dream of racial equality. On this historic occasion, the civil rights movement was transformed from a Southern regional struggle into a national one. Before a live audience and all the major news networks, King declared 1963 the year to open the doors of social and economic opportunity. In retrospect, his speech and the March on Washington during which it was delivered formed a pinnacle in the 1960s quest for civil rights.

Events in History at the Time of the Speech

King's emergence as a civil rights leader. On a December afternoon in 1955, Rosa Parks, a black seamstress, boarded a Montgomery City Lines bus. The bus had a special segregated sec-

> ### THE LITERARY WORK
> A speech made in front of the Lincoln Memorial in Washington, D.C.; delivered on August 28, 1963.
>
> ### SYNOPSIS
> In his landmark speech, King cites a one-hundred-year history of denial of equal rights to blacks in the United States, and he calls on both blacks and whites to turn the dream of social equality into a reality.

tion for blacks behind the white passengers, and Parks took a seat in the first row of the black section. Sitting in the same row was a black man next to her and two black women across the aisle. When more whites boarded the bus, one was left standing. The driver told the blacks in Parks's row to rise so the white passenger could sit there. While the three other blacks finally obliged him, Parks refused to stand up. This insubordination led to her getting arrested, which roused the black community into action. What began as a one-day boycott of the city's bus system by its black riders ended up lasting for more than a year.

Born in Atlanta, Georgia, and educated in various states, King had moved to Montgomery, Alabama, the previous year to serve as pastor at the Dexter Avenue Baptist Church. When leaders of the black community organized themselves into the Montgomery Improvement Association, they unanimously elected King president, and he became the spokesman-leader of the boycott movement. Although a popular minister with a large following, King was not yet a nationally known figure. The boycott proved pivotal in this regard; afterward it would become difficult, if not impossible, for him to remain a private man.

The boycott began on December 5, 1955. On February 1, 1956, four black women lobbied a federal court to issue a ban on segregation in public transportation in Montgomery. On June 4, the court ruled in favor of the women, outlawing such segregation there. Although Alabama officials appealed the decision, on November 13 the United States Supreme Court upheld the district court's ruling. The Supreme Court's written order to desegregate the city's buses arrived on December 20, and the following day the boycott ended. The civil rights movement had won a landmark victory.

Throughout the remainder of the decade, King rose in national stature as he crusaded for civil rights. With the election of President John F. Kennedy in 1960, King increased his efforts to involve the federal government in his proposed political, economic, and social changes. He saw in the young president "a leader unafraid of change" (King in Bennett, p. 119). In an article entitled "Equality Now," published in *Nation* in February of 1963, King laid out his proposals. He stated that the new administration had the best chance in one hundred years to extend civil rights to black America. King asked for "recognition by the federal government that it has sufficient power at its disposal to guide [the country] through the changes ahead" (King in Bennett, p. 120). During a White House meeting, King urged President Kennedy to develop a plan for a nationwide realization of civil rights. Although the 1960 Civil Rights Act had increased voting protection for black Americans, to King this step signaled only a beginning.

Eventually King's efforts, along with those of other activists, paid off. They marched, staged sit-ins, and defied local segregation laws. The activists suffered greatly for their efforts, enduring beatings, jailings, the bombing of black churches, and even some murders. In April 1963, just a few months before the March on Washington, King led a nonviolent demonstration in Birmingham, Alabama. City police used gushing firehoses, electric cattle prods, and fierce police dogs against the protesters, some of whom were schoolchildren. Television stations broadcast the brutal treatment of the nonviolent protesters to a shocked nation, a sight that roused much of the nation's sympathies for the black civil rights struggle. Following on the heels of this horror, King's "I Have a Dream" speech was, in essence, a demand for action by Congress.

Finally, in 1964, the United States Congress passed the strongest civil rights act since Reconstruction. It ordered public businesses such as restaurants and hotels to serve all patrons equally, regardless of race or national origin. The act also barred employers from discriminatory practices. A year later it was followed by the 1965 Voting Rights Act, which put an end to poll taxes, literacy tests, and other methods employed to prevent blacks from voting. These achievements could not have been realized without King's efforts to elevate the civil rights movement from the local to the national arena.

King's speechmaking style. Beginning with the Montgomery boycott, King's speeches were an instrumental part of his civil rights efforts. Scholars point to the various tools of language King used, perhaps the most basic of which is metaphor. In his "I Have a Dream" speech, for example, King compares the March on Washington to cashing a check, suggesting that civil rights are owed to the black citizens of America and it is time to pay up. A second tool used by King is repetition, including the repetition of the same sound within a line and of the same phrase across a series of lines. The speech in question ends with two such series, the "I have a dream" sequence and a "let freedom ring" sequence, whose rhythms stem largely from repetition. Also King typically used language that is both religious and patriotic, thereby elevating his cause into a holy as well as a national crusade. Finally, he used inclusive grammar, like the pronoun *we,* to enlist white as well as black listeners in his struggle and convince them that "*his* dream was *their* dream too" (Lischer, p. 10).

The March on Washington. The civil rights movement gained much of its national following from the historic March on Washington of August 1963. Contrary to popular perception, King did not initiate the plans for this rally. On July 2, 1963, six civil rights leaders of varied backgrounds met at New York's Roosevelt Hotel. They were Roy Wilkins of the National Association for the Advancement of Colored People (NAACP), Philip A. Randolph of the Brotherhood of Sleeping Car Porters, James Farmer of the Congress of Racial Equality, Whitney Young of the Urban League, John Lewis of the Southern Christian

Dr. King giving his "I Have a Dream" speech during the March on Washington.

Leadership Conference (SCLC), and King, also representing the SCLC. Randolph opened the meeting, stating that he had held the dream of a march on the nation's capitol for over twenty years. After some discussion, the team decided that Randolph should head the effort, aided by another civil rights activist, Bayard Rustin. They set the date, August 28, 1963. With sixty days to pull the march together, the six men then set out to organize this massive effort.

Preparations began across the nation. In Harlem, a predominantly black section of New York City, Rustin distributed his *Organizing Manual No. 1* to two thousand interested leaders. These, in turn, amassed their own followers. King and Wilkins, the two most prominent public figures of the group, appeared jointly on television ads. Despite some interpersonal tensions between them, the men collaborated successfully on the national undertaking. While those planning to participate in the march showed optimism, the city hosting the event clearly felt apprehensive. Authorities in Washington, D.C., took precautions to safeguard the capital against possible rioting—local liquor stores, for example, stopped all alcohol sales. President John F. Kennedy and his military chiefs of staff stood ready for violence with 4,000 troops located in the suburbs and another 15,000 paratroopers on alert in North Carolina. Local hospitals canceled all nonemergency surgeries for the day in case their services were needed, while city courthouses prepared for an evening of all-night criminal hearings.

Meanwhile, Rustin was determined to avert all unrest. He led a staff of two hundred volunteers to the Mall, a famous area of Washington containing national monuments, setting up several hundred portable toilets, twenty-one temporary drinking fountains, and twenty-four first aid stations. In New York's Riverside Church, another group of volunteers prepared eighty thousand sack lunches for those traveling overnight to make the march. Rustin not only handled the logistics of meeting the visitors' needs but also organized the speakers. He allowed each orator only seven minutes on the podium, believing that a timely evacuation of the crowd would diminish the chances for violence.

The speakers at the event realized that it was an opportunity for the struggle for civil rights to reach further than the black community. With this in mind, they sought to write speeches that outlined common grievances rather than pointing at particular enemies. John Lewis, an ac-

complished orator and friend of King's, helped each of the speakers to add a few lines that outlined common black ideologies. Other aides assisted with the inclusion of language that would sharpen the political points of each address.

King did not begin to write his own speech until the day before the event. In a Washington, D.C., hotel room, he penned his opening line. He completed his address by morning, but the speech he delivered departed from his prepared manuscript midway. He delivered the rest of the speech impromptu, coming up with the inspired second half on the spot. As the last speaker of the day, King took the podium after the attentiveness of listeners had waned. Nonetheless the crowd fell silent as he began.

In his distinctive baritone, King had begun to speak verbatim from his script. Toward the end of his speech, however, he felt himself caught in the momentum of the crowd. Unable to hold fast to his prepared text, King began to preach as his vocation had taught him. Behind him, on the speech platform, gospel singer Mahalia Jackson urged the speaker, "Tell 'em about the dream, Martin" (Jackson in Branch, p. 882). Although King could not later recall whether or not he had heard the woman, at this point he began introducing his ideas with the words, "I have a dream."

With a steady, solemn cadence, somewhat restrained in keeping with the serious tone of the occasion, King continued. He listed his variations on the American dream—such as that some day even the state of Mississippi would be transformed into an oasis of freedom—and that other such visions would come to pass. Only when King reached his final words, "Let freedom ring" (King in Branch, p. 882), did he allow himself to smile.

King and the Black Baptist Church. There was a precedent for King's impromptu, almost sermon-like performance at the March on Washington. King's father, like his maternal grandfather, served as pastor of the Ebenezer Baptist Church in Atlanta, Georgia. From an early age, King had been exposed to preaching. After his own college training, King joined his father for a time in serving the parish of the family church. From his first day at work, King stressed community involvement to his followers, urging all members to register as voters and to join the National Association for the Advancement of Colored People (NAACP). A natural leader, King also understood the important role the church played in any black community.

Historically, blacks and whites did not always worship in separate houses. A winter morning in 1787, however, helped change this fact. Two black men received reprimands for praying in the whites-only section of the St. George Methodist Episcopal Church in Philadelphia. As a result of this incident, the men organized the Bethel African Methodist Episcopal Church. Their success in the North sparked a chain reaction of black churches being established across the United States. Blacks would gradually stop worshipping with whites except in places where the black community was not large enough to support its own congregation.

Although Methodists initiated this revolution, the Baptists in the South quickly joined the movement. The church became not only a house of God, but a cornerstone of the black community. Church buildings acted as schoolhouses where black children barred from whites-only public schools received an education. During the peak years of American slavery, between 1800 and 1865, the churches also served as stations for the underground railroad, a network of safe havens that helped runaway slaves. When the practice of slavery ended, in the confusion of the post-Civil War era, the emancipated blacks turned again to the stable symbol of hope that they had relied on in the past—the church. In turn, its leaders provided guidance to their flock in more ways than just spiritual—acting as a community center, providing welfare to the sick and poor, and job training for the able-bodied.

Between the years of 1936 and 1962, the population of the Baptist denomination increased from about 3.8 million to over 7.6 million. The role of the church grew during the civil rights movement of the 1960s. Inspired by the Montgomery bus boycott and the role that church leaders had played in organizing the effort, King and one hundred Southern ministers founded the Southern Christian Leadership Conference (SCLC). As president of the organization, King led the SCLC in a nonviolent campaign to end racial discrimination in the United States.

The Speech in Focus

The speech. Delivering his speech from the steps of the Lincoln Memorial, King opened with a reference to his surroundings. Recalling Abraham Lincoln's **Gettysburg Address** (also covered in *Literature and Its Times*), King began, "Five score years ago, a great American, in whose symbolic shadow we stand, signed the Emancipation Proclamation. This momentous decree came as a

great beacon light of hope to millions of Negro slaves" (King, "I Have a Dream," p. 110). The speech went on to highlight the fact that in spite of the end of slavery, black Americans still did not live as a free people. Although one hundred years have passed between the signing of the Emancipation Proclamation and the March on Washington, a black man "still finds himself an exile in his own land" ("I Have a Dream," p. 110).

"In a sense we have come to our nation's Capital to cash a check," King stated ("I Have a Dream," p. 110). Referring to the **Declaration of Independence**, (also covered in *Literature and Its Times*), he noted that the founding fathers promised each American citizen "the unalienable rights of life, liberty, and the pursuit of happiness" ("I Have a Dream," p. 111). He insisted that America has defaulted on its promissory note to its black citizens with regard to these pursuits. At this point in the address, King told his audience, "Now is the time to lift our nation from the quicksands of racial injustice to the solid rock of brotherhood" ("I Have a Dream," p. 111). He urged them not to rest until such equality has been attained. In keeping with his nonviolent philosophy, however, King asked that the quest for freedom not lead to bitterness and hatred toward the oppressors. He told his audience to maintain dignity, to fight physical force with the force of the soul. Along with this seemingly passive resistance, however, King urged his listeners to not be satisfied "until justice rolls down like waters and righteousness like a mighty stream" ("I Have a Dream," p. 112). Building to a crescendo, the civil rights leader exhorted the members of the audience to return to their homes knowing that the situation of blacks in America could be changed.

At this point in his address, King abandoned his written text and began what is perhaps the most widely recognized portion of his speech. "On a surge of emotion, more inspired than he had ever been in his life, [he] spoke from his heart" (Oates, p. 260). "I say to you today, my friends, that in spite of the difficulties and frustrations of the moment I still have a dream" ("I Have a Dream," p. 112). For the remainder of his speech, King repeated the phrase "I have a dream," instilling in his listeners the same hope for freedom. His dream stemmed from the American dream, the simple belief that all are created equal. This equality, according to King, should translate into a nation where children "will not be judged by the color of their skin but by the content of their character" ("I Have a Dream," p. 112). King remarked that in order for America

Another view of Dr. King giving his speech in front of the Lincoln Memorial.

to become a truly great nation, true freedom must ring throughout its land. Echoing the patriotic lyrics of the song "America" (sometimes called "My Country 'Tis of Thee") he asked that freedom be allowed to ring from every mountainside. He cited various mountain ranges across the United States from whence the bells of freedom must ring. Concluding his address, King envisioned a nation of multicultural citizens holding hands singing, "Free at last! Free at last! Thank God almighty, we are free at last" ("I Have a Dream," p. 113).

Two speeches in one. King originally shied away from the profession that his father had chosen as a Baptist pastor. An avid scholar, the son had hoped to enter into academia in his professional pursuits. King sought a different vocation than one infused with the vivacious hand-clapping and vocal "amens" of the African American church. While studying for his undergraduate degree at Morehouse College, however, he met two professors who changed his mind. Both Dr. George D. Kelsey and Dr. Benjamin E. Mays were seminary-trained ministers. In their classrooms, they proved to King that religion and academia could mix. With their intelligent, socially relevant sermons, the two men inspired King to follow their examples and become a "real minister" (King in Bennett, p. 27).

Although King successfully mixed the two worlds of spirituality and the intellect, this dichotomy manifested itself in many of his oral addresses. Nowhere was the duality more obvious than in his "I Have a Dream" speech. As previously mentioned, King had prepared a written draft of the speech. The first half of the address reflected the meticulous research that any professional academic would undertake. With its multiple references to historical events, the speech read like a lesson in the struggle for civil rights. Beginning with a reference to the Emancipation Proclamation, King reminded his audience of the historical roots beneath black America's struggle for full equality.

The speech then moved from the Emancipation Proclamation to another historical document, the Declaration of Independence. King declared that it was obvious that America had defaulted on its promise of equality to its citizens of color, that it has given his people a bad check that has come back marked "insufficient funds." He stated, "Those who hope that the Negro needed to blow off steam and will now be content will have a rude awakening" ("I Have a Dream," p. 111). With this King quelled rumors that the Kennedy administration had tamed the civil rights movement. Even in this minor rebuttal, however, King maintained a slow cadence and an absence of emotion in his voice. He stuck to his rehearsed script.

When he reached the halfway point of his address, however, the minister in King overruled the statesman and the academic in him. As he took leave of his written speech, his allusions changed from the historical to the religious. He spoke of "waters of righteousness" and of "God's children" ("I Have a Dream," pp. 112-13), eliciting the very "amens" and applause that he had shunned in his career. King also wove folk references into his spontaneous speech. He played with the lyrics of "America," repeating the refrain "Let freedom ring" ("I Have a Dream," p. 113) several times over. In this manner, he connected with his audience not as a formal speaker, but rather as the minister that he had been for several years. Behind him on the podium, Mahalia Jackson cried out loudly, "My Lord! My Lord," responding to the religious pitch of the address (Jackson in Branch, p. 882). In testament to his

success as a preacher, the most memorable portion of King's speech remains, to this day, the second half. King's speech would not be limited by the restraint of unemotional intellect. As he had done in his choice of a vocation, in his address, King simply followed that inspiration that "came to [him]" (King in Branch, p. 882).

Sources. Most immediately King drew on his own written draft of the speech, which he revised and departed from as described in the contents section above. Here is a segment from the delivered speech, followed by the same segment from a draft:

The Delivered Speech

There are those who are asking the devotees of civil rights, "when will you be satisfied?" We can never be satisfied as long as the Negro is the victim of the unspeakable horrors of police brutality. . . . We can never be satisfied as long as the Negro's basic mobility is from a smaller ghetto to a larger one. We can never be satisfied as long as a Negro in Mississippi cannot vote and a Negro in New York believes he has nothing for which to vote. ("I Have a Dream," p. 12)

The Draft

I read a newspaper editorial recently which speculated upon when the leaders of this civil rights movement would become "satisfied" so that America could return to normalcy. We can never be satisfied as long as a Negro boy in Albany, Georgia attends an all-Negro school. . . . We can never be satisfied so long as a Negro in the District of Columbia is restricted to a housing ghetto. We can never be satisfied so long as a Negro in Mississippi cannot vote and a Negro in New York believes he has nothing for which to vote.
        (King, "Normalcy—Never Again," p. 3)

The remainder of this draft, the part King did not deliver because he abandoned his text and veered into an impromptu speech, continues in the same vein, speaking about the importance of rejecting the normalcy that has become racism and embracing "a new, creative positive normalcy; a normalcy in which we recognize the brotherhood of man on Monday as clearly as we acknowledge the Fatherhood of God on Sunday" (King, "Normalcy—Never Again," p. 4). As the momentum builds, the draft reminds listeners about the work left to be done and encourages them that "freedom is in sight," especially now that the movement has "annexed millions of allies whose skins are untouched with color but whose hearts have been touched with compassion and guilt (King, "Normalcy—Never Again,"

p. 4). Although King later refined the writing and then, by this point, diverged from the written text when delivering the speech, his final climax built on this same uplifting tone.

King also drew on his own previous speeches and on historical sources in the speech that he finally delivered. He had, for example, earlier used a series of "I have a dream. . ." phrases with great impact in a speech in Detroit. Drawing on historical sources, the speech he delivered in Washington echoes the opening of the Gettysburg Address and names both the Emancipation Proclamation and the Declaration of Independence. By recalling these landmarks in American history, King was reminding his audience to bear the burden of social struggle until the national ideals declared so long ago had been met. He was not, however, supporting a violent social coup. In fact, King tells the audience, "We must not allow our creative protest to degenerate into physical violence," an admonition he repeats throughout his speech ("I Have a Dream," p. 111).

KING AND HIS SOURCES

One biographer cautions against focusing too much attention on King's sources: "I will insist that we do King a disservice to evaluate his originality according to his use of written sources. He practiced the creativity of a preacher and a poet. He had . . . the gift of metaphor, and fretting about sources must not distract us from its appreciation. In King's vision of the world, ordinary southern towns became theaters of divine revelation. . . . This is what the Kingdom of God will *look like,* he promised a quarter million people at the Lincoln Memorial: like white people and black people from Georgia sitting at table together and acting like kin." (Lischer, p. 10)

King's ideas and oratory were influenced over the years by the arguments and styles of other African Americans. Additional influences include the essayist Henry David Thoreau (1817-62), author of **"Civil Disobedience"** (also covered in *Literature and Its Times*), and the Indian leader Mohandas Gandhi (1869-1948), whose nonviolent philosophy deeply impressed King. In protest of the British rule of India, Gandhi led his people in two campaigns of civil disobedience (1919-22 and 1930) that employed nonviolent measures such as marches and hunger strikes. Introduced

to Gandhi's philosophy at Morehouse in 1950, King immediately purchased half a dozen books on the recently assassinated leader—Gandhi had been killed two years earlier by a Hindu fanatic who objected to the leader's tolerance of Muslims.

King believed in the impact of a nonviolent movement and encouraged his own followers to fight with such dignity. In 1959 King traveled to India, where he encountered Gandhians of various backgrounds—"Muslims, mystics, rich industrialists, Communist governors, and cynical bureaucrats" (Branch, p. 252). Despite their differences, these men and women all embraced the peaceful philosophies of their former leader. King attempted to infuse their tactic of nonviolent protest into the civil rights struggle in the United States. Tragically, after advocating nonviolence for years, King, like Gandhi, met a violent death after being struck by an assassin's bullet on April 4, 1968.

Reception of the speech. The crowd roared its approval in shouts and applause after King stepped down from the podium. Overcome with emotion, he heard SCLC colleague Ralph Abernathy express the view that the Holy Spirit had taken hold of King in his delivery of the speech. King himself took satisfaction in the thought that "millions of whites had heard his message for the first time, heard what he'd been trying to say since Montgomery" (Oates, p. 263). President Kennedy voiced his approval too. After hearing him speak, Kennedy said of King, "He's damn good" (Kennedy in Branch, p. 886).

While many newspapers ran headlines such as "'I Have a Dream' Peroration by Dr. King Sums up a Day the Capital Will Remember" (*New York Times* in Branch, p. 886), others made no mention of King's success. The *Washington Post,* for example, featured Randolph's speech and made no mention of King's. The black press, however, more than atoned for this oversight. Its papers praised King as an unequaled orator. Southern mainstream papers made mention of the speech too. Even Atlanta's *Daily World* relaxed its prejudices and ran pictures of King on its front page.

Yet the South remained resistant to the advancement of civil rights for blacks. Before the march, President Kennedy had sent to Congress a civil rights bill that would prohibit segregation in public places. The march had been organized to press for the passage of this bill, but Congress failed to vote in favor of it that year, despite King's stirring speech. Only after Kennedy was assassinated and President Lyndon Johnson promoted the bill would it finally pass into law as the far-reaching Civil Rights Act of 1964.

For More Information

Bennett, Lerone. *What Manner of Man.* Chicago: Johnson, 1976.

Branch, Taylor. *Parting the Waters: America in the King Years, 1954-63.* New York: Simon & Schuster, 1988.

King, Martin Luther, Jr. "I Have a Dream." In *The Civil Rights Reader.* Edited by Leon Friedman. New York: Walker, 1967.

King, Martin Luther, Jr. "Normalcy—Never Again." Draft of Dr. Martin Luther King, Jr. Address of August 28, 1963. Library and Archives, Martin Luther King, Jr., Center for Nonviolent Social Change, Atlanta, Georgia.

Lischer, Richard. *The Preacher King: Martin Luther King, Jr. and the Word that Moved America.* New York: Oxford University Press, 1995.

Meshack, B. A. *Is the Baptist Church Relevant to the Black Community?* San Francisco: R & E Research Associates, 1976.

Oates, Stephen B. *The Life of Martin Luther King, Jr.* New York: Harper, 1982.

Sobel, Lester A. *Civil Rights: 1960-66.* New York: Facts on File, 1967.

I Heard the Owl Call My Name

by

Margaret Craven

Margaret Craven was born in Bellingham, Washington, in 1898, and attended Stanford University. She began her writing career as a newspaper journalist, and in fact it was a story she wrote for the *Saturday Evening Post,* based on the experiences of a minister in the Queen Charlotte Islands of British Columbia, that was the genesis of her novel *I Heard the Owl Call My Name.* For much of her life Craven had struggled with a career as a fiction writer, experiencing only nominal success, but at the age of sixty-nine her quietly moving book about life in a Kwakiutl Indian village would become the culmination of her career.

Events in History at the Time of the Novel

Kwakiutl Indians. The Kwakiutl people live in and around the Queen Charlotte Strait, which is on the central coast of British Columbia, Canada; they formerly inhabited the northeastern part of Vancouver Island as well. The word *Kwakiutl* means "beach on the other side of the river," and at first designated a very specific place and group, though the term has been extended to apply to all tribes who share a common linguistic heritage. Contact with Europeans seems to have occurred in 1786, when an English trader by the name of James Strange first made his way along the strait. Sources seem to indicate no further contact with whites occurred until 1792, when a veritable flood of foreigners sailed through the area—Americans, British, and even Spanish. About

THE LITERARY WORK	

A novel set in the mid-1960s in the Kwakiutl Indian village of Kingcome, British Columbia; published in 1967.

SYNOPSIS

A young Anglican vicar finds peace in life and death among the Kwakiutl tribe.

thirty years later, the English-based Hudson's Bay Company established trading posts all over the area, and the Kwakiutl became economically linked with the outside world.

The Kwakiutl built permanent villages of wooden houses, generally alongside a river or other shoreline, with secondary seasonal structures located in other places close to rich sources for food gathering. There were three social classes, roughly approximating the European classes of nobility, commoner, and slave. Nobility was not extended to entire families, but to the member of the family, generally the eldest son, who would one day assume guardianship of the emblems and rights of the family's primal ancestor. Commoners were sometimes responsible for contributing toward the upkeep of the noble head of their family, giving him a certain portion of their food, for example. The Kwakiutl—both nobles and commoners—in the past sometimes kept slaves, who were usually captured members of other tribes. If the person was not ransomed by his or her family, he or she lost all social status and became a slave for life, able only to marry another slave and produce children born into slavery. The life of Kwakiutl slaves was not necessarily harsh; they often lived with the family they served and, if useful or skillful, could become a valued member of that family unit. Also it was possible for a slave to be released from bondage upon the word of his master. In *I Heard the Owl Call My Name,* the behavior of Sam, the unlucky drunkard who mistreats both his wife and his daughter, is explained by his heritage:

> Sam was descended from slaves and in the old days to be a slave was to be worse than a nothing. He had no pride. His boats burned under him. When he reached the fishing grounds, the fish had not come yet, or they had seen him and fled.
>
> (Craven, *I Heard the Owl Call My Name,*
> p. 24)

The Kwakiutl Indians have traditionally supported themselves largely by fishing for halibut, cod, and salmon, by digging for clams, and by hunting for bear, wolf, beaver, and seal. In more recent years, as the mythic power of their art has become popular far beyond their coastal home, the production of native handiwork has probably surpassed all other forms of enterprise.

Missionaries. In 1881 the Anglican Church of Canada set up a mission with a school in Alert Bay, the Queen Charlotte region's major center of commerce, health services, and government. The school would become the main center of education in the entire area, right up until the time that Craven was writing her novel. The Anglican Church of Canada made an impact on the Indians in the Queen Charlotte Strait, but it was only at Kingcome, the setting of *I Heard the Owl Call My Name,* that the Anglicans set up a permanent church, St. George. Other Indian villages received monthly visits from Anglican churchmen; every six weeks the Anglican hospital boat would arrive offshore and offer basic health services. The Pentecostal Church was also very active in the area at the time Craven was writing, and was perhaps the more popular because of its novel approach; the formal Anglican services were in English (although the Anglicans did issue a translation of the Book of Common Prayer in Kwakwala, the language of the Kwakiutl), while the Pentecostal services were often held in the native Kwakwala tongue and were more spontaneous, with a lot of "yelling and jumping around and shouting" (Sewid, p. 175). Despite the enthusi-

A Kwakiutl, wearing a basketry hat and button blanket, visiting a British ship in 1873.

asm evident in its church services, the Pentecostal Church was strictly against dancing, gambling, and drinking, and such taboos tended to make it less popular than it might have been among native populations. In 1969 (two years after *I Heard the Owl Call My Name* was published), the autobiography of the Kwakiutl Indian James Sewid appeared, in which he wrote of a conflict between the Anglican Church and the Pentecostal Church in the very village of Kingcome about which Craven wrote:

> I had to take a trip up to Kingcome one time because the Pentecostals had gone up there and that whole village was divided. The fathers and sons were divided, the mothers and fathers, they were not on good terms, and the way I saw it it was not a good thing.
>
> (Sewid, p. 178)

Despite all the flurry of Western religious activity conducted in their communities, the Kwakiutl maintained their ancient religious traditions. These ancient traditions continue to be observed and generally exist alongside Christianity.

Nawalakw. According to the Kwakiutl world view, everything in nature contains a supernatural aspect, known as nawalakw, which people address in thanks while they perform daily tasks, such as hunting, picking berries, or fishing. In *I Heard the Owl Call My Name,* the nawalakw of the salmon is particularly prominent, not just because fishing was such an important part of daily life at Kingcome, but also because the character Mark is associated with the salmon, for reasons that become clear during the course of the novel. Mark himself knows a version of the salmon prayer, and recites it to Jim, his Indian helper, on the day that the two of them see a silver shoal of salmon moving with secret urgency to their spawning beds. The anthropologist Franz Boas recorded a version of the salmon prayer at the

---

CANDLEFISH

In *I Heard the Owl Call My Name,* the Indians of Kingcome hold an annual ceremony at the end of March in preparation for the coming of the oolakan, or candlefish, the mainstay of their economy and diet. As the novel relates, like other ceremonies of the season, this one was taken quite seriously.

> [In fact, this was a] season so deep in the tradition of the people that all the taboos and superstitions were remembered, and followed. No pregnant woman must cross the river. No body must be transported upon it. The chief of the tribe must catch the first fish.
>
> (*I Heard the Owl Call My Name,* p. 65)

The oolakan, or eulachon, run for about five weeks every spring. The fish is a sort of salmon, but tiny—only eight inches in length. Its great value is not its flesh, but its oil, which females of the species have in greater abundance. The eulachon has so much oil, in fact, that when dried and stood on its end, it actually burns—like a candle. The Kwakiutl used the oil for cooking.

---

turn of the century while he was among the Kwakiutl:

> We have come to meet alive, Swimmer. Do not feel wrong about what I have done to you, friend Swimmer, for that is the reason why you come that I may spear you, that I may eat you, Supernatural One, you Long-Life-Giver, you Swimmer. . . . Now call after you your father and your mother and uncles and aunts and elder brothers and sisters to come to me also, you, Swimmers, you Satiater.
>
> (Boas, p. 207)

After such a prayer, the speaker answers back to himself in the place of the animal or fruit— "yes," or an affirmation of another sort. Craven's novel links the "Yes, my Lord," that Mark utters to his own god, in acceptance of his call to minister to the Kwakiutl, with the response of the salmon who affirms the rightness of his capture by the Indians.

Cannibal Dance. In the novel, before he moves to Kingcome, Mark is given some sage advice by his predecessor, an aged cleric named Caleb: "Don't call them cannibals. It was never true literally. No one alive has seen the famous dance in which the young man, maddened by the cannibal spirit, returns to his village crying for flesh and carrying a body taken from a grave tree" (*I Heard the Owl Call My Name,* p. 5). What Caleb is referring to is the *hamatsa,* or Cannibal Dance, a winter ceremony that marks the initiation of a young man into the Cannibal Society, one of the many secret societies to which Kwakiutl people, both men and women, belong. The Kwakiutl seem to have developed the Cannibal Dance after contact and marriage with nearby Indians, the Bella Bella and Oowekeeno, probably after having killed a number of Bella Bella nobility sometime around 1856.

The secret societies—altogether there were apparently eighteen of them—each honor a mythical ancestor, supposedly each group's founder. Group members, who protected the "secrets" of their societies, were generally of the same age and gender; the Crow society was for young women, the Sea Lion society for older men, for example. In the winter, the most sacred time of the year, people no longer went by their everyday names, but by the sacred names given them in their societies.

There were many different kinds of dances that could be performed, with the *hamatsa* being the most terrible. The general theme behind the dances was that the dancer had been abducted by the spirits, who gave the dancer horrible powers or qualities; it was up to the other members of the tribe to capture and tame the person through ceremonial dance. "The public ceremonial was the performance and taming of the possessed dancer, who had disappeared from the village some time before, often under dramatic circumstances, and had been in seclusion in the woods or in a special room" (Codere, p. 373).

The *hamatsa* dancer was cured over a period of four days; at his first appearance, the dancer was wild, having acquired the taste for human flesh. He snarled at, clawed, and bit the people gathered to sing and dance him back to health. To appease him, a woman danced in front of him with what appeared to be a corpse in her arms; his appetite led him to follow her around the room, a first sign of being tamed. Eventually, the young man, who had first appeared naked, put on clothes, stood up straight and began to become more social. Some anthropologists believe that one of the purposes of such displays of ferocity was to frighten non-members of the society into believing that Cannibal Society members—generally drawn from the potential nobility—were really in touch with the spirit world and were not to be challenged.

Burial rites. *I Heard the Owl Call My Name* is a book about death—not just that of the hero but of several members of the young vicar's flock. Consequently the novel is rich in discussions about traditional burial rituals. Mark, the vicar, distinguishes himself by his tolerance and support of such traditions as he attends his first burial in the village: "Did you notice that at the graveside he left quietly and asked no questions? . . . He respected our customs" (*I Heard the Owl Call My Name*, p. 23). Upon death, a Kwakiutl's body was immediately put into a wooden box made from local materials, the hands and face washed and then painted red. Traditionally the open box was hoisted into a tree top belonging to the family of the dead person so that the body could be eaten by birds—usually ravens—and thus the person's spirit, passing into the bodies of creatures of this earth, would remain in the world of human beings, and have the chance of being reborn once again into a human body upon the death of the animal. It was thought that if a person were buried underground, his or her spirit would pass only into the creatures who inhabit the soil and would have no hope of being reborn into the human community. Another traditional burial form was to put the body into an above-ground wooden tomb apart from the village. In both cases, tradition has given way to a more generally acceptable custom. Government and missionary church pressure have now compelled the Kwakiutl people to bury their dead underground.

The Novel in Focus

The plot. Mark Brian, a twenty-seven-year-old Anglican ordinand, has three years before he will die. Unaware of this, he is sent by his bishop to live among the Kwakiutl Indians in their remote coastal village of Kingcome (in the Kwakwala

tongue, *Quee,* or "inside place"). On his first day in the village, he confronts the task of burying a small boy who has drowned ten days earlier. The people have been unable to bury him not just because they have been without a vicar, but because the Royal Canadian Mounted Police (RCMP) have not yet arrived to investigate and issue a death certificate. After the insensitive officer has come and gone, Mark accompanies the tribe to the burial ground separated from the village by a section of heavy forest. Giving a traditional Anglican funeral service, Mark is moved by how appropriate the ceremony seems to him, here in this remote and alien part of the world. When he is finished, he senses that the people themselves are not yet through, and he leaves, with a Kwakwala lament echoing through the burial glade behind him. His sensitivity to their customs impresses the Indians.

OLD TALES

Whether or not the Cannibal Dance, which enacts the eating of dead bodies, ever really involved actual cannibalism remains a matter of debate. Craven's novel, however, gives an explanation by Peter, the ceremonial totem carver, that suggests the cannibal dances actually involved human remains: "In my father's day when the hamatsa entered on the second night of the dance carrying a real body taken from the old burial ground, the women were afraid, and they said, 'Is the body from my family's tree? Is it one of ours?' When I was a boy the hamatsa carried no body because the government forbade it, and he only pretended to bite people, holding a piece of seal liver in his mouth. As a boy I saw the scars on the arms of the old men, and I heard the tales" (*I Heard the Owl Call My Name,* pp. 100-01).

The following day he awakes from his first sleep in the village to discover by the broad light of day that his vicarage is a shambles and his church a dark and dank ramshackle place. Rejecting an offer from the bishop to have a prefabricated house sent up to Kingcome to replace the crumbling vicarage, Mark begins to clean and set things right; he wants to wait to build the vicarage until his people offer to help him with the difficult task. The Indians watch him politely, shyly, and Mark feels keenly that he is an alien in their home.

A collection of goods to be given away at a potlatch, or ceremonial feast, c. 1900.

One late September afternoon Mark and his Indian helper, Jim, take a trip together up the river that runs past the village. Mark wants to see the "death of the swimmer," the last moments of the salmon that swim upstream to spawn and die. They meet some of the other villagers there, near a small group of cabins where they dry salmon and pick berries; among the other villagers are Marta Stephens, an ancient woman who has been kind to the young vicar, and Keetah, a young woman who alone among the villagers does not have an English nickname. They all picnic together and discuss the puzzle of death, debating whether it is a tragedy or a triumph. Keetah weeps at the death of the salmon, but Marta and Mark both feel that death is a moment of culmination, when one achieves what one was born to do.

The men of the tribe, and especially Jim, come to like and respect the vicar for his tenacity and his curiosity about their way of life. A spirit of love is even evident between them by Christmas, although Mark still feels the Kwakiutls' reservation about accepting him as one of them. Christmas vacation, however, brings with it a spirit of unrest. The older children of the village have returned home from the native church school in Alert Bay; they speak English almost exclusively, can no longer converse fluently in the Kwakwala

tongue, and are filled with the "superior" technologies of the white man's world. Old Mrs. Hudson, Keetah's grandmother, nearly has a heart attack when she learns that her granddaughter (Keetah's sister) is going to marry a white man. Her foreboding turns out to be justified. At the yearly potlatch, the outsider gets his fiancee's uncle drunk and buys from him a priceless ceremonial mask for the paltry sum of $50. Out of their shame that such a thing could have happened, the old people of her family depart, Keetah with them, for a deserted village elsewhere to live for a time.

Mark takes it upon himself to find out what has happened to the sister, for the villagers are certain that the white man took advantage of her just to get the family's treasure. A kindly Canadian police officer looks into the matter, and discovers that she was indeed abandoned in Vancouver and, totally unfamiliar with city life among white people, she soon turned to drink and drugs and died of an overdose. Mark feels that he has begun to share in the sadness that he sees in the eyes of so many of his flock. Because he suffers with his people over the death, they welcome him among them fully; they offer to help him put up a new vicarage and he gladly accepts.

While his vicarage is being built, Mark goes to live with Marta, where he sees a lot of Keetah.

He encourages the girl, whom he has come to love, to write down the old stories that are slowly being forgotten, now that the children are being educated in the white man's world. In the fall, Mark takes four of the village boys to Vancouver, to help them prepare for their new life in the city of Powell River, where they will board with white families and attend a white school. They are the first in the tribe to do such a thing, and when he accompanies them to the city, the vicar is aware of how much he himself has changed, how alien he finds the life he once led.

When Gordon, the most promising and well-loved of the boys, comes back, he also realizes how much he has changed and that he can no longer live in the village. He takes Keetah with him, breaking the hearts of their families, who see in their departure the end of the old life. But unable to bear life away from her home, Keetah returns to the village, alone. She has waited to return until she was pregnant, but not, as Mark suspects, to make Gordon return; rather, she wants to bring something of him back to the village to comfort his family and herself for their great loss.

The following spring, after a terribly hard winter, old Marta notices on the face of the young vicar a look that she knows all too well. She sends a quiet note to the bishop, who arrives in a season of high celebration. He tells Mark—who still has no idea that he is fatally ill—that he is seeking a replacement for him. One night after burying an old friend on a remote promontory, Mark hears an owl call twice—the traditional Kwakiutl sign of impending death. Mark begins to realize that he has not been formally told something that deep inside himself he knows full well. His impending departure from the village fills him with grief—he will die, he realizes, in a strange city far from the peace he has found among the Indians. But in their own quiet way, the Indians have taken matters into their own hands and asked the bishop to allow Mark to wait out his death among them. Keetah, who loves him, brings him the news.

One afternoon Mark and Jim are at sea when a terrible accident happens; their boat is caught in a slide coming down the mountain at the foot of which they are sailing. Mark is killed and the villagers grieve at his passing. The book closes on the night of Mark's funeral, as the villagers privately hold Mark in their thoughts; Peter, the ceremonial carver, is certain that the spirit of the young man will return to the village he loved:

Past the village flowed the river, like time, like life itself, waiting for the swimmer to come

again on his way to the climax of his adventurous life, and to the end for which he had been made.

(*I Heard the Owl Call My Name*, p. 138)

Potlatch. When Mark, the young Anglican vicar, first comes to live among the Kwakiutl, he knows a few set "facts" about the people, and one of them is that potlatches, the traditional ceremony of gift-giving, "were based on a chief's desire to shame his rival, even if it meant his tribe and his children went hungry" (*I Heard the Owl Call My Name*, p. 59). The Northwest Indian tradition of potlatch is probably the most famous of all Indian rituals, written of extensively by the renowned anthropologist Franz Boas, who worked among the Kwakiutl in the late 1800s and early 1900s. Essentially, potlatch is the ceremonial redistribution of wealth, which among the tribes of the Northwest became a complex web of debt and obligation. At its height, potlatch obligated the receiver of property to double the value of what he received in what he himself gave away at potlatch. The extreme lengths to which certain chiefs would go was a matter of power and pride, but also had the effect of binding tribes more closely together. In 1915 the Canadian Parliament passed a law forbidding potlatch, partly on the grounds that it was ruining Indian tribes financially. The law was enforced by the Royal Canadian Mounted Police, who instructed the Kwakiutl people to hand over all the ceremonial trappings pertaining to the potlatch; such regalia included a lot of valuable copper shields and artwork that were never returned to their owners. The practice of potlatch did not abruptly disappear; it remained underground in certain areas. According to one anthropologist's research, a potlatch held in 1921 saw a chief give away pool tables, sewing machines, engine-powered boats, and furniture (Codere, p. 369). But the Depression of the 1920s and 1930s further discouraged the ceremony. Financial hardship, added to the legal prohibitions, more or less militated against the general practice of potlatch among the Kwakiutl for forty-odd years. A revision of The Indian Act in 1951 lifted the ban against the ceremony, but still it was not resumed. Finally, in the late 1960s—a period of Indian activism and strong assertion of native identity all over North America—the potlatch was once again revived among the Kwakiutl.

Sources. Margaret Craven visited the Kwakiutl village of Kingcome, setting of *I Heard the Owl Call My Name*, and based many of the characters and incidents in the book on composites of the people she came to know there during her four-month stay. The opening scene, in which a church organ is being transported to Kingcome on a pair of canoes, actually happened on her voyage there, and Craven herself appears in the novel as the physical model for the annoying English anthropologist, with her tight wool skirts, huge shoes, and inability to pronounce words in the Kwakwala language.

Craven modeled the young Anglican vicar, Mark Brian, upon Eric Powell, an Anglican vicar in his mid-thirties who had broken his back as a young man and faced eventual paralysis. When she was writing the novel, she had a terrible time creating the episode in which Mark Brian would be killed because he was based on Eric, who had become very important to Craven.

Reviews. Craven, an American, originally sought an American publisher for *I Heard the Owl Call My Name* with little success. She was, however, able to interest a Canadian house in the manuscript, and upon its publication her novel became an instant bestseller. The American market took notice eventually, and the novel has now sold well over a million copies worldwide. In her autobiography, *Again Calls the Owl,* Craven writes:

> There was an astounding deluge of mail. . . . From the rich and the poor, the House of Commons, boys in jail, Arabs, Africans, a headhunter village in New Guinea, from Australia, New Zealand and of course from Canada and my own country. . . . The vast majority of readers . . . said the same thing in almost the same words: I have read the 'Owl'

four times and I feel I must write and tell you what it means to me.
> (*Again Calls the Owl,* p. 116)

Reviews by critics were generally favorable. "It is hard to imagine," wrote Elaine Moss in the *Times Literary Supplement,* "a more complete and fulfilling book than this" (Moss in Gunton, p. 80). In the view of another critic, the novel tends "to idealize life in a Kwakiutl village" but manages nevertheless to create "an entrancing chemistry" between the Indians and the dying vicar (Lewin in Gunton, p. 79).

For More Information

Boas, Franz. *Kwakiutl Tales.* New York: Columbia Univerity Press, 1910.

Codere, Helen. "Kwakiutl: Traditional Culture." In *Handbook of North American Indians.* Vol. 7: *Northwest Coast,* ed. Wayne Shuttles. Washington, D.C.: Smithsonian Institution, 1990.

Craven, Margaret. *I Heard the Owl Call My Name.* Toronto: Clarke, Irwin, 1967.

Craven, Margaret. *Again Calls the Owl.* New York: Dell, 1980.

Gunton, Sharon R., ed. *Contemporary Literary Criticism.* Vol. 17. Detroit: Gale Research, 1981.

Rohner, Ronald, and Evelyn C. Rohner. *The Kwakiutl Indians of British Columbia.* New York: Holt, Rinehart & Winston, 1970.

Sewid, James. *Guests Never Leave Hungry: The Autobiography of James Sewid, a Kwakiutl Indian,* ed. James Spradley. New Haven, Conn.: Yale University Press, 1969.

Walens, Stanley. *Feasting with Cannibals: An Essay on Kwakiutl Cosmology.* Princeton, N.J.: Princeton University Press, 1981.

I Never Sang for My Father

by

Robert Anderson

Born in New York in 1917, Robert Woodruff Anderson graduated from Phillips Exeter Academy and Harvard University before serving in the U.S. Navy. He afterward wrote radio and television scripts, taught playwriting, and endured the death of a wife before writing some of his best-known works. *I Never Sang for My Father* was originally conceived as a film script, and, after a brief Broadway run, it made its screen debut in 1970. At heart a drama about survival, *I Never Sang for My Father* pits father against son in the struggle to live independently in the face of death and aging. Reflected in the relationship are conflicting influences of the two characters' times.

THE LITERARY WORK

A two-act play set in New York City and a town in Westchester County, New York, in the mid-1960s; written in 1966 and first performed in 1968.

SYNOPSIS

An elderly father and son struggle with the deaths of their wives and their own lifelong animosity toward each other.

Events in History at the Time of the Play

Old West. Midway through Act 1 of *I Never Sang for My Father,* Gene Garrison, the hero, steps forward and addresses the audience, confiding to them his father's lifelong addiction to television Westerns: "[W]e hurried through [dinner] to rush home to one of my Father's rituals . . . [t]he television Western. . . . He would sit in front of them hour after hour . . . falling asleep in one and waking up in the middle of the next one . . . never knowing the difference . . ." (Anderson, *I Never Sang for My Father,* p. 19). The Western, always a popular American film genre, found a new home on television in the 1950s after falling out of favor somewhat among film audiences, who by then

had come to prefer star-studded Hollywood extravaganzas.

On television the genre developed into the Western-themed series, whose shows differed from their film counterparts in several respects. Violence, for example, had to be kept to a minimum on television, and the characterization of the hero differed too. On film, the Western hero was a loner, an outcast, the mysterious stranger; on television, the hero was often a family man.

In the mid- to late 1960s, the most popular television Western series were *Bonanza* and *Gunsmoke,* both of which starred a distinctly paternal hero. *Gunsmoke* began as a radio drama in 1952 and appeared as a television series in 1955; within three years, 17 million homes tuned in weekly to the show, which ran until the early 1970s. *Gunsmoke*'s main character, Matt Dillon, is the heroic, paternal guardian of the town of which he is the marshal. *Bonanza* (1959-73),

Michael Landon and Lorne Greene as Joe and Ben Cartwright, in a scene from the popular television western *Bonanza.*

which traces the fortunes of the Cartwright family and their Ponderosa ranch, located in Nevada near Lake Tahoe, is also at heart a family drama. *Bonanza* was headed by Pa (Ben) Cartwright, who governed the Ponderosa as well as his own three sons with intelligence and good-heartedness. The actor Lorne Greene, who played Pa, suggested that it was this essential "happy family" quality that made *Bonanza* so successful: "The Cartwrights happen to be a family that other families want to be like. [Everybody] . . . wants to love and be loved. The Cartwrights love each other" (Greene in Parks, p. 149). In *I Never Sang for My Father,* the manipulative and sometimes cold father, Tom Garrison, ignores his real family to share in the fantasy family life proffered him by television Westerns.

Rotarians. The play's Tom Garrison is a member of the Rotary Club International, a service club for businessmen (and later, businesswomen) and professionals. The Rotarians meet each week to discuss and implement community projects in education, citizenship, and social programs, as well as to participate on the international level in encouraging peace between nations. They are called "Rotarians" because originally their meetings would rotate between members' places of business week by week. The

first Rotary Club was started in 1905 by a Chicago lawyer named Paul Harris; today, the Rotary Club International has members in nearly every country in the world. In 1967, the Rotarians celebrated the 50th anniversary of the Rotary Foundation, a fund that was designed to promote understanding and friendship between people of different nations through charitable, educational, or otherwise philanthropic projects. At the time of the play, the Rotary Foundation sponsored overseas travel, study, and work for approximately 450 people per year.

The graying of America. It was in the 1960s that people started to take note of the general aging of American society; as one textbook on aging from 1960 notes, "there will soon be . . . *almost 50 million of us beyond 50 years of age*" (Tibbits and Donahue, p. xiv; original emphasis). Sociologists and economists began to speculate on the profound changes that a significant population of seniors might have on the American way of life—the changes, more specifically, that might transpire in employment patterns, pension benefits, recreational facilities, health care, and family life. Researchers recognized that American notions of social usefulness and status stem from roles as parents and breadwinners; when these roles are no longer serviceable, problems of identity and self-worth arise. *I Never Sang for My Father* dramatizes just such a crisis, as Tom Garrison struggles to maintain a sense of usefulness and dignity by insisting upon his role as father and provider to his children who no longer require such things of him. To further complicate matters of generational adjustment in America, a new burden of obligation began to settle upon the shoulders of the middle-aged (represented in the play by the characters Gene Garrison and his sister Alice), who suddenly were going to be responsible not just for children and their welfare, but also for the welfare of parents who could now be expected to live perhaps twenty-five years beyond retirement.

Golden years? In *I Never Sang for My Father,* it is not just the father-son relationship between Tom and Gene that has broken down, but also in many respects the marital relationship between the older Garrisons themselves. Tom's wife, Margaret, reflects sadly on the fact that she was often abandoned for a golf game or Tom's buddies, or an entertaining television show. Many sociologists in the 1960s and early 1970s suggested that such a deterioration in the perceived quality of marriage was not uncommon among older couples. A study conducted in 1960 of just over nine hundred women in Detroit, for example, showed that less than 10 percent of them were satisfied with their marriages twenty years into them, and that couples still married after the retirement of the husband were especially unfulfilled. The researchers pointed at the husband's loss of power and sense of identity following his retirement as a major cause of marital discontent.

Generation gap. The conflict between the father and children in Anderson's play can be traced at least in part to shifting tendencies in the nation as a whole. In the play the father expels his daughter from the family for marrying a Jewish man. His anti-Semitism is a holdover from previous decades rather than a typical attitude of the 1960s era in which the play is set. In fact, anti-Semitism in the United States diminished in the 1950s and early 1960s, and relations between Christians and Jews improved. This was partially a result of sympathies for the survivors and victims of the Holocaust, Nazi Germany's effort to eliminate Europe's Jewish population through systematic murder during World War II.

Occupational barriers to hiring Jews in various businesses began to disappear in the 1950s, a trend that continued into the next decade. At the same time, the overt social discrimination by which Jews were excluded from certain resort areas and so-called "restricted" (non-Jewish) neighborhoods also began to decrease. Jews started moving to suburbs that had formerly been closed to them. However, social discrimination lingered in some areas and in the attitudes of people like the play's Tom Garrison. In real life, some employment agencies continued to write "no Jews" on job applications, and a number of private housing developments still refused to sell to Jews. Behind such policies was a stubborn set of Christian-biased prejudices dating back to medieval times that regarded Jews as untrustworthy outsiders.

OASIS

One of the compelling features of television's *Bonanza* is the sense of security and calm offered by the Cartwright family's Nevada homestead, the Ponderosa. Regardless of what might be taking place in the real world, at the Ponderosa there is security, peace, and tradition. This sense of calm must have been reassuring to Americans made anxious by the urban sprawl and inner-city problems that rose to new heights in the 1960s. One writer compares the two environments: "The Cartwright ranch is surrounded by a world of chicanery, violence, and treachery in almost the way the harmonious American middle-class suburb is threatened by the explosive forces of the expanding city. But the cohesiveness, mutual loyalty, and homogeneous adjustment of the Cartwright family always turns out to be capable of throwing back, or blunting the edge of, the invading forces" (Cawelti, p. 76). In Anderson's *I Never Sang for My Father,* the once-quiet New York town of which the father was formerly the mayor has degenerated into a grimy urban landscape. The sense of decay and loss that Tom expresses over and over again may also explain his fascination with the Western dramas played out on his television.

Tom Garrison, the father, who grew up in an environment less accepting of Jews than the one in the play, may have been influenced by anti-Semitic views more common in his youth. His daughter, on the other hand, a product of the newly tolerant post-World War II era, goes so far as to break the ultimate social barrier by marrying a Jew. Along with changing prejudices, attitudes in the play reflect newer thinking about the role of the American family. The 1960s was a decade of rebellion in which notions about the ideal family—breadwinner father, mother, and dutiful children—were called into question and self-fulfillment became a major concern.

> Even in the early 1960s, marriage and family ties were regarded by the "human potential movement" as potential threats to individual fulfillment as a man or a woman. The highest forms of human needs, contended proponents of the new psychologies, were autonomy, independence, growth, and creativity, all of which could be thwarted by "existing relationships and interactions."
>
> (Mintz and Kellog, p. 206)

In the play Tom's forty-year-old son refuses to sacrifice his own desires—to marry and move to California—for the sake of his father. Yet, having grown up in an earlier era, when the family still took priority over the individual, he nevertheless feels tempted to step into the self-sacrificing role of the dutiful son who gives up his own happiness to please his father.

The Play in Focus

The plot. Act 1 opens at a train station, where forty-year-old Gene Garrison has come to pick up his aging parents, Tom Garrison (nearly eighty) and Margaret Garrison (seventy-eight) who have returned from Florida to their New York State home. Tom is a domineering man who believes that he is the only one who has a sense of what is really happening around him; he has a terrible cough, is more or less deaf, and obviously ill. He feels concerned for his wife rather than himself, however; she needs a wheelchair from time to time and has a bad heart.

The three go out to Westchester County, to the once-elegant town where Gene's parents live that has become part of the urban blight surrounding New York City. Tom tells Gene that he and Gene's mother are a little upset that Gene has been seeing a woman in California, only one year after his wife, Carol, has died. They are worried that Gene will move out to the West, which would break his mother's heart. The three of them eat dinner at a local restaurant, where the men have a little argument about who will pay for the meal. Gene is on sabbatical from his teaching job and his father wants to pay for his own dinner rather than accept the night out as a gift from his son.

It becomes clear that money is a point of tension in the family—Tom has been reluctant to see a doctor in Florida because he is certain that he will be overcharged; he has his diamond ring appraised habitually, and orders dinner according to what is cheapest on the menu. His wife accuses him of being interested only in watching Westerns on television and of rehashing his own tragic childhood over and over again. Tom's father abandoned the family when Tom was nine; a year later, when his mother died, the father showed up drunk at the funeral. Tom threw his father out and continued to hate him vehemently right up until the old man died of alcoholism. The memories kill Tom's appetite and he starts flirting with the Irish waitress, another old habit, which irritates Margaret. They leave the restaurant in a rush so that Tom can get home in time to catch a Western on TV that night.

Gene's mother recalls memories from their life together, praising Gene for being so attentive to her at parties when Tom was off dancing and carousing with other people. She abruptly brings up the subject of the California woman whom Gene now loves. Contrary to what Tom has suggested, Margaret encourages Gene to take the big step into another marriage, and, with considerable embarrassment, the two talk obliquely about sex and whether or not they have been happy in their marriages. Margaret impresses upon Gene how grateful she is to have had such a good son and hopes that she has been a good mother. She also tries to impress upon her son what a good father Tom has been, a subject that the two have addressed countless times before. Gene clearly remains unconvinced, but his mother continues in this vein. She confides that Tom makes a great fuss about his relationship with his son, boasting that the two are very close. This stretching of the truth saddens Gene. As he prepares to leave them to return home, Margaret tells her son to go ahead and marry in California; she and Tom will be fine together and they can all keep in touch over the phone. Tom, however, reiterates his earlier statement, that Gene's move west would surely kill his mother.

As he leaves, Gene reminisces about his father's controlling nature, which manifested itself most devastatingly in his expulsion from the family of Gene's sister Alice for marrying a Jew. When Gene arrives home, his father telephones him with some bad news—Margaret has had a heart attack and is in the hospital. The two men visit her the next day but do not stay long, since she needs rest. They eat some supper at the Rotary Club to which Tom belongs and have an argument about whether or not Gene should spend the night with his father or go back home. Gene insists on going home, but Tom makes him feel guilty for wanting to do so. They part on awkward terms and, the next morning, Gene learns his mother has died.

Act 2 opens with Gene in conversation with Dr. Mayberry, his parents' physician, who tells him frankly that his father should not be living alone. Gene takes his sedated father to talk to Mr. Scott, the mortician, and the two of them wander through a showroom of coffins. Gene is agitated by his father's businesslike analysis of costs and expenses. Tom quibbles with the mortician over how much coffins cost and how well they stand up to things like seepage and intrusive tree roots. At one point Tom comes to stand before a tiny child's coffin, which brings back his mother's funeral—she was "a little bit of a thing"—and he rehashes the old story of throwing his father out at her funeral (*I Never Sang for My Father*, p. 40). Finally he settles on the coffin he wants—making sure that the tax is included in the price tag.

The action shifts to a bar where Gene is sharing a few drinks with his older sister Alice. The two of them discuss their father, his sterling reputation in the town, and also his selfishness; Gene also acknowledges that his father's famous fighting edge, though dulled, remains a part of the deaf, forgetful old man's character:

> Still, wait till you see him. There's something that comes through . . . the old Tiger. Something that reaches you and makes you want to cry. . . . He'll probably be asleep when we get home, in front of television. And you'll see. The Old Man . . . the Father. But then he wakes up and becomes Tom Garrison.
>
> (*I Never Sang for My Father*, p. 43)

The scene shifts to the graveyard, in which Margaret has just been laid to rest in the family plot where Carol, Gene's wife, was buried a year earlier. Irate, Tom walks away, to find the caretaker and complain about the state in which the plot is being kept. Gene and Alice discuss what to do as a memorial for their mother, and also what to do about their father, who clearly should not be left alone, but who, equally clearly, cannot come to live with either of his children. Alice sees her father as a selfish old man who neglected their mother, beat Gene, and threw her out of the house because of her choice of spouse. His frailty does not wring much compassion from her, but for Gene matters are more complicated. He feels an enduring sense of obligation and guilt because his father has done well for the family, and because he has never been able to love the old man.

The two later broach the idea of getting a live-in housekeeper for Tom, but he resists, insisting that Gene can look in on him a couple of times a week. Tom still refuses to understand that Gene wants to move to California, or to acknowledge that his own health is so bad that he might need constant supervision. The three of them have a terrible fight, in which Tom's hatred and jealousy of his children appears nakedly. He hates their freedom and independence. Alice bluntly tells Tom that Gene wants to move away and Tom receives the news with chilly sarcasm, insisting that he doesn't want to ruin anyone's life. After the old man has left the room, Alice remarks that he already has ruined people's lives and that if Gene is smart he'll cut himself loose from the weird bonds of guilt and compulsion that tie him to his ungrateful father. Gene and Alice reconcile before she leaves; he knows that what she says is true, that the image of the eternally bereaved husband and the dutiful son—and the pull to live up to it—is hard to overcome.

Alone again, Gene goes to his father's bedroom, where the old man kneels and prays, as he does every night. The two men share some tender moments as the father reveals that he has saved a drawerful of keepsakes from Gene's childhood, including a Glee Club program. Tom remembers that he was always coming into rooms just in time to hear Gene finish singing (hence the title of the play). Gene is softened sufficiently that he invites his father to move to California to live near him and Peggy, his fiancée. Tom refuses, preferring that Peggy and her children move into Tom's house and they all live together. Gene refuses this option and Tom's tone becomes chilly; he informs his son that from this moment on he can consider his father dead and never bother another second about him. Gene leaves, never to return, with his father screaming "GO TO HELL" behind him (*I Never Sang for My Father*, p. 62). At the end of the play, Gene tells the audience that his father did come to California and had to be put into a hospital there because of his hardening arteries and the onset of senility. The play closes with the sight of Tom in a wheelchair, as Gene states that his father died watching television:

> Death ends a life . . . but it does not end a relationship, which struggles on in the survivor's mind . . . towards some resolution which it never finds.

Alice said I would not accept the sadness of the world. . . . What did it matter if I never loved him, or if he never loved me? . . . Perhaps she was right. . . . But, still, when I hear the word Father. . . . It matters.

(*I Never Sang for My Father,* p. 62)

Roosevelt. "'[G]o through [obstacles] or over them, but never around them.' Teddy Roosevelt said that, I took it down in shorthand for practice. . . . Any young man in this country, who has a sound mind and a sound body, who will set himself an objective, can achieve anything he wants within reason" (*I Never Sang for My Father,* p. 38). Teddy Roosevelt is one of Tom Garrison's heroes, a model of behavior to which the old man has clung for his whole life. During Roosevelt's presidency (1901-1908), the United States enjoyed unparalleled prosperity and the comfort of living under a president who was a hero, a social reformer, and an inspired motivational speaker to boot. More to the play's point, however, Theodore Roosevelt—an intellectual from a wealthy and powerful Eastern family— was indelibly associated with the lure of the West in America's imagination. In 1884, after the death of his wife and a major political disappointment, Roosevelt packed up and moved to the Dakota Territory, to try and prosper in the burgeoning beef industry there. He wrote three books about his experiences, books that were to a large extent responsible for the creation of the "Old West" myth of rugged individualism and vast open spaces that became part of American popular culture. Naturalist notes on bighorn sheep, tips on hunting grizzly, and character sketches of the wild and wonderful people that Roosevelt encountered made his books immensely popular. He also wrote a four-volume series called *The Winning of the West.* Upon his return to New York City, he ran for mayor. The "Cowboy Candidate," as he was popularly known, experienced a sound defeat in that particular election, but he would, of course, rise eventually to the presidency.

Production. *I Never Sang for My Father* began as a film script entitled *The Tiger,* which was completed in the summer of 1962. It was then sent upon a convoluted journey in an attempt to bring it to stage or screen, a process so arduous it seemed unlikely to ever see production. Anderson first offered the film script to Fred Zinneman, who praised it and stated that he would love to work on the movie as long as Spencer Tracy would play the role of Tom Garrison. Tracy declined the offer and meanwhile another director, Elia Kazan, expressed the de-

President Theodore Roosevelt

sire to perform *The Tiger* as a play. Months passed, and Kazan finally admitted that he could find no suitable actor to take on the difficult part of the bitter old man. Producer after producer turned down the play—now entitled *I Never Sang for My Father*—and then, in a climactic moment of confusion and competition, Anderson had two offers at the same time. It turned out that Spencer Tracy would do the movie after all, on television, and could probably be counted on to bring Katherine Hepburn along with him to play the role of the mother. Simultaneously, another television producer, who had never done any performance on Broadway, expressed an interest in attempting the play in the theaters. Just as Anderson gave permission for the Tracy-Hepburn production, Zinneman called to say that CBS found the play too grim and that they wouldn't run it after all. Finally, on January 25, 1968, almost six years after the original script was finished, *I Never Sang for My Father* made its debut with a different cast at the Longacre Theatre in New York City. On the success of the play, a Hollywood production was launched; the film version premiered in 1970, starring Gene Hackman as Gene, and Melvyn Douglas as Tom.

Reviews. *I Never Sang for My Father* ran for a mere 124 performances as a stage play in New York, then went to London where it was hoped it would fare better. Clive Barnes reviewed the play in the *New York Times,* commenting that "the poignancy of the situation, real enough and believable in all conscience, is constantly betrayed by the over-obviousness and sentimentality of the writing" (Barnes in MacNicholas, p. 43). One of the reviewers in London called it "sensitive, intelligent, patently honest—and very stale and familiar"; "we have met these people before," said another (Adler, p. 133). Still *I Never Sang for My Father* was held by some to be one of the best Broadway plays of the season: "[N]ot only a powerful experience of theatre, it was also a triumph of American playwriting combined with Broadway stagecraft" (Guernsey, p. 20). In 1970 Anderson won the Writers Guild of America Award for the screenplay, which he adapted from the stage version of 1968.

For More Information

Adler, Thomas P. *Robert Anderson.* Boston: Twayne, 1978.

Anderson, Robert. *I Never Sang for My Father.* New York: Dramatists' Play Service, 1968.

Brubaker, Timothy H., ed. *Family Relationships in Later Life.* Beverly Hills, Calif.: Sage, 1983.

Cawelti, John G. "The Gunfighter and Society." *The American West* 5, no. 2 (March 1968), 30-5, 76-7.

Guernsey, Otis L., Jr., ed. *The Best Plays of 1967-68.* New York: Dodd, Mead, 1968.

MacNicholas, John. *Dictionary of Literary Biography.* Vol. 7. Detroit: Gale Research, 1981.

Miller, Nathan. *Theodore Roosevelt: A Life.* New York: William Morrow, 1992.

Mintz, Steven, and Susan Kellog. *Domestic Revolutions: A Social History of American Family Life.* New York: Free Press, 1988.

Parks, Rita. *The Western Hero in Film and Television.* Ann Arbor, Mich.: UMI Research Press, 1982.

Tibbits, Clark, and Wilma Donahue, eds. *Aging in Today's Society.* Englewood Cliffs, N.J.: Prentice-Hall, 1960.

Imagining Argentina

by
Lawrence Thornton

Lawrence Thornton (1937-) earned his Ph.D. at the University of California and was a visiting professor at its Santa Barbara and Los Angeles campuses from 1984 to 1988 when he wrote his first novel, *Imagining Argentina.* Thornton, an English professor, became interested in a story he saw on the CBS television news magazine *60 Minutes* about Argentina's "dirty war." From 1976 to 1983, Argentina was ruled by a group of generals who targeted thousands of their own citizens, attempting to snuff out political opposition and free speech by kidnapping, torturing, and murdering any Argentines suspected of liberal or antigovernment views. Thornton's novel tells the story of the victims of this dirty war—known as *desaparecidos,* or "disappeared ones"—through the eyes of a fictional journalist, Martín Benn, and his friend Carlos Rueda, whose wife is among the *desaparecidos.*

Events in History at the Time the Novel Takes Place

A century of chaos. From 1930 to 1983, Argentines lived in a continual state of political instability. The army's 1930 overthrow of President Hipólito Yrigoyen set a pattern that was to be repeated incessantly throughout the following decades. Leaders replaced one another sometimes as often as every few months, and elections, if held, were as likely to be fixed as fair. In 1946, in a rare, relatively clean election, army colonel Juan Perón was elected; his stint in of-

> ## THE LITERARY WORK
> A novel set in Argentina in the late 1970s and early 1980s; published in 1987.
>
> ## SYNOPSIS
> After his wife suddenly disappears one day, Carlos Rueda discovers that he can use his powerful imagination to learn the truth about the Argentine government's kidnapping, torture, and murder of thousands of its own citizens.

fice would last nearly ten years. His second wife, Eva Duarte de Perón, won for him enormous popular support among the working classes; she also solidified his ties to the country's powerful trade unions. This unusually long regime came to an abrupt end, however, when Perón resigned rather than wage a civil war against the group of military officials who challenged his rule. Between Perón's resignation in 1955 and the democratic election of Raúl Alfonsín in 1983, Argentina was ruled by sixteen different governments—an average of one new government every eighteen months.

Fake war, real violence. Juan Perón spent most of those intervening years in exile, but returned in 1971 and won Argentina's 1973 presidential election. Unfortunately the aged Perón died the following year, and presidential duties were taken over by his third wife, Maria Estela "Isabel" Perón. During her reign, terrorist activity increased. In March 1976, she was forced out of power by a group of Argentine generals. Justifying their takeover as an attempt to rescue Argentina from impending civil war, the generals quickly dismissed the congress, replaced other elected officials and judges with military officers, and, ignoring the Argentine constitution, declared that the death penalty could be used in sentencing crimes against the state. There were two leftist rebel groups who appeared to threaten the junta's hold on the country, the Montoneros and the ERP (People's Revolutionary Army); both were actively working to seize control of the government. Yet the generals themselves were well aware that such a coup would be extremely unlikely—the rebel groups were too small and too weak to be a real threat. In fact, to convince the public that a military government was necessary in Argentina, the generals actually faked hundreds of terrorist acts—acts that they then said were committed by the rebels.

The real goal of these Argentine generals was much bigger than winning a war against disorganized, relatively powerless rebel groups. What they attempted to do in the years between 1976 and 1983 was create a country in which any aberrant political or social views were eliminated. Although their major targets were labor unions, liberal priests, and politically active students and intellectuals, the ultra-conservative generals could easily become suspicious of almost anyone, from the distant cousin of a labor leader to the teenage son of a nosy reporter. These suspicions alone were often enough for innocent Argentines to become *desaparecidos*.

What happened to every *desaparecido* is not known, but the cases that have come to light are shocking. One victim of the dirty war, Pablo Díaz, was sixteen when he was kidnapped for protesting a rise in student bus fares. Suspecting that he and his fellow protesters might have links to the rebel Montoneros, military authorities brought them to what they called the "truth machine," an electric prod used for torture. "They gave it to me in the mouth, on my gums and on the genitals," Díaz said later.

> They even pulled out a toenail with a tweezers. Often we were hit with billyclubs, fists and kicked. . . . They asked all of us about the school fare, why we participated, what motivated us to ask for the reduction, who was guiding us. . . . We had to sleep on the floor. Us guys were in our underwear, because they had taken our clothes from us. Almost all of us ended up in rags, almost nude.
>
> (Díaz in Andersen, p. 201)

This was only the beginning of months of torture for Pablo Díaz and his classmates. When it was finally over, only three of the fifteen kidnapped students had survived.

The brutal treatment of these students for such a seemingly innocent act was not unusual in the days of Argentina's dirty war. It was not unusual for Argentine citizens to disappear for committing such "subversive" acts as teaching modern math or setting up cooperative farms for poor peasants. As more and more people vanished, a feeling of great fear swept over the country, and most Argentines felt powerless to stop the horrors that they suspected (or knew) their government was responsible for.

A PHONY BATTLE

A common practice of the Argentine military during the dirty war was to stage phony battles between their forces and communist rebels. One former U.S. intelligence agent tells the story of "having arrived at the scene of a supposed 'shoot-out' between the security forces and leftist guerrillas in 1976 to find the former splashing chickens' blood around the locale before admitting local reporters and photographers" (Andersen, p. 3).

Government news vs. real news. Journalists were equally at risk during the years of repression between 1976 and 1983. When the military seized power, it also seized control over the Argentine press, torturing or killing writers like the novel's fictional Cecilia, who tried to report on stories independent of the official government news agencies. Such control of the press was necessary for the junta to protect the basic lie of its regime—the façade that it was fighting a war against terrorist rebels, not innocent citizens.

The Mothers of the Plaza de Mayo. Despite their fears of retaliation, one group of Argentine citizens managed to protest the government's brutality throughout the dirty war. This group, the Mothers of the Plaza de Mayo, staged its first demonstration in front of the government headquarters (at the Plaza de Mayo) in April 1977 to demand that their "disappeared" children, friends, and relatives be returned alive. Every Thursday afternoon for the next ten years, the

Eva and Juan Perón

Mothers returned to the Plaza de Mayo carrying pictures of their kidnapped loved ones and demanding information about their whereabouts. They also made lists of the disappeared, the most recent numbering over eight thousand. Although Argentina's military government sent a spy to investigate the Mothers and kidnapped and killed a number of them, the group stayed intact well into the 1980s, working to insure that those responsible for the disappearances were identified and punished.

Nazis in Argentina. After the defeat of Germany in World War II, a number of key Nazi figures escaped from Europe and the subsequent war crimes trials. Most settled in somewhere in South America under an assumed name. In the late 1940s and early 1950s, Argentina's President Perón welcomed thousands of Nazi war criminals, issuing fake passports that protected the identities of these new immigrants. One such beneficiary was Adolf Eichmann, who headed the Jewish section of the Gestapo and thus oversaw the murder of millions of Jews in Europe's concentration camps during the war years. Perón claimed that he was most interested in the technical skills of these Nazi immigrants, which would help him build new factories and improve Argentina's military hardware. What he welcomed to Argentina, however, was more than

technological know-how. Many of the same Nazis listed by the U.S. Army as war criminals began serving in the Argentine military, leading one Nazi immigrant to comment: "There are now so many former Gestapo men in the intelligence service here that it is riskier to tell a joke about Argentine Government personages in German than in Spanish" (Hunt, p. 148).

The mingling of exiled Nazis with Argentine military and government officials in the decades following World War II may also have resulted in a fusion of harmful ideas and practices. Many Jewish Argentines—especially those who had immigrated after surviving Hitler's concentration camps—noticed the similarities between the Nazi past and the Argentine dirty war. One such Argentine explained, "I was held in Germany's concentration camps, I was persecuted during the [military regime], and my daughter was kidnapped here. The only difference was that there they cremated people and here they threw them in the river" (Andersen, p. 205).

The Novel in Focus

The plot. Carlos Rueda's life as playwright for a children's theater in Buenos Aires is suddenly interrupted one afternoon when his wife, Cecilia, disappears. A journalist, Cecilia has written one too many editorials critical of Argentina's military government; her husband and daughter, Teresa, assume that she has been taken on the orders of government officials.

Soon after Cecilia's abduction, Carlos discovers that he has a strange new ability: after hearing the stories of other *desaparecidos* from their loved ones, he can imagine where they are, what has happened to them, and what is still in store for them—and these imaginings turn out to be true. Deciding to use this gift of extrasensory perception to combat the lies told by the government about the *desaparecidos,* Carlos begins holding sessions in his garden with the mothers he meets in the Plaza de Mayo to hear their stories and to tell how they end.

Although Carlos is able to bring comfort to a number of families with his gift, he cannot use it to find his wife; he sees passing images of her but none that tell him where she is or whether she is alive. These images lead Carlos to the pampas, or grasslands, of southern Argentina. There he finds an old Jewish couple, the Sternbergs, who survived a Nazi concentration camp and give him this advice: "If you are forced to live in a nightmare, you survive by realizing that you can reimagine it, that some day you can return to reality" (Thornton, *Imagining Argentina,* p. 79).

After his visit to the pampas, Carlos completes a play for his theater called *The Names.* This play, about the erased names of the disappeared, is performed to a packed audience that includes government officials. In retaliation for what they see as an act of subversion, the officials board up the theater, knock Carlos unconscious, and kidnap Teresa. Dizzy but enraged, Carlos follows one of the generals home from his government office with a gun, but when he sees him with his family he is not able to pull the trigger.

Left now without his wife or daughter, Carlos continues searching his imagination for traces of both. In one of his garden sessions, he describes the images of Teresa that come to him, but when his vision ends in a blinding light, he believes that she is dead—a belief that is confirmed later in the novel. Unable to tell any more stories and unable to stop reliving Teresa's death, Carlos leaves Buenos Aires. For a few weeks, he lives on a beach, uncertain of whether Cecilia is alive or whether he should go on living. By the end of his stay, though, he is able to sense her presence and returns to Buenos Aires to tell her story.

In his garden, Carlos tells of how Cecilia was taken from home and moved from place to place, always blindfolded. He tells of how eventually she was kept in the same building as Teresa and, as part of a soldiers' game, was forced to choose her daughter's rapists. Then he tells of how she survived by writing in her head and how she memorized her words by matching each thought to a place on her cell's wall. Finally, he describes how she escaped by killing a guard. This story and the images that follow gradually lead Carlos to discover Cecilia's whereabouts; she has been hiding with a family in the pampas since her escape. It is not until Argentina's generals themselves start disappearing and the dirty war reaches its end that Cecilia returns to Buenos Aires and is reunited with her husband. There they watch the trial of the generals who brutalized their country, and there they both return to the reality that was interrupted by a true nightmare.

A WORD ABOUT LATIN AMERICAN FICTION

In an essay called "Latin America: Fiction and Reality," the Peruvian writer Mario Vargas Llosa argues that Latin Americans have a hard time differentiating between fiction and reality, and this difficulty can be traced to the days of Spanish colonization. Because novels were forbidden in the Spanish colonies of Latin America by the strict Spanish Inquisition, the natural human "appetite for lies" emerged in other parts of life. As Vargas Llosa explains, "the inquisitors achieved the exact opposite of their intentions: a world without novels, yes, but a world into which fiction had spread and contaminated practically everything: history, religion, poetry, science, art, speeches, journalism, and the daily habits of people" (Vargas Llosa, p. 5). This theory perhaps sheds some light on how a regime based on lies and terror could last so long in Argentina—and why it took so much time for the truth about the dirty war to emerge.

The uses of imagination. *Imagining Argentina* tells the story of a government that has taken control of almost everything in the country, even deciding what constitutes truth. One of the only things beyond its reach is the imagination of its citizens. For the "disappeared" characters in the novel, imagination provides an escape from the nightmare of torture, as it had for the Sternbergs during the Holocaust. For Carlos Rueda, however, imagination assumes even greater meaning.

The Mothers of the Plaza de Mayo.

It is both an escape from a painful reality of uncertainty as well as a window into the truth. It enables him to sense true stories that otherwise might never be heard.

Although Carlos is used to writing fictional plays for children, he discovers after his wife's disappearance that to help his community and himself, he must also start dealing in facts—the facts that have been distorted by Argentina's military government. Through his imagination, Carlos gains access not only to information about the *desaparecidos*, but to the feeling of power that comes from knowing things for certain—a rare feeling during the fearful and unpredictable era of the dirty war. In *Imagining Argentina*, Carlos shows that imagination is not just the tool of an artist, but a necessity for surviving these times. "We have to believe in the power of imagination," Carlos says, "because it is all we have, and ours is stronger than theirs [the generals']" (*Imagining Argentina*, p. 65). In a country ruled by terror, suspicion, and lies, imagination ends up being a powerful weapon for self-defense.

Sources. Lawrence Thornton had never been to Argentina when he began writing his first novel. He had been following the disturbing news reports about Argentina's dirty war and was especially moved by a *60 Minutes* television interview with the Mothers of the Plaza de Mayo in the early 1980s. This interview prompted him to think about the word "disappeared," and his thoughts led to the writing of *Imagining Argentina*.

The novel borrows heavily from the real history of Argentina's dirty war. For example, Cecilia works at a real Buenos Aires newspaper, *La Opinión*, whose publisher, Jacobo Timmerman, was abducted during the dirty war. Other details from the novel are also taken straight from history: the green Ford Falcons used as getaway cars during kidnappings were a common sight in Argentina at that time. Listed below are a few of the most shocking events from the novel, events that actually happened in Argentina between 1976 and 1983:

- Fifteen high school students are abducted and tortured, most eventually killed, for protesting high bus fares.

- A government spy, disguised as the mourning brother of a *desaparecido*, infiltrates the Mothers of the Plaza de Mayo, planning the abduction of some key members. In the novel, the spy's plan is foiled by Carlos, who senses his dishonesty. In reality, the plan succeeded.

- In the Naval Mechanics School and in other facilities used for torture around the country, innocent victims of a suspicious government, like Carlos's friend Silvio, endure weeks or months of electric shocks and beatings, finally being thrown out of helicopters and into the sea, where they disappear forever.

Events in History at the Time the Novel Was Written

A final injustice. Economic trouble and a failed attempt to win back control of the British-held Malvinas (Falkland) Islands finally ended the rule of the generals in 1983. Sensing their loss of any popular support—their lies had become less credible after the lost war with Britain—and their inability to solve the economic problems brought on by high military spending and financial mismanagement, the generals yielded power to civilians, scheduling a presidential election for October 1983.

A month before their planned departure, the generals passed a law protecting all military personnel from being prosecuted for acts committed during the dirty war. This attempt at protecting themselves failed, however, when newly elected president Raúl Alfonsín nullified the law soon after taking office. Two years later, after dozens of unmarked mass graves had been discovered and torture had been declared a crime equivalent to murder, the nine generals who had run the country from 1976 to 1983 were put on trial for genocide. However, despite the stirring words of their prosecutor, who claimed to be working in the name of "10,000 *desaparecidos*" (Andersen, p. 11), many of the generals received light sentences, with four acquitted and only two sentenced to life imprisonment. In 1990 the three generals still in prison and all others convicted for participating in the dirty war were pardoned by President Carlos Menem.

Reception. *Imagining Argentina* won numerous book awards and received praise from reviewers for its powerful storytelling and effective blending of the supernatural with the realistic—a style known as "magical realism," popular among Latin American writers. It inspired a number of screenplays and a flamenco production called "Garden of Names." Criticism of the novel focused on its unconvincing portrayal of Argentina, noting signs of Thornton's unfamiliarity with the look and feel of Buenos Aires and the pampas. Thornton himself dismisses these criticisms, explaining that writing novels is not just about telling or re-telling stories but changing reality. "I believe," he says, "that fiction plays an important social function, and while novelists can't expect their works to change the world, we have to believe it's possible" (Thornton in Trosky, p. 421).

For More Information

Andersen, Martin Edwin. *Dossier Secreto: Argentina's Desaparecidos and the Myth of the "Dirty War."* Boulder, Colo.: Westview, 1993.

Hodges, Donald C. *Argentina's "Dirty War": An Intellectual Biography.* Austin: University of Texas Press, 1991.

Hunt, Linda. *Secret Agenda: The United States Government, Nazi Scientists, and Project Paperclip, 1945 to 1990.* New York: St. Martin's, 1991.

Levy, Alan. *The Wiesenthal File.* Grand Rapids, Mich.: William B. Eerdmans, 1993.

Rock, David. *Argentina, 1516-1982: From Spanish Colonization to the Falklands War.* Berkeley: University of California Press, 1985.

Thornton, Lawrence. *Imagining Argentina.* New York: Doubleday, 1987.

Trosky, Susan M., ed. *Contemporary Authors.* Vol. 132. Detroit: Gale Research, 1991.

Vargas Llosa, Mario. "Latin America: Fiction and Reality." In *Modern Latin American Fiction.* Edited by John King. London: Faber & Faber, 1987.

In Nueva York

by

Nicholasa Mohr

Nicholasa Mohr was born to Puerto Rican parents in 1935 in a neighborhood of New York City known as *El Barrio,* or Spanish Harlem. She grew up in the Bronx in New York during the Great Depression, facing economic and social challenges associated with the time, the place, and her ethnicity. Mohr used adversity to fuel her creativity and imagination, first as a visual artist, painting the community scenes that she saw around her, and then as a writer. Her novel *In Nueva York* portrays the lives of several families living in the Puerto Rican neighborhoods of the Lower East Side of New York City around 1970. The eight vignettes that comprise the novel look at the community from several perspectives, bringing into relief both its cruelties and its joys.

Events in History at the Time of the Novel

Puerto Rico: A brief history. Puerto Rico was originally called *Borinquen,* meaning "the land of the brave lord" in the language of the natives (the Arawak or Taino Indians, Taino being the Spanish name for them). In 1492 Christopher Columbus encountered a thriving native population of some 40,000. A few years later, in 1505, the Spanish founded a settlement on the island, after which the numbers of natives shrunk rapidly. Some 6,000 rebelled and were punished by being shot to death in 1511. Faced with a sudden labor shortage, the Spanish began to import African slaves on boats that also brought small-

pox to the island. By 1515 only about 4,000 Taino Indians, or one-tenth of the original population, were left (Novas, p. 147).

Puerto Rico became the gateway to the Spanish empire in South and Central America and soon sported an imposing fortress. Spanish ships making the long trip from America to Europe stopped at the island for supplies. At first, the African slaves worked fields of sugar cane, coffee, and spices, to which were later added tobacco and ginger. Most of the money that people made in Puerto Rico came from illegal trade with other European nations, a practice that Spain had forbidden, of course, but could not seem to control. In 1765, Major Alejandro O'Reilly, a Spanish official, arrived on the island and started a cultural overhaul of the place. He gave free farm land to Spaniards willing to till it; he oversaw the building of Spanish schools and communities—in short, he tried to turn Puerto Rico into a little piece of the motherland, in the hopes that stronger cultural and political ties would bring economic ties with them.

But it would prove to be too late—the Puerto Ricans (now a mixture of Taino, African, and Spaniard) already considered themselves a separate people from the Spanish, and began a long process of negotiating for independence. On July 17, 1898, Spain finally gave in and granted the Puerto Ricans the right to be governed not by Spaniards, but by locally elected officials. This system lasted just one week—and then the United States, at war with Spain since April 1898, arrived in force on the island and ruled it thereafter. Official notice of the change in leadership dragged behind the actual fact. Spain ceded Puerto Rico to the United States in the Treaty of Paris, signed December 10, 1898, which brought the Spanish-American War to an official end.

To the dismay of Puerto Ricans, the American victory did not bring about independence. Instead the United States ruled the island through a military government, until pressure for increased autonomy produced the Jones Act. Passed in 1917, the Act declared Puerto Ricans to be citizens of the United States—a move widely resented by the general population, in part because Puerto Rican men were now subject to the American draft during World War I (17,000 were actually drafted). As American citizens, Puerto Ricans were subject to federal laws, but they could not vote in U.S. elections and did not pay federal taxes unless they lived on the mainland. Still Puerto Ricans agitated for greater reform. In 1946, Jesús Piñero (1897-1952) became the first Puerto Rican-born governor of the island, and in 1952, Puerto Rico became an *estado libre asociado,* or free associated state (in English, a "Commonwealth"), which allowed Puerto Ricans to live and work in the mainland U.S. and travel freely between the U.S. and Puerto Rico.

Migration. After the Spanish-American War, Puerto Ricans began the massive migration to America and especially to New York City that continued into the time during which Mohr was writing *In Nueva York.* During and after World War I, Puerto Ricans settled in Brooklyn, near the Navy Yard, where many served during the war. However, by the 1930s (the period during which Old Mary, the character at the beginning of *In Nuevo York,* first came to America), the largest Puerto Rican community was in Harlem. After World War II and the passage of legislation making Puerto Rico a United States commonwealth, Puerto Ricans began to migrate by the thousands to the mainland, and especially to

New York City, seeking greater economic prosperity. Puerto Rico was at that time experiencing widespread unemployment along with a population boom; America, on the other hand, was more prosperous than ever. The migrants came to New York City in particular because it was relatively easy to find work in the massive service industry and in the Garment District, especially for Puerto Rican women.

STEREOTYPES

When Nicholasa Mohr was a high school student, "she was mortified by her guidance counselor's insistence that she, as a Puerto Rican girl, did not need a solid academic education" and would be well served by attending a school where she could learn to sew. (Telgen, p. 275)

One historian notes that the Puerto Ricans "constitute the first airborne migration to the United States"; with mid-century airfare between San Juan and New York costing as little as $50 and with travel agencies willing to accept monthly installments on the price of the six-hour flight (about three hours today), the Puerto Ricans have not had to undergo the terrible ordeals that other migrating peoples have had to suffer in coming to America (Fitzpatrick, p. 15). By 1973, nearly 5 million Puerto Ricans migrated to the mainland annually. Not all of them would stay, however; a great many Puerto Ricans return to the island once they have established themselves financially in New York, or have managed to save enough money to fund an extended return home. As of 1970, one of the biggest problems nagging the New York Puerto Rican community was the absence of wealth and prestige, for as soon as these were achieved, people tended to go back to Puerto Rico. In Mohr's novel, for example, Old Mary's friend, who puts her in touch with her long-lost son, William, retires to Puerto Rico after spending his working life in New York City.

In 1970, according to the U.S. Census, 817,712 Puerto Ricans resided in New York—the largest Puerto Rican population of any city in the world, including San Juan, Puerto Rico. In the same year, 1970, the average per capita income of Puerto Ricans, the poorest group of people in New York City, was $5,575—almost half the citywide median of $9,682. One-third lived

Children playing in a vacant lot on the Lower East Side of New York.

below the poverty level and were the poorest of all Latino groups in the United States. There are signs of this poverty throughout Mohr's novel.

"Nueva York." After World War II—during the most active Puerto Rican migration period—Puerto Ricans in New York spread from their original settlements near the Navy Yards into East Harlem, the South Bronx, the Upper West Side, the Williamsburg section of Brooklyn, and the Lower East Side (where *In Nueva York* is set). The Lower East Side was previously a Jewish neighborhood before the arrival of the Puerto Ricans, and the Jews had been preceded by many other groups. The area was in an advanced state of dereliction, but some of its areas were a step up from the East Harlem Puerto Rican neighborhood known as El Barrio, the neighborhood in which Mohr was born. This community of Spanish Harlem remains the heart of the Puerto Rican community in New York.

El Barrio had first begun to attract Puerto Ricans as early as 1917. In the following decade, the Puerto Ricans slowly displaced the Russian-Jews, Irish, and Italians who had been living there; the original inhabitants were not thrilled with what was happening, and a plague of youth gangs formed to dispute territory. But change was inevitable, and East Harlem became a solidly Puerto Rican neighborhood. An observer of the

neighborhood in roughly 1970 describes the place as follows:

> Life begins to stir in the Barrio at 6:30 in the morning, for the poor are early-risers. They must do the jobs nobody else wants, those with very early hours or very late hours . . . the Puerto Rican women set out for the garment factories. Later, the children pass by on their way to school. Still later, unemployed men gather on the sidewalks to chat. . . . Old people and housewives lean from their windows to watch the passers-by.
>
> (Tovar, p. 38)

Despite the obvious problems of poverty, the Puerto Rican community in New York is tight-knit and culturally active. It has its own Spanish-language newspaper, *El Diario de Nueva York,* which Mary is reading as *In Nueva York* opens. *El Museo del Barrio,* located alongside the city's other museums on Fifth Avenue, showcases the work of Puerto Rican and other Latino artists. The community has had several theatre companies that produce Puerto Rican plays, perhaps the most innovative of which was the *Teatro Rodante Puertorriqueño* (Puerto Rican Theatre on Wheels), which traveled to the poorest of neighborhoods to put on performances. *La Marqueta,* an open air market, is the social center of the community.

Drugs. In one of the novel's vignettes, "I Never Even Seen My Father," a teenage girl, Yolanda, explains to her friend, Lil, how it was that she wound up in rehabilitation:

> Look, maybe I started on drugs because of a lotta things that might be wrong with me. Right? First of all, drugs are out there, available for anybody who wants to get high. . . . When you're high, it's beautiful, because you got no worries, man. You feel fabulous, you ain't scared of nothing and nobody. Your problems are over because you don't see where you live and you don't see what you ain't got and what you look like, and you don't miss what you can't see.
>
> (Mohr, *In Nueva York,* pp. 40-1)

Yolanda is describing a problem that, in New York City in the late 1960s and early 1970s, afflicted a disproportionate number of Puerto Ricans. Between 1964 and 1968, 23 percent of the 62,938 people in New York City whose names were on the Department of Health's Narcotics Register were Puerto Rican; in 1969 alone, 689 Puerto Ricans died of drug abuse in the city (Fitzpatrick, p. 172).

It is generally agreed that one of the major causes of drug addiction among New York's Puerto Rican poor is environmental: peer pressure and the high visibility of drug users in the neighborhood. Children and youth, like Yolanda in Mohr's novel, are particularly susceptible. *In Nueva York* describes the neighborhood as infested with drug pushers and addicts—this is one of the main reasons that Mary wishes to move away. In the same year in which *In Nueva York* was published, the *New York Times* (February 27, 1970) ran a story about a twelve-year-old Puerto Rican boy who had become a heroin addict. The boy stated that his decline into addiction was purely a matter of conforming: "nobody taught me, nobody forced me, but I didn't want to be left out when I saw my friends use drugs" (Fitzpatrick, p. 173).

The education factor. *In Nueva York* illustrates that lack of education and its attendant economic opportunity are major obstacles facing the Puerto Rican community. Primarily because New York City schools did not offer bilingual education until 1975, there was a high dropout rate among Puerto Rican immigrants who spoke little English. In 1970 the average twenty-five-year-old Puerto Rican had completed 8.6 years of school, compared to a national average of 12.1 years, and just 2 percent had finished college. Contributing to the high dropout rate was an opposition in the community to becoming "Americanized"; many

Puerto Ricans felt that learning English and being exposed to an American/Eurocentric education would compromise loyalty to their culture, homeland, and language. The disproportional dropout rate led to a class action lawsuit against the New York City Board of Education in 1975. Filed by Aspira, a Puerto Rican educational association, the lawsuit (*Aspira v. NYC Board of Education*) demanded bilingual education for the city's significant Spanish speaking population.

ASPIRA

From the Spanish word meaning "to strive," Aspira was founded in New York City by Antonia Pantoja in 1961 to help Puerto Rican youth obtain a higher education, whether academic, artistic, or otherwise. Not only does it solicit scholarship funds for deserving students, it also promotes Puerto Rican culture. In 1970 Aspira clubs existed in many high schools in New York's Puerto Rican community, encouraging students to achieve academic and personal success.

Following the lawsuit, district schools began providing instruction in Spanish for regular curriculum classes such as math and history, and implementing multicultural studies programs. As a result, there has been an increase in college enrollment among Puerto Rican youth. Furthermore, the proportion of second-generation Puerto Ricans attending adult education classes is now higher than for any other ethnic group in the nation, and a Puerto Rican Studies Center has been established at the City University of New York. Meanwhile, many Puerto Ricans have joined the ranks of New York State and City educators and administrators—including Mohr, who began teaching in 1967 and publishing books in 1973.

The Novel in Focus

The plot. The novel opens with "Old Mary," the story of an elderly Puerto Rican woman living in the Puerto Rican ghetto of Lower East Side New York City. Mary had come to New York from Puerto Rico nearly forty years before to make a better life for herself. She had always planned to return to her homeland but, still struggling to make ends meet, that is no longer a realistic possibility for her. Out of the blue, Mary receives a letter from her long-lost son, William. As a poor teenager in Puerto Rico, she bore her employer's child and left the baby behind when she came to America. She had vowed to send for him once she had made enough money, but her plan fell through; her husband did not want the child to come to them, and once they had started a family with children of their own in America, she could not save enough to send for William.

William's letter is a welcome surprise, which Mary feels must be a sign from God that her prayers have been answered. Her son writes that he is coming to New York to be with her; she plans a joyful reunion with her beautiful baby and dreams about the two of them moving out of the barrio together. She waits anxiously for his arrival, as do her other (grown) children, who go to pick him up at the airport. When William steps out of the car, Mary does not recognize him: William is a little person, 3'11" tall. At first family and friends are taken aback by his size, but quickly realize that he will be a good provider and great company for Old Mary.

The second vignette, "I Ain't Never Seen My Father," records the reunion of two high-school friends several years after graduation. They are eating at Rudi's Luncheonette, the local gathering spot, where Mary's son William now works. Yolanda and Lillian, who grew up together, used to be inseparable, but their adult lives have taken very different turns. In despair over her poverty and lack of opportunity, Yolanda has turned to drugs and prostitution; Lillian, however, has gone to college, where she is majoring in psychology. Lillian is trying to explain Sigmund Freud's theory about the "Oedipus Complex" to her friend, whose court-mandated psychiatrist told her that subconscious hatred for her mother and desire for her father have made her act in a self-destructive manner. Yolanda does not understand this concept at all and is appalled that anyone would think she wanted to sleep with a father she has never seen. Lillian tries in vain to explain to Yolanda that it is precisely because she has never seen her father that she takes drugs and works as a prostitute. Clearly education has separated the pair of friends forever. The two part company, and it is clear they will soon lose contact for good.

In "The English Lesson," Mary's son William (nicknamed Chiquitin) attends a local night school in order to strengthen his English. He takes with him Lali, the young wife of his boss, Rudi. Fresh off the plane from Puerto Rico, Lali is from a small village in the mountains and is used to the customs of her tropical island home—a stark contrast to the concrete jungle of New York City. Lali speaks very little English and feels extremely alienated in New York City; William is sure that learning English will help her overcome her feelings of being alone and he convinces Rudi that it is a good idea. She and Chiquitin share the bond of being recent immigrants from Puerto Rico and become fast friends.

The English class is filled with people from all over the world who have come to New York in search of a better life: a Polish professor of music, a Dominican man, and a Chinese man as well as Puerto Ricans. Their stories provide a backdrop and larger context for the tales of Puerto Rican experience in the city.

"The Perfect Little Flower Girl," the next story in the series, is about two gay couples who stage a wedding. Johnny Bermudez has just been drafted and has six weeks before he must report for boot camp; the Vietnam War wears on in Southeast Asia and, despite the fact that the army will not allow gay soldiers, Johnny seems to have strong personal reasons for wanting to join up and will keep his orientation a secret. His partner, Sebastian Randazzo, is ill and unable to work regularly. With Johnny gone and no one to support him, Sebastian's situation will be bleak. But Johnny and Sebastian have come up with a plan: Johnny will marry Sebastian's lesbian friend, Vivian, so that he can collect the salary of a married soldier and continue to support his mate, Sebastian. Vivian will help look after Sebastian while Johnny is away.

The simple Catholic wedding comes off without a hitch, despite its underlying unconventionality; the priest clearly has no idea what the real situation is as he unites Johnny and Vivian in the presence of their respective mates. The reception is catered by a neighbor, Raquel, whose daughter, Hilda, is the flower girl. Friends, family, and neighbors join in the celebration. At the end of the reception Hilda, who has always wanted to be a singer, performs "You've Got a Friend" (by James Taylor), and moves her audience to tears.

"The Operation" tells of a little girl who stays out late playing one evening. Her parents are frantic and immediately think she has been abducted by an old white man who has raped and killed three neighborhood girls, according to graphic newspaper accounts. Angie, the panic-stricken mother, is overwhelmed by guilt—for letting her child play outside, for living in such a poor neighborhood, and for not being able to do anything about it. The neighbors are all

Nicholasa Mohr.

alerted to the girl's absence and everyone comforts Angie. As it turns out, her daughter, Jennie, has been distracted by a young cat that a local stray, an orange cat that figures in all the vignettes, has chased off. The little girl follows the young cat up onto the roofs of some nearby buildings, trying to give it some affection. The cat eludes her, but she bumps into "Captain Nate," a former tugboat captain who lost his union card in 1954 because he was a communist. Captain Nate has just had an operation for lung cancer and has no where to go to recuperate—he lives on the street. He takes Jenny back to her street and she arrives home hours late. Her parents are of course overjoyed to see her and to learn that her brush with this particular old man did not lead to tragedy, as it might have.

The next vignette, "Lali," follows Rudi's wife as she struggles with her feelings for William's brother, Federico. Rudi has broken his leg and cannot work. Federico takes his place at the luncheonette and soon he and Lali begin an affair. As the day of Rudi's return dawns, Lali realizes that she is trapped in a loveless marriage and pleads with Federico to take her away. He is obviously reluctant, but he finally gives in. The two plan to bankroll their flight with some of the luncheonette's profits. Lali will do anything to escape from the husband she doesn't love and the city she hates and will do anything for Federico, with whom she has fallen hopelessly in love. Federico, however, has a history of instability and has left a trail of broken hearts behind him. Lali goes through with her half of the plan and gives

Federico $2,000, but he leaves without her. When William brings her the letter revealing that he is gone, the two make love for the first and only time.

"The Robbery" takes place in the luncheonette six months later. Rudi is back at work and so is Lali; relations were strained between them because of what transpired with Federico, but things are now more or less back to "normal"— Rudi and Lali hardly speak. Near closing time, two young boys come in and rob the store at gunpoint; one of them shoots William, wounding but not killing him. Rudi gives chase and corners the two, shooting and killing one of them. From that day forward, the deceased boy's mother pickets the luncheonette in an effort to get Rudi to pay for a headstone for her son's grave. She cannot afford to mark it and has a large family to support.

GARBAGE RIOTS

~

The eight stories in *In Nueva York* are linked by the common image of a scruffy orange cat picking through garbage on the street. Prior to the late 1960s, New York City had been slow to provide full sanitation, health care, and other social services to the most impoverished neighborhoods; Mohr's characters are always commenting on how much garbage is lying around rotting the streets and how irregularly the city picks it up. The situation came to a head in 1969 during the so-called "garbage riots," when the youth group known as the Young Lords, a former street gang, grabbed headlines for their part in the protest. They not only drew attention to the filth and squalor of the streets in their neighborhood, but occupied a local run-down hospital, agitating for improved health services, among other things.

The final vignette, "Coming to Terms," returns to Old Mary on her stoop and shows life as usual in the barrio. The cagey orange cat that is forever rummaging through the garbage bins outside Rudi's luncheonette is once again making a mess of the place. Rudi, who has vowed repeatedly to kill the infamous neighborhood fixture, grabs something in the store and runs toward the animal. But instead of shooting the cat, he offers it a saucer of milk, saying: "I can't shoot you . . . we come to terms already, eh? Anybody who lasts as long as you don't die easy" (*In Nueva York*,

p. 192). The novel closes as the cat laps up the milk and then finds a warm, dry place to sleep.

Citizens. In "The English Lesson," Mohr stages a confrontation between a man from the Dominican Republic, Diego Torres, and his classmates, who seem uniformly delighted with the prospects of being, or becoming American citizens. Through this character the novel suggests that, although the Latino characters look upon it as a good opportunity, their huge migration to America is something of an outrage, necessitated as it is by poverty and ambition. Torres is in New York because he feels he has no choice; American conglomerates control all the industry in his deeply impoverished homeland and it is impossible for him to find work:

> O.K., I prefer live feeling happy in my country, man. Even I don't got too much. I live simple but in my own country I be contento. Pero this is no possible in the situation of Santo Domingo now. Someday we gonna run our own country and be jobs for everybody. My reason to be here is to make money, man, and go back home buy my house and property. I no be American citizen, no way. I'm Dominican and proud!"
> (*In Nueva York*, p. 57)

Torres is also upset when an Italian student thinks that he, like William, is Puerto Rican. William can vote because he is an American citizen, but Torres does not believe this is such a great privilege; it hardly alters the basic fact that William has had to leave Puerto Rico in order to find work, for example.

The Dominican Republic has had a long history of dictatorship and civil war; in 1963, U.S. Marines landed to prevent war from escalating between the country's left- and right-wing factions. The turmoil involved has not been conducive to economic prosperity for most Dominicans. Consequently many try to cross the eighty-mile Mona Passage to Puerto Rico, and from there to catch a domestic (and hence uncontrolled) flight to the United States. Political and economic necessity, in short, compels people from the Dominican Republic to try and pass as Puerto Ricans.

Sources. *In Nueva York* is based on the author's experiences as a resident of the Puerto Rican barrio. She patterned the characters and incidents on real people and events, drawing on her imagination and creative talent to expand upon these sources. Mohr's mother taught her as a young girl that "by making pictures and writing letters I could create my own world . . . like magic"

(Mohr in Tardiff and Mbunda, p. 555). Heeding this advice, Mohr studied art at the Art Students' League in New York and then in Mexico City, where she was profoundly influenced by the works of muralists Diego Rivera and José Clemente Orozco. This exposure was "to shape and form the direction of all [her] future work" (Mohr in Tardiff and Mbunda, p. 555). Both her illustrations and stories reflect the influence of the muralists, and nowhere is this clearer than in her book of vignettes, *In Nueva York,* which has been called a "vivid tapestry of community life" (Telgen, p. 275).

Reviews. First published in 1977, *In Nueva York* won rave reviews and garnered several awards from young adult and from adult organizations. The *Bulletin of the Center for Children's Books* praised the work as "tough, candid, and perceptive," complimenting Mohr for creating a remarkably realistic mix of community life and of individual characters (Telgen, p. 276). The work won the Best Book Award from *School Library Journal* and the Best Book Award in Young Adult Literature from the American Library Association. This widespread approval persisted, with the selection of the novel as one of the *New York Times*'s "New and Noteworthy" paperbacks in January 1980.

For More Information

Fitzpatrick, Joseph P. *Puerto Rican Americans: The Meaning of Migration to the Mainland.* Englewood Cliffs, N.J.: Prentice-Hall, 1971.

Jennings, James, and Monte Rivera, eds. *Puerto Rican Politics in Urban America.* Westport, Conn.: Greenwood Press, 1984.

Mohr, Nicholasa. *In Nueva York.* Houston: Arte Publico, 1993.

Novas, Himilce. *Everything You Need to Know about Latino History.* New York: Plume, 1994.

Tardiff, Joseph, and L. Mpho Mabunda, eds. *Dictionary of Hispanic Biography.* Detroit: Gale Research, 1996.

Telgen, Diane, and Jim Kamp, eds. *Notable Hispanic Women.* Detroit: Gale Research, 1993.

Tovar, Federico Ribes. *El libro puertorriqueño de nueva york / Handbook of the Puerto Rican Community.* New York: Plus Ultra Educational Publishers, 1970.

Wagenheim, Kal, ed. *The Puerto Ricans.* New York: Praeger, 1973.

Inaugural Address

by
John F. Kennedy

On the sunny, snow-covered afternoon of January 20, 1961, forty-three-year-old John F. Kennedy assumed the office of the President of the United States. While twenty thousand shivering guests crowded onto the Capitol Plaza in below-freezing temperature, the inaugural team assembled on the dais. The poet Robert Frost recited a piece from memory, since the glare of the sun prevented him from reading the verse he had composed for the occasion. Following the reading, Chief Justice Earl Warren swore in the new president. Kennedy then stepped up to the microphone to deliver a memorable address, which focused on international issues. Keeping the speech short, as was his wont, he had made last-minute changes up until that morning. His text was a collaborative work, composed with Ted Sorensen, his main speech writer since 1954.

Events in History at the Time of the Speech

The road to the inauguration. John F. Kennedy's inauguration as president of the United States marked the pinnacle of his political career. The first president to be born in the twentieth century, Kennedy brought with him a new era in American politics. He was the youngest elected president in history and the country's first Roman Catholic head of state as well. With his youth, wit, charm, and Hollywood looks, the president captivated the nation. It has been argued that no leader could better live up

THE LITERARY WORK

A speech delivered in Washington, D.C., on January 20, 1961.

SYNOPSIS

In his address to the nation on the day of his inauguration as president of the United States, John F. Kennedy outlines his hopes for the future in a world threatened by Cold War hostilities.

to the phrase in Kennedy's own inaugural address, "the torch has been passed to a new generation of Americans" (Kennedy, Inaugural Address, p. 12). Since outgoing President Dwight D. Eisenhower was seventy, the oldest man ever to hold the office up to that time, and Kennedy was the youngest, the phrase indeed seemed apropos.

Despite his youth, Kennedy had substantial political experience. His career in public service began in 1946 when he won the election for the Eleventh Massachusetts Congressional District in Boston. In 1952, after his three terms in the U.S. House of Representatives, Kennedy ran for a seat in the Senate. While popular within his district, he campaigned as the underdog in the statewide senatorial contest against incumbent Henry Cabot Lodge Jr. His surprising victory over Lodge proved the influence of both the Kennedy campaign money and the young politician's charisma.

The following year Ted Sorensen joined Senator Kennedy's team of assistants, and in 1954 he became Kennedy's chief speech writer, a role that he would retain for close to a decade. Intimate friends, the men resembled each other in their quick wit and intelligence, sober judgment, and frank verbal expression. The two were so in tune that "when it came to policy and speeches, they operated nearly as one," said another of Kennedy's advisers (Schlesinger, p. 208). The drafting of speeches became Sorensen's most difficult job as Kennedy moved up the political ladder, for Kennedy took his speeches very seriously. "He believed in the power and glory of words—both written and spoken—to win votes, to set goals, to change minds, to move nations" (Sorensen in Kennedy, *"Let the Word Go Forth,"* p. 1). In 1958 Kennedy easily won reelection to the Senate; two years later he announced his intention to campaign for president.

At a National Press Club meeting in January of 1960, the young candidate declared, "We will need in the sixties a President who is willing and able to summon his national constituency to its finest hour—to alert the people to our dangers and our opportunities—to demand of them the sacrifices that will be necessary" (Kennedy in Giglio, p. 16). It was a theme to which Kennedy would return throughout his campaign and in his inaugural address.

Kennedy quickly won a succession of primary elections, and at the Democratic National Convention in Los Angeles in July 1960, he earned the nomination of his party. His acceptance speech spoke of standing at a New Frontier of opportunities and perils. This New Frontier, he said, "is a set of challenges. It sums up not what I intend to offer the American people, but what I intend to ask of them" (Kennedy, *"Let the Word Go Forth,"* p. 101).

Facing then-vice president Richard M. Nixon as his Republican opponent, Kennedy embarked on his national campaign. Television had recently become a major cultural influence in America, and the medium proved to be a potent political influence in his campaign. During televised debates, young Kennedy proved himself an equal to the more experienced Nixon. It was said that Nixon lost many votes due to his poor appearance in the first televised debate while Kennedy's grace and charisma charmed the nation. One survey found that 4 million people made their decisions based on the televised debates; of these, 3 million voted for Kennedy (Giglio, p. 18).

Kennedy nonetheless faced a close election. Out of 68 million votes cast, he won by less than 120,000. This would prove to be the narrowest victory in the history of presidential elections. Prior to the inauguration, Kennedy was well aware of the reservations among some Americans—that he was too young or weak for the job. For this reason, his inaugural address emphasized strength in the face of adversity and commitment to the future. It did so in a speech using techniques that Kennedy had refined over his past fourteen years in politics, techniques that Sorensen identified and employed in his role as Kennedy speech writer.

Speechmaking—the Kennedy style. According to Sorensen, Kennedy never just accepted or delivered a speech without seeing and editing it himself first. "[H]e always upon receiving my draft, altered, deleted or added phrases, paragraphs or pages" (Sorensen, p. 60). There were several rules connected to Kennedy speechmaking. Kennedy was a stickler for keeping his speeches simple and short. He disliked wordy messages, double talk, or tentative words such as *suggest*. He avoided contractions, elaborate metaphors, and hackneyed or overused expressions, although Sorensen points out that Kennedy had a weakness for one "unnecessary" lead-in: "The harsh facts of the matter are . . ." (Sorensen, p. 61). At the same time, Kennedy had a keen sensitivity to the rhythm of his speeches. Key words would sometimes rhyme or a sentence would use alliteration, beginning several words with the same sound for the effect on listeners's ears and to embed his reasoning in their minds.

Kennedy had definite goals in mind for the inaugural address. He wanted it to be short and focused on foreign policy and to respond to a recent speech by Soviet leader Nikita Khrushchev that seemed to call for communist revolution throughout the world. He wanted to offer the Soviets a choice between peace and conflict, to inspire his own people to greatness, and to sound eloquent. Inviting suggestions, he told Sorensen to gather input from everyone. He also asked Sorensen to study Lincoln's **Gettysburg Address** (also covered in *Literature and Its Times*) to determine the secret of its success (Sorensen concluded that Lincoln never used a long [two- or three-syllable] word when a short [one-syllable] one sufficed).

The drafting of the address did not begin until about a week before the inaugural. Suggestions had come flooding in by then, "[b]ut however numerous the assistant artisans," declared Sorensen,

President John F. Kennedy and Vice President Lyndon B. Johnson review the inaugural parade.

"the principal architect of the Inaugural Address was John Fitzgerald Kennedy" (Sorensen, p. 241). This is perhaps best illustrated by the fact that Kennedy was unhappy with all attempts to mention domestic issues; they all, to his mind, sounded too divisive. So he decided to "drop the domestic stuff altogether" (Kennedy in Sorensen, p. 242). The draft was too long anyway, he said. And, while there were serious domestic troubles plaguing the nation at the time, clearly the Cold War and the threat of nuclear destruction were the pre-eminent issues of the day.

The Cold War—the olive branch approach. Much of Kennedy's speech held out the olive branch, that is offered peace in international relations. In adopting this approach, the president aptly evaluated his audience. Tensions between the United States and the Soviet Union had overshadowed most foreign policy of the 1950s. During World War II, the United States and the Soviet Union had fought alongside each other as allies. But afterward the two superpowers clashed as the United States tried to prevent further communist inroads into a war-ravaged Europe.

The westernmost edges of the Soviet Union were bordered by lands buffering it from the remainder of Europe, including Finland, Estonia, Latvia, Lithuania, Poland, and the Balkan countries. By the end of World War II, Soviet troops had occupied these lands and areas beyond them, which the Nazis had formerly occupied—for example, Hungary, Austria, Romania, Bulgaria, Czechoslovakia, Poland, Yugoslavia, and eastern Germany. The Soviet Union, the world's only communist nation at that time, subsequently ascended to a position of enormous influence across this portion of Europe, as shown by political developments in the region. Between 1945 and 1948, communist regimes (supported by the presence of Soviet troops and advisors) were installed in Poland, Romania, Bulgaria, Czechoslovakia, and Hungary. Communism had by the end of 1948 clearly become a leading political force in the world.

The United States, the world's chief defender of democracy, warily eyed Soviet expansion and set out to contain it from spreading any further. U.S. leaders established a program of economic aid (the Marshall Plan) to war-ravaged countries in Europe, infusing them with capital for defense and rebuilding. In 1949 North America and western Europe forged even closer ties by entering into a mutual defense pact—the North Atlantic Treaty Organization (NATO). NATO's members vowed that an attack against one of them would be regarded as an attack against all, to be repelled with joint force.

Meanwhile, the Soviets exploded their first atomic bomb in 1949, and the same year Mao Zedong (Tse-tung) led the communists to power in China. The next decade saw Soviet advancements in technology—the Soviet Union tested a hydrogen bomb in 1953 and successfully orbited a satellite (Sputnik) in outer space in 1957. By the decade's end, the Soviets appeared capable of sending nuclear warheads into the heart of the distant United States. The Americans had earlier demonstrated their own command of technology by dropping the atomic bomb in World War II, and detonating a hydrogen bomb in 1952, but U.S. leaders, despite their country's strength, were anxious about the Soviet Union's growing military strength. The destruction of all humanity appeared to hang in the balance.

This concern remained in the forefront during the struggle for world leadership between the United States and Soviet Union. Known as the Cold War, it was a struggle that differed from previous conflicts because the opponents refrained from direct combat with each other (hence the term "cold" war). Instead, they competed indirectly in hostile actions outside their own lands. The worst of these actions drew U.S. soldiers directly into battle against Soviet-supported troops—war broke out in Korea (1950-53), for example, and in Vietnam (1957-75), with the Soviet Union and the United States backing opposite sides. Still the two superpowers refrained from fighting each other directly, since each possessed atomic arsenals that could theoretically annihilate the other side.

Kennedy's address boldly asked both sides to "formulate serious and precise proposals for the inspection and control of arms—and bring the absolute power to destroy other nations under absolute control of all nations" (Inaugural Address, p. 14). This point certainly touched an emotional chord in his audience. Because of the political tension between the United States and the Soviet Union, most Americans lived in fear of an eventual nuclear war. Public buildings such as schools erected fallout awnings over their windows to protect the occupants from an atomic blast. A few private citizens even built and maintained their own backyard fallout shelters in anticipation of an eventual nuclear holocaust. When he assumed the presidency, Kennedy knew that he was about to lead a people who feared the possibilities of a Soviet takeover of the United States or their own nuclear destruction.

The Cold War—the militant approach. Kennedy's address walks a delicate balance.

While it offers peace, it also assures the world of America's military readiness to resist aggression. In his address, Kennedy specifically states, "Let all our neighbors know that we shall join with them to oppose aggression or subversion anywhere in the Americas. And let every other power know that this Hemisphere intends to remain master of its own house" (Inaugural Address, p. 13). This quote summarizes Kennedy's intentions in relation to the potential spread of communism in the West. Although parts of Europe had been brought under Soviet control, Kennedy intended to keep the balance of power in the West tipped toward capitalist democracy. The area that concerned Kennedy most at the time was the island nation of Cuba, which sat just ninety miles off the coat of Florida.

Cuba's leader, Fidel Castro, had seized power in 1958, assuming control of property, businesses, labor unions, and the press, as well as the government. Cuba had not yet declared itself a communist nation at the time of Kennedy's inaugural (it would soon become the first to do so in the Western Hemisphere). It had, however, entered a period of economic and social upheaval, during which Castro singled out the United States as a target, convincing Cubans that the U.S. government sought to invade their tiny island and enslave its inhabitants. Tensions between the two nations mounted until Castro ordered the expulsion of all but eleven members of the American Embassy in the capital city, Havana. In retaliation, the United States reduced the quota of sugar that it purchased from Cuba, further weakening Cuba's already fragile economy. Left with little choice, Castro turned for aid to Nikita Khrushchev, the Soviet president. Khrushchev was, of course, quick to respond to this potential ally in the West. The Soviet Union promised not only economic support, but in 1960 Khrushchev declared, "Soviet artillery can support the Cuban people with its rocket fire if aggressive forces in the [U. S.] Pentagon dare to start an intervention against Cuba" (Khrushchev in Halle, p. 402). Russian technicians and advisors poured into Cuba to assist the tiny country in various areas of development.

Meanwhile, scores of Cuban refugees left their homeland. Fleeing Castro's rule, the refugees came to Florida at the rate of about a thousand per week. U.S. leaders had been calling for a response to the Soviet influence in Cuba, and a number of them began to view these refugees as a potential rebel army that could overthrow Castro. During the winter of 1960-61, President

Eisenhower's last and President Kennedy's first days in office, preparations were begun for the invasion of Cuba. U.S. Central Intelligence Agency (CIA) operatives secretly armed and trained several hundred Cuban refugees, expecting that once they landed in Cuba, the locals would join the anti-Castro struggle and shore up the rebel army.

On January 3, 1961, before Kennedy took office, the U.S. State Department announced that it had severed all diplomatic ties with Cuba because of the seizure of several American firms there. A few months later, on April 17, 1961, President Kennedy authorized the invasion at the Bay of Pigs. It was a disaster—contrary to expectations, local citizens did not join the uprising, and the United States quickly withdrew its support. Almost all the invaders were captured on the beachfront. Far from ending the communist crisis in the Western Hemisphere, the incident only fueled the fires of U.S.-Soviet antagonism, giving Khrushchev further reason to step up a military presence on the island. The tension proceeded to escalate, climaxing in the Cuban Missile Crisis of October 1962, which brought the world to the brink of nuclear war, a possibility Kennedy had foreseen in his inaugural address, delivered twenty-one months earlier. Under U.S. pressure, the withdrawal of Soviet missiles would diffuse the deadly crisis.

The Speech in Focus

The contents. On the National Mall in Washington, D.C., having laid down his tophat and overcoat, the newly inaugurated President Kennedy faced his audience. He began his inaugural address with a declaration: "We observe today not a victory of party, but a celebration of freedom—symbolizing an end as well as a beginning—signifying renewal as well as change" (Inaugural Address, p. 12). The statement set the tone for the remainder of the speech, which renews the commitment to liberty made by the founders of the American nation and acknowledges how the world has changed.

The speech notes that humankind's scientific achievements inspire awe and hope—society now possesses the power to abolish all human poverty and at the same time, with nuclear weapons, to abolish all human life. Pronouncing a willingness to help the nations of the world defend democratic rights, the President proclaimed that

> the torch has been passed to a new generation
> of Americans . . . unwilling to witness or permit

the slow undoing of those human rights to which this nation has always been committed, and to which we are committed today at home and around the world.

Let every nation know, whether it wishes us well or ill, that we shall pay any price, bear any burden, meet any hardship, support any friend, oppose any foe to assure the survival and the success of liberty.

> (Inaugural Address, p. 12)

He focused in the remainder of his address on foreign policy, making various pledges to the nations of the world. To America's allies, the speech swears continued support. To republics emerging from colonial control, it pledges respect for their newfound independence. To the millions struggling for survival, it promises to lend a helping hand for however long such a hand is needed:

> To those peoples in the huts and villages of half the globe struggling to break the bonds of mass misery, we pledge our best efforts to help them help themselves, for whatever period is required—not because the communists may be doing it, not because we seek their votes, but because it is right.
>
> (Inaugural Address, p. 12)

To the countries of Latin America, the president offered "a new alliance for progress," then went on to affirm America's strength. The United States would oppose aggression in the Americas, Kennedy declared in no uncertain terms to the Soviets as much as his fellow citizens. The Western Hemisphere intended to remain master of its own domain. To the United Nations, Kennedy promised support of its ideals. Finally, to those nations "who would make themselves our adversary," he requested a pursuit of peace, "before the dark powers of destruction unleashed by science engulf all humanity in planned or accidental self-destruction" (Inaugural Address, p. 13). It is at this point that Kennedy asked both sides in the Cold War to generate proposals for the inspection and control of arms.

All this work, cautioned Kennedy, would not be finished in the first one hundred days of his administration, nor in the first one thousand, but it had to be begun and not by him alone. In fact, said Kennedy, "In your hands, my fellow citizens, more than mine, will rest the final success or failure of our course" (Inaugural Address, p. 14). Democracy had reached its hour of greatest danger, he continued. The challenge was for every American to rise to the defense of freedom in this perilous time, a role that Kennedy said he him-

President John F. Kennedy

self welcomed. He then began his now-famous conclusion:

> And so, my fellow Americans: ask not what your country can do for you—ask what you can do for your country.

> My fellow citizens of the world: ask not what America will do for you but what together we can do for the freedom of man.

> Finally, whether you are citizens of America or citizens of the world, ask of us here the same high standards of strength and sacrifice which we ask of you. With a good conscience our only sure reward, with history the final judge of our deeds, let us go forth to lead the land we love, but knowing that here on earth God's work must truly be our own.
>
> (Inaugural Address, pp. 14-15)

Those who heard the speech. With the single sentence "ask not what your country can do for you—ask what you can do for your country," the president attempted to unite his diverse audience into one people committed to preserving American ideals. Although Americans were united behind the effort to contain communist expansion, they were divided on the domestic front.

At home, the new president faced an array of problems. The civil rights movement had led to violence on the part of Southern law enforcement authorities and a bitterly divided populace. In fact, the day before the inauguration, twenty-three black students had demanded service at segregated lunch counters in department stores in Richmond, Virginia. "You can't do this," objected Professor Harris Wofford when Kennedy showed him an advance copy of his inaugural address (Wofford in Reeves, p. 39). Wofford objected because at this point the address did not refer at all to the civil rights struggle at home, whereupon Kennedy, agreeing that he must acknowledge the domestic strife, added the words *at home* to a sentence in his speech ("those human rights to which this nation has always been committed . . . at home and around the world"). Those two words were all he added, though. Aware of the issues that divided Americans, Kennedy sought to unite them with nationalist pride. Domestic affairs therefore had little place in his address.

Kennedy further attempted to unify Americans in foreign affairs by taking a militant stand while at the same time offering the prospect of peace. This dual approach succeeded, appealing to both sides of America's power base—war-ready hardliners and liberals who wanted to ease tensions with the Soviet Union. Republicans who feared that the young president might cave in to Soviet pressures found solace in his strong commitment to American interests abroad. At the same time, Democrats were soothed by Kennedy's apparent intention to reduce Cold War tensions.

Sources and composition. Though Sorensen drafted the inaugural address, the ideas for it came from Kennedy. Sorensen credits the president with its authorship. "[A]ccuracy, not modesty or loyalty, compels me to emphasize once again that John Kennedy was the true author of all his speeches and writings. They set forth *his* ideas and ideals, *his* decisions and policies, *his* knowledge of history and politics" (Sorensen in Kennedy, *"Let the Word Go Forth,"* p. 2). In the case of the inaugural, however, the phrasing was largely Sorensen's, though some of the wording came from Kennedy and others. John Kenneth Galbraith recommended using "cooperative ventures" rather than "joint ventures." Walter Lippman suggested referring to the communist bloc as America's "adversary" rather than its "enemy." Dean Rusk advised having the world ponder "what together we can do for freedom" instead of "what you can do for freedom" (Sorensen, p. 243). These were some of the final changes in a labor-intense process that entailed draft after draft of the speech.

First Draft
We celebrate today not a victory of party but the sacrament of democracy.

Next Draft
We celebrate today not a victory of party but a convention of freedom.

Final Text
We observe today not a victory of party but a celebration of freedom.

Kennedy made stylistic as well as content decisions along the way. "Let's eliminate all the 'I's', he said. "Just say what 'we' will do" (Kennedy in Sorensen, p. 243). Also he kept reworking the ask-not sentence until the morning of the inaugural. Kennedy had used the idea in earlier speeches, such as the July 1960 acceptance speech cited at the beginning of this entry. Thus, his sources were his own words and ideas as well as those of others.

Kennedy's inaugural drew on past as well as present sources for some of its ideas. The line "In your hands, my fellow citizens, more than mine, will rest the final success or failure of our course" harks back to a line in Abraham Lincoln's inaugural: "In your hands, my dissatisfied fellow countrymen, and not in mine, is the momentous issue of civil war" (Lincoln in Reeves, p. 39).

Kennedy never memorized his speeches. But once the inaugural address was drafted, he familiarized himself with the speech, and practiced reading it aloud. In the end, all the effort—Kennedy's, Sorensen's, and the suggestions of others—paid off. Kennedy's inaugural was hailed as one of the most remarkable in American history.

Reception of the speech. While reading Thomas Jefferson's inaugural address, Kennedy quipped, "Better than mine" (Kennedy in David, p. 6). The president, however, proved to be his own worst critic. The *New Republic,* the *National Review,* and the *New York Times* all lauded the speech for its attempt to assuage U.S. and Soviet relations. Members of both political parties also voiced their approval, as indicated by a *New York Times*

headline:

> Kennedy Sworn in, Asks "Global Alliance"
> Against Tyranny, Want, Disease, and War,
> Republicans and Democrats Hail Address
> (Reeves, p. 41)

"That speech he made out there was better than anything Franklin Roosevelt said at his best," said Congressman Sam Rayburn, "it was better than Lincoln" (Rayburn in Martin, p. 12). Foreign heads of state responded in equally kind terms. Soviet Premier Khrushchev, Harold Macmillan of Great Britain, and France's Charles de Gaulle all expressed satisfaction with Kennedy's words. Perhaps most important was the effect the address had on America's citizens. "It seemed to me," remembered Sorensen, "as I watched the faces of the crowd that they had forgotten the cold, forgotten party lines, and forgotten all the old divisions of race, religion and nation" (Sorensen, p. 248). At least for the moment, Kennedy's speech had achieved what it set out to do—it had unified the American people.

For More Information

David, Jay, ed. *The Kennedy Reader.* New York: Bobbs-Merrill, 1967.

Giglio, James N. *The Presidency of John F. Kennedy.* Lawrence: University Press of Kansas, 1991.

Halle, Louis J. *The Cold War As History.* London: Chatto & Windus, 1967.

Kennedy, John F. *"Let The Word Go Forth": The Speeches, Statements and Writings of John F. Kennedy, 1947 to 1963.* Selected and with an introduction by Theodore C. Sorensen. New York: Delacorte, 1988.

Kennedy, John F. Inaugural Address. In *"Let The Word Go Forth": The Speeches, Statements and Writings of John F. Kennedy, 1947 to 1963.* New York: Delacorte, 1988.

Martin, Ralph G. *A Hero for Our Time: An Intimate Story of the Kennedy Years.* New York: Macmillan, 1983.

Reeves, Richard. *President Kennedy: Profile of Power.* New York: Simon & Schuster, 1993.

Schlesinger, Arthur M., Jr. *A Thousand Days: John F. Kennedy in the White House.* Boston: Houghton Mifflin, 1965.

Sorensen, Theodore C. *Kennedy.* New York: Harper & Row, 1965.

The Joy
Luck Club

by

Amy Tan

T he years following World War II brought a surge in immigration from the Chinese mainland to the West Coast of the United States. This was in part due to the 1943 repeal of the Chinese Exclusion Act, and was later compounded by civil war in China and its eventual communist takeover in 1949. Once in America, many Chinese immigrants families began to produce a generation of American-born children. Amy Tan, born in Oakland, California, in 1952, was part of this wave. She wrote *The Joy Luck Club* in 1989, by which time Tan was married and had begun to write fictional stories after forgoing a career as a technical writer. Her novel reflects the real-life experiences of postwar Chinese immigrants and their daughters.

Events in History at the Time of the Novel

The Chinese Revolution. By the turn of the twentieth century, China, under the leadership of the Qing dynasty, had been weakened by corruption, economic stagnation, and the rebellion of the poor. Many Chinese intellectuals of the day questioned the ancient monarchical system of government that had been in place for centuries. In the opinion of many of these intellectuals, China needed to follow the example of Western powers and move toward a modernized republic system of government.

One advocate for such a new Chinese republic was Dr. Sun Yat-sen, whose call for the overthrow of the Qing dynasty drew devoted sup-

---

> ### THE LITERARY WORK
> A novel set in present-day San Francisco and China, and through a series of flashbacks, also set in China from 1918-49; published in 1989.
>
> ### SYNOPSIS
> Discussion at the mahjong table diverges into the histories of four Chinese women who immigrate to America and their fully assimilated American-born daughters. A series of vignettes highlights the differences between the mothers and their daughters.

---

port. After years of less successful revolts throughout southern China, the central cities of Hankou, Hanyang, and Wuchang became sites of a 1911 revolt that would sweep across most of the country. Within a year, the Qing emperor, a six-year-old child, abdicated and put an end to 268 years of Qing rule, and more than 2,500 years of imperial rule. The period that followed, 1912-49, would come to be known as China's Republican Era.

Japanese occupation of China. China suffered the violence of Japanese occupation during the Republican Era. In 1915 Japan made its infamous "Twenty-one Demands," which required China to make major concessions in land and power. Some of the specific demands included Japanese supervision of police departments in important cities, the development of Japanese schools, hospitals, and churches in China, the right of the Japanese to circulate religious propaganda in China, and a merging of the Japanese-Chinese armed forces. China was outraged, and protest and violence swept the nation, but eventually it was forced to agree to a modified version of the demands. This modified settlement did not include the major points listed above. Instead, Japan was granted some Chinese holdings as well as limited control of certain regions in China.

By 1931 Japan had occupied the mineral-rich northern province of Manchuria. In 1937 Japanese aggression escalated when its forces overtook the port city of Shanghai and much of the country's northern railways, launching the Sino-Japanese War. China's Nationalist army, though weak, disorganized, and lacking in resources, put up a surprisingly strong defense. The Japanese had not taken into account the tremendous level of national pride and unity of the Chinese during this period. Chinese forces were prepared to fight the Japanese to the death, and they often did. The war persisted from 1937 to 1945, inadvertently strengthening China's new sense of unity and nationalism.

FOOT-BINDING IN IMPERIAL CHINA

Women with large feet were considered a disgrace in imperial China. The painful process of foot-binding, it was thought, was a remedy for this. Through the tight wrapping of fabric around the foot, the feet of a young girl were compressed into as small an area as possible. The practice could cause infection and even loss of life, yet it persisted for generations. A girl's feet would not stop growing but, during the six- to ten-year period in which they were bound, would grow into a deformed shape. The custom was practiced by the better classes; peasant women normally did not have bound feet. In the time leading up to and during Republican China, the practice ended altogether, but at least one author declared that all women he saw of middle age or older in China during the early 1930s had bound feet (Fairbank, p. 173).

On December 7, 1941, Japan's attack on Pearl Harbor brought the United States into World War II. Now China and the United States faced a common enemy. In August of 1945, the United States dropped atomic bombs on Hiroshima and Nagasaki in Japan. Japan officially surrendered

on September 1, 1945, bringing World War II to an end; Japanese forces began a massive retreat from Chinese soil that very day. A new wave of strife dawned as the forces of China's Nationalist Party, the Guomindang (Kuomintang), found themselves embroiled in a civil war with the Chinese communists. From 1945 to 1949, this civil war brought further destruction to China and instigated large-scale Chinese immigration to America. It would, in the end, be won by the communists.

Women in Republican China. Under imperial rule, and into the early years after the overthrow of the Qing dynasty, women were tremendously limited in terms of opportunity, social status, and education. Under the old Chinese rule, women were largely viewed as deserving of lower status than men:

> Girls were generally regarded as much less valuable than boys, and sayings in common circulation appraised sons as infinitely preferable to daughters. One such proverb stated in effect that the most beautiful and gifted girl is not so desirable as a deformed boy.
> (Latourette, p. 574)

In marriage, a wife was often regarded "as a sex object, as a labor power, or as a machine for producing sons . . . a thing, not a person" (Kazuko, p. 145). The right of divorce was at first enjoyed only by men. In 1931 the Republican government instituted a new Family Law that finally gave women the right of divorce but made it extremely difficult for them to exercise this right. The wartorn 1940s were a period of intense activism in which Chinese women farmed on their own, transported food, nursed the wounded, and even fought. Their status improved, and after the war, the Marriage Law of 1950 at last guaranteed to women as well as men the rights of divorce and freedom of choice in marriage.

The anti-Chinese movement. As the United States entered the industrial age in the mid-nineteenth century, demands for cheap labor brought with it successive waves of foreign immigration—and, in leaner times, periods of sometimes violent discrimination. The Chinese laborers recruited to help in the newly created mining and railroad industries in the West were one such group that suffered as a result of this. A legislative war of sorts was waged against the Chinese immigrants through a series of local and state initiatives, especially in California. In certain places Chinese children were not allowed in public schools. Chinese were no longer admitted to San

Anti-Chinese demonstration by the Workingmen's Party in nineteenth-century San Francisco.

Francisco City Hospital. Special taxes were levied against them. A $50 tax was levied on Chinese ship passengers. And a new foreign miner's tax of $3 to $20 monthly per miner forced most Chinese out of the industry. Along with blacks and Indians, the Chinese could not legally testify in court cases involving whites. This anti-Chinese campaign peaked in 1882, with the Chinese Exclusion Act, which banned all immigration of Chinese laborers for ten years and was renewed thereafter, though exclusion would never be total. An average of 1,500 Chinese immigrants per year managed to enter the United States during the exclusion periods, many of them former residents of the United States who were returning from China. Altogether, this period of exclusion would last from 1882 to 1943.

A new era. During World War II, conditions began to change for Chinese immigrants. China became an ally of the United States in its fight against the Japanese. As U.S. allies, the Chinese gained stature in the eyes of Americans and public opinion began to change. Long-standing discrimination against the Chinese began to slowly taper off. The new attitude was perhaps best illustrated by the 1943 repeal of the Chinese Exclusion Act.

The 1943 legislation allowed for some Chinese to apply for citizenship and dictated a quota of 105 new immigrants from China per year. However, female immigrants fell outside the limitation of quotas if they qualified for entrance under the War Brides Act or the G.I. Fiancées Act. The War Brides Act allowed the spouses and children of active or honorably discharged servicemen who married abroad to be brought permanently into the United States as nonquota immigrants, and the Fiancées Act allowed fiancées of active or honorably discharged servicemen into the U.S. as temporary visitors, giving them three months to get married and thereby achieve permanent resident status. Largely because of these new acts, Chinese immigration temporarily skyrocketed in the postwar years. Almost ten thousand of the Chinese newcomers were women in less than a decade after the war. Settling down to a new life in the United States with their American husbands, many of these women started families. At the same time, Chinese American society underwent a major shift during the 1940s. Instead of being a society whose focus was on the old world— Asia—it became one whose major focus was on life in the United States.

The next generation. American-born children of Chinese immigrants in this postwar period showed a general pattern of ready assimilation into larger society in terms of language, education, housing, and marriage. One such example was a rising trend among younger Chinese Americans to choose their own spouse, rather than allow marriage to be arranged by one's parents. This sometimes led to disagreements and strained parental relationships. Many children of immigrants even married non-Chinese mates. In fact, as early as 1970, in the sixteen to twenty-four age group, 30 percent of Chinese American husbands and 22 percent of Chinese American wives had non-Chinese spouses.

MAHJONG

Mahjong, also spelled mahjongg, is an ancient Chinese game consisting of 144 small tiles. By arranging the tiles in certain ways, players can earn points and win. In 1920, the game was patented and introduced in the United States.

At least one historian speaks of the "increasing self-confidence" that many Chinese Americans began to feel in the 1960s and 1970s (Daniels, p. 326). Such a change, suggests this historian, was due in part to a greater sense of belonging and acceptance in America itself, as opposed to feeling a sense of connection to the land of their parents. Improved diplomatic relations between the two countries, especially with the early 1970s visit to China by President Richard Nixon, perhaps contributed to this sense of Americanization. The feeling of belonging to two separate societies—China's and America's—was the unique experience of the first, not the second, generation of Chinese Americans. The result was a chasm between the generations that the characters in *The Joy Luck Club* attempt to bridge.

The Novel in Focus

The plot. *The Joy Luck Club* introduces us to four Chinese women who fled their war-torn homeland in the 1940s and their four American-born daughters.

The Mothers	The Daughters
Suyuan Woo	June Woo
An-mei Hsu	Rose Hsu Jordan
Lindo Jong	Waverly Jong
Ying-ying St. Clair	Lena St. Clair

Their club, which the women hope will bring joy and luck, is a regular social gathering consisting of mahjong contests (an ancient Chinese tile game) and joint investments in the stock market. One of the mothers, Suyuan Woo, has died, and her daughter Jing-mei (June) is asked to take her place at the mahjong table. As she sits for the first time in her mother's place, she hears the often tragic tales of the four mothers' lives in China. The stories of the four pairs of mothers and daughters convey a sense of the cultural barriers and strong emotional ties that exist between the two generations.

The first mother whose story unfolds is the Joy Luck Club's founder, Suyuan Woo. During the Japanese invasion of China, she is forced to flee to the city of Chongqing with little more than her twin daughters, some food, and clothing. Along the way, exhaustion forces her to abandon all her possessions, and finally leaves her infant daughters on the roadside as well. She prays that they will be saved. A devastated Suyuan Woo eventually boards a boat to San Francisco. She meets a fellow Chinese immigrant, marries, and has a daughter named June Woo.

June, the daughter who has taken her mother's place at the mahjong table, has long been in competition with another second-generation daughter, Waverly Jong. June feels inadequate compared to Waverly. As a child, while Waverly impressed everyone as a chess prodigy, June embarrassed herself by plunking out wrong notes at a piano recital. As an adult, June thinks she's on a lackluster career path. "I realized I was no better than who I was. I was a copywriter. I worked for a small ad agency. . . . I was very good at what I did, succeeding at something small" (Tan, *The Joy Luck Club,* p. 207). She at first considers the Chinese silk dresses worn by the women of the club funny-looking and "too strange" for American parties.

Another mother in the club is An-Mei Hsu. Born in 1914, An-mei grew up in the home of her uncle and aunt under the strict supervision of her domineering grandmother, Popo. As a young girl, she learned that her absent mother was a disgrace, a third concubine to the wealthy Wu Tsing. Her mother is called "a ghost," someone whose name is not to be mentioned. During Popo's last days, as the grandmother lay dying, young An-mei gets a lesson in the unbreakable bond between a mother and child. An-mei's mother, the exiled concubine, returns home and prepares a healing soup for her dying mother, Popo. She takes a knife and cuts a piece of flesh

Kiev Chinh in a scene from the film adaptation of *The Joy Luck Club.*

from her arm to cook in the soup. The soup, it is believed, will help cure her mother.

An-mei's American-born daughter is Rose Hsu Jordan. As a child, Rose was charged with keeping an eye on her four-year-old brother, Bing. While she was distracted, Bing drowned. Rose talks about her disillusionment and sadness. She grows into an adult without much direction. She marries Ted Jordan, a Caucasian man whom she meets in college. Never able to make decisions for herself, she earns Ted's resentment because of her indecisiveness. He wants a divorce and decides that he will keep the house. Heeding the council of her mother, Rose demands to keep the house for herself. For the first time, she seems to value her own needs and rights. She stands up for herself and intends to fight her husband for a divorce settlement.

The third mother is Lindo Jong. At the age of two, Lindo was pledged as a future wife to the son of a neighboring family, the Huangs. Later, floods destroy her family's home and she is left with the Huangs. Her young husband refuses to consummate their marriage. For months, Lindo is mistreated by an abusive mother-in-law and husband for not producing a son. Despite her mistreatment, and the marriage arrangement that has made her the property of the Huangs, she vows to herself to never forget who she is. She devises a plan to leave the bad marriage without shaming her parents' pledge. She says that an ancestor visited her in a dream. The marriage is a mistake. The true wife of her husband is an already pregnant servant girl. Believing the story, the Huang family sets her free. She travels to San Francisco where she meets her next husband while working at a fortune cookie factory. Lindo bears three children, one of them a daughter named Waverly.

Waverly emerges an impressive child and chess prodigy, achieving great acclaim for winning against players older than herself, and she becomes a source of great pride to her mother. Embarrassed by her mother's constant bragging about her skills, she accuses her mother of exploitation and refuses to play. After giving up the game for a while, Waverly resumes playing, but never as well as before. She has lost the gift. As an adult, she elopes with a Chinese man and has a daughter, Shoshana. The marriage fails and Waverly next marries a Caucasian man named Rich. The conflicts between Waverly and her mother grow. Lindo Jong feels that her daughter is embarrassed by her, and doesn't want to be like her. Waverly feels that nothing she does is ever good enough for her mother.

The fourth mother is Ying-ying St. Clair. Born into a wealthy family, Ying-ying vainly thinks

SOME INCIDENTS IN THE NOVEL AND THEIR REAL-LIFE COUNTERPARTS

Fictional Incident	Real-Life Source
June Woo's mother dies of a brain aneurysm.	When Amy Tan was fifteen, both her father and brother died of brain tumors.
In 1944, Suyuan Woo is forced to abandon her twin daughters in China due to Japanese attack.	In 1949, Tan's mother, Daisy, was forced to abandon her three daughters in China.
June Woo travels to China with her surviving parent to meet her Chinese-born half sisters.	Tan travels to China with her surviving parent to meet her Chinese-born half sisters.
The Joy Luck Club is formed for mahjong and joint stock investments.	Tan and friends form a social group that shares investment tips. The club is called "A Fool and His Money."

that she is too pretty for any of the village boys. As a child, she plays with a valuable jade vase as if it were made of cheap paper. She is wild and rebellious, seemingly full of spirit. She marries a flashy young man and becomes pregnant. After a brief period, her husband leaves her for another woman, an opera singer. Heartbroken, she induces an abortion, killing her unborn son. She feels like a ghost, a body who has lost its spirit, and just stays in bed for days at a time. Finally Ying-ying remarries, this time to an American—a Caucasian named Clifford St. Clair, and moves to the United States. At the immigration station, her husband renames her "Betty" St. Clair, further obscuring her identity. They have a child, Lena, but the mother's depression persists.

Lena, who has her mother's "Chinese eyes," sees her mother's condition and despairs that there is nothing she can do. She envies a neighboring mother and daughter, who share a volatile yet loving relationship. Lena grows up to marry an architect named Harold who is miserly and cold. When the marriage seems to be headed for divorce, her mother decides that she must make herself available to support Lena. Only by being strong, Ying-ying realizes, can she pass on strength to her daughter. Ying-ying vows to make herself whole again, for Lena's sake.

At the conclusion of the novel, as if to take readers full-circle on this journey of mothers and daughters, June Woo travels to China with her father to meet her half-sisters, and to tell them of her mother's death. She feels herself becoming Chinese as she arrives in the land. Then, ful-

filling her mother's lifetime wish, June meets her sisters and learns that the three of them look alike, and that they look like their Chinese mother. The knowledge fills her with pride.

Ethnic identity and the daughters of *The Joy Luck Club*. In just one generation, tremendous changes occurred in the lives of the Chinese American women featured in the novel. These differences become evident when comparing the experiences of the mothers to those of the daughters.

The daughters enjoy greater opportunities in terms of education, career, and general social success in Western culture. Yet readers are left to wonder about what the daughters do not have. Gains have been made, but at what cost? The question of ethnic identity, and the price paid for assimilation, is posed by the third mother, Lindo Jong, "I think about our two faces. . . . Which one is American? Which one is Chinese? Which one is better? If you show one, you must always sacrifice the other. . . . So now I think, What did I lose? What did I get back in return?" (*The Joy Luck Club,* p. 266). Her daughter, Waverly, marries a Caucasian man. Clearly the daughter feels less torn between two cultures than the mother, but she has her own emotional obstacles to overcome.

For the daughters, assimilation and the gaining of American acceptance, affluence, and even spouses, seemingly entails a concomitant loss of ethnic identity, pride, and confidence to some degree. *The Joy Luck Club* mothers see their daughters as having more opportunity in life. But the daughters seem to be lacking a type of Chinese spirit or strength that served the mothers through their severe hardships.

Lindo Jong best describes the hopes and frustrations of the mothers, "I wanted my children to have the best combination: American circumstances and Chinese character. How could I know these two things do not mix?" (*The Joy Luck Club,* p. 254).

The mothers may come from a landscape of concubines, foot-binding, and female subjugation, but they nevertheless maintain a firm sense of self-worth and determination. On the other hand, the daughters, perhaps victims of their own good fortune, struggle to gain a sense of themselves. Many times in the novel, the daughters appear spiritually lost. Rose lacks self-esteem and the ability to make decisions. June also lacks self-confidence. Waverly feels unaccepted by her mother, and Lena suffers an eating disorder and an emotionally abusive husband. The novel suggests, though, that there is a remedy for the disorientation that seems to plague the second generation. The story ends hopefully, with June Woo arriving in China and claiming as her own the Chinese part of herself. At the start of the novel June calls the mothers' traditional Chinese garb odd. At the end she feels herself "becoming Chinese" and gaining new vision: "[N]ow," says June, "I see what part of me is Chinese. It is so obvious. It is my family. It is our blood" (*The Joy Luck Club,* p. 288).

Sources. Originally, Tan penned a short story about a child chess prodigy and her strained relationship with her mother. The piece, called "Endgame," was submitted to a writing mentor of Tan's. The mentor thought the short story was wonderful, and encouraged Tan to expand it with additional short stories in a similar vein. The result was *The Joy Luck Club,* Tan's first novel.

The daughters' journey toward ethnic identity seen in the novel is something that Tan herself says she experienced in real life. "Chinese food was wonderful when it was just family. But when my friends came over, I was embarrassed," Tan admits (Tan in Reynolds, p. 1). As a freelance writer, Tan took the non-Asian-sounding pseudonym May Brown. She also speaks of having worn a clothespin at night to make her Asian-appearing nose more narrow. With time and maturity, Tan says, she gained a sense of pride in her heritage and formed a connection with her mother that resulted in this novel.

Reception. Upon its release, *The Joy Luck Club* was greeted with nearly universal acclaim by critics and the public alike. Michael Dorris of the *Chicago Tribune* called the book "rare," and "mesmerizing," adding that it was "a pure joy to read" (Dorris in Matuz, pp. 90-1). Writing for the *Los Angeles Times Book Review,* Carolyn See declared "*The Joy Luck Club* is so powerful, so full of magic, that by the end of the second paragraph, your heart catches" (See in Matuz, pp. 90-2).

Some exception was taken to the fact that a few characters were less than fully developed and to the novel's storytelling technique. "*The Joy Luck Club,*" asserted Rhonda Koenig in *New York,* "is lively and bright but not terribly deep. The stories resolve themselves too neatly and cozily, and are often burdened with symbols (a . . . weed-choked garden for an unhappy marriage) that flatten them out. One cannot help being charmed, however, by the sharpness of observation . . ." (Koenig in Matuz, p. 94). Other critics praised her descriptive ability and the novel's feat of "showing the tragi-comic conflicts of cultures and generations, and never telling a word" (Gates in Matuz, p. 95).

The book's mostly favorable reviews were matched by sales. In its first year alone, *The Joy Luck Club* sold more than 275,000 hard-cover copies and remained on the *New York Times* bestseller list for seven months. It was translated into seventeen languages. The U.S. paperback rights alone sold for $1.23 million.

For More Information

Daniels, Roger. *Asian America: Chinese and Japanese in the United States since 1850.* Seattle: University of Washington Press, 1988.

Fairbank, John King. *China: A New History.* Cambridge, Mass.: Belknap, 1992.

Kazuko, Ono. *Chinese Women in a Century of Revolution.* Edited by Joshua A. Fogel. Stanford, Calif.: Stanford University Press, 1989.

Latourette, Kenneth Scott. *The Chinese: Their History and Culture.* New York: Macmillan, 1962.

Matuz, Roger, ed. *Contemporary Literary Criticism.* Vol. 59. Detroit: Gale Research, 1989.

Reynolds, Moira Davison. *Coping with an Immigrant Parent.* New York: Rosen Publishing Group, 1993.

Takaki, Ronald. *Strangers from a Different Shore: A History of Asian Americans.* New York: Penguin, 1989.

Tan, Amy. *The Joy Luck Club.* New York: Putnam, 1989.

The Left Hand of Darkness

by
Ursula K. Le Guin

U rsula Kroeber was born in Berkeley, California, on October 21, 1929. Her parents were Alfred Kroeber, an anthropologist of international repute, and Theodora Kroeber, who later became a successful writer. The Kroeber household was filled with books and interesting visitors, including graduate students, anthropologists, scientists, and Native Americans. As a girl Ursula was exposed to Norse mythology and Native American legend and literature of all kinds. She went on to earn degrees from Radcliffe College and Columbia University, marrying Charles Le Guin in 1953. Le Guin published her first novel, *Rocannon's World,* in 1966; it would become the initial work in the science fiction series that was to include *The Left Hand of Darkness.* This later novel appeared at the close of a decade fraught with conflict in the United States and abroad.

Events in History at the Time of the Novel

Civil rights movement. Marches, sit-ins, and freedom rides made headlines during the first half of the 1960s. Determined to end the unconstitutional segregation of blacks and whites that had long been a hallmark of Southern society, civil rights activists converged in the region in record numbers. Though nonviolent themselves, the protesters experienced bombings, physical beatings, and murder for their pains. Among those killed in the first five years were well-known personalities, such as Medgar

THE LITERARY WORK

A science fiction novel set on the fictional planet Gethen in the distant future; published in 1969.

SYNOPSIS

Genly Ai has come from Earth as an envoy to the planet Gethen to persuade its inhabitants to join the Ekumen League of Worlds, a peaceful interplanetary organization. Ai soon discovers his task is all the more difficult given the fact that Gethenian leaders are unable to trust one another, let alone an outsider. Ultimately the future of the planet depends on whether he can reciprocate the trust that one of them has in him.

Evers, and the lesser known, including four black girls in a church bombing in Birmingham, Alabama. Racial tensions eventually surfaced across the country as the decade wore on and came to a head in the long, hot summer of 1967, when race riots erupted in Newark and Detroit as Le Guin was writing *The Left Hand of Darkness.* Race, though an issue in her novel, is treated as a minor matter there: "Are they all as black as you?" the king asks the envoy, who replies "Some are blacker; we come in all colors," dismissing the issue of race and moving on to the matter of gender (Le Guin, *The Left Hand of Darkness,* p. 39).

Eastern religions in America. The late 1960s saw an unprecedented explosion of interest in alternative faiths, and Eastern religions were among the most popular. Such exploration into other cultures may have been the result of a relaxation of immigration laws, but the susceptibility of Americans to Eastern ideas lies primarily in the counterculture of the 1960s. During this cultural revolution, young adults and teenagers rebelled against traditional philosophical systems and sought out new ways to view the world. Among the Eastern belief systems that made inroads in the West during this time was Daoism (also spelled Taoism). This is a Chinese philosophy derived chiefly from the *Daodejin* (or *Tao-Te-Ching)*, a book usually ascribed to Laozu (Lao-Tze), a legendary philosopher said to have been born in 604 b.c; later scholarship dates the work instead to the third century b.c. *Dao* is translated as "the path" or "the way"—meaning the path taken by natural events. The *Daodejin* teaches an attitude of noninterference and a general antidote to the more formal structure of Confucianism, another ancient Chinese faith that espouses the values of obedience, obeisance, and observance of rites.

In her essay "Dreams Must Explain Themselves" (1973), Le Guin says that her attitude toward literary creation is linked to her interest in Daoism. In her creative work she feels that she is discovering places and people rather than inventing them. To her, Daoism implies a similar discovery of the way things work. Order, in other words, is not imposed on life from without or above; rather the true laws of life just exist in things and are there to be discovered. Furthermore, in Daoism dual forces, though different, are seen as being complementary. Western society, by contrast, tends to view life from the perspective of opposing dualities—black vs. white, man vs. woman, United States vs. Soviet Union—which Le Guin saw as one of her society's fundamental problems:

> Our curse is alienation, the separation of yang from yin. . . . Instead of a search for balance and integration, there is a struggle for dominance.
>
> (Le Guin in Cummins, p. 70)

Women's liberation movement. After World War II, the majority of American women returned to their traditional roles as wives and mothers. Marriage rates rose and the average age of brides fell. The concepts of equal employment opportunities and fair pay were almost nonexistent at the time, and two-thirds of all women dropped out

of college before graduating. According to a famous 1962 Gallup poll, 96 percent of American women were happy being housewives, yet most interviewees admitted that they wanted their daughters to have more education and to marry later. In 1963 Betty Friedan gave voice to this lurking sense of dissatisfaction in *The Feminine Mystique,* a book widely credited with launching the modern American feminist movement.

The situation would begin to brighten for women during the decade. In 1960 President John F. Kennedy appointed Esther Peterson as the first female head of the Women's Bureau of the Commerce Department, a subagency designed to monitor women's issues in the workplace. In 1961 the Presidential Commission on the Status of Women was formed, and debate was renewed on the Equal Rights Amendment (ERA), a controversial amendment to the U.S. Constitution guaranteeing equal treatment for women under the law. Although the amendment was eventually defeated, American women did achieve some legislative victories—for example, the equal-pay bill (1963) and Title VII of the Civil Rights Act (1964), which was amended to prevent discrimination in employment of women as well as African Americans.

However, the federal Equal Employment Opportunity Commission (EEOC) refused to enforce the sex discrimination clause in Title VII, spurring Betty Friedan to join with other activists in founding the National Organization for Women (NOW) in 1966. As the 1960s progressed, feminist ideas gained widespread support and the ratification of the ERA and decriminalization of abortion became significant issues. By the end of the decade NOW's efforts had been joined by those of more radical feminist groups such as Women's International Terrorist Conspiracy from Hell (WITCH), whose aim was to topple white-male hegemony. It was believed that attaining this goal demanded nothing less than social revolution.

In Le Guin's novel, the inhabitants of Gethen—which has also come to be known as the planet Winter—have, instead of continuous sexuality, periods called "kemmer" in which any partner might assume either male or female sexuality. In between the kemmer periods they are androgynous—they have both male and female characteristics. This means that anyone can bear children, which makes for a society of greater equality than might otherwise be the case.

> The fact that everyone between seventeen and thirty-five or so is liable to be . . . "tied down

President Kennedy (left) meeting with Secretary of Defense Robert McNamara (center) and others to discuss an appropriate response to the construction of Soviet missile sites in Cuba, October 1962.

to childbear," implies that no one is quite so thoroughly "tied down" here as women, elsewhere. . . . Burden and privilege are shared out pretty equally. . . .

There is no division of humanity into strong and weak halves, protective/protected, dominant/submissive, owner/chattel, active/passive. In fact the whole tendency to dualism that pervades human thinking may be found to be lessened or changed on Winter.
(*The Left Hand of Darkness*, pp. 93-4)

Meanwhile, Genly Ai, the envoy from Earth, is at a loss for words when asked to explain how women differ from men on his planet. It is a question that brings to mind the controversies in the women's movement of the 1960s:

[Ai:] It's extremely hard to separate the innate differences from the learned ones. . . .

[Estraven:] Are they mentally inferior?

[Ai:] I don't know. . . . I can't tell you what women are like. I never thought about it much in the abstract. . . .
(*The Left Hand of Darkness*, p. 223)

The Cold War. The ideological battle between the Soviet and American spheres of influence known as the Cold War continued on into the 1960s. In June 1961, President Kennedy and So-

viet Premier Nikita Khrushchev reached a stalemate over the status of the divided German city of Berlin. Two months later, East Germany attempted to stem the tide of citizens leaving for better pay and more excitement in the West by sealing off its borders and starting construction on a wall that would separate the Soviet-controlled sector of Berlin from the sectors controlled by the United States, Great Britain, and France. (The entire city of Berlin was located about 100 miles inside East Germany.) Tensions between the United States and the Soviets reached their peak in October 1962 when photographs taken by an American U-2 spy plane discovered nuclear missile launch sites under construction in Cuba. The result was a thirteen-day standoff between Kennedy and Khrushchev that many feared would end in a nuclear attack. Finally, on October 28, Khrushchev agreed to withdraw his missiles in exchange for a promise from Kennedy not to invade Cuba.

The Cuban missile crisis was a pivotal event in U.S.-Soviet relations. The realization that the world had come so close to nuclear war had a sobering effect on relations between the two countries. A hot line was established between the two superpowers at the Kremlin (Soviet headquarters) and the White House (U.S. headquarters) to prevent any potentially fatal miscommunication. Despite their differences over the Six-Day War involving Israel, Syria, Jordan, and Egypt in June, 1967; over the invasion of Czechoslovakia by the Soviet Union in 1968; and over the escalation of U.S. troops in Vietnam, the superpowers were able to negotiate two significant arms control agreements during the 1960s. On January 16, 1967, the United States and Soviet Union numbered among the sixty-two nations that signed a treaty prohibiting the military use of space. During the rest of the decade relations between the United States and Soviet Union remained reasonably stable and paved the way for the policy of détente, or relaxation of tensions, espoused by Richard Nixon when he became president in 1969.

Parapsychology. At the same time that nontraditional religions were gaining popularity in the West, there was a growing interest among the scientific community in parapsychology, broadly defined as the study of mental phenomena not explainable by accepted principles of science. The use of scientific discipline in the investigation of paranormal and supernormal phenomena is comparatively modern, dating back to the founding in London of the Society for Psychical Research in 1882. A great deal of study in the field has centered around extrasensory perception, or ESP, a term coined by Joseph Banks Rhine at Duke University to denote telepathy and precognition.

Telepathy, which refers to apparent communication between two persons that occurs outside of the usual sensory processes such as sight or sound, has implications in both religion and in science, and is often described as a "shared spiritual experience" similar to the psychologist Carl Jung's concept of the shared unconscious. Telepathy plays an important role in *The Left Hand of Darkness,* where it takes the form of "mindspeak," a mystical form of speechless communication in which dishonesty is impossible. At the time the novel was written, telepathy was receiving increasing attention from researchers, as is illustrated by such publications as Alister Hardy's *The Challenge of Chance* (1973), which documents elaborate experiments designed to test the scientific validity of telepathy.

Precognition, defined as foreknowledge of randomly occurring future events not based on inference from presently available data, appears in *The Left Hand of Darkness* in the form of the "Foretellers," supernatural clairvoyants in an "East Karhidish story" included by Genly Ai in his report to the Ekumen. As Jule Eisenbud points out

in his 1982 book *Paranormal Foreknowledge,* precognition "would seem to be opposed by the very pillars on which our [traditional] science rests" (Eisenbud, p. 4). Nevertheless, there was an increase in the study of precognition in the late 1960s and early 1970s—particularly in the study of dreams and visions—that even included advanced laboratory work.

Women writers and science fiction. Science fiction is a literary genre in which a background of science or pseudoscience is an integral part of the story. Strictly speaking, its beginnings are generally traced back to the late 1800s with the novels of Jules Verne and of H. G. Wells. The field was still in its infancy when Hugo Gernsback founded the pulp magazine *Amazing Stories* in 1926. *Amazing Stories,* which Le Guin read as a child, was devoted exclusively to science fiction. In 1937, John W. Campbell Jr. founded *Astounding Science Fiction,* and is credited with discovering such important science fiction writers as Isaac Asimov, Theodore Sturgeon, Fritz Leiber, and Robert Heinlein. After declining somewhat in popularity during World War II, science fiction rode the wave of public excitement over recent technological discoveries to subsequently reach unprecedented levels of popularity in the late 1940s and 1950s, a period now referred to the genre's golden age.

THE GULAG

In the novel Genly Ai is imprisoned in the Orgoreyn labor camp, which bears a striking resemblance to the actual Soviet prison camps known by their Russian acronym "gulag." The gulag system had been in place since 1918 and was perfected during the regime of Josef Stalin, but it continued on after his death in 1953. Inmates of the gulags—which were often located in remote corners of the Soviet Union—were considered by Soviet authorities to be a threat to their government, as Ai is in the novel.

This golden age of science fiction was known for its use of technological puzzles, physics, chemistry, and engineering. Few women appeared in, or wrote, such works. In the 1960s, however, science fiction underwent a transformation, largely at the hands of women writers such as Joanna Russ, Alice Sheldon, and, of course, Ursula Le Guin. Le Guin's novels represented a departure from adventure stories and hard science, focusing instead on anthropological, ethnological, and psychological concerns. *The Left Hand of Darkness* includes myths to help explain the beliefs and culture on the planet Winter. And far from conquering nature with technology, the novel's characters must adapt to survive.

It took time, however, for women writers of science fiction to gain recognition. Despite exceptions such as Mary Shelley, author of *Frankenstein,* they have lagged behind their male counterparts in prestige. In Robert Silverberg's *Science Fiction Hall of Fame* (1970), an anthology subtitled "The Greatest Science Fiction Stories of All Time," only one of the twenty-six stories is by a woman. Le Guin's work has helped to remedy this problem. Her tales have garnered respect for both herself as a writer as well as her genre. According to one critic, "Le Guin wrote elegant, cogent, subtly-structured English, thus helping to make science fiction aesthetically respectable" (Maddern, p. 117).

The Left Hand of Darkness is one of a series of works by Le Guin referred to collectively as the Hainish cycle, all of which share a common historical background. Included in the cycle are the novels *Rocannon's World* (1966), *The Left Hand of Darkness* (1969), *Planet of Exile* (1966), *City of Illusions* (1967), *The Dispossessed* (1974), and *The Word for World is Forest* (1976), as well as four short stories. The cycle is named after the original race of humanity who arose on the planet Hain and colonized other planets, including Earth, until galactic war isolated the various human settlements. All of the Hainish stories take place after the war and a subsequent dark age. The collected tales cover a time span of about twenty-five hundred years, during which contact is gradually being reestablished among the colony worlds. In the meantime, most of these colonies have forgotten their origin, and their humanoid inhabitants vary widely from planet to planet biologically as well as culturally. Their development has been altered by time and independent evolution and perhaps, as is suspected of the so-called "menwomen" in *The Left Hand of Darkness,* by biological experiments conducted by the ancient Hainish.

The Novel in Focus

The plot. The protagonist and principle narrator of *The Left Hand of Darkness* is Genly Ai, a young black man who has been sent from Earth

Ursula K. Le Guin

to a planet on the farthest edge of the known universe. The planet, Gethen, is also called Winter because it is in the midst of an ice age. Ai is the lone envoy of an organization called the Ekumen League of Worlds, an interplanetary organization whose goal is to unite the far-flung planets comprising the former Hainish colonies in a voluntary union for free commerce and exchange of information. The novel is presented as his retrospective report to the Ekumen, which also includes not only of his own accounts but also reports by a previous envoy, Gethenian myths, and passages from the diary of his principle ally on Gethen, Therem Harth rem ir Estraven.

Ai arrives first in Karhide, one of two principle civilizations on Gethen. His only confidant there is Therem Harth rem ir Estraven, the prime minister. Ai does not trust Estraven, but when Argaven, the king, suddenly declares Estraven a traitor and exiles him from Karhide, Ai feels deserted because he had come to rely on Estraven in his mission to win the king's participation in the interplanetary league. King Argaven, we discover, is fearful of the Ekumen, and wants nothing to do with Ai's mission.

After wandering around Karhide for some time, Ai travels next to Orgoreyn, the other Gethenian civilization. Unlike the cordial, disorganized Karhide, Orgoreyn is a highly oppressive bureaucracy run by a political body called the Commensals. By the time Ai reaches the Commensals, Estraven has already arrived in Orgoreyn. At first Ai is supported by an Orgoreyn political faction, but it later disowns him. He is then sent by the Sarf, or secret police, to the Pulefen Commensality Third Voluntary Farm and Resettlement Agency, a labor camp at the extreme edge of the habitable zone of Orgoreyn. Genly nearly succumbs to the harsh conditions there, but is rescued in dramatic fashion by Estraven, whereupon the two of them set out across the Gobrin Ice, a huge expanse of frozen wilderness separating Orgoreyn from Karhide. The journey is long and very dangerous, and over time a genuine trust and love develops between them as Ai learns to accept his friend as a "manwoman." "Until then," Genly Ai admits, "I had rejected him, refused him his own reality" (*The Left Hand of Darkness*, p. 234).

When at last they reach Karhide, Genly Ai signals to the starship, where his companions are waiting for him. News of Ai's return to Karhide and of the imminent arrival of the ship induces King Argaven to accept membership in the Ekumen, although his decisions are still based on fear—in this case the fear that the Orgoreyns will join the Ekumen first, thereby gaining some advantage. Ai, it appears, has succeeded in his mission at last. His success, however, is tainted, for Estraven has been killed trying to cross the border back into Orgoreyn. Ai feels the loss very deeply. Visiting Estraven's family, he speaks to them of the heroism of his lost friend and so brings the novel to a close.

A study in rivalry. Le Guin's imagined world of Gethen is made up of two separate civilizations—Karhide and Orgoreyn—that share a single planet. Despite their proximity and genetic similarities, the Karhide and Orgoreyn are in constant conflict with each other. Although on the surface the rivalry concerns a disputed stretch of border land, the land itself is almost never mentioned. The conflicts are shaped largely by forces within the two societies themselves rather than by credible conflicts of interest between them. Fear and distrust are the true causes. It is fear and distrust that prevent King Argaven or the Commensals from joining the Ekumen, a federation of eighty-three other worlds, including Earth, that is reminiscent of the United Nations. Ironically, it is only by playing each civilization's fear of the other against

them that Ai manages to recruit anyone from the planet into the Ekumen.

The fictional climate in which the rivalry between two civilizations affects every aspect of life is reflective of political realities at the time the novel was written. In the late 1960s, the fate of much of the world was dominated by the hostility between the United States and the Soviet Union. In Le Guin's fictional world, the two nations of Gethen never actually engage in combat, yet psychologically and politically they carry out a cold war of sorts. The comparison, however, is not a literal one. Although certain aspects of Orgoreyn society do resemble the Soviet Union—the rigid political structure, the secret police (Sarf), the frigid work camps—the lack of other correlations, particularly between Karhide and the United States, suggest that *The Left Hand of Darkness* is not about any nation in particular but about the nature of hostility and conflict and its consequences. Like Le Guin's fictional civilizations, the United States and the Soviet Union never actually met in battle but rather existed in a state of perpetual stalemate. Moreover, as Miroslav Nincic states in his book *Anatomy of Hostility,* "There is little evidence to suggest that either superpower was intent on bringing about the downfall of the other system" (Nincic, p. 5). Viewed in this light, the enmity of the Cold War era was founded less on aggression than on fear. There is, in fact, no word for war in the languages of Gethen. The whole fictional atmosphere brings to mind the nuclear stalemate of the 1960s, which thwarted actual military engagement, despite a climate of hostility and confrontation.

The novel goes beyond portraying such tension, however, suggesting that a solution lies in respecting each other's differences. The protagonist, Genly Ai, is black, but his racial identity becomes merely incidental to the story; the dominant difference is between Ai's single sexuality and the Gethenians's dual sexuality. And it is Ai's acknowledging this major difference, his being "unable to ignore Estraven's double sexuality," that leads to the "final breakdown of barriers" between them (Cummins, pp. 83-4). Ai arrives in the alien world inflamed with conviction about the benefits of cooperation and comes away with the knowledge that for it to succeed he must both acknowledge and respect differences.

Sources. In her 1976 essay "Is Gender Necessary?" Le Guin argues that the true subjects of *The Left Hand of Darkness* are betrayal and fidelity. She began with these subjects as well as gender, then went on to eliminate gender so she could discover what would be left. As Le Guin explains, it was the prospect of experimenting with an androgynous fictional universe that prompted her to write the book.

> In the mid-1960s the woman's movement was just beginning to move again, after a fifty-year halt. . . . I considered myself a feminist . . . but I had never taken a step beyond the ground gained for us by Emmeline Pankhurst and Virginia Woolf.
>
> I began to want to define and understand the meaning of sexuality and the meaning of gender, in my life and in our society. . . . But I was not a theoretician, a political thinker or activist, or a sociologist. I was and am a fiction writer. The way I did my thinking was to write a novel. That novel, *The Left Hand of Darkness,* is the record of my consciousness, the process of my thinking.
>
> (Le Guin, *The Language of the Night,* pp. 161-62)

Reaction. Although Ursula Le Guin's early work had been well received, *The Left Hand of Darkness* won tremendous acclaim and earned her a degree of attention and respect rarely seen in the world of science fiction. It won both the Hugo and Nebula Awards for best science fiction novel of the year. The opinion of one critic, George Slusser, was representative:

> The early novels, however skillfully written, remain bare skeletons, too stylized and bound by the conventions of the space adventure to be truly effective. In *The Left Hand of Darkness,* Le Guin takes a bold step. . . . [It] is far more complex than its predecessors; in terms of sheer technical skill, it is Le Guin's most satisfying work to date.
>
> (Slusser, p. 16)

Not every critic received the novel with such enthusiasm. David Ketterer, for example, objected to what he saw as Le Guin's over-reliance on mythical structures. "*The Left Hand of Darkness* is a skillfully integrated . . . piece of work, although my criticism that the plot is unfortu-

nately subordinate to the overly conscious use of mythic material remains" (Ketterer in Gunton, p. 267). Others complained that the androgynes were not associated with enough female traits and that the novel kept using the pronoun "he" to refer to them. This bothered Le Guin, who left the novel as originally written but added several appendixes to the 1994 edition that experiment with, for example, using the invented pronouns "e" and "en" instead of "he" and "him" on a few pages from the novel. Despite this criticism the novel was a critical as well as a commercial success, and the general consensus among readers—even those who do not care for science fiction—was that *The Left Hand of Darkness* constitutes a work of unquestionably high standing.

For More Information

Cummins, Elizabeth. *Understanding Ursula K. Le Guin.* Columbia: University of South Carolina Press, 1990.

Eisenbud, Jule. *Paranormal Foreknowledge: Problems and Perplexities.* New York: Human Sciences, 1982.

Gunton, Sharon R., ed. *Contemporary Literary Criticism.* Vol. 22. Detroit: Gale Research, 1982.

Hardy, Alister. *The Challenge of Chance: A Mass Experiment in Telepathy and Its Unexpected Consequences.* New York: Random House, 1973.

Kyle, Richard. *Religious Fringe: A History of Alternative Religions in America.* Downers Grove, Ill.: InterVarsity, 1993.

Le Guin, Ursula K. "Is Gender Necessary?" In *The Language of the Night.* New York: Putnam, 1979.

Le Guin, Ursula. *The Left Hand of Darkness.* 1969. Revised edition, New York: Walker, 1994.

Maddern, Philippa. "True Stories: Women's Writing in Science Fiction." *Meanjin* 44, no. 1 (March 1985): 110-23.

Nincic, Miroslav. *Anatomy of Hostility: U.S.-Soviet Rivalry in Perspective.* San Diego: Harcourt Brace Jovanovich, 1989.

Slusser, George Edgar. *The Farthest Shores of Ursula Le Guin.* New York: Borgo, 1976.

Love Medicine

by
Louise Erdrich

Louise Erdrich belongs to the Turtle Mountain Band of Chippewa. She was born in Little Falls, Minnesota, in 1954 and raised in Wahpeton, North Dakota, a region near the Turtle Mountain Chippewa Reservation, the setting for *Love Medicine*. Erdrich began her writing career as a young girl, encouraged by her father, who paid his daughter a nickel for each of her completed stories. She graduated from Dartmouth College, earned a master's degree in creative writing from Johns Hopkins University, and married the writer Michael Dorris, with whom she collaborated when writing. *Love Medicine,* her first novel, won the National Book Critics Circle Award in 1984. In 1993 Erdrich reorganized and expanded the novel, adding an additional four stories.

Events in History at the Time of the Novel

The Chippewa. The Chippewa (also known as the Ojibwa in eastern Canada or as the Plains-Ojibwa or Bungi on North America's plains) originally occupied a large territory that ranged from northern Ontario eastward to Quebec, southward to Michigan, Wisconsin, and Minnesota; later that territory expanded westward into Manitoba, Saskatchewan, and the Dakotas. Known to themselves as the Anishinaubae ("original men," or "good men"), they were given the name "Chippewa" by the Cree Indians, who speak a closely related language. "Chippewae" means "he or she who mumbles, stammers or slurs," a ref-

erence to the Chippewa custom of speaking extremely rapidly (Johnston, p. 241).

The Chippewa came into early contact with the French, English, and Spanish explorers who roved over eastern North America in the seventeenth to the nineteenth centuries. These Indians quickly becamed involved in trading furs with the Europeans, a practice that forever changed their Indian way of life. As they became more and more dependent upon the goods—notably the guns—that they received in exchange for beaver pelts and the hides of other animals, the Chippewa began to hunt farther and farther west from their traditional home in the woodlands on the shores of the Great Lakes. Eventually, their involvement in the fur trade led them to the prairies. Formerly hunters of deer, moose, and beaver in the eastern forests, the "plains" Chippewa now began to hunt buffalo and pronghorn antelope as their primary means of sustenance. When the buffalo herds were depleted, circumstances forced the plains Chippewa into a sedentary existence, and their culture began to diverge from that of their woodland ancestors: they started to live in tipis, began riding horses instead of paddling canoes, and even developed new religious ceremonies. So greatly did the plains Chippewa differ from their woodland relatives that some anthropologists have questioned how appropriate it is to identify these Indians as Chippewa at all. Erdrich's characters, however, routinely describe themselves as Chippewa.

Métis. Once on the plains, the Chippewa were heavily influenced by the presence of French and British traders in the area. Unions between these Europeans (generally the French) and the Chippewa resulted in the rise of a sizeable population of mixed-blood people. This new group became known as the *métis* (French for "mixed"), although its members were once referred to as the *bois brulés,* French for "burnt wood," a reference to their color. The métis held themselves to be a separate people from both their Indian and their European ancestors, adopting and criticizing different aspects of both cultures. The European influence manifested itself especially in the matter of religion; specifically, Catholicism took strong root among the métis, and proved to be a point of contention between them and their full-blooded Indian relatives. One historian points out that the métis were more willing to adopt European ways than the full-blooded Chippewa and therefore welcomed the French Catholic missionaries who roamed the west of what is now Canada and the United States (Camp, p. 64). The full bloods, on the other hand, saw in the Catholic missionaries white men who rode on the buffalo hunt with the métis, and held them partly responsible for the dramatic depletion of the native food source, the bison.

The Turtle Mountain Chippewa, who are central to *Love Medicine,* had significant dealings with the French Catholics; the Turtle Mountain area in northern North Dakota is heavily populated by métis on both sides of the U.S.-Canada border. In the novel, the nuns at the Sacred Heart convent, where Marie Lazarre stays for a brief time, are French, and many of Erdrich's characters, from the Lamartines to the Lazarres, bear French names. Some of the hostilities between the Lazarres and the Kashpaws might perhaps be attributed to the historical tension between the métis and the full-blood Chippewa.

Turtle Mountain. Most of the characters in *Love Medicine* live on or near the Turtle Mountain reservation in North Dakota. The Turtle Moun-

tains are actually a group of wooded hills surrounded by prairie; the North Dakota-Manitoba border runs through the middle of the area. By 1960, roughly 7,000 Chippewa lived on the 70,240-acre Turtle Mountain Reservation near Bellcourt, North Dakota. Unlike other native American tribes, the Turtle Mountain Indians actually agitated for the creation of a reservation; alarmed by the intrusion of white settlers into the Red River Valley of the North in the mid-nineteenth century, the plains Chippewa appealed to the government that land be set in reserve for their exclusive use. Typically, the federal government acted shabbily in its dealings with the Turtle Mountain Chippewa—at various times, the size of their reservation shrank drastically, they were paid poorly for land they were asked to give up to white settlement, and parts of the tribe were forced to scatter as far away as Montana when it became clear that not enough land was available for them on the North Dakota reservation.

In 1892 the Turtle Mountain Band of Chippewa agreed to exchange their claim to 9 million acres of land for a cash settlement of $1 million, a 70,000-acre reservation (at Turtle Mountain), and land elsewhere on the plains (primarily in Montana and the Dakotas) for members of the tribe who were not able to live on the main reservation. In 1980 slightly more than 4,000 American Indians lived at the Turtle Mountain reservation, along with some 300 non-native residents, in a community of 1,095 homes. Tribal members had, on average, eight years of education and most, like Henry Lamartine in Erdrich's novel, worked at the William Langer Jewel Bearing Plant in Rolla, North Dakota. The tribe earned $10,000 a year by leasing out portions of the reservation's agricultural property (Confederation of American Indians, p. 210).

Life on American Indian reservations has always been and continues to be harsh, although the 1980s and 1990s have seen something of an improvement. In most instances the land that the government assigned to the Indians was barren and without modern amenities. Unemployment was rife, education was minimal, and the rate of disease and alcoholism were high. Communication between the generations suffered because of the introduction of mainstream American methods of schooling and the insistence that children be educated in English. Furthermore, schools that the government set up for American Indian children were often so far from their homes that the youngsters had to board at school, which

Rocky Boy (Stone Child), a Chippewa chief.

took them away from their parents and family traditions. In *Love Medicine*, Marie Lazarre Kashpaw sends one of her sons, Nector, off to the government school, but keeps her other young son, Eli, at home where he can learn the traditional ways.

Social problems linked to reservation life emerge in *Love Medicine;* yet equally apparent in the novel are a strong sense of survival and a determination to pull together as a family. In particular, Erdrich draws attention to the enterprising spirit of present-day reservation dwellers; in one of the added stories in her 1993 revision of *Love Medicine*, "Lyman's Luck," Lyman dreams of turning an "Indian artifact" factory into a lucrative gambling enterprise. This enterprising spirit is manifested in modern real-life gains. Statistics indicate that reservation Indians today are more highly educated and healthier than ever before and that their tribes are now economically stronger.

Manitou. The concept of *manitou* encapsulates the Chippewa understanding of spirituality. *Manitou* does not mean only "spirit," as the word was interpreted rather simplistically by certain Christian missionaries, but "mystery," "transcendence," "deity," "matter" and "essence," among other things (Johnston, p. 242). Kitchi-Manitou (or "great spirit") created the world and all the other manitou in it. Some manitou govern plant and animal life; some, like Sky-Woman, governed things beyond the earth—virtue and luck, for example. Other manitou walk the earth in the shape of human beings. Nanabozho, or Nanapush is the son of the West and a human woman, Winonah, and represents human nature in all its frailty and complexity. While Nanabozho is generally (though not always) a comic figure, other manitou are fearsome indeed. Missepeshu, the Great Lynx (or sometimes panther) who lives underwater, is one of the fearsome manitou (he recurs in the lives of the Turtle Mountain people in Erdrich's sequel to *Love Medicine, Tracks*). The most terrible of the manitou to stalk the earth, however, is the *windigo,* whose name recurs in *Love Medicine* whenever people go a little mad. A huge cannibalistic ice-giant who hunts men and eats them raw, the *windigo* may be intended to signify human selfishness, for it is driven by a hunger that only increases the more it eats. Human beings can become *windigo,* particularly in winter, when hunger sets in; tales of North American Indians in the United States and Canada are filled with people who suddenly turn into cannibals and eat their family members. In *Love Medicine* Rushes Bear warns Lulu Lamartine not to go near Moses Pillager because he is *windigo*—"his grandfather ate his own wife!" (Erdrich, *Love Medicine*, p. 75). A primal horror that dwells in the darkness at the edge of human settlements, the *windigo* represents the danger of venturing away from home alone. *Love Medicine* uses the ghastly figure of the *windigo* to emphasize the power of family to keep one safe and the importance of not severing ties with the community.

Bureau of Indian Affairs. In 1824 the Bureau of Indian Affairs (BIA) was born. A division of the Department of the Interior, the BIA was to train native people to develop their resources and manage their own affairs. BIA executives were generally white people, with Indian staff members serving in subordinate positions; run by those who sometimes had little knowledge of or love for the Indian peoples, the Bureau was regarded with suspicion by many of those it was ostensibly supposed to help. "The Bureau has done a terrible job; it has compromised the Indian time and again; it has permitted, tolerated, even assisted in the erosion of Indian rights and the whittling away of the Indian land base," writes one critic (Cahn in Josephy, p. 143). And yet, this same critic notes that the BIA is important to Indian life; in 1969 the American Indian Task Force, including Mary Cornelius of the Turtle Mountain Chippewa, released a proposal not to dismantle the BIA but to reorganize it. In Erdrich's novel, the two sides—the Bureau and the Indians—are at odds, resulting in a hilarious but also serious riot in a souvenir factory on the reservation.

Taking AIM. During the 1960s, when the civil rights movement and anti-Vietnam War activism surged to the forefront of American politics, prominent American Indian activists also began to protest unjust government policies toward Indians. One of Erdrich's characters, Lyman Lamartine, who works as a BIA representative on the reservation, makes a mental catalogue of some of the abuses heaped upon American Indians by the government:

> They gave you worthless land to start with and then they chopped it out from under your feet. They took your kids away and stuffed the English language in their mouth. They sent your brother to hell [Vietnam], they shipped him back fried. They sold you booze for furs and then told you not to drink.
>
> (*Love Medicine*, p. 326)

Clyde Bellecourt, one of the founders of the American Indian Movement.

In 1968 three Chippewa Indians—Dennis Banks, George Mitchell, and Clyde Bellecourt—founded the American Indian Movement (AIM). AIM was a spokesgroup especially for urban Indians—they aimed to receive the same government services as reservation Indians—but the group also promoted civil rights for all Indian peoples. In 1972 members of AIM occupied the offices of the BIA in Washington, D.C., in order to draw national attention to their complaint that traditional tribal councils were being controlled by federal bureaucrats. In the following year, in a bloody confrontation, AIM took over the small community of Wounded Knee, South Dakota (the historic site of an Indian massacre by the American cavalry in 1890), and demanded reforms in tribal government and a restructuring of the system by which American Indians negotiated with the federal government.

Needless to say, not all American Indians agreed all of the time with the methods of AIM, even the nonviolent methods. AIM began to associate itself with traditional Indian ways, which some saw as taking a step backward or as stereotyping Indian people. A number of AIM activists took to wearing traditional Indian clothing and hairstyles. In the novel, Lyman refers to such people as the "back-to-the-buffalo type" (*Love Medicine,* p. 303). He also looks askance at his mother, Lulu, who has become a local AIM leader, adopting a curious habit of speech all of a sudden. Looking out at the plains where buffalo once roamed, Lulu reflects:

> "The four-legged people. Once they helped us two-leggeds."
>
> This was the way her AIM bunch talked, as though they were translating their ideas from the original earth-based language. Of course, I knew very well they grew up speaking English. It drove me nuts.
>
> She went on musing, and I tried to listen. "Creation was all connected in the olden times."
>
> "It's pretty much connected now," I said. "As soon as my plumbing's hooked in I'll be part of the great circle of life."
>
> (*Love Medicine,* p. 307)

The Novel in Focus

The plot. *Love Medicine* is a collection of eighteen overlapping stories narrated by three generations of the Kashpaw and Lamartine families. The collection is framed by reflections upon the fate of June Kashpaw, whose life gradually spirals into a drunken procession of men and failed opportunities off the reservation. In the bleak opening story, "The World's Greatest Fishermen," June gets out of the car in which she has just had sex with a drunk and walks across the plains in the face of an oncoming snowstorm. That she is walking to her death is certain, but to June, walking away from her empty life is the best thing she can imagine to do. In the final story, "Crossing the Water," June's illegitimate son, Lipsha Morrissey, a healer of sorts, finally learns who his mother was; he is able to contemplate the good things that she achieved even in her headlong plunge into disaster.

Over the course of some fifty years, the Kashpaws and Lamartines (and some Lazarres, Nanapushes, and Morrisseys) experience imprisonment and injustice, infidelity, sickness, poverty, suicide, the effects of the Vietnam War on their young men, and conflicts between traditional Indian lifestyles and white religion, language, and schooling practices. Despite these harships however, the people in Erdrich's novel remain bound in a strange extended community where everyone seems to be somehow related to everyone else and hence responsible to and for each other. *Love Medicine* is first and foremost a book about love.

At the center of the story is the stormy love triangle formed by Nector Kashpaw, Lulu Nanapush Lamartine, and Marie Lazarre. Marie, a poor white girl, flees from the clutches of a sadistic nun and runs smack into Nector, who intends to marry Lulu. A strange, sexual connection happens between Nector and Marie, and the two of them get married. Nector tries to forget about Lulu, who does her best to forget about him. Lulu goes on to have eight children by eight different men, eventually driving her husband to suicide. Marie starts taking in unwanted babies after her own son and daughter die in their infancy. She is ambitious for Nector; she keeps him on the straight and narrow, off the bottle, and out of trouble, seeing to it that he becomes the tribal leader. After some seventeen years of marriage, however, Nector is drawn back to Lulu; they begin a secret affair that results in the birth of a son, Lyman. As tribal leader, Nector is one day compelled to inform Lulu that the land on which she lives is needed for the building of a factory. She is furious with him and refuses to let him in the house, the first time in many years that she has declined to receive him. He accidentally burns her house down while trying to leave her a proposal of marriage, having already written a goodbye note to Marie. Marie pretends not to have read the note, and when Nector comes home shaken from having watched Lulu's house

burn down, she takes him back as though nothing has happened.

In time Nector grows senile, and he and Marie move into a senior citizens' home on the reservation. Lulu is also there. Marie instantly gets jealous and asks her grandson, Lipsha, to help her concoct a love medicine to win back Nector's heart. They settle upon geese hearts as suitable for the traditional recipe, but when Lipsha is unable to shoot geese, he buys frozen turkey hearts at the grocery store. Marie eats hers raw and tries to make Nector eat his, but he knows she is up to something and, making fun of her, he accidentally chokes on the heart and dies.

After Nector's death, Lulu and Marie make peace with each other, and even work together in the tribal souvenir factory established by Lyman through the Bureau of Indian Affairs. They have their fallings-out from time to time, but basically learn to care for and respect each other.

The extended families of Lulu and Marie fill the pages of *Love Medicine;* their complicated relationships and fates are developed gradually throughout the book. What follows are some key details about members of the families and their interconnections:

Albertine Johnson: daughter of Zelda; struggles through university to be a doctor, after having a troubled youth.

Zelda Bjornson: daughter of Marie; marries Swede Johnson, a white man, who abandons her shortly after marriage; mother of Albertine.

Eli Kashpaw: brother to Nector; the family bachelor; raises June.

Henry Lamartine, Jr.: Son of Lulu and her husband, Henry; returns devastated from Vietnam; drowns in a local river, possibly a suicide.

Lyman Lamartine: Henry's brother; illegitimate son of Lulu and Nector; works for the BIA; dreams of opening a casino.

Gordie Kashpaw: Son of Nector and Marie; marries June; they have a stormy relationship and she leaves him from time to time.

June Morrissey Kashpaw: Marries her cousin Gordie; she has a son, King, with Gordie, and another illegitimate son, Lipsha, with Gerry (one of Lulu's boys); June dies drunken and desperate in a snowstorm.

Gerry Nanapush: An escape artist and AIM activist; accused (possibly unjustly) of murder; Lipsha's father (with June).

Lipsha Morrissey: Possessed of a mystical healing touch, Lipsha learns at the end of the novel that he is June and Gerry's son.

King: Son of June and Gordie; a wife-beating drunkard who snitches on Gerry while both are in prison.

Love medicine. In the story that gives the novel its name, Lipsha Morrissey, who has a mystical healing touch, tries to concoct a love medicine that will make his grandfather, Nector, fall in love once again with his wife, Marie. Working on the principles of ancient Chippewa medicine, Lipsha, in accord with his grandmother, looks for an appropriate cure in nature. According to traditional Chippewa belief, all things, whether living or nonliving, had spirits one could tame for the purpose of helping the sick or harming enemies. Love medicine, however, was not traditionally considered to be benign medicine; because it "subvert[s] the autonomy and welfare of other animate beings," love medicine was held to be "bad medicine," along with hunting medicine, which increases the likelihood of bringing down prey (Brown, p. 181). George Nelson, an early nineteenth-century trader who had extensive contact with the Northern Ojibwa and Cree, reports that love medicine—sometimes made from powdered hyssop—was often smeared on a sleeping person and had various effects, from "arousing spontaneous desire to incurring hypnotic dependency and sexual aggressiveness" (Nelson in Brown, p. 181). Nelson also reports that fear of this medicine pressured women especially to accept suitors. In the novel Lipsha settles upon the hearts of wild geese, who mate for life, as appropriate for the age-old medicine. He fails, however, in his attempt to shoot a pair of geese and instead brings his grandmother the hearts of two frozen turkeys that he has bought at a local store. Disaster follows. His grandfather chokes to death on a turkey heart. Lipsha believes that he has messed around with powers much greater than his understanding, and is thus responsible for his grandfather's death:

> I told myself that love medicine was simple. I told myself the old superstititions was just that—strange beliefs. . . . And here is what I did that made the medicine backfire. I took an evil shortcut.
>
> (*Love Medicine*, p. 245)

Lipsha learns something about the conflict between tradition and modernity as he puzzles over the strange death of his grandfather. But when Nector's spirit does not seem to actually have departed to the afterlife, appearing to both Marie and Lipsha, the youth decides that love medicine transcends historical situations and is at work in both the world of Indian custom and the world where the hearts of fowl are found in the frozen food section. Comforting his grieving grandmother, who believes that Nector cannot rest because the love medicine she and Lipsha concocted was too strong, Lipsha tells her what he has come to understand:

> Love medicine ain't what brings him back to you, Grandma. No, it's something else. He loved you over time and distance, but he went off so quick he never got the chance to tell you how he loves you, how he doesn't blame you, how he understands. It's true feeling, not no magic. No supermarket heart could have brung him back.
>
> (*Love Medicine*, p. 257)

Love medicine, then, the power of love to cure hurt, is found in the human heart, a conclusion that affects the entire set of stories. The work manages to merge the traditional idea of Chippewa love medicine with the restorative powers of a not always appealing but ultimately healing community of love.

NANAPUSH, CREATOR OF EARTH

Known by the same name as one of the families in *Love Medicine*, Nanapush (or Nanaboozoo or Nanabozho) plays a key role in Chippewa legend. According to various stories, Nanapush is held to be either a manitou or the first man. He created the earth by blowing on a small piece of dirt until it grew to its present size, and then formed people, animals, and trees from clay. The central figure in the mythology of the plains-dwelling Chippewa, Nanapush represents the human potential for both good and evil, but he is generally a force for good, having at one point staged a huge battle with the underwater lynx (sometimes refered to as a panther) who killed his brother.

Sources. Louise Erdrich hails from a mixed Chippewa heritage. She attended boarding schools run by the Bureau of Indian Affairs and often visited her maternal grandparents on the Turtle Mountain Chippewa Reservation, the setting for the stories in *Love Medicine*. The set of interwoven stories is one of Erdrich's first attempts to focus on her Indian heritage in fictional form. "I [previously] tried to write about [my Chippewa roots]," Erdrich recalls, "but I wasn't able to address that part of me, to speak in that voice. It was difficult. [Writing *Love Medicine*] forced me to come to terms with who I am" (Erdrich in Hall, p. 128).

Erdrich's prize-winning short story "The World's Greatest Fishermen" became the basis for and first chapter of *Love Medicine*. Two other chapters, "The Red Convertible" and "Scales," were also published previously. Erdrich developed them into her novel, meanwhile working in close consultation with husband Michael Dorris, author of *A Yellow Raft in Blue Water* (also covered in *Literature and Its Times*).

Reviews. *Love Medicine* was accepted for publication when Louise Erdrich was twenty-eight years old. Some readers were confused by the book's overlapping stories and myriad characters. The *New York Times Book Review* wondered why Erdrich did not fully develop stories in which younger characters are closer to success than the older generation. Overall, however, *Love Medicine* met with a generally positive response. A review in *Booklist* called the novel "[a] beautifully written, realistic account of the lives of two Chippewa Indian families" (Kooi in Hall, p. 129). "The stories, beautifully crafted, lead to the conclusion that in not knowing this people before we have truly impoverished our land," wrote a critic in *Best Sellers* (Kinney in Hall, p. 129). In a review that was broadcast, Jascha Kessler commented that the "the two dozen or so relatives [in *Love Medicine*] come through to us, full of surprises and full of disasters that are, it seems, typically Indian, and a world away from the usual life of Americans. And yet that world is here . . . and very much part of our national consciousness, or it should be" (Kessler in Hall, p. 131). In 1984, Erdrich won the National Book Critics Circle Award for *Love Medicine,* which turned out to be the first in a series of four books continuing the saga of the Kashpaws and Lamartines.

For More Information

Brown, Jennifer, and Robert Brightman. *"The Orders of the Dreamed": George Nelson on Cree and Northern Ojibwa Religion and Myth, 1823.* St. Paul: Minnesota Historical Society Press, 1988.

Camp, Gregory Scott. *The Turtle Mountain Plains-Chippewas and Métis, 1797- 1935.* Ann Arbor, Mich.: UMI, 1987.

Confederation of American Indians, New York. *Indian Reservations: A State and Federal Handbook.* Jefferson, N.C.: McFarland, 1986.

Erdrich, Louise. *Love Medicine.* 1984. Revised edition. New York: HarperPerennial, 1993.

Hall, Sharon K., ed. *Contemporary Literary Criticism.* Vol. 39. Detroit: Gale Research, 1985.

Howard, James. *The Plains-Ojibwa or Bungi: Hunters and Warriors of the Northern Prairies with Special Reference to the Turtle Mountain Band.* Vermillion: South Dakota University , 1965.

Johnston, Basil. *The Manitous: The Spiritual World of the Ojibway.* New York: HarperCollins, 1995.

Josephy, Alvin M., Jr. *Red Power: The American Indians' Fight for Freedom.* New York: American Heritage Press, 1971.

Nineteen Eighty-Four

by

George Orwell

Eric Arthur Blair was born in Motihari, Bengal, India on June 25, 1903, to English parents. Though offered a university scholarship, Blair instead opted to serve in the Indian Imperial Police in Burma. On leave in England in 1927, he dropped out and decided against returning to Burma. Troubled by the caste and racial barriers that had prevented him from getting to know a wider cross-section of the populace there, he began mixing with the downtrodden of Europe, gathering material for *Down and Out in Paris and London.* He changed his name upon the publication of this first book (1933) to George Orwell after the Orwell River in Suffolk, England. In his fiction and essays, Orwell stresses the importance of intellectual and human liberty, attacking imperialism, totalitarianism, and left-wing hypocrisy as its enemies. These convictions found perhaps their ultimate literary expression in his last novel, *Nineteen Eighty-Four.*

Events in History at the Time of the Novel

Utopia. In 1516, Sir Thomas More published a book that criticized the injustice of his own society and at the same time portrayed an ideal state in which peace and order reign and poverty and misery are erased. Its title was *Utopia,* referring to the name of its imaginary island setting, a word of Greek origin that literally translated as "no place." Since that time, the term has been adopted as a general term for various ideal states in works such as Plato's *Republic* and St.

> ## THE LITERARY WORK
>
> A satirical novel set in London in the fictional future year 1984; published in 1949.
>
> ## SYNOPSIS
>
> Winston Smith lives in a society in which "the Party" keeps a ruthless stranglehold on power through total control over the thoughts and actions of its members. When Winston and his lover Julia defy the Thought Police and join an underground resistance movement, they soon discover the powerlessness of the individual in the face of absolute political oppression.

Augustine's *City of God.* Other famous pre-nineteenth-century utopias include François Rabelais's description of the Abbey of Thélème in *Gargantua and Pantagruel* (1532), Tommaso Campanella's *The City of the Sun* (1632), and Francis Bacon's *The New Atlantis* (1627). The concept of utopia changed in the eighteenth century with the popularization of philosopher Jean Jacques Rousseau's idea that a primitive, uncorrupt society existed before the development of civilization. This faith in natural order and the innate goodness of humankind became the ideological foundation of utopian socialism, the notion that class divisions and competition could evolve into a new classless cooperative society, whose inhabitants live under ideal conditions.

Proponents of the notion included the nineteenth-century social theorists Pierre Joseph Proudhon and Robert Owen.

The mid-nineteenth century saw the rise of the utopian romance. These novels depicted the sometimes glowing, sometimes frightening social implications of the new industrialism. Among the more prominent titles are Samuel Butler's *Erewhon* (1872), Edward Bellamy's *Looking Backward* (1888), and H. G. Wells's *A Modern Utopia* (1905). In *Looking Backward,* the hero Julian West falls asleep in 1887 and awakens in the year 2000 in a utopia achieved peacefully through the operation of one huge national trust run by the government. All of the nation's citizens aged twenty-five to forty-five work in an industrial army, after which they retire to read, pursue hobbies, and provide the little leadership needed in the povertyless and crime-free society.

THE ATOMIC BOMB

The history of atomic warfare in Orwell's novel begins with the first detonation in the 1940s, followed by a full-scale atomic war about ten years later, in which hundreds of bombs are dropped on industrial centers in European Russia, Western Europe, and North America. Orwell published *Nineteen Eighty-Four* four years after the destruction of Hiroshima—the dawn of the nuclear age. After World War II, the United States submitted a proposal to the United Nations to form an international regulatory body with the right to send atomic weapons inspectors into countries and enforce sanctions against any country found guilty of unauthorized use of atomic power. But the Americans at that time were the sole possessors of the bomb, and the Soviets rejected the proposal and proceeded with their own atomic research. By the time of the novel's publication in 1949, the Soviets were equipped to conduct atomic warfare, and the arms race had begun.

The utopian romance was followed in the early to mid-twentieth century by a number of novels that portrayed negative utopias, sometimes called dystopias. These dystopias are imaginary places wracked by misery and wretchedness; the people lead dehumanized and often fear-ridden lives. Examples include Yevgeny Zamyatin's *We* (1924), Aldous Huxley's **Brave New World** (1932; also covered in *Literature and Its Times*), and Orwell's *Nineteen Eighty-Four*

(1949). These books reflect to varying degrees the sense of general disillusionment experienced in the first half of the twentieth century. After undergoing two wars and their attendant mass destruction, a severe international economic crisis, the genocide of the Holocaust, the totalitarian terror in the Stalinist Soviet Union, and the advent of the atomic bomb, it seemed as if Western civilization was on the brink of certain collapse. Negative utopias express the powerlessness and hopelessness of modern man just as the early utopias expressed the self-confidence and hope of postmedieval humankind. *Brave New World,* for example, portrays a scientifically balanced state that permits no individual emotions or responses, considers art disruptive, and forbids the use of "mother" or "father" since all the inhabitants belong to one another.

Propaganda. In the novel Winston's job at the Ministry of Truth consists of falsifying historical documents in such a way as to make the Party, or administration, appear infallible. This kind of systematic eradication had precedent, most notably during the Stalinist era in the Soviet Union of the 1930s. After Josef Stalin consolidated power, the names of once-revered leaders of the Russian Revolution—men like Leon Trotsky, Nikolai Bukharin, and Lev Kamenev—were deleted from the history books, their faces obliterated even on historical photographs. The articles devoted to them were eliminated from the official encyclopedia and new pages were supplied to replace those that subscribers were ordered to cut out (Esslin, p. 128).

But the Soviets were not alone in engaging in such practices. The British government undertook its own propaganda efforts as well, of which Orwell himself was both a witting and later unwitting participant. From 1939 to 1941, Stalin was portrayed in the British press as an arch-villain who had sacrificed Poland by signing a nonaggression pact with Germany's Adolf Hitler. But on the day Hitler invaded the Soviet Union, Stalin was instantly remade into a hero and friend of Britain. In its radio broadcasts, the British Broadcasting Corporation (BBC) stressed the fortitude of the Russian people and the heroism of the Red Army. Orwell worked for the BBC during this period in which Stalin was so lionized; at the same time, Orwell's satirical novel *Animal Farm,* which condemned Stalin as a despot, was steadily rejected by British publishers. Only two years later, after the war came to an end and Stalin was no longer an "ally," did Orwell find a house willing to publish the book.

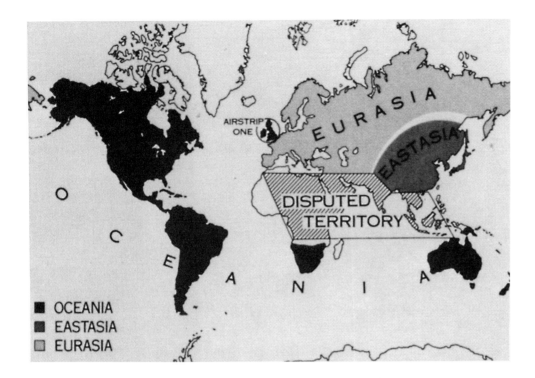

The world as depicted in *Nineteen Eighty-Four*.

In Orwell's fictional Oceania, radio broadcasts consist of special announcements of victories and large doses of martial music and fanfares. This bears a distinct resemblance to the successful tactics used by Germany's minister of propaganda under Hitler, Joseph Goebbels. Additionally, Orwell's concept of the "Newspeak" language, which plays such a critical element in the debasement of society in *Nineteen Eighty-Four,* bears a striking resemblance to Goebbels's *Sprachregelung* ("language manipulation"). In Sprachregelung, for example, Churchill was referred to by officials as "that brandy-sodden alcoholic Winston Churchill," and Roosevelt "that syphilitic degenerate Roosevelt" (Esslin, p. 129).

International political alignment after World War II. In *Nineteen Eighty-Four,* the world is divided into three great powers—Oceania (the United States and Britain), Eurasia (continental Europe and Russia), and Eastasia (China and Southeast Asia). This scenario is grounded in the actual political realignments that followed World War II. At a conference in the Iranian city of Tehran in December 1943, Roosevelt and Churchill met with Stalin and discussed, among other things, the postwar occupation and demilitarization of Germany. Not wishing to lose the cooperation of the Soviets in the war against the

Germans, Roosevelt put off confrontational territorial issues until victory was assured. At the Tehran meeting it was agreed that a secret Allied assault on German-occupied France would take place in the spring of 1944. This would force Germany to fight a war on two fronts, both east and west; since 1941 it had been trying to take over the Soviet Union. A grateful Stalin promised to launch a simultaneous offensive effort on the eastern front. This is the strategy that would win the war in the next eighteen months, but it was also a plan that all but guaranteed the Russian domination of eastern Europe. By the time the leaders met again at Yalta in February of 1945, Stalin's armies had driven the Nazi forces back to within forty miles of Berlin, and were in control of Poland and nearly all of eastern and central Europe.

Fearful that the Soviets would impose a totalitarian political system on this vast area, Roosevelt and Churchill pressed Stalin to pledge the earliest possible establishment of sovereign governments in the region through free elections. Stalin conceded verbally, but he refused to allow international supervision of the elections. In the decade following the war's end, a ravaged Europe became a battleground for the two ideologies, and nowhere was their inability to agree more evident than in the political division of Germany into East and West, and indeed even within the former capital of Berlin itself. At Yalta the leaders had also agreed to a founding conference for the United Nations, set up that same year to maintain international peace and security. Yet even a multinational cooperative coalition had little substantive effect on the growing rift between the United States and the Soviet Union. From 1945 to 1955, obstructing the progress of concerted international action, the Soviets used their veto in the United Nations seventy-five times, the Americans three times. The ongoing diplomatic and ideological clash of interest between these two nations came to be known as the Cold War.

WHAT ORWELL IS ATTACKING

The question arises why Orwell, a socialist himself, would write a novel that attacked English socialism. Socialism had been promoted in England since the late 1800s, with men such as science-fiction writer H. G. Wells calling for gradual reform through government intervention in social areas for the benefit of the people. In fact, Orwell contended that *Nineteen Eighty-Four* was not an antisocialist novel at all, but rather a warning against totalitarianism, as explained by Michael Sheldon in his biography:

> "The scene of the book," he [Orwell] explained, "is laid in Britain in order to emphasise that the English-speaking races are not innately better than anyone else and that totalitarianism, *if not fought against,* could triumph anywhere." (The italics are Orwell's.) He also made it clear that he did not see his book as a specific assault on socialism. . . . "My recent novel is NOT intended as an attack on Socialism . . . but as a show-up of the perversions to which a centralised economy is liable and which have already been partly realised in Communism and Fascism."
>
> (Sheldon, p. 433)

The third great power to emerge out of World War II was the People's Republic of China. The triumph of Mao Zedong's (Tse-tung's) Red Army was the final episode in a long civil war between the Guomindang (Kuomintang), or Nationalists, and the Communists that had begun in 1927. The uneasy alliance formed between the two groups in 1937 to fight the Japanese barely held together through the war years. After the war, fighting broke out and continued from 1946 to

1949. Despite the aid given to the Nationalists (who were themselves undemocratic, but at least not communist) by the United States, the Red Army emerged triumphant in 1949, forcing the defeated Guomindang to withdraw to the island of Taiwan. Mao then reestablished the national capital in the ancient city of Beijing, and for the next twenty-seven years proceeded to rule the People's Republic of China.

Totalitarianism. When Vladimir I. Lenin, the leading force behind the Russian Revolution in 1917, died seven years later, his obvious successor appeared to be Leon Trotsky, a companion of Lenin's during the revolution. But unlike Lenin, Trotsky was essentially an intellectual, uncompromising in his devotion to the ideals of the revolution and outspoken in his contempt for what he perceived to be the recent erosion of those ideals. At the party congress elections in 1927, he was displaced by a figure who wielded much less political clout, Josef Stalin. Not long afterwards, Trotsky was exiled to Siberia, and later banished completely from the Soviet Union. With the rise of Stalin, the Communist Party underwent a drastic purge. A third of its membership was expelled for allegedly sympathizing with Trotsky (who in this respect bears a striking resemblance to Goldstein, the traitor vilified by the Party in *Nineteen Eighty-Four*). During the 1930s, large numbers of political insiders and common citizens alike were accused of crimes against the state. In such show trials, the accused confessed in full to their crimes. Many—including Bukharin and Kamenev—were summarily executed. The news that all had confessed seemed highly suspect to the rest of the world, causing it to doubt the honesty of the proceedings.

More than a decade later, these grisly events were to some extent repeated in China. Soon after Mao Zedong's Communists captured power from the Nationalists in 1949 and established the People's Republic of China, totalitarianism again appeared in the newly formed communist state—although its appearance seems less indicative of communist ideology than a long history of despotic rulers in both Russia and China. Mao and his lieutenants manipulated all organs of information for indoctrination purposes. Political education was accompanied by mass arrests and executions, forced labor, and the liquidation of anticommunist opponents. Later, Mao would admit that in the first five years of the revolution hundreds of thousands of opponents had been purged. As the years passed, repression continued, but coercion was often less important in China than the mobilization of social pressures for conformity. Political opponents were rehabilitated rather than liquidated, and often permitted to return to positions of responsibility. The fact that the majority of these events, which are strikingly similar to those recounted in *Nineteen Eighty-Four,* occurred after the publication of the book is a testament to the novel's uncanny prescience.

The Novel in Focus

The plot. It is the year 1984, and the world is divided into three superstates—Oceania, Eurasia, and Eastasia. The novel takes place in London, portrayed as a drab city in a province known as Airstrip One in a place called Oceania. Although the superstates are perpetually at war with one another, the atomic devastation of the past has been replaced by distant conventional warfare over border disputes in far-flung lands.

Oceania is governed by an oppressive totalitarian regime known simply as the Party. The Party's ideology is called English Socialism, or Ingsoc, the slogans of which are "War is Peace," "Freedom is Slavery," and "Ignorance is Strength" (Orwell, *Nineteen Eighty-Four,* p. 7).

Symbolized by the ubiquitous image of Big Brother, the Party controls every conceivable aspect of human action and thought. Even language falls under its control. "Standard English" is being systematically replaced by "Newspeak," a language "which has been devised to meet the ideological needs of Ingsoc, or English Socialism," and at the same time "to make all other modes of thought impossible" (*Nineteen Eighty-Four,* p. 246).

Winston Smith is a thirty-nine-year-old minor official and Outer Party member who works in the Records Department of the Ministry of Truth, where he falsifies historical documents. At heart, Winston is an enemy of the Party because he questions hierarchical authority and because he cannot help but retain some semblance of his "ancestral memory," which provides him with some understanding of the present—and therefore an awareness of his own individuality. When he comes across a photograph at work proving that the Party falsely accused and executed three innocent men, he begins to write down his thoughts in a diary—an act that qualifies him as a criminal.

Winston grows progressively preoccupied with the past; not the official past, but "what it was like in the old days, before the Revolution"

(*Nineteen Eighty-Four,* p. 76). In a society in which individuality has all but ceased to exist, Winston becomes an outcast. He walks the streets aimlessly, wandering into the section of town reserved for the "proles," the underclass that make up 85 percent of the population. When he runs across an old man in a pub, he asks him about the past, but the man can't seem to answer his question, or perhaps doesn't understand what he means. In defiance of the Thought Police, who monitor every movement of every Party member, Winston enters a junk shop run by a prole named Mr. Charrington. There he buys a paperweight, which he carries home with him. Although it appears to be a worthless object, the paperweight is valuable to Winston because it is old, and therefore provides a link to the past.

Winston finds little comfort in his patriotic workmates Parsons and Syme, but does seem to have an unspoken connection with a man named O'Brien. Before Winston can find the courage to approach O'Brien, though, a young woman named Julia approaches Winston, handing him a secret note that says "I love you." In Julia, Winston finds a sympathetic companion and someone who has mastered the art of deceiving the Party. Not only does she perform her perfunctory Party duties, she volunteers additional time as well, all in order to throw the Thought Police off her track. In private, she despises the Party and everything for which it stands. Winston and Julia become lovers, and eventually they rent a room above Charrington's junk shop to use as a meeting place. For the first time since he was a little child, Winston is happy.

Having found each other, Winston and Julia wonder if there are more people out there like them and speculate again about the existence of the Brotherhood. The Brotherhood, according to Party propaganda, is a guerrilla organization dedicated to overthrowing the Party, and is led by a legendary enemy of the party named Goldstein. Soon afterwards, O'Brien discreetly approaches Winston, and just as Winston suspected, O'Brien turns out to be a member of the Brotherhood. He initiates the couple into the secret society and gives them a book written by Goldstein called *The Theory and Practice of Oligarchical Collectivism* that details the methods by which the Party exercises complete control over the population. Before Winston can finish reading the book, however, he and Julia are ambushed in their private room by the Thought Police, who beat them into submission and drag them away.

John Hurt in a scene from the 1984 film adaptation of *Nineteen Eighty-Four*.

Winston wakes up in a jail cell in the windowless Ministry of Love, where he is greeted by O'Brien, who is not really a genuine member of the Brotherhood but is actually a member of the Inner Party. O'Brien proceeds to systematically torture Winston within an inch of his life, and although Winston confesses every crime he can think of, including those he did not commit, O'Brien is not satisfied. According to O'Brien, the torture is not meant to punish or elicit a confession. The Party, he explains, wants no martyrs. The ignorant proles must never have a leader to rouse them. It is not enough to obey Big Brother, you must love him too. "We do not merely destroy our enemies," O'Brien explains, "we change them" (*Nineteen Eighty-Four,* p. 209). In the end, Winston is taken to the mysterious "Room 101," where prisoners are confronted with their worst fear. In Winston's case, that fear is rats. As a cage filled with hungry rats is being strapped to his face, the terrified Winston finally commits the ultimate betrayal, crying, "Do it to Julia! Do it to Julia! Not me! Julia!" (*Nineteen Eighty-Four,* p. 236).

Winston is released a changed man. Nothing interests him beyond the petty duties of his new job, his Victory Gin, and his daily chess game (in which the white pieces must always win). Even his chance encounter with Julia is characterized by indifference. Each admits having betrayed the other under torture, and then they part. One day in the tavern the telescreen announces that Oceania has won a critical military victory, and something snaps inside Winston. He starts to cry. Now finally he can be put to death, for at last he loves Big Brother.

Living conditions in Britain after World War II. The world in which Winston Smith lives is a spartan one. Luxury items such as chocolate are rationed by the Party, and even common items are scarce: "At any given moment there was some necessary article which the Party shops were unable to supply. Sometimes it was buttons, sometimes it was darning wool, sometimes it was shoelaces; at present it was razor blades. You could only get a hold of them, if at all, by scrounging more or less furtively on the 'free' market" (*Nineteen Eighty-Four,* pp. 43-4). Products sponsored by the party, such as "Victory Cigarettes" and "Victory Gin," are very poor quality. "Regulation lunch" consists of the following: "metal pannikin of pinkish-gray stew, a hunk of bread, a cube of cheese, a mug of milkless Victory Coffee, and one saccharine tablet" (*Nineteen Eighty-Four,* p. 44). As unappealing as this life may sound, it is in fact a fairly accurate representation of the standard of living in Britain at the time the novel was written. The conclusion of World War II did not bring an end to the suffering of the British. The war had cost a quarter of the nation's wealth, and for several years afterward life in postwar Britain was dismal. Basic goods and services were limited. Certain foods and industrial products were rationed, and in the winter of 1946-47 fuel shortages were so severe that the government was forced to impose drastic rations on the use of power for both industrial and private consumers. Orwell himself, though he was not poor, ran out of coal that winter and was forced to burn peat in his fireplace to keep warm.

Sources. Orwell wrote *Nineteen Eighty-Four* as he was dying. In the spring of 1947 he rented a secluded house in the Scottish island of Jura, where he began to compose the novel. He was hospitalized in December for tuberculosis, from which he had suffered for many years. Six months later, in spite of the warnings of his physician, he returned to Jura and resumed his work. He collapsed almost immediately upon completing the manuscript and never completely recovered.

Many critics point to the circumstances of Orwell's illness to account for the dark tone of the work, and indeed the author himself is rumored to have said that the novel "wouldn't have been so gloomy if I hadn't been so ill" (Orwell in Poupard and Person, p. 296). But regardless of how readers choose to interpret *Nineteen Eighty-Four*, it is clear that Orwell himself saw it as a political work. In his 1946 essay "Why I Write," Orwell states, "In a peaceful age I might have written ornate or merely descriptive books, and might have remained almost unaware of my political loyalties. As it is I have been forced into becoming a sort of pamphleteer" (Orwell, *A Collection of Essays,* p. 313).

There is evidence as well to support the claim that *Nineteen Eighty-Four* is also a personal novel, for much of its content can be traced to Orwell's own experiences. For two years Orwell produced propaganda materials as a member of the Indian section of the BBC's Empire Service. The first outline of *Nineteen Eighty-Four,* entitled "The Last Man in Europe," can be dated close to the end of 1943, about the time Orwell left the BBC. Martin Esslin, in his essay "Television and Telescreen," points out that the "hive of propaganda activity" in the offices of the Empire Service bore a striking resemblance to the propaganda efforts of Winston Smith's Ministry of Truth in the novel (Esslin, p. 127). The media's manipulation of the masses in *Nineteen Eighty-Four,* then, is drawn not only from Soviet and Nazi propaganda tactics, but also from Orwell's own experiences as a propagandist in the BBC's English-language service to India as well.

Reception. *Nineteen Eighty-Four* was published in Britain and the United States in June of 1949 and received tremendous acclaim. Within a year of its publication, 50,000 copies had been sold in Great Britain and 170,000 in the United States. Mark Schorer, writing for the *New York Times,* called it "the most contemporary novel of this year and who knows how many past and yet to come" (Schorer, p. 16). The English writer V. S. Pritchett said "I do not think I have ever read a novel more frightening and depressing; and yet, such are the originality, the suspense, the speed of writing and withering indignation that it is impossible to put the book down" (Pritchett in Poupard and Person, p. 301). A month after the novel's publication, the *New York Times Book Review* stated that of the sixty reviews in American publications, 90 percent were "overwhelmingly admiring, with cries of terror rising above the applause" (Poupard and Person, p. 430).

Nevertheless, there were some dissenting voices. Julian Symons asserted that the book emphasized ideas at the expense of depth of character. In his review, Symons characterized the trajectory of Orwell's career as one marked by an increasing tendency to ignore characterization in favor of ideas: "in *Nineteen Eighty-Four,* [characterization] has been as nearly as possible eliminated. We are no longer dealing with characters, but society" (Symons in Poupard and Person, p. 298). But doubtless the most virulent response of all came from Samuel Sillen in the communist magazine *Masses and Mainstream:*

> Like his previous diatribe against the human race, *Animal Farm,* George Orwell's new book [*Nineteen Eighty-Four*] has received an ovation in the capitalist press. The gush of comparisons with Swift and Dostoyevsky has washed away the few remaining pebbles of literary probity. . . . Indeed, the response is far more significant than the book itself; it demonstrates that Orwell's sickness is epidemic. . . . The literary mouthpieces of imperialism have discovered that crude anti-Stalinism . . . is not enough; the system of class oppression must be directly upheld and any belief in change and progress must be frightened out of people.

> (Sillen, pp. 79-81)

For More Information

Esslin, Martin. "Television and Telescreen." In *On Nineteen Eighty-four*. Edited by Peter Stansky. Stanford, Calif.: Stanford Alumni Association, 1983.

Orwell, George. *A Collection of Essays*. New York: Harcourt Brace Jovanovich, 1946.

Orwell, George. *Nineteen Eighty-Four*. 1949. Reprint. New York: Signet, 1981.

Poupard, Dennis, and James E. Person Jr., eds. *Twentieth-Century Literary Criticism*. Vol. 15. Detroit: Gale Research, 1985.

Reilly, Patrick. *Nineteen Eighty-Four: Past, Present, and Future*. Boston: Twayne, 1989.

Schorer, Mark. "An Indignant and Prophetic Novel." *The New York Times Book Review* (June 12, 1949): 1.

Sheldon, Michael. *Orwell: The Authorized Biography*. New York: HarperCollins, 1991.

Sillen, Samuel. "Maggot of the Month." *Masses and Mainstream* 2, no. 8 (August 1949): 79-81.

Ordinary People

by

Judith Guest

First-time novelist Judith Guest made a stellar debut in 1976 with the publication of *Ordinary People.* Guest was born in Detroit, Michigan, in 1936, and raised there as well. She would later reside in Minnesota with a family of her own. Having lived all of her life in the Midwest, Guest was able to lucidly depict the type of upper-middle-class suburban community in which *Ordinary People* is set. Being the mother of three boys as well as an elementary school teacher further aided Guest in creating her fictional portrait of a troubled adolescent boy. The novel focuses on the boy's battle with severe mental distress and his experience in psychotherapy as he comes to terms with his suppressed feelings of guilt over the accidental death of his brother.

THE LITERARY WORK

A novel set in suburban Illinois in the mid-1970s; published in 1976.

SYNOPSIS

After an attempted suicide following the death of his only brother, a seventeen-year-old boy returns home from a psychiatric hospital and has difficulty adjusting to both his family and school life.

Events in History at the Time of the Novel

Teen suicide and depression. According to studies, the rate of suicide among teenagers in the United States increased dramatically among the later baby boom generation. Additionally, the rate of attempted suicide increased from 1,300 a year in 1960 to over 5,000 a year in 1980. Statistics also show that white teenage males kill themselves far more than any other groups of teenagers, accounting for more than 70 percent of all teen suicides.

Although not all attempted suicides are successful, the attempt itself, whether halfhearted or not, can be regarded as a sign of severe depression on the part of the individual, who is calling attention to himself or herself with such a destructive act. In *Ordinary People,* Conrad is unable to deal with the accidental death of his brother, Buck, and the way in which it affects the emotional equilibrium of his supposedly happy family. Conrad slices his wrists in the bathroom but is found by his parents before bleeding to death. Teenagers who attempt suicide in such a way as Conrad's character did, in the home with at least one parent nearby, are not considered as serious about dying as they are about using suicidal behavior to express their extreme unhappiness.

There are a few main reasons why people commit suicide, including the physical and emotional stress of a terminal illness, overwhelming feelings of guilt after committing a crime or harming a loved one, or mental illness. Of the latter category, depression is widely accepted as the most common motive behind suicide attempts for adults as well as teenagers. In clinical terms, depression is defined as a psychoneurotic or psychotic disorder in which an individual is overcome with extreme feelings of sadness, hopelessness, and dejection. Depending on the individual and his particular set of circumstances, this affliction can strike at any age and can be triggered by any number of different factors.

There are different types and degrees of depression. According to Emery Nestor in his book *Depression: Finding Hope and Meaning in Life's Darkest Shadow,* the most common type is called "reactive depression." Reactive depression is based on environmental factors and is most often a reaction to a meaningful loss—for example, the loss of a loved one, of a job, or of one's home.

In adolescence, an individual undergoes an emotionally challenging transformation from child to adult. The emotional transition during this period of life can be intense, and it is common for teenagers to feel somewhat depressed on occasion. Moreover, feelings of depression can be heightened in an adolescent by additional significant changes in one's life circumstances, such as a breakup with a boyfriend or girlfriend, the divorce of one's parents, or, as in Conrad's case, the pain of a death in the family. There are usually warning signs long before the depressed teen decides to take suicidal action. They include mood swings, irritability, frustration, fatigue, and withdrawal from people and regular activities. In the novel Conrad displays many of these symptoms, but only in hindsight does his father recognize them as classic signs of severe depression.

While many teens experience varying degrees of depression, not all of those diagnosed with depression attempt suicide. It cannot be sociologically explained why some teens are better able to handle emotional stress than others. Individual psychology would seem to be a major factor. It is widely believed in the medical community, based on an early theory by Sigmund Freud, that suicide itself is an acting out of an individual's anger turned inward. It was Freud's theory that suicide is an example of self-inflicted aggression in which a suicidal person attempts to kill a hated trait or image of a parent that he/she recognizes within the self. In *Ordinary People,* Cal Jarrett comments to Dr. Berger about his son Conrad and Conrad's mother:

"I see her," Cal says, "not being able to forgive him."

"For what?"

He shrugs. "For surviving maybe. No, that's not it, for being too much like her."

(Guest, *Ordinary People,* p. 147)

During his therapy, Conrad comes to realize that he has been unable to forgive himself for his brother's death or his own suicide attempt, forgiveness being a trait that both he and his mother have difficulty incorporating. Conrad seems to intimately understand this inability in his mother, and a Freudian psychologist might have said that his attempt at suicide was perhaps a way of trying to rid himself of the inability. Conrad refers to his suicide attempt when explaining to Dr. Berger why it is that his mother won't forgive him:

"Once I tried to kill myself. . . . I am never going to be forgiven for that, never. . . . She fired a goddamn maid because she couldn't dust the living room right, and if you think she's ever going to forgive me. . . . I think I've just figured something out," he says.

"What's that?" Berger asks.

"Who it is who can't forgive who."

(*Ordinary People,* pp. 119-20)

Adolescent psychotherapy. Originating with Sigmund Freud at the turn of the twentieth century, psychoanalysis would later become the basic method of treating mental illness. This approach features a psychiatrist or analyst helping a patient to discover and confront the causes of his/her mental distress or illness. The therapist listens carefully while the patient is encouraged to speak freely and confidentially about feelings and thoughts that are severely disturbing or significant to him or her. The therapist asks relevant questions specifically designed to help the patient understand how the troubling emotional state came into being. *Ordinary People* illustrates this in Berger's sessions with Conrad. Although others have challenged and even disagreed with Freud's theories on the causes of mental illness, the practice of psychotherapy remains one of the most widely accepted treatments for mental disorders. Over the years, various methods of analysis have been developed based on Freud's basic structure for treatment.

Only in the 1950s did adolescents gain a distinct identity as a subgroup in society, separate from children and adults. In subsequent years the specialty of adolescent therapy came into practice. It was recognized that teenagers were at a different stage of development than children or adults and that they had their own particular sets of problems within their subculture of peers. Us-

Mary Tyler Moore and Timothy Hutton in a scene from the 1980 film adaptation of *Ordinary People*.

ing the same framework that Freud established for adult psychoanalysis, therapists employed special guidelines to gear their therapy to teenagers. For example, because teenagers can be prone to mood swings during adolescence, therapists who treat them need to keep in mind that they are still developing emotionally. The therapist must differentiate between demonstrations of normal emotional maturation and signs of a severe mental illness in the adolescent. Because of the increasing rate of teen suicide and other developments in society, more therapists began specializing in treating teenagers for mental and emotional disorders. The most common of these disorders is depression.

There is no set time period for undergoing therapy, either for adolescents or adults. The length and frequency of treatment varies from patient to patient and is determined by the individual therapist. Conrad Jarrett undergoes several months of therapy from the time he attempted suicide, and is still in the midst of his therapy process when the novel ends.

In *Ordinary People*, we only get a few flashbacks of Conrad's experience in the mental hospital where he resided after his attempted suicide. In the hospital, Conrad supposedly underwent both individual and group analysis, but when he returns home he still has a difficult time facing his feelings and is referred to a Dr. Berger to continue his therapy. It is in Conrad's sessions with Dr. Berger that the process of analysis is depicted.

In the course of his sessions with Berger, Conrad progresses from an unwilling patient unable to cope with his depression to one who gradually opens up about feeling responsible for his brother's accidental death. The therapy sessions eventually reveal that Conrad harbors extreme guilt about having survived an accident that his popular and well-loved brother did not. Unable to accept the pain of losing his brother and feeling that fault must be placed on someone, Conrad blames himself. At the same time, he wants desperately to be forgiven for something he was never responsible for in the first place. Dr. Berger approaches Conrad's inner distress by asking him questions about matters that would concern a young man his age, questions about school, girls, his friends, and, of course, his relationship with his parents. Berger listens to Conrad's thoughts and feelings, and he poses alternative perspectives for Conrad to consider. However, the doctor takes care to never advise or suggest how Conrad should or shouldn't behave. His aim is to encourage his patients to make healthy choices for themselves.

Suburban life. *Ordinary People* takes place in a suburb outside Chicago, Illinois. This area was carefully chosen by the author; she wanted the members of her fictional family, the Jarretts, to be representative of the type of people who generally inhabit a comfortable suburban community. In the decades that followed World War II, suburban enclaves grew rapidly outside major U.S. cities, and the Chicago area's growth ranked at the top of the list.

Compared to the inner cities, the suburbs are thought to be particularly good places to raise children. Schools there are considered better and the streets safer and less crowded. During the 1970s, Northfield, Hinsdale, and other suburbs of Chicago competed to have the best-ranked schools in the Midwest. Additionally, such suburbs saw unprecedented new housing development during the postwar years, making them attractive places in which to raise a family comfortably. The federal highway program, which helped link such outlying suburbs to urban centers of finance and commerce, allowed people such as the novel's Cal Jarrett to work in the city but reside in a suburb.

The Jarretts reside in Lake Forest, near Evanston, Illinois. Evanston lies ten miles north of downtown Chicago and is home to Northwestern University. As a larger suburban city, Evanston contains a population that varies in terms of race and economic status. However, the greater population of smaller suburban communities, such as Lake Forest, are largely comprised of neighborhoods of specifically white, upper-middle-class families. The novel takes place in the 1970s, when many heads of suburban households worked in Chicago proper, and a large percentage were professionals such as lawyers, doctors, and businesspeople. The incomes were typically upwards of $55,000 a year for single-income households, and $100,000 or more for double-income households.

The Jarretts are an example of the kind of family and lifestyle of the people who live in such a Chicago suburb. Cal Jarrett is a lawyer with a practice in Chicago, and his wife Beth is a homemaker whose other activities include participating in the social events in her local country club and working as a volunteer with charitable organizations. The Jarretts reside in a large two-story single-family dwelling and take expensive vacations during the holiday season. They can easily meet and exceed the financial demands of their everyday lifestyle. In short, they seem to represent the typical upper-middle-class Midwestern suburban family.

The Novel in Focus

The plot. *Ordinary People* is a story about a family whose underlying and deep-seated problems emerge in the aftermath of a tragic accident. The Jarretts seemed, by all appearances, to be a perfectly normal family living in an upper-middle-class suburb of Chicago, until the death of eighteen-year-old Buck Jarrett. The tragedy undermines the façade of this seemingly happy family, and the deterioration harshly exposes its problems.

As the novel opens, Conrad Jarrett has just returned from the mental hospital where he spent time after a suicide attempt that occurred several months after the accidental death of his brother, Buck. Buck was less than a year and a half older than Conrad, and they were close. In contrast to Conrad, Buck received a great deal of attention. He was handsome, possessed a lively, outgoing personality, excelled in sports, and was popular at school. Conrad Jarrett, though also a good student and an athlete like Buck, lacked the same outward confidence. After a tragic boating accident in which Buck drowned, Conrad became deeply and severely depressed. Still in shock themselves about Buck's death, and not knowing enough to detect oncoming signs of mental illness, Beth and Cal Jarrett found their son Conrad bleeding to death on the bathroom floor after having slit his wrists.

While Cal becomes overly concerned with his son's well-being to the point of obsession, Beth removes herself from Conrad emotionally, as if his suicide attempt was a personal act of hostility toward her. Conrad battles extreme feelings of guilt for having survived the accident in which Buck died, and for alienating his mother by attempting to commit suicide. When Conrad returns from the mental hospital, he finds that he cannot go back to living life as before, especially with Buck now missing. In Conrad's struggle to adjust to being the only surviving child, the family's inner dysfunctional core slowly surfaces. As the father begins his own journey down the path toward healing, he recognizes the emotional limitations of his wife, and his marriage begins to fall apart. Conrad works with his therapist, Dr. Berger, to regain his emotional footing and forgive himself because he harbors unfounded guilt over Buck's death. He also learns to forgive his mother for not being emotionally capable of dealing with anything of an extraordinary nature, such as death.

The stigma of mental illness. Mental illness is a subject of much controversy in American so-

Judith Guest

ciety. While psychoanalysis has become widely accepted as a form of treatment in the medical community, some still find it difficult to admit that they need help resolving mental or emotional problems. The fear has been said to stem from the belief that receiving treatment for mental illness or distress is an admission of abnormality and is likely to be largely frowned upon by peers and loved ones. While the fear has abated somewhat with the passing of the years, it still was a reality for many in the 1970s, when the novel takes place. In *Ordinary People* the stigma attached to mental illness and its treatment manifests itself in the characters of Conrad's mother, Beth Jarrett, and his swim coach, Mr. Salan. At a dinner party that Beth and Cal Jarrett attend, Cal admits to another guest that his son Conrad is seeing a psychiatrist. Later, during the drive home, Beth tells Cal that she thinks that admitting that Conrad is seeing a doctor was in bad taste, not to mention a violation of privacy. However, Beth does not answer when Cal asks whose privacy she feels he violated. Clearly she was embarrassed to admit that her son was still having mental or emotional problems. One day after swim practice, Conrad is questioned by Coach Salan about the treat-

ment he received while in the hospital. Salan reacts disapprovingly and says, "I'm no doctor, but I don't think I'd let them mess around with my head like that" (*Ordinary People,* p. 22). Even though Conrad's father makes a wholehearted attempt to understand what his son is going through, the father also admits to Dr. Berger in his own therapy session that he doesn't necessarily believe in psychiatry as a solution for everyone.

Shattering the façade. The Jarretts, as well as the community in which they reside, appear to be more concerned about the healthy outer image of suburban family life than about the reality of possible problems within it. During the mid-1970s, when *Ordinary People* was written, many Americans began to question the outward appearance of a seemingly honest, well-run government when the Watergate scandal—the burglary of Democratic party headquarters by respected Republicans—became common knowledge. The scandal helped undermine the public's faith in the integrity of government officials and their elected leaders. Similarly, the Jarretts only seem to be an upstanding family of nice, well-adjusted people. In the wake of a tragic accident, however, the true dysfunctional elements of the family reveal themselves. The novel's first chapter points to the façade by revealing Conrad's thoughts about his parents:

> This house. Too big for three people. Straining, he can barely hear the early-morning sounds of his father and mother organizing things, synchronizing schedules at the other end of the hall. It doesn't matter . . . they would certainly not be talking about anything important. They would not be talking, for instance, about him. They are people of good taste. They do not discuss a problem in the presence of the problem. And, besides, there is no problem.
> (*Ordinary People,* p. 4)

This attitude of preferring ignorance to the knowledge of an unpleasant reality was changing in the 1970s, which became known as the "Me" generation. Turning away from the political activism of the preceding decade, many Americans began to concentrate on improving the inner self. Self-help movements and the general focus on the individual during these years made it possible for an increasing number of people to confront even unhappy truths.

Sources. Judith Guest maintains that *Ordinary People* was not based on any real-life models or experiences. The story was pure fiction. She did, however, draw on her experiences as an older sister of two brothers, a mother of three sons, and an elementary school teacher to portray her main character, the teenaged Conrad Jarrett. She referred also to memories of her own adolescent experience in structuring Conrad's character.

When Guest was writing *Ordinary People* she was living in Palatine, Illinois. Though Palatine was a suburban community outside Chicago, Guest carefully chose nearby Lake Forest for her novel's setting because she had a friend who lived there and felt that it contained just the right kind of white upper-middle-class community in which the Jarretts might reside.

Reviews. Judith Guest submitted *Ordinary People* as an unsolicited manuscript, and it was published by Viking Press, a house that hadn't published an unsolicited work in twenty-seven years. The novel quickly became a bestseller, and it was generally well reviewed, although critics found fault with some aspects of the work while praising others. They, for example, applauded the realistic language of the novel's teenagers but criticized the lack of voice given to some of its adult characters. Appearing in the *New York Times Book Review*, an article by Lore Dickson mixes praise with criticism:

> Guest portrays Conrad not only as if she has lived with him on a daily basis . . . but as if she has gotten into his head. The dialogue Conrad has with himself, his psychiatrist, his friends, his family, all rings true with adolescent anxiety. This is the small hard kernel of brilliance in the novel; the rest is deeply flawed. . . . Guest has a raw, unpolished talent, but she also has a passionate honesty and sensitivity.
>
> (Dickson, pp. 14-18)

Ordinary People would go on to be adapted into an Academy-Award winning film in 1980.

For More Information

Baker, Don, and Emery Nester. *Depression: Finding Hope and Meaning in Life's Darkest Shadow.* Portland, Ore.: Multnomah, 1983.

Colton, Mary Ellen, and Susan Gore. *Adolescent Stress: Causes and Consequences.* New York: Aldine De Gruyter, 1991.

Dickson, Lore. Review of "Ordinary People." *The New York Times Book Review* (July 18, 1976): 14-18.

Freedheim, Donald K. *History of Psychotherapy: Century of Change.* Washington, D.C.: American Psychological Association, 1992.

Gilbert, Sara. *What Happens in Therapy.* New York: Lothrop, Lee & Shepard, 1982.

Goldman, Nikki. *Life Issues: Teen Suicide.* New York: Marshall Cavendish, 1996.

Guest, Judith. *Ordinary People.* New York: Viking, 1976.

Schwartz, Barry. *The Changing Face of the Suburbs.* Chicago: University of Chicago Press, 1976.

The Outsiders

by

S. E. Hinton

Born in Tulsa, Oklahoma, in the late 1940s, Susan Eloise Hinton began writing *The Outsiders* when she was fifteen years old. Hinton loosely based the novel on her high school experiences and published it when she was seventeen. She is credited as one of the first authors of modern young adult fiction.

Events in History at the Time of the Novel

S. E. Hinton and young adult literature. Although critics had acknowledged the genre of young adult fiction in one form or another for thirty years prior to *The Outsiders*, many credit S. E. Hinton as one of the first modern writers for young people. The genre rapidly expanded during the 1940s and 1950s, but was limited and predictable. Young adult fiction generally consisted of animal tales, mysteries, science fiction, career, and sports stories. Romances for young girls—which focused on problems of popularity, first dates, high school proms, and best friends—proliferated. Such antiseptic, didactic stories compelled critic Frank G. Jennings to dismiss the genre in 1956 as "mealy-mouthed, gutless, and pointless" (Jennings in Cart, p. 26).

S. E. Hinton agreed with this perspective. She notes: "There was no realistic fiction being written for teenagers. It was all Mary Jane goes to the prom, that kind of stuff. I'd been to a few proms and they weren't anything like that. There weren't any books that dealt realistically with teenage life so I wrote *The Outsiders* to fill that

gap" (Hinton in Garrett and McCue, p. 66). Hinton's characters, as Ponyboy himself notes at the end of the novel, are people whose stories had not yet been told. In the novel Ponyboy and the rest of the greasers are worried not about the prom, but about their own survival. *The Outsiders* was one of the first novels to portray their world and the anxieties it generated.

Hinton's novel helped launch a movement called "realism" or "new realism" in young adult literature. Authors in the movement sought to portray difficult, serious, and thoroughly contemporary teenage issues. After *The Outsiders* it became popular to write, in the words of Richard Peck, "books about young people parents thought their children didn't know" (Peck in Cart, p. 45). This trend mushroomed, spawning "a veritable avalanche of young adult works some of which focus on heretofore taboo topics: teenage pregnancy, homosexual relationships, brutality and sadism, divorce, abusive parents, corrupt public officials, gang violence, murder, substance abuse, and so and on. The 'New Realism' . . . has been broadly characteristic of the young adult fiction ever since, now spanning a quarter century" (Simmons, p. 434). In comparison to these later books in the movement, *The Outsiders* now seems mild and romantic, but it continues nevertheless to appeal to many teens.

FROM *THE OTHER AMERICA*

The poor, concludes Michael Harrington in *The Other America,* are three times as emotionally depressed as the wealthy. They have a fatalistic outlook that is not confined to personal experience alone, to expectations about job and family. It literally permeates every aspect of an individual's life. . . .

This pessimism is involved in a basic attitude of the poor: the fact that they do not postpone satisfactions, that they do not save . . . it is the logical and natural pattern of behavior for one living in a part of American life without a future. It is, sad to say, a piece of realism, not of vice.

Related to this pattern of immediate gratification is a tendency on the part of the poor to "act out," to be less inhibited, and sometimes violent. . . . In the first place, this violence . . . is a product of human density and misery. . . . [I]t is one more way in which the poor are driven [by their environment] to hurt themselves. (Harrington, pp. 133-35)

War on poverty. In the novel *The Outsiders,* greasers are tough, street-wise kids from the poor side of town. The main character, Ponyboy, says, "the term 'greaser' . . . is used to class all us boys on the East Side. We're poorer than the Socs [socials] and the middle class. I reckon we're wilder, too" (Hinton, *The Outsiders,* p. 6). The greasers' underprivileged condition vexes Ponyboy throughout the book. Several chapters later, for example, he angrily comments that life is unfair because the greasers have all the rough breaks, "while the Socs had so much spare time and money that they jumped us and each other for kicks, had beer blasts and river-bottom parties because they didn't know what else to do. Things were rough all over, all right. All over the East Side. It just didn't seem right to me" (*The Outsiders,* p. 40).

In the early 1960s over 35 million people in America lived in poverty. Although the 1950s are generally portrayed as a time of increasing wealth and affluence, many people remained poor despite the expanding postwar economy. Most of mainstream America did not notice the economic troubles of the poor, however, until a small but vocal group of anthropologists and sociologists began studying poverty seriously. Anthropologist Oscar Lewis, for example, published *Children of Sanchez* in 1961, an influential ethnographic study of poverty in the Puerto Rican and Mexican immigrant communities in the United States. According to this study, poverty in America was not only an economic condition, but also a psychological one. Michael Harrington's 1962 best-selling book, *The Other America,* generalized Lewis's controversial hypothesis to include more groups and focused national attention on the subject by suggesting that perhaps one quarter of the nation's population were poor. Furthermore, he proposed that Lewis's "culture of poverty" determined the world view of some people. Whether or not Hinton's greasers maintain this alleged world view cannot be determined. At the very least, however, her characters conceive of themselves as an underprivileged group of people and purposefully maintain particular behaviors, ways of speech, and manners of dress that identify them as boys from the East Side. As Ponyboy wistfully notes before cutting his hair, "Our hair labeled us greasers—it was our trademark. The one thing we were proud of. Maybe we couldn't have Corvairs or madras shirts, but we could have hair" (*The Outsiders,* p. 64).

Publications such as *The Other America* combined with various events of the early decade to influence the national political agenda. In 1964 the eradication of poverty became an important part of President Lyndon B. Johnson's "Great Society" program, in which the government assigned itself an active role in improving citizens' lives. In his State of the Union address Johnson announced, "This administration today, here and now, declares unconditional war on poverty in America" (Johnson in Nash et al., p. 924). His administration proceeded to create an Office of Economic Opportunity, designed to help the poor successfully compete in the economy by focusing on civil rights, job training, education, and the rehabilitation of juvenile delinquents such as the characters in Hinton's novel.

Family. The gang members in *The Outsiders* are on their own. Neglected and abandoned by their parents and society, many, such as Dallas, have grown accustomed to daily lives without adult guidance. Dallas professes not to care about this neglect: "Shoot, my old man don't give a hang whether I'm in jail or dead in a car wreck or drunk in the gutter. That don't bother me none" (*The Outsiders*, p. 78). A second character, Johnny, lives with both parents, who either abuse or ignore him depending on their mood. He often prefers to spend the night on the streets rather than return home. Three other characters—the brothers Darrel, Sodapop, and Ponyboy Curtis—have been orphaned for eight months at the time of the story. Yet despite these circumstances, or more likely because of them, the ties that bind the characters are as strong as any kinship relations. The gang members form a family among themselves, connected by loyalty, affection, and mutual respect, rather than blood. As Ponyboy explains throughout the novel, they need one another.

Families in the 1960s were rapidly changing. A decade earlier, the ideal family was characterized by a stay-at-home mother, a breadwinner father, and more or less obedient children. Some semblance of such an arrangement still characterized over 70 percent of white middle-class households in 1960. Yet that decade ushered in an era of rapidly changing family structure that continues into the 1990s. After 1967, for example, the birth rate plummeted while the divorce rate soared, and there was a corresponding increase in the number of households headed by women. An increasing number of these and other women, moreover, joined the work force. The 1960s also witnessed a widespread change in sexual mores. Premarital sex became more widely accepted, and the number of births by unmarried couples increased. Such changes would eventually lead to a radical rethinking of what constitutes a "family." The term would in time be expanded to include single mothers and children, stepfamilies, unmarried partners, and gay couples. Although conceptions of family structure were still fairly conventional at the time of the novel's publication, the role of the gang as a familial unit heralds the inception of one of the most important social revolutions of the twentieth century.

The Novel in Focus

The plot. The term "outsiders" refers to a group of neglected, abandoned, and abused kids who live in the impoverished part of town in Tulsa, Oklahoma. Known as "greasers," they are tough

characters who wear their hair long, dress in well-oiled, lived-in jeans and T-shirts, and drive souped-up old cars. Occasionally some of the greasers rob gas stations or have gang fights, and all are perceived by the rest of society as hoodlums. Most possess little in life of their own beyond their hair and their reputation. Opposing the greasers are the Socs, which stands for "socials." The Socs are the wealthy kids from the west side of town who sometimes beat greasers up for fun.

The novel centers around a particular greaser gang. Ponyboy, the narrator, is a fourteen-year-old greaser who enjoys sunsets and lives with his brothers, Sodapop and Darrel. A good-looking and merry high-school dropout, Sodapop works at a local gas station; Darrel gave up college to roof houses so he can support his brothers. Other gang members include Two-Bit, a wisecracking trickster who shoplifts for fun; Dallas, a cold, tough, part-time jockey who spent three years "on the wild side of New York" (*The Outsiders*, p. 13); and Johnny, Ponyboy's best friend.

The opening of the story finds Dallas, Ponyboy, and Johnny at a drive-in movie. Dallas harasses two good-looking Soc girls in front of them until Cherry, a red-haired cheerleader, throws a drink in his face. "That might cool you off, greaser," she retorts. "After you wash your mouth and learn to talk and act decent, I might cool off, too" (*The Outsiders*, p. 24). When Johnny, who worships Dallas, nervously orders him to leave the girls alone, Dallas stalks off, leaving the boys to spend the evening with Cherry and her friend Marcia, who have abandoned their drunken dates, two Soc boys.

Two-Bit, who showed up halfway through the movie, offers everyone a ride home when it is over, but a blue Soc Mustang trails them as they walk to his car. In the Mustang are the two drunk Soc boys, who threaten Two-Bit, Johnny, and Ponyboy, and the girls leave with the Socs to avoid a fight. Cherry says quietly to Ponyboy, "If I see you in the hall at school or someplace and don't say hi, well, it's not personal or anything" (*The Outsiders*, p. 42). As Ponyboy bitterly watches them leave, Johnny notes, "It seems like there's gotta be someplace without greasers or Socs, with just people. Plain ordinary people" (*The Outsiders*, p. 44). Together Ponyboy and Johnny watch the stars and fall asleep in an abandoned lot.

Later that night, Ponyboy and Johnny again encounter the drunken Socs in the park. Some insults pass between a Soc named Bob and Pony-

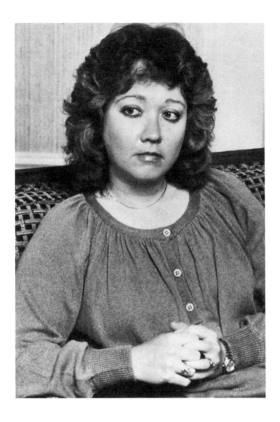

S. E. Hinton

boy. Ponyboy spits at the Socs angrily, and they shove him into a nearby fountain and hold him underwater until he blacks out. When he recovers, Johnny is beside him, his switchblade covered with blood. Bob lies dead on the ground. "I killed that boy," says Johnny simply (*The Outsiders,* p. 51). Dallas gives them money and a gun and instructs them to hide in an abandoned country church for the next week.

In the country, they cut their hair and Ponyboy reluctantly dyes his blond. The boys spend the week smoking cigarettes, eating baloney, playing poker and reading **Gone with the Wind,** (also covered in *Literature and Its Times*), bought at the local grocery store to help pass time. Johnny admiringly compares Dallas to the gallant old Southerners. Neither boy has spent much time in the country, and after watching a sunset together Ponyboy recites a poem by Robert Frost that ends with the line "Nothing gold can stay."

Dallas arrives a week later with the most recent news. The murder has spawned violence all over town, and the greasers and Socs will rumble tomorrow night. After a brief trip to a nearby town for food, they return to the church and discover it has caught on fire. A school crowd has gathered and children are trapped inside.

Johnny and Ponyboy save them, but the burning roof crashes on Johnny and breaks his back. Dallas crawls in after him and both end up in the hospital.

The next night, the greasers and Socs rumble. Ponyboy participates, although he feels ambivalent about the event. Dallas escapes from the hospital, in time to join the fray, and the greasers win the fight. Ponyboy and Dallas run to the hospital to tell Johnny the good news. Johnny, who is dying, informs them that fighting is useless and, before he dies, tells Ponyboy to "stay gold."

Dallas runs out of the hospital, leaving Ponyboy to walk home in a stupor. When Ponyboy arrives home, he wonders about Dallas's and his own reactions:

> Why can I take it when Dally can't? And then I knew. Johnny was the only thing Dally loved. And now Johnny was gone. "So he finally broke." Two-Bit spoke everyone's feelings. "So even Dally has a breaking point."
> (*The Outsiders,* p. 133)

Dallas robs a store after leaving the hospital, then calls to say that the police are after him and that he will be in the abandoned lot in a few minutes. The gang arrives at the lot in time to see him purposefully wave an unloaded gun at the police. As their shots ring through the air, Ponyboy realizes that Dallas wants to die, and in his view it is an honorable death, a death worthy of Dallas. "He died violent and young and desperate, just like we all knew he'd die someday. . . . But Johnny was right. He died gallant" (*The Outsiders,* p. 134).

Ponyboy becomes physically ill and mentally unstable. Every time he looks at *Gone with the Wind* he thinks of "Southern gentlemen with big black eyes in blue jeans and T-shirts, Southern gentlemen crumpling under street lights" (*The Outsiders,* p. 137). He begins to fail school. When his English teacher suggests that he write a composition for extra credit, Ponyboy thinks of his friends: "Someone should tell their side of the story, and maybe people would understand then and wouldn't be so quick to judge a boy by the amount of hair oil he wore" (*The Outsiders,* p. 155). He sits down, and begins to write.

Conflict and teen life. The popularity and notoriety of *The Outsiders* stems from the fact that it was one of the first books to acknowledge teenage violence and portray real-life conflicts that existed in the lives of many teens during the 1960s. Like the decade in which it is set, *The Outsiders* is replete with confrontations. Themes of strife and discord permeate the story, and violence between greasers and Socs commonly occurs. As the novel opens, for example, a group of Socs jumps Ponyboy. "Need a haircut greaser?" they sneer and hold a switchblade knife to his throat. "How'd you like that haircut to begin just below the chin?" (*The Outsiders,* p. 8). Later in the novel, Ponyboy and Johnny are again jumped, and the affair ends in the murder of the young Soc named Bob. The murder spawns a rumble that ends in only temporary victory for the greasers. Although they chase the Socs off, both Ponyboy and Johnny recognize that the victory will not end the existing antagonism.

Moreover, this antagonism does not stop with the greasers' relation to the Socs; instead, conflict defines and pervades their lives. Greasers also fight among themselves. When Dallas slashes another greaser's tires, the event leads to a brawl. Family hostilities are also common. Johnny is a nervous wreck because his parents fight all the time and because they beat him. Even Darrel, Sodapop, and Ponyboy often quarrel. Ponyboy acknowledges the role of conflict in the greasers' lives at the beginning of the novel by explaining that greasers are kind of wild. They steal things, have gang fights, and get into trouble with the police. Conflict is an integral part of a greaser's identity—they see being "tough" as an admirable, sought-after quality. Such a perspective differs greatly from the images of teens in previous young adult books, which had portrayed adolescents as remorseful when they got in trouble. Certainly the perspective is representative of a decade famous for its political and social turmoil. Civil rights violence, urban race riots, and assassinations of a number of political leaders, for example, all transpired during the decade, and being able to weather such violence became a grave concern not only for youths but also for activists in the larger population.

Sources. Much of the setting in *The Outsiders* is based on real places in Tulsa, Oklahoma. As in the novel, Tulsa in the 1960s had both a "good" and "bad" side of town; also the novel's drive-in movie is based on a real drive-in theater called the Admiral Twin.

Although some parts of the novel, such as the church fire, are pure invention, much of the plot is loosely based on Hinton's high school experiences during the mid-1960s. The opposing camps of greasers and Socs, for example, represent part of the social structure of Will Rogers High School. Hinton remembers: "The Socialists and the Greasers were actually just the extremes.

There were all kinds of middle groups like the "artsy-craftsy" people, the "student council" people. . . . It was a complicated social situation" (Hinton in Senick, p. 133). Although not a greaser herself, Hinton recalls that she carried a switchblade knife, occasionally ran from the police, and once chipped a tooth because she was hit in the face with a bottle. She compares herself to Ponyboy, and claims that his experiences are based on events that happened to some of her friends. Since she published the book while still in high school, most likely those experiences were fresh in her mind when she wrote the story.

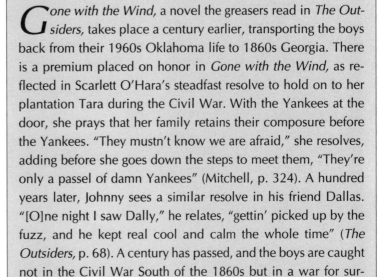

FROM *GONE WITH THE WIND* TO *THE OUTSIDERS*

Gone with the Wind, a novel the greasers read in *The Outsiders,* takes place a century earlier, transporting the boys back from their 1960s Oklahoma life to 1860s Georgia. There is a premium placed on honor in *Gone with the Wind,* as reflected in Scarlett O'Hara's steadfast resolve to hold on to her plantation Tara during the Civil War. With the Yankees at the door, she prays that her family retains their composure before the Yankees. "They mustn't know we are afraid," she resolves, adding before she goes down the steps to meet them, "They're only a passel of damn Yankees" (Mitchell, p. 324). A hundred years later, Johnny sees a similar resolve in his friend Dallas. "[O]ne night I saw Dally," he relates, "gettin' picked up by the fuzz, and he kept real cool and calm the whole time" (*The Outsiders,* p. 68). A century has passed, and the boys are caught not in the Civil War South of the 1860s but in a war for survival as have-nots in 1960s Oklahoma; still, the concept of honor is much the same.

Reviews. In the adult world, *The Outsiders* was recognized as an important piece of literature. In 1967, the novel was chosen as the *New York Herald Tribune*'s Children's Spring Book Festival Honor book, and won both the *Media & Methods* Maxi award and the American Library Association's Best Young Adult Book in 1975, as well as the Massachusetts Children's Book Award from Salem State College in 1979.

At the time of the novel's publication, critics occasionally rebuked Hinton for her lack of subtlety and finesse. They attributed such shortcomings, however, to her youth and inexperience and praised her descriptive insights. In 1967 Lillian N. Gerhardt noted that Hinton was "a writer not yet practiced in restraint perhaps, but nevertheless seeing and saying more with greater storytelling ability than many an older hand" (Gerhardt in Senick, p. 70). Thomas Fleming, writing for the *New York Times Book Review*, also praised Hinton's abilities:

> By almost any standard, Miss Hinton's performance is impressive. At an age when most youngsters are still writing 300-word compositions, she has produced a book alive with the fresh dialogue of her contemporaries and has wound around it a story that captures, in vivid patches at least, a rather unnerving slice of teen-age America.
>
> (Fleming in Senick, p. 70)

Among young adult readers, *The Outsiders* was not widely read at the time of publication, probably because teens were not yet aware of its existence. Knowledge of the book was passed along mostly by word of mouth, and therefore it took some years before the book was commonly circulated in that age group. Once discovered, Hinton's novel became extremely popular among young people, and continues to appeal especially to at-risk teens, who often identify with the characters in her books. Hinton is one of the most widely read young adult authors today. *The Out-siders* alone has sold more than 4 million copies in the United States.

For More Information

Cart, Michael. *From Romance to Realism: 50 Years of Growth and Change in Young Adult Literature*. New York: HarperCollins, 1996.

Garrett, Agnes, and Helga P. McCue, eds. "S. E. Hinton." In *Artists and Authors for Young Adults*. Vol. 2. Detroit: Gale Research, 1989.

Harrington, Michael. *The Other America: Poverty in the United States*. New York: Macmillan, 1969.

Hinton, S. E. *The Outsiders*. 1967. Reprint. New York: Dell, 1989.

Kaplan, Marshall, and Peggy L. Cuciti, eds. *The Great Society and Its Legacy*. Durham, N.C.: Duke University Press, 1986.

Mitchell, Margaret. *Gone with the Wind*. New York: Macmillan, 1936.

Nash, Gary, et al. *The American People*. Vol 2. New York: Harper & Row, 1986.

Senick, Gerard J., ed. *Children's Literature Review*. Vol. 23. Detroit: Gale Research, 1978.

Simmons, John S. "A Look inside a Landmark: *The Outsiders*." In *Censored Books*. Edited by Nicholas J. Karolides, Lee Burress, and John M. Kean. Metuchen, N.J.: Scarecrow, 1993.

The Pigman

by

Paul Zindel

P aul Zindel was born in 1936 in Staten Island, New York, where he and his sister were raised by his mother. He began writing plays in high school and eventually pursued a chemistry degree at nearby Warner College. In college he took a creative writing course by playwright Edward Albee, who became a primary influence on the young writer. Zindel taught chemistry and physics at a Staten Island high school for ten years (1959-69), meanwhile pursuing his creative writing. *The Pigman*, Zindel's first novel, was based on a friendship he shared with a rebellious male high school student who lived near his home in Staten Island.

Events in History at the Time of the Novel

Youth protest against the Vietnam War. During the late 1960s the explosion of a youth culture—marked by rock music, new clothing and hair styles, a less inhibited attitude toward sex and drug use, and opposition to the Vietnam War—distanced many postwar baby boomers then coming of age from their parents' generation. An "us against them" mentality prevailed, and on both sides. The anger that many teenaged and young adults held toward their parents' generation found voice at the growing number of protest demonstrations against the Vietnam War. College-age students considered the idea ludicrous that young American men should be drafted in large numbers to fight a war against communism in the jungles of a far-off land, in marked

---

> **THE LITERARY WORK**
>
> A novel set in an American suburb in the late 1960s; published in 1968.
>
> **SYNOPSIS**
>
> An elderly widower befriends two troubled high school students.

---

contrast to the willing sacrifices their parents had made during the years of World War II.

The conflict between the generations peaked at the Democratic National Convention in 1968, the year *The Pigman* was published. Thousands of young people gathered in a Chicago park near the convention to protest U.S. involvement in Vietnam. The protesters' signs attacked not just the war but many forms of establishment authority. One sign, which read "Kill the Pigs," referred to the police—perhaps the ultimate symbol of authority. The demonstration turned ugly when the protesters released a giant pig balloon and the police began to attack the crowd. According to one historian, "The cops swung out with a fine indifference at demonstrators, male or female, and news reporters. Shortly after midnight, with the help of tear gas, most of the crowd was finally driven from the park" (Viorst, p. 454). Television cameras broadcast images of this war at home into America's living rooms.

Long hair and generational conflict. Although the riots outside the Democratic National Con-

Chicago police struggle with antiwar protesters in Grant Park during the 1968 Democratic National Convention.

vention were perhaps the most graphic illustration of the conflict between generations, the tension was obvious in everyday life as well. Clothing styles of the young changed drastically in the 1960s. Long, loosely worn hair became a symbolic gesture of defiance, a way to reject ties to one's parent's generation for both young women and men. "Hippie" became both a term of self-identification and derision, depending on who used it. Ronald Reagan—who had been elected governor of California in the mid-1960s after pledging not to tolerate youth rebellion—attacked the youth style when he declared that a hippie was someone who "dresses like Tarzan, has hair like Jane, and smells like Cheetah" (Reagan in Gitlin, p. 217). Such sentiments were typical among parents of baby boomers. The conflict in style between "establishment" and "hippie" segments of society during this time is illustrated in *The Pigman* by John's father, a clear representative of the older generation. He screams at John to "Be yourself! Be individualistic! . . . But for God's sake get your hair cut. You look like an oddball" (Zindel, *The Pigman*, p. 60).

Changing sexual morality. Although it could be argued that premarital sexual activity has always existed, before the late 1960s few publicly admitted to having sex out of wedlock, and even fewer defended this as a legitimate activity. The

late 1960s, however, saw dramatic changes in attitudes toward sex. Young people no longer shied away from sex as a topic, the way their parents had, and many began openly to advocate engaging in sexual activity. The late sixties saw the flourishing of a "free love" movement, whose proponents claimed that sex could and should exist in a casual relationship. Encouraging this movement was the availability of a recently developed oral contraceptive, the birth-control pill. Introduced in 1955, the pill had become readily available by this generation, and it seemed to its young people to remove the threat of pregnancy from sexual experimentation.

In a group of interviews about the differences between the early 1960s and the late 1960s, Joan Morrison and Robert Morrison asked a group of women what their experiences were like during the "sexual revolution" of the late 1960s. One participant, Lynn Ferrin, explained, "I was among the women in that whole *avant-garde* of sexual freedom who were very excited by being free women. You can have lovers. You don't have to be married. You can have different men, and experience different men's lovemaking . . . The suburbs and the station wagon full of Cub Scouts became something you didn't want anything to do with" (Ferrin in Morrison and Morrison, p. 176).

The fact that Paul Zindel writes openly about the beginnings of a sexual relationship between two high school students in a book for high school students is evidence of this changing sexual morality. In the 1950s, sex was often considered a taboo topic in mainstream adult novels and certainly would have been very controversial in a book aimed at young adults. Zindel, however, was one of the first to begin writing realistically about the lives of young people. His honesty was welcomed by many reviewers. One writer raved in the *Times Literary Supplement* that while Zindel's subjects "are not the stuff that teenage novels used to deal with . . . the stuff of teenage life is not what it used to be either, and what counts is the way Paul Zindel handles it, with a delicacy at once funny and heartfelt, outspoken and sensitive" (Quigley in Lesniak, p. 483).

The changing family. The 1950s is often recalled as the era when the "nuclear" family predominated—breadwinner father, stay-at-home mother, obedient children. By the late 1960s, however, this model and the values that went along with it had begun to disintegrate. In the 1950s over 70 percent of American families consisted of a father who worked, a mother who was a housewife, and children. By the 1990s less than 15 percent of families in America had this stay-at-home mother and breadwinner father structure (Mintz, p. 184). The breakup of the nuclear family began in the late 1960s when, according to one study, "popular attitudes towards marriage and divorce underwent a dramatic change" (Mintz, p. 188). Some states revised divorce laws that had been on the books for generations, making it somewhat easier and less costly to dissolve a marriage. Popular culture began to reflect these changes, and novelists such as Zindel explored issues that could have been familiar ones to readers. In *The Pigman,* instead of clinging to an idealized picture of the American family, Zindel's novel addresses one adolescent's (Lorraine's) relationship with her single-parent mother and the other's (John's) dislike of his "typical" family. Lorraine's parents have divorced, and the novel is quite graphic in laying the blame on Lorraine's father's infidelity. Lorraine explains, "I don't think she'll ever be able to forgive what he did to her . . . when she was pregnant her doctor called and told her my father had some kind of disease, and she shouldn't let him touch her until he got rid of it. It turned out that he had a girlfriend on the side, and that's when she filed for a legal separation" (*The Pigman,* p. 87). Such openness about divorce, infidelity, and venereal disease was virtually revolutionary in young adult literature. Meanwhile, although John's parents are still together, it is clear that their family has problems. John refers to his father as "the bore" and is constantly criticizing his parents. The relationships that Zindel describes capture the transition from 1950s idealism about the nuclear family to late 1960s realism about divorce, infidelity, and less-than-ideal family life.

Old age and depression. Among elderly people, such as Mr. Pignati in the novel, depression is widespread. Like Mr. Pignati, many seniors have experienced the loss of a spouse. Such a grave personal loss, combined with retirement from the workplace, often brings about a tremendous sense of isolation in senior citizens. Whereas younger people usually have friends to rely upon and a social network associated with work or educational pursuits, older people often find themselves alone. According to many doctors who specialize in working with the elderly, this isolation inevitably brings about depression. One such gerontologist explains, "work is gone, and so are friends. . . . Self-disdain has replaced self-esteem. Hope has disappeared. There is a sense of passivity and helplessness . . . loss and isolation" (Friedan, p. 205).

Serious depression as a result of the loss of a spouse tends to affect white males more than any other group. Among the elderly between the ages of seventy and seventy-four, white men commit suicide at nearly three times the rate of nonwhite men and five times the rate of women their age. Studies have shown that depression causes death in less direct ways than suicide as well. These studies indicate that serious illness is often a result of depression. This emotional problem surfaces again and again in the studies, in clinical data and in interviews with old age specialists—"no matter what the symptom or disease . . . one finds behind it depression or despair" (Friedan, p. 449).

The Novel in Focus

The plot. *The Pigman* is the story of a friendship between two teenagers and a lonely widower told from the narrative perspective of each of the two main characters, John and Lorraine. Through the different styles of writing that the two characters employ in their narration, the reader comes to understand their different personalities. John is a bit arrogant. "Like Lorraine told you," he explains, "I really am very handsome and do have fabulous eyes" (*The Pigman*, p. 14). He is also a self-confessed "smart-aleck" who admits, "I hate school, but then again I hate everything" (*The Pigman*, p. 10). Although Lorraine is John's best friend, she is more intellectual. Her comments are filled with references to the writings of great thinkers like the famous psychologist Sigmund Freud. Through these two very different characters, the story of their friendship with the Pigman begins to unfold.

John and Lorraine explain that they met the Pigman while playing their favorite game, "the telephone marathon." The object of this game, John informs the reader, is to dial a random number on the phone and keep whoever is reached on the phone as long as possible. One day while playing, Lorraine dials the number of a Mr. Pignati. In order to keep him on the phone she poses as a charity worker soliciting donations. Although Lorraine explains early in the novel, "I have compassion," she is convinced by John that they should go to Mr. Pignati's house and pick up his "donation" (*The Pigman*, p. 8).

Although the two originally go to Mr. Pignati's house to take advantage of him, they find him to be fascinating and develop a friendship. While John cannot get along with his parents and Lorraine has a hard time relating to her mother, both are very fond of the Pigman. He is spontaneous, charming, and talks to them both as if they were adults. At one point Mr. Pignati purchases roller skates for the three of them and encourages John and Lorraine to skate through a department store. When they come to visit him, he gives them wine. The two affectionately nickname Mr. Pignati "the Pigman" because he has a large collection of model pigs.

The friendship seems to be the perfect cure for Mr. Pignati's depression over the death of his wife, and for John and Lorraine's frustration with their parents. Ultimately, however, the two teenagers betray their older friend. When Mr. Pignati is hospitalized, John and Lorraine decide to throw a party in his house. Just as the party is getting out of control and Mr. Pignati's prize collection of model pigs is being destroyed, the old man returns to the house. Feeling rejected and betrayed, he throws all the teenagers out of the house and becomes depressed once again. He passes away shortly after. A friendship that had brought happiness to the lives of a lonely old man and two teenagers angry at the adult world ends in complete disaster.

The Pigman as a timeless character. In Zindel's novel the relationship that John and Lor-

raine have with Mr. Pignati stands in glaring contrast to the relationship both characters have with their parents. John and Lorraine argue with their parents in a manner that reflects the larger generational conflict of era. Their relationship to the Pigman, however, seems to be outside of time. The Pigman does not criticize the two teenagers' way of dressing or their rebelliousness. He is also refreshingly free of any of the awkwardness that often occurs in an attempt to bridge a generation gap.

In contrast to Mr. Pignati, John's parents are caricatures of the 1950s family. His father continually stresses the need for John to get a "real job" and ridicules the notion that there is value in pursuing anything but a business career. Both parents are extremely concerned with material success and are unable to relate to their son. When John informs his father that he wants to be an actor, his father ridicules him and argues that he needs to be more like his brother, who has a Wall Street job. John reacts to their constant nagging about the need to make a lot of money by labeling his father "the bore" and his mother "the old lady" (*The Pigman*, pp. 29, 27). He continually criticizes them for being completely out of touch with his concerns.

While John's parents are simply distant from the concerns of their son and his generation, Lorraine's mother is fear-stricken about the dangers the new social trends have brought with them. Having separated from her husband because he had an affair with another woman, Lorraine's mother is convinced that all men are only after sex from women. She constantly discourages her daughter from all relations with men.

In stark contrast to these relationships with their parents, John and Lorraine enjoy the Pigman's company because he lacks any awareness of the tensions of the time. Unlike other older people who pretend to understand the ways of the new generation, the Pigman (as John explains) is timeless. Particularly annoying to John is his English teacher, who calls him a "card" and makes, in John's eyes, lame attempts to show that she is in touch with the ways of the young. He writes, "A card she calls me, which sounds ridiculous coming out of the mouth of an old-maid English teacher who's practically fifty years old. I really hate it when a teacher has to show that she isn't behind the times by using some expression which sounds so up-to-date, you know for sure she's behind the times" (*The Pigman*, p. 14). The Pigman, by contrast, does not attempt to prove that he is aware of current trends. His

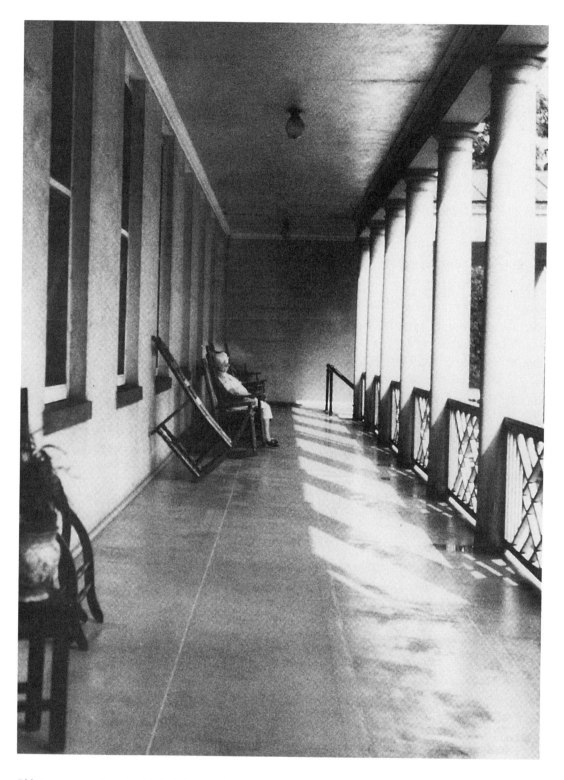

Old age can sometimes lead to isolation and loneliness.

charm, John believes, lies precisely in the fact that he is not caught up in the trends and tensions of the period. John explains, "In fact, the thing Lorraine and I liked best about the Pigman was that he didn't go around saying we were cards or jazzy or cool or hip. He said we were delightful, and if there's one way to show how much you're not trying to make believe you're not behind the times, it's to go around saying people are delightful" (*The Pigman*, p. 14). Unlike all the other older people in John and Lorraine's life, the Pigman was a genuine friend.

OTHER PIGMAN PROJECTS

Although *The Pigman* was written very early in Paul Zindel's writing career (he was still a high school chemistry teacher when he wrote the novel), it became the basis for several other projects that he completed later on. Zindel wrote *The Pigman's Legacy*, a sequel to the original novel, in 1980. For this second novel, Zindel received multiple awards, including the American Library Association's Best Young Adult Novel award. In addition, Zindel's autobiography *The Pigman and Me* focuses on the relationship between Zindel and the real-life Pigman. Throughout this autobiography, the reader finds real-life inspiration for various details in the original novel. Zindel's mother, like Lorraine's mother, was abandoned by her husband, for example.

Sources. Paul Zindel has written several explanations of the bases for the characters in *The Pigman*. In the back of the 1978 edition of the novel, Zindel published answers to a number of questions he had gotten from teenagers. When asked who inspired him to write *The Pigman*, Zindel explained that it was the real-life John. He writes, "I was living in a fifty-room haunted ex-convent when a boy by the name of John came across the side lawn and I went out to yell at him for trespassing. He was ready to sock me, but instead we decided to talk things out, and it turned out he was a fascinating fifteen-year-old with parents, teachers, and truant officers who never took the time to understand him" (Zindel, Postscript to *The Pigman*, p. 155).

Zindel also explains that Lorraine's mother was based on his own real-life mother, adding that "my mother had a nice side too, I didn't seem to write about that in the book" (*The Pigman*, p. 156). Zindel wrote more about his real-life

mother and the man on whom he based the character of the Pigman in his autobiography entitled *The Pigman and Me*. When Zindel was young, he lived in a house with his mother and another family. A man named Nonno Frankie, a grandfather in the family that shared Zindel's house, was the basis for the character of the Pigman. Zindel describes Nonno as a kind and spontaneous man who taught him songs and jokes and was always laughing. Zindel explains, "I should have suspected that Nonno Frankie was becoming my Pigman, but I didn't know then what a Pigman was. One of the things a Pigman does is help you, but sometimes someone can be helping you in a lot of little ways and then suddenly one day it all adds up and you're able to say to yourself, 'This person is my Pigman'" (Zindel, *The Pigman and Me*, p. 80).

The rise of realism in young adult fiction. *The Pigman* has often been noted as one of the first young adult novels to address the real-life concerns of teenagers. Many novels written earlier for young adult readers focused on issues of popularity or sports competitions. *The Pigman*, by contrast, dealt with depression, divorce, and parental conflict in an honest and open manner. Zindel realistically portrayed the changing family structures of society and the conflict between generations. One reviewer of *The Pigman* wrote, "*The Pigman* was a groundbreaking event because . . . it transformed what had been called the teen 'junior novel' from a predictable, stereotyped story about high school sports and dances to one about a complex teenage protagonist dealing with real concerns" (Cart, p. 55). Earlier "romantic" young adult novels tended to ignore the real problems of teen life. In contrast, Zindel's focus on the complexity and anxiety of teenage life was realistic. Much of the realism stemmed from his use of the first-person, and in both sets of narratives providing an accurate sense of how teenagers like John and Lorraine actually talked. By writing the novel from the perspective of two young adults, Zindel was able to capture the real-life problems of this generation in their own words.

Reviews. Reviewers showered Zindel's realistic style with effusive praise. Weary of earlier novels with naive plots and superficial characters, many critics were excited by what was seen as a daring attempt to capture the actual lives of teenagers. John Weston, a writer for the *New York Times Book Review*, commented that the novel was an "epic" that "makes a very funny book at one level because Mr. Zindel catches the bright, hyperbolic sheen of teen-age language accurately and with humor" and added that it is still "a serious book" (Weston in Lesniak, 483). Diane Farell also praised the novel's realistic style and commented, "few books that have been written for young people are as cruelly truthful about the human condition" (Farell in Lesniak, p. 483).

For More Information

Cart, Michael. *From Romance to Realism: 50 Years of Growth and Change in Young Adult Literature.* HarperCollins, New York, 1992.

Friedan, Betty. *The Fountain of Age.* New York: Simon & Schuster, 1993.

Gitlin, Todd. *The Sixties: Years of Hope, Days of Rage.* New York: Bantam, 1987.

Lesniak, James, ed. *Contemporary Authors New Revision Series.* Vol. 31. Detroit: Gale, 1991.

Mintz, Steven. "New Rules." In *American Families.* Edited by Joseph Hawes and Elizabeth Nybakken. New York: Greenwood, 1991.

Morrison, Joan, and Robert Morrison. *From Camelot to Kent State.* New York: Times Books, 1987.

Viorst, Milton. *Fire in the Streets: America in the 1960s.* New York: Simon & Schuster, 1979.

Zindel, Paul. *The Pigman.* 1968. Reprint. New York: Bantam, 1978.

Zindel, Paul. *The Pigman and Me.* New York: HarperCollins, 1991.

Pilgrim at Tinker Creek

by
Annie Dillard

In 1974 *Pilgrim at Tinker Creek* earned Annie Dillard the distinction of being the youngest person (at age thirty-one) ever to win the Pulitzer Prize for nonfiction. Combining theological, scientific, and literary inquiry, the book offers insight into the everyday world. As national and international conflicts (the Watergate break-in and the Vietnam War) prompted controversy in America, Dillard, secluded in the Roanoke Valley of Virginia, looked to the earth and its creator for clues about how to live a fully human existence.

Events in History at the Time of the Essay

Naturalism in Virginia. *Pilgrim at Tinker Creek* takes place in the Roanoke Valley of Virginia, in the southeast Appalachians along a range known as the Blue Ridge Mountains. This geographical area is home to Virginia's highest peaks, which are also some of the most ancient mountains in the world, and it holds some of the most beautiful natural scenery in America. Located in the valley is Tinker Creek, on the banks of which Annie Dillard wrote her essay in wilderness areas so remarkable that two major conservation and recreation projects were instituted there.

The area was opened up after World War II by the construction of the Blue Ridge Parkway, a 575-mile recreational highway that creeps along the tops of the Blue Ridge Mountains. Construction of the Parkway began in 1935 as a part of a massive public-works program instituted by

the federal government to alleviate unemployment during the Great Depression. It was completed in 1959. Though the Parkway vastly improved the local economy, it was constructed at considerable cost to the environment. At the same time, the Parkway project intended to promote conservation. It aimed not only to bring motorists into the rugged natural landscape, but also to teach them about the history, flora, and fauna that distinguish the area; along the length of the Parkway are naturalist information centers and historical markers. A Harvard study found that "of the 1,032 genera of seed-bearing plants indigenous to eastern North America, over half—557—occur in the southern Appalachians" (Ogburn, p. 27), which makes the area a treasure-trove for nature lovers.

The second project, in the immediate vicinity of Tinker Creek, is the 2,031-mile-long Appalachian Trail, a footpath that links New England to the South. The brainchild of Benton MacKaye, the trail was first proposed in 1921 and quickly gained momentum and support.

Called a "Footpath for those who seek Fellowship with the Wilderness," the trail runs from Springer Mountain, Georgia, north through fourteen states to Maine's Mt. Katahdin (Ogburn, p. 91).

The Walden movement. Annie Dillard wrote her master's thesis at Hollins College (in Roanoke, Virginia) on Henry David Thoreau, author of *Walden* and America's most famous naturalist. *Walden* recounts Thoreau's two years on the shores of Walden Pond; the writer spent his days observing his natural surroundings, reducing his life to its most simple routines, and reflecting on human society. The work became synonymous with American Utopianism, the search for the ideal society. B. F. Skinner's 1945 book, *Walden Two*, picked up on Thoreau's social questioning and described life in a commune, in which positive reinforcement and love, rather than fear of punishment, provided the rules for social behavior. In the 1960s and early 1970s, the combined utopian visions of *Walden* and *Walden Two* helped launch many back-to-nature communes, which shared the goal of redefining society on the basis of friendship, shared work, and the free exchange of ideas. Communes of this sort sprang up all over the country, from Neverland in California to Walden Three in Providence, Rhode Island. Some of these communes were "hippie" retreats—loosely organized groups of mostly young people who experimented with Eastern philosophies, radical politics, vegetarianism, free love, and sometimes drugs as well.

Other communes of the time were organized formally around certain codes of social behavior. Of the latter sort was the Twin Oaks colony in Louisa, Virginia, about 100 miles northeast of Roanoke. Founded in 1967 by Kathleen Kinkaid, Twin Oaks based its goals on the vision of society put forth in *Walden Two*. The newsletter of the community, "Walden Pool," states among its goals: "The placing of the purposes of the individual above property or profit, and also above the purposes of any technology. . . . Equality among all members. . . . The expansion of community to provide for the people of this country an alternative to the corporate state" (*Journal of a Walden Two Community*, p. 9).

At Twin Oaks and at most of the rural Walden communes across the country, people lived from the land and tried to do without such environmentally destructive objects as cars. Characterizing the movement were a radical retreat from the city and a quest for spiritual as well as social enlightenment, attributes that are associated with

Dillard's work. Although *Pilgrim at Tinker Creek* is by no means associated with the Walden commune movement, the essay manifests the same 1970s focus on the environment, on individual development, and on spirituality held by many of the communes.

EARTH DAY

America's first Earth Day was held on April 22, 1970. This official day of protest and education about environmental issues was organized in response to people's fears about ecological destruction. The Environmental Protection Agency administrator at the time, William Reilly, summed up conditions at the time as follows:

> In the late 1960s, a series of environmental horror stories gave rise to the first Earth Day. Rivers caught on fire. Whole cities were routinely shrouded by thick black clouds of industrial pollution. Raw sewage was discharged into rivers, and automobiles released ten times the emissions of today's [1990] cars.
>
> (McGuire, p. 3)

Virginia, the state in which Dillard lived while writing *Pilgrim at Tinker Creek*, routinely appeared, and continues to appear, near the top of the list of states with environmental problems.

Space in the 1970s. *Pilgrim at Tinker Creek* delves into a variety of scientific disciplines, including entomology, physics, and botany. The book also returns time and again to issues of astronomy and cosmology, as Dillard ponders humanity's place on an earth that is spinning through space:

> At this latitude I'm spinning 836 miles an hour round the earth's axis. . . . In orbit around the sun I'm moving 64,800 miles an hour. The solar system as a whole, like a merry-go-round unhinged, spins, bobs, and blinks at the speed of 43,200 miles an hour along a course set east of [the constellation] Hercules. . . . I close my eyes and I see stars, deep stars giving way to deeper stars, deeper stars bowing to deepest stars at the crown of an infinite cone.
> (Dillard, *Pilgrim at Tinker Creek*, p. 21)

Throughout the book, Dillard contemplates the earth's moon, the moons of other planets, showers of shooting stars, comets, and other heavenly messengers. This is not at all surprising—in the early 1970s, while she was writing

The space probe Mariner X, launched November 3, 1973.

Pilgrim at Tinker Creek, the conquest of space seemed a very real possibility. American and Soviet satellites circled the earth, and the two nations competed for primacy in space through a series of lunar launches. Even further from home, an American probe launched in 1972, Pioneer 10, was sending back photographs of Jupiter and its mysterious red spot by 1973, and, by 1974, of Jupiter's moon, Callisto. The American Skylab project, which sent manned research craft into space to perform scientific experiments and to photograph both the earth and the sun, began in 1973, the year Dillard wrote her work. Mariner IX completed a year-long mapping mission of Mars in 1972, and two years later, Mariner X sent back pictures of Venus's atmosphere. In 1972 the Russians landed Venera 8 on the surface of Venus, where it remained for an entire 50 minutes before it burned up, and they also landed a probe on Mars in 1973. The heavens no longer seemed to be unfathomable territory.

Thomas Merton. Throughout *Pilgrim at Tinker Creek,* Dillard refers to many different religious traditions from Christianity, Islam, and Judaism. There is one devout figure in particular who exerted a strong influence upon her hermit-like existence upon the banks of Tinker Creek: the Roman Catholic theologian Thomas Merton (1915-68). His works in fact influenced others

to retreat from society as well. Merton, whom Dillard quotes several times in her book, was a poet, a Trappist monk, and a pop culture figure who became a millionaire author (and gave away all his money), an ardent pacifist, and America's most famous hermit. In 1948 Merton published his spiritual autobiography, *The Seven Storey Mountain,* which became a touchstone for Christians and non-Christians alike: "[I]t was a confrontation of the basic alienation of man with society, with the natural and supernatural forces that had nurtured him over the centuries. . . . It became a symbol and a guide to the plight of the contemporary world" (Rice, p. 88). Later, in the 1960s, Merton became the most outspoken Catholic theologian regarding Christian moral responsibilities and the subject of war—nuclear war, to be exact. For a large portion of his life, he was a Trappist monk in Gethsemani, Kentucky. Trappists, a monastic order that originated in France in the mid-1800s, take vows of silence, vegetarianism, and manual labor; part of Merton's labor was to write. Eventually, Merton persuaded his superior to allow him to live as a hermit within the monastery, and set up shop in an unheated cement house in the nearby woods. There he lived a life of contemplation, but also took strident literary stands against war. He became increasingly interested in Eastern philosophies and set out for the Orient in 1968; he died

world around her; the result is a work of ecstatic description and theological/philosophical speculation on the nature of the universe and humanity's place within it.

Annie Dillard

DILLARD CONTEMPLATES THE UNIVERSE

What else is going on right this minute while ground water creeps under my feet? The galaxy is careening in a slow, muffled widening. If a million solar systems are born every hour, then surely hundreds burst into being as I shift my weight to the other elbow. The sun's surface is now exploding; other stars implode and vanish, heavy and black, out of sight. Meteorites are arcing to earth invisibly all day long.

(*Pilgrim at Tinker Creek*, p. 97)

---

later that year of accidental electrocution in Bangkok, Thailand. In 1973 Merton's *Asian Journal* was published to great public acclaim; it records his encounter with Buddhism and other Eastern religions and philosophies. The journal both participated in and contributed to American culture's turn toward the East for alternate systems of spirituality in the 1960s and 1970s.

The Essay in Focus

The contents. The fifteen chapters of *Pilgrim at Tinker Creek* describe and reflect upon the amazing abundance and intricacies of life in the vicinity of the author's home in Virginia's Blue Ridge Mountains: insects, birds, beasts, trees, atomic particles, microscopic compartments of the human kidney, solar wind, the warmth of the moon: "I propose to keep here what Thoreau called 'a meteorological journal of the mind,' telling some tales and describing some of the sights of this rather tamed valley, and exploring, in fear and trembling, some of the unmapped dim reaches and holy fastnesses to which those tales and sights so dizzyingly lead" (*Pilgrim at Tinker Creek*, p. 11). In the book, Dillard recounts her day-by-day curriculum of learning to see the

According to Dillard, the structure of the book is very deliberate, and is meant to duplicate the two ways of knowing God that characterize medieval mysticism. The first seven chapters, which proceed from observation of the teeming life around her, seek to understand the divine by noticing its presence in things of this world; this is the intellectual and spiritual discipline of the "via positiva," "the journey to God through action & will & materials" (Dillard in Johnson, p. 5). The last seven chapters focus on the "via negativa," "the spirit's revulsion at time and death" (Dillard in Johnson, p. 5), which is characterized by attempts to empty oneself of consciousness, to allow things to happen as they will, and to reflect on those things that cannot be seen but that nevertheless point to the presence of a creator. The difference between the two approaches, via positiva and via negativa, becomes apparent in the chapter "Stalking," in which Dillard observes the elusive muskrats that inhabit Tinker Creek.

I can stalk them in either of two ways. The first is not what you think of as true stalking but it is the *via negativa,* and as fruitful as actual pursuit. When I stalk this way I take my stand on a bridge and wait, emptied. . . . Something might come, something might go. . . . Stalking the other way [the via positiva], I forge my own passage seeking the creature. I wander the banks; what I find, I follow. . . .
(*Pilgrim at Tinker Creek*, p. 134)

Seeing, according to Dillard, is potentially the most important action a person can take; seeing deeply, clearly, and precisely is both a scientific tool, "analytical and prying," and a spiritual discipline that leaves the viewer "transfixed and emptied" (*Pilgrim at Tinker Creek*, p. 31). Both kinds of seeing, which are respectively more active and more perceptive than the daily habit of just looking, can reveal what the world truly is.

WHY TAKE A PEN NAME?

Dillard originally intended to assume a male pen name for *Pilgrim at Tinker Creek* because "she couldn't think of a single book about theology written by a woman other than Simone Weil" (Smith, p. 9), the French social philosopher and World War II Resistance activist.

Throughout the course of the book, Dillard passes through winter, spring, summer, and fall, and describes the seasonal changes in her own life as well as that of the plants and animals around her. Spiders, mantises, muskrats, a sycamore tree, microscopic paramecia—all of these denizens of Tinker Creek come under scientific and spiritual scrutiny. The final purpose is not so much to amass a fortune of interesting facts about nature, nor to seek to understand why creatures act as they do; the deepest wonderment in *Pilgrim at Tinker Creek* is the supernatural: who or what is the god that made all this, and how does a human being partake of the divine? "We are people; we are permitted to have dealings with the creator and we must speak up for the creation" (*Pilgrim at Tinker Creek*, p. 264). In other words, one must hallow creation by calling it constantly to mind and noticing everything about it—its complexity, the wonders of it, and its horrors as well as its beauties. As Dillard explains, people must do this because "the universe was not made in jest but in solemn incomprehensible earnest. By a power

---

WHAT IT ALL MEANS

What I aim to do is not so much learn the names of the shreds of creation that flourish in this valley, but to keep myself open to their meanings, which is to try to impress myself at all times with the fullest possible force of their very reality. (*Pilgrim at Tinker Creek*, p. 137)

---

that is unfathomably secret, and holy, and fleet" (*Pilgrim at Tinker Creek*, p. 270). To appreciate it, as she says elsewhere in the essay, is the least she can do.

J. Henri Fabre. "Fish gotta swim and bird [sic] gotta fly; insects, it seems, gotta do one horrible thing after another" (*Pilgrim at Tinker Creek*, p. 63). A good part of *Pilgrim at Tinker Creek* is devoted to the bizarre and sometimes stomach-churning habits of the insect world. Dillard's fearless leader through the fields of entomology is the French scientist Jean Henri Casimer Fabre. Born in 1823, Fabre spent much of his life as an impoverished science teacher in Avignon, France, and used his weekends and holidays to wander along fields and roadsides, observing local insects. He was considered a strange man, and when he allowed girls to attend his science lectures in 1870, it proved to be the last straw and he was fired. With a loan from his friend, the English philosopher, John Stuart Mill, Fabre set upon a writing career and within nine years had sold enough books (mostly science books for the young) to buy himself a small plot of land. There he found more than enough insects to keep him occupied for the rest of his life.

The books Fabre produced on the subject of entomology ran to ten volumes and eventually brought him international fame. His method is one that Dillard shares, that of studying living creatures—their habits, their diet, their mating rituals. Both fascination and horror run through his account of the daily routines of such creatures as red ants, the cicada, the praying mantis, and the hunting wasp. Comparing his own approach to the study of insects with that of more established scientists, Fabre says:

> You rip up the animal and I study it alive; you turn it into an object of horror and pity, whereas I cause it to be loved; you labour in a torture-chamber and dissecting-room, I make my observations under the blue sky to the song of the Cicadas. . . . [I]f I write for men of learning, for philosophers . . . I write also, I write above all things for the young. I want to make them love the natural history which you make them hate.
>
> (Fabre, pp. 3-4)

Fabre has been described as a Thoreau-like character, living alone in nature according to his own rules and pondering the mysteries not only of the animal kingdom but of humanity as well. So it is not just with his subject material that Dillard shares an interest, but with Fabre's approach to life in general.

Sources. *Pilgrim at Tinker Creek* is fundamentally about sight—how to train oneself to notice one's surroundings and how to articulate what has been seen in a way that accurately captures the complexity and the wonder of the universe. In the second chapter, entitled "Seeing," Dillard recounts her indebtedness to a 1932 German work by Marius von Senden, translated in 1960 as *Space and Sight.* As von Senden himself relates in the preface to the English translation, in the post-World War II era it became practically impossible to find congenitally blind adults for whom to restore sight, because such operations were now routinely performed upon infants. It is thus increasingly difficult to talk to people before and after blindness, to discover how the world seems to them. The book provides case studies of blind adults who, through surgery, become sighted; it records the patients' emotional and cognitive reactions to a startling new world. Dillard uses this unusual collection of stories to suggest how different the world can look when one discovers the gift of seeing; she suggests that for all intents and purposes many of us are congenitally blind. To see—the shocking ability to experience and to know—is treated in a mystical way throughout the book, as a gift of profound value:

> It is possible, in deep space, to sail on solar wind. Light, be it particle or wave, has force: you rig a giant sail and go. The secret of seeing is to sail on solar wind. Hone and spread your spirit till you yourself are a sail, whetted, translucent, broadside to the nearest puff.
>
> (*Pilgrim at Tinker Creek,* p. 33)

Principle of Indeterminacy, 1927. "The present is an invisible electron; its lightning path traced faintly on a blackened screen is fleet, and fleeing, and gone" (*Pilgrim at Tinker Creek,* p. 79), says Dillard in the chapter entitled "The Present." The full force of this quotation and others like it emerges gradually in the work; Dillard returns frequently to the mysteries of atomic particles throughout *Pilgrim at Tinker Creek,* and gradually the reader understands that the events conducted at the most minute level of life serve as a model for the higher functions of all creatures. One episode in the history of physics particularly fascinates her, for it yokes together philosophy and science. In 1927, Werner Heisenberg (1901-76), a German physicist, presented the Uncertainty Principle, or the Principle of Indeterminacy. He won the 1932 Nobel Prize in science for this theory, which basically states that it is impossible to know both the velocity and the position of an atomic particle. It is impossible, as

Dillard clearly understands, not because we are not yet able to know such a thing, but because the thing itself is unknowable. There is no rule or formula that will tell us with certainty both where and how fast an atomic particle is; Dillard quotes Heisenberg, who says "there is a higher power, not influenced by our wishes, which finally decides and judges" (*Pilgrim at Tinker Creek,* p. 203). The natural and the supernatural are one and the same.

LIVING IN THE PRESENT

In the sixth chapter of *Pilgrim at Tinker Creek,* Dillard recalls a Hasidic Jewish tradition in which each individual helps redeem the creation by "hallowing" it. Hallowing is to think upon created life, to invest it with the full force of human spirituality. But to notice the life around one is the real trick: "I am sitting under a sycamore by Tinker Creek. . . . But under me, directly under the weight of my body on the grass, are other creatures, just as real, for whom also this moment, this tree, is 'it.' Take just the top inch of soil, the world squirming right under my palms. In the top inch of forest soil, biologists found 'an average of 1,356 living creatures present in each square foot, including 865 mites, 265 springtails, 22 millipedes, 19 adult beetles and various numbers of 12 other forms . . .'" (*Pilgrim at Tinker Creek,* p. 94).

Heisenberg's suitability as a role model for Annie Dillard is immediately apparent: not only was he one of the most important physicists of the twentieth century, but he was also a lover of the arts and something of a philosopher as well. The son of a professor of Greek in Munich, he became interested in atomic particles when reading Plato on a break from his duties as a soldier during World War I. "Heisenberg has shown us in striking fashion what it means to seek, to enquire, to understand and to know: that it means to dedicate oneself to a task without reservation; to reach toward the difficulties by laborious detailed work; to try to separate the essential from the inessential; and not to succumb to the temptation of sacrificing content to form" (Durr in Heisenberg, p. 139).

Reviews. From its first excerpted appearance within the pages of *Harper's* and *Atlantic* magazines, *Pilgrim at Tinker Creek* was heralded as a masterwork. When Larry Freundlich, editor of

Harper's Magazine Press (which published *Pilgrim at Tinker Creek*) first read the manuscript, he marvelled at it: "I never expected to see a manuscript this good in my life. . . . The chance to publish a book like this is what publishers are here for" (Freundlich in Smith, p. 1). A few critics complained that the style of the book was heavy-handed, and others found the theological discussions hard to stomach. In the March 24, 1974, edition of the *New York Times Book Review,* Eudora Welty wrote that Dillard seemed to be "a voice that is trying to speak to me out of a cloud instead of from a sociable, even answerable, distance on our same earth" (Welty in Johnson, p. 3). Such criticisms failed to drown out the more prevalent enthusiasm for Dillard's work, though. On May 5, 1974, *Pilgrim at Tinker Creek* was awarded the Pulitzer Prize for nonfiction.

For More Information

Dillard, Annie. *Pilgrim at Tinker Creek.* New York: Harper's Magazine Press, 1974.

Fabre, J. Henri. *The Insect World of J. Henri Fabre.* Translated by Alexander Teixeira de Mattos. Introduction and interpretive comments by Edwin Way Teale. New York: Dodd, Mead, 1966.

Heisenberg, Werner. *Encounters with Einstein, and Other Essays on People, Places, and Particles.* Princeton, N.J.: Princeton University Press, 1983.

Johnson, Sandra Humble. *The Space Between: Literary Epiphany in the Work of Annie Dillard.* Kent, Ohio: Kent State University Press, 1992.

Journal of a Walden Two Community: The Collected Leaves of Twin Oaks 1, nos. 1-15. Yellow Springs, Ohio: Community Publishing Cooperative, 1972.

McGuire, E. Patrick. "Environmental Progress since Earth Day 1970." *Conference Board Research Bulletin* 243 (1990).

Ogburn, Charlton. *The Southern Appalachians: A Wilderness Quest.* New York: William Morrow, 1975.

Rice, Edward. *The Man in the Sycamore Tree: The Good Times and Hard Life of Thomas Merton.* Garden City, N.Y.: Image, 1972.

Smith, Linda L. *Annie Dillard.* New York: Twayne, 1991.

The Prince of Tides

by
Pat Conroy

Framed by a series of flashbacks, *The Prince of Tides* actually takes place in two separate settings and two different eras. When Tom Wingo visits his sister's psychologist in modern-day New York, he only intends to provide emotional support for Savannah. Through his retelling of childhood memories, however, Tom uncovers a past that hurt both his sister and himself. Conroy, born in Atlanta, Georgia, in 1945, recalls the Southern setting of his own past as he records the Wingos' childhood in the small town of Colleton, South Carolina.

> ## THE LITERARY WORK
> A novel set in both Colleton, South Carolina, and New York City from the 1940s to the 1980s; published in 1986.
>
> ## SYNOPSIS
> In an effort to save the life of his suicidal twin sister, Savannah, Tom Wingo revisits his childhood through psychotherapy.

Events in History at the Time of the Novel

Rural South Carolina life. Much of the novel focuses on a contrast between the lazy pace of a small town in South Carolina and the frenetic energy of New York City. Even after spending a summer discovering New York, its main character opts to return to the comforts of the South. Conroy, a native Southerner himself, paints a vivid picture of rural South Carolina. While the modern era brought rapid urban growth to the state, South Carolina nonetheless boasted a rural population greater in proportion than that of the rest of the country. A 1980 census reports that rural residents constituted 46 percent of South Carolinians, while they represented only 27 percent of the population of the nation as a whole. However, the rural population of South Carolina grew at about only one-third the rate of the remainder of the state between 1950 and 1980.

This would account for the impression that the novel's town of Colleton seems to change little over the course of Tom's life.

Tom's father, a lifelong shrimper, has a profession shared by many South Carolinians. In 1982 the commercial seafood industry in South Carolina earned over $24 million, and shellfish accounted for about three-fourths of this total. The shellfish industry, however, is not merely a product of modern times. Both Native Americans and early European settlers used oysters and shrimp as food staples. During the 1930s, the industry exploded with shrimping fleets, docks, and icehouses popping up across South Carolina's Sea Islands. Today shrimping represents one-half the value of South Carolina's seafood catch. While modern shrimpers still rely on old-fashioned instinct and experience, they now also employ such technologically advanced equipment as radar and electronic navigators. Other advances in the shrimping industry involve aquaculture, or the farming of sea creatures. In 1984 the South Carolina Wildlife and Marine Resources Department opened a center for aquaculture development in Colleton County. Although still in the experimental stages, some predict that such farming could represent the future of Southern shrimping.

South Carolina and nuclear development. In *The Prince of Tides* Tom and Savannah Wingo experience several harrowing events over the course of their lives. Perhaps none of these touches them so deeply as the death of their older brother, Luke. Luke Wingo might have lived a peaceful life in Colleton, South Carolina, had the federal government not annexed the county for the building of a plutonium plant. Firmly against the production of such a lethal substance and concerned about its effects on the local marshlands, Luke leads a one-man crusade against the governmental developers. In the end, he loses his life to this cause.

While in real life the production of plutonium never actually sparked such a contentious situation in South Carolina, the question of nuclear energy and its environmental dangers did provoke the community. During the 1950s and 1960s, atomic energy emerged as a source of cheap power. South Carolina's first nuclear power plant, the Carolinas-Virginia test reactor, opened in 1963. Closed only four years later, the plant nonetheless marked a new era in South Carolina's energy production. By the late 1980s, nuclear energy provided approximately 45 percent of the state's electrical power. This figure outdistanced the national average by three and one-half times.

Along with its growth in popularity, however, nuclear energy raised questions concerning environmental safety. The problem of nuclear waste soon became an issue of heated debate. While such agencies as the Nuclear Regulatory Commission monitored the handling of debris, South Carolina never designated a site on which to store high-level nuclear waste. Instead, plants stored their own byproducts on their business grounds. This, in turn, led to concerns over the possible contamination of areas located near nuclear power stations.

Communities also worried about the cost of nuclear power. Three units built at the Oconee Nuclear Station during the 1970s, for instance, cost South Carolina some $493 million. Nonetheless, with nuclear power providing half the state's energy, the production of it could not be abandoned. Profitable businesses depended on this energy in real life. And, as Luke sardonically remarks in the novel, "Whenever Big Money goes up against the Environment, Big Money always wins" (Conroy, *The Prince of Tides*, p. 637).

Fears such as Luke's about the danger of nuclear power to people were validated, although not in the United States. On April 26, 1986, a massive explosion and fire occurred at a Soviet nuclear power plant in Chernobyl, Ukraine. Killing thirty persons immediately, the event is said to have hospitalized or killed some five hundred others in the following weeks; other estimates blame as many as eight thousand deaths on the human-error accident. The Soviet government evacuated citizens living within a eighteen-and-a-half-mile radius of the plant. There were global consequences as well. It was predicted that Western Europe would experience 5,000 extra cancer deaths in the next fifty years because of the accident and that it would cause genetic problems and mental retardation in those years as well (Medvedev, p. 212). The radiation spread, contaminating lambs in the United Kingdom, reindeer in Sweden, leafy vegetables in Austria, and milk produced by cattle that grazed on contaminated plant life in several countries, including Sweden, Italy, Austria, Hungary, and Poland.

The Chernobyl accident, and its devastating effects, roused anti-nuclear feeling in the United States. A *Washington Post*-ABC poll published in 1986 (also the year of the accident and of the publication of *The Prince of Tides*) reported that 78 percent of those surveyed opposed building new nuclear plants in the United States (up from 67 percent in 1985); 40 percent wanted existing plants to be phased out. Thus Luke Wingo's antinuclear stance—while singling him out in Colleton—was by no means an unusual or inexplicable one at the time.

Divorce and the modern American family. In the novel, not one of the Wingos maintains what society would call a normal or healthy marriage. Mr. Wingo abuses his wife and their children, while Mrs. Wingo forces emotional and psychological repression upon the family. Although Tom does not have such overt problems in his own marriage, his inability to communicate drives his wife into the arms of another man. With a divorce rate of 50 percent in the United States during the 1980s, the Wingos hardly represent a social aberration.

Society had become far more accepting of divorce by the 1980s. In the novel, Tom's grandmother divorces his grandfather during the Great

A May 9, 1986, photograph showing the damage to the Chernobyl nuclear power station.

Depression of the 1930s. Divorce was a rare occurrence in those days, and she finds herself ostracized from her community. By the time that the marriage of Tom's parents ends some forty years later, however, a broken marriage seems to shock no one. A more tolerant attitude toward divorce had become prevalent in American society by that point. Back in the 1960s, domestic relations court judges rotated quickly out of divorce assignments because they considered these sessions too emotional and vindictive. By the 1980s, however, a new perception had emerged, as shown by the attitude of one divorce court judge. He regarded his work as critically important. "The future of families and children" he said, "depends on what I do" (Bohannan, p. 24). The government also began to accept the likelihood that a fair number of marriages would end in divorce at this time. By 1985 only two states, Illinois and South Dakota, still required the establishment of "marital fault" in the granting of divorce. All other forty-eight states simply acknowledged "irreconcilable differences" as a legitimate reason to terminate a marriage. While in the novel Tom goes home to repair his own failing marriage, he also entertains the possibility of divorce. This candid attitude reflects only too well the realistic alternatives for troubled marriages of the time.

The growing acceptance of divorce and divorced people reflects a more fundamental change in American society over the time span covered by the novel (1940s-1980s). During the 1960s and 1970s in particular, attitudes toward sex, marriage, and divorce became considerably more liberal. The infidelity committed by Tom's wife in the novel seems indicative of this trend. There was a new frankness about sex in books, movies, and advertising, and the rate of adultery skyrocketed. A 1983 study by Philip Blumstein and Pepper Schwartz, *American Couples,* reported that 21 percent of women committed adultery after a couple years of marriage.

In tandem with changing attitudes about sex, marriage, and divorce came psychological therapies that stressed self-fulfillment and personal growth. They superseded earlier theories that had promoted adjustment and compromise as the solution to a person's problems. These earlier theories—formulated and popularized by Alfred Adler and Dale Carnegie, among others—called for people to suppress their impulses, avoid confrontation, and defer to the wishes of others. In contrast, newer philosophies—championed, for example, by Abraham Maslow and Erich Fromm—called for people to "get in touch with their feelings and freely voice their opinions, even if this generated feelings of guilt" (Hawes and Nybakken, p. 188).

Further support for this approach to life came from the women's liberation movement of the 1970s, which attacked the notion that wives should defer to the needs of their husbands and children at the expense of fulfilling themselves. Their arguments were bolstered by evidence they uncovered of unhappy families who, behind the image of unity, hid some gruesome realities, such as the ones suffered at the Wingo household in *The Prince of Tides*.

The Novel in Focus

The plot. The opening of *The Prince of Tides* finds Tom Wingo at home in Sullivans Island, South Carolina, with his wife and their three young daughters. Although the family portrait seems cheerful at first, the reader soon discovers the dysfunctional underside of the Wingos' marriage. When Tom's estranged mother calls to notify him that his twin sister, Savannah, has attempted yet another suicide, Tom's life begins to unravel. Within the same twenty-four-hour span, his wife, Susan, tells him that she has been having an affair with another man. She cites Tom's emotional coldness and self-pity as her reason for seeking affection outside their marriage. Fired from his coaching and teaching job over a year earlier, Tom has yet to locate new employment. He eventually alienates himself from his wife through his own guilt and frustration. Unable to piece together his broken life, Tom leaves for New York in an attempt to help Savannah put her own life in order.

Although Savannah has lived in New York for over two decades, her brother rarely comes to the city. Compared to his native South, New York seems cold and distant. Nonetheless, Tom prepares himself to stay throughout the duration of Savannah's recovery. During his first day in New York, Tom visits with his sister's psychologist, Dr. Susan Lowenstein. A serious woman, Lowenstein seems to have nothing in common with Tom, nor does she warm up to his casual, sarcastic manner. As Savannah has not maintained any type of relationship with either of her parents, however, Lowenstein has no one else to whom she can turn. While at Lowenstein's office, Tom hears an audio tape of Savannah's mental breakdown. A famous poet, Savannah recites fantastic imagery and figures, even in the midst of a psychological collapse. Unable to understand her patient's references, Lowenstein asks Tom's

aid in picking apart the tape. With Savannah in a catatonic state, her brother is the only person in a position to aid in her recovery. Although he does not really like the doctor, Tom agrees to meet with Lowenstein once a week in order to help his sister.

During these sessions, Tom recalls memories from his and Savannah's childhood. He tells of their upbringing on Melrose Island in Colleton County, South Carolina. The children of a poor shrimper and a housewife, Tom and Savannah knew no real material wealth. With their older brother Luke, however, they found their own entertainment among the local marshes and woodlands. Were it not for their parents, the Wingo children's lives might have been quite pleasant. Unfortunately, Mr. Wingo was prone to abusing his wife and children. On more than one occasion, they suffered physical injury at his hands and feared for their lives. Mrs. Wingo, a strong woman in many respects, never summoned the courage to leave her husband. Practical by nature, she realized the improbability of a single, uneducated woman raising three children on her own in the American South. She instead created a household of denial in which the children were forbidden to discuss the abuse, even with each other. Mrs. Wingo operated on the belief that if one told oneself something never happened, then in fact it never did.

Despite this odd, even harmful arrangement, the Wingo children still might have led relatively normal lives had they not become the victims of a heinous, violent attack. One day three escaped convicts broke into the Wingos' home while Mr. Wingo and Luke were away. The men raped Mrs. Wingo, Tom, and Savannah, and would have killed them had Luke not returned early from work. Luke surprised the attackers with his own assault, and the Wingos eventually killed the three men. Under Mrs. Wingo's direction, they buried the bodies in the woods and erased all evidence of the crime. She forbade the children to speak of the event, even to their father. Realizing the social stigma attached to rape, she feared becoming an outcast in the town and possibly in her own home. Forced into silence, Savannah made her first attempt at taking her own life that afternoon.

A few months after the attack, Tom left for college and Savannah moved to New York. Luke stayed in Colleton to join his father in the shrimping business. With the children grown and out of the house, Mrs. Wingo left her husband and filed for divorce. A social climber, she managed to marry the richest man in Colleton, and she gave to him Melrose Island, the property she had acquired in the divorce. Mrs. Wingo's new husband then sold his property holdings in Colleton to the federal government. With plans to build a plutonium plant in the county, the government paid handsomely for the land. It quickly bought out all other residents and forced the entire town to relocate. Everyone went along with the government's wishes except for Luke Wingo. Dedicated to his homeland, Luke fought for the small South Carolina county. He began a one-man revolution, blowing up construction sites and bridges, ambushing the government's efforts. Although his family pleaded with him, he refused to surrender. Eventually, a Marine sniper's bullet ended Luke's crusade and life. In his memory, Savannah penned a poem she entitled "The Prince of Tides." She wanted the public to know of the lengths to which her brother went in order to save their corner of the world.

Tom retells this injured family history to Lowenstein over the course of an entire summer. As the sessions go on, the two eventually become friends and lovers. Lowenstein helps Tom to face his painful past, making it possible for him to open up to people once again. Together, they help Savannah leave the psychiatric institution and take steps toward healing. Neither Tom nor Savannah blame their parents for the imperfections that they handed down to their children. At the summer's end, Tom returns to South Carolina to try to repair his broken marriage.

Long-term impact of childhood abuse. In the novel, Savannah Wingo's past haunts her with vivid hallucinations and imagined voices. Although an adult, she still cannot escape the abuses that she suffered as a child. The attack by the three escaped convicts only added to her torment. Tom and Savannah's mother, a Southern woman who feared small-town gossip, later forbade mention of the rapes. During the time when they occurred, the early 1960s, sexual abuse was not yet an appropriate topic of conversation. Only later, as adults, could the Wingos begin to explore their traumatic pasts.

While in the novel all three family members suffer sexual abuse, it is Savannah who emerges most traumatized by it later in life. Her reaction to her earlier physical abuse is not uncommon. Contemporary psychotherapy posits that the effects of childhood abuse can be broken down into four parts: *traumatic sexualization, betrayal, powerlessness,* and *stigmatization.* Savannah's

Pat Conroy

problems in the novel can be classified into these categories. More specifically, "traumatic sexualization" refers to the inappropriate development of a child's sexuality—possibly an association of sex with painful memories. As an adult, Savannah maintains no close sexual relationships. She connects sexual encounters only with pain and suffering. "Betrayal," according to psychologists, means the discovery that a loved one has caused harm. A child experiences betrayal from either the offender or a family member who does not protect or believe the child. Mrs. Wingo's insistence on "forgetting" the rape could easily be viewed as betrayal in Savannah's eyes. As an adult, she does not even communicate with her mother. The third portion of the dynamic, "powerlessness," refers to the notion that the child victim of abuse feels no control over his or her environment. Powerlessness becomes an element of Savannah's later life in the form of mental hallucinations over which she has no control. "Stigmatization" of the child, the final element, refers to society's ostracism of victims of sexual abuse and the corresponding negative self-image of the victim. Researchers find that these feelings often multiply when the abuse is kept secret. Certainly this holds true for the Wingo children. While, eventually, they do begin to heal, both Tom and Savannah find difficulty in escaping the effects of their childhood trauma. Only through modern counseling procedures can the Wingos attempt to put their pasts behind them.

Sources. Though born in Atlanta, Georgia, Pat Conroy grew up in various homes along the southeast coast of the United States. Having spent a great portion of his childhood in Beaufort, South Carolina, the author certainly drew from his own past in his creation of *The Prince of Tides*. Like Mr. Wingo, Conroy's father, a Marine Corps fighter pilot, was ill-tempered and ornery. Likewise, the author described his mother as socially ambitious, a characteristic that he gave to the novel's Mrs. Wingo.

In fact, Conroy used other elements from his past in his work. Like his main character, Tom Wingo, Conroy taught high school English on an island just off the South Carolina coast. For his use of unorthodox teaching methods and his disrespect for school authorities, Conroy was fired from his post. More significantly, however, Conroy too had a poet sister who lived in New York. In a manner similar to that of Savannah Wingo's, Conroy's sister suffered a mental collapse.

Reception of the novel. Although Conroy used to be quite close with the sister referred to above, she refused to speak with him after the publication of the novel. In fact, many of the author's relatives expressed shock at the work. Conroy noted, "I'm saddened, but when you write autobiography, this is one of the consequences. They're allowed to be mad at you. They have the right" (Conroy in Ryan, p. 680).

Critically, Conroy's novel met with mixed reviews upon publication. While a review in the *Chicago Tribune* proclaimed, "Pat Conroy has fashioned a brilliant novel that ultimately affirms life" (Bass in Ryan, p. 679), others were not so complimentary. One article, which appeared in the *Los Angeles Times Book Review,* complained that "the characters do too much, feel too much, suffer too much, eat too much, signify too much, and above all, talk too much" (Eder in Ryan, p. 679). Regardless of the critical debate, however, *The Prince of Tides* found wide acceptance among the reading public.

For More Information

Auerbach Walker, Lenore E., ed. *Handbook on Sexual Abuse of Children.* New York: Springer, 1988.

Bohannan, Paul. *All the Happy Families.* New York: McGraw-Hill, 1985.

Conroy, Pat. *The Prince of Tides.* New York: Bantam, 1986.

Hawes, Joseph M., and Elizabeth I. Nybakken, eds. *American Families: A Research Guide and Historical Handbook.* New York: Greenwood, 1991.

Kovacik, Charles E., and John J. Winberry. *South Carolina: A Geography.* Boulder, Colo.: Westview, 1987.

Medvedev, Zhores A. *The Legacy of Chernobyl.* New York: W. W. Norton, 1990.

Ryan, Bryan, ed. *Major Twentieth Century Writers.* Vol. 1. Detroit: Gale Research, 1991.

The Right Stuff

by

Tom Wolfe

THE LITERARY WORK

A nonfiction narrative of space travel set in the United States from 1945 to 1963; published in 1979.

SYNOPSIS

The Right Stuff is a history of the early years of the U.S. space program. Starting with an account of the lives of military pilots and their wives, the book progresses to the selection of the first seven astronauts, their grueling training, their relationship with the press and public, and the Project Mercury flights themselves.

Tom Wolfe was born in 1931 in Richmond, Virginia. He decided to become a writer at the age of six in emulation of his father, an editor, whom he often saw writing at his desk. After graduating with a Ph.D. in American studies from Yale, Wolfe went to work as a journalist. In 1963, based on his research of a California customized car and hot rod show, Wolfe published "There Goes (Varoom! Varoom!) That Kandy-Kolored Tangerine-Flake Streamline Baby" in *Esquire* magazine. The article was the first of many accounts by Wolfe covering the lifestyles of unconventional groups and public figures in contemporary culture. *The Right Stuff* is his seventh such book.

Events in History at the Time of the Narrative

NASA. The National Aeronautics and Space Administration (NASA) is a civilian agency of the U.S. federal government whose mission is to conduct research and develop operational programs in the areas of space exploration, satellites, and rocketry. Officially launched on October 1, 1958, NASA replaced the National Advisory Committee on Aeronautics (NACA). NACA had been a relatively small organization, focusing primarily on research and cooperating closely with the military and other governmental agencies. When the Soviet Union launched Sputnik I, the first artificial satellite, on October 4, 1957, a general panic over America's perceived unpreparedness led to the creation of NASA, a far more powerful organization in which the resources of the various military branches were pooled together. Soon after its inception, in addition to taking over several research centers from NACA, NASA acquired the U.S. Army Jet Propulsion Laboratory in Pasadena, California, and, later, the Army Ballistic Missile Arsenal in Huntsville, Alabama. The best-known NASA facilities became the Lyndon B. Johnson Space Center near Houston, Texas, from which the Apollo and other manned flights were coordinated, and Cape Canaveral midpoint on the Atlantic Coast of Florida, where the launches actually took place. Cape Canaveral was renamed Cape Kennedy in 1963 to honor President Kennedy after his assassination that year, but the original name was restored in 1973.

John Glenn, one of the original Project Mercury astronauts.

The space race. When the USSR launched its first artificial satellite, Sputnik I, there was tremendous political pressure in the United States to equal or exceed the accomplishments of the Soviets. This international competition became popularly known as the "space race." A few months later, the U.S. launched their own satellite, Explorer 1, in early 1958. But this did little to diminish the sense of urgency among the American public to beat the Soviets in the space race. NASA embarked on Project Mercury, whose mission was to put a man in space as soon as possible—it was essentially a political endeavor. On April 12, 1961, the Soviet cosmonaut Yuri Alekseyevich Gagarin, traveling in Vostok 1, became the first man to reach space. Nevertheless, when Mercury astronauts Alan Shepard and John Glenn successfully completed suborbital and orbital flights later that spring, American morale was given a tremendous boost, and the astronauts were embraced by the public as heroes of the struggle between the United States and Soviet Union for world leadership.

Even while Project Mercury held the attention of the nation, NASA and President Kennedy were focusing on a still greater goal—a lunar landing.

After taking office in 1961, President Kennedy committed the United States to the goal of landing Americans on the moon and bringing them back safely to earth by the end of the decade. The resulting Apollo program was the largest scientific and technological undertaking in history. In the decade following Sputnik I, the United States and the USSR between them launched about fifty unmanned space probes to explore the moon. Meanwhile, manned space flight progressed steadily, with the Soviets maintaining a slim lead. In the first multipassenger flight, three Soviet cosmonauts were launched in a Voskhod spacecraft in October 1964. In March 1965, another Voskhod cosmonaut left the capsule to take the first "walk in space." The first launch of the Gemini program, carrying two American astronauts, occurred a few days after the Soviet spacewalk. The Apollo program, however, had become the primary focus at NASA, and the program finally realized its goal when Neil Armstrong and Edwin E. ("Buzz") Aldrin, Jr. set foot on the lunar surface on July 20, 1969.

The Cold War. The Cold War is a term used to describe the mutual suspicion and shifting struggle for world leadership between the Western powers and the Communist bloc starting after World War II and lasting until the end of the 1980s. The global conflict had its roots in the ideological differences between communism and capitalist democracy. After the war, the West felt threatened by the continued expansionist policy of the Soviet Union; meanwhile, traditional Russian fear of incursions from the West also continued. The United States formulated a positive national policy to "contain" the spread of communism. In 1947 it initiated the European Recovery Program, also known as the Marshall Plan, which helped to restore economic stability and prosperity in Europe and thereby preempt any possible Soviet encroachment.

After the Soviets blockaded the western sectors of Berlin, Germany, in 1948, the United States reversed a policy of avoiding permanent alliances and in 1949 signed the North Atlantic Treaty Organization (NATO) with eleven other nations. In turn, the communist countries would form an alliance of their own, the Warsaw Treaty Organization, in 1955. In 1949 communist leader Mao Zedong (Tse-tung) gained control of mainland China, and the following year communist forces from North Korea attacked South Korea, precipitating the Korean War.

Hopes for an end to the Cold War were raised when long-time Soviet leader Josef Stalin died in

1953 and was replaced by new premier Nikita Khrushchev. These hopes were dashed, however, by the launch of the Soviet artificial satellite Sputnik I in 1957, which introduced a new international competition in space exploration and missile capability. In 1961 East Germany erected the Berlin Wall to check the embarrassing flow of its citizens to the West. In 1962 U.S. intelligence discovered the presence of Soviet missile installations in Cuba, and a tense naval confrontation ensued, controlled by Kennedy and Khrushchev, before the Soviet premier finally called home his vessels at the last moment. Though the Cuban Missile Crisis was perhaps the most direct standoff between the two nations, tensions would remain high for decades and figure in many foreign policy decisions. The Cold War would not end, in fact, until the Soviet empire weakened and dissolved in the late 1980s and early 1990s.

The New Journalism. The New Journalism is a form of nonfiction writing that combines traditional newspaper reportage with fictional techniques such as stream-of-consciousness, shifting points of view, extended dialogue, character description, and a strong sense of the writer's presence. The term first caught on in the 1960s and 1970s as a label for the nonfiction work of writers such as Tom Wolfe, Gay Talese, Norman Mailer, Terry Southern, George Plimpton, and Truman Capote. Tom Wolfe has been identified as the quintessential New Journalist. "One working definition of the New Journalism is that it's what Tom Wolfe writes. If not exactly the founder of the movement . . . Wolfe has for some years now been its major theorist and of course among its most visible practitioners" (Weber, p. 13). In 1973 Wolfe published an anthology of nonfiction entitled *The New Journalism,* in which he includes an essay of his own on the subject.

The Narrative in Focus

The contents. *The Right Stuff* opens with the gruesome death of U.S. Navy pilot Bud Jennings. What follows—the grim task of notifying the wife and the military funeral—are common rituals in the world of military aviation. Readers are then taken to Maryland's Patuxent River Naval Air Station, the Navy's prime test center. Now that the Korean War has ended, and with it the opportunities for combat flying, the best alternative (and the most dangerous) for daring young pilots is "flight test." The reader soon discovers that one of the unwritten prerequisites for pilots and their wives who spend each day

under the specter of imminent death is to not talk about it: "Like many other wives in Group 20 Jane wanted to talk about the whole situation, the incredible series of fatal accidents. . . . But somehow the unwritten protocol forbade discussions of this subject, which was the fear of death" (Wolfe, *The Right Stuff,* p. 15). Having the right stuff means keeping your fears to yourself, and if there is one man among all the others who represents toughness and coolness under pressure, it is Chuck Yeager.

JOHN F. KENNEDY AND THE SPACE RACE

President Kennedy (1961-1963) was a vocal supporter of space projects, as is evident in these pre-election remarks made in 1960: "Because we failed to recognize the impact that being first in outer space would have, the impression began to move around the world that the Soviet Union was on the march, that it had definite goals, that it knew how to accomplish them, that it was moving and we were standing still. That is what we have to overcome. . . . If the Soviets control space they can control Earth, as in past centuries the nation that controlled the seas has dominated the continents" (Kennedy in Baker, p. 81).

A West Virginia boy, Yeager joined the Army Air Force in 1941 at the age of eighteen and in 1943 flew planes over France and Germany. He is a tough young man, says *The Right Stuff,* but his most remarkable quality is his hollow, deadpan, Appalachian drawl, and his composed demeanor even in the direst of life-and-death situations. After the war Yeager worked as a test pilot at Wright Field in Dayton, Ohio, where he impressed his instructors with his stunt-flying and his utter fearlessness. He was then chosen to go to Muroc Field (later called Edwards Air Force Base) in California for the X-1 project. The X-1 project was the Army Air Force's effort to reach the speed of Mach 1, thereby breaking the "sound barrier," which at 40,000 feet in the air, where the temperature is at least 60 degrees below zero, is about 660 miles an hour. The speed of sound had become known as "the sound barrier" or "the sonic wall" because aircraft approaching that speed had started shaking uncontrollably and then disintegrated, which led some scientists to speculate that the g-forces (gravitational pressure) became infinite at Mach 1.

MANNED SPACE FLIGHT HIGHLIGHTS

Mission	Launch	Country	Remarks
Vostok 1	4/12/61	USSR	First manned space flight
Mercury Redstone-3	5/5/61	USA	First U.S. flight (suborbital)
Mercury Atlas-6	2/20/62	USA	First U.S. manned orbital flight
Vostok 3	8/11/62	USSR	Dual flight with Vostok 4
Vostok 6	6/16/63	USSR	Carried first woman into space
Voskhod 1	10/12/64	USSR	Carried first three-man crew
Voskhod 2	3/18/65	USSR	Supported first space walk
Gemini-Titan-4	6/3/65	USA	First U.S. space walk
Soyuz 1	4/23/67	USSR	First man killed in space
Apollo 8	12/21/68	USA	First orbit of moon
Soyuz 4	1/14/69	USSR	First docking of two-man ship
Apollo 9	3/3/69	USA	First manned test of moon lander
Apollo 11	7/16/69	USA	First moon landing (7/20/69)

When other pilots opt out of the test, Yeager eagerly steps in. Not being an engineer, he doesn't believe such a "barrier" exists at all. And he is right. On October 14, 1947, Yeager flies the X-1 aircraft through the sound barrier at 700 mph. As his speed approaches Mach 1, the aircraft shakes, after which a sonic boom reverberates over the desert floor and the aircraft smoothes out. As soon as Yeager lands, it is made clear that his accomplishment is to remain a military secret. The military does a very poor job of handling the press, though. Instead of releasing the story on their own terms, they insist on keeping it a secret long after word has dribbled out, and the result is that the story of Chuck Yeager's record-breaking test flight leaks out gradually, undramatically, and inaccurately.

Plans are already under way for the X-15, an aircraft designed to achieve an altitude of 280,000 feet, just above fifty miles, which is generally considered the boundary where the atmosphere ends and "space" begins. Despite these plans, the launching of Sputnik I in October 1957 creates a sense of panic in the world of tactical weaponry, and an almost superstitious obsession with controlling the heavens. The urgency to put a man in space grows so great that there is no time to design the rockets necessary to send the X-series aircraft into space as

planned. Instead a simpler task is chosen: put a man in a capsule atop a Redstone (70,000 pounds of thrust) or an Atlas (367,000 pounds) rocket and shoot him straight up until he reaches space. This new project, called Project Mercury, is given to the newly instituted National Aeronautics and Space Administration (NASA).

The next logical question, of course, is who will go? It is thought that the cream of the aviator crop, the test pilots, might not be interested because the Mercury capsule will be completely automated, which means that the astronaut will not be doing any actual flying. This situation is underscored by the fact that a monkey is going to be sent up in place of an astronaut for a test flight. Pilots refer to the program derisively as "spam in a can." However, a large number of test pilots apply for the job anyway, and after a grueling selection process, seven men are chosen: L. Gordon Cooper, M. Scott Carpenter, Alan B. Shepard, Virgil I. "Gus" Grissom, Donald K. "Deke" Slayton, John H. Glenn, and Walter M. Schirra.

As soon as the astronauts are selected, they are presented to the press, and the nation goes wild. The astronauts are greeted as heroes, as a new breed of cold warrior. Meanwhile, back at Edwards Air Force Base, the "true brethren" still believe they, as test pilots, are at the top of the

Apollo 11 astronaut Edwin E. Aldrin, Jr. walks on the surface of the moon.

heap. The astronauts' mission is not as dangerous, nor does it demand as much skill, as missions that require the services of the very finest test pilots. But regardless of this insiders' view, the astronauts command an extraordinary degree of public attention. Whereas test pilots receive little money, the seven astronauts have signed an exclusive deal with *Life* magazine and suddenly are able to buy large houses. They are given sports cars for free and treated like royalty by businessmen, politicians, and reporters. It is becoming apparent that the age of a whole new breed of hero, the astronaut, has arrived.

After a series of test flights, and an endless string of invasive medical tests in which the astronauts are treated like lab animals, Alan Shepard is chosen to make the first Mercury flight. His successful suborbital flight gives him a place in history as the first American in space, and he is greeted as a hero. Gus Grissom is next in line. His flight proceeds much the same as Shepard's, except that he exits early during the sea rescue and the capsule sinks. The third Mercury mission sends John Glenn into the earth's orbit. This is considered a still greater achievement, and Glenn is embraced by the nation with a desperate warmth and gratitude that no astronaut has ever received since, including the other members of Mercury team that followed.

For the duration of the space flights, it is unclear who is under more pressure, the man trapped in a tiny capsule up in space, or his wife. The media, hungry for the human interest angle, descend upon the wives in their living rooms with ferocious intensity. Although the wives enjoy many of the benefits of their husbands' new status as national heroes, they also pay a heavy price for it, especially during those horrific hours spent waiting helplessly for their husbands' return while being hounded by the press.

"The right stuff." The essence of Wolfe's book is not the record of military flight tests or NASA's space program in itself. As the author himself explains in his 1983 foreword, it is about "what makes a man willing to sit up on top of an enormous roman candle . . . and wait for someone to light the fuse . . . which is to say, courage" (*The Right Stuff,* p. ii). But even that word is too simple. After all, the book points out, any fool can throw away his own life.

> The idea here . . . seemed to be that a man should have the ability to go up in a hurtling piece of machinery and put his hide on the line and then have the moxie, the reflexes, the experience, the coolness, to pull it back in the last yawning moment—and then to go up again the next day, and the next day, and every *next day,* even if the series should prove infinite— and, ultimately, in its best expression, do so in a cause that means something to thousands, to a people, a nation, to humanity, to God.
> (*The Right Stuff,* p. 24)

There are some other curious aspects to this elusive quality of "the right stuff." For example, it is never spoken of directly; it is simply understood. Indeed, it was Wolfe's curiosity at the reticent responses of the pilots to his questions about their courage that drove him to write the book in the first place. One of the things that makes "the right stuff" difficult to identify is that there is no single litmus test. Instead there is an endless series of tests. Having the right stuff means having the will to constantly prove it. Those with the right stuff are set apart as gifted and unique. "A man either had it or he didn't! There was no such thing as having *most* of it" (*The Right Stuff,* p. 29). How does death figure into it? After all, a military test pilot always runs the risk that their next flight will be their last. The answer, simple and somewhat shocking, is that if one dies, that is evidence that he did not have the right stuff.

It seems that almost anyone, for any reason, can be dismissed for lacking the right stuff. A person who is too tall to be admitted to the elite group, or who has fallen arches, lacks the right stuff. A person who suffers from claustrophobia and is assigned to fly jet transports lacks it. Only those who are assigned to fighter squadrons— the "fighter jocks," as they call one another—are in the fraternity. The right stuff is about courage, about manhood, about stoicism. In these respects, it resembles the traditional warrior codes of various cultures throughout history. Yet it is also about luck, about being the right height, about not having an irregular heartbeat or corrective lenses or any other physical imperfection. Men with the right stuff exhibit peripherally and even morally dubious behavior, such as drinking, womanizing, and driving fast cars. In the air, fighter jocks who have the right stuff engage in the dangerous practice of mock dogfighting— that is, a reckless type of vying between planes to best each other in the air. Though officially forbidden, dogfighting is in fact a kind of necessary test of manhood for each and every aviator coming up through the ranks. If something goes wrong and the pilot has to bail out, he has a ready explanation for his superiors: "I don't know what happened, sir. I was pulling up after a target run, and it just flamed out on me" (*The Right Stuff*, p. 31).

Sources. Tom Wolfe may be America's preeminent documenter of American subcultures, and his style depends heavily on meticulously observed physical details, slang, and personal habits. Like any good journalist, Wolfe spent a great deal of time talking with the pilots, their families, technicians, journalists, and a host of other figures who participated in or had information on his subject.

In his 1983 foreword to the book, Wolfe points out that the fashion among writers in Europe and the United States after the First World War was to portray war as "inherently monstrous, and those who waged it—namely, military officers—were looked upon as brutes and philistines" (*The Right Stuff*, p. i). Primary among the culprits promoting this view were, he claimed, great works of literature: Erich Maria Remarque's **All Quiet on the Western Front** (also covered in *Literature and Its Times*), Louis-Ferdinand Céline's *The Journey to the End of the Night*, and Jaroslav Hasek's *The Good Soldier Svejk*. According to Wolfe, the only sympathetic military character one sees in such books is the enlisted man, the man who is little more than a pawn in the great struggle for power, and thus a ready symbol for all victims of war. What's missing from these books, Wolfe argues, is "the old fashioned tale of prowess and heroism (*The Right Stuff*, p. i)." *The Right Stuff* can therefore be viewed as an effort to alert an otherwise oblivious literary world to the fact that not only do heroes still exist, but they exist right under our noses, in the cockpits of our aircraft and in the capsules of our rockets. Wolfe's book is the result of his effort to understand why men were willing to risk their lives to become heroes "in an era literary people had long since character-ized as the age of the antihero" (*The Right Stuff*, p. ii).

Reaction. Tom Wolfe is no stranger to controversy. His unusual style and strong opinions always seem to elicit emphatic critical response, both positive and negative. *The Right Stuff* is generally considered to be his most widely respected book. Wolfe's journalistic style, however, was attacked by some:

> Tom Wolfe does not have a likable persona, and *The Right Stuff* is not a likable book. . . . Wolfe's book is not a history; it is far too thin in dates, facts and source citations to serve any such purpose. It is a work of literature which must stand or fall as a coherent text.
> (Powers in Mooney, p. 1382)

Most reviewers, however, lauded the book for its thoroughness and its unusual approach: "[This] is Tom Wolfe at his very best, better in fact than he's been before. [The book] is technically accurate, learned, cheeky, risky, touching, tough, compassionate, nostalgic, worshipful, jingoistic—it is superb" (Williamson in Mooney, p. 1382).

For More Information

Baker, David. *The History of Manned Space Flight*. New York: Crown, 1982.

Mooney, Martha T., ed. *Book Review Digest*. Vol. 75. New York: H.W. Wilson, 1980.

Weber, Ronald, ed. *The Reporter as Artist: A Look at the New Journalism Controversy*. New York: Hastings House, 1974.

Weisberger, Bernard A. *Cold War Cold Peace; The United States and Russia since 1945*. New York: American Heritage, 1984.

Wolfe, Tom. *The New Journalism*. New York: Harper & Row, 1973.

Wolfe, Tom. *The Right Stuff*. New York: Farrar, Straus & Giroux, 1979.

Roots: The Saga of an American Family

by
Alex Haley

Born in Ithaca, New York, in 1921, Alex Haley was raised in Henning, Tennessee, by his maternal grandmother. Haley heard stories during his childhood about his heritage from his grandmother and from other elderly female relatives. As a young adult he joined the Coast Guard, and when he left the service he landed a job writing biographical stories for *Reader's Digest,* a journal that would eventually sponsor some of the research and travel that made *Roots* possible.

Events in History at the Time of the Biography

Life in Juffure. *Roots* begins with the mid-eighteenth century birth of Haley's ancestor, Kunta Kinte, in the small village of Juffure in the Gambia, a land in West Africa. The Gambia stretches along a narrow fertile belt (295 miles in length and between 15 and 30 miles wide) on both sides of the Gambia River. In modern times the continent's smallest nation, the Gambia abuts the Atlantic Ocean on the west, while its other three sides border Senegal. Juffure is situated more than 100 miles upstream from the mouth of the Gambia River. Daily life for residents in Juffure had, by the time when Haley visited there in the 1970s, changed little since 1750; lack of modern conveniences such as telephone service and electricity had preserved traditional ways of life there more easily than in cities, although items such as Western-style clothing and portable radios were not uncommon.

Gambians are comprised of three ethnic groups: Mandingo, Fula, and Wolof. Peanuts grown for export provide almost all of the country's income. Ninety percent of Gambians are practicing Muslims. Many still live in huts made from a material called banco, which is a mixture of straw and sun-dried clay and is similar to adobe brick. Silk-cotton tree branches form the roof beams, the roof itself being thatched from long grasses and millet straw. The most common food staple is couscous, which the women of the village pound with mortars; the men still paddle pirogues (dugout canoes) to work in the distant couscous and cotton fields.

Oral tradition. *Roots* is based on the oral tradition that Haley's family handed down through seven generations. He heard the history of his ancestors from his grandmother and his cousin,

Several generations of a slave family, 1862.

who "had talked the family narrative on the . . . front porch" (Haley, *Roots*, p. 670). Correlating what he had been told with the facts he found in libraries and other repositories of official data, Haley discovered how accurate the information was that his relatives had passed down to him. Later, on a trip to the Gambia inspired by his research into his family's past, Haley met an elder from the village of Juffure who told the story of Haley's ancestors through many centuries, up until the time when a man named Kunta Kinte, whom Haley knows is his great-great-great-great grandfather, disappeared one day when slave-gathering ships were in the area.

In the West African culture of which the villagers of Juffure are part, history is passed from generation to generation orally instead of in writ-

ten form; men called griots fill the role of both storyteller and historian and are able to recount the tales of generations long past: "The griot is musician, poet, historian, and paid publicity agent—working on a fee basis or annual salary. . . . He is the village's memory, its newspaper" (Vollmer, p. 8). Although they had no "official" function in the black American community, Haley's grandmother and the other old women from whom he learned of his ancestry were themselves American griots, keeping alive the old stories that one day enabled Haley to rediscover the African branch of his family.

Haley's insistence throughout *Roots* on writing the speech patterns of his ancestors in dialect is another reflection of his debt to the African oral tradition. Most of the information in the novel is transmitted not through standard narration but through conversations among the characters, who, in effect, are replicating the griot's role. In the 1960s and 1970s, this attention on the part of African American writers to the oral tradition was part of a general cultural movement in which blacks in the United States looked to the land of their ancestors for literary and social influence.

The civil rights era. The civil rights era of the 1960s and 1970s, during which Alex Haley was researching and writing *Roots,* had its beginnings in the massive migration undertaken by hundreds of thousands of Southern blacks to the industrial cities of the North beginning around 1910. Disillusioned with the strict segregation laws in the South and in search of better employment, African Americans moved to and settled their own communities in such cities as Chicago and New York. The "Harlem Renaissance," a movement of the 1920s in which black New York artists broke new ground in music, literature, and the visual arts, served to consolidate feelings of community among African Americans and helped inspire the more radical political outcry of later decades.

WHO WE ARE

In the acknowledgements section at the beginning of *Roots,* Alex Haley states how greatly he is indebted to the tribal storytellers, the griots, who made it possible for him to know his own history: "I acknowledge immense debt to the griots of Africa—where today it is rightly said that when a griot dies, it is as if a library has burned to the ground" (*Roots,* p. viii).

In 1964, about the time that Haley started to research his family history, the contemporary civil rights movement was finally scoring some successes. Nonviolent protests, undertaken by both blacks and sympathetic whites, won the support of the federal government and led to the Civil Rights Act of 1964, which outlawed racial discrimination in public places. More civil rights efforts followed—the Mississippi Summer Project (1964) to register black voters and Dr. Martin Luther King Jr.'s march from Selma to Montgomery in Alabama (1965) to protest local opposition to registering black voters. After the march, pressed by President Lyndon Johnson,

Congress passed the Voting Rights Act of 1965, which permitted federal officials to register black voters in areas where local authorities were obstructing this process.

Despite these gains and other apparent victories—James Meredith forced the University of Mississippi to enroll a black student (1966) and Thurgood Marshall became the first black justice of the U.S. Supreme Court (1967)—advancement did not match the governmental promises of the decade. Black activism split into two factions, with one committed to continuing the nonviolent protest of Martin Luther King, and the other turning to more radical means of securing power. A leader of this second group was Malcolm X, whom Alex Haley helped to write ***The Autobiography of Malcolm X*** (also covered in *Literature and Its Times),* one of the most influential black autobiographies ever written. During the time that Haley was working with him, Malcolm X became interested in re-establishing ties to Africa as a means of securing the civil rights of African Americans; with the political clout of African nations behind the struggle of American blacks, Malcolm felt that the cause would be that much stronger.

Links to Africa. Haley states that the research for *Roots,* which was published in 1976, took him twelve years; the mid-1960s era in which he began the project was a time when some African Americans were forging links with the continent of their forebears. In 1964, the Student Nonviolent Coordinating Committee (SNCC), a political action group for young black Americans, was invited to Africa by the government of Guinea. Members of the group toured Guinea, Ghana, Liberia, Zambia, Kenya, Ethiopia, and Egypt, meeting with foreign leaders, diplomats, and Malcolm X, who was in Africa on a public relations mission. Upon their return, the students drafted a set of proposals, including one to establish an African Bureau within the SNCC, which would bring foreign pressure from Africa and elsewhere to bear upon American governments—both federal and state—unwilling to take the necessary measures to ensure black citizens their full rights.

As black Americans became more politically conscious, they also began focusing more on their African heritage. An increasing number studied African culture, history, art, and languages, and wore African-style clothes and hairdos. This identification with the continent was also expressed in the African American literature of the time. For example, Clarence Reed's work "Song from the Wasteland" and Jon Eckel's poem

AFRICAN AMERICAN TIMELINE

(Events in bold print are mentioned in *Roots*)

1619: Twenty Africans first arrive in Virginia as indentured servants, who would be freed after a requisite number of years of service.

1766-1767: The British ship *Lord Ligonier* sails from the Gambia with a cargo of slaves (including Kunta Kinte) and African goods.

1774-1804: All Northern states abolish slavery.

1775: In one American Revolution incident, Lord Dunmore (English governor of Virginia) offers to free all slaves who join the English cause.

1776: Declaration of Independence signed.

1791: Slave rebellion establishes nation of Haiti.

1793: Invention of cotton gin increases demand for slave labor in South; cotton replaces tobacco as main crop.

1800: Gabriel Prosser Rebellion is attempted in Richmond, Virginia.

1800-1860: Price of slaves quadruples at slave markets.

1804: The Underground Railroad, abolitionist activity helping slaves reach the North or Canada, begins in earnest.

1808: It becomes illegal to import African slaves into America.

1822: Denmark Vesey Rebellion is attempted in Charleston, North Carolina.

1830s: Abolitionist movement begins in North.

1831: Nat Turner's Rebellion occurs in Southampton Co., Virginia.

1859: John Brown and militant force seizes U.S. Armory at Harpers Ferry, Virginia, in antislavery protest.

1861-1865: American Civil War is fought—the Northerners are victorious; Thirteenth Amendment is ratified, freeing all slaves.

1896: In *Plessy v. Ferguson* the U.S. Supreme Court rules that racial segregation is legal under the Constitution, provided facilities for blacks and whites are equal.

1914-1918: World War I draws thousands of black Americans to Northern industrial cities and into the armed forces; Haley's father, Simon, fights in France.

1939: Alex Haley joins Coast Guard; World War II begins in Europe.

1954-1955: In *Brown v. Board of Education* U.S. Supreme Court reverses *Plessy v. Ferguson;* civil rights movement gains adherents in bus boycott in Montgomery, Alabama.

1976: Publication of *Roots* in year of American Bicentennial.

"Home Is Where the Soul Is" both focus on Africa. Toni Morrison's *Song of Solomon* is concerned with African American folklore and the "quest for the family roots," which in turn, "is linked to the search for Afro American cultural heritage" (Bruck and Karrer, p. 290). Morrison and other African American writers—for example, Ernest Gaines, author of ***The Autobiography of Miss Jane Pittman*** (also covered in *Literature and Its Times*)—also turned to oral tradition in their works, replicating the patterns of black speech. Published in 1976, *Roots* contributed to the literary trends of the day.

Nation of Islam. In *Roots,* Kunta Kinte is Haley's only Islamic ancestor, and his master allows him to retain his religion, an action atypical of most plantation owners. Generally, masters and preachers urged slaves to embrace Christianity. Slaveowners often expressed the view that slavery had been ordained by God as a moral means of introducing Christianity to Africans. In fact, the insistence on spreading Christianity among the slaves served another, less noble, purpose: Christianity was used to "bind the slave to the will of the master in the name of Jesus Christ" (Earl, p. 38). Not surprisingly, then, for many the religion of the slaveowners became a symbol of the repression suffered by black Americans.

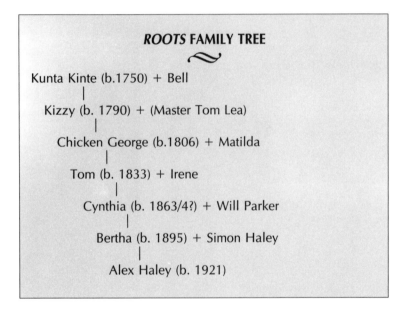

ROOTS FAMILY TREE

Kunta Kinte (b.1750) + Bell
|
Kizzy (b. 1790) + (Master Tom Lea)
|
Chicken George (b.1806) + Matilda
|
Tom (b. 1833) + Irene
|
Cynthia (b. 1863/4?) + Will Parker
|
Bertha (b. 1895) + Simon Haley
|
Alex Haley (b. 1921)

In the 1960s, a growing number of black Americans turned away from Christianity and embraced the religion of Islam. Founded in the 1930s, the organization of African American Muslims called the Nation of Islam experienced tremendous growth later under the influence of Malcolm X. Haley himself does not practice Islam, although in his newly discovered "hometown" of Juffure he is taken to the village mosque and prays with the other men. The book thus opens and closes with Haley's ancestral religion.

The Biography in Focus

The plot. In 1750 a boy is born in the village of Juffure, located four days upriver from the coast of the Gambia in West Africa. The infant is given the name Kunta Kinte. Kunta spends the first seventeen years of his life in Juffure, where he is surrounded by his parents, grandmother, three brothers and the extended family of the tribe. During his youth, he is taught African tribal customs and rituals as he receives an African education, which includes lessons in hunting and the Islamic religion.

One day when Kunta is seventeen, he goes downstream to chop wood to make a drum. Here he is captured by slave traders who put him on a ship headed for the American colonies. The male slaves are beaten, made to lay naked on wooden boards, and shackled together in pairs. Many die on the voyage from ill treatment and from dysentery. Kunta arrives in Annapolis, Maryland, in 1767, and is purchased by "Massa" John Waller, who owns a plantation in Spotsylvania County, Virginia. Kunta cannot reconcile himself to his fate and tries to run away several times. On his fourth attempt, he is caught by professional slave-hunters and is given the choice of punishment: castration or amputation of one of his feet. He chooses the latter. "Massa" John's brother, Dr. William Waller, is appalled by the inhumane action of his brother. He helps Kunta recover and then buys him, assigning him to tend the vegetable garden, a relatively easy job for the maimed man.

On Dr. Waller's plantation, Kunta Kinte meets and marries a slave woman named Bell and they have a daughter named Kizzy in 1790. Kizzy grows up hearing about her father's life and his African heritage. When she is sixteen, she helps a young male slave, with whom she is in love, run away. The Underground Railroad, a network of safe places where runaway slaves can rest as they flee northward, has been launched in earnest by then; Kizzy's young man has heard that certain white people will help him escape. Unfortunately he is caught and she admits to the crime of having drawn him an escape map. Dr. Waller punishes Kizzy by selling her on the slave market, separating the family forever.

Kizzy is bought by Tom Lea, a violent man who owns a small plantation in North Carolina. He rapes her and in 1806 she bears him a son named George. George grows up listening to his mother's stories of his grandfather, Kunta Kinte. Like his father/master, George enjoys chicken fighting and earns the nickname "Chicken George"; Tom Lea and his son develop a fairly close relationship over the years, and George accompanies him on his gambling junkets. In

Alex Haley on the lawn of his boyhood home in Henning, Tennessee.

1827 Chicken George marries Matilda, who bears him eight children. With the birth of each child, Chicken George gathers his family around the slave cabin and tells them the story of Kunta Kinte. Shortly after the birth of George and Matilda's third son in 1831, Master Lea learns of Nat Turner's Rebellion in Southampton County, Virginia, in which revolting slaves murdered 55 whites, and in his fury he rifles through the meager belongings of every one of his slaves, destroying what little they have in his search for concealed weapons. Shortly thereafter, Matilda and Chicken George decide to scrape and save to buy the freedom of the entire family.

When George and Matilda's fourth son, Tom, is apprenticed as a teenager to a blacksmith on another plantation, he comes into contact with news from the North. At Thanksgiving dinner, he tells his family about former slaves who had bought their freedom, and of the improved lives of free blacks in the North. In particular he tells them about Sojourner Truth and Frederick Douglass, blacks who gave public lectures about the evils of slavery, lectures attended by white people opposed to slavery. Chicken George tells Tom about his plan to buy the freedom of the family, and Tom agrees to help by saving all his earnings for the next fifteen years.

In 1856 Tom Lea goes bankrupt, having lost a bet on his chickens. To pay his debt to an English lord, Lea sends Chicken George to England with the victorious Englishman. Matilda and her children are meanwhile sold to the kindly "Massa" Murray, who owns a tobacco plantation in Alamance County, North Carolina. Tom, Matilda's and George's fourth son, becomes a blacksmith and in 1857 marries a half-Indian slave named Irene. Because white men patronize Tom's smithy, he frequently hears news about what is happening in the nation. The Civil War is approaching, and rumors of war abound. One day, Chicken George arrives back unexpectedly; he has just received his freedom and the family is reunited. However, the euphoria does not last long—the sheriff discovers that George is free and informs Murray of a North Carolina law that a free black can remain only sixty days in the state, or face re-enslavement. Everyone is unwilling for the only free member of their family to be re-enslaved, so Chicken George leaves once again.

In 1860, the Murray slaves hear that Lincoln has been elected president and, shortly thereafter, that North Carolina has seceded from the Union. On April 12, 1861, war breaks out between the North and South, and the slaves begin a long anxious period of waiting to see which side will emerge victorious. In 1863 they hear that Lincoln has signed the Emancipation Proclamation, freeing all the slaves in rebel territory, and they rejoice. Over the next months, however, it becomes obvious that the Proclamation will not have much effect upon their lives, and it is not until 1865, when the South surrenders, that they actually achieve liberation. The Murrays offer to partition the plantation and let their former slaves sharecrop. They accept the arrangement for a time. Chicken George again returns, bearing news that Henning, Tennessee, is a hospitable place, and the family moves there.

The family prospers in their new home, and Tom and Irene's good fortune is capped when their youngest daughter, Cynthia, marries a promising young lumber company owner. In 1895, Cynthia and Will have a daughter named Bertha, who grows up to marry Simon Haley in 1920. Alex Haley is born in 1921. The long tale of this child's roots ends with the death of his father, Simon.

OUT OF AFRICA

Haley's search for his roots was inspired by a visit to the British Museum in London, where he saw the famous Rosetta Stone, a mysterious ancient text from Africa. On the stone are three separate inscriptions: one in Greek, one in Egyptian hieroglyphics, and one in a cursive version of the hieroglyphics. Surmising that the three passages were translations of one another, linguists used the well-known Greek passage to crack the "code" of Egyptian hieroglyphics, which had previously been unknown.

Black autobiography. The autobiography has been a favored form of literary expression in African American culture; slave narratives of the nineteenth century—such as Harriet Jacobs's *Incidents in the Life of a Slave Girl* and Douglass's *Narrative of the Life of Frederick Douglass* (both covered in *Literature and Its Times*) helped establish this powerful literary tradition. *Roots*, though a fictionalized account, fits into this genre. The roots sought in the work are those of the writer, who in his effort to unearth his family's history also attempts to deepen his self-knowledge. In this last respect, the work achieves similarities with efforts of other minority groups during the 1960s and

1970s to discover themselves, to better establish their own identities through an examination of their heritage. It builds on an already well-established genre, the African American biography.

The trials of Kunta Kinte form the first part of *Roots,* just as the slave narrative marks the first epoch of black biography and autobiography. Meant to be a social document, and to convey the horrors of slavery to white Northerners insulated from seeing it firsthand, the classic slave narrative takes the moral high ground against slavery, appealing to the Christian goodness of the white readership and condemning the slaveowner for betraying the virtues he claims to possess.

A secondary movement in black writing, arising at the turn of the twentieth century, explores the contradictions of living in a society that had officially abolished slavery but remained virulently racist. Prime examples of this second generation of black autobiography include Richard Wright's **Black Boy** (1945; also covered in *Literature and Its Times*), and Chester Himes's *The Quality of Hurt* (1972) and *My Life of Absurdity* (1976).

The mid-1960s brought yet another wave of black autobiography, as black activists told the story of the civil rights movement and the more militant branches of black activism. Most influential among this generation of black autobiographies are James Baldwin's *Nobody Knows My Name* (1961) and **The Autobiography of Malcolm X** (1965; also covered in *Literature and Its Times*), both of which helped prompt other black Americans to write their own stories, as Haley did his.

Sources. According to Alex Haley, *Roots* was directly inspired by his family's oral history, which led him on a twelve-year search to uncover its details. Haley is quoted as saying, "To the best of my knowledge and my effort, every lineage statement within *Roots* is either from my African or American families' carefully preserved oral history, much of which I have been able conventionally to corroborate with documents" (*Roots,* p. 686). In a *New York Times* interview on September 26, 1976, Haley wanted to call his book a "faction," a term that has been defined as a literary social document resulting from intense research that presents facts in history through fictional dialogue.

Reception. Though critics found literary and historical flaws in *Roots,* they praised it as the "most important civil rights event since the 1965 march on Selma" (Bryfonski, p. 206). Some questioned Haley's accuracy; according to the historians

Mills and Mills, for example, "those same plantation records, wills, and census cited by Mr. Haley not only fail to document his story, but they contradict each and every pre-Civil War statement of Afro American lineage in *Roots*!" (Mills and Mills, p. 6). In an article in the *New York Times* (April 10, 1977), Haley conceded that *Roots* has dozens of errors; his purpose, though, was not to write a history but a work of fiction based upon factual events. Other critics faulted the limited treatment of Haley's more recent ancestors—113 of the book's 120 chapters deal with pre-Reconstruction events, and little attention is paid to the civil rights movement of the 1950s and 1960s. Nevertheless, *Roots* was roundly commended. A review in *Library Journal* asserted, "A brief review cannot do justice to the power of this book" (Samudio, p. 489). Haley received special citations from both the National Book Award and Pulitzer Prize committees for his work.

Roots was transformed into an acclaimed and widely seen twelve-hour television miniseries broadcast in 1977. This greatly enhanced the book's reputation and by the end of that year, 2 million copies had been sold. Its popularity among blacks was connected to a mutual concern at the time. As Haley explained, many of them were searching, as he had been, for a cultural history with which to identify.

For More Information

Aptheker, Herbert. *American Negro Slave Revolts.* New York: International, 1943.

Bruck, Peter, and Wolfgang Karrer, eds. *The Afro-American Novel since 1960.* Amsterdam: B. R. Gruner, 1982.

Bryfonski, Dedria, ed. *Contemporary Literary Criticism.* Vol. 10. Detroit: Gale Research, 1979.

Cashman, Sean Dennis. *African-Americans and the Quest for Civil Rights, 1900-1990.* New York: New York University Press, 1991.

Earl, Riggins R. *Dark Symbols, Obscure Signs: God, Self, and Community in the Slave Mind.* New York: Orbis, 1993.

Haley, Alex. *Roots.* New York: Doubleday, 1976.

Henige, David P. *The Chronology of Oral Tradition.* Oxford: Clarendon Press, 1974.

Mills, Gary B., and Elizabeth Shoun Mills. "*Roots* and the New 'Faction'." *Virginia Magazine* 89, no. 1 (January 1981): 1-26.

Rawley, James A. *The Transatlantic Slave Trade.* New York: W. W. Norton, 1981.

Samudio, Josephine, ed. *Book Review Digest.* Vol. 72. New York: H. W. Wilson, 1977.

Vollmer, Jurgen. *Black Genesis: African Roots.* New York: St. Martin's, 1980.

The Runner

by
Cynthia Voigt

Cynthia Voigt was born in 1942 in Boston, Massachusetts. A high-school teacher of English, Voigt began her writing career in 1981 and produced a string of ten bestselling, acclaimed young-adult novels within the next five years. Voigt insists upon the sophistication of younger reading audiences, refusing to sugarcoat difficult issues like loss, family conflict, death, and pain. *The Runner,* one of several books about the Tillerman family, takes on the issue of the Vietnam War from the perspective of a rebellious boy who makes the complicated choice to enlist in the army.

THE LITERARY WORK

A novel set in Crisfield, Maryland, from 1967 to 1969; published in 1985.

SYNOPSIS

An independent loner confronts family conflict, racial tension, and the Vietnam War.

Events in History at the Time the Novel Takes Place

The Vietnam War. United States military forces were officially involved in Vietnam from 1964 to 1972. The history of America's involvement with this country, however, reaches back to the close of World War II. Before the war, France counted Vietnam among its colonies. The situation changed, though, in 1945 at the war's end. Vietnam was proclaimed a republic, and France signed an accord with its president, Ho Chi Minh, while the Japanese occupied the greater Indochina area. After the war, America wanted France to join the North Atlantic Treaty Organization (NATO), an alliance for mutual defense against the Soviet Union and other communist nations. To get the French to join, America agreed to support them in their quest to reinstate themselves in Vietnam and the rest of In-

dochina. However, an ardent group of Vietnamese nationalists under Ho Chi Minh, who were supported by the Soviet Union, fought hard against the return of the French. In 1954 the French forces were dealt a sizeable blow at the Battle of Dien Bien Phu; thereafter, in an effort to contain the conflict, a cease-fire was arranged by an international committee in Switzerland. The regions of North and South Vietnam were created temporarily until an election could be held. America, however, decided that the danger of the communists' winning control of the whole country was too great a risk to take. The fear was that if South Vietnam fell to the communists, nearby countries would fall prey one by one to the same fate. The United States therefore lavished economic support on South Vietnam's leader, Ngo Dinh Diem, and signed a pact with members of the Southeast Asian Treaty Organization (SEATO) guaranteeing protection from aggressors. By 1954 France received enough financing from the United States to support 80 percent of its war effort. This same year the United States replaced the French presence in Vietnam.

In 1961 U.S. President John F. Kennedy sent advisors to South Vietnam to determine what further assistance was needed, and to teach Diem how to wage a successful war against the North Vietnamese. In late 1964 U.S. military involvement in Vietnam escalated when Kennedy's successor, Lyndon B. Johnson, initiated a bombing campaign against North Vietnam. By 1968, 40,000 American soldiers were dead and 250,000 wounded, with no end to the war in sight. (Vietnamese losses were several times this number.) By 1969 there were more than 550,000 U.S. troops in South Vietnam.

Efforts toward negotiated peace began in 1969, but U.S. military operations continued until 1972. In January 1973 a peace treaty was finally signed by South Vietnam, the United States, North Vietnam, and the National Liberation Front (the communist provisional revolutionary government in South Vietnam). The treaty provided for the withdrawal of U.S. forces. Fighting between South Vietnam and the communists continued, however, until the South Vietnamese government fell to the communists in May 1975.

Working-class war. Some 80 percent of the American soldiers who fought in Vietnam came from poor and working-class families. Bullet Tillerman's choice in *The Runner* conforms to a general cultural pattern: "America's most unpopular war was fought primarily by the nineteen-year-old children of waitresses, factory workers, truck drivers, secretaries, firefighters, carpenters, custodians, police officers, salespeople, clerks, mechanics, miners, and farmworkers" (Appy, pp. 6-7). As the child of a poor farmer in a rural community, Bullet's chances of serving in the Vietnam War were high; a disproportionate number of children from farming families served in the American forces in Southeast Asia in the 1960s. At the time of the Vietnam War, Selective Service, the process by which certain men were drafted into the armed forces, was heavily influenced by class: people enrolled in college—in most cases, the middle and upper classes—were exempt from military service on the grounds that they were training for professions vital to American interests. Also in the mid-1960s the selection criteria for serving in the armed forces changed dramatically. A program called "Project 100,000" sought to admit into the military many of the men who would previously have been rejected on physical or mental grounds. The result was that the Vietnam contingent was populated liberally with men who were mentally or physically unfit for service, or who came from America's poorest and most broken homes. The death rate of Project 100,000 men was twice that of the average American forces, probably because the 100,000 men were trained largely as combat soldiers (Appy, p. 33).

Protesting the draft. In part because of the high rate of casualties and brutality, and because of the prominence of televised reports of the battlefield, the Vietnam War sparked unparalleled protest at home. At the time of the war, U.S. law dictated that the Selective Service could draft all young men between the ages of eighteen and twenty-six. Some men avoided military service by remaining enrolled in universities, by claiming conscientious objection to the war, by getting married, or by claiming 4-F status (a disability exemption). Some men deliberately mutilated themselves, going so far as to chop off one or more fingers in order to avoid the draft. Most recruits, however, were assigned 1-A status, requiring them to report for active duty.

WHY DID THEY GO?

Historians speculate that many American men enlisted for military service during the Vietnam War because for America's lower classes jobs were scarce and prospects dim. A 1968 study of seventy-six white, working-class Vietnam veterans revealed the following reasons for enlisting:

Nothing else to do	14
Draft-motivated	13
To avoid trouble, police	11
To get away from home/family	9
No stated reason	9
To do duty like friends	8
To prove manliness, self	6
Sick of school, hassles	4
For the security of a job	2

(Appy, p. 48)

Around 1967 the antiwar forces were organized to such an extent that young men began en masse to refuse to register for the draft, or to reject military induction if called. Black heavyweight boxing champion Muhammed Ali, for

In the 1960s demonstrations against the war in Vietnam sometimes led to violent clashes between police and protesters, as shown in this photograph from the period.

one, refused to serve in what he described as a white man's war. Other young men flocked to Canada during this time to avoid being drafted into military service. One of the high school students in *The Runner* sees this option as the most attractive for him: "I'll be in Canada before they get a chance at me," Jackson proclaims (Voigt, *The Runner*, p. 31).

Chanting "We Won't Go!" draft opponents who had already registered with the Selective Service burned their draft cards to protest what they believed was an unjust war that America had no business fighting. In October 1967 "there were draft-card 'turn-ins' all over the country; in San Francisco alone, three hundred draft cards were returned to the government" (Zinn, p. 187). By 1970 peace rallies were drawing hundreds of thousands who opposed the war in Vietnam.

Women and antiwar protest. When Bullet, the main character in Voigt's *The Runner*, comes to tell his mother, Abigail, that he has signed up to go to Vietnam, she merely nods and tells him that she has been expecting him to do so. Abigail is so browbeaten by her domineering husband that she perhaps is not capable of doing what many other mothers did during the Vietnam War: protesting the draft. Middle-aged, middle-class mothers achieved a level of politi-

cal notoriety during the war. The nationwide Women Strike for Peace (WSP) movement was well in stride by the time the events in *The Runner* take place. These women, and the men who worked along with them, realized that their middle-class white sons had many advantages over rural and black young men, who often did not know what their options were in relation to the draft or where to seek help. The WSP set up counseling centers in poor communities to show men how to pose a legal challenge to draft laws. They also came to the aid of those who resisted the draft, visiting them in prison, writing them letters, and encouraging them in their stance. In 1967 WSP marched on the White House under the slogan "Not My Son, Not Your Son, Not Their Sons." They kept up strident protest for the duration of the war and, when American forces finally pulled out of Vietnam, WSP continued to agitate for amnesty for draft-dodgers, deserters, and American men in exile in Canada.

Counterculture and the protest generation. The term "counterculture" refers broadly to a social movement of the 1960s that was generally composed of young, white, middle-class Americans who rejected "traditional" American values. Members of the movement set themselves against the standards of their parents, choosing to in-

THREE VOLATILE YEARS IN AMERICA

1967

- U.S. planes drop bombs on Hanoi, capital of North Vietnam; Vietnam War heats up

- Almost half a million American soldiers stationed in Vietnam

- Martin Luther King Jr. leads anti-Vietnam War protest at the United Nations building in New York City

- Summer of racial violence erupts across the United States

- Muhammed Ali, who refuses to fight in Vietnam, is stripped of his heavyweight boxing title

- Thousands turn in or burn their draft cards at nationwide "ceremonies"

1968

- January: In the "Tet offensive," North Vietnamese troops attack throughout South Vietnam and take the U.S. Embassy in Saigon

- Civil rights bill signed into law in the United States

- Supreme Court orders all U.S. public schools to make immediate desegregation plans

- April 4: Assassination of Martin Luther King, Jr.

- June 6: Robert Kennedy dies from an assassin's bullet

- Richard Nixon promises to end the Vietnam War and is elected president

- Feminists storm the stage at the Miss America pageant

1969

- First American troops withdraw from Vietnam

- Commission on Civil Rights castigates the Nixon administration for poorly planned desegregation policy

- November: "March against Death" in Washington, D.C., protests the Vietnam War for thirty-eight hours

dulge in drugs and sex to an unprecedented degree; theirs was the "hippie" culture that embraced rock-and-roll, the birth-control pill, and environmental activism. While some historians insist that this was a fundamentally apolitical movement that should not be associated with the antiwar movement and related political protests that swept the nation, others note that the counterculture youth were making a political statement by rejecting the values of their parents, and that some of them were politically active. Whether or not they were part of the rebellious counterculture, many young people publicly protested the Cold War, the Vietnam War, and

the ongoing gender and racial discrimination, including the segregation of blacks and whites in schools (an issue in *The Runner*).

To certain factions of the counterculture, the government seemed an oppressive and sometimes sinister authority. In *The Runner*, Tommy, who has just been kicked out of his position as editor of the school paper by the school principal, suggests that his treatment is indicative of a larger conspiracy to silence and control America's youth. He speaks of closely guarded records and files that contain secret information on every student; he proposes violent solutions; and, as Bullet sees it, Tommy switches crusades in the blink of an eye, turning from the Vietnam War to America's own battle for racial and civil rights. For all his talk of conspiracy and rebellion, Tommy fails to see what Bullet himself can see—that getting even is not the same as rectifying what has gone wrong.

The Novel in Focus

The plot. Samuel "Bullet" Tillerman is a high school senior who lives near the eastern shoreline on a farm in Crisfield, Maryland, with his tyrannical father and his mother, Abigail. The father has already driven off Bullet's elder brother and sister, Johnny and Liza, and has completely alienated Bullet, but Abigail endures her husband's bullying with a silent acquiescence. Although her husband will not allow her to have a driver's license, she escapes temporarily from time to time in a leaky boat that her son Johnny left behind. Bullet's main complaint against his father is that the "old man" tries to "box" him in (*The Runner,* p. 3). The boy copes by running; when the book opens, he is on his nightly ten-mile cross-country course.

On his way home from his run, Bullet thinks about how to respond to his father's latest despotic demand: that he cut his long hair because it makes him look like a girl. The boy fantasizes about the bizarre hairstyles he might develop but then settles at last on the idea of shaving his head. When he returns from his run, he and his mother share a charged moment—she knows he is about to do something, but is simply too resigned to the constant tension in her family to even ask what.

The next day at school, Bullet joins some friends for lunch. They are discussing two hot topics of the day—women's liberation and the Vietnam War. The liberal aphorisms they trade back and forth irritate Bullet, who knows that for all their political posturing, they are simply afraid of the war. He knows what fear is and how to deal with it. He has been fighting all of his life—with his brother, his father, and with the kids who want to humiliate him further because he failed a grade.

Bullet is the school's cross-country star; people are even talking about his trying out for the Olympic team one day. At track practice that afternoon, Bullet meets Tamer Shipp, a black student trying out for the team as a cross-country runner. Bullet acts cold toward him, which Tamer reads as racism: "I read you, Whitey," he says; what he doesn't realize is that Bullet dis-

likes almost everyone, regardless of race (*The Runner,* p. 42). Just the same, Bullet is full of platitudes about what "colored" people are and are not like, lumping them all into a group, sharing (as it turns out) many of the racist assumptions of his classmates.

When Bullet returns home at the end of the day with no hair whatsoever, his father refuses to lay eyes upon him, and Bullet is no longer allowed to join his parents for dinner. This moment of rejection is blunted, as usual, by the company of Patrice, a French crab-fisherman for whom Bullet works. Patrice treats the boy like a son. The Frenchman has named his boat Fraternité, a word meaning "Brotherhood," which formed part of the slogan of the eighteenth-century French revolutionaries: *Liberté, Egalité, Fraternité* (Liberty, Equality, Brotherhood). Though a rebel himself, Bullet shares little else with the French revolutionaries; his form of protest is singular, not community-based.

One day at school Bullet sits with some other boys who have rejected Tamer Shipp from the football team on the sole grounds that he is black. The Vietnam War is raging and the boys talk about wanting to avoid getting drafted. Later five masked white boys beat Shipp badly because he entered the student lounge, which, by tacit agreement, is for whites only. The entire school grows electric with tension as white students and black students react to the heightened racial hostility. One lunch period when a white student trips Shipp in the cafeteria, Bullet intervenes to stop an armed fight. The white boy has a switchblade, so things might otherwise have gotten very ugly.

Just the same, Bullet is not a racially tolerant person. He flatly refuses to help Shipp learn how to be a better cross-country runner: Shipp is "colored" and Bullet doesn't "mix" (*The Runner,* p. 119). The coach therefore drops Bullet from the team, but Bullet hardly cares. He runs not because he is on a team, but because his body is built for running. Now, because he no longer has to practice, he has more time to spend with Patrice, who has begun an arduous task—restoring an abandoned boat that has washed ashore.

Frank Verricker, the sailor with whom Bullet's sister, Liza, ran off years before, appears at Bullet's high school one afternoon. He is driving a sportscar and is with a woman who is not Bullet's sister. The three of them drive to a nearby bar. According to Verricker, he and Liza never got married—at her insistence—although they are about to have their second child. He himself comes and goes as he pleases, and she doesn't seem to mind. Bullet, who greatly misses his sister, hates hearing this information.

One day, while hunting in the woods, Bullet accidentally shoots Liza's dog. The accident shocks Bullet into facing his grief (about Liza) and responsibility (for the death of her dog). He begins to empathize with others, realizing how alike he and his father are, how his mother is trapped in a loveless marriage, and how the standoffs between Bullet and his father increase her pain.

Visiting Patrice the next day, Bullet learns that when the Frenchman was a boy he was a runner—a courier—for the French Resistance. He was captured by the Germans, who tortured him by cutting off several of his fingers. Under torture, he revealed the whereabouts of his comrades, and the Germans planned to ambush them. Patrice thought he could reach his friends in time to warn them of the ambush, but he did not arrive in time, and many men died. The Resistance fighters understood but sent him away. Patrice points out that his child's body and its pain had forced him to make a compromise that hurt others; Bullet, he feels, is like him in this respect, except that it is his rebellious spirit that betrays him into hurting others. Then, when Bullet tells him why he was kicked off the track team, Patrice shares the shocking news that he himself is one-eighth black. Confused and ashamed, Bullet reports for track practice the next day, after offering to help Tamer Shipp.

Bullet's friend Tommy, who is the editor of the school paper, writes an editorial about the incident in which Tamer Shipp was beaten by white students. The faculty considers the editorial inflammatory and Tommy is relieved of his duties. Bullet is absolutely disgusted by the heavy-handed tactics of the school principal, who sees to it that Tommy is fired.

At the state track championship Bullet meets his first real competition, a runner from Baltimore. Running the race of his life on the toughest course he has ever traversed, Bullet wins. He looks into the crowd and spots his mother just getting up to leave. Bullet marvels at her coming all this way by bus and boat just to watch his race, appreciating her support for him. On the third day of the track meet, Bullet faces a dilemma. The track coach wants him to participate in the relay race with Tamer and two other black runners so that the team can be guaranteed of state ranking, but that would mean running on a track, something he won't do. After some persuading from Tamer, Bullet decides to

acquiesce if Tamer promises to stay out of Vietnam. Tamer consents to the condition.

Bullet himself does not want to be boxed into fighting the war at someone else's bidding, and so he decides to take matters into his own hands. On March 21, 1968, when he turns eighteen, Bullet buys Patrice's refurbished boat for his mother, who until now has had to sail to town in the leaky old boat. He then proceeds to enlist in the army. Nine months later, the young man's mother receives a phone call. Her son Samuel Tillerman has been killed in action.

High school protest. The high school students in *The Runner* are intimately involved in protest against the war, sexism, and racism. In fact, during the late 1960s America's high schools were the site of legal controversy regarding the rights of students to free speech. The Supreme Court was debating the rights of high school students to protest the war and racial inequality on school property and during school time. The case of *Tinker vs. Des Moines* pitted students who wore black arm bands to school in protest of the war against high school officials who warned them that public school was not an appropriate forum to express such political beliefs. The Supreme Court weighed the students' right to free speech against the potential for disruption of normal school activities and decided in favor of the students, ruling that "School officials do not possess absolute authority over their students" (Small and Hoover, p. 229). Another case, *Zucker vs. Panitz* in New York State, recalls the episode in *The Runner* in which the antiwar editor of the school's newspaper is ousted from his job by a principal who disagrees with his writing an editorial about racial intolerance. In *Zucker,* a high school principal refused to run an ad in the student newspaper that protested the war. Again the Court ruled in favor of the students:

> This lawsuit arises at a time when many in the educational community oppose the tactics of the young in securing a political voice. It would be both incongruous and dangerous for this court to hold that students who wish to express their views on matters intimately related to them . . . may be precluded from doing so by that same adult community.
> (Small and Hoover, p. 230)

Lest it be thought, however, that it was easy for teachers during this time of protest, it should be mentioned that those who voiced strong opinions one way or another, on the war or other contentious issues, faced being fired. The courts were concerned that students not be unduly influenced by their teachers on matters that did not strictly have to do with the curriculum. In *The Runner,* a student teacher is extremely careful not to come right out and make judgmental statements about controversial issues—he encourages the students to think things through for themselves.

Sources. *The Runner* is the fourth book in the Tillerman family saga. The other stories deal with the family of Dicey, who appears in *The Runner* as Liza's infant daughter. Voigt explains that she knew right from the beginning of the series that she would write about the uncle who was lost in Vietnam. Like other books about the Tillermans, *The Runner* deals with high school students, a population Voigt herself has taught. The novel is also set along Maryland's eastern shore, near where the author once lived. Finally, Voigt, who was in her mid- to late twenties in the years the novel takes place, observed firsthand the issues it raises.

Events in History at the Time the Novel Was Written

The Vietnam Veterans Memorial. There were differences between veterans of the Vietnam War and those of the earlier conflict from their parent's era, World War II. One difference concerns age, with the average for soldiers in World War II being 26 years in contrast to 19.2 years for American soldiers in Vietnam. Another difference lies in how veterans were received after the end of the increasingly unpopular Vietnam War. Research indicates that they did not feel as warm a welcome home as had veterans of earlier wars, particularly from people their own age. In fact, according to the research, the public in general felt the veterans deserved the country's respect despite having been part of a war that was unsuccessful. Over the years this public sympathy for the veterans increased, as reflected in the 1982 dedication of a Vietnam veterans war memorial in Washington, D.C.

Before a crowd of 250,000, the Vietnam Veterans Memorial was officially dedicated on November 13, 1982, on a site granted by Congress in the vicinity of the Washington Monument. A glossy black wall in the shape of a *V,* engraved with the names of the 57,939 American men and women declared killed or missing in the Vietnam War, the memorial was designed by a female architect, Maya Yang Lin. It came under hostile criticism by those who felt that it was too bleak or that it seemed critical of the American war ef-

Maya Lin at the Vietnam Veterans Memorial, which she designed.

fort in Vietnam—they called it a "black ditch" (MacPherson, p. 606). The overall reaction, however, seems to be massively in favor of the wall; families of the dead as well as veterans of the war have flooded the monument from the moment of its unveiling. In 1984, the year in which *The Runner* was published, a bronze sculpture of three soldiers was added to the memorial, to honor those who fought in and lived through the Vietnam War.

Reviews. Many reviewers dwelled on whether or not Bullet is a likeable character. Bullet "is so thoroughly bitter, so sure of himself, so competent and mature, that he is almost a bore," wrote a reviewer in *School Library Journal.* "Bullet's ready acceptance of Vietnam when he has rejected so many other things is not clear" said another (Unsworth in Mooney, p. 1643). More substantive criticism centered on Voigt's treatment of the race issue: "[T]he portrayal of Black characters is simple and one dimensional," complained a reviewer in *Interracial Books for Children Bulletin* (Goodwin in Senick, p. 237). At the same time, however, *The Runner* was widely praised for making readers care about a character like Bullet, who is cold and aloof. "[Voigt] breaks all the old conventional rules of the adolescent novel, and forces us to follow her in the investigation of this strange, remote, inaccessible young man in his loneliness and vulnerability," wrote a reviewer in *The Junior Bookshelf* (Crouch in Senick, p. 237).

For More Information

Appy, Christian G. *Working-Class War: American Combat Soldiers and Vietnam.* Chapel Hill: University of North Carolina Press, 1993.

Glazer, Nathan. *Remembering the Answers: Essays on the American Student Revolt.* New York: Basic Books, 1970.

MacPherson, Myra. *Long Time Passing: Vietnam and the Haunted Generation.* Garden City, N.Y.: Doubleday, 1984.

Mooney, Martha T., ed. *Book Review Digest.* Vol. 81. New York: H. W. Wilson, 1986.

Senick, Gerard J., ed. *Children's Literature Review.* Vol. 13. Detroit: Gale Research, 1987.

Small, Melvin, and William Hoover, eds. *Give Peace a Chance: Exploring the Vietnam Antiwar Movement.* Syracuse, N.Y.: Syracuse University Press, 1990.

Voigt, Cynthia. *The Runner.* 1985. Reprint. New York: Scholastic, 1994.

Zinn, Howard. *The Twentieth Century: A People's History.* New York: Harper & Row, 1984.

Shoeless Joe

by
W. P. Kinsella

William P. Kinsella grew up in western Canada, later moving to Iowa to earn a master's degree in fine arts. He also grew into an avid baseball fan as an adult. Once married and settled in rural Alberta, Canada, he and his wife began touring America's major league baseball parks every season. In 1980, by then an established writer of short fiction, Kinsella published a story, "Shoeless Joe Comes to Iowa," about the famous Chicago White Sox player of the 1920s. Two years later, this story became the first chapter in a full-length novel about the centrality of baseball to the American way of life.

Events in History at the Time of the Novel

The business of baseball. "Shoeless Joe" Jackson was a Chicago White Sox outfielder who was accused, along with seven other players, of conspiring to deliberately lose the 1919 World Series against the Cincinnati Reds. The conspiracy was cooked up by Sox first baseman Chick Gandil, who may have been motivated by revenge against Sox owner Charles Comiskey, a notorious cheapskate who paid his players very little—he was so cheap, in fact, that he refused even to pay the laundry bill for his team's uniforms. Comiskey's team renamed themselves the "Black Sox" in recognition of their filthy uniforms—a name that would later stick to the players who agreed to take money in exchange for losing to the Reds.

All notions of sportsmanship aside, in the context of 1920s baseball history, "throwing" (or deliberately losing) the World Series might have seemed like a sound business decision. It made economic sense. Baseball had begun as an amateur sport; by the 1860s a loose association of teams governed by the players oversaw schedules and the general management of the game. But the popularity of the sport and its need for a stable financial base soon attracted savvy business managers, who, in March 1871, organized a National League of Professional Baseball Players. This league, however, dwindled in popularity in part because of economic depression and in part because gamblers could buy off players to lose games, a shadow that was to haunt the game of baseball for a good many years.

In 1876 the National League of Professional Baseball Clubs was formed, with teams in the cities of Boston, Louisville, St. Louis, Hartford, Philadelphia, Cincinnati, New York, and Chicago. The earlier player-operated association had produced some stars who now fetched comparatively high salaries for the time—up to $2,000 a year. The powerful owners of National League teams would have none of that; they drew up binding contracts that reduced salaries to as little as $800 a year and restricted player movement. The five best players on any team were obligated to remain on the team with which they had signed contracts and could not be traded; this was known as the reserve clause and was not removed from baseball's rule books until 1975.

Even though their employment situation was constricting, most players knew that even poorly paid work was still work, something that was hard to come by at the time. By the end of the 1880s, players were locked into salary schedules that still paid the best of them only $2,500 a year. In 1890, John Montgomery Ward, a player with the New York Giants and a recent graduate of Columbia Law School, began to challenge the reserve clause, likening it to the fugitive slave law: "The reserve clause," he wrote, denied the ballplayer "a harbor or a livelihood, and carried him back, bound and shackled, to the club from which he attempted to escape" (Ward in Ward and Burns, p. 39). The player rebellion that he inspired achieved only minor changes; the reserve clause and salary restrictions remained intact.

The stranglehold on players was, if anything, tightened at the turn of the century, when another eight-club league, the American League, emerged. The two leagues formally agreed to stage a World Series each year beginning in 1903. Bickering between the leagues prevented a 1904 World Series but it resumed the next year. Club owners loved the idea of the World Series, recognizing its lucrative potential; the players, on the other hand, were asked to play not for a share in the money, but mostly for pride. While the salaries of American entertainers grew astronomically, especially during and after World War I, baseball players were paid as sportsmen rather than as entertainers. Consequently the temptation was strong to supplement the meager salaries in whatever way possible—and the 1919 Chicago White Sox did just that.

The World Series scandal of 1919. At first, the 1919 match between the Chicago White Sox and the Cincinnati Reds appeared easy to predict. The Sox were heavily favored (5-1) against the Reds. As noted earlier, the scandal seems traceable to the actions of Chick Gandil, who apparently approached a small-time gambler acquaintance of his with the information that the Series could be bought—at the right price. While it remains uncertain who actually came up with the $100,000 that Gandil demanded, most likely the money came primarily from a big-time New York gambler by the name of Arnold Rothstein. The first of the nine games in the series started out with a 9-1 loss for Chicago, and certain sportswriters began to wonder whether the ugly rumors that had been circulating about a fix weren't true after all. The second game also ended in Cincinnati's favor, 4-2. Chicago won game three 4-0, perhaps its way of reminding the gamblers who

---

THE CONFESSION

In 1920, Jackson confessed to a grand jury that he had helped fix the 1919 World Series. The following comes from the transcript of his conversation with Assistant State Attorney Harley Replogle:

> Replogle: Did anybody pay you any money to help throw that series in favor of Cincinnati?
>
> Jackson: They did.
>
> Replogle: How much did they pay?
>
> Jackson: They promised me $20,000, and paid me five. . . .
>
> Replogle: Does [Mrs. Jackson] know that you got $5,000 for helping throw these games?
>
> Jackson: She did that night, yes. . . .
>
> Replogle: What did she say about it?
>
> Jackson: She said she thought it was an awful thing to do. . . . She felt awful about it, cried about it a while
>
> (Ward and Burns, p. 143)

Jackson served no time for his part in the scandal—in fact, no one did since there was no law in Illinois against throwing a game. He also escaped being convicted of fraud because the transcript of his testimony disappeared into thin air and could not be produced in court.

---

were backing the fix that payment was due or the series would not turn out as planned; at this point, it appeared that the promised payment had not been forthcoming or had been much less than originally stated. Game four was won by Cincinnati; Hugh Fullerton, a sportswriter, noted then that "there is more ugly talk and more suspicion among the fans than there ever has been in any World's Series. The rumors of crookedness, of fixed games and plots, are thick" (Fullerton in Ward and Burns, p. 139). The Sox also lost game five, at which point the crooked Chicago players, who had seen next to nothing of the money they had been promised, decided to give up on the idea of throwing the series. They won the next two games, bringing the series score to 4-3. Then Rothstein in New York supposedly sent a thug to threaten Chicago pitcher Lefty Williams, promising violence against him and his family if Cincinnati did not win the next game. Williams was scared enough to accede to the thug's wishes—the game was to all intents and purposes lost in the first inning, when the terrified pitcher gave up three runs. Since the series score was now 5-3 in favor of Cincinnati, a ninth game was unnecessary. The Chicago White Sox had thrown the series, and the Cincinnati Reds had won.

Fallout. "Say it ain't so, Joe"—these are the famous words that characterize the nation's disappointment when the fact that the Chicago team had thrown the series finally became public knowledge. The investigation into the 1919 World Series occurred the next season, when the White Sox were playing the Cleveland Indians for the American League title. Some of the Chicago White Sox players, who were already wracked with guilt about their role in Chicago's loss to Cincinnati, came clean shortly after their names were published as being suspected of conspiracy in the 1919 World Series. Shoeless Joe Jackson himself had felt so terrible that following the series he had sent a letter to Comiskey, confessing to what had happened and asking his advice about what to do with the $5,000 that he had "earned" from the gambling consortium. Comiskey, who did not want to deal with the besmirching of baseball, or the besmirched reputation of his own club, ignored Jackson. The 1920 baseball season opened and proceeded without incident until September, when a grand jury summoned the Chicago Sox players to testify.

Along with other teammates, Jackson confessed to a grand jury; he became one of the first to talk on September 27. The next day Jackson would deny his confession. None of the seven players involved in the scandal went to jail for their part in the plot, but they were all banished from baseball for life by outraged baseball commissioner Kenesaw Mountain Landis. The conservative Landis held fast to the belief that baseball represented everything that was decent,

Arnold Rothstein, the New York City gambler who probably financed the fixing of the 1919 World Series.

moral, and upright about the American way of life. Men who had thrown a baseball game tore at the fabric of American society; in his view Landis had no choice but to turn them out of the game forever. Shoeless Joe Jackson went on to play ball for small teams in the South under an assumed name, but soon grew tired and quit the sport for good.

Players' rights. The economic abuses suffered by players in baseball's early days improved vastly over the years; by the 1970s, baseball players had their own union and negotiated their own individual contracts through agents, just like other entertainers did. In 1973, a few players decided to play the year without a contract and then to declare themselves free agents. The issue went to the courts and the 1976 season finally saw changes in the reserve clause. Some players then became free to play for any team, and salaries grew proportionate to an agent's ability to barter on his client's behalf. George Brett, the most valuable player in the American League in 1980, earned $140,000 for that year. His counterpart in the National League, Mike Schmidt, obviously had a better agent—he earned $560,000 that same year. Reggie Jackson, who had come into the major leagues in 1969 at an annual salary of $20,000, was able to negotiate a long-term contract for 1977-82, under the conditions of which he would receive $512,000 each year. On the other hand, Willie Stargell, the National League's most valuable player for 1979, never signed a contract for more than $100,000 a year—the same salary supposedly paid Babe Ruth in 1927.

Changes in baseball. The sport of baseball had changed along with the status and salaries of its players. By the early 1980s, speed had reentered the sport as equal in value to power hitting. The base-stealing wizardry of Maury Wills and Curt Flood brought a new dimension to a game long enamored of big sluggers at bat. Pitchers were no longer required to throw a full nine innings, with "relief pitchers" more often than not replacing tired starters and finishing the game. This change made pitching consistently stronger. To balance this new pitching power and give aid to the batters, major league rules redefined the strike zone (the physical area through which the pitched ball must pass in order to make the pitch a strike, rather than a ball), making it smaller and lower. Shoulder-high pitches that had once been strikes now were balls.

The tenor of the times. *Shoeless Joe* is set in a generation that contended with material as well as spiritual difficulties. Economically the United States endured a recession that resulted in a climbing unemployment rate throughout the 1970s, culminating at 10.8 percent in 1982. By then the American economy had sunk to levels not seen since the Great Depression of the 1930s. Some 12 million Americans were out of a job by 1982, which helps explain Ray Kinsella's inability to find work as an insurance salesman in the novel. The economic malaise was compounded by a nagging disillusionment left over from the debacles of the 1970s. Early in the decade, the United States pulled out of the Vietnam War and admitted large-scale military defeat for the first time in its history. There was internal cause for despair too, when Richard Nixon became the first U.S. president to resign from office. His resignation was a result of the Watergate scandal, which involved a burglary of the Democratic National Headquarters and a subsequent coverup at the highest government levels. Americans sometimes asked themselves if the nation's preeminence as a world power was in decline, and if its moral fiber was unredeemably tarnished. "An unclarified sense of defeat and moral disaffection troubled many. Between Vietnam and Watergate the most cynical of Americans lost faith in the in-

tegrity and judgment of the national leadership" (Gordon and Gordon, p. 473).

There was, however, a hopeful dimension in society too. The 1960s had been a decade in which rebels challenged the materialistic values and conformity of mainstream America. This decade had also witnessed the launching of President Lyndon Johnson's "Great Society" program, which helped usher in progressive legislation such as the Civil Rights Bill of 1964 and the War on Poverty. There was, it seemed, a desire in America to fulfill the nation's basic ideals of equality, justice, and a fair share of America's riches for all. By the 1970s this desire had found its way into mainstream American thought.

A PRESENT FOR J. D. SALINGER

Socked away in my suitcase lies a baseball—but a very special baseball. I can only imagine what it will mean to a dedicated fan of the game like J. D. Salinger, to have someone turn up on his doorstep . . . and present him with a baseball, shiny and fragrant as new, but with a signature and construction that labels it as being from the 1920s.

"'This is a home-run ball hit by Shoeless Joe Jackson,' I'll tell him. . . .

"What I won't mention, right away, is that the ball was hit over the left-field fence of *my* stadium, clubbed by Shoeless Joe off a ghostly relief pitcher during an extra-inning game. (*Shoeless Joe*, pp. 46-7)

During the 1970s, the United States as a whole also seemed better able to own up to its past prejudices and foibles. There was a "new candor" that enabled the American public to "confront genuine social issues," and so revisiting the 1919 baseball scandal in the form of a novel like *Shoeless Joe* did not seem farfetched (Gordon and Gordon, p. 475). In the end, the novel reaffirms American ideals, long connected to the game, and the possibility of realizing them despite past errors—an attitude very much in keeping with the mood of the 1970s.

The Novel in Focus

The plot. Ray Kinsella, an uninspired insurance salesman with a college degree in a field in which he can find no work, leases some land in Iowa from an ex-baseball player, Eddie Scissons, and becomes a farmer. Ray turns out to be not very good at this career—he spends more time fantasizing about baseball than doing any farming. With his wife Annie's encouragement, Ray lives out a lifelong fantasy; responding to a mysterious announcer's voice that only he can hear, which tells him "If you build it, he will come," he converts a corner of his cornfield into a beautifully manicured baseball diamond in the hopes of luring long-dead baseball great Shoeless Joe Jackson to his magical field (Kinsella, *Shoeless Joe*, p. 3). Gradually, as he adds to it area by area, Ray's ball park is visited by some of the most famous ballplayers of the past, many of them former members of the infamous Chicago White Sox who fixed the World Series of 1919.

LITERARY HEROES AND THEIR GENERATIONS

In the 1950s J. D. Salinger had created a character, Holden Caulfield of **Catcher in the Rye** (also covered in *Literature and Its Times*), who dropped out of mainstream society for a time to do his own thing. Caulfield felt alienated from the mainstream, as did many real-life rebels who dropped out to find themselves in the 1960s. In fact, novels of the era portrayed heroes who were victims of mainstream society and fled it to escape this victimization. Ken Kesey's **One Flew Over the Cuckoo's Nest** (also covered in *Literature and Its Times*), shows such a victim of mental hospitals; Joseph Heller's **Catch-22** (also covered in *Literature and Its Times*), features a victim of military bureaucracy. Set in the 1970s, *Shoeless Joe* features a different kind of hero. Ray Kinsella progresses beyond dropping out of society to interacting with it in a way that aims to rekindle some long-dormant ideals in himself as well as in other Americans.

One day, Ray hears the announcer once again; this time, the command is "Ease his pain" (*Shoeless Joe*, p. 31). Ray knows instantly what the voice means—he is to find and help the famous American writer and recluse, J. D. Salinger. Easing Salinger's pain, Ray feels, means to take Salinger to a baseball game, something that Salinger has not done for years, which pains the author of *Catcher in the Rye,* at least according to an article that Ray has read. In the article, an interview, Salinger claims that his childhood dream

was to play at the Polo Grounds, home of the New York Giants, which was torn down in 1964, some years after the Giants moved to San Francisco. To further strengthen the bond that Ray feels stretches across America between them is the fact that one of Salinger's stories features a man by the name of Ray Kinsella, and yet another stars a man named Richard Kinsella, the name of Ray's long-lost twin brother. So off he goes to New Hampshire, from where he kidnaps Salinger and drives him to Boston's Fenway Park to see a game.

Despite initial reservations, Salinger—known now to Ray as "Jerry"—agrees to accompany his former captor on a mission to "go the distance," as they both hear the announcer's voice tell them. For some mystical reason, they both understand that going the distance means heading off to Cooperstown's Baseball Hall of Fame and then to Minnesota in search of "Moonlight" Graham, who had the shortest baseball career in history—one inning. In Graham's hometown, the questions that the two of them ask about the former ballplayer spur a kind of Graham renaissance, with folks staying up all night to trade memories of the man who became a pillar of their community. When Jerry and Ray leave the place, they take Graham with them—like all former ballplayers in the novel, Graham is written of as if still alive—and head off in search of the "oldest living Chicago Cub"—Eddie Scissons, from whom Ray leased his Iowa farm, and who lives in Iowa City.

The four men return to the farm, where the next day Ray makes the horrid discovery that Eddie Scissons has reluctantly sold the farm; the men to whom he has sold it know that Eddie in fact never played baseball and use it against him. But Ray fights back and, aided by Annie and his identical twin, Richard, he wins the right from creditors to keep the farm and the ballpark. Meanwhile, on Ray's baseball diamond, the Chicago White Sox of 1919, along with Ray's dad, who once played semipro ball and was the biggest Chicago White Sox fan in the country, are playing ball just like in the good old days. The novel ends as J. D. Salinger himself is invited to pal around with the ghostly players, to walk through the door in the right field wall through which the players of the past disappear at the end of every game. No one knows what lies behind that door, but Salinger is willing to find out, in the hopes of finding his own dream of playing ball at the Polo Grounds.

riety of spoofs in popular magazines, and one enterprising journalist even attempted to sell a fake interview with the author to *People* magazine. Salinger sued. Kinsella's own work went without any comment from Salinger.

Sources. Kinsella, an ardent baseball fan—many of his short story collections and several of his novels are devoted to the game—fills his novel with characters drawn from real-life participants in the Chicago White Sox scandal of 1919. These include Chick Gandil, Happy Felsch, Buck Weaver, Swede Risberg, Fred McMullin, Eddie Cicotte, Lefty Williams, and "Shoeless" Joseph Jefferson Jackson, perhaps the greatest baseball hitter of all time. Kinsella's development of Shoeless Joe's character in the novel fits with the many contemporary descriptions of the man. Illiterate and feisty but ultimately conscientious, "Shoeless Joe" got his nickname for once playing outfield in his stocking feet because his new shoes pinched.

In his novel, Kinsella often refers to Jackson's famous bat, Black Betsy, which leaves a "darkish bruise" on a ball that Jackson hits out of Ray's ballpark (*Shoeless Joe,* p. 47). The bruise was the result of the unique treatment Jackson gave his legendary bat—he coated it with tobacco spit.

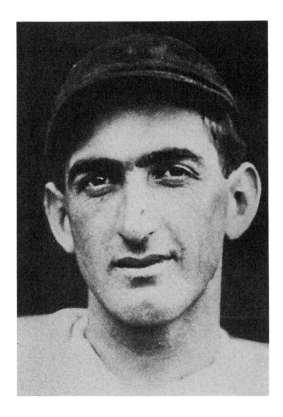

Shoeless Joe Jackson

J. D. Salinger. Kinsella's choice of J. D. Salinger as the object of baseball's redemptive powers is not as strange as it might seem at first. In a novel about dead baseball players who are actually not quite dead yet, and one in which life and death become blurred whenever the subject of baseball is brought up, it makes perfect sense to introduce the reclusive New Hampshire author, who has been described as "invisible, as good as dead, and yet for many . . . still [holding] an active mythic force" (Hamilton, p. 4). Salinger published his most famous work, *Catcher in the Rye,* in 1951; the protagonist of the book, the alienated teenager Holden Caulfield, became an American cultural icon. Before that, Salinger had written a number of magazine stories and articles, one of which openly stated that he was fond of baseball. *Catcher in the Rye* was controversial, even banned in some places for its frank depiction of juvenile sexuality. The novel aroused much discussion in literary circles, and made Salinger one of America's best-loved writers, though he refused steadfastly to take part in any debate about his work. Salinger was indeed as reclusive as his fictional counterpart in *Shoeless Joe.* Other authors have played with the mystique of Salinger's hermit genius; there have been a va-

---

THE SLUGGER

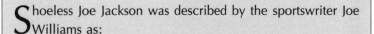

Shoeless Joe Jackson was described by the sportswriter Joe Williams as:

"[P]ure country, a wide-eyed, gullible yokel. It would not have surprised me in those days to learn he had made a down payment on the Brooklyn Bridge. . . . He was a drinker and a heavy one. He carried his own tonic: triple-distilled corn. And on occasions he carried a parrot, a multi-colored pest whose vocabulary was limited to screeching 'You're out!'" (Williams in Ward and Burns, p. 134).

Reviews. W. P. Kinsella was widely recognized in Canada and elsewhere for his short stories before "Shoeless Joe Jackson Comes to Iowa" grew into the novel *Shoeless Joe.* While the critics' reviews bore some mixed reactions, the novel was a bestseller. In the *Christian Science Monitor,* Maggie Lewis lavished praise on the novel for being such a pleasurable read:

[Kinsella] does wonders in the book: The visual fantasies are so rich that whether you believe them or not, you can't help imagining them. . . . [Kinsella] has a rare talent for conveying pure joy. He waxes corny and nostalgic, but it doesn't matter, because by then the thrill of seeing all the old baseball stars is yours, too.

(Lewis in Mooney, p. 732)

William Plummer in *Newsweek* wrote that while the "wonderfully hokey" novel does have its flaws—"the language sometimes melts in the hand rather than the heart, the subplots are a hasty pudding, the Salinger of the book is not smart or quirky enough"—such criticisms ultimately fade in contrast with "the novel's lovely minor music" (Plummer in Mooney, p. 732). *Shoeless Joe* was awarded the Houghton Mifflin Literary Fellowship Award. Kinsella's novel also became the inspiration for the successful motion picture *Field of Dreams*.

For More Information

Chadwick, Bruce, and David M. Spindel. *Boston Red Sox.* New York: Abbeyville, 1992.

Gordon, Lois, and Alan Gordon. *Seven Decades in American Life: 1920-1989.* New York: Crown, 1990.

Hamilton, Ian. *In Search of J. D. Salinger.* New York: Random House, 1988.

Kinsella, W. P. *Shoeless Joe.* Boston: Houghton Mifflin, 1982.

Kinsella, W. P. "Shoeless Joe." In *Shoeless Joe Jackson Comes to Iowa.* Toronto: Oberon, 1980.

Mooney, Martha T., ed. *Book Review Digest.* Vol. 78. New York: H. W. Wilson, 1983.

Scheinin, Richard. *Field of Screams: The Dark Underside of America's National Pastime.* New York: W. W. Norton, 1994.

Seymour, Harold. *Baseball, The People's Game.* New York: Oxford University Press, 1990.

Ward, Geoffrey C., and Ken Burns. *Baseball: An Illustrated History.* New York: Knopf, 1994.

Stranger in a Strange Land

by
Robert A. Heinlein

Robert Anson Heinlein was born on July 7, 1907, in Butler, Missouri. He dropped out of the University of Missouri in 1925 to enlist in the U.S. Navy, in which he served as an officer on several ships, including the first U.S. aircraft carrier, before taking a medical discharge in 1934 because of tuberculosis. Afterwards he studied physics and mathematics at the University of California in Los Angeles, going on in 1939 to publish his first short story, "Life Line," in the magazine *Astounding Science Fiction*. Heinlein proceeded to write many short stories and several novels. His *Stranger in a Strange Land,* the first science fiction novel to make the *New York Times* bestseller list, appealed to readers not only as a fantasy but also as a reflection on social attitudes and change.

Events in History at the Time of the Novel

The space race. In *Stranger in a Strange Land,* Heinlein parodies the rivalry between the United States and the Soviet Union that began in 1957 when the Soviet Union launched the first satellite into the earth's orbit. Whereas the powerful nations of Heinlein's earth vie for control of distant Mars, the United States and the Soviet Union competed first to send a manned spacecraft into orbit around the earth and then to land a human on the moon.

In 1957 the Soviet Union launched Sputnik, a satellite about 22 inches in diameter, into orbit around the earth. The successful launch as-

---

THE LITERARY WORK

A novel set in the first decades of the twenty-first century; published in 1961.

SYNOPSIS

The child of space explorers who perished during the first mission to Mars is brought to Earth, where he struggles to both adapt to and reform human social habits.

---

tonished and alarmed U.S. scientists, who had misled the American public into believing that the United States would be first in space. The success of the Soviet mission prompted many U.S. citizens to panic. Not only did they conjure up vague visions of Soviet satellites launching missiles at U.S. cities, but they began to doubt the technological superiority of the United States. The *New Republic* warned that Sputnik was "proof of the fact that the Soviet Union has gained a commanding lead in certain vital sectors of the race for world scientific and technological supremacy" (Divine, p. xv).

During his presidential campaign of 1960, John Fitzgerald Kennedy capitalized on this distress by reprimanding his opponent Richard Nixon, who had served as vice president under Dwight Eisenhower, for having "allowed" the Soviets to lead the quest into space (Breuer, p. 2). In a dramatic confrontation with Soviet president Nikita Khrushchev, Nixon had once responded,

Alan B. Shepard

"You may be ahead of us in rocket thrust, but we are ahead of you in color television" (Nixon in Breuer, p. 2). Kennedy profited from this hasty remark. "I will take my television in black and white," he declared before a cheering crowd. "I want to be ahead in rocket thrust" (Kennedy in Breuer, p. 2). Kennedy won the 1960 election by a slim margin. He immediately established a committee headed by his scientific advisor, Jerome Weisner, to win support for his proposals to fund space exploration. Among them was a proposal by Kennedy to land a man on the moon. Then, on April 12, 1961, the Soviet Union dealt another blow to faith in American ingenuity. Yuri Gagarin, a Soviet Army major, was launched into space and orbited the earth for more than one hundred minutes. Khrushchev proclaimed Gagarin "the new Christopher Columbus" (Khrushchev in Breuer, p. 3).

Less than three weeks after Gagarin had returned to earth, *New York Times* headlines proudly boasted "U.S. Hurls Man 115 Miles into Space" (Breuer, p. 3). Alan B. Shepard Jr. had become the first U.S. citizen to leave the earth's atmosphere. Although the entire flight lasted a mere fifteen minutes, it indicated that the United States was making substantial advances.

Kennedy resolved to take the lead in the space race in spite of the Soviet Union's unquestion-able head start. On May 25, 1961, he declared before Congress, "this nation should commit itself to achieving the goal, before this decade is out, of landing a man on the moon and returning him safely to earth. No single space project in this period will be more impressive" (Kennedy in Breuer, p. 4). Congress responded to Kennedy's speech by agreeing to double the funding for space exploration. The space race against the Soviet Union would proceed for the remainder of the decade, beyond the assassination of Kennedy in 1963, until it reached his goal. In 1969, Neil Armstrong would finally make the famous giant leap for mankind onto the surface of the moon, carrying with him an American flag.

The 1950s. The 1950s are often referred to as a decade of both economic prosperity and social contentment. Certainly the nation enjoyed economic growth bolstered by marketing innovations such as the installment plan, which allowed customers to purchase goods and pay for them over time, paying less interest than they would to a bank. In 1954, the earnings of the General Electric corporation rose 68 percent over a nine-month period, and Westinghouse, a rival corporation, boasted a 73 percent increase. The percentage of white-collar workers grew to exceed that of blue-collar workers.

Levittown, New York, the first of the sprawling, mass-produced suburbs in the United States.

As the nation's economy prospered, the standard of living rose as well. Contractors built lush suburban neighborhoods to house the burgeoning middle class. Consumers took advantage of low interest rates to purchase labor-saving devices like washing machines and dryers as well as sleek new cars. Sales of barbecue pits with matching patio furniture, popular items in the suburban home, rose from 53 million in 1950 to 145 million in 1960.

Yet beneath the veneer of contentment lurked simmering anxieties. The adults who enjoyed the economic prosperity of the 1950s were children of the 1930s. Having lived through both the Great Depression and World War II, they were not only attracted to material success, but also anxious about the stability of their lifestyles.

To quell these anxieties the adults of the 1950s sought comfort in conformity. Identically dressed businessmen left their jobs to return to similar suburban homes tended by their stay-at-home wives. From the mass media came broadcasts that promoted images of the contented mother and the hardworking and successful father.

It was no doubt natural for this generation to stress the merit of teamwork and cooperation as well as to defend the image of their country, which had emerged as the only real victor of the Second World War, given the damage the others suffered and America's development of atomic weaponry. Yet the zeal with which the conservative elements in the country lashed out against nonconformists in the 1950s was dangerous. Senator Joseph McCarthy exploited these fears by denouncing his political opponents and many others as communists. Although McCarthy offered little evidence to support these allegations, the mere accusation sufficed to ruin many people's careers. McCarthy seemed to succeed simply because the public was overly suspicious of anyone who did not conform to a rigid definition of "American."

Children of the fifties: seeds of social upheaval. If, for the adult generation of the 1950s, the term *nonconformist* was a nasty epithet, it was for their children a compliment. Many of the white middle-class youths coming of age at the time had never known economic deprivation and did not have the same apprehensions that troubled their parents. Whereas the older generation took pride in conformity, the youths delighted in challenging accepted norms.

The popularity of certain media icons reflects the frustrations of the youth of the 1950s. Movies like *The Wild One* and *Rebel without a Cause* glamorized the social deviant who chose nonconformity. J. D. Salinger's novel **Catcher in the Rye** (also covered in *Literature and Its Times*), the popular adolescent classic, told the story of a middle-class boy disgusted with a world of materialistic "phonies." Many of these youths longed to shatter the narrow molds cast by their parents. "The only people for me," proclaimed popular author Jack Kerouac, "are the mad ones . . . the ones who never yawn or say a commonplace thing, but burn, burn, burn" (Kerouac in Stevens, p. 99). The generation that would come of age in the following decade would see the rise of a much larger group of young rebels, which became known as the counterculture. Again made up largely of young, middle-class whites, its adherents found much to criticize in the various manifestations of what they called the "establishment." New expressions in art, music, politics, and even value systems would all coalesce to give evidence to the progressiveness of the counterculture, and to grow into a major movement by the end of the decade. Vehement protests against U.S. involvement in the war in Vietnam were also a major component. Much larger and more outspoken than the nonconformists of the 1950s, the members of the counterculture staged a music festival at Woodstock, New York, in 1969 attended by 400,000. It was the culmination of years of protest and nonconformity, a fitting end to a decade that had begun shortly before *Stranger in a Strange Land* was published. The decade would be remembered in history as one in which nonconformist elements in society not only voiced protest, but also inaugurated change.

The sexual revolution. In 1948 sociologist Alfred Kinsey published an extensive statistical report on the sexual habits of American citizens. The report, based on thousands of interviews, revealed not only that 60 percent of married men and 40 percent of married women confessed to having sex with someone other than their spouses, but also that homosexuality, promiscuity among adolescents, and masturbation were far more common than previously suspected. Although the report stirred noteworthy controversy among sociologists and psychologists, it did not by any means convince the public to question conventional values and customs regarding sex.

Although it is unlikely that the majority of adolescents growing up in the 1950s read Kinsey's research, it is certain that they questioned their parents attitudes toward sex. When the Food and Drug Administration approved the oral contraceptive pill in 1960, the youth of the United States began to fling aside the staid faith in monogamy professed by their parents' generation. Premarital sex started to seem less of a taboo.

The sexual revolution did not really begin, however, until after the publication of Heinlein's novel. Heinlein's fictional man from Mars, who advocates casual sex and group cohabitation, anticipates the cult leaders of the 1960s who would exhort their adherents to relish promiscuity. During the 1960s even married couples would, like some of the couples in Heinlein's novel, swap mates and experiment with the concept of group marriage. In the mid-1960s some students from the University of California at Berkeley would, like the followers of the man from Mars in Heinlein's novel who casually commingle in the nude, organize a nude wade in San Francisco Bay.

Lysergic acid diethylamide. The popularity of lysergic acid diethylamide (LSD), a hallucinogenic drug, in the late 1950s and 1960s again reflects the desire of youths to escape what they perceived as the dull world of middle-class suburbia. First synthesized in 1938 by Albert Hofmann, a Swiss chemist, LSD was used during the 1950s first by the Central Intelligence Agency as a potential truth serum and then by psychologists as a promising treatment for both schizophrenia and depression.

By 1960 the use of the drug had become a popular pastime among artists, writers, and other progressive intellectuals. Some followed the advice of men like controversial Harvard professor Timothy Leary and British novelist Aldous Huxley and volunteered to serve as subjects for experiments with LSD. Popular counterculture poet Allen Ginsberg described his use of LSD as an attempt to "resurrect a lost art or a lost knowledge or a lost consciousness" (Ginsburg in Lee and Shlain, p. 60). Actors like Cary Grant took LSD at the advice of their therapists. "All my life," Grant stated, "I've been searching for peace of mind. . . . Nothing really seemed to give me what I wanted until this treatment" (Grant in Lee and Shlain, p. 57).

The declarations of proponents of LSD are remarkably similar to the phrases used by Heinlein's protagonist to explain his philosophy. Whereas the man from Mars pleads with his fellow humans to believe that "Thou art God" (Heinlein, *Stranger in a Strange Land,* p. 406) and "[love] is the greatest gift we have" (*Stranger in a Strange Land,* p. 397), Timothy Leary wrote "Listen! Wake up! You are God!" (Leary in Stevens, p. 133), and Huxley asserted that his experience with LSD convinced him that "Love

[is] the primary and fundamental cosmic fact" (Huxley in Lee and Shlain, p. 48). LSD did not become a widely used drug until after the publication of *Stranger in a Strange Land,* however, so while Heinlein's protagonists seems to echo advocates of LSD like Leary and Huxley, the similarities merely reflect the intellectual climate of the times.

The Novel in Focus

The plot. Toward the end of the twentieth century humans launched the first manned craft bound for Mars. Four married couples were chosen to make the journey of almost three earth years. Before the end of their journey, one of the women was pregnant, but not by her husband. The doctor, her husband, delivered the infant boy by cesarean section and the woman died on the operating table. The doctor proceeded to slit the throat of the child's father, then his own. The rest of the crew died on Mars and only the boy, raised by Martians, survived.

Two decades after the first mission to Mars a technological advance allowed humans to make the journey to Mars in nineteen days. A second expedition to Mars was planned with the goal of determining whether or not Mars was inhabited and whether or not there were any survivors of the first mission. The crew returned both with startling reports concerning native life on Mars and with Valentine Michael Smith, the survivor of the first mission.

Smith is brought to earth, where he is kept under guard by the government. Maladapted to earth's stronger gravity and ignorant of the English language, he is a docile guest and relies on the help of the doctors. Armed guards spare him the ordeal of having to speak to the crowds of eager reporters outside the hospital.

Smith is not only physically unsuited to earth; he has grown up among Martians, who are cerebral creatures, and is perplexed and frightened by human displays of emotion. Should he perceive that he has offended anyone, he closes his eyes, slows his breathing, reduces his heartbeat, and "discorporates." Because he is so sensitive, doctors recommend that he be sheltered from the flash cameras of inquisitive reporters.

The government is particularly interested in Smith's fate not merely because he may serve as a wellspring of scientific information, but also because, as the first living human to have been on Mars, he can, under legal precedent, claim ownership of Mars. Smith himself does not realize

this, nor will he ever fully understand the concept of ownership, but the many countries of the globe recognize him as having a rightful claim to the planet. The government hopes to force Smith to cede to them his claim to Mars, but in the meantime it fears that rival nations may be plotting his assassination.

Jill Boardmen, a nurse, and Ben Caxton, a muckraking journalist, kidnap Smith and spirit him away to the Pocono Mountains. He arrives at the home of Jubal Harshaw, a cynical attorney who gave up law because he found writing sensationalist novels more amusing. Acting as Smith's attorney, Jubal relinquishes all claims to Mars to the Martians themselves, thus saving Smith from the danger of being kidnapped by countries hoping to colonize Mars.

> ## CLAIMS TO MARS
>
>
>
> When Jill discovers that the nations of the earth are squabbling over legal claims to Mars just as they had over the legal claim to the moon, she protests that Mars, unlike the moon, is inhabited. It is absurd, she contends, for human nations to vie for dominion over territory that belongs to the Martians. Ben pointedly argues that European powers like Britain, Spain, and France fought for control of North America in spite of the fact that this continent was already inhabited.

Jubal, Jill, and Ben begin teaching Smith the tricky ceremonies humans have concocted to complicate communication. Smith begins to grasp sarcasm but is unable to comprehend either humor or the vague word "God." Although he reads several volumes of the *Encyclopedia Britannica* a day, the outsider relies on his friends to explain the mysteries of human conduct.

In turn Smith explains to them that he can control his metabolism to such an extent that he can voluntarily grow muscle or hair. He can also survive for hours without oxygen and days without food. These abilities seem trivial, however, when Smith demonstrates that, without even lifting his hand, he can make objects, guns, cars, even people, vanish.

Having spent many months with Jubal, Smith finally leaves with Jill so that he can sample life among strangers. The couple joins a carnival, where Smith performs as a magician, levitating Jill or making objects disappear. They leave the

Stranger in a Strange Land

carnival, however, because he cannot seem to entertain an audience.

Jill and Smith linger in various places. While he has accepted that God is a vague abstraction meaning different things to different people, Smith has not yet grasped humor. Jill takes him to a zoo, where he notices for the first time the similarity between apes and humans. Smith erupts with laughter. Jill is troubled and hurries him out of the zoo. Later Smith explains, "I had to laugh. I looked at a cageful of monkeys and suddenly I saw all the mean and cruel and utterly unexplainable things I've seen and heard and read about . . . and suddenly it hurt so much I found myself laughing" (*Stranger in a Strange Land,* p. 300).

Believing that he has grasped the causes of human joy and anguish, Smith resolves to explain to the human race its folly. He hopes to convince mankind that one need not invent a vague abstraction like God to stifle fears of the unknown. Rather, all living things are God and there is nothing to understand apart from oneself.

Smith founds a church. With Jill's help he leads services that resemble both a carnival magic act and a Catholic sermon. Dedicated disciples struggle to learn the Martian language, because this is the only path to self-realization. As they learn they find that not only does their health improve, but they, like Smith, can communicate telepathically.

Smith's success provokes the rancor of other churches. Angry mobs denounce him as the anti-Christ. His church is burned and the congregation is forced to relocate to another city. When crowds mob his new establishment, Smith resolves to confront them. Standing before the mob he banishes the clouds from the overcast sky, bathes himself in sunlight, and announces that he is a son of man. Someone hurtles a brick against his face, but he continues. "Hear the truth, you need not hate, you need not fight, you need not fear." "Blasphemer," the mob answers (*Stranger in a Strange Land,* p. 405). Someone takes off one of Smith's arms with a shotgun. "Give him the other barrel," the mob jeers (*Strange in a Strange Land,* p. 406). The crowd overwhelms Smith and smashes his rib cage. As Smith smiles and whispers once more "Thou art God," they douse him in gasoline and set his body aflame (*Stranger in a Strange Land,* p. 407).

The stranger's perspective. Michael Smith views American society without the blinders of conventional prejudice. He is the ultimate stranger in a strange land. Not merely a foreigner who judges Americans by the moral code of his nation, Smith is an alien with no preconceptions to hamper his perception.

Seen through Mike Smith's eyes, some of the habits and mores of American culture seem absurd or even hypocritical. For example, Mike astounds his new acquaintances when he reveals that when a Martian dies, its friends express their love by devouring the corpse. When an earthling scoffs at this "cannibalism," Jubal comes to the Martian's defense, likening the practice to participating in the sacrament of the Eucharist in the Catholic church. "Tell me," he chides, "how did you feel when you took part in the symbolic cannibalism that plays so paramount a part in your church's rituals?" (*Stranger in a Strange Land,* p. 126).

Smith's introduction to human sexuality, for which there was no counterpart among Martians, convinces him that physical love is "the source . . . of all that makes this planet so rich and so wonderful" (*Stranger in a Strange Land,* p. 397). He is confounded to discover that human children are "brought up to think that sex [is] 'bad' and 'shameful' and 'animal' and something to be hidden and always distrusted" (*Stranger in a Strange Land,* p. 398). "This lovely perfect thing," he laments, "[is] turned upside down and inside out and made horrible" (*Stranger in a Strange Land,* p. 398).

Yet Smith perceives that the puritanical ethics of American society do not effectively conceal the nation's preoccupation with sex. He is aware that "[i]n the twentieth century . . . nowhere on earth was sex so vigorously suppressed—and nowhere was there such deep interest in it" (*Stranger in a Strange Land,* p. 277). Like the cult leaders of the 1960s, Smith rejects the conventions of chastity and monogamy.

Sources. Heinlein made some use of his experience as an engineer when devising his science fiction fantasies. In fact, his wife alleged that he often drew graphs and charts to determine how long space travel between two planets might last, or even how long an expedition might have to tarry on the surface of Mars before the planet was realigned with earth.

Heinlein, however, asserted that there were only two basic types of science fiction story, the gadget story and the human interest story. His writing, he insisted, was human interest fiction. His purpose in writing *Stranger in a Strange Land,* said Heinlein, "was to examine every major axiom of Western culture, to question each axiom, throw doubt on it—and, if possible—to make the antithesis of each axiom appear a possible and perhaps desirable thing" (Heinlein in Panshin, p. 98). He playfully mocks the space race between the United States and the Soviet Union, corrupt legal systems, manipulative politicians, religious practices, and even conversational habits. The most daring of Heinlein's challenges, however, was his critique of the nation's attitudes toward sex. He anticipated the social upheaval that postdated the publication of the novel. "I saw [the mores of America] changing," he wrote, "and my timing was right" (Heinlein in Stover, p. 54).

Reception. *Stranger in a Strange Land* was Heinlein's greatest commercial success, selling well over a million copies. While cynical critics contended that the popularity of the novel was due to the host of female characters who frolicked in the nude, others insisted that Heinlein had addressed fundamental issues at the heart of the unrest of the 1960s. "The values of the sixties," said one review, "could hardly have found a more congenial expression" (Scholes and Rabkin in Stine, p. 166).

Critics fond of science fiction disputed the merit of the novel. Some complained that Heinlein had ruined a delightful and imaginative tale by proselytizing. "[A]s Heinlein the preacher has come to the forefront," one critic lamented, "the quality of his fiction has declined" (Parkin-Speer in Metzger and Straub, p. 223). Other critics, however, praised Heinlein for having "suggested to the public that the genre had possibilities for objects other than adventures in outer space" (Samuelson in Stine, p. 167).

For More Information

Breuer, William. *Race to the Moon*. Westport, Conn.: Praeger, 1993.

Divine, Robert. *The Sputnik Challenge*. New York: Oxford University Press, 1993.

Heinlein, Robert. *Stranger in a Strange Land*. New York: G. P. Putnam's and Sons, 1961.

Kirkendall, Lester, and Robert Whitehurst. *The New Sexual Revolution*. New York: Donald W. Brown, 1971.

Lee, Martin, and Bruce Shlain. *Acid Dreams*. New York: Grove Weidenfeld, 1985.

Metzger, Linda, and Deborah Straub, eds. *Contemporary Authors New Revision Series*. Vol. 20. Detroit: Gale Research, 1987.

Panshin, Alexei. *Heinlein in Dimension*. Chicago: Advent, 1968.

Stevens, Jay. *Storming Heaven: LSD and the American Dream*. New York: Atlantic Monthly Press, 1987.

Stine, Jean, ed. *Contemporary Literary Criticism*. Vol. 26. Detroit: Gale Research, 1983.

Stover, Leon. *Robert A. Heinlein*. Boston: Twayne, 1987.

Sweet Whispers, Brother Rush

by
Virginia Hamilton

Virginia Hamilton was born in 1936 in Yellow Springs, Ohio, where years earlier a fugitive slave on her mother's side of the family had settled. The family grew, working at farming and indulging in storytelling, a skill shared by both of Hamilton's parents. Hamilton moved to New York after college, where she wrote and began a family of her own before moving back to Ohio some fifteen years later. Meanwhile, in her fiction, family became an important element. *Sweet Whispers, Brother Rush,* one of over a dozen books Hamilton wrote for young people, features the family of an adolescent named Tree. Forced to raise her children alone, Tree's mother struggles to earn a living at a job that keeps her away from home too often. The novel exposes the desperation and isolation that poverty often brings but also offers hope that through struggle, hardships can be overcome.

Events in History at the Time of the Novel

Single parents and the crisis of the black family. In the early 1980s two-thirds of adult African American women were single or living away from their husbands. In addition, the majority of African American children did not live with their fathers (Anderson, p. 273). The reason for the predominance of single-parent families in the African American community has been a subject of intense debate among researchers and historians. Some have claimed that the black community is a "matriarchal" society, one that is domi-

THE LITERARY WORK

A novel for young adults set in an urban ghetto during the early 1980s; published in 1982.

SYNOPSIS

A young girl learns of her family's secret past when she and her brother are visited by the ghost of her uncle, "Brother Rush."

nated by women. One group of scholars points to this as evidence that the African American community has still not recovered from the brutal effects of slavery: about one-third of slave families were broken up as children, fathers, and mothers were sold to separate owners, and the remainder lived under the constant threat of such a forced separation. There are researchers who argue that the specter and reality of this forced breakup has contributed to contemporary family breakdown. Others have argued that matriarchy has its roots in African traditions.

In addition to these theories, many researchers have argued that the economic hardships African Americans have endured throughout history, often as a result of racism, are responsible for the large number of single mothers in the African American community. These researchers note that the fact that many African American men have had to struggle to find well-paying jobs has taken a toll on their self-confidence. They point to the fact that the number of single mothers increased when African Americans migrated from farms to cities at the beginning of this century. This change brought with it massive unemployment in the African American community; all of a sudden, large numbers of men found themselves without jobs and unable to support their families. According to one writer, the loss of self-esteem that comes with unemployment is largely responsible for African American men having a lack of commitment to women. The writer explains that "as a hedge against masculine failure, many poor black men attempted to limit their affective ties and economic commitments to families" (Anderson, p. 273).

The theory that the large number of single mothers in the African American community is due to economics is strengthened by the fact that in middle-class African American families with gainfully employed men, there are much fewer single mothers than there are in African American communities that have high male unemployment (Anderson, p. 275).

The burden of raising children alone. Regardless of the causes of the large number of single-parent African American families, the reality is that through much of American history many African American children have been raised alone by single mothers. Often these women were forced both to work long hard hours and to fulfill the roles played by two parents in many families. This obviously difficult task has taken a toll on many children. In addition, even with hard work, single mothers who do not have the benefit of a second income are often unable to pull their families out of poverty. According to Anderson, African American economic success or mobility "rests firmly on the two earner family" (Anderson, p. 275). In the novel Tree's mother works many hours to keep her family from slipping into deep poverty. These many hours keep M'Vy from being with her children. In fact, Tree is left alone for days at a time to care for her brother Dab, and her mother does not even appear until the middle of the novel. The cause for this absence is largely economic. "Poor honey—my baby. . . . Know I'd be here every moment if I could," M'Vy explains as she tries to comfort Tree (Hamilton, *Sweet Whispers, Brother Rush*, p. 90). However, her job is far away and she claims that there is little hope of finding a closer one. "I got to work where I can and hope for somethin closer to home" (*Sweet Whispers, Brother Rush*, p. 95). M'Vy copes as best she can and more positively than once was the case. At first,

when she gave birth to Dab, M'Vy was poor, single, and very young. These conditions were too much for her to handle at the time, and although she would later regret it, she abused Dab.

Ronald Reagan and the increase in urban poverty. Politically, the early 1980s are remembered as a very conservative period. Ronald Reagan, who was elected president in 1980, set out to cut social programs and lower welfare benefits. Reagan won popularity with many Americans by verbally attacking single "welfare mothers" who lived in America's urban ghettos. This type of attack led one writer to lament, "what sets my teeth on edge is . . . its apparent hostility to the female poor, who form a majority of the population known colloquially as 'welfare cheats'" (Ehrenreich, p. 192). Reagan's policies in the early 1980s resulted in the poorest citizens of the country getting poorer while the richest citizens grew richer. This increase in the poverty of those living in the ghetto only put further pressure on poor African American families, already struggling to stay together.

CHILD ABUSE AND SINGLE PARENTS

Single mothers face some persistent pressures in raising their children. Those who must support their families without the extra income of a spouse must often contend with difficult financial circumstances. Having to raise a child alone is another obvious pressure. These concerns can cause immense frustration in single-parent mothers, frustration that may be taken out on the children. Studies indicate that single parenthood combined with poverty has often led mothers to abuse their children and that the likelihood of child abuse increases among teenage single mothers. According to one long-term study, "in the period 1979-1988 about 2000 child deaths were recorded annually in the United States as a result of abuse and neglect. . . . The most vulnerable children are those under two years of age whose parents are single or were very young at their first pregnancy" (Fontana and Besharov, p. 13).

Kinship ties and the African American community. Despite the high number of large single-mother families, the African American community at large has historically exhibited a strong sense of commitment among its members. According to historian Steven Mintz and anthropologist Susan Kellogg, this commitment has existed since slavery. They write, "Despite the frequent breakup of marriages and families by sale, Afro-Americans managed to forge strong and durable family and kinship ties within the institution of slavery" (Mintz and Kellogg, p. 67). If children were sold and separated from their parents, often other slaves would take on the burden of raising them. "Whenever children were sold to neighboring plantations," Mintz and Kellogg explain, "grandparents, aunts, uncles, and cousins often took on the functions of parents. When blood relatives were not present, strangers cared for and protected children" (Mintz and Kellogg, p. 69).

Despite the strains that economic hardship, racism, and unemployment have placed on the contemporary African American family, kinship ties, as during slavery, remain strong. Although single-mother families are predominant in the African American community, often neighbors or other family members fulfill needs commonly taken care of by mothers and fathers. According to Mintz and Kellogg, in "present-day urban ghettoes, networks of kin or 'fictive kin' often share resources and responsibilities" (Mintz and Kellogg, p. 79). This is certainly the case in *Sweet Whispers, Brother Rush*. Silversmith, who is M'Vy's boyfriend, provides a great deal of emotional support to Tree, even though the two have not known each other very long.

Virginia Hamilton and magical realism. In the 1970s and 1980s writers from around the world began writing in a style that has been called "magical realism." Writers such as Toni Morrison and Gabriel García Márquez began to intertwine elements of the supernatural with otherwise realistic plots. In Morrison's *Beloved* the vengeful spirit of a murdered baby is present throughout the novel. In García Márquez's *One Hundred Years of Solitude* a ghost inhabits a room in a family house and helps direct the course of strange events in the village. In contrast to science fiction—in which the reader is always aware of the fact that he is reading a work of fantasy because all the characters are placed in completely strange environments—in works of magical realism strange happenings mingle with realistic events.

Sweet Whispers, Brother Rush presents the reader with a supernatural world in which a ghost joins characters who are portrayed very realistically. Although it is quite common for authors to include the dreams or fantasies of an individual character in realistic novels, in *Sweet Whispers, Brother Rush* Hamilton makes it clear

Virginia Hamilton

that the ghost of Brother Rush is real. Not only does Tree's brother see the ghost, but so does the cleaning lady Miss Pricherd. If sightings of the ghost were limited to just one character, it could be seen as fantasy, but Hamilton portrays the ghost as a real character who interacts with several people.

The African roots of Hamilton's magical realism. Hamilton has written that she uses the supernatural to portray the "mysteriousness" of African and African American culture. She sees her writing as a chance to "convey the magic, fetishes, to bring across the Africanness I've described. . . . It is a magic they [the Africans] brought with them. It is spells. It is everything they believed that we couldn't understand" (Mikkelson, p. 67). Hamilton's views on the African origins of connection with the supernatural world are shared by her character M'Vy. M'Vy explains to Tree that she is able to see ghosts because of her African heritage. She tells her, "I never seen the mystery. . . . But I remember the talk. . . . There was one who'd look at me and say 'Afrique! Afrique!' And say some kind of words that rolled out of her like dancing on drums. And she told of mysteries, the way you learn them and see and feel them" (Hamilton, p. 130).

Bucking the trend in children's literature. The early 1980s saw a large increase in the number of books published for teenagers. Many of these novels were part of what has been labeled the "romantic revival." Novels such as *Sweet Valley High* and *Sweet Dreams* were set in the suburbs and focused on the love lives of white middle-class high school students. These novels ignored serious social problems like poverty, single-parent families, and death. The romance novels of the 1980s were attacked by many concerned critics for not addressing the struggles that many young people faced. Michael Cart contended that these books "teach girls that their primary value is their attractiveness to boys; devalue relationships . . . depict middle-class, white, small-town families as the norm; and portray adults in stereotypical sex roles" (Cart, p. 101). *Sweet Whispers, Brother Rush,* by contrast, was praised by many critics for providing an alternative to the suburban romance novel. Hamilton refused to follow the trend of the time and instead wrote about a community often ignored by writers for teenagers.

The Novel in Focus

The plot. *Sweet Whispers, Brother Rush* focuses on the life of Theresa Pratt as she struggles to take care of her ailing brother, Dab, to confront the changes of adolescence, and to come to terms with her family's horrible secrets. It is only with the help of her uncle, Brother Rush, that Theresa, or "Tree" as she is called, is able to cope with all that confronts her.

Tree first sees Rush as she is leaving school. Immediately she is attracted to him. "It was love at first sight in a beating of her heart that took her breath" (*Sweet Whispers, Brother Rush,* p. 1). After her initial sighting of Rush, he was nowhere to be seen. Suddenly, however, he appears in her living room, floating through the hardwood table, holding an oval mirror. As Tree watches Rush, she realizes that he is a ghost. Rush beckons her to come forward and invites her to enter into what turns out to be a magic mirror.

Inside the mirror Tree finds dead relatives and her mother as a young child. She has entered the world of her family's past. Tree witnesses events that happened while she was very young. She rides around with Rush in his car at one point and is quite content. However, later on she witnesses a younger version of her mother beating her brother, who is only a baby. Tree then sees her mother tying young Dab to a bed.

In the real world, Tree and Dab are left to fend for themselves most of the time because their mother, M'Vy, works far away. Since Dab is mentally impaired and gets very sick during the course of the novel, Tree must often serve as nurse to her elder brother. M'Vy arrives home midway through the novel after Tree has already taken several trips into the mirror. Upon hearing of her daughter's supernatural experiences, M'Vy informs them that she knows about the ghost of her dead brother, Brother Rush. Although M'Vy cannot see Brother when he appears, she certainly believes that Tree has seen him. "I didn't see him. I felt him though. It was Brother. . . . He come visit my Tree" (*Sweet Whispers, Brother Rush,* p. 132). M'Vy is further convinced that her daughter has seen a real ghost upon hearing that Miss Pricherd, the cleaning woman, has also seen Brother. M'Vy's conviction that Tree has seen her dead brother is confirmed when Tree confronts her with the abuse that Dab suffered as a child. Emotional but relieved that the truth is out, M'Vy admits that she treated Dab horribly as a child and apologizes.

Toward the end of the novel, Dab's illness, a fatal genetic disease, intensifies and eventually he dies. After Dab's death Brother Rush invites Tree for one last trip into the mirror. Inside, she sits in the back seat of Brother's car while he and Dab ride in the front. Although Tree is somewhat comforted by the knowledge that her brother is with Brother Rush, she is still angry at her mother for letting Dab deteriorate throughout his life. With M'Vy's promise that she will become more of a mother, Tree begins to forgive.

Memories and the magic mirror. The magic mirror that Brother Rush allows Tree to enter is both mystical and filled with memories. By having Tree experience the world inside the mirror, Hamilton is able to explore the history of Tree's family and to expose secrets that her mother has tried to hide. In addition to exposing the past abuse that M'Vy has wrought upon her family, the mirror also forces her to acknowledge the current abuse she has forced Tree to endure. The mirror serves not only to enlighten Tree and her mother about the past, but it forces them to confront present problems.

When Tree first confronts M'Vy with the news that she is aware that Dab was abused as a child, M'Vy is visibly shaken. Hamilton writes, "M'Vy's legs quivered. She was sliding" (*Sweet Whispers, Brother Rush,* p. 97). Overcome with guilt, M'Vy attempts to explain to Tree that she was young and could not deal with having to raise children alone, and M'Vy took her frustrations out on Dab.

Although the mirror focuses on bringing out events of the past, these memories serve to show both M'Vy and Tree that something is wrong with the present. M'Vy's abuse of Dab was obviously horrible, and when she is confronted with these memories, she recognizes this. M'Vy, however, has also been abusive in another way; she has left her young daughter alone for days and weeks at a time to tend to her older brother. M'Vy is unable to recognize this neglectful abuse until the end of the novel. Tree blames M'Vy's neglect for the death of her brother and her own intense depression. After Tree has related how kind and good Brother Rush could be to her and her brother and how important it is to her to be surrounded by family, M'Vy begins to recognize the damage her neglect has caused. If her family is to be free from abuse, M'Vy realizes, they must be together. At the end of the novel she cries, "All these years I've been wrong. I admit it. I should have taken less money and stayed with you and your brother. . . . I'm gone put it together" (*Sweet Whispers, Brother Rush*, p. 211). By being confronted by her wrongs of the past, M'Vy is made to realize the seriousness of the problems of the present.

Sources. As a child, Virginia Hamilton had little in common with her character Tree. She grew up in a small middle-class Ohio town and was raised by both her mother and her father. Her novels, however, are deeply influenced by her own memories of childhood. She believes that her stream-of-consciousness or dreamlike style of writing—in which she composed the chapters that describe Tree's adventures inside the magic mirror—reflects the way that many children actually think. She explains in an interview, "I believe kids think in stream-of-consciousness. . . . If you look at some of the young writings, you'll find it just keeps running on and on. . . . It's as if the mind were talking in a stream" (Hamilton in Lesniak, p. 210).

Hamilton also credits her father, a musician, for influencing her style of writing, which has often been labeled musical or melodic. She explains, "I come from a rather musical family. My father was a musician, and I suppose my interest in music as it relates to fiction comes from him. . . . And I love music anyway so a lot of it enters my writing" (Hamilton in Lesniak, p. 208).

Reviews. The reviews for *Sweet Whispers, Brother Rush* were tremendously positive. It was awarded a John Newbery Honor Book Award and a Coretta Scott King award. Reviewer Geraldine Wilson praised the book's use of African culture when she compared the book to an African quilt, "finely stitched, tightly constructed and rooted in cultural authenticity" (Wilson in Lesniak, p. 208). In *The Horn Book Magazine*, Ethel Heins describes the novel's characters as "complex, contradictory, and ambivalent as is life itself: sometimes weak, sometimes attractive, always fiercely human" (Heins in Stine, p. 158). Although some reviewers claimed that the book might be hard for children to understand because of its stream-of-consciousness style and because it is written in the dialect of an African American ghetto, Katherine Paterson disagreed. Published in the *New York Times Book Review*, her evaluation set forth a challenge: "To the more timid reader, young or old, who may feel inadequate to Miss Hamilton's always demanding fiction, I say: 'Just read the first page, just the first paragraph, of "Sweet Whispers, Brother Rush." Then stop if you can'" (Paterson in Stine, p. 159).

For More Information

Anderson, Karen. "African American Families." In *American Families*. Edited by Joseph Hawes and Elizabeth I. Nybakken. New York: Greenwood Press, 1991.

Cart, Michael. *From Romance to Realism: 50 Years of Growth and Change in Young Adult Literature*. New York: Harper Collins, 1996.

Ehrenreich, Barbara. *The Worst Years of Our Lives: Irreverent Notes from a Decade of Greed*. New York: Harper Collins, 1990.

Fontana, Vincent, and Douglas J. Besharov. *The Maltreated Child*. Springfield, Ill.: Charles C. Thomas, 1996.

Hamilton, Virginia. *Sweet Whispers, Brother Rush*. New York: Avon Books, 1982.

Lesniak, James, ed. *Contemporary Authors New Revision Series*. Vol. 20. Detroit: Gale Research, 1991.

Mintz, Steven, and Susan Kellogg. *Domestic Revolution: A Social History of American Family Life*. New York: Free Press, 1988.

Mikkelsen, Nina. *Virginia Hamilton*. New York: Twayne, 1994.

Stine, Jean C. *Contemporary Literary Criticism*. Vol. 26. Detroit: Gale Research, 1983.

The Time of
the Hero

by
Mario Vargas Llosa

Mario Vargas Llosa was born in Arequipa, Peru, in 1936. His parents separated before his birth, and shortly after he was born his mother moved with the infant to Bolivia. After ten years in Bolivia, Vargas Llosa's mother was reconciled with his father and took her son back to Peru, to reunite the family in Lima, the capital. Disturbed by his twelve-year-old son's literary efforts, Vargas Llosa's father enrolled the boy in the Leoncio Prado Military School in an attempt to change his direction. Vargas Llosa hated the school and left after three years to spend his last year in a civilian high school. Inspired by his experience at the Leoncio Prado, Vargas Llosa used the school as the setting for his first novel, *The Time of the Hero*.

THE LITERARY WORK

A novel set in Lima, Peru, in the 1950s; published in 1962.

SYNOPSIS

An adolescent boy from a middle-class background comes of age as a cadet in a military school. When the death of one of his classmates during a training exercise is covered up by the school officials, the cadet tries to expose the truth.

Events in History at the Time of the Novel

Peruvian politics. Throughout the twentieth century, the state of affairs in Peru has seen almost constant upheaval, with a succession of rulers and regimes that ranged from moderate to dictatorial. Throughout the 1920s a U.S.-supported president, Augusto Leguia, served primarily the interests of the local oligarchy and foreign investors. Poor economic conditions for the working classes and rising inflation led to the formation of two powerful populist movements. The leftist APRA, (American Popular Revolutionary Alliance) was founded in 1924 by Raul Haya de la Torre as a response to postwar inflation. Another populist leader, Sanchez Cerro, founded the Union Revolucionaria, a right-wing and nationalistic party that, like the APRA, gained most of its support from the working class. Cerro took power in 1931 only to be assassinated in 1933, quite likely by a supporter of the APRA.

The two decades following the assassination were plagued by political strife and economic instability. The government of José Luis Bustamente, a moderate liberal elected in 1945, gave power to Haya de la Torre and the *apristas* (APRA supporters), but General Manuel Odria took over the government in 1948 with the backing of the country's elite, who had been distanced by leftist tendencies in the Bustamente government. According to Mario Vargas Llosa, "With Odria, barbarism reigned once more in Peru" (Vargas Llosa in Williams, p. 9). Odria's regime was brutal, oppressive, and rife with corruption. Under his presidency, APRA members were forced to remain underground; Haya de la Torre himself fled to the Colombian embassy in Lima in hopes of gaining political asylum, but he was forced to remain inside for five years. Odria permitted elections in 1956, which resulted in the presidency of Manuel Prado, who won the contest with APRA support. Toward the end of Prado's second term in 1962, new elections were held. The three candidates consisted of Odria, Haya de la Torre, and Fernando Belaúnde, a leader of APRA. After a period of political and military maneuvering following the elections, as well as a brief military junta, Belaúnde was elected. Vargas Llosa attended the Leoncio Prado Military School during Odria's presidency and wrote the novel during the political turmoil of the 1962 elections.

Peru's corruption. Throughout modern Peru's history, corruption has been a constant factor. This is evident in the questionable political and economic influence of the country's major banks, as well as in the state's clandestine provision of key pieces of information to powerful businessmen, who in turn wield an imposing influence on the government and the economy. Such corruption and its stultifying effect on Peru would become one of Mario Vargas Llosa's greatest inspirations for writing. For Vargas Llosa, much of the corruption stems from the prevalent masculine values in the country. One Vargas Llosa biographer, Dick Gerdes, points out that Peruvian society tends to exalt masculinity and male chauvinism. Vargas Llosa—not unlike other intellectuals—views this cultural determinant as an overpowering and destructive force. He also condemns Peru's middle class, blaming them for many of the country's problems; Vargas Llosa described Peru's middle-class as "the worst thing under the sun: an absolutely noxious class, infected with prejudices, ignorant, and hypocritical" (Vargas Llosa in Gerdes, p. 2).

Vargas Llosa realized early that he wanted to attempt to cure some of Peru's problems through his writing. "I had discovered, in my last year of high school," he explains, "that the country had severe social problems. I wanted to be identified with the poor and to be part of the revolution that would bring justice to Peru" (Vargas Llosa in Gerdes, p. 3).

Many of the country's social problems have involved the stratified society and the extreme prejudice directed toward the native Indian population, who live in impoverished conditions in rural mountain areas. Other troubles involved Peru's political sphere. Popular elections have been nullified by the military, as in the case of Odria's seizure of power in 1948; accusations of voter fraud occurred during the 1962 elections; and members of specific political parties were harassed mercilessly in society, namely the *apristas* during Odria's presidency. In the novel, Lieutenant Gamboa comments on Peru's problems, believing the military to be exempt from the problems. "Why is our country the way it is?" he asks. "Lack of discipline. Lack of order. The only part of it that stays strong and healthy is the army, because of its structure, its organization" (Vargas Llosa, *The Time of the Hero*, p. 310). Despite Gamboa's belief in the army, it becomes apparent that the army is corrupt in its own right when Captain Garrido tells Gamboa to stop his search for truth in the death of Arana because "A clean conscience might help you get into heaven, but it won't help your career" (*The Time of the Hero*, p. 351). Gamboa finally realizes this after his diligence in looking for the truth brings him nothing but disdain from other officers and reassignment to a remote military outpost. In the novel, injustice goes unpunished and virtue unrewarded, underscoring the author's belief that Peru's society is in desperate need of moral improvement. With this in mind, it is not surprising that Vargas Llosa would opine, "Literature in general and the novel in particular are expressions of discontent. Their social usefulness lies principally in the fact that they remind people that the world is *always* wrong, that life should *always* change" (Vargas Llosa in Williams, p. 8).

Peruvian ethnic groups and prejudice. The principal ethnic groups in Peru are the Indians, Hispanicized *mestizos* (of mixed Spanish and Indian blood), and whites. There is also an influential Japanese presence in the country; Peru has even seen the election of a president of Japanese descent, Alberto Fujimori, in 1990. Whites, or *criollos* as they are also known, are the elite of Peruvian society. Their claim to social superiority comes not only from their control of the country's resources but also from their heritage of aristocracy; many whites trace their descent to the early Spanish settlers of Peru. Mestizos are also sometimes called criollos. This ambiguous terminology reflects the ambiguity of ethnic group membership in Peru. To say someone is white is to attribute elite status to that person. To call someone a mestizo is to assign him or her to the middle or lower class. Despite this distinction, mestizos and whites share similar legal status and both have traditionally held power over the Indian majority.

A family of the Ashaninca tribe in Peru.

The contrast between mestizo and Indian in Peru exists in various dimensions of life. Culture, economics, ethnicity, class, and language all play a part in defining the relationship between mestizos and Indians. Mestizos speak Spanish and are integrated into the Peruvian political and economic systems, but most Indians speak Indian dialects (Quechua and Aymara) as their native language and enjoy little involvement in politics or the economy. Geography also plays a part in the distinction between mestizos and Indians. Mestizos generally live in Peru's major cities along the coastal area, while Indians inhabit the Andes Mountains, where they raise crops and cattle. Other minority groups in Peru include a small black population and descendants of Chinese immigrants who moved to Peru in great numbers in the nineteenth century.

Various ethnic distinctions of Peru appear throughout the novel, and the Leoncio Prado student body seems to mirror the prejudices of the country as a whole. At the school, the Indians are considered "peasants" and are stigmatized with countless negative stereotypes. When Boa thinks about Cava's suspension from the school, several of these stereotypes emerge. He muses that "the peasants have bad luck, something's always happening to them. . . . The peasants are kind of stupid. . . . It's good luck not to be born a peasant" (*The Time of the Hero*, p. 173). Later, Boa thinks about Cava again: "That poor peasant Cava, he's had a bad time . . . now he'll go back to the mountains and won't ever study again, he'll just stay up there with the Indians and the llamas, he'll just be a stupid field hand" (*The Time of the Hero*, p. 218). These stereotypes are common throughout Peru, as reflected in the Peruvian expression "The Indian is the animal closest to man" (Nyrop, p. 73). Other prejudices about Indians include the beliefs that they are drunken, lazy, dirty, superstitious, pagan, and addicted to coca.

The Novel in Focus

The plot. As the novel begins, four cadets at the Leoncio Prado Military School in Lima, Peru, play dice in the barracks bathroom. The four boys are Alberto Fernandez—also known as "the Poet"—Porfirio Cava, Boa, and Jaguar. Their dice game will determine who among them will have to steal a chemistry examination from a locked classroom. Cava loses the game and must steal the test. During the theft, he accidentally breaks a window; the school officials discover the theft and confine the cadets who were on guard duty to the barracks. The cadets are to stay there until the culprit comes forward to take responsibility for the crime.

Through their various narratives, the cadets describe events from their lives before coming to the Leoncio Prado. Alberto Fernandez and Ricardo Arana, a cadet known as "the slave" because of his submissive nature, fantasize about romances with neighborhood girls and think about their families. The Jaguar, who is the toughest cadet in the academy, recalls a childhood spent working for a ring of thieves.

After several weeks without any weekend leave, Arana can no longer cope with the confinement and tells the officers that Cava stole the exam. In exchange for his information he receives an afternoon leave. Cava is suspended from the academy, and the Jaguar vows revenge on the unknown "squealer." A few days later during a combat training exercise, Arana is shot in the head from behind and dies.

The preliminary investigation reveals little about the death. To minimize scandal as local elections approach and to protect the reputation of the school, the academy officers attribute the death to Arana's own negligence, stating that he was clumsy and shot himself with his own weapon. Alberto, who was Arana's only friend in the school, believes that the Jaguar is the killer. Desiring justice for his dead friend, Alberto decides to tell Lieutenant Gamboa, one of the officers, that the Jaguar killed Arana. He also tells Gamboa about other illicit cadet activities on the campus, namely the countless thefts, fights, drinking, smoking, and escapes without leave. Gamboa is shocked and feels morally obligated to investigate the allegations. As a result of Gamboa's prompting, the school officials search the barracks and find an abundance of alcohol, cigarettes, and gambling paraphernalia. However, the officials would rather let Arana's death go unsolved than create a scandal. Gamboa is even reprimanded for his attempt to uncover the truth.

Alberto is likewise blackmailed into complicity after school officials discover incriminating evidence against him; Alberto has written pornographic stories for the other cadets in exchange for cigarettes and money. When they are placed in a cell together, Alberto accuses the Jaguar of Arana's murder and tells him that he has told the school officials. The two cadets fight viciously, and the Jaguar beats Alberto severely. When they return to the barracks, the other cadets think the Jaguar is responsible for the shakedown that has resulted in heavy punishment for all of them. The

Jaguar does nothing to admit or deny his guilt; his code of honor forbids him from "snitching" on another person.

Finally, the Jaguar admits to Lieutenant Gamboa that he did shoot Arana, but by this point it is too late. Gamboa has been reassigned to a remote outpost because of his quest for the truth and is too disillusioned to pursue the incident further. By dropping his accusations, Alberto is permitted to graduate and returns to civilian life. As the novel ends, the Jaguar goes unpunished, marries his boyhood sweetheart, and becomes a bank clerk.

Masculine values in the novel. One of the most prominent issues in the novel is the recurring theme of masculinity that is so much a part of life for the cadets at the Leoncio Prado. The interactions and conversations of the cadets center around their attempts to prove their masculinity. As the cadets joke with each other, they constantly challenge each other's masculinity and sexuality. In one episode, one of the cadets, Vallano, calls Alberto a "fairy" (*The Time of the Hero*, p. 142). Alberto turns the jest back on Vallano to the delight of the other cadets, raising the ire of Vallano, who shouts, ". . . I'm more of a man than any of you and if somebody wants to prove it, come on over" (*The Time of the Hero*, p. 142). When Boa wonders what's happening, the cadets draw him into the jocular dispute by saying, "He [Vallano] said it's obvious you're a queer" (*The Time of the Hero*, p. 143).

In fact, many of the cadets are in the academy as a result of the masculine values of their fathers. Just after Arana is shot, Alberto talks with Arana's father outside the infirmary. Arana's father describes his motivation for sending Ricardo to the academy, "It did him good, it changed him, it made a man out of him" (*The Time of the Hero*, p. 211). He goes on to say, "His mother thinks I'm to blame, that's a woman for you. . . . But I've got a clear conscience, absolutely clear. I wanted him to be a man" (*The Time of the Hero*, p. 212). Alberto thinks back to a conversation with his own father about enrolling at the academy. "It's for your own good," his father told him. "They'll make a man out of you. They'll give you a strong body, a strong personality" (*The Time of the Hero*, p. 215). As if to prove his own masculinity, Alberto's father has numerous girlfriends even though he is married. Almost every night he comes home late, or fails to come home at all. When Alberto tells his neighborhood friends about a fight his parents had over his father's indiscretions, one of the friends says, "He's a killer,

all right. He's got rafts of women" (*The Time of the Hero*, p. 221). Instead of being disappointed in this behavior, Alberto's friends admire Alberto's father for his proficiency as an adulterer.

The best definition of masculine values in the novel appears during a discussion between the officers of the Leoncio Prado. When Gamboa tells Captain Garrido about the illicit activities of the cadets and demands severe punishments and an investigation of Arana's death, the captain is less anxious to take action. He tells Gamboa, "We'll have to punish them for the liquor and the exams. But remember, the first thing you learn in the army is to be a man. And what do men do? They smoke, they drink, they gamble . . ." (*The Time of the Hero*, p. 310). He continues, telling Gamboa, "The cadets all know they get expelled if they're discovered. . . . But the smart ones don't get caught. If they're going to be men, they have to take chances, they have to use their wits" (*The Time of the Hero*, p. 310). At the Leoncio Prado, the cadets certainly do learn to become men according to Garrido's definition. Outside educational and military training, the cadets occupy much of their time with sex, drinking, gambling, and fighting, the very values that appear in Garrido's assessment of typical masculine behavior. When Gamboa suggests that he will "make better men of them" (*The Time of the Hero*, p. 311) by teaching them discipline and honesty, Garrido tells him, "You talk like a religious fanatic. Do you want to wreck your career?" (*The Time of the Hero*, p. 311). With such an attitude prevalent at the highest level of the school's leadership, the cadets are doomed to the same codes of masculinity that have been taught to their fathers and destined also to pass them on to their own sons.

Sources. Much of Mario Vargas Llosa's *The Time of the Hero* comes from his own experiences as a cadet at the Leoncio Prado Military School. Vargas Llosa writes, "Ever since I was in the Leoncio Prado I wanted to write about it. . . . It was an outlet for my revolt against the Leoncio Prado. Also something hidden. Because in school one didn't dare show any sign of that" (Vargas Llosa in Gerdes, p. 2). Much of the description of the masculine values shaping the lives of the cadets at the Leoncio Prado comes directly from Vargas Llosa's own life. As Vargas Llosa describes, his father had found out that he was writing poems, feared for his future (believing that poets were doomed to die of hunger), and also feared for his manhood since it was generally believed that poets were homosexual. It seemed to the father that the perfect antidote was the Leoncio Prado Mil-

Mario Vargas Llosa

itary School. There is obvious similarity between the attitude of Vargas Llosa's father and that of Ricardo Arana's and Alberto's fathers in the novel, who have enrolled their sons at the academy to make men of them.

Alberto's discontented life in Lima also bears a relation to Vargas Llosa's own experiences as a boy. Vargas Llosa describes his introduction to the city: "I went to Lima for the first time when I was just growing out of childhood. I hated the city from the beginning because of the unhappiness I felt there. My parents had been separated and then reconciled after ten years" (Vargas Llosa in Williams, p. 10). His parents' separation may have also served as a source for the novel. Several of the cadets at the school describe marital problems between their parents as major causes of concern.

Critical response to the novel. The publication of *The Time of the Hero* in 1963 gave rise to a wide variety of responses. The most dramatic response came from the Leoncio Prado Military School, which Vargas Llosa had used as the setting for the novel. Vargas Llosa describes the reaction of the school officials: "The book had a brilliant reception: one thousand copies were ceremoniously burned in the patio of the school and several generals attacked it bitterly. One of them said that

the book was the work of a 'degenerate mind,' and another, who was more imaginative, claimed that I had undoubtedly been paid by Ecuador to undermine the prestige of the Peruvian army" (Vargas Llosa in Williams, p. 13).

A more significant response, however, was the immediate critical praise from reviewers and Latin American writers. The novel was lauded for its clever use of slang and taboo vocabulary, and for its complex narrative strategies. The fact that Jaguar is one of the narrators is not revealed until late in the novel. One critic, J. J. Armas Marcelo, applauds the secret narratives of the novel during which the reader is uncertain as to who is speaking. Marcelo writes, "This functionality of the concept of secrecy in the formal structure of the novel constitutes, without a doubt, one of the fundamental characteristics and, at the same time, one of the most outstanding stylistic features of *The Time of the Hero*" (Marcelo in Bryfonski, p. 500). Another assessment of the novel commended Vargas Llosa's ability to create a complex narrative while maintaining fluidity in his prose:

> He [Vargas Llosa] will write around a scene until he feels he has wholly encompassed it. There is, of course, the danger that too many devices will draw attention to themselves and defeat his whole purpose by running interference. They do sometimes. But he is skillful enough not to get caught in the quagmire.
> (Harss and Dohmann in Bryfonski, p. 493)

Vargas Llosa's success in creating a narrative in his first novel, *The Time of the Hero,* that defies conventions without detracting from the story instantly established him as one of Latin America's foremost novelists. Vargas Llosa himself ran unsuccessfully for his country's presidency in 1990.

For More Information

Bryfonski, Dedria, ed. *Contemporary Literary Criticism.* Vol. 10. Detroit: Gale Research, 1979.

Gerdes, Dick. *Mario Vargas Llosa.* Boston: Twayne, 1985.

Martin, Luis. *The Kingdom of the Sun: A Short History of Peru.* New York: Scribner's, 1974.

Nyrop, Richard F., ed. *Peru: A Country Study.* Washington, D.C.: American University Press, 1981.

Vargas Llosa, Mario. *The Time of the Hero.* New York: Grove, 1966.

Werlich, David P. *Peru: A Short History.* London: Feffer & Simons, 1978.

Williams, Raymond Leslie. *Mario Vargas Llosa.* New York: Ungar, 1986.

Understand This

by

Jervey Tervalon

Jervey Tervalon's family moved from New Orleans, Louisiana, to Los Angeles, California, when he was four years old. They settled among other working- and middle-class black families in a community-oriented, predominantly black neighborhood a mile west of the Los Angeles Memorial Coliseum. In high school, Jervey tried his hand at writing horror and kung fu stories as well as poetry. He finished his first novel, *Understand This,* when he was in his early thirties, basing it on his experiences as a student and an English teacher in the inner city.

Events in History at the Time of the Novel

Inner-city poverty core. Researchers have identified an inner-city poverty core of about 105 square miles in the Los Angeles area (Scott and Brown, p. 7). Along with other areas in the poverty core are South Central, Watts, and parts of Compton, for example. Despite its specific meaning, the term "South Central" is sometimes used loosely to refer to the poverty core as a whole. The largest populations in the poverty core are Latino (62 percent) and African American (22 percent), with African Americans predominant in some of the over 280 tracts, or neighborhoods, that comprise the core.

Most blacks in the poverty core live in single-family homes that are one or two stories tall, but apartment-style project housing shelters some of the poorest residents. In response to an overall increase in violent crime, many homeowners have

---

> **THE LITERARY WORK**
>
> A novel set in parts of Los Angeles, Santa Cruz, and Santa Barbara, California, in the early 1990s; published in 1994.
>
> **SYNOPSIS**
>
> Other lives are intertwined with those of two black high school students who are preparing for drastically different futures.

---

taken precautions like installing bars on their windows and fencing their yards. Simple pleasures that most people take for granted—sitting on the front porch, going for a jog, letting children play outside—are denied residents who fear street violence, break-ins, and harassment by police.

In the novel, the comforts enjoyed by people who live on the Westside are contrasted with the harsher reality in South Central. A young black man named François makes the following observations on a trip to an apartment complex on the Westside, just twenty minutes from his home:

> Five-story apartment buildings on both sides and in the center where we're walking, hot tubs and pools and brick ponds, cool and blue in front of each building. Ahead I see tennis courts. It's like Disneyland. We pass two white people soaking in a hot tub, their conversation dies as we get close. Must scare them like hell. Pay all that money to live behind twenty-foot walls and they still got to see us.
>
> (*Understand This,* p. 17)

The National Guard was called out to restore order in Los Angeles during the 1992 riot.

The tension in this encounter recalls the riots and looting that ravaged Los Angeles in the spring of 1992. Unrest and rebellion were specific names given to the response provoked when a jury acquitted four white police officers charged with civil rights violations, despite a videotape that showed them taunting and severely beating black motorist Rodney King, who lay motionless on the ground. Seventy-two hours of rioting followed the verdict.

The riots brought a rush of attention to inner-city problems like police brutality, unemployment and falling incomes, inadequate business investment, substandard schooling, and hostility between different ethnic groups. Suddenly it became common knowledge outside of South Central that its residents resented the presence of a liquor store on every corner and the absence or scarcity of banks, offices, shopping malls, and other businesses capable of creating jobs and generating revenue that would remain in the community. News programs and talk shows spent weeks discussing how the same problems and hopelessness that had prompted the Watts riots in 1965 seemed to have persisted almost unchanged.

Many people worked to improve the crisis-like conditions in South Central and the surrounding areas. Local church leaders and House Representative Maxine Waters had devoted themselves to addressing local problems for decades already. At this point, the challenge was also taken up by young people, such as the members of the South Central/Watts chapter of Americorps. President Bill Clinton's nationwide Americorps program was designed to encourage higher education through stipends and put young people to work in new and pre-existing local programs. In the South Central/Watts area, black and Latino Americorps members in their late teens and early twenties made full-time, nine-month commitments to serve their community through health education, tutoring, gardening, and violence prevention projects.

Violence. "It's like a war out there," thought Tervalon after one of his favorite students was shot to death and another suffered a nervous breakdown, also the result of a shooting (Tervalon in McLellan, p. 2). In the novel, at least two characters are murdered, and others are shot or threatened; many of them have accepted the role that violence plays in gang- and drug-related activities.

Around the time of the novel, Los Angeles's black and Latino youth ran a considerably higher risk of becoming homicide victims than young whites did. One study revealed that the overall homicide rate among blacks was roughly nine times higher than that of whites, while the rate among Latinos was about four times higher than that of whites. A 1993 study showed that homicide was in fact the leading cause of death among the city's young black men and women. It was furthermore found that more than 90 percent of these killings were committed with firearms, the weaponry used in the novel.

The media and many statistical records sometimes assume that homicides and lesser crimes committed by minorities in the inner city are gang-related even when they are not. Gang violence does in fact account for a significant share of crime, but none of the murders in *Understand This* is gang-related. Still the largest Los Angeles gangs—the Bloods and the Crips—make their presence felt in the novel by wearing gang colors. This practice is consistent with real life: Bloods wear red, and Crips wear blue, in the style of Mexican immigrant gang members who used to wear blue bandannas.

The spring of 1992 witnessed an unusual and welcome development: a gang truce negotiated in meetings between Crips and Bloods. Gang leaders met behind closed doors and reached an agreement, despite the frustration of having their peaceful meetings broken up by police on a regular basis. The truce resulted in a dramatic decrease in the number of drive-by shootings, but it did not prevent all gang-related violence, since some factions of the two gangs were unwilling to accept the truce. The fact that a unity movement came together at all is remarkable, given that an estimated 219 Crip gangs and 84 Blood gangs existed, each with its own leadership, rules, and interests. As the months passed, however, those participating in the truce were frustrated by the fact that the media seemed to focus on violations of the truce rather than the positive impact it was having. At the same time, many had expected that the government would recognize their efforts and come through with educational, economic, and recreational opportunities as an alternative to gang activity or at least as a show of good faith. But no such recognition was forthcoming, and the failure brought deep disillusionment. One young man described the failure:

> These brothers have done the part that society asked them to do. We ought to be ashamed of ourselves to let such a historic event go unanswered.
>
> (ex-gang member Fred Williams in Katz, p. 22)

In addition to gang-related aggression, among the other causes of injury and death by violence have been the need to settle personal disagreements, support drug habits, and do business as a drug dealer. Whatever the motivation, local hospital emergency rooms have received a steady stream of victims of shootings, stabbings, or similar injuries. The load placed on hospital staff members in real life helps the reader understand why Ann, a registered nurse in the novel, feels overwhelmed working in the emergency room.

Drug dealing and use. One of the ironies of life in the inner city is the fact that drug dealers often feel superior to the desperate users they supply. This reflects the self-concept many dealers have of themselves as respectable businessmen, as well as the fact that few lucrative, mentally challenging jobs exist in the inner city. The status, strategy, and financial gain involved in being a dealer attract many young people willing to take enormous risks.

DISNEYLAND VISITS THE INNER CITY

Frustration with the lack of job opportunities and corporate investment in inner-city areas contributed to the 1992 Los Angeles riots. In the months following the unrest, Disneyland was one of the companies to make a good-will gesture toward inner-city youth, traveling to South Central to interview job applicants aged 17 to 22 for 200 summer jobs. Company officials were surprised when over 600 young men and women showed up. They were also surprised to see that the applicants did not match the negative images of inner-city youth usually presented by the media. "They were wonderful kids, outstanding kids," said one spokesman. "We didn't know they were there" (Rimer, p. 20). The jobs paid only $5.25 an hour, but one young woman voiced the applicants' desire for any acceptable work: "A job's a job! Disneyland's Disneyland. It's not like Popeye's or McDonald's [fast food restaurants where she had worked for the last three years]. It's like, 'Hey girl, how'd you get that job at Disneyland?'" (Rimer, p. 20).

Understand This presents both major and minor players on the drug scene. A relatively small-time dealer named François reflects on the disapproval of his girlfriend Margot, his reasons for dealing, and the greed of a fellow dealer:

> Margot don't know, don't see it or she doesn't want to see it, what I have is because of what I do, and if I didn't have it, if I was a scruffling,

half-assed fool working at some bullshit job she wouldn't gone out with me. My mama works hard for money. She don't need me begging off of her. In this world you gotta get up off of it, gotta get your own, work for it and not be a fool. I'm not a fool. . . . Tommy's a fool cause he needs too much. I only need a little.

(*Understand This,* p. 44)

The characters in the novel deal mainly in marijuana and the rock form of cocaine called crack. In the real world, law enforcement, legislators, and the court system were creating and applying tough laws to deter even the smallest drug transactions. In one highly publicized case in 1989, a twenty-two-year-old black man, Richard Winrow, was made an example of when he was sentenced to life in prison without possibility of parole for possessing just 5.5 ounces of crack. Critics complained the sentence was harsher than that given some murderers, but authorities were pleased. The Assistant U.S. Attorney and chief of the Los Angeles Gang Drug Task Force even planned to put up posters in South Central, advertising details of the young man's case as a warning to others.

In addition to drug dealing, Tervalon's novel focuses on users by including scenes of young women trading sex for a quick fix and an addict shooting a dealer at point-blank range in order to steal his supply. Needle-sharing and this kind of sexual contact had devastating consequences for real addicts, since such behavior put them at extremely high risk for contracting sexually transmitted diseases such as AIDS.

Life in school. Mr. Michaels, a teacher at fictional Bolt High School in the novel, tries hard to capture his students' attention with facts about safe sex and HIV transmission leading to the AIDS disease, for example. Since few of his students display interest in the academic curriculum, he wants to wedge in a few practical lessons when he can. The lack of interest and the disciplinary problems he encounters on a daily basis reflect a real-life lack of concern for education on the part of many students. The list of reasons is long, including poverty, deprivation, negative teacher expectations, lack of parental involvement, and a curriculum that seems unrelated to the limited opportunities students will face upon completing or abandoning school.

The underachievement of inner-city youth in school is well documented, although many students like Margot in the novel manage to keep their sights on college against all odds. Before attending the University of California at Santa Cruz, Margot takes part in a transition program like those designed to help real students from underprivileged areas deal with the fact that they have not been as well prepared for college as most other high school students.

Starting in the 1970s, "affirmative action" programs required university admissions committees to admit (and federal and state agencies to hire) a percentage of women, blacks, and other minorities in proportion to the presence of these minorities in the general population. The novel mentions affirmative action, which may have played a role in Margot's acceptance to the university.

In the years immediately following the publication of *Understand This,* two new developments began to reshape the debate about what was best for black students in California's high schools and universities. First, the constitutionality of affirmative action was called into question when the state's voters approved a 1996 initiative banning special consideration for any person on the basis of race, gender, or other factors. At the end of that same year, the Alameda County School District provoked controversy by announcing plans to recognize the nonstandard English spoken by its black students as a language of its own, called Ebonics, and to use this form of English to engage students in learning. Questions surrounding the issue sparked national debate about how best to reach out to America's black students, a group showing overall improvement in academic achievement but still behind by a significant margin. Furthermore, it has been confirmed that many more black youths drop out of school than whites. National statistics show only 67 percent of blacks finishing high school in contrast to 87 percent of whites (Taylor, p. 129). As many as a third of African American youths drop out before acquiring their high school diplomas.

The Novel in Focus

The plot. The chapters of *Understand This* contain a series of overlapping observations about the same events, told from eight different points of view.

A young black man named François is the first narrator. He and his good friend, Doug, had been tossing a football on 54th Street in South Central Los Angeles until Doug's light-skinned girlfriend Rika showed up. She and Doug are engaged in a heated argument, when she suddenly draws a gun and shoots her boyfriend twice, killing him. Though not at the scene himself, Doug's younger brother, Ollie, suspects Rika is the assassin, but François pretends not to know who the murderer is or where Rika lives.

François confides in his girlfriend, Margot, and the second chapter is told through her eyes. A confrontational young woman, she makes François consider the possibility that Rika was high on drugs and therefore might not have planned to kill Doug. Margot engages in routine power struggles with her father and passes time in the classroom of Mr. Michaels, watching him teach and discipline his students. Ollie, for one, seems determined to cause trouble.

The perspective shifts back to François as he attempts to deal with his family, Ollie, Margot, and a drug-dealing acquaintance named Tommy. François is already a small-scale drug dealer in Los Angeles, but he is reluctant to join Tommy in cultivating a market in Santa Barbara. Still unsure what to do about Rika, he hopes that going to her house and looking her in the face will help him decide. She turns out not to be home. Haunted by thoughts of Doug's drug use and dysfunctional relationship with Rika, François runs for miles on the beach in an effort to clear his head.

The next perspective is that of Mr. Michaels, who reflects on his permissive classroom environment and his fascination with Margot, whom he regards as "the class of a sorry act," meaning the class act of a sorry environment (*Understand This*, p. 51). He feels like an outsider now, even though he grew up nearby and the students accept and like him.

Unfortunately for Ollie, whose perspective next dominates the story, a high-rolling drug wholesaler named Cowboy telephones and demands the Mercedes belonging to Ollie's dead brother, Doug, as payment for a $20,000 debt that Doug had left behind. Ollie refuses. He searches for Rika and tries to take over Doug's drug business, with limited success. Later, Cowboy's men ambush and severely beat him, and he is rushed to the hospital by his sister, Sally.

The novel continues from the point of view of François's mother Ann, a nurse who has seen plenty of gang-related injuries and deaths at the hospital where she works. "This isn't no way to live," she thinks to herself, "seeing more and more Françoises in the emergency room in various states of dying" (*Understand This*, p. 80). Her pride in her responsible young daughter, Mary, is counterbalanced by her worry over her son. The three of them attend Doug's funeral,

where François spots Rika watching from a distance.

The next chapter opens with Rika at the cemetery and at home, talking to Doug in her mind. She is frequently high, and her inner monologue reveals an ongoing desire to taunt the boyfriend she killed. At one point, Rika starts to trade sex for crack, but she shoots and robs the dealer instead. She is pregnant with Doug's baby and determined to destroy it by smoking crack. Her family tries to get her professional help, but she runs away.

In a chapter narrated by François, he and Margot argue about whether or not they should have a baby and discuss the fact that she will soon leave to attend college in Santa Cruz. Aware that Margot disapproves of the business he does with Tommy, he feels ambivalent about being involved in drug dealing and seems to despise Tommy and Ollie's conduct as dealers.

Margot takes a week-long trip to Santa Cruz in order to participate in a transition program and familiarize herself with the area. She has considerable trouble relating to anyone, including the black students she meets, and is convinced college life will be miserable. Her return to Los Angeles disappoints her too: the fact that François does not meet her at the airport means he has gone to Santa Barbara with Tommy against her wishes.

Tommy continues the story in Santa Barbara. He is sure that dealing drugs provided by Cowboy and getting together with white women is the life for him. François could not be less enthusiastic, and he finally decides to quit the partnership and go home. The whole venture ends in disaster when one of Tommy's women makes off with $30,000. Tommy flees north after telling Cowboy that François stole the money.

A chapter narrated by Ann begins with the police's arresting François late one night in front of their house. Her son seems paranoid since returning from Santa Barbara, and Ann has taken steps toward moving the family to Atlanta. François is released, but he does not discuss his problems.

The perspective shifts to the teacher Mr. Michaels again: Ann's coaxing has convinced him to try to talk with her son. François says little, but he does express interest in driving Margot to Mr. Michaels's upcoming wedding, and she consents.

In the next chapter, François tells how he seeks out Cowboy and sets the record straight about what happened in Santa Barbara. François starts working for Cowboy at a check-cashing store that he runs in addition to his drug-wholesaling business. Later François and Margot drive to Santa Barbara for Mr. Michaels's wedding and spend the night together, probably for the last time.

The next chapter is told from the point of view of Sally, the sister of Ollie and Doug. While feeding homeless people at her church, she sees Rika and realizes that Doug must be responsible for the pregnancy. Sally enlists the aid of Ann in an effort to help Rika with prenatal care. François drives Sally and Ann to the shelter where Rika now lives so that they can take her to a hospital. Ollie has followed them, and before he sees Rika he starts screaming and waving a gun at François, with whom he has had a falling out earlier in the story. At one point, the gun goes flying, and Rika slowly picks it up and shoots Ollie to death.

Mr. Michaels, who has quit his teaching job and become a law student, catches up on local news through Margot six months later. Michaels learns of Ollie's death and observes François sitting on the front porch with Rika's baby.

A mind for business. One of the background characters in *Understand This* offers a troubling example of a young black man who has succeeded despite the limits typically placed on young black men's potential in the inner city. He is Cowboy, the wholesale drug dealer who looms above the novel's other dealers in wealth, status, and power.

When Cowboy's knees gave out after two semesters of playing sports at a university, one traditional avenue to success for young black men closed to him. He left the university and became a businessman in the most profitable business in his community: drug dealing. By the time the reader meets him, he has developed the talents and strategies common to any high-powered, law-abiding executive. He surrounds himself with intelligent, hardworking people, whose respect and loyalty he commands. In dealing with his employees, Cowboy rewards the professionalism and ethical behavior displayed by François, while rebuking Tommy for his incompetence and unreliability. He is a shrewd judge of human nature and skilled in testing the character of his subordinates. His barren office and conservative approach to entering the drug market in Santa Barbara attest to his ability to manage money and make wise business decisions.

Looking back, Cowboy realizes that no one saw potential in him and muses that it took time for him to come around and make something of himself. In François, he recognizes, "the kinda brother who gets it together when he's little older," adding, "I was like that but nobody could see" (*Understand This*, p. 171). The result was that Cowboy set about applying his talents illegally, doing damage to his community in the process. From his point of view, the realistic alternative was a dull minimum-wage job in a local fast-food restaurant.

Sources and writing. Jervey Tervalon based *Understand This* on his own experiences in Los Angeles, where he attended and taught high school. One of his students was shot to death after basketball practice by gang members who had mistaken him for someone else. Another suffered a nervous breakdown after his cousin was murdered. And Tervalon could not forget the scene that a friend had witnessed and told him about years earlier, while Tervalon was enrolled at Dorsey High School: during an argument in the street, a boy's girlfriend had shot him in the face after he slapped her. These actions find parallels in the murders and other violent incidents in the novel, as well as the characters' feelings about killing.

There are similarities between the English teacher in *Understand This* and the novelist himself. Suffering from burnout yet reluctant to leave his job, the fictional Mr. Michaels resembles Tervalon in the late 1980s at the end of five years of teaching at Locke High School in South Central. Both eventually moved on to graduate school.

The inspiration for the novel came primarily from the lives of Tervalon's students and the author's desire to portray the psychology that might be behind their actions. As he saw it, society usually overlooked the suffering that lay beneath the tough exterior presented by many of these young people. He returned to an unsatisfactory first draft of *Understand This* while attending a graduate writing workshop at the University of California at Irvine. Told that his characters did not talk like real blacks, Tervalon resolved to revise his manuscript and make the dialogue truer to that spoken in Los Angeles. He explained later that when he read from the new passages, the other students in the writing workshop, who were white, "didn't understand a lot of the dialogue, but they liked it. And I liked that reaction: They were sort of intimidated by it, so I continued to write at a pretty quick pace" (Tervalon in McLellan, p. 2). He finished the novel while in the writing program. Once the manuscript was given to an agent, it sold within three weeks.

Reception. Hailed as a gritty and powerful novel, *Understand This* offered readers a compelling story told from several points of view not commonly included in discussions about the inner city. Critics pointed out that the type of events in the novel had been portrayed in fiction before, yet Tervalon's treatment of characters marked the novel as a bold, unusual look at modern urban life. One reviewer appreciated the novel's authenticity in the following terms:

> Tervalon takes his audience beyond the violence to a place viewers of Black inner-city films and readers of books about Black inner-city life rarely get to go: Through the crack, crime and craziness that overwhelms much of today's writing about the inner city and obscures what life is really like there.
>
> (Monroe, p. 61)

Other reviewers shared this sentiment, praising the novel's multidimensional characters and recognizing the insight and integrity needed to present them so sensitively and honestly.

For More Information

Katz, Jessie. "Violence Punctuates Truce between Bloods and Crips." *Los Angeles Times* (September 13, 1992): sec. A, pp. 1, 20, 22.

McLellan, Dennis. "'It's Like a War Out There': Teacher-Novelist Gives an Eloquent, Gritty Voice to the Struggles of Black Youth in Los Angeles." *Los Angeles Times* (April 4, 1994): sec. E, p. 2.

Monroe, Sylvester. "'Understand This' Explores Tough Life and Death Choices." *Emerge* 5, no. 6 (March 1994): 61.

Rimer, Sara. "Job Opportunities Bring Out Young People (and Their Idealism) in Riot Area." *The New York Times* (June 18, 1992): sec. A, p. 20.

Scott, Allen J., and E. Richard Brown, eds. *South Central Los Angeles: Anatomy of an Urban Crisis.* Los Angeles: Lewis Center for Regional Policy Studies. Working Paper No. 6., June 1993.

Smith, Anna Deavere. *Twilight: Los Angeles 1992.* New York: Anchor, Doubleday, 1994.

Taylor, Ronald L., ed. *African-American Youth: Their Social and Economic Status in the United States.* Westport, Conn.: Praeger, 1995.

Tervalon, Jervey. *Understand This.* New York: Anchor Books, Doubleday, 1994.

Watership Down

by
Richard Adams

THE LITERARY WORK

A novel set in England's countryside in the mid- to late twentieth century; published in 1972.

SYNOPSIS

A small group of rabbits flee their warren to escape poisoning by men and to attempt to establish a new warren without the unfair hierarchy of their original home.

While working as a civil servant in Great Britain's Department of Environment, Richard Adams began writing *Watership Down*. The novel developed from stories that Adams told to amuse his two young daughters. At their insistence, Adams began writing the novel and finished it two years later. After numerous rejections, he finally found a publisher who agreed to print a small number of copies. The book became an immediate success with both juvenile and adult audiences.

Events in History at the Time of the Novel

Rabbits in fiction and the wild. Rabbits are believed to have been brought to England by the Normans in the eleventh century and to have been abundant there ever since. They prefer to place their warrens in dry areas that allow for easy digging and comfortable shelter. Their diet consists of grasses and plants and any vegetables that can be obtained from nearby gardens. Typically rabbits live in small groups that are dominated by a single male. This dominant male will have clearly marked territory as well as claim to one or more female rabbits. Other powerful males will have their own smaller territories and usually one of their own mates. The males mark their territories with excretions from a gland on their chins, which they rub on the ground bordering their space. If another male intrudes on the dominant male's territory, the intruder will be attacked and chased away.

Female rabbits, called does, typically dig the warrens; in rare instances the male helps, but usually only for a few minutes at a time. Does can produce a litter approximately once every thirty days. The offspring, though born furless and blind, are on their own at the end of thirty days, when their mother must begin nursing the next litter. A phenomenon in female rabbits is the process of resorption, through which they reabsorb their embryonic litters if the area is overpopulated. The process only takes two to three days and occurs most often in subordinate does, who typically are the younger ones in a community. In the novel, the younger Efrafan female rabbits want to leave their overpopulated warren because they have been reabsorbing their young.

Richard Adams used R. M. Lockley's *The Private Life of the Rabbit* as his primary source for *Watership Down,* and several of his rabbit characters seem modeled after Lockley's examples.

The major difference between Lockley's and Adams's rabbits (aside from the fanciful ability of Adams's rabbits to speak to one another in English) is the mostly peaceful interaction among the male rabbits within a warren. In reality, a large group of male rabbits would not live together for such a long period of time without quarrels. None of the territoriality of real rabbits appears in the novel, and the rabbits of *Watership Down* rarely fight among themselves, except for one or two minor squabbles over a doe. Despite this difference, Adams's portrayal of his rabbits is consistent with many of Lockley's descriptions; the basic behavior of Adams's rabbits, as they eat, play, and hide from enemies, is true to reality, except for a few creative embellishments that develop them as characters for the story.

Man vs. rabbit. In the 1950s British farmers began taking a serious look at the damage to their crops caused by rabbits. Some estimates stated that rabbit infestation was costing British agriculture as much as £40 million per year. The problem had little to do with the rabbits themselves but rather came as a result of changes in human society. For centuries, the abundant human rural population had kept rabbit populations in check, capturing rabbits for their fur and as a food source. As more and more people left rural areas for the cities, the rabbit population began to grow unchecked. The introduction of the spring gin trap, a device consisting of two saw-edged semicircles of iron that close on a powerful spring, also caused the rabbit population to flourish. Though the traps caught numerous rabbits, they also captured and critically injured other animals, especially the rabbits' natural predators: fox, badger, weasels, cats, and wild birds. These animals had served as a natural control on the rabbit population, and their deaths caused it to rise dramatically. Ultimately the traps were outlawed by the Pests Act of 1954, thanks to efforts by humanitarians and farmers who understood the long-term effects of the gin traps.

In 1953 scientists began spreading a deadly disease to control the rabbit population. The disease, myxomatosis, causes the rabbit's eyelids to swell, and from there the inflammation quickly spreads to the ears, forehead, and nose. An animal usually dies about twelve days after becoming infected. As a rule the disease is carried by fleas that make their homes on the soft skin of rabbits' ears. Myxomatosis succeeded in its goal, severely reducing rabbit populations and saving British farmers millions of pounds. In the novel, myxomatosis has been experienced by some of the rabbits, who call it "white blindness" (Adams, *Watership Down*, p. 122).

In addition to myxomatosis, England's rabbits have also suffered at the hands of Rabbit Clearance Societies. These groups provide teams of experts that come on to agricultural lands to kill overabundant rabbit populations. They exist as a result of the Pests Act of 1954, through which the British Minister of Agriculture may give notice to a landowner to destroy rabbits that breed or live on his lands. By joining a Clearance Society and paying a small monthly fee, a landowner can obtain the use of the removal experts. These experts may remove rabbits legally by using ferrets or dogs to flush them out of their holes, gassing the holes, snaring the rabbits with a wire trap, netting them, or shooting them. In the novel, several of these removal methods are used against the rabbits. Their first warren is gassed, most likely with calcium cyanide dust, which produces hydrocyanic acid gas when blown into the burrow. The novel's Bigwig is caught in a wire snare, though he escapes, and Hazel narrowly avoids getting shot.

RABBIT FIGHTING

Despite their reputation as soft and timid animals, rabbits are fierce fighters among themselves. They employ their teeth and forepaws to fight, but their most powerful weapon is their clawed hindlegs, which they use to kick and scratch their opponents. With these hindleg kicks, one rabbit can rip open the stomach of a weaker opponent, killing it. In *Watership Down*, several rabbits are killed in attacks by other rabbits.

Social and economic issues in England. The 1960s and 1970s were a turbulent period in Great Britain's social and economic history. Some of the last vestiges of the Victorian era were cast aside during this time. During that age—which stretched across most of the nineteenth century and left its imprint on the twentieth century as well—people regarded adherence to laws and social codes as a matter of personal responsibility, which helps explain the era's reliance on class hierarchy and social stratification. Though Richard Adams specifically states that his novel is not meant to parallel human history or society, a strong connection appears nonetheless. Just as the social hierarchies of Victorian England continued to fade away during the 1960s and 1970s,

Photograph of an adult buck (right) and an immature rabbit (left), from R. M. Lockley's *The Private Life of the Rabbit,* Adams's source for *Watership Down.*

the strict hierarchies of the rabbits in the novel decline as they change warrens. The rabbits of *Watership Down* eventually lead a life devoid of hierarchy, where all aspects of life are strictly democratic and no member of the society remains subordinate to another.

Another parallel between British society and the rabbits of *Watership Down* can be found in relation to the issue of population decline. In the early 1970s, Great Britain was experiencing a decline in population for the first time in history. Not only was the birth rate falling, but since 1964 the number of people emigrating from the country had exceeded the number of people immigrating to it. Various demographic factors partially explained this trend, such as the availability

of reliable birth control methods, access to abortion, and changing attitudes in women toward having children—many saw a wider range of opportunity for themselves outside the home. In the novel, the rabbits begin to complacently settle in to live at Watership Down but then suddenly realize that their community will become extinct without female rabbits to raise litters. This realization prompts the dangerous expeditions to Efrafa from which they finally acquire the does necessary to the continuation of their society.

The Novel in Focus

The plot. Hazel is a young male rabbit living in a warren ruled by Threarah and his "Owsla," a group of powerful rabbits who reserve all privileges for themselves. While looking for food, Hazel and his brother Fiver find a newly erected sign near the warren. Fiver, a small rabbit who was the runt of the litter, immediately has a bad feeling about the sign. Hazel has seen Fiver's predictions of danger come true in the past and takes his premonitions seriously. He and Fiver gain an audience with the Threarah, and Fiver explains his feelings about the impending danger. Though he listens patiently, the Threarah dismisses Fiver's bad feelings and refuses to evacuate the warren as Fiver suggests.

Confident that Fiver is right, Hazel decides to take all willing rabbits away from the warren. Ten rabbits gather that night, including, to Hazel's surprise, two members of the Owsla—Bigwig and Silver. As they prepare to depart, Holly, the captain of the Threarah's Owsla, arrives with two Owsla soldiers to arrest Bigwig for inciting a mutiny against the Threarah. Bigwig instantly attacks Holly, and other rabbits join the fray, eventually chasing Holly and his henchmen away. Knowing that more of the Owsla will come after them, the small group flees the warren.

After several dangerous days in the open, the rabbits find another warren. They are surprised when Cowslip, a member of the new warren, greets them and invites them to join the community. After their initial suspicion wears off, Hazel's group enters the warren and are delighted to find that the rabbits are friendly and incredibly healthy, though surprisingly few in number. They are even more excited to find that a nearby farmer puts out vegetables for the rabbits and kills most of the rabbits' predators, making life quite safe and comfortable. Hazel and the other rabbits immediately begin enjoying this new lifestyle; only Fiver is uncomfortable, refusing to stay in the warren and wanting to leave immediately. One day, while roaming for food, Bigwig is caught by a snare. Hazel and the other rabbits are horrified, but stay with Bigwig and chew through the peg holding him. From this experience Hazel and the others realize that the farmer protects the rabbits only so that he can snare them for his own selfish aims. In terror, Hazel leads his rabbits away. Strawberry, a rabbit from the new warren, joins them, not wanting to live in fear any longer.

Hazel leads the rabbits to Watership Down, a high, sandy hill. The rabbits settle in and begin digging their new warren, happy to have found such a perfect location. A few days later, they are surprised to see Captain Holly approaching with Blueball, another rabbit from their first warren.

The rabbits are further dismayed when Holly tells how the entire warren was exterminated by men with poison gas and then dug up with a tractor. Holly and Bluebell are fully accepted into the new warren and join in constructing it.

As the warren takes shape, Hazel realizes that they will need does, or female rabbits, if their community is to last. About this time the rabbits find a wounded seagull recuperating nearby. Though it had never been done before, Hazel proposes befriending the bird and helping him to recover from his injuries. The bird, Kehaar, recovers in one of the tunnels of the warren and is grateful to the rabbits for sheltering and feeding him while he was weak. In return for their help, Kehaar agrees to scout out the surrounding territory from the air to see if there are any nearby rabbit communities where does might be found. Kehaar easily finds a community a few miles away. Holly leaves with three other rabbits, Silver, Buckthorn, and Strawberry, for the neighboring warren.

Meanwhile, an impulsive Hazel mischievously decides to investigate a rabbit hutch at a nearby farm. He hopes the group of tame rabbits might include some does that could be freed and brought back to Watership Down. After a dangerous adventure, Hazel and his comrades manage to avoid the farmer's two cats and dog and rescue three rabbits. Two new females and a male are brought back to the warren.

Holly and the other rabbits also return to the warren, exhausted and wounded. They describe the neighboring burrow, called Efrafa, and their horrible experience there. The warren is governed by a tyrannical leader called General Woundwort and his Owsla of incredibly powerful and merciless rabbits. When Holly and the others reached the warren, they were captured and forbidden to leave again. After a brief captivity, they managed to escape. Holly tells Hazel that the warren is overpopulated with does, but Woundwort would not even consider giving any of them up.

Hazel comes up with a plan and leaves for Efrafa with most of the rabbits. Bigwig approaches Efrafa posing as a refugee from a warren destroyed by men. Because of his power, size, and ability, Bigwig is immediately recruited into the Owsla, which rules Efrafa with an iron fist. Bigwig then plans an escape with some young does who are anxious to leave Efrafa. When it seems as though his deception has been discovered, he escapes with the does; a male rabbit, Blackavar, also comes along. Woundwort and his Owsla pursue them relentlessly, but Hazel gath-

Richard Adams

ers the male rabbits and the does in a boat, gnaws through the rope holding it, and escapes downriver from the Efrafan rabbits.

The rabbits of Watership Down finally have everything they need for a successful community; shortly after their return, several of the does are pregnant. Their temporary happiness is, however, broken by the arrival of Woundwort and an entire army of Efrafan rabbits. The rabbits of Watership Down seal the entrances to their warren and prepare to defend themselves against Woundwort's siege. All seems lost as Woundwort's troops dig into the burrow, but Hazel has an idea and charges out a side entrance with two rabbits, Dandelion and Blackberry. Hazel reaches the nearby farm and chews through the rope holding the dog. Dandelion and Blackberry play decoys and lead it back toward the warren. As Hazel watches them go, he is attacked from behind by the farmer's cat. Meanwhile, Bigwig faces Woundwort in a narrow tunnel and severely injures him, though Bigwig also suffers heavy wounds. At the most desperate moment the dog from the nearby farm charges into the Efrafan rabbits, ripping several of them to pieces and sending the others running for their lives back to Efrafa. Miraculously, Hazel is saved by the farmer's young daughter, who cleans him up and releases him. Bigwig recovers from his injuries,

and the rabbits finally settle in and begin living normal lives at Watership Down.

The rabbits' view of man. A recurring idea of the novel is the great danger to the rabbits from humankind. In the beginning of the novel, Fiver and Hazel see a sign, and Fiver realizes that it is the source of his bad feelings for the future. He says to Hazel, "This is where it comes from! I know now—something very bad! Some terrible thing—coming closer and closer" (*Watership Down,* p. 15). Fiver's premonitions prove accurate when the men kill the rabbits and bulldoze Fiver's first warren to make room for a housing development. When one of the rabbits suggests that the men destroyed the warren because the rabbits had been raiding a nearby garden, another rabbit, Toadflax, tells him, "That wasn't why they destroyed the warren. It was just because we were in their way. They killed us to suit themselves" (*Watership Down,* p. 163). Fiver concludes. "There's terrible evil in the world," and Holly elaborates on the evil: "It comes from men. All other elil (enemies) do what they have to do and Frith (the sun-god) moves them as he moves us. They live on the earth and they need food. Men will never rest till they've spoiled the earth and destroyed the animals" (*Watership Down,* p. 157).

Throughout the novel, human dangers threaten the rabbits. Bigwig is almost killed in a trap; they later realize that the farmer who appears benevolent toward them is interested only in trapping them for food. The cars, tractors, and trains of men also terrify the rabbits; the vehicles literally paralyze them with fear.

When Strawberry and Holly first visit the Efrafan warren, they try to use their common distrust of men as a bond to persuade the tyrannical leader Woundwort to let them leave with the does or to just let them leave peaceably. Holly describes his conversation with Woundwort to the other rabbits, saying, "Strawberry tried all he could to help me. He spoke very well about the decency and comradeship natural to animals. 'Animals don't behave like men,' he said. 'If they have to fight, they fight; and if they have to kill, they kill. But they don't sit down and set their wits to work to devise ways of spoiling other creatures' lives and hurting them. They have dignity and animality'" (*Watership Down*, p. 243). In an era during which land development was peaking and poisons and diseases were concocted to destroy rabbit populations, Strawberry's speech contains much truth about human attitudes toward the animal kingdom.

Composition and sources. Adams was first inspired to create a story about rabbits after he had read R. M. Lockley's *The Private Life of the Rabbit*. From this, Adams began telling stories to amuse his two young daughters and at their insistence he began writing the novel. In the process, Adams returned to Lockley's nonfiction book and used its detailed scientific descriptions to create his own fictional rabbits. Information about rabbit sicknesses, their leisure activities, and the various actions of the does comes directly from Lockley's work.

Some traits and interactions of the rabbits in the novel seem to have been drawn from the behavior Lockley witnessed in his rabbit test subjects. This use of Lockley's rabbits appears to be especially prominent in the depiction of the warrens of the Threarah and General Woundwort. The government by violence practiced by these two leaders, especially Woundwort, appears as normal rabbit behavior in Lockley's study. In his research the most powerful male rabbits would secure the best food sources and the majority of the does while the weaker male rabbits could neither lay stake to any desirable territory nor acquire any does. Though the novel seems to have drawn from these examples of tyranny and violence, its rabbits are much more likable and intriguing than any of Lockley's subjects. Adams's ability to give each of his rabbits distinct personalities while making their basic animal behavior realistic captivated readers and eventually made the novel an astounding success.

Adams also drew on personal experience to write *Watership Down*. Through his job with Great Britain's Department of Environment, he gained personal familiarity with the countryside setting used in the novel. The various places that appear in the course of the novel are real.

Critical reaction. Richard Adams received the Guardian Award and the Carnegie Medal for *Watership Down*. Critics praised him for creating an entire world of rabbits with its own language, mythology, and culture, and also praised him for his success in maintaining excitement and suspense in a novel about rabbits. "There are a lot of things that make this book work," wrote Eliot Fremont-Smith, "including the traditional and here expertly employed device of cliff-hanging chapter endings. But mainly it is Richard Adams's wonderfully rich imagination, together with an extraordinary and totally disarming respect for his material" (Fremont-Smith in Lesniak, p. 3). Another critic, Janet Adam Smith, lauded Adams for dignifying the action of the novel and making it not just the journey of a group of rabbits "but a movement of creatures who are no less part of nature than we are, and whose humble disasters and migrations have a claim to the attention of men, for all the greater scale of *theirs*" (Smith in Lesniak, p. 3). Lastly, Charles Thomas Samuels spoke of the lesson to humankind: "Among the pleasures offered by Adams' book is the implication that some of man's victims are clever enough to keep us from getting away with it, and that we might even learn from them something about escaping the beastliness of ourselves" (Samuels in Riley, p. 7).

For More Information

Adams, Richard. *Watership Down*. New York: Avon, 1972.

Bedarida, François. *A Social History of England, 1851-1990*. New York: Routledge, 1991.

Havighurst, Alfred F. *Britain in Transition: The Twentieth Century*. Chicago: University of Chicago Press, 1985.

Lesniak, James G., ed. *Contemporary Authors New Revision Series*. Vol. 35. Detroit: Gale Research, 1992.

Lloyd, T. O. *Empire to Welfare State: English History, 1906-1985*. New York: Oxford University Press, 1986.

Lockley, R. M. *The Private Life of the Rabbit*. New York: October House, 1966.

Riley, Carolyn, ed. *Contemporary Literary Criticism*. Vol. 4. Detroit: Gale Research, 1975.

The Woman Warrior: Memoirs of a Girlhood among Ghosts

by
Maxine Hong Kingston

Born in Stockton, California, in 1940, as a first-generation Chinese American, Maxine Hong Kingston grew up under the sometimes competing influences of Chinese and American cultures. As both a female among Chinese and as a Chinese American among other ethnic groups, she found herself devalued and limited in her opportunities. Her memoir *The Woman Warrior* includes contrasting images of female power and female oppression. Published in a decade that saw the growth of an active women's movement in the United States, Hong Kingston's memoir was immediately embraced by the feminist community.

Events in History at the Time the Memoir Takes Place

Gold Mountain. When the *Woman Warrior* opens, it refers to the 1924 emigration of Hong Kingston's father from China to Gold Mountain in California. The destination, by then, had been attracting Chinese men for around seventy-five years. After gold was discovered at Sutter's Mill, California, in 1848, men from China raced to the area to make their fortune through mining. As far away as Hong Kong, tales of the "gum shan" or "mountain of gold" in California enticed would-be prospectors onto ships heading for the West Coast. Aside from the potential rewards of mining, the highest wages in the world

> **THE LITERARY WORK**
>
> A fictionalized memoir set in China and San Francisco from approximately 1924 to 1975; published in 1976.
>
> **SYNOPSIS**
>
> A Chinese American woman struggles against the confinements of Chinese and American culture.

were to be had in the mining communities of California, by launderers and railway workers as well as other laborers. The money drew a flood of Chinese immigrants, attracted by the high pay ($30 a month for a railroad job in 1860s America, in contrast to $3 to $5 a month for a job in South China). The immigrants were almost exclusively male. In China, a woman was raised to "obey her father as a daughter, her husband as a wife, and her eldest son as a widow. As a daughter-in-law, she was expected to take care of her husband's aging parents" (Takaki, pp. 36-7). So married women stayed home, while single women were taught not to travel to faraway places alone.

Coming to America. Hong Kingston's mother arrives in the United States in 1940, sixteen years after her husband. *The Woman Warrior* is, in fact,

U.S. POLICY ON CHINESE IMMIGRATION

1882: Chinese Exclusion Act bans immigration of all laborers from China to the United States until 1892.

1892: Chinese Exclusion Act is renewed for ten more years.

1902: Chinese Exclusion Act is renewed indefinitely.

1924: Johnson-Reed Act imposes quotas on all nationalities desiring to enter the United States; the system favors immigrants from Western Europe.

1943: Chinese Exclusion Act repealed; 105 Chinese per year allowed to enter the United States.

1946: Chinese wives of American citizens may immigrate freely. The number of Chinese women admitted climbs from 64 in 1945 to 986 in 1947 to 3,317 in 1948.

1965: Immigration Act of 1965 does away with quota system by nationality; sets up a limit of 170,000 immigrants per year from the Eastern Hemisphere, allowing immediate relatives to be admitted without regard to this limit.

full of arrivals—Hong Kingston's father and mother, her uncle, her cousin, and her aunt all arrive in America at different times. Historically, the conditions of immigration differed during these various periods. Apart from the years immediately following the gold rush of 1848, it has not been easy for Chinese people to immigrate to the United States. Until recently, laws and quotas have been enacted to keep the numbers of Asian immigrants to a minimum.

Hong Kingston's father was one of the lucky few who gained entry to America from China in 1924, the year quotas were imposed on all nationalities desiring to enter the country. Hong Kingston herself seems unsure whether or not he entered legally or as a stowaway. While the Chinese Exclusion Act forbade the entry of laborers from China, it did not apply to merchants, students, citizens by birth, and the children of citizens, so a few Chinese could still lawfully immigrate. Also, some exceptions were made for women to immigrate during the exclusion period (1882-1943), since the Chinese Americans consisted mainly of males at first. Between 1906 and 1924 the government made provision for a number of Chinese men to send for their wives; 150 women a year were legally admitted to America during this period. Such a policy was later adopted again. Under the 1930 Immigration Act, Chinese women were allowed to immigrate if they had married men now residing in America before May 26, 1924 (the date on which the 1924

Immigration Act became law). Only sixty such women were allowed entrance a year, however. It is during this period of limited immigration that Hong Kingston's mother, the character identified in the memoir as Brave Orchid, joins her husband in New York.

When the 1965 Immigration Act finally did away with the quota system and admitted immediate relatives without subjecting them to numerical limits, more Chinese families were reunited. Immigrants from other parts of the Eastern Hemisphere also came to escape their war-torn homelands. Moon Orchid, Hong Kingston's aunt in *The Woman Warrior,* arrived in California about 1969, six years before the Vietnam War would start driving hundreds of thousands of Asians to America. Meanwhile, U.S. troops, including Chinese Americans, found themselves fighting overseas in this war. Hong Kingston's brother, for example, served with the American contingent in Vietnam.

The land they left. *The Woman Warrior* takes place against the backdrop of Chinese history: the tides of emigration from China to America relate just as much to events in Asia as to what was happening in the United States. Hong Kingston reminisces at different points in the memoir about various historical wars, about Chinese social institutions (such as marriage and family structure), about Maoist communism and the Cultural Revolution, and about how these events affect the people in her life.

Mao Zedong and adoring followers.

The political and economic climate in China made emigration from that country very attractive in the mid-nineteenth century. The gold rush in America coincided with floods and famine in China that destroyed crops and endangered the livelihood of peasant farmers (who comprised the bulk of the population). A violent civil war, known as the Taiping Rebellion (1851-64), was ravaging southern China. The "Opium Wars" (1839-42 and 1856-60) with Great Britain, which were begun when the Chinese destroyed vast stores of Western European-owned opium, and which China lost, opened the country's previously closed ports to Western influences. China was forced to concede Hong Kong to Great Britain and to pay a $21 million reparation fee to the British government. This was, of course, economically devastating to the nation, but even more importantly for Chinese immigration, the influx of Western goods and Western ideas made the Chinese people consider the possibility of escaping economic and political hardships at home by sailing for America.

The Boxer Rebellion of 1900, an antiforeigner nationalist movement in China, sought (and failed) to expel all foreign (mostly British and American) people and influences from the nation, leading to a military invasion and then occupation of China by Western powers. The Chinese Republic was proclaimed in 1911, as the last Qing emperor abdicated, ending three thousand years of rule by Chinese monarchs. Uproar ensued in 1916-28 as opposing warlords, who were backed by different imperial powers, struggled for control. It was during this period of unrest that Hong Kingston's father departed China for New York.

The years 1917-23 saw an intellectual revolution in China, in which activists called for the acceptance of Western science and democracy as the basis of a new way of life. The period is sometimes called the May Fourth Movement because of a huge student demonstration held on May 4, 1919. About 5,000 demonstrators gathered in Beijing to protest a verdict of the World War I Versailles Peace Conference. The verdict awarded to Japan control of the Chinese province of Shantung. Idealistic about democracy when the talks began, many Chinese were sorely disappointed by this turn of events. Some felt so disillusioned that they rejected democracy and began to embrace Marxist socialism or communism. Shortly thereafter, in 1921, the Chinese Communist Party was founded. It would take more than two decades for it to seize power. The country first came under the control of the Guomindang Nationalist Party, then was invaded by Japan in 1937. The Communists pledged their support to the Nationalists in the Sino-Japanese War, taking advantage of the opportunity to move into central China and set up Communist bases there (Hsü, p. 589).

Plagued by overlapping wars—the Sino-Japanese War (1937-45) and World War II (1939-45)—China's Nationalist government did not attend to the distress of its own people, who were in dire need of social and economic reforms. This distress contributed to the subsequent outbreak of Civil War (1945-49) between China's Communists and Nationalists. Emerging victorious, the Communists quickly took control of the government, with Mao Zedong declaring the establishment of the People's Republic of China on October 1, 1949.

As Hong Kingston herself relates, one of the first things the Chinese communists did, inspired by their Russian counterparts, was to make women equal to men. Less happily, and as Hong Kingston also relates, the government immediately "redistributed" land among the Chinese peasantry, killing and imprisoning people who had once been landowners. Many of Hong Kingston's relatives were executed for the crime of owning property in pre-Communist China.

Women in China. The Communists in China killed members of Hong Kingston's family simply for owning land. Yet her memoir does not completely condemn them, for upon taking power, they granted Chinese women more equality than they had ever enjoyed previously. Customarily, women were second-class citizens. Female infanticide had always been common, because girls were generally considered an economic burden and a social shame. In *The Woman Warrior,* Brave Orchid describes how female babies were often killed immediately after being born; the doctor would take a bowl of ashes kept by the labor bed in case the baby was a girl and, holding the back of the child's head, would turn the face into the pile of ashes until the infant suffocated. If females were not killed as babies, they were sold into servitude by many families or married off as soon as possible into other families. Marketplaces were filled with girls for sale and with infants who were given away at no cost. As *The Woman Warrior* relates, Hong Kingston's mother herself eventually bought a slave girl, for approximately $50.

The Memoir in Focus

The contents. Told in five sections, *The Woman Warrior* examines the torments and indignities of being a female in Chinese culture and of being Chinese American in mainstream American so-

ciety. The book combines personal memoir, family history, traditional Chinese legends (given a new twist) and pure fantasy, in the creation of a literary genre that is unique. However, it is more often considered a valid family history than a fictionalized tale.

LIGHT UP THE HOUSE

Hong Kingston relates her childhood thankfulness for the communist takeover in China, since it means that she will never have to return there with her family, where she would surely be sold into slavery. "[W]hile the adults wept . . . I was secretly glad. As long as the aunts kept disappearing and the uncles dying after unspeakable tortures, my parents would prolong their Gold Mountain [Californian] stay" (Kingston, *The Woman Warrior,* p. 190). She is also grateful for the Communist stance on women, and hopes that under their rule, the birth of a girl will cause the house of the parents to be lit up with festive lights as it traditionally was only for the birth of boys.

The Woman Warrior opens with the tale of Hong Kingston's aunt, known only as "No Name Woman." In compliance with Chinese tradition, her marriage was arranged; shortly thereafter her husband immigrated to America. The two were almost strangers to each other, having spent less than a year together and many years apart. Nevertheless, women were expected to remain faithfully married for their entire lives, even in the absence of their husband, and so when the aunt became pregnant by another man, she and her family were punished for her crime. Jeopardizing the delicate balance of social relations in the small village by her adultery and producing a child out of wedlock at a time of famine and hardship, Hong Kingston's aunt is portrayed as being treated to a village-wide display of hatred and revenge. On the night on which it seemed likely she would give birth, the family house was ransacked, livestock were slaughtered, crops razed, and personal goods destroyed. The aunt left the ruined house and gave birth alone in the pigsty, in a small brave attempt to provide some protection for her child. In the morning she drowned herself and the baby in the nearby well, poisoning the drinking water. No one in the family ever mentioned her again, except as a warning. Hong Kingston's mother would say: "Don't tell anyone you had an aunt. Your father does not want to hear her name. She has never been born" (*The Woman Warrior*, p. 15). In telling the story of this nameless woman, Hong Kingston gives a voice to a woman who could not speak for herself, but still she feels guilty for having participated in her relative's punishment: "In the twenty years since I heard this story I have not asked for details nor said my aunt's name; I do not know it" (*The Woman Warrior*, p. 16).

THE SLAVE MARKET

In *The Woman Warrior,* following her graduation from medical school, Brave Orchid decides to buy herself a slave. Such girls were readily available in the market, where their parents tried to sell them, or where professional slave traders who had already bought them from their parents haggled for their price with potential buyers. "'Open your mouth,' [Brave Orchid] said, and examined teeth. She pulled down eyelids to check for anemia. She picked up the girls' wrists to sound their pulses." (*The Woman Warrior*, p. 80)

The second part of the book, entitled "White Tigers," contrasts a heroic fiction about a woman warrior with the decidedly unheroic business of being an average Chinese American woman in a family in which females have no worth. The story of the woman warrior begins when a Chinese girl is magically drawn up a mountain away from her parents and into the presence of an old man and woman, who offer to train her in the skills of being a warrior, an avenger for her family and village of all the wrongs done to them by rich and powerful men. Her family misses her but knows that she has been picked out by fate for a very important purpose, and they wait eagerly for her return. For fourteen years, the woman remains with the old couple, from whom she learns survival tactics, combat skills, and the art of meditation and mind control. When she reaches adulthood, she returns to her village to lead an assault against the ruling elite that is threatening her family and community. She disguises herself as a man and becomes one of the most heralded leaders in China, a savior of her village. Everyone loves and feels gratitude toward her, especially her husband, who respects and adores his powerful wife.

Hong Kingston contrasts this fantasy of female power with her own experiences as a girl. She perpetually endured sexist comments and behavior from her Chinese neighbors and family: "Better to raise geese than girls" (*The Woman Warrior*, p. 46), she heard once, and records that the Chinese word for the female "I" is also the word for "slave" (*The Woman Warrior*, p. 47). Her parents will not take her and her sister out in public because other Chinese people shake their heads in pity for the family that has no sons. As the section ends, Hong Kingston, who now lives far away from her family and the Chinese community that knows her, expresses the wish that they might accept her as a warrior woman and not as just another disappointing female, so that she can return from self-imposed exile and live among them in peace.

"Shaman" is the third part of *The Woman Warrior;* it tells the story of Brave Orchid, Hong Kingston's mother, who enrolls in medical school after her husband departs for America. Because she is so much older than the other students (a fact that she keeps carefully hidden), she studies much harder and garners respect for her great mind. Upon graduation she returns to her village, where she is greatly admired as an excellent doctor. With her she has brought a slave whom she purchased to act as her nurse. Hong Kingston dwells upon the fact that her mother once had a female slave, seeming torn between the horror of the slave market and the conviction that her mother valued the slave girl more than she ever did her own daughter.

"Shaman" goes on to reveal that Brave Orchid immigrated to New York in January 1940, and that she bore a child, Hong Kingston, during the World War II years. Although Brave Orchid derived self-respect from her own advanced education, with her daughters she was primarily concerned that they learn skills that would win them a husband, convinced they could not support themselves. Hong Kingston tried continually to impress her mother with good grades and scholarships, but her mother never outwardly voiced her approval. Instead she told her daughter endless ghost stories and spoke often about the terrible "ghost country" in which they lived. Hong Kingston's mother called Americans ghosts, partly because of their lack of history and their propensity to speak about insubstantial matters. Traditional Chinese speak little and do not waste breath on trivial matters, so Hong Kingston's mother considered most Americans insubstantial and ghostlike. By inference, Hong Kingston, a Chinese *American* herself, fell into this ghostlike group.

The fourth section, "At the Western Palace," is about another of Hong Kingston's aunts, Moon Orchid, her mother's sister. Moon Orchid's husband had immigrated to America decades ago, and, while he did send money regularly to her, he never returned to China or requested that she join him in Los Angeles. Brave Orchid decides that her sister must come to America and reclaim what is hers. Although the husband has remarried, Brave Orchid fantasizes about bullying both him and his second wife and about installing her sister into the home that is rightfully hers. Moon Orchid moves to California and slowly but surely Brave Orchid gets her to confront her husband in Los Angeles. It turns out that the husband is a successful brain surgeon married to one of his young nurses, and Brave Orchid has to orchestrate a fake accident scene to get the doctor down to the street where his first wife waits in the car. Needless to say, he is hardly glad to see her and confesses that she seems like something out of a story that he once read. He promises to continue to send her money, but he refuses to do anything else for her and never wants to see her again. Devastated, Moon Orchid moves in with her daughter, who had immigrated to America five years previously and also lives in Los Angeles. But Moon Orchid cannot adjust and begins to imagine a Mexican conspiracy against her. Brave Orchid sends for her once again, and the family watches the aunt decline into madness. Every time someone leaves the house, she is convinced that they will never return. Moon Orchid dies soon after being committed to a mental hospital.

The final section, "A Song for a Barbarian Reed Pipe," begins with a traditional Chinese story about a poetess named Ts-ai Yen, who was born in A.D. 175 and abducted twenty years later by foreign raiders. Hong Kingston allies herself with this writer who is forced to make the best of being trapped in a culture that is not hers. Writing of herself as a woman seeking to reconcile her cultural divergences and identities, the author confronts her mother, her community, and society at large in an effort to break free from the restrictions she feels have been placed on her as a Chinese American woman. Far from home and uprooted from her culture, Ts-ai Yen similarly struggles to live successfully in her new society, yet remains firmly tied to the Chinese culture of her homeland. Her children never learn to speak Chinese, and she never learns to speak the tongue of her captors. But when she finally returns home, she brings with her songs with Chinese words and alien music, which signifies a certain level of cultural integration. The book ends simply with the observation that one of the songs from this alien experience, "Eighteen Stanzas for a Barbarian Reed Pipe," has endured in Chinese culture because "[i]t translated well" (*The Woman Warrior*, p. 209).

Giving voice. *The Woman Warrior* breaks ground by shattering myths about Chinese American women and stereotypes of them. Hong Kingston relates previously "secret" stories of women in her family and society, stories of women who could not speak for themselves. By telling their stories she gives power to their memories and to all women who are repressed and unable to speak for themselves.

The most powerful image of the silence imposed upon women occurs in the final section of the book. Hong Kingston tells the odd story about how her mother cut—or said she did—her daughter's frenum (fold under the tongue) so that she would not be tongue-tied and could speak in any language. The daughter, however, sees this act of mutilation as a cause of her inability to speak English in public. Her childhood is spent in almost utter silence at English school; she is so quiet, in fact, that the teachers worry about her mental health and call her parents in for a discussion. One evening, all the anger and bitterness that she has suppressed finally erupts, and out comes a torrent of language, in which the narrator accuses her mother of trying to silence her. According to the mother, though, this was not her intention. Brave Orchid counters her daughter's verbal onslaught with the observation that much of Hong Kingston's sense of being stifled comes from within and from her childhood misunderstanding of Chinese culture:

> "You turned out so unusual. I fixed your tongue so you could say charming things. You don't even say hello to the villagers."
>
> "They don't say hello to me."
>
> "They don't have to answer children. When you get old, people will say hello to you."
>
> "When I get to college, it won't matter if I'm not charming. And it doesn't matter if a person is ugly; she can still do schoolwork."
>
> "I didn't say you were ugly."
>
> "You say that all the time."
>
> "That's what we're supposed to say. That's what Chinese say. We like to say the opposite."
> (*The Woman Warrior*, p. 203)

Although *The Woman Warrior* does not shy away from pointing a finger at older Chinese and

Chinese Americans for the repression of Chinese women, the memoir here suggests that part of the problem originates within these young women themselves. Because she has not properly understood her parents' culture, Hong Kingston has suffered from a lifelong misunderstanding of her mother's intentions. Looking back on her girlhood outburst, the author suggests that "giving voice" does not involve merely protesting what has been done to one, but also communicating so that mature understanding can take place. Her memoir itself signals a desire for communication.

Sources. *The Woman Warrior* is based on Hong Kingston's own life and the history of her family, both in China and America; it also makes use of traditional Chinese legends, although it does not always represent them in strict accordance with tradition. The book has been described as a blending of "myth, legend, history, and autobiography into a genre of her own invention" (Currier in Metzger, p. 289). The work draws from Hong Kingston's ethnic heritage and incorporates her personal experiences from growing up in Stockton, California, and attending college at the University of California at Berkeley in the 1960s. Much of the book is reconstructed from tales told to Hong Kingston by her mother, each recounted as "a story to grow up on" (*The Woman Warrior,* p. 5).

The figure of the woman warrior for which the book is named is based in part on Fa Mu Lan, a legendary Chinese warrior woman. Said to have lived in the 400s A.D., she is a daughter who served as a substitute for her ill but conscripted father, donning male clothes in order to pass for a man. Fa Mu Lan fought for twelve years in the army, never revealing her female identity. Despite great military success, as soon as she returns from war, she happily dons female clothing and promises to bring up sons for her husband's family. There have been other warrior women in Chinese history, though none so famous as the legendary Fa Mu Lan. The warrior woman that Hong Kingston longs to emulate in the memoir is also reflected in its purely fantastic story of a group of women that she (as woman warrior) has released from servitude. Unlike Fa Mu Lan, these women are not model daughters—once freed, they form a band of renegade mercenaries who save infant girls from death and other women from the bondage of unhappy marriages. Not wholly positive, they also ride around killing men and boys. For a woman to be a warrior, then, does not only entail changes for the better.

Events in History at the Time the Memoir Was Written

Generations. Throughout *The Woman Warrior,* Hong Kingston battles with her mother and other older family members for recognition and understanding. Historians point out that such conflicts between first- and second-generation Chinese Americans were common. As members of the second generation began to adopt the ways of the Americans around them, they formed expectations about education, language, marriage, and even places to live that differed from those of their parents, and these differences tended to strain family relationships. The children often felt torn between two cultures. Their anxiety, however, seems not to have been shared to the same extent by their parents, many of whom felt more like Chinese people in America than like Chinese Americans

This anxiety eased somewhat in the 1970s. The decade saw an increase in self-confidence among many of the younger generation when America's President Richard Nixon made his historic visit to China in 1972. More or less shut off from the West since the country's communist revolution in 1949, China had since been seen by the West largely as a communist enemy, and many people of Chinese extraction felt a corresponding unease. As their ancestral country was gradually welcomed back into the world community, these Chinese Americans tended to feel more secure in the United States.

American feminism. In the 1970s, when Hong Kingston was writing *The Woman Warrior,* the women's movement was gaining momentum in America. Led by women who wanted to increase their opportunities in education and employment, the "Women's Liberation" movement publicized the discrepancies between male and female roles in society and the glaring disparity of pay and job advancement between men and women. In 1968, the salaries of women were only 58 percent of those of men, for example (Banner, p. 238). As more women received college degrees and entered the work force in professional capacities, changes in pay and advancement began to take place.

In 1972 the Equal Rights Amendment was passed by Congress, guaranteeing equal treatment of all under the law regardless of race or gender. Though the amendment was never ratified, it had reverberating effects throughout the country, helping to force the public and the government to take women's issues seriously and to make changes in the way women were treated and paid. *The Woman Warrior* was embraced by the newly militant feminist community in America; Hong Kingston's tale of personal rebellion and her description of the lifetime of cultural oppression that she underwent was an experience shared, to varying extents, by women the nation over.

Reviews. Although feminists applauded *The Woman Warrior*, the response from literary critics was less universally positive. Some argued that the book should not have been published as nonfiction when it contains so much obvious storytelling and so many embellishments on Chinese history and legend. The book nevertheless earned generally high acclaim. A reviewer in the *Washington Post* called the work "a wild mix of myth, memory, history and a lucidity which verges on the eerie" (Allen in Metzger, p. 289). It received the National Book Critics Circle award for nonfiction in 1976, and in 1979 *Time* magazine named *The Woman Warrior* one of the top ten nonfiction books of all time.

For More Information

Aria, Barbara. *The Spirit of the Chinese Character.* San Francisco: Chronicle, 1992.

Banner, Lois W. *Women in Modern America: A Brief History.* New York: Harcourt Brace Jovanovich, 1974.

Cheung, King-Kok. *Articulate Silences: Hisaye Yamamoto, Maxine Hong Kingston, Joy Kogawa.* Ithaca, N.Y.: Cornell University Press, 1993.

Hoexter, Corinne. *From Canton to California.* New York: Four Winds, 1976.

Hong Kingston, Maxine. *The Woman Warrior.* New York: Alfred A. Knopf, 1976.

Hsü, Immanuel C. Y. *The Rise of Modern China.* 4th ed. Oxford: Oxford University Press, 1990.

Metzger, Linda. *Contemporary Authors New Revision Series.* Vol. 13. Detroit: Gale Research, 1984.

Takaki, Ronald. *Strangers from a Different Shore: A History of Asian Americans.* New York: Penguin, 1989.

A Yellow Raft in Blue Water

by
Michael Dorris

M ichael Dorris was born in Louisville, Kentucky, in 1945. Of Modoc Indian descent, Dorris was actively involved in a variety of American Indian issues. Also, he taught anthropology and American Indian studies in his career as a professor. As a writer, Dorris authored first nonfiction and then fictional works dealing with the American Indians. *A Yellow Raft in Blue Water,* his first novel, features three generations of Indian characters, bringing into focus some of the difficulties in contemporary Indian life.

THE LITERARY WORK

A novel set mainly in Montana and Washington State in the 1980s; published in 1988.

SYNOPSIS

Three generations of American Indian women recount their differing perspectives on the single story into which their lives are braided.

Events in History at the Time of the Novel

Life on the reservation. *A Yellow Raft in Blue Water* takes place for the most part on and around an unnamed Indian reservation in northern Montana. There are 90 million acres of reservation land in the United States, roughly half of which are situated in Alaska. When reservation land was assigned to the American Indian population, beginning in the mid-1800s, most of it was considered barren, useless, or unnecessary to the rest of the population. Even today, much of this land is still isolated, inhospitable country. For the majority of the 755,000 American Indians currently living on reservations, poverty is a fact of life. Removed from the rest of the country, some of the reservation population still live without electricity or running water.

A vast disparity separates Indian and non-Indian living conditions across the country; for ex-

ample, a 1985 survey of the Pine Ridge Sioux Reservation in South Dakota estimated unemployment at 87 percent, while the state of South Dakota as a whole had a 5.9 percent unemployment rate. Given these figures, it is understandable that the average income of American Indians is substantially lower than that of the rest of the American population. In 1984 the Navajo per capita income was $2,214 while the per capita income for the nation was $7,731. American Indians are the poorest minority group in the country, yet they receive the least financial aid. In 1980 the average per capita federal government spending for all U.S. citizens was $3,688, but was only $2,948 for American Indians, 20 percent less than the average.

Many tribes are working hard to create industries utilizing the natural resources on their reservations and to otherwise stimulate an increase in the number of jobs they have to offer tribal members. A few groups have succeeded in starting enterprises linked to mineral and timber rights, for example, and in encouraging tourism, but most reservation dwellers are still very poor. A 1984 study found that of the 182,000 Indian families living on or near reservations, 33,097 were homeless, many living in tents, tipis, and cars. Of those who had homes, many were doubling and tripling up with other families in single family dwellings. Now, as before, overcrowding is the rule rather than the exception. When fellow tribal or family members have no place to live, others often welcome the homeless into their own houses. These dwellings quickly become overcrowded, and with already inadequate sanitation and water supply, unhealthy conditions prevail. A statistical comparison again tells the story. While only 1.9 percent of all Americans live in overcrowded housing, 27.6 percent of American Indians suffer overcrowding.

Indian alcoholism. *A Yellow Raft in Blue Water* takes a hard look at one of the greatest difficulties in American Indian life: alcoholism. In the novel, Christine's binge drinking leads to her health problems; according to her doctors, she is going to die as a result of her alcohol abuse. Rayona's teenaged cousin Foxy is already an alcoholic, whose drinking ruins his chances of competing as a rodeo rider. Aunt Ida's father, Lecon, turns to drink when his domestic problems overwhelm him. More than 35 percent of all American Indian deaths in the United States are directly related to alcohol; a 1985 study showed that three times as many Indians as non-Indians die from alcohol-related causes. Among Indians, the occurrence of Fetal Alcohol Syndrome (FAS)—when alcohol consumed by a pregnant mother damages the unborn child—is as much as six times higher than the national average. FAS can cause clumsiness, behavioral problems, stunted growth, and mental retardation in a child. Michael Dorris himself witnessed the terrible effects of FAS in his adopted son, Adam, an Indian boy whose mother drank heavily while pregnant with him.

Several reasons have been suggested for the disproportionate alcoholism among American Indians. One of the most widely accepted is that the massive disruption of their traditional way of life has led to tremendous feelings of powerlessness and hopelessness, from which alcohol provides an escape. Another possible cause for alcohol abuse among Indians has been the strict regulation of alcohol in and around reservations. For many years alcohol could not be sold on Indian reservations, and there were strict limita-

tions on its sale in surrounding areas. On some reservations, possession of alcohol was prohibited, and alcoholic beverages could be confiscated. As a result of these regulations, many Indians became binge drinkers, consuming alcohol as quickly as possible off the reservation, or drinking it quickly on the reservation, knowing it might soon be confiscated. A third explanation is that there is a biological element involved, which makes Indians particularly susceptible to alcohol. But there is disagreement among scientists over whether or not this is so.

ROCKY BOY'S CHIPPEWA-CREE RESERVATION

The novel *A Yellow Raft in Blue Water* mentions by name just one Indian nation—the Cree. There is, in fact, a genuine Cree reservation in Montana, the Rocky Boy's Reservation. Rocky Boy's encompasses 107,612 acres on which about 1,500 American Indians live. Most of the income for the Indians now living at Rocky Boy's comes from farming, mineral rights, and forestry. The only commercial establishment on the reservation is a gas station and store operated by a non-Indian, which brings to mind the gas station operated by Sky in the novel.

Catholic influence on the reservation. Almost half of the American Indian population claims some type of Christian affiliation, and most Indian reservations have Christian missions on them. The largest such mission is the Roman Catholic Church, which in 1970 reported a baptized membership of 177,651 American Indians. Historically, the main function of the Catholic Church on the reservations was to educate American Indian children. In the twentieth century, the Bureau of Indian Affairs (BIA) has taken over this function, but despite their waning influence, Catholic clergy remain on many reservations. Dorris's novel shows both the compassion and success of Father Hurlburt in past generations, as well as the contemporary decline of the Catholic influence, as the "God Squad" fails to generate interest among the reservation's young people. It has been suggested that one of the problems with the Catholic Church's presence on the reservations has been the failure to bring Indians into the clergy. Even today there are very few American Indians in the Catholic clergy, a state of affairs that has caused resentment on many reservations.

View of Rocky Boy's reservation in Montana.

Another important issue involving the efficacy of the Catholic Church among Indian populations has been that on many reservations the teachers at the mission schools have generally known little about Indian culture. There has been a high turnover rate among non-Indian teachers—as high as 90 percent from year to year. The education that Indian children receive has often been based on an alien white culture and its expectations, rather than on improving the existence and broadening the horizons of American Indians from the standpoint of their own values and lifestyles.

Rodeo. In the novel Lee George, raised as Christine's younger brother, is a talented rodeo rider. Even as a teenager, Lee is beginning to acquire a reputation at rodeos throughout eastern Montana. The next step for him is to start attending the professional rodeos, like those in Cheyenne, Wyoming, and Calgary, Alberta. Aunt Ida is against this, however, arguing that rodeo contestants hurt themselves so badly and so often that they wind up practically crippled by the time they are thirty. She's right: rodeo is a very dangerous sport. Depending on the event, the cowboy is susceptible to a wide variety of injuries, from whiplash to broken bones, pulled muscles, and the loss of fingers. The most notorious case of rodeo injury is that of "Wild Horse Bob"

Crosby who, during his career, broke every bone in his body, with the exception of his backbone and his left leg. He broke his right leg five times (Fredriksson, p. 123). The bareback-bronc—the event in which Lee's niece, Rayona, rides—consists of trying to ride an unbroken horse (that is, a horse that has not been trained to accept a rider). Among the dangers that threaten riders are getting caught in the rope used to hang on with, dislocating vertebrae with the shock of the horse's bucking, and getting kicked by the horse, not to mention the injuries associated with impact when the rider is thrown to the ground or against a fence.

Warriors. In all three sections of *A Yellow Raft in Blue Water,* American Indians appear as veterans of war; they have fought in either World War II, the Korean War, or the Vietnam War. It is the Vietnam War that is most central to the novel; Christine's brother, Lee, dies in Vietnam, and a long-term rift opens up between her and Dayton and between her and Aunt Ida, since Christine was the one who pressured Lee into enlisting. Some 42,000 American Indians went to war in Vietnam between 1966 and 1973, many for the same reason that Lee goes—to gain respect within the Indian community. A study conducted between 1985 and 1988 reveals that, to 35.3 percent of American Indian Vietnam veterans, gaining "respect from Indian people" was "very important"; it was "somewhat important" to another 27.1 percent (Holm, p. 59). Even higher is the percentage of men who went to Vietnam because the "family tradition" included making war—51.2 percent of Indians who served in Vietnam said this was "very important" to them (Holm, p. 59). The United States military used this tradition to its advantage, and recruited American Indians on that basis, claiming that they were natural warriors with superior battle skills. Of all American Indians in Vietnam, roughly half wound up serving in the infantry, where they were regularly given the most dangerous jobs of scouting and tracking because of the belief that they were naturally good at it.

While the postwar trauma that affected many Vietnam veterans also took hold of American Indians who served in the war, a certain healing power was more readily available to Indians who belonged to tribes with ceremonies designed to bring men from the state of "peace to war and back again" (Holm, p. 60). These healing ceremonies, while based on traditional rituals, have, among certain Indian tribes, become associated with service in the American military. The funeral service that is held for Lee on the Indian reservation illustrates this point:

> [T]he three World War II veterans [came] out of the boys' locker room and pause[d] on the sideline. They were dressed in their powwow costumes, polka-dotted colored-ribbon shirts, ruffs, cowbells on their high moccasins. They waited for the drum to start the honor song, then began. The one in the middle, Willard Pretty Dog, was sour and scar-faced as he supported a fringed American flag. . . . [O]n either side of him, Vernon LaVallee and Sam Garcia, Sr., did a slow toe-heel progression as they made a circuit in front of the fold-out bleachers.
>
> (Dorris, *A Yellow Raft in Blue Water*, pp. 214-15)

The Novel in Focus

The plot. As the novel opens, Rayona, a teenage girl who is half black and half American Indian, is visiting her mother, Christine, in a Seattle hospital, where she has once again ended up after a drinking binge. Rayona's father, Elgin, briefly visits the two and upsets Christine when he refuses to make another attempt at living with her. After leaving the hospital, Christine, now both romantically and financially bankrupt, decides the only place she can seek refuge is at the house

Michael Dorris

of the woman who is ostensibly her mother, on the Montana reservation where she grew up. Unfortunately, the homecoming is a failure. Before she even sets foot in the house, Christine argues with her "mother," whom she calls Aunt Ida, and flees, leaving Rayona with the older woman. Rayona sees her own mother get into a passing truck but has no idea where Christine goes after this point.

Rayona is uncomfortable around Aunt Ida, who rarely speaks and does little but watch television. Yet the girl stays with Aunt Ida for a while. Tormented at local reservation school because of her mixed Indian-black ancestry and upset by her mother's departure, Rayona allows herself to be befriended by Father Tom, a young Catholic priest in charge of the reservation's Catholic youth group. On the way to a weekend youth camp, Father Tom makes sexual advances toward Rayona, to which the lonely girl very briefly responds. The priest immediately realizes his mistake, and, fearing that she might mention what has happened between them, supports her decision to leave for Seattle, where she claims her father awaits her return. Only too happy to see her leave, Father Tom gives Rayona some money and drops her off at the train station.

But Rayona has no intention of returning to Seattle and trying to hunt down her elusive and half-hearted parent. After spending the night sleeping beside the railroad tracks, uncertain of what to do next, she wanders into a service station owned by Sky, an affable former Vietnam War draft-dodger whose wife, Evelyn, works at a local campground. Sky and Evelyn take Rayona in, find her a job, and refuse to accept rent money from her. To explain what she is doing alone at the campground, Rayona invents a fantasy life, based on the life of a beautiful and wealthy college student who works as a swimming instructor at the campground, starring loving parents who are vacationing in Europe. When the girl's deception is finally unmasked, Evelyn insists that she and Sky drive Rayona to a local rodeo in Havre, Montana, where Rayona thinks that her mother may show up.

INDIAN HORSE CULTURE

The Plains Indians, including the Cree tribe, had strict rules regarding the care and use of horses dating from shortly after the time of the introduction of horses to the tribes in the seventeenth century. These rules dictated what activities horses could be used for, how they should be ridden, and how to care for them. After the near-extinction of the buffalo and the end of the wars between tribes and whites, Indians still maintained close bonds with horses as they moved into ranching and farming. In the novel, this closeness can be seen in the Indian rodeo, which is an important entertainment for the Montana tribes as well as a way for young men to earn prestige. The rodeo, in fact, holds widespread importance among American Indians, who by 1990 had established a dozen associations in the United States and Canada that sponsor rodeos.

Christine is not at the rodeo, but Foxy, Rayona's mean-spirited cousin from the reservation, is. Foxy is too drunk to compete in the bareback bronc riding event and badgers Rayona to stand in for him, disguising her as a man with his coat and hat. Rayona is almost immediately thrown from the horse, but refuses to be beaten and climbs right back on. The crowd has rarely seen anything like this—a cowboy who will not concede defeat, even when pitched into the dirt more than once. Her tenacity earns her a special award, and as she accepts it she causes a sensation by revealing to the judges and crowd that she is a

girl. Dayton, an old friend of Christine's and the owner of the horse Rayona rode, takes Rayona back to his house on the reservation, where Christine has been living. Rayona forgives Christine and is excited by the prospect of learning to ride after Dayton tells her she has a natural talent, like her now-dead uncle Lee.

Christine tells the next segment of the novel, which describes her life before and after having Rayona. Christine and her little half-brother, Lee, grow up with Aunt Ida, never knowing who their fathers are. Christine and Lee are practically inseparable until Dayton Nickles moves onto the reservation. Almost exactly Lee's age, Dayton idolizes Lee and the two become close friends. Jealous of their friendship, Christine grows bitter toward both young men, even more so after Dayton rebuffs her romantic overtures. She accuses him of being in love with Lee, an accusation that stands between them for years. Despite the fact that her brother does not wish to fight in the Vietnam War, Christine pressures him to enlist, finally convincing him that military service is crucial for his aspirations to become a leader in the tribal council. She is indeed ambitious for him, but she also wishes to tear him from Dayton, who, as the sole surviving son in his family, is not obligated to—and will not—serve in Vietnam.

After Lee leaves for Vietnam, Christine and Aunt Ida have a serious falling out. Christine leaves the reservation and takes a job in Seattle. After receiving a telegram that Lee is missing in action, a badly shaken Christine meets Elgin, a sympathetic black soldier, in a neighborhood bar and falls into a passionate affair with him. She soon becomes pregnant. Christine and Elgin get married, but discover that they are compatible only sexually; living together for any length of time is clearly impossible. When the pregnant Christine receives word that Lee has been killed in Vietnam, she goes into immediate labor and bears a daughter. Christine goes about life like a single parent, raising Rayona, always hoping that Elgin will come back for good, but he never does. Periodically Christine goes on drinking binges, and when she reaches the moment at which Rayona's earlier story commences, the hospitalized Christine knows that she is dying. Aware that Elgin will not accept responsibility for his daughter, Christine takes Rayona—who does not know of her mother's condition—to the reservation. Christine then reconciles with Dayton, who allows her to stay in his home, where they take care of each other.

A Yellow Raft in Blue Water concludes with Aunt Ida's narrative. The first information she reveals is how she came to be known as Aunt Ida, and why she is so touchy when Rayona calls her "Gramma" or when Christine tries to call her "Mother." Long ago, Ida's mother fell gravely ill. The mother's younger sister, Clara, moved into the house to help take care of her and the family. But Clara takes care of more than is right and proper, and becomes pregnant by her sister's husband (Ida's father). Because she adores her aunt deeply, Ida agrees to the following plan: The baby will be passed off as Ida's after making it known that she has been raped by an unknown vagrant; Ida will leave, and when the baby is born, she will return and raise the child as her own. Outside of the family, only a Catholic priest, Father Hurlburt, knows the truth about baby Christine. Ida returns to discover her family shattered: her sister, Pauline, has moved into a foster home, her father has spiraled into alcoholism, and her mother is still terribly ill. Ida struggles to raise Christine alone, and loves the child with all her heart. At one point, Clara returns, trying to wheedle Christine away from Ida, who refuses to hand the child over, knowing that Clara intends to sell the girl to a childless couple. Father Hurlburt helps her manufacture paperwork that states that Ida is Christine's mother. Just the same, the newly talking Christine has been told that Clara is her mother, and uses the word exclusively for her. Ida becomes "Aunt" Ida, forever.

Two years later Ida becomes involved with Willard Pretty Dog, formerly the most handsome boy on the reservation, but now hideously scarred from wounds suffered in World War II. The plain Ida, who has long desired Willard, offers him comfort. He moves in with her and they have an affair until a successful operation repairs his facial scarring. Restored to his former beauty, Willard is at last the prize that Ida always thought him, but she cannot live with a man who considers her second-best (his mother is distraught at the idea of her precious son with a woman of ill repute). Ida sends him back to his mother, and never tells anyone that she is carrying his baby, Lee, who will be raised as Christine's brother. Ida's apparent coldness, then, which both Rayona and Christine feel so deeply, has its roots in a lifetime of selfless giving, vanished dreams, and love. The misunderstandings that run throughout the novel are cleared up only for the reader. The characters remain in the dark as to all the secrets that are revealed, but they manage nevertheless to reconcile with one another before the close of the novel.

End of the world. A Yellow Raft in Blue Water is, in part, about betrayals and forgiveness; one wrong that is never righted, however, is that perpetrated upon the teenager Christine by the Catholic Church. The episode is both funny and sad, underlining the conflicted relationship between the American Indians and many of the Catholic missionaries who have taught and counseled them. As Christine tells Rayona, she suffered a fatal crisis of faith brought on by the failure of a famous prophecy to come about, and she has never gone to a Catholic church since.

LITTLE BIG MAN

On her flight from Seattle, Christine makes one last stop to obtain a present for Aunt Ida. She settles on a couple of videos, one of which is "Little Big Man." Christine chooses it for sentimental reasons—she once dated one of the men who acted in it—but the film has a stronger resonance in the context of A Yellow Raft in Blue Water as a whole. The film is based on the classic Western written in 1964 by Thomas Berger, which deals with the history of the American West at the time that the Plains Indians were finally defeated by the American government and by white settlers. The narrator, the 111-year-old Jack Crabb, spent part of his youth among the Cheyenne Indians, and hence has an understanding of and sympathy for them. While they are not written of in strictly glowing terms at all points in the novel, the Indians are described as valuing personal freedom, as having little fondness for political power of any sort, and as having tolerance for strangers, children, and homosexuals (Bakker, p. 177). All of these issues are raised in A Yellow Raft in Blue Water.

One of the Catholic nuns who taught at the reservation school was a devout believer in the cult of Our Lady of Fatima, part of which involves a secret message to the world delivered in 1917 by the Virgin Mary to a young Portuguese child named Lucia. The Virgin Mary appeared six times from May to October 1917, alighting upon a tiny tree and speaking to Lucia and her two young cousins—and increasing thousands of onlookers—of the need for prayer in order to secure peace, convert Russia from communism to the Roman Catholic cult of Our Lady of Fatima, and avert worldwide disaster. The cult became a nationalist symbol in Portugal, which suffered from terrific political upheaval at the time. One of the major concerns of the Portuguese was the possible spread of Marxism from neighboring Spain. The Virgin Mary apparently addressed this concern directly, and ever since, the cult of Our Lady of Fatima, which has achieved worldwide popularity among Catholics and anti-Russian forces of many stripes, has been associated with the defeat of Soviet-style communism.

Lucia claimed that the Virgin Mary told her three secrets, two of which she revealed early on: Mary prophesied the Bolshevik Revolution and World War II. In December 1940, Lucia, now a nun, wrote to Pope Pius XII and informed him in part of the third secret that Mary had told her. Lucia also asked him to consecrate Russia to the Immaculate Heart of Mary so that the country might be saved. If this did not happen, she feared, communism would spread throughout the earth and many nations would be punished. The third secret, sealed in an envelope in possession of the papacy in Rome, was long kept quiet, conjuring up worldwide speculation; as Dorris's novel reveals, some people believed that the letter said something about nuclear holocaust, the end of the world, or another violent chastisement of sinful humanity. Her eye on the unchanged situation in Russia, Christine expects the worst, and is certain that the world will end on New Year's Eve of 1960.

> The whole time I was growing up, all I heard was The Letter, The Letter, The Letter. The Pope was supposed to unseal it in 1960. Either Communist Russia was going to be converted or the world would come to an end, one or the other. In school at the Mission, we prayed constantly about that letter. . . .
> (*A Yellow Raft in Blue Water*, p. 135)

In 1960 Pope John XXIII did open and read this letter. The world—at least the Catholic world—waited in breathless anticipation. The Pope, however, said nothing at all about the contents of the letter, and Lucia's words were never made public. Christine is not alone in her feelings of having been let down: worldwide, the Marian cult suffered in popularity as a result of the Pope's silence.

Sources. Part American Indian himself, Michael Dorris had firsthand familiarity with issues central to Indian life. His research as an anthropologist took him to numerous reservations, where he observed the living conditions of American Indians.

Another major influence on the novel was Dorris's own experience with his adopted son Adam, an Indian boy born with Fetal Alcohol Syndrome. After the adoption, Dorris learned that Adam's mother died from alcohol poisoning in 1973.

Reviews. *A Yellow Raft in Blue Water* has enjoyed widespread critical success, winning the National Book Critics Circle Award. According to a review in the *New York Times,* "It doesn't matter that there's little conventional plot. . . . Good writing can always be counted on to torture characters into significance. . . . This book is mighty good" (Broyard in Mooney, p. 460). Austin MacCurtain admires the narrative complexity of the novel—"[the three women] narrate in turn their versions of the experiences that connect them, and this Faulknerian device gives a density and richness of texture to the story"—but argues that the three characters all speak in essentially the same voice, and that their sophisticated narratives are "not how such people see themselves, or tell their stories" (MacCurtain in Mooney, p. 460). Cathi Edgerton finds no such problem in the novel and instead sees Dorris's threefold narrative technique as the book's strongest point: "Dorris skillfully weaves the reader into his faultless prose as each thread of story binds the heart with the riddle of our common humanity and our insistence on separateness" (Edgerton in Mooney, p. 460).

For More Information

Bakker, J. *The Role of the Mythic West in Some Representative Examples of Classic and Modern American Literature.* Lewiston, N.Y.: Edwin Melle, 1991.

Beaver, Dr. R. Pierce, ed. *The Native American Christian Community.* Monrovia, Calif.: Missions Advanced Research and Communication Center, 1979.

Dorris, Michael. *A Yellow Raft in Blue Water.* New York: Warner, 1988.

Frederiksson, Kristine. *American Rodeo: From Buffalo Bill to Big Business.* College Station: Texas A & M Press, 1985.

Harlan, Judith. *American Indians Today: Issues and Conflicts.* New York: Franklin Watts, 1987.

Holm, Tom. "Forgotten Warriors: American Service Men in Vietnam." *Vietnam Generation* 1, no. 2 (Spring 1989): 56-68.

Mooney, Martha T., ed. *Book Review Digest.* Vol. 84. New York: H. W. Wilson, 1989.

Perry, Nicholas, and Loreto Echeverria. *Under the Heel of Mary.* London: Routledge, 1988.

Index

Index

Index

O

R

global commercial and cultural influence 1:223; 3:92

"heroes" as powerful and nonconformist 4:262, 292, 381–82

inflation and anxiety 4:109–10

mass culture and influence of television 4:111, 379, 398

postwar boom, prosperity 4:109–10, 328

teenage culture 4:391–93, 394–95

War Brides Act 4:124, 127; 5:231

white male economic dominance 4:397

women and cult of domesticity 4:237, 240–41

women as sex objects 4:393

United States in 20th century: 1960s

appeal of Eastern religions 5:237, 281

civil rights protests. *See* Civil rights movements

counterculture, hippies, and protesters 5:37, 64 (sidebar), 83, 158, 237, 272, 279, 308–10, 323–25

cults, iconoclasm, rebels as heros 5:83–84, 318 (sidebar), 323–24

decade of tumult 5:309 (sidebar)

environment, concern for 4:337–42; 5:85–86, 279

feminism. *See* Women's rights movement (and feminism)

"free love" movement 5:272

"graying" of America 5:202–4

Johnson's Great Society and War on Poverty 3:324; 5:68, 150, 266

riots 2:97–98; 3:324; 4:207; 5:112 (sidebar), 340

self-fulfillment and human potential movement 5:204, 287–88

(*See also* Vietnam War)

United States in 20th century: 1970s–1980s

antibusing incidents 3:324

disillusion with government after Nixon and Watergate 3:99; 5:158–59, 263, 317

environment, concern for 5:279 (sidebar)

feminism. *See* Women's rights movement (and feminism)

judicial opposition to civil rights legislation 5:1–2

"me" generation and self-help movements 5:263, 287–88

official apology and monetary compensation to Japanese Americans for WWII internment 4:143, 195

probusiness conservatism (Reagan presidency) 5:1

recession, unemployment, and welfare cuts 5:1, 329

rise of New Right and religious fundamentalists 5:136–39

sexual revolution 5:151

(*See also* Vietnam War)

U.S. Army. *See* Military

United States Military. *See* Military

U.S.S.R. *See* Soviet Union

Up From Slavery, Washington, Booker T. 2:410–15

Urbanization

in 19th-century America 2:125, 195, 301–4

of 19th-century England 1:106, 217, 417; 2:118, 353, 354, 358

in 19th-century France 2:103–4, 209

in 20th-century America 3:25, 73, 88–89; 4:171–72

in 20th-century South 5:91

in 20th-century South Africa 4:95

by American Indians in 20th century 4:186

in Chile 5:164

cities viewed as hotbeds of sin 3:69

of colonial America 1:102

department stores made possible by 2:303

with immigration 2:302, 327; 3:101, 102, 166

and Mexican Americans 4:171

promoting individualism 2:302

replacing rural, agrarian society 2:312, 327; 5:91

rise of crime and police detectives 2:153–54

(*See also* Ghettos; Housing)

USS *Somers* 1:56

Usury (moneylending) 1:103–4, 182–83, 243, 247

Utopian societies

depicted in literature 5:251–52

in novel *Looking Backward* (1888) 2:423

of 1840s 2:418

Shakers 3:95–99

Twin Oaks colony 5:279

Walden movement 5:279

V

Valdez, Luis 5:172

Zoot Suit 4:403–10

Van Dine, S. S. 3:227

Vargas Llosa, Mario 5:211 (sidebar)

Time of the Hero, The 5:333–38

Veblen, Thorstein 3:169

Venice, Italy 1:242–46, 295–97

Verne, Jules

Twenty-Thousand Leagues under the Sea 2:384–90

H. G. Wells compared to 3:410

Verona, Italy 1:344–45

Verrall, Richard 4:40

Vesey, Denmark 2:94–95

Veterinarians 3:1

Victor Emmanuel III, King of Italy 4:66, 67

Victoria, Queen of England 2:28, 335

Victorian Age

agricultural depression 2:353

charity 2:264

circuses and freak shows 2:33, 120, 329

class divisions and social stratification 2:152–53, 157, 358

crime in London 2:262–64

debt, bankruptcy, and poorhouses 2:211–12, 261–62, 266

emancipation of

   negative portrayals in detective fiction of
      1920s 3:228–29
   new freedoms of 1920s 3:147
   opponents and proponents 3:167
   single mothers of 1950s as "irrational"
      4:169 (sidebar)
employment for 2:326; 3:271; 5:138
   as chorus girls 2:329
   as midwives 4:218
   as repugnant to Religious Right 5:137
   in wartime and afterwards 4:21–22, 74,
      166–67, 196 (illus.), 197–98
fashions for. See Fashions
importance of marriage 3:168
Jewish 3:427–30
in Maoist thought 3:136
Mexican 3:197–98, 200–202
participation in Progressive Era's reform
   movements 3:75, 76
protesting Vietnam War 5:308
rural life
   isolation of 3:271
   for sharecropper families 3:370–71
   on Texas frontier 3:246
as sexual goddesses, sex objects 4:74, 393
as single heads of households 2:65; 3:80, 423;
   4:2; 5:68, 117, 136, 138, 267, 328–29
subject to sexual double standard 4:38, 74, 395
and suicide 4:22–26
(See also African American women)
Women's rights movement (and feminism)
   abortion and Roe v. Wade 5:51, 136
   advocating self-determination 5:138–39
   antifeminist backlash 5:136
   authors active in
      Gilman 2:424
      Le Guin's take on 5:237–38
      Morrison 2:64
      Renault's sympathy with 1:62
      Woolf 3:330–32
   battered wives shelters 5:136
   and black feminism 2:64; 3:86–87, 354–55;
      5:92–93, 117
   in Britain 3:359
   Chicana women's movement 3:202
   in czarist Russia 2:37, 39
   educated women at core of 5:135
   hiatus between 1918 and 1960s 5:135–36
   legislation affecting
      Civil Rights Act (1964), Title VII 1:35;
         5:136
      Equal Pay Act (1963) 1:35; 5:237
      Equal Rights Amendment (ERA) 3:79; 5:51
         (illus.), 136, 358–59
      Higher Education Act (1972), Title IX
         5:136
   in Mexico 3:201–2
   National Organization of Women (NOW)
      1:62; 4:22, 394; 5:136, 237

in Norway 2:112–13
origins in
   19th century 2:22, 24, 25, 27, 55, 204, 423;
      3:16
   abolitionist movement 2:24, 204
   civil rights movement of 20th century 1:35;
      2:58
   discontent of women in 1950s 4:167–70;
      5:136
   EEOC's refusal to enforce Title VII 5:237
   Friedan's Feminine Mystique 1:62; 2:58;
      3:430; 4:11 (sidebar), 167, 241, 394; 5: 136
   gender discrimination in workplace 1:35;
      5:136
   myths of women's selfless inclination to serve
      and nurture 5:136, 288
   objections to sexual double standard 4:38,
      74, 395
   oppression and discrimination 2:23–24,
      355–56, 380, 422, 423–26
   sexual harassment in workplace 1:35
   women's subordination to men 4:169,
      170
rape crisis centers 5:136
role of women's clubs 2:336; 3:16–17, 287
   (sidebar)
in Victorian England 2:335
women's studies programs resulting 5:117
Women's rights and roles, discussion pertaining to
   Antigone 1:14–21
   Canterbury Tales, The 1:68–69
   Ethan Frome 2:126–27, 128–29
   Left Hand of Darkness, The 5:237–38, 239–40,
      242
   Lottery, The 4:237
   Macbeth 1:226
   Maltese Falcon, The 3:228–29
   Midsummer Night's Dream, A 1:259–60, 261–64
   Noon Wine 3:246–47
   Odyssey 1:282, 285
   Of Mice and Men 3:271–72
   Passage to India, A 3:301–2
   Sweet Whispers, Brother Rush 5:329
   Turn of the Screw, The 2:378–83
   Worn Path, A 3:420–21
Women's rights and roles, literary works
   emphasizing
   "Ain't I a Woman?" 2:22–27
   Anna Karenina 2:34–40
   Awakening, The 3:15–20
   Beauty: A Retelling of the Story of Beauty and the
      Beast 1:30–36
   Bell Jar, The 4:21–27
   Belle of Amherst, The 2:54–58
   Beloved 2:59–65
   Bluest Eye, The 4:49–57
   Carrie 5:46–52
   Color Purple, The 3:80–87
   Daisy Miller 2:105–10
   Doll's House, A 2:111–17

Z